CONSTRUCTING MEANING

Balancing Elementary Language Arts

Fourth Edition

Joyce Bainbridge

UNIVERSITY OF ALBERTA

Rachel Heydon

THE UNIVERSITY OF WESTERN ONTARIO

Grace Malicky

UNIVERSITY OF ALBERTA

With a Chapter on Drama by Linda Lang

NELSON EDUCATION

NELSON / EDUCATION

Constructing Meaning: Balancing Elementary Language Arts, Fourth Edition
by Joyce Bainbridge, Rachel Heydon, Grace Malicky, and Linda Lang

Associate Vice President, Editorial Director:
Evelyn Veitch

Editor-in-Chief, Higher Education:
Anne Williams

Executive Editor:
Cara Yarzab

Marketing Manager:
Heather Leach

Developmental Editor:
Lily Kalcevich

Permissions Coordinator:
Vicki Gould

Content Production Manager:
Imoinda Romain

Production Service:
Macmillan Publishing Solutions

Copy Editor:
Rodney Rawlings

Proofreader:
Barbara Storey

Indexer:
Maura Brown

Senior Manufacturing Coordinator:
Joanne McNeil

Design Director:
Ken Phipps

Interior Design:
Olena Sullivan

Cover Design:
Olena Sullivan

Cover Image:
Jeff Smith/Getty Images

Compositor:
Macmillan Publishing Solutions

Printer:
RR Donnelley

Library and Archives Canada Cataloguing in Publication

Bainbridge, Joyce, 1944-

Constructing meaning : balancing elementary language arts / Joyce Bainbridge, Rachel Heydon, Grace Malicky ; with a chapter on drama by Linda Lang. -- 4th ed.

Includes bibliographical references and index.

ISBN: 978-0-17-644133-3

1. Language arts (Elementary)
2. English language -- Study and teaching (Elementary) II. Heydon, Rachel, 1971– I. Malicky, Grace, 1944– III. Title.

LB1575.8.B34 2008

372.6'044   C2008-902574-1

ISBN-10: 0-17-644133-6
ISBN-13: 978-0-17-644133-3

PREFACE

Research has long shown that children develop their language abilities through interacting meaningfully with people in their daily lives—in story-time, at mealtimes, during chores, and at play. When children enter school, they continue this process through using language in purposeful ways across the entire school curriculum. Learning is enhanced through interactions with teachers, parents, peers, and other people both within and outside the school context. In the school setting, teachers play a crucial role in maximizing children's language development. They serve as language models, providing a stimulus for thinking and for exploring ideas, and they practise literacy in action.

This textbook is an introduction to teaching elementary language arts from an integrated, balanced, and social constructive perspective. It is intended for both pre-service and in-service elementary school teachers. As in the first three editions, we provide a comprehensive theoretical framework accessible to beginning teachers and a range of ideas related to different areas of the language arts. New in this edition, however, is more explicit reference to the work of specific teachers whose classroom practice has provided us with inspiration, and who demonstrate the teaching strategies, classroom organization, and practical professional knowledge this book is founded upon.

Another significant change in this edition is the integration of electronic media (new literacies/new media) throughout all the chapters. We made this change partly as a result of the rapidly developing nature of this field, and partly because provincial programs of study are structured the same way. In most programs of study, Information Communication Technology outcomes are "infused" throughout all curricular areas. We have also increased our focus on teaching literacy within a critical literacy framework. We have updated all chapters in the textbook, providing additional information on current teaching strategies that can provide varying levels of support to learners from guided to independent practice. In addition, we have enhanced the design of the book, switching from a black-and-white to a full-colour format.

We continue to introduce each chapter with a graphic organizer that provides readers with an overview of topics and subtopics to be considered. We present scenarios of teacher practice at the beginning of each chapter, include teachers' opinions and advice in sections entitled "Teacher Wisdom," and we pose questions based on teacher practice in "Talking Points" at the end of every chapter. Definitions of terms in boldface type are presented in the Glossary at the end of the book. Included in many chapters are book lists, examples of teaching/learning activities, and samples of children's reading, writing, and oral language. We end each chapter with a summary and a short annotated list of teacher-recommended professional resources for readers who wish to pursue an area further. We rely more heavily on web resources in this edition than in previous ones, and frequently include them in our lists of suggested professional resources for teachers. The end-of-book Appendix contains publishing information for all the children's books mentioned in the chapters, along with additional titles, both fiction and nonfiction, that we recommend for students at various grade levels.

In **Chapter 1**, we present our theoretical framework and encourage readers to reflect on their notions of how children learn. We also introduce the dimensions of language learning included in most language arts programs: speaking, listening, reading, writing, viewing, and representing. Because we hold a social constructivist view of learning, we devote considerable attention in this chapter to the social context of learning. We end the chapter with an indication of what we mean by balance in language arts classrooms.

Chapters 2 through **9** provide specific suggestions for assessment and instruction in speaking, listening, reading, and writing. In chapter 2, we briefly describe the structure of language and explore how language functions in different social contexts and in learning in particular. We then present suggestions for enhancing listening and speaking in classrooms and for assessing children's oral language abilities.

The focus of **Chapter 3** is early literacy. In this chapter, we begin by describing perspectives on early literacy development. We then provide suggestions for assessing young children's literacy development and for planning appropriate programs to be responsive to their needs. We end the chapter by describing specific balanced instructional strategies to foster early literacy development.

Reading is the focus of **Chapters 4** through **6**. We begin in Chapter 4 by describing various theoretical perspectives on reading and strategies for assessing children's reading abilities and needs. In Chapters 5 and 6, we suggest specific instructional techniques to support children in becoming lifelong, purposeful, and strategic readers.

In **Chapter 7** we focus on the role of literacy in learning across the curriculum. We use this as a framework for discussion of instruction and issues in new media and Information Communication Technologies. We describe strategies for reading in the content areas, teaching text structures, reading and researching information, as well as working with journal writing, learning logs, research reports, and study skills.

Chapters 8 and **9** are devoted to teaching writing. In Chapter 8, we examine models and forms of writing, the process of composing, and guidelines for implementing a writing workshop. Chapter 9 deals with techniques for assessing children's writing as well as for teaching the conventional aspects of writing.

We believe that children's literature has a critical role to play in children's language development. In **Chapters 10** and **11**, we provide lists of children's books (with a heavy emphasis on Canadian content), as well as information on selecting children's literature and on responding to literature through a range of activities involving response groups, journals, drama, and visual arts.

Chapter 12, written by Linda Lang, introduces various forms of drama, such as dramatic play, process or improvisational drama, interpretive drama, and performance, and shows how these can be used in the classroom to help children represent meaning and more fully understand their world. The chapter also addresses issues of assessment in drama work.

the biases and viewpoints of the assessment tools they are using, and acknowledging the potential mismatch between these and the funds of knowledge of their students. The second step is adjusting assessment so that children are able to show what they know and are able to do.

Curriculum Documents: Part of the Assessment Dialogue

Complicating matters further when teachers are trying to assess is that the goals of assessment (and instruction) can be influenced by agendas from administrators, policymakers, parents, and taxpayers. To deal with these competing agendas, we suggest that teachers go back to the notion of curriculum as a dialogue. Teachers can then think about how this dialogue includes assessment: what we teach and what we assess, how we teach and how we assess, all affect each other. To highlight a few of the voices in this dialogue, we now turn to a brief overview of regional curriculum documents and demonstrate how they may relate to assessment.

With an increased focus on accountability in education in the 1990s, many Canadian provinces and regions began to redevelop their curriculum documents to explicitly include "clear learning outcomes and high learning standards" (Alberta Learning, 2000, p. 1). Most documents across the country (see Chapter 1 for a list of websites containing these documents) now include outcomes, standards, expectations, and/or objectives for elementary children, nearly always organized by grade levels. For example, British Columbia specifies three broad categories of curriculum organizers: Oral Language (speaking and listening), Reading and Viewing, and Writing and Representing. These categories are further subdivided into purposes, strategies, thinking, and features (Ministry of Education, Province of British Columbia, 2006). These documents become part of the assessment (and curriculum) conversation through two main pathways: provincial or territorial achievement tests and teachers' reporting procedures.

Most provinces and territories have developed achievement tests based on the outcomes stated in curriculum documents, and often administration of these achievement tests is mandatory. The most frequent scheduling of provincial and territorial achievement testing in reading for elementary students is at the ends of grades 3 and 6, although scheduling is different in some provinces (e.g., in British Columbia elementary students are assessed at the end of grades 4 and 7). The most recent list we could find of Canadian assessment practices is available at http://www.apecneted.org/knowledgebank/index.cfm?action=dsp_byType&type=3.

Provincial and territorial reading achievement tests are similar across the country (see Erin's description of her EQAO reading test at the beginning of this chapter): students read a number of passages and answer multiple-choice questions to determine whether they have met the expectations/outcomes specified in curriculum documents. Some provinces also require students to answer a small number of open-response questions. Tests generally include both narrative and informational passages and sometimes also poetry.

Most provinces and territories identify a standard or expected level of student performance in their curriculum documents. This standard is used to mark the achievement tests.

The Ontario Ministry of Education (2006), for example, has set out four levels of achievement that are related to expectations in four areas of knowledge and skills: Knowledge and Understanding (i.e., "Subject-specific content acquired in each grade (knowledge), and the comprehension of its meaning and significance (understanding)"), Thinking (i.e., "The use of critical and creative thinking skills and/or processes"), Communication (i.e., "The conveying of meaning through various forms"), and Application (i.e., "The use of knowledge and skills to make connections within and between various contexts") (pp. 20–21). Level 3 is the provincial standard, representing the expected level of achievement at each grade level. Level 1 represents achievement below the standard; Level 2, achievement approaching the standard; and Level 4, achievement surpassing the standard. In addition to the **evaluation** of the achievement test being conducted and communicated in these ways, the Ontario government also mandates a provincial report card that is correlated with these achievement levels.

Results on provincial and territorial achievement tests are widely distributed and generally broken down by school district and sometimes by school. Many school districts also administer reading tests at the end of each grade, providing even more data on reading achievement levels of children in specific schools. Taylor's experience with CASI is such an example. The data collected can significantly affect the viability of some school programs when financing is provided on a per-pupil basis. The next section examines high-stakes assessment and its potential to help and to hinder the reading achievement of children in our schools.

High-Stakes Assessment

Many of you may recall year-end reading tests when you were in school. Were you ever aware of what these tests were for or what happened with the results? Sometimes the results were simply placed in your file and not much else happened. Other times, the results were used by your teacher to determine a mark on your report card. In a small number of instances, the results were used as a basis for grade repetition or placement in a special class. The stakes were much higher in the last than in the first instance. Hence the term *high-stakes assessment*: there is a lot riding on one test, as a gambler might have a lot of money riding on one hand of blackjack. In North America, for instance, one assessment is often used to make important and complex decisions involving such things as promotion or retention in grades, graduation, entrance into an educational institution, teacher salary, or a school district's autonomy (e.g., Ontario requires students to pass a literacy test in grade 10 to earn an Ontario Secondary School Diploma). The most common high-stakes tests are standardized norm-referenced and criterion-referenced tests.

Nature of Standardized Tests

Standardized tests have been used in North American schools for many decades as one way to gather information about children's reading. Such tests are "administered, scored, and interpreted in a standard manner" and, as mentioned, may be norm- or criterion-referenced (Council of Chief State School Officers, n.d., n.p.). Standardized, criterion-referenced tests are those in which children are given the same set of questions or tasks in the same way and their performance is judged against a standards-based set of criteria, such as curricular outcomes or expectations. Standardized, norm-referenced tests are also tests that are implemented in a standard way, but they go a step further in that they are scored against a "norm." Such tests are developed by selecting items at a range of difficulty levels and administering them to children at various grade and age levels. Tables of norms are then developed, providing teachers with percentiles, grade equivalents, and/or standard scores corresponding to the number of items a child completes correctly. When a norm-referenced standardized test is administered, it determines how well the children in the class perform on the test in relation to the children in the standardization sample.

The primary reason school systems and provincial governments administer both kinds of standardized tests is accountability—to show that the programs provided in the school system are producing the desired results. Administrators compare the scores of one class, school, or system with those of the standardization sample (in the case of norm-referenced tests) and/or of other classes, schools, and systems. Sometimes scores are compared across provinces, states, and even nations. At this point you might have many questions regarding the potential benefits and disadvantages of such assessment. As educators working within a social-constructive perspective who understand literacy as a broad and complex set of situated practices, we have many concerns with standardized tests and high-stakes assessment.

Some Problems with High-Stakes Testing

High-stakes tests have come under considerable criticism in recent years (e.g., Kohn, 2002). One common criticism involves the extent to which a single assessment, as well as a standardized assessment, can be consistent with the language arts programs being implemented. Because curriculum is a dialogue, one test cannot "represent the curriculum and instructional diversity among teachers" (Paris & Hoffman, 2004, p. 205). As Erin's description of the reading passage in her EQAO test shows, such tests also fail to address the multifaceted, rich types of texts that balanced literacy teachers promote. Often, the passages used to assess comprehension tend to be short and contrived rather than high-quality children's literature; and even when a reasonably well-written text is used, because the tests are standardized, students must read the same materials and there is no accounting for the role of background knowledge or engagement in the reading process. Think, for example, about Taylor's situation with the CASI. In the year when she read about figure skating, something she knew about and enjoyed, she did well. In the year where she had to read about basketball, she found the text long and hard going. The roles of background knowledge and engagement affected her scores on these tests. As such, a single, standardized assessment cannot "capture the variety of skills and developmental levels," not to mention funds of knowledge of "children in most ... classes" (p. 205).

Another feature of many standardized, high-stakes tests is their reliance on multiple-choice items. Multiple-choice items fail to measure what really counts in reading when reading is considered to be a meaning-making process (e.g., critical thinking, construction of meaning, collaborative learning), and it tends to reinforce the notion of one right answer, which can be offputting for children who have developed more robust notions of what reading is about. For instance, consider this quote about one of her students from a teacher in a study about the effects of high-stakes testing:

> He sat down to take the test and tears were coming down his face and he looked up at me and he said—I was teaching third grade—and he said, "*I thought I could read.*" And I thought, from that minute on, that's never going to happen to me again. My kids are all going to feel comfortable. No one is going to look at this test and start crying. (Valli & Chambliss, 2007, p. 57)

Unfortunately, many aspects of high-stakes assessment have been hurtful to children. High-stakes assessment has been found, for instance, to highlight children's deficits, rather than their funds of knowledge or strengths (Heydon & Iannacci, 2005). Indeed, this is a feature of norm-referenced assessments.

In the construction of the norm, test items are deliberately selected "to produce failure among some and success among others" (Field, 1990, p. 108). How does this happen? When items are being selected for inclusion on a particular test, those items that all students get right or all students get wrong are eliminated because they do not help to differentiate among children. In other words, unless a set percentage of children fail an item, it is not included. And by linking scores on these tests to grade equivalents, it is predetermined that some children will be at grade level, some will be above, and some will be below. In other words, when norm-referenced tests are used, half of the children will succeed and half will fail. This leads to a basic contradiction between the goals of schooling and the use of standardized tests. On the one hand, most people believe that an appropriate goal of schooling is to ensure that all children are able to read at a level appropriate to their grade. On the other hand, the use of standardized tests means that this will never be achieved.

Another problem with standardized tests is that, through them, some children are identified very early as reading below expectations, the emphasis being on what they cannot do rather than what they can do. Many educators are, therefore, greatly concerned about the potentially negative impact that test results can have on individual children by marginalizing them and telling them that they are not good enough. Particularly problematic is that the children who are most often marginalized by these types of tests, because of built-in bias in test items, are the poor and those from minority groups (Kohn, 2002; Shannon, 1998; Sloan, 2007). Indeed, it appears that these students are being forced out of schools by high-stakes testing in some regions in order to increase overall results (Kohn, 2002; Voke, 2002). To make matters worse, because the assessments are high-stakes, test results are usually communicated publicly. This practice has been found to "undermin[e], even stigmatiz[e] the reputations of the local community, the school, the principal, the teachers, and the students" (Sloan, 2007, p. 29).

Because teachers like the one quoted in the Valli & Chambliss (2007) study care so much about their students and hate the pain that certain kinds of assessment practices create, many teachers have resorted to altering their teaching to teach specifically to the test. This has resulted in stilted teaching that oversimplifies literacy and leads children to develop a form of literacy that is itself overly simple (Valli & Chambliss, 2007). Rather than standardized tests measuring what is taught, the opposite is often the case—what is taught is determined by what is tested. This is particularly the case in high-poverty schools that tend to have the lowest test scores. The use of high-stakes tests accelerates an emphasis on lower-level skills and drill-and-practice activities rather than higher-level thinking (Kohn, 2002). Additionally, there is now the concern that **culturally and linguistically diverse (CLD)** students

> may be put at greater risk of disengagement from school and from literacy development because of high-stakes testing programs. That finding is particularly ironic because many [governmental] content and performance standard programs were adopted to address gaps in the performance of students from diverse ethnicities. Self-determination theorists and researchers argue that reward- and punishment-oriented approaches that pressure students cannot succeed. (Unrau & Schlackman, 2006, p. 99)

Finally, we must include in this list of problems with standardized assessments that another, related problem involves the amount of time testing takes away from instruction. It is not only the time spent in actual testing, but also the time for preparation and recovery (Johnston, 1998; Voke, 2002). The International Reading Association (1999) argues that the "consequences of lost instructional time, particularly for low-performing students, are too great for information that can be gathered more efficiently" (p. 4). Just think, for instance, of all the instructional time that was lost for Taylor and Erin.

Despite the bad-news story that we've just laid out, teachers in Canada, unlike their colleagues in the United States, still have some flexibility to see high-stakes tests and other assessment issues that we've just discussed as part of a dialogue, rather than a wholesale takeover of their professional autonomy. So what might a balanced perspective on reading assessment look like? This is the central concern of the rest of this chapter.

BALANCED ASSESSMENT

Just as there is no one right way to bring children to literacy, there is no one best reading assessment. Professional teachers need to have at their disposal a range of assessment tools and procedures. When they are selecting how and when to assess, teachers need to take into consideration the counsel of the Language and Literacy Researchers of Canada that literacy assessment should

- be part of the teaching and learning process,
- incorporate multiple and varied sources of data,
- when designed for one purpose, should not be used for another,
- reflect the complexity of literacy processes,
- be developmentally and culturally appropriate,
- not use one measure in making decisions regarding certification or access to programs or resources,
- encourage student and family participation. (2006, n.p.)

Just like the principles of assessment that we explored regarding young children in Chapter 3, reading assessment in social constructive frameworks should always consider the context in which the assessment is being conducted. Insofar as possible, assessment should be classroom-based. In the next section we lay out three different major reading assessment strategies that can all become part of a teacher's balanced literacy repertoire (observation,

TABLE 4.1 Assessment Strategies

Strategy One: Observation	
Contexts	Recording
• interactive read-aloud, shared reading, guided reading, independent reading, reader response activities, explorations, mini-lessons • oral reading/retelling • drama	• checklists • anecdotal records • reading logs • audiotapes • running records • videotapes
Strategy Two: Conferencing	
Contexts	Recording
• teacher/student conferencing • conferences with families (including student-led conferences)	• conference logs • anecdotal records • questionnaires • surveys • story collection
Strategy Three: Work Samples	
Contexts	Recording
• interactive read-aloud, shared reading, guided reading, independent reading, reader response activities, explorations, mini-lessons	• artifacts from contexts (e.g., Venn diagrams, character maps) • anecdotal records • portfolios

work samples, and conferencing). Table 4.1 (adapted from Hibbert, 2005) is based on Kathy Hibbert's classroom practice and understanding of key pieces of assessment literature (e.g., Cooper & Kiger, 2005; Vacca, Vacca, & Begorary, 2005). The table lays out the strategies, the contexts in which they might be conducted, and the ways in which assessment information can be recorded. As you can see in this table, teachers can mix and match strategies, contexts, and ways of recording information to suit their needs. When interpreting assessment results, teachers can triangulate their data, that is, they can check to see how the information they've collected from various sources compares to each other and whether it is consistent.

Strategy One: Observation

As noted in Chapter 3, teachers are continuously and implicitly assessing their students' reading every time they interact with them. Many educators identify classroom observation as a core tool in reading assessment (e.g., Simmons, 2000). Observation can provide great information about reading achievement and process, including how well a child is reading, how they are reading, and what types of activities and texts engage them. The reading checklist in Table 4.2 is designed to help teachers observe and interpret children's reading behaviours during daily classroom reading instruction.

TABLE 4.2 **Reading Checklist**

Aspects of Reading	Reading Strategy	Comments
Positive attitude to reading	— Is able to name favourite books and authors. — Enjoys reading silently in class time. — Engages in extensive independent reading.	
Integrates knowledge and text to construct meaning	— Is able to set a purpose for reading. — Is able to predict what a story or text will be about from the title. — Is able to predict what will happen next in a story. — Uses both knowledge and text information to answer inference questions. — Retellings include inferences as well as text information.	
Uses knowledge of story structure to construct meaning	— Is able to answer questions about the setting, characters, events and ending of stories. — Includes information from setting, events, and ending in retellings of stories. — Retells stories in sequence.	
Uses knowledge of expository text structure to construct meaning	— Is able to answer questions involving main idea, sequence, cause/effect, and comparison/contrast relationships. — Retellings reflect organizational patterns of informational texts (enumeration, cause/effect, sequence, comparison/contrast).	
Uses context cues to identify words	— Oral reading miscues make sense and sound right in relation to prior text. — Gives real-word rather than nonsense-word responses when reading. — Corrects miscues that do not make sense.	
Uses print cues to identify words	— Oral reading miscues look and sound like the words in the text. — Most sounds are represented in inventive spellings. — Identifies words by processing letter groups, syllables or words within other words. — Corrects miscues that do not "look right."	
Integrates context and print cues to identify words	— Most miscues both make sense and look right. — Corrects most miscues that change the author's meaning.	
Reads with automaticity	— Identifies high-frequency words immediately. — Reads fluently and at an appropriate rate. — Completes silent reading assignments in a reasonable time.	

The headings in the left-hand column reflect those aspects of reading that are used to organize the teaching/learning techniques discussed in Chapter 6. So, if a child does not display reading behaviours associated with a particular aspect of reading, you can go directly to the appropriate section in Chapter 6 to select the teaching/learning techniques to use with that child. For example, a child who is not yet able to include information from the setting, events, and endings of stories in retellings may benefit from work on narrative text structure. A child who is not yet representing most letters in inventive spellings and whose **miscues** bear little resemblance to words he or she is reading may benefit from work on **phonemic awareness** and letter sounds.

Strategy Two: Conferencing

Conferencing can provide teachers with information about students' interests, their attitudes to reading, and the strategies they use and/or know about. It can also be a means of engaging students in their own goal setting and self-assessment. Interests, attitudes, and engagement are all critical areas of concern for assessment. Cambourne (1988), of course, instructs us that engagement is a necessary condition of learning, and literacy researchers like Richard Allington (2006) teach that unfortunately more children *can* read than *do* read. Because, Allington explains, reading volume is positively correlated with reading achievement, the more teachers can learn how to engage children in reading (e.g., by finding out what books they would be interested in), the more effective instruction is likely to be. Given that good readers have strategies for dealing with text when it gets rough, it is also important to find out what students do or do not know about strategies. Assessment experts Michael McKenna and Steven Stahl (2003) have found that conferencing in the form of interviews is an excellent way of ascertaining students', especially older students', understanding of strategies.

Conferencing can take many forms. During classroom interactions, teachers can encourage children to talk about what they read, why they read, and how they read. The interview schedule outlined in Table 4.3 is designed to help teachers collect more specific information about a child's reading interests, habits, and knowledge about reading and strategies. Despite the plethora of new publications on reading assessment, many reading assessment interviews continue to rely on tried-and-true interview protocols. We are no different in this regard. Hence, our interview schedule is made up of old favourites (Atwell, 1987; Goodman, Watson, & Burke, 1987; Lipson & Wixson, 1991).

Note that in the interview you will not likely ask any child all of these questions in one sitting. Instead, you will think about what you need to know about a particular child and select those questions that might help gather this information. For example, if a child rarely chooses books to read independently, you might ask the questions about interests and attitudes. If a child appears to have few strategies for making meaning as he or she reads, you might ask the last four questions in the reading strategies section.

Strategy Three: Work Samples

Just as we described in Chapter 3, teachers can save samples of children's reading throughout the school year to assess growth. Here are some forms that these samples can take:

TABLE 4.3 Reading Interview

Area	Questions
Interests	• What kinds of things do you like to do in your spare time? • What is your favourite subject at school? Why? • What kinds of books do you like to read? • Name two books you have read recently that you liked.
Attitudes	• If you could read a story or watch it on television, which would you choose? Why? • How much time do you spend reading each day at home? At school? • How many books do you own? Do you go to the library to get books? • How do you feel about reading?
Knowledge about reading Functions of reading Reading strategies	• What is reading? • Why do people read? • Think of someone who is a good reader. How do you know he/she is a good reader? • How would you help someone who was having trouble reading? • What do you think about as you read? • What do you do when you are reading and come to a word you don't know? • What do you do when you are reading and something doesn't make sense? • What do you do to help you remember what you read (e.g., in social studies)? • Do you ever read something over again? Why? • Do you read some things faster than others? Why?
Self-appraisal	• How would you describe yourself as a reader? • Is learning to read easy or hard? Why? • What's the easiest thing about reading for you? What's the hardest thing? • What kind of help to you think you need with your reading?

■ Reading logs provide information on what children read and are commonly kept in their reading **portfolios**. In their logs, children keep a list of books they have read during the year, and make note of the amount, genre, and level of material read. Children can include the date each book was selected and completed, along with comments about the book. These entries help teachers determine children's growth in voluntary reading behaviour.

Response to literature is another way to sample children's reading. It is crucial to examine children's written responses in terms of their ability to *retell* (e.g., identify main ideas and story structure) *relate* (e.g., connect the text to other texts, the world, and themselves), and *reflect* (e.g., evaluate ideas, ask questions) (Schwartz & Bone, 1995). Children's responses to text illustrate how they transact with a given text rather than their specific use of reading strategies. It is also important to keep in mind when examining responses that they are often as much a reflection of expressive ability (i.e., writing, representing, and speaking) as reading comprehension.

Running records, which we described in Chapter 3, can be used to collect samples of children's oral reading, to determine what level of material is appropriate for instruction and to examine their growth in using meaning and print cues to identify words. As with young children, running records can be kept of children reading stories from basal texts, books, or passages specifically designed for this purpose. However, recently many educators have turned to **levelled texts** to obtain running records.

When taking running records with levelled texts, the teacher selects a book he or she thinks will be easy for the child to read and asks the child to read orally. While the child reads, the teacher notes any miscues that the child makes, and when the reading is completed, the teacher calculates the percentage of words read accurately (including miscues corrected by the child). By having the child read progressively more difficult books, the teacher attempts to determine what level is "just right" for instructional purposes. Some teachers decide that a text is at an independent level of reading when the child reads 90 to 95 percent of the words correctly. Teachers can then analyze children's miscues to determine how the child is using cues to identify words. Balanced literacy teachers, however, may want to pair up the information they glean from running records with information they have collected through other assessments. In this way, teachers acknowledge that reading is about more than just accurately being able to "word call."

The coding system described below for informal reading inventories can be used for running records as well. While it is more authentic to gather running records on materials actually being used in the classroom, teachers may wish to use informal reading inventories with older students and when leveled texts are not available.

Informal Reading Inventories

Informal reading inventories usually consist of two components: a series of word lists, and a number of passages with comprehension questions at increasing levels of reading difficulty. The word lists included on the inventories are used to estimate the reading level at which to begin administering reading passages. That level is the one at which children can identify all or most of the words. This ensures that children do not spend time reading passages that are much too easy or much too difficult for them.

The teacher then has the child read passages orally and silently and answer the questions about them. The child continues to read passages of increasing difficulty until he or she is no longer able to identify 90 percent of the words or answer 70 percent of the questions correctly. As the child reads orally, the teacher keeps a running record of oral reading miscues and writes down the child's answers to comprehension questions. The marking system used for taking a running record with early readers is also an appropriate means of recording miscues for more independent readers.

Many teachers choose to use informal reading inventories, because the passages and questions are all in one place and the teacher does not have to search out a series of books at a range of reading levels and design tasks to assess comprehension of passages in these books. Informal inventories are designed to be administered individually, so they are used primarily with children when the teacher is puzzled and needs more information to plan appropriate instruction. A wide range of informal reading inventories is available, including the *Informal Reading Inventory* (Burns & Roe, 2002), *Classroom Assessment of Reading Processes* (Swearingen & Allen, 2000), and the *Qualitative Reading Inventory—3* (Leslie & Caldwell, 2001). The last two inventories include both narrative and expository passages. Please note that when using "graded" or "levelled" passages, the grades and levels need to be taken with a grain of salt. This quantitative information can give us a ballpark idea of where children are, but grades and levels are never absolute.

Interpreting Informal Reading Inventories

Teachers can get two major types of information from an informal reading inventory: achievement and diagnostic information. The child's level of reading achievement is the highest level at which the child meets the criteria set in the test for instructional reading level.

Although tests vary, the instructional reading level is generally the level at which the child is able to identify 90 percent or more of the words accurately *and* answer 70 percent or more of the comprehension questions correctly. The child is able to read material independently if word identification and comprehension are close to 100 percent. Material is probably too difficult for a child if he or she reads with less than 90 percent accuracy *or* less than 60 percent comprehension. It is important to remember that informal inventories provide only a rough indication of the level of material children can handle. Children may be able to understand more difficult material if they know a great deal about the content or are very interested in it. On the other hand, if the topic in a narrative or informational passage is unfamiliar, children may have difficulty with it even if it is at their instructional reading level as determined on an informal reading inventory.

Many informal reading inventories include an activity for children to do before they read each passage, to assess their background knowledge. On the *Qualitative Reading Inventory*, for example, children are asked to associate meanings with key concepts in passages to be read. On other inventories, they are asked to read the title and predict what passages will be about. Still others ask children to rate their knowledge about the content of the passage after they have finished reading it. From a social constructive perspective, a reader's background knowledge is a critical component in the reading process.

How the reader uses this knowledge along with print and text information is even more important. Unfortunately, because we cannot get inside children's heads to see reading as it occurs, we have to rely on indirect evidence to interpret what they are doing. Two major sources of diagnostic data from informal reading inventories that provide this evidence are oral reading miscues and answers to questions.

Miscues

As we discussed in Chapter 3, when working with readers who are beyond an early stage in their reading development, teachers can analyze oral reading miscues according to the two major cuing systems—meaning and print. The major difference when conducting miscue analyses with more proficient readers is that the criteria for coding miscues are more stringent. We present the criteria, as well as examples of miscues of a grade 4 child named Paul in Box 4.3. Take a look at this passage and, just as you did for David in Chapter 3, think of what you can tell about the student's reading from the information provided by the assessment.

BOX 4.3   ORAL READING MISCUES OF A GRADE 4 BOY

Marking System for Miscues

▷ A substituted word or mispronunciation is written above the text word.

▷ An omission is indicated with a circle around the word.

▷ A T is written above words provided by the teacher.

▷ An insertion is indicated with a caret.

▷ SC indicates that a miscue was corrected.

Coding System for Miscues

▷ M (meaning-based): Miscue makes sense in relation to prior text and the rest of the sentence as the child reads it.

▷ P (print-based): Miscue contains half or more of the same letters as the text word.

▷ I (integrative, both print and meaning): Miscue contains half or more of the same letters as the text word *and* makes sense in relation to prior text and the rest of the sentence.

Excerpt from a "Grade 4" Passage

      I   I

Johnny   for

John first gathered bags of apple seeds. He got many of his seeds from farmers who squeezed apples to make a drink called cider. Then, in the spring, he left

                    P

        front tire SC

for the western frontier.

              I

        trees

He planted seeds as he went along. Also, he gave them to people who knew how valuable apple trees were.

John walked many miles in all kinds of weather. He had to cross dangerous rivers and find his way

|

cool

through strange forests. Often he was hungry, cold, and wet. Sometimes he had to hide from unfriendly Indians. His clothes became ragged and torn. He used

M

his

a sack for a shirt, and he cut out holes for the arms. He wore no shoes. But he never gave up. He guarded his precious seeds and carefully planted them where they

P

strange SC

had the best chance of growing into strong trees.

Source: From **AMERICA'S HISTORY** B. B. Armbruster, C. L. Mitsakas, V. R. Rogers © 1986 by Schoolhouse Press. Used by permission of Pearson Education, Inc. All Rights Reserved.

When we looked at the sample we found that, given the number of miscues for this passage, the "fourth-grade" material is at Paul's instructional level. He showed that he was able to effectively use both print and context cues to predict words that made sense, sounded right, and checked out with the print. He was able to integrate print- and knowledge-based cues to construct meaning as he read. Like many good readers, he corrected miscues when they did not make sense. He did not correct his substitution of *for* for *of* because this miscue was consistent with the meaning that he constructed. He was able to answer seven of the eight questions he was asked about this passage, confirming that he was able to effectively construct meaning when reading this passage. Our hypothesis that this passage was at Paul's instructional level was confirmed when Paul was asked to read material a level above and he made well over the acceptable number of miscues.

Now what do you make of the miscues of Kyla, a grade 3 student, identified in Box 4.4?

In our estimation Kyla met the criteria for instructional reading level for both miscues and comprehension questions on the grade 2 passage shown. The most obvious thing about Kyla's miscues is the number she corrected. This shows that she was aware of when at least some of her miscues did not make sense or look right. Her self-corrections also indicate that she has developed some effective strategies for word identification. However, these strategies are not yet well enough developed to enable her to handle material at a "third-grade" level. This was confirmed for us when Kyla was asked to read a more difficult passage and demonstrated behaviour consistent with frustration.

BOX 4.4   ORAL READING MISCUES OF A GRADE 3 GIRL

Excerpt from a "Grade 2" Passage

It was a Saturday morning. John looked at the toys in his room. They were all old and he wanted something new. John went to his mother. "All my toys are old," he said. "I want something new to play with."

His mother looked at (him). "John, we don't have

SC

All

the money to buy you anything new. You'll have to find a way to make something new." John went back to his room and looked around at the toys. There were many toys that were fun. But he had played with them so much that they weren't fun anymore.

SC

They

Then he had an idea. His friend Chris wanted a truck

M

one   SC

just like his red truck. And John wanted a car like the (one) Chris got for his birthday. Maybe they could trade. John ran down the street to Chris's house. "Hey, Chris would you like to trade your car for my truck?" "Sure," said Chris. "I'll trade. Later we can trade something else.

P   P   SC

They   well   away

That way we'll always have something new to play with."

What We Know About Effective Readers and Miscues

Effective readers use cues both in context and within words as they read. Miscues help teachers determine where to place the instructional focus at any point in time. For example:

- If children focus almost exclusively on print cues in material at their instructional level, they need less attention to cues within words for a while and a heavier focus on using context cues.

- If their miscues make sense but are not consistent with print cues, they need instruction on strategies for processing cues within words.

As soon as children begin to show more effective use of the cuing system that is the focus of instruction, it is crucial to provide a balanced program so that children learn to use multiple sources of information to identify unfamiliar words.

Questioning

Teachers can use question data to determine how a child might be constructing meaning from text. If children are successful in answering factual questions, they appear to be able to use text information to construct meaning. If they are successful in answering inferential questions, they appear to be able to integrate their world knowledge with text information to construct meaning as they read.

Children who are able to answer factual but not inferential questions may think reading is a meaning-getting rather than meaning-making enterprise, or they may not know how to use their knowledge along with text to construct meaning. They could then benefit from the teaching/learning strategies described in Chapter 6 in the section on integrating knowledge-based and text-based information.

Children who are able to answer inferential questions better than factual ones may be relying too much on their background knowledge to construct meaning. Often, if they're asked to retell what they have read, they demonstrate limited processing of text information. They frequently benefit from teaching/learning strategies designed to help them use the structure of narrative and expository texts to construct meaning.

Portfolios

Portfolios have been defined as "collections of artifacts of students' learning experiences assembled over time" (Valencia, Hiebert, & Afflerbach, 1994, p. 14). Reading portfolios provide information on children's reading, including strategies that they use in a range of everyday reading activities. The process of developing and discussing the portfolio is also intended to help children develop **metacognition** as they reflect on their reading (Wiener & Cohen, 1997).

While there are many different kinds of portfolios, two of the major types are the working portfolio and the showcase portfolio (Christie, Enz, & Vukelich, 2003). The items in the working portfolio represent a child's typical, everyday performance. From the working portfolio, children and their teachers can select pieces to include in the showcase portfolio that contains the child's best work.

Take a moment to consider the interview we conducted with upper elementary teacher John Guiney Yallop about his use of portfolios (see the next Teacher Wisdom box). When you read John's responses, think about the following:

- What goes in the portfolio?
- Who decides what goes in?
- What is the process of putting artifacts in the portfolio?
- What are the various ways that the portfolio is used?
- How might portfolios be directly linked to assessment and to student improvement?

Content of Portfolios

The content of reading portfolios reflects the reading theories of teachers, the reading programs in classrooms, the type of portfolio, and children's interests, goals, and strategies. Hence, there

TEACHER WISDOM

JOHN GUINEY YALLOP

What do you see as the benefits of portfolios?

The main benefit I think is that they give students ownership of their learning and the assessment of that learning as well. They take responsibility. They can look back on their work and see their journey as a learner. That, for me, is the most exciting. Students are able to say, I read this book or I read this chapter or I read this section aloud in class and here is how I feel about my reading now and here's how I felt about my reading before.

What do you notice about your students' ability to self-assess?

Sometimes students feel uncomfortable even giving themselves a pat on the back and maybe from having come from a more formal environment where they have been evaluated they got used to the idea that the teacher tells me if I'm good or not. The teacher tells me if I can read or not. So my goal is to get them to a point of being able to say, I make decisions about how well I'm reading. I'm noticing my progress. I'm reading better this month than I did last month, because here's what I'm noticing I can do now that I didn't do before.

Do you require the students to reflect on their journey as a component of the portfolio?

Yeah. For every piece that goes in, they write a reflection. Over the years, I've borrowed some reflection sheets and other times I develop them to tailor them to my students' needs. The sheets ask students to answer a couple of questions: What is this piece? What growth is it showing? What subject area? I also have them answer the questions: Why am I putting this in my portfolio? What do I like about this piece?

I often saw on the borrowed forms the question: "What can I improve?" And I grew to dislike that question because it always gave the message that this work is never good enough. So I tended to drop that question, and instead I ask them, "If you were showing this work to another student or someone else, what would you like to draw their attention to?" What I try to do with this question is to make the students aware or help them to talk about what particularly is attractive to them about this piece of work or something that they wanted to build on in a future piece of work. I also sometimes just want students to stop and celebrate a success.

What sorts of things do the students include?

We talk about the idea of a showcase portfolio, where you have these final pieces. That tends not to be the kind of portfolio that I do. The students have the option, of course. Final pieces are included there as well, but sometimes pieces along the way showing the journey are included. The idea is to show progress and growth.

How are the items in the portfolio organized?

One is to organize by the subject area of the report card. Another option is to organize them chronologically. And my use of the portfolio evolved over time as well. I started basically with shoeboxes, and just about everything went in there. Then I noticed that having folders would be helpful, so I went to hanging folders as portfolios in a filing cabinet. That's probably the one that I find most useful, because it is easier to organize in terms of classroom space.

How do you use the portfolios?

I use them by sitting with students and talking to them about their work and their learning journey. Usually the last day of the week in a six-day cycle I have a period or two where we say this is our portfolio time. It is important to put it in the timetable, because if I don't put it in the timetable the message would be given that it's not valued. During this time the students have time to select a piece and reflect on it and then to put it in the portfolio. During that time I conference with students who are having some difficulty finding a piece of work. I help them to find it, or if they aren't sure what to write about the piece, I chat with them to help them find a way to reflect on the piece.

I also use them when it comes time for report cards. I sit with the portfolios, just one at a time. It gives the feeling of being with a student's body of work. It allows me to be able go back and forth and make connections in the comments that I make about their work.

The other way I use them that is probably one of the most effective is in student, parent, teacher conferences. I introduce the process by saying, your child is going to show you some of their work and talk about their work, and then I'll make a few comments about what I've noticed and what I may have said in the report card already, or most importantly if you have some comments about the work, you know you can direct those to your child, or if you have some questions for me, I can answer that as well. What is really powerful is when children share their work with their parents. Often parents are getting the work going home, but they're unaware about how much their children accomplish during the day, and often the students themselves are unaware of how much they accomplish during the day as well. Because sometimes if a project is unfinished it feels like we're not making any progress. But you need to go back and look at your journey.

The other way we use portfolios is for portfolio parties. I try to do them once a term, but sometimes it ends up being twice a year, where we basically put the desks in a circle around the room, with the fronts of the desk facing into the circle, and have some spaces there for people to enter. Students are behind their desks and this is where they select pieces, because this is a very public showing of their portfolios. So it isn't the whole portfolio that is on display, although some chose to do that, but I explain to them that you could leave in whatever you want to leave in and take out anything you don't want to show. We invite other classes. Teachers come in with their students and circulate around the room and look at the portfolios, and the students are there showing their work. I invite parents to the showing

(Continued)

day as well. The administration is invited and anyone who had been involved in our learning that term. For example, if we did a unit on cities or if it was an election year and we had had a politician in they would be invited back. I found those portfolio parties really festive times: the students were celebrating and others were celebrating their work as well. So they were really proud.

What else do you notice about how your students use portfolios?

I don't do this every year, but I sometimes have students do their own report card—before I do one. I tell them to sit with your portfolio and just get a sense of yourself, so now you're reporting on your progress. Create a report card using the model we have to use. You make the decisions about what you think you've learned, how you learned, and how you've grown.

is considerable diversity in the nature of portfolios across children and classrooms. In addition to information obtained from observations, interviews, and reading samples as outlined above, portfolios often include

- anecdotal notes
- learning logs
- reading response artifacts
- family information
- (sometimes) the results on standardized reading tests

In short, portfolios can contain the range of data that we've described in this chapter.

When trying to determine what to include in a portfolio, teachers should reflect on the purpose of the portfolio they are building. One of the strengths of portfolio assessment is that it can be used to promote teachers' (and students') reflections concerning children's understandings, attitudes, and reading achievement and abilities (Serafini, 2000/2001). When we take seriously a social constructive approach to reading, we find that children must be included in the assessment process. This involves much more than a change in how assessment is done. It suggests a fundamental change in the way power relationships are constituted between teachers and children. Children participate in decisions not only about what goes into portfolios but also about what counts as "good" reading.

Many teachers ask children to select at least some of the reading samples included in their portfolios. They sit down with children periodically to look at and talk about the reading growth shown in their portfolio samples. Children share their portfolios with their parents when they visit the school. When teaching a new reading **strategy** in the classroom, teachers invite children to comment on whether the strategy works for them and why or why not. These and other comments are included in learning logs in portfolios.

Learning logs are used by children to keep a record of their learning in the classroom. Students' logs generally focus on what they have learned, what they didn't understand, and what they did or didn't like. Teachers use this information to modify plans for subsequent lessons. Teachers can also have students complete their own learning and goal charts to include in the portfolio. For instance, teachers can make a table in which they list in the first column the areas of reading that they are addressing in their teaching (e.g., **fluency**, vocabulary). This list can come from conferencing with students, curriculum guidelines, and/or assessment data. Next to this, children can complete a column entitled "Things I Can Do" (e.g., "I can read chapter books") in which they list what they can do and indicate where there is evidence to demonstrate this ability (e.g., reading response journal). The next column is entitled "Things I Am Working On" (e.g., "I am working on reading informational text"), and the final column is entitled "Goals" (e.g., "I want to be better at understanding what I read in informational books"). In this last column students can also provide a plan for how they will accomplish this goal (e.g., "What I will do: Look at important words and find out what they mean") (Barone & Taylor, 2007, p. 134).

In addition to learning logs, students and/or teachers can complete little forms that they attach to each piece that they enter into the portfolio. On this form the person making the submission can indicate why they've selected this entry, what it is showing, the date, and any other pertinent information that could provide a context and rationale for its inclusion as assessment data. Portfolios can then be used to guide teacher/student conferences and conferences with parents (which can be led by the students themselves).

SUMMARY

Before we can teach someone to read we must first assess what they know, what they are able to do, and what they value. Before we can assess, we must have a clear definition of what it means to read. You have begun to think about your definition of reading, and you have juxtaposed it against some of the key definitions in the field (top-down, bottom-up, interactive, and social constructive perspectives). Recognizing the importance of social interactions and social contexts in learning underlies social constructive theories of reading. We define reading in this book as the active construction of meaning from cues in the text and from the reader's background knowledge within a social context.

Reading assessment is part of a teacher's curricular dialogue. Also part of this dialogue are objectives and standards in provincial and territorial curriculum documents and the forms of assessment (including standardized assessments) that are promoted in a given region.

Teachers need different information to serve as a basis for daily planning, and performance assessment is widely employed for this purpose. This type of assessment focuses on what children do as they read. Checklists and interviews can be used to assess how children use print-based and knowledge-based cues to construct meaning as they read, as well as to assess children's interests. Reading logs are records of what children have read, response journals provide an indication of how children interpret and react to literature, and running records indicate what level of text is "just right" for instruction. Samples of children's oral and silent reading can be collected using informal reading inventories and results provide an indication of their instructional reading level. Examining answers to comprehension questions and oral reading miscues reveals information on children's use of print-based and knowledge-based cues as they read.

Portfolios are collections of artifacts documenting children's reading growth and development over a period of time. Some of these artifacts include checklists, interview data, anecdotal notes, reading and learning logs, written responses to literature, running records, completed projects, and sometimes results on standardized tests. Portfolio assessment can either be completed within a procedural framework, where the focus is on the collecting and scoring of information, or within a process framework, where the focus is on reflection concerning children's understandings, attitudes, and reading abilities.

Assessment must always be multifaceted, reflect the complexity of one's definition of reading, and be focused on student improvement. Teachers must be careful to select assessment measures that are balanced and see children as at-promise.

TALKING POINTS

> Upper elementary teacher Jane Edwards has conducted student-led conferences for years. Read what she has to say about how she and her colleagues organized this practice, and then consider the questions that we pose at the end.

Jane Edwards

While there may be a variety of interpretations within the structure of student-led conferences, this is how our grade 7 teaching team planned for them: The conferences were held during the week leading up to the day when report cards went home in first term. The conferences were held throughout the day as well as one evening during that week. The parents within our school community represented a variety of working hours and we needed to honour that reality.

In our school we had large hallways immediately outside our classroom doors, so a few classroom desks and chairs lined the one side of the hallway during conference week (as well out of the way of daily student hallway traffic as we could provide).

Our vision of a student-led conference was a specific interview time set aside where the student and parent(s) could meet in a one-to-one setting and review the student's portfolio, work folders, art folders, projects, notebooks, electronic portfolio, learning styles, Annual

Education Plan, etc. that the student had worked on throughout the first term. Portfolios were a key component, and we focused on portfolios as an assessment tool in our classroom. In order to feel comfortable with this conference presentation, I would rehearse the prepared agenda with the students. It was usually a four-to-five-page agenda with questions, topics, etc. that the students would address within the conference. It would cover all the subject areas and activities within our program, and allowed spaces for the students to fill in their own ideas, specific project topics, etc. in order to personalize the agenda. The students were more at ease with a prepared agenda/script that allowed for them to share their learning. The agenda also included a space for the parents to make written comments about the conference.

My role as the teacher was to make sure the parents felt welcomed at our conferences. We always had a schedule posted in the classroom to know when each conference was to be held so that the students were ready for their parents' arrival. At the end of the conference I would thank the parents for coming. I did not sit in on the actual conference between the parent and student. Parents knew that having these conferences did not eliminate the parent–teacher conferences that were always held after the report cards went home. I found that parents were far more informed and prepared for the report card and any parent–teacher interviews that followed, and that most importantly the student was at the centre of this process.

All students were required to participate in student-led conferences. My school community was highly multicultural, and it was amazing to see and hear conferences being held in a variety of languages as students shared their work with their parents. If parents were not able to attend we encouraged grandparents, aunts, uncles, older siblings, etc. to attend in their place. We also had staff members who were always eager to be surrogate parents and attend a conference for a student. Because of the conference being a requirement of all students, the approach to participation and engaging students in the process was very positive and encouraging.

Reflecting on Jane Edwards's Student-Led Conference Practice

▷ What learning opportunities do you think this practice might have created for students, families, and teachers?

▷ What role does the portfolio play?

▷ How does the use of the portfolio here compare with the one in John Guiney Yallop's class?

▷ How do the practices of portfolios and student-led conferences compare to the forms of assessment and evaluation that you experienced as a student?

▷ As a teacher, what aspects of these practices are attractive to you? What hesitations might you have? What logistical questions do you have? What more do you want/need to know?

SELECTED PROFESSIONAL RESOURCES

Kathy Hibbert recommends ...

Barone, D. & Taylor, J. M. (2007). *The practical guide to classroom literacy assessment.* Thousand Oaks, CA: Corwin Press.

As the title suggests, this is a very practical guide to conducting a variety of reading assessment protocols. Importantly, the book looks at reading within the totality of all the language arts. Written in an accessible and friendly tone, this is one of those books that teachers might like to keep close to their hip.

Murphy, S. (2001). "'No one has ever grown taller as a result of being measured' revisited: More educational measurement lessons for Canadians." In J. P. Portelli & R. P. Solomon (Eds.), *The erosion of democracy in education: From critique to possibilities* (pp. 145–168). Calgary, AB: Deselig.

Sharon Murphy from York University in Ontario is one of the most authoritative figures working in reading assessment today. To really get at the issues, read her foundational book *Fragile Evidence: A Critique of Reading Assessment* (1998), visit one of her current articles on the web: "Assessment Allegories: A Reflective Essay," in *Language & Literacy*, 8(1). It is available at http://www.langandlit.ualberta.ca/archivesDate.html, or read the chapter listed above. What you'll be sure to leave with after reading Murphy's work is a deepened respect for the complexity of assessment and a heightened awareness of why it's so important.

Swope, K. & Miner, B. (Eds.). (2000). *Failing our kids: Why the testing craze won't fix our schools.* Milwaukee, W: Rethinking Schools Ltd.

This is part of the Rethinking Schools collection that is bound to expand your thinking on teaching and learning. Rethinking Schools began as a grassroots organization made up of a variety of educators who were concerned with certain trends in schools, such as standardized testing, textbook-dominated curricula, and the proliferation of basal readers. Today, they publish wonderful, low-cost educator resources like the one mentioned here. Check out their website at http://www.rethinkingschools.org.

Balanced Reading Instruction: Major Components

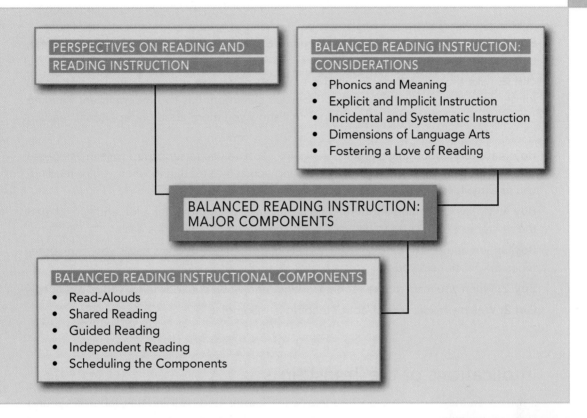

PERSPECTIVES ON READING AND READING INSTRUCTION

BALANCED READING INSTRUCTION: CONSIDERATIONS

- Phonics and Meaning
- Explicit and Implicit Instruction
- Incidental and Systematic Instruction
- Dimensions of Language Arts
- Fostering a Love of Reading

BALANCED READING INSTRUCTION: MAJOR COMPONENTS

BALANCED READING INSTRUCTIONAL COMPONENTS

- Read-Alouds
- Shared Reading
- Guided Reading
- Independent Reading
- Scheduling the Components

STUDENTS' VIEWS OF READING AND READING INSTRUCTION

Long-time teacher Sharon Taberski (1996) has some older, but terrific videos that document her language arts program. The end of the last video shows her students talking about reading and how she has helped them with it. Whenever we listen to children read and talk about their reading, we are offered a "window" into their "literacy" (Rhodes & Shanklin, 1993) and into some of the experiences that may have brought about their learning. We have transcribed some of Taberski's students' comments below. As you read these comments, consider: What are the children illustrating that they know, are able to do, and value about reading?

Child engaged with book

Sharon Taberski's Students on Reading

Girl 1: Sometimes when I have [reading] conferences with Sharon, she helps me so much. It's like she gives me really good books to read.

Boy 1: I think I'm reading better, because I'm not just staying on one book. I'm going on to different levels, and trying my best.

Boy 2: Sharon helps me by like, giving me a hint, or she helps me by telling me to skip the word, or look at the period and stuff. That really makes it go clearer to me, and I understand the book more.

Boy 1: Sometimes when a book is too hard, Sharon reads it first, it's like better for me, because she's read it.

Girl 2: I like the second reading we have, because you can read more in that time; it's a longer period of reading. [Note that Taberski's classroom has two Independent Reading periods, one short and the other long. We'll show you more about independent reading later in this chapter.]

Boy 3: It's very important to practise reading, because you're supposed to learn, because when you're learning, you're actually teaching yourself to read, and when you're reading, you're actually learning, learning a lot, a lot, a lot.

Boy 4: My favourite thing about reading is that I really like mysteries a lot, and when I read the mysteries I have clues to do, so it helps me read more mysteries easier.

Boy 3: Sometimes skipping a word helps you. Sometimes phonics helps you, but sometimes they both help you.

Boy 2: When you read, you're reading writing, and when you're writing, you're reading.

Girl 2: Well my favourite part about reading is *reading*!

Implications of the Transcripts

If you review the list of what good readers do in Chapter 4, you will find that Taberski's young students are exhibiting many of these values, as well as an awareness of a number of these skills and **strategies**. Note that a strategy is an overall, conscious plan for performing a task (e.g., reading) that readers can apply across contexts, while skills may be unconscious, are more context-bound and used in the service of a strategy. Examples of strategies include summarizing and monitoring comprehension. In terms of values, skills, and strategies, in the transcript Taberski's students show

- an appreciation of reading and literature
- the ability to self-assess and to see one's reading progress
- the ability to read progressively more challenging material
- an engagement with reading
- a knowledge of a variety of reading strategies and the use of a variety of cuing systems
- an emphasis on comprehension
- the ability to use oral language (in this case, listening) to help support reading
- the ability to engage in sustained periods of reading

■ the recognition that reading is purposeful and that we learn when we read

■ the ability to use the conventions of a genre for comprehension

■ a recognition of the reciprocal relationship between reading and writing

In looking at this list, the critical questions become: What clues does the transcript offer about what Taberski did with the children that led them to develop these understandings? Furthermore, what could you do with your own students to help them achieve these ends? This chapter is designed to introduce you to a number of the components of balanced reading instruction and to expand on some of the components that you've already encountered. It begins with a look at perspectives on reading and reading instruction and then explores the instructional strategies of Read-Aloud, shared reading, guided reading, and independent reading. □

PERSPECTIVES ON READING AND READING INSTRUCTION

In the last chapter we discussed various perspectives on the nature of reading. What you believe learning to read is like will affect how you decide to teach reading. Think about how you would finish this sentence: Learning to read is like . . . (e.g., building a tower, riding a bike, baking a cake, or dancing) (Weaver, Gillmeister-Krause, & Vento-Zogby, 1996).

When Rachel was a teacher candidate, she got partway through her teacher education program and thought, "I still don't know how to teach reading." She assumed that reading instruction would be something that she could clearly identify as a sequential process that probably focused on phonics and built up to more complex parts of language. She believed that learning to read was like building a big tower, where you put one thing on top of the other and each child's tower was built in the same way. Her own early reading instruction had obviously been from a bottom-up perspective, and she kept looking for this familiar course of instruction. Ironically, Rachel did not actually learn to read through this form of instruction.

Recently, Rachel found a dogeared copy of one of her kindergarten report cards. The report card consisted of a list of criteria next to which the teacher wrote either a "yes" (yes, the criterion had been achieved), a dash (to indicate that the criterion had not been achieved), or an "OK" (which we take to mean progressing toward a "yes"). We've listed some of the highlights from this report below. Rachel's teacher indicated that Rachel

■ recognized at least half the alphabet

■ could write her first name from memory

■ had an "OK" expression of ideas

■ had no phonetic understanding of letters

■ could not rhyme

■ had listening ability and could follow directions

- was "OK" in terms of courtesy
- was "OK" in terms of self-control

Like all report cards, the structure of this report, including what it includes and what it excludes, reflects the dominant views of what were important predictors of reading achievement at a the time that it was written. It also reflects the expectations of what a child of this age could do. What the report never asked and therefore couldn't convey, was that at the time it was written, Rachel was reading whole books independently—something she had learned to do at home through means that looked very much like Cambourne's (1988) conditions for learning. In fact, Rachel's nickname at home was "Rachel Books" as she could always be found with a book tucked under her arm or under her nose. Rachel is not sure if her kindergarten teacher ever recognized that she could read books. She, like all others in her classroom, received the same instruction and learning opportunities at school—regardless of her **funds of knowledge**. So instead of being given books to read during class time, Rachel was given a tedious list of **phonics** sheets (which might explain her struggle with courtesy and self-control!).

This story clearly indicates some of the limitations of the "tower" model of teaching reading and one of its features, which is that every child is treated as though he or she is the same. Through her pre-service language arts program, and then progressively as Rachel began to teach and to think like a teacher, she came to believe that learning to read is not at all like building a tower, but instead akin to learning to swim. The metaphor of swimming is apt given that reading and swimming are both processes where the "whole" is accomplished by a number of different component parts working synergistically. To illustrate, consider Victoria Purcell-Gates's take on the metaphor:

> While moving one's arms in designated ways (termed *swimming strokes*), kicking one's legs in designated ways, and breathing out of the water in designated ways are all component processes of swimming, not one of them alone can be termed *swimming*. Nor can swimming be learned and mastered by practicing and mastering any one of these parts alone [or] by mastering all of these parts separately and then putting them together. Swimming must be learned by actually swimming, all the while coordinating the processing of the component processes so that swimming—and not sinking—is achieved.
>
> Reading and writing are also processes . . . while they are for the most part mental processes . . . they still require the synergistic coordination of component processes to achieve the goal processes of reading and writing. . . . So while the component processes (or skills) of reading—like eye movements, letter and word perception and recognition, decoding, comprehension, and so forth—can be isolated and practiced, they must be used in process for the synergistic workings of each to result in *reading*, defined as comprehension of print. Since the workings of each part of a process look and act differently in process, the individual processes involved in reading and writing must be, and are, learned in process. (2001, pp. 121–122)

Reading instruction, then, must involve numerous opportunities to engage in the actual process of reading, and when the situation demands, opportunities for students to engage in "side-of-the pool" (p. 123) learning, where they are provided with explicit instruction in skills.

In the case of swimming, side-of-the-pool learning might involve improving one's kicks. In reading, it might involve phonics, comprehension strategies, and the like.

Unlike swimming, however, reading is not just a process: it is also a socio-cultural *practice*. Subsequently, teachers must consider the context in which children are learning to read, their funds of knowledge, including the extent to which they have developed the "big picture" of literacy (Purcell-Gates, 1996), and reading engagement. The suggestions for balanced reading instruction that we offer are designed to address this view of learning to read. Please note that these suggestions must be considered within the larger definition of literacy and the balanced literacy framework that is offered in *Constructing Meaning*.

BALANCED READING INSTRUCTION: CONSIDERATIONS

There can be a lot of anxiety tied up with teaching reading. Part of this anxiety comes from the fact that learning to read is usually considered to be one of the most important outcomes of schooling, and we teachers hold a great deal of responsibility for whether children achieve this outcome. It is no wonder that many teachers, particularly new ones, would like a "recipe book" to tell them exactly how to teach reading. Yet this desire for "the answer" can be another source of anxiety, because what professional educators know is that where reading is concerned there is "no quick fix" (Allington & Walmsley, 1995), and any program or model claiming otherwise is just selling "snake oil" (Larson, 2001). Instead, what experts like the International Reading Association tell us is that there is no one way to teach reading, and one of the best opportunities that children have of learning to read is to have knowledgeable teachers who can responsively draw on a variety of methods:

> We believe that there is no single method or single combination of methods that can successfully teach all children to read. As a result, teachers must be familiar with a wide range of instructional methods and have strong knowledge of the children in their classrooms in order to provide the most appropriate instruction for all learners.
>
> Numerous large-scale research studies support the position that children can learn to read from a variety of materials and methods. Though focused studies show that various methods "work," no one of these methods is necessarily better than others.
>
> Controversy about the "best" way to teach reading cannot be resolved by prescribing a single method. Because there is no clearly documented best way to teach beginning reading, educators who are familiar with a wide range of methodologies and who are closest to children must be the ones to make decisions about what instructional methods to use. And further, these professionals must have the flexibility to modify those methods when they determine that particular children are not learning. (n.d., n.p.)

Though there may not be a best way to teach reading, there are a number of key considerations that teachers must balance, and educators have also identified some essential methods to have in one's reading instruction "toolkit." Thus we offer you some issues to consider in the teaching of reading, followed by foundational instructional components from which you can pick and choose as the situation demands. The components are outlined in Figure 5.1, and in this chapter we focus on Read-Aloud, shared reading, guided reading, and independent reading.

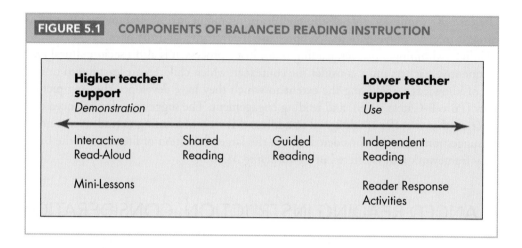

FIGURE 5.1 COMPONENTS OF BALANCED READING INSTRUCTION

TABLE 5.1 **Considerations in Balanced Reading Instruction**

Ownership and Control	
Hierarchical relationships	Collaborative relationships
Teacher ownership	Student ownership
Competition	Cooperation
Phonics and Meaning	
Focus on words	Focus on meaning
Teaching from parts to wholes	Teaching from wholes to parts
Teaching and Use of Language	
Explicit instruction	Creating conditions for learning
Systematic	Incidental
Aspects of Language Arts	
Focus on reading	Focus on all aspects of language
Level of Difficulty	
Common expectations	Different expectations
Relatively easy tasks for automaticity	Challenging tasks for new strategies
Independent learning	Scaffolding

When balance is applied to reading instruction, there are a number of factors that teachers need to consider in their programming (see Table 5.1).

In her study of teacher candidates, Deborah Britzman (2003) identified a number of "cultural myths of teaching." One of these myths is that teachers must absolutely control students' behaviour in class or no learning can happen. It is, therefore, not uncommon for classrooms to be set up so that the major role of students is to listen and the major role of teachers is to tell. For instance, in Chapter 4, teacher John Guiney Yallop talked about how his students found it difficult at first to gauge their own reading progress, because they were used to someone else telling them "if" they could read, and teacher candidate Natalie discussed her experience of being told exactly what she would read in class when she was an elementary student. Social constructivists understand, however, that children's identities, funds of knowledge, and interests are all important mediators of their learning. Cambourne's (1988) conditions also remind us of the importance of children being able to take "responsibility" for their learning. This necessitates that children be given some amount of choice.

What might the role that a teacher takes in balanced reading instruction look like? It is obviously a multifaceted one, including at least the following dimensions, all of which correspond with Cambourne's conditions:

- The teacher is a *provider* of reading resources and an *organizer* of space and time so that children have the opportunities and materials they need for learning (Lindfors, 1987).

- In the role of *demonstrator* (Smith, 1983; Cambourne, 1988), the teacher shows how reading is done (e.g., through a think-aloud in shared reading).

- Reading should be a lifelong activity, and it's important for children to see the teacher's own enthusiasm, process, and questioning as a reader. Thus again in the role of *demonstrator,* teachers need to share their reading lives with their students (Routman, 2003).

- The teacher is a *responder.* When we are reading something new, exciting, or confusing, it is helpful to share it with another. This person can respond to our questions, question us further, support our learning, and let us know how we are doing. That is not the same as judging our performance. Response is productive and occurs as the teacher actively follows what children are trying to do and attempts to further that learning. This is why assessment is a constant in balanced reading instruction.

- In the role of *observer* or "kidwatcher" (Owicki & Goodman, 2002) the teacher gains insight into the children's reading processes and comes to understand what children know, can do, and value.

- In observing, teachers can also learn how to be *catalysts* for engagement (Cambourne, 1988): leading children to want to read and to feel like reading is accessible to them and can be attempted without risk.

As teachers' roles become more consistent with **social constructivism**, children take increasing responsibility for their own reading, moving from Read-Aloud to independent reading and the relationship between teachers and children becomes more collaborative and less hierarchical (Vygotsky, 1978). By working collaboratively in classrooms, children can develop a sense of ownership of both their knowledge and language. By making choices about their reading, children are provided with opportunities to feel like readers—like they belong to the "literacy club" (Smith, 1988).

Phonics and Meaning

Sometimes skills instruction (e.g., explicit phonics instruction) and meaning-based approaches to teaching reading are positioned as a dichotomy—you must do one or the other. In the version of balance that we espouse, however, we take meaning making as the centre of reading, and at the same time recognize the importance of skills, such as phonics skills. In Chapter 2, we discussed cuing systems and demonstrated how the graphophonic system is a primary tool for reading. Teachers must help students acquire all cuing systems and use them in tangent with one another. In fact, most educators now recognize that part of what children need in reading instruction is a context-specific balance between a focus on words and a focus on meaning (e.g., Cunningham & Allington, 2007; Gambrell, Malloy, & Mazzoni, 2007). Purcell-Gates (2001) advocates that teachers consider teaching through a "whole-part-whole" structure, in which children are provided with a context (the focus on meaning) from which teachers can demonstrate how a part of language (e.g., a sound of a particular letter) operates or a specific reading skill (e.g., using the knowledge of the sound of a particular letter) can help one create meaning before showing how the part/skill relates to the whole. For example, using the swimming metaphor, this would mean that children swim (i.e., engage with the "whole" practice), the instructor or swimmer identifies the skill swimmers need to strengthen (e.g., kicks), swimmers go to the side of the pool to strengthen their kicks (the "part"), then return to swimming to implement the improved kicks (i.e., reengage with the "whole"). We presented a sample early literacy lesson plan that used this format in Chapter 3.

Explicit and Implicit Instruction

Teachers also need to strike their own balance between explicit and implicit teaching. Explicit instruction involves teachers presenting knowledge and then having students use that knowledge in new situations (e.g., moving from shared reading to independent reading). Classroom Activity 5.1 shows how explicit instruction can work when applied to strategy instruction. In addition to explicit instruction, teachers need to create the conditions within their classrooms in which children can learn inductively or they can learn the rules or big ideas about reading by experiencing reading in use and then building generalizations. Cambourne's (1988) conditions apply here as well, in particular his condition of immersion.

Ultimately teachers should balance explicit and implicit instruction according to their assessment of what the situation at hand demands. Moreover, we should never assume that children will "just know" how to do something unless we have created the conditions in which they can learn it. Some children, particularly those who are **culturally and linguistically diverse (CLD)**, may require more explicit instruction so that all expectations are clear (Delpit, 2006). On the basis of understandings of social constructivism, however, we know

> ## CLASSROOM ACTIVITY 5.1
>
> ### Example of Explicit Instruction as Applied to Strategy Instruction
>
> 1. Teachers identify what a specific strategy is, explain why the students are learning the strategy and when and where they should use it, and model the strategy to make the mental processes visible to the students. This modelling can be done in a shared reading situation or even in a Read-Aloud.
>
> 2. Teachers involve students in guided practice (e.g., during guided reading) during which teachers provide support but require students to take more and more responsibility for the strategy.
>
> 3. Teachers provide students with opportunities for independent practice and application, monitoring their performance and reinstating support if necessary (e.g., in independent reading time).

Source: Armbruster and Osborn, 2002, p. 70.

too that children need time to explore, experiment, and learn alongside the teacher. Also, even when teachers decide to use explicit instruction, they should expect that no two children will develop exactly the same understanding of what's being taught.

Incidental and Systematic Instruction

Another major question faced by teachers is the degree to which reading skills and strategy instruction should be provided incidentally in mini-lessons or sequentially in a systematic set of planned lessons. Should practice be provided on an occasional basis or on a continuous basis? The answer will depend, as it did for implicit and explicit teaching, on each child's needs.

Sometimes incidental instruction or occasional practice will be sufficient, but often it is not. Many times it is possible to teach skills *as* children read, but again, this is not always the case. Once more, balance is needed. By carefully observing children in the classroom, teachers decide when and how to provide instruction at any point. They also decide how much practice children need in order to generalize skills and strategies to other reading and writing contexts.

Dimensions of Language Arts

Each language art can help to support the development of the others: Reading is no exception. In a study of researchers who had divergent views of how to teach, reading, one of the points that Rona Flippo (2001) found these researchers could agree on was that, insofar as possible, teachers should "use every opportunity to bring reading/writing/talking/listening together so that each feeds off and feeds into the other" (p. 35). You'll note that representing and viewing are missing here, but there is emerging research that demonstrates how representing and viewing also help to support the development of print literacy (Kress, 1997; Pahl, 1999) as well as support students' engagement in literacy practices (Malloy & Gambrell, 2006). Within their curricular dialogue, teachers must decide what is important to emphasize and when.

Many children in language arts classrooms experience daily frustration and are unable to engage in reading learning opportunities, because they are unable to complete tasks that are too difficult for them. Others are not sufficiently challenged to maximize their learning. Only by having learning opportunities at an appropriate level of difficulty will children experience success *and* reach their potential. There are three major ways teachers can achieve this type of balance:

- by adjusting their expectations for performance during the initial stages of learning something new
- by setting different expectations for different children on the same learning task
- by providing different levels of materials and tasks for different children

Each of the reading instruction components that we present in this chapter attempts to provide differing levels of teacher support—ranging from the greatest amount of teacher support (Read-Aloud) to the least amount of teacher support (independent reading). Most components also allow for a degree of **differentiation**—that is, a lesson or activity can allow for children to perform differently on the same learning task. For example, in a kindergarten class, following a Read-Aloud, the teacher might have very different expectations for what children will be able to do with a predictable book once it is read to them. That is,

- Some children will be able to identify words in the book as they reread it.
- Other children may point to the words as another child reads them, developing an understanding of the one-to-one relationship between words in oral and written language.
- Still other children may listen to the book on tape and chime in, developing an understanding of how written language sounds.

In other words, different children do different things with the same book in order to achieve different objectives.

Sometimes, however, the teacher needs to adjust the level of materials and tasks for different children and different situations. For example, an important goal for all children is to become fluent, automatic readers. One way of helping children to achieve this is to create opportunities for them to read and reread texts that they can easily handle independently. At the same time, children will not progress without engaging with texts that challenge them. At least some of the time they need to be working in their **zone of proximal development** (Vygotsky, 1978), that is, a level that is just beyond where they can work independently. Such texts are perfect to use in a guided reading setting. This type of support is frequently referred to as **scaffolding** to refer to interaction between young children and their mothers, in which the mothers support their children "in achieving an intended outcome" (Bruner, 1975, p. 12). The children decide to do something and the mothers provide the assistance (such as a helping hand, gesture, or word) that allows the children to manage to do it. In schools, teachers use scaffolds as temporary supports to help children extend their skills and knowledge to a higher level of competence (Dorn & Soffos, 2001).

We encourage you to think about the reading instruction components in Figure 5.1 as a gradual "handover of responsibility" (Routman, 2003, p. 44) from teacher to student. Read-Aloud offers the highest degree of teacher support and is consistent with Cambourne's (1988) immersion (e.g., being immersed in language) and demonstration. Shared reading is a "shared demonstration" (Routman, 2003, p. 44) and allows students to "approximate" the demonstration and to receive important "response" on their attempts (Cambourne, 1988). Guided reading marks a shift to a greater amount of responsibility for the students, and this transitions into independent reading, in which there is the least amount of teacher support and the greatest opportunity for readers to "use" (Cambourne, 1988) or "practice" (Routman, 2003, p. 44) what they have been observing and approximating. Thinking about the components in this way can help teachers plan and carry out important learning opportunities for students. For instance, upper-elementary teacher Cory Woodrow (see Teacher Wisdom box) uses the components in a handover of responsibility fashion to structure her language arts program.

Fostering a Love of Reading

A final important consideration here is that for children to read and to keep on reading, they have to feel that the practice is forwarding the purposes of their lives (Cambourne, 1988). Cambourne's notion of engagement tells us about the importance of pleasure, and

TEACHER WISDOM

CORY WOODROW AND PLANNING FOR INSTRUCTION

How do you plan for language arts in your classroom?

Literacy is rooted in who children are within their community. How they communicate is based upon how they view themselves and is connected to their prior experiences and culture. It becomes essential, then, that teachers know who their students are to teach and assess them. It is vital that upper elementary teachers have a sense of where their students have come from and what they bring with them. The [provincial curriculum I use] is certainly a continuum of skills, and [middle and upper elementary teachers] should see themselves as building upon the work of primary teachers.

When I started teaching, I had a gut feeling that, more [significant] than any [instructional] strategy I could implement, students would need to feel safe and supported within their learning environment to become literate. This was based on my own school experiences, and I certainly feel it has been backed up by the professional reading I have done in the last few years. It seems to me that regardless of the curriculum we follow, or the trends in education we are trying to implement, we need to remember that we are teaching children [first], not skills. We need to provide a safe place for children to develop, and to consider that we are fostering literate learners for life. Contemplating the bigger picture can sometimes make my job seem overwhelming, but also exciting and meaningful at the same time.

At the beginning of the year I gather data on my students from Developmental Reading Assessment scores (DRA) (Beaver, 2001), past report cards, and by speaking with previous classroom and resource teachers. In terms of curriculum, I group expectations that naturally fit for oral communication, reading, writing, and media literacy [which includes viewing and representing], and then align them with texts I plan to use. I also look for connections to other subjects. For example, skills required for writing nonfiction texts could be developed in language time in preparation for [an] animal research for a unit.

When I get to specific planning, I consider the gradual release of responsibility. That is, for each required skill, first I model it, then the students practise it in a shared experience, then I support the development of the skills by guiding students, and finally I give them independent practice.

our instructional strategies must never forget this principle. For, as Louise Spear-Swerling, a professor of special education, and Robert Sternberg, a professor of psychology, have found,

> Children must indeed acquire accurate and automatic word-recognition skills in order to progress in reading acquisition. … But their engagement with text and their interest in reading also push forward their decoding skills. … Children become "hooked" not on phonics, but on stories, books, and ideas. (Spear-Swerling & Sternberg cited in Gangi, 2004)

> **BOX 5.1**   **WHAT TEACHERS CAN DO TO FOSTER A LOVE OF READING**
>
> ▷ Find texts that you love and get "caught" reading by students (demonstration) (Routman, 1991).
>
> ▷ Make a high volume of texts accessible to readers (immersion) (Allington, 2006).
>
> ▷ Give readers ample time to read (use) (Allington, 2001).
>
> ▷ Give readers chances to share what they're reading and to respond to their reading (response) (Daniels, 2002).
>
> ▷ Allow readers choices that are high-quality and that suit them and the situation (e.g., difficult texts for Read-Alouds and shared reading, slightly challenging-level texts for guided reading, and easier texts for independent reading) (responsibility & engagement).

Source: Daniels, 2002; Taberski, 2000.

Box 5.1 offers a quick glance at some of the ways teachers can foster a love of reading in their students. This list also includes in parentheses the conditions from Cambourne (1988) that the various strategies can fulfill.

BALANCED READING INSTRUCTIONAL COMPONENTS

Read-Aloud

In Chapter 3 we discussed Read-Alouds within the context of early literacy. We now build on that information to demonstrate how Read-Alouds can be used across the elementary panel. All the reasons for conducting Read-Alouds that we listed in Chapter 3 remain for children in middle and upper elementary. In fact, research shows that readers of all levels and ages can benefit in a variety of ways from participating in Read-Alouds (Blessing, 2005; Lesesne, 2006). It seems that, even beyond teachers modelling for students *how* to read (Routman, 2003) and giving them exposure to new texts and content that they might not otherwise choose to read or be able to read independently, Read-Alouds can also demonstrate that we teachers have a passion for reading. This sharing of our "reading lives" with others can help to bond us to students (Routman, 2003) and illustrate our "expectation" (Cambourne, 1988) that reading is a lifelong endeavour that can be pleasurable and enriching. To illustrate the "real-life" importance of Read-Aloud, consider the case of David and Jacquie, two upper elementary students whom Betsy Reilly (from Chapter 1) taught in first grade.

Recently we asked David and Jacquie about some of their views on reading instruction and learning (see Box 5.2). In grade 1, one student found reading easy, while the other needed some time and extra teacher support for reading to "click." Despite their different reading profiles, these students expressed similar views about the kinds of experiences that helped them to become avid readers. As you read through our interviews with the students, think about what kind of foundation Betsy must have established for her class, and notice what David and Jacquie draw our attention to through what they decide to include (and exclude) in their responses. From this, you might want to think about the implications for your own teaching of reading.

In Chapter 1 we met teacher Betsy Reilly. We asked two of her former students, David and Jacquie, who are now in upper elementary, to respond to a survey and to talk about their reading experiences. Here is some of what they shared with us. Note that while we have listed the students' responses together, David and Jacquie were not together when they responded to these questions.

1. What experiences have you benefited from most in language arts?

   David: Our teachers reading aloud—if they are good readers. . . . Ms. Reilly read [*The*] *Secret Garden* (Burnett, 1962) to us, and I loved that.

   Jacquie: Read-Aloud. I have benefited the most from the books that were read to me.

2. What is one pet peeve you have about what teachers do (that teachers should avoid)?

   David: When you read a book to the class make it interesting: it should be a good book and the teacher should be a good reader to bring the characters to life.

3. What started you on your literacy journey or were you always interested in reading?

   David: My mom started me. I loved when stories were read aloud to me, and I wasn't so interested in reading myself at first. I listened to stories on CD at night and still like to do that. For example, I listened to [*Lemony Snicket*] (Snicket, 2002).

   Jacquie: [I remember] really wanting to be able to read "little books" at home by myself, and I will [always] remember grade 1 and [being read] *The Secret Garden* and *The Trumpet of the Swan* (White, 1970).

Conducting Read-Alouds

Out of all of the experiences that David and Jacquie have had around reading, they both identified being read to as significant; and out of all of the teachers they have had and texts they have been exposed to, it is Betsy's Read-Alouds that they remember and share. So what might it be about how Betsy conducted Read-Alouds that stuck with David and Jacquie, and how can you conduct Read-Alouds to similarly entice your students?

Read-Alouds can be conducted throughout the elementary years in the ways that we suggested in Chapter 3. Additionally, Read-Alouds can be used to highlight one or a combination of the following:

- to introduce students to a new unit or topic (Lesesne, 2006)
- to introduce students to a new author, series, or genre
- to highlight the aesthetic quality of a text

- to simply provide pleasure to listeners (Lesesne, 2006)
- to model specific skills and strategies (e.g., context clues, word attack skills, or main idea) (Lesesne, 2006)
- to demonstrate a proficient reader's thinking as s/he reads (Routman, 2003)
- to create an effect in students such as to settle them after recess or get them excited for a new lesson or activity

While Read-Alouds are usually done with a whole group, they can be conducted with a small group. They can also take the form of students listening to a book on tape or CD or MP3 (Lesesne, 2006).

Here are a few more tips on how to conduct Read-Alouds:

- Always pre-read a text that you are planning to read for a Read-Aloud, and be sure to plan out how you will read it (e.g., what you want to emphasize, what kind of voice you will use if you are going to switch into character, and where you're going to leave off so that you finish with your students wanting more) (Reid, 2007).
- Practise how you will show any illustrations (Braxton, 2007a).
- When you're reading to older students, you'll likely need to talk with them about why you're reading aloud to them, as this might be an unfamiliar practice for them (Blessing, 2005).
- Be sure to let students get physically comfortable for the reading. Younger students may appreciate being able to cuddle up with a stuffed toy (Braxton, 2007b). Many students, even those beyond the early elementary years, might also like to get together on the carpet for the reading. Middle elementary teacher Kathy Gillies, for instance, keeps a specific read-aloud space in her classroom that is carpeted and contains a rocking chair (see photo).

Rocking chair in a Read-Aloud space

- Signal in some way to your students that it is time for Read-Aloud. You can do this in a variety of creative ways, including: "Light a candle or a soft-globe lamp at the beginning of the story so that the children know that they cannot speak unless invited, until the candle flame is blown out"; "Create a short verse or a finger play … in which the children can join in as they settle"; "Put on your storytelling cloak and hat" (Braxton, 2007b, p. 56); play the beginning of some music or introduce an interesting prop that goes with the text.
- Some students are better listeners when they're allowed to doodle. If students are doodling, you can encourage them to draw what they're hearing (Blessing, 2005).
- Some students may need the accommodation of having the text in front of them. Be ready to allow this (Reid, 2007).

▨ If this is the first time in a long while that your students have been read aloud to, begin with something short like a short story, magazine article, or poem (Blessing, 2005).

▨ While you're reading, be sure to monitor your students' reactions so that you can adjust your reading if you're not getting the response you had hoped for (Blessing, 2005).

▨ Watch the tempo of your reading. Your students will be able to better follow you if you read slower than your normal speaking voice (Braxton, 2007b).

▨ Use every opportunity to allow students to interact with the text during the Read-Aloud. Identify if there is a line or phrase that they might repeat; pause when and if appropriate and have students predict what might come next; and think aloud about your own predictions and indicate what clues are leading you to think in this way (Braxton, 2007b). Be sure, however, not to interrupt the text too often or this could ruin the flow of the reading (which is something that seven-year old Rene Haller told us when she was describing why she prefers Read-Aloud at home to Read-Aloud at school).

▨ Finally, have fun, and don't worry too much about a perfect reading. You can use any blooper as an opportunity to demonstrate your own process as a reader, which will undoubtedly serve your students well (Braxton, 2007b).

Selecting Materials

When selecting materials for Read-Alouds, teachers have many options and their situation can help guide their choices. First is the need for teachers to select high-quality texts that represent a variety of genres "with which students can identify" (Routman, 2003, p. 20). Think about your students' background knowledge and pay attention to what texts can "expand this knowledge" (p. 20), while also allowing opportunities for some degree of accessibility so that students can understand what is being read to them. As you survey a selection, question what kinds of learning opportunities or experiences the text might create. Then ask yourself: Is the text's content and language appropriate? How might the text relate to the demographics and funds of knowledge of my group? (E.g., "Is the gender of the protagonist likely to appeal to most of the group?") (Blessing, 2005, p. 44.) Consider whether you can engage with the text; if you can't, chances are you will not be a very engaging reader for your audience. You'll also want to select your texts on the basis of whether you're reading to early, middle, or late elementary students.

Many early elementary children, librarian Barbara Braxton (2007a) tells us, enjoy "rhyme and repetition" and "themes of families, friends, pets, animals, toys, and teddies" (p. 52). When selecting theme-based texts, consider what kinds of issues your students are experiencing and draw on texts with these themes. Note that many fiction texts for children of this age will anthropomorphize animals and have these characters play out the concerns of young children. Think, for instance, of books like *The Bike Lesson* (Berenstain & Berenstain, 1964), part of the classic Berenstain Bears series. Learning to ride a two-wheeler is certainly a topic that will be on the mind of much of the class! (For more on the Berenstain Bears, see their official website at http://www.berenstainbears.com). Routman (2003) also reminds us of Betsy Reilly's lesson that young children can benefit from Read-Alouds of chapter books. While Braxton doesn't disagree outright with this, she does suggest that it might be best to select texts that can be completed in one session. She also, however, offers a compromise by saying,

> Publishers are now very aware of the needs of students who want more than a picture book but are not quite ready for serializations read over time, so there are many series now available in novel format where each chapter is a complete episode within itself. (2007a, p. 52)

Teachers should use their own best judgment when using longer texts with their students. Just imagine what David and Jacquie would have missed if Betsy had not read them chapter books in grade 1. When selecting longer books, consider which have natural breaks or good places to pause between one reading session and another, and consider when your students might be ready for such an experience.

Another consideration when selecting materials for young children is the quality of the illustrations or other visual information to accompany the print. Young, inexperienced, and/or CLD learners, for instance, can be offered great support for comprehension when the picture matches the oral story. Strong visuals can, in fact, "orient" (Braxton, 2007a, p. 52) readers and provide a concrete reference point for what might be an unfamiliar concept.

Middle elementary students can benefit from slightly more sophisticated material than their younger counterparts. Braxton has found that these children still like animals, but their interest in them has shifted. Instead of stories where animals are anthropomorphized, middle-years students tend to prefer to learn *about* animals. This is where nonfiction texts can find a natural place. Adventures and mysteries can be favourites, provided their plots are not too complicated. Horror and fantasy can also be favourites, but children tend to prefer to "identify with the characters or visualize themselves in the story" in such a way that "the underlying theme is one of a vicarious empowerment that readers do not have yet in real life" (p. 52).

Upper elementary students, like students of all ages, can benefit from Read-Alouds of texts of all genres. This, however, can be slightly more challenging, as Routman (2003) has discovered that many upper elementary students have come to "believe that if it's not a chapter book, it's not acceptable" (p. 21). Braxton (2007a) also notes that finding a text for a whole class at this age is difficult, because most students' tastes are now fairly well established. Nonetheless, Routman (2003) includes picture and poetry books in her repertoire, but she selects them carefully. One of her favourites to read aloud is *Jorge: On Both Sides of the River* (Median, 1999), which she describes as "a touching book of poems in English and Spanish that deals with respect for one's culture" (Routman, 2003, p. 21).

In general, Braxton (2007a) has found that teachers conducting a Read-Aloud with upper elementary students are likely to find success with texts that deal with time travel (both forward and back) and historical fiction that can tie in with other areas of the curriculum. Humour can also be a popular choice. Unfortunately, humorous texts are hard to come by, and when teachers do find them they need to proceed with caution: some of the material, while funny to students, might need to be edited when you're reading aloud to a whole class. Librarian Rob Reid (2006) has a whole list of potentially useful titles. Some of his favourites include: a collection of short stories entitled *First French Kiss and Other Traumas* (Bagdasarian, 2002) and a collection of tabloid stories called, *Bat Boy Lives! The Weekly World News Guide to Politics, Culture, Celebrities, Alien Abductions, and the Mutant Freaks That Shape Our World* (Perel, 2005).

Braxton (2007a) also points out that many upper elementary students are quite aware of world issues (both current and historical), and might find texts that are issues-oriented very appealing. Accounts of the Holocaust, for example, would fall into this category. These kinds of texts can be very important for us to expose our students to, as

> What is at stake in these texts is not just the provision of information and the humanization of impersonal historical accounts and statistics. . . . Our hope is that stories of persecution and suffering will become part of a remembrance that will have some progressive, moral force. This hope is based on the familiar assumption that literature has the power to facilitate an ethical sense which enhances a concern for others, responsibility to the values of diversity and human rights, and a sense of hope that, while developing the capacity to look life in the face, maintains a vigilance against injustice. (Simon & Simon, 1995, p. 27)

At the same time, we must remember that many of these texts are "risky" (Simon & Simon, 1995), in that they may deal with difficult and sensitive subjects (e.g., violence) that can be traumatic for children to witness and can be easily misconstrued. When considering using risky material, teachers need to use their own critical literacy skills to ask questions about the text, the readers, and the context in which they are going to be conducting the Read-Aloud. They need to

- consider the developmental level and background knowledge and experience of the readers
- select texts that are historically accurate
- select texts that avoid vivid descriptions of violence and cruelty
- select texts that focus on the strength of the human spirit and people's incredible efforts to preserve human dignity and life (Simon & Simon, 1995)

Two classic examples of fiction that fit this bill are:

- *The Diary of a Young Girl: Anne Frank* (Frank, 1952). This book confronts the reader with "individual death and suffering," yet "there are no scenes directly dealing with the Nazi practices of systematic degradation and genocide. . . . The focus is on Ann's sensitivity, intelligence and hopeful outlook, without any direct confrontation with the realities of genocide that lead to her death" (Simon & Simon, 1995, p. 28).
- *Sadako and the Thousand Paper Cranes* (Coerr, 1977), which is about a child who develops leukemia as part of the aftermath of the A-bomb being dropped in Hiroshima. This "is a story through which children can celebrate human courage and optimism while keeping the realities of mass destruction contained in the abstractions of 'war' or 'the bomb'" (Simon & Simon, 1995, p. 29).

Text selection is, of course, only one part of the equation when dealing with risky texts. The context you set as a teacher will also guide their appropriate use. For that reason, consider the following when you're thinking about using a risky text within any reading instruction component:

- Use the book when the class feels like a community (e.g., you've gotten to know each other and you feel safe with each other).
- Use the book when you have time to really deal with the issues.
- Prepare children by providing a context for the content of the text (e.g., embedded within a unit of study).

- Be ready for the fact that risky texts may disrupt the practices of school that children normally experience (Simon & Simon, 1995).

- Structure opportunities for readers to respond to the text.

- Structure response activities to allow responses at a variety of levels.

- Anticipate the kinds of questions that children will ask.

- Take the time to debrief the response activities.

- Help your students to read critically, that is, with an eye to putting the text and its reading in context and questioning how equity and social justice operate within these.

- Think about the kinds of experiences that your students are likely to have had in the past (e.g., experiences with war) or the present (e.g., experiences with violence in the home) that might make certain texts or issues particularly risky for them, and consider if you are able to offer the degree of support that might be necessary to deal with their needs.

Shared Reading

As we discussed in Chapter 3, shared reading is very similar to Read-Aloud. Both are usually conducted with a text that would be at a frustration level if the child were to attempt to read it alone (Rog, 2003). Different, however, is that shared reading involves the teacher reading *with* rather than *to* students. During shared reading, children may read aloud with the teacher, follow along silently, or chime in at appropriate points (e.g., teachers can conduct an oral cloze where they pause and have students fill in the gaps) (Routman, 2003). This requires that everyone can see the text. Early elementary grades typically use Big Books or charts for this reading. Older elementary grades normally use overheads or Smartboard (though, of course, these too are appropriate to use with early elementary students). If students have their own copies of the text, be sure to still use a master copy that everyone can see so that when appropriate you can draw their attention to specific features of the text (e.g., you might want to use the example of a compound word to talk about strategies for decoding unknown words, or you might want to show how different levels of headings work in an information text).

The goals of shared reading are for teachers to support children in reading the text and to model what good readers do when they are reading and the going gets a bit tough (e.g., "What do I do when I come to a word I don't know?"). Shared reading is therefore an opportunity to share with students how to use reading strategies in the construction of meaning. Sharon Taberski (1996; 2000) uses Read-Aloud and shared reading to work with the whole class before she meets in guided reading groups, where students have the chance to practise using these strategies in smaller, targeted groups. Again, think of how to demonstrate what you would like children to do, then move into giving them the chance to do this with a gradual handover of responsibility. In the Teacher Wisdom box below, Graham DeVeber, whom you met in Chapter 4, talks about the importance of making explicit and concrete the various strategies that can help children become better readers.

Ironically, Graham's advice to read like nobody's listening is given in a context where he's happy that his students are listening to his think aloud. What we understand from Graham is that teachers need to abandon their self-consciousness and share their processes with their students. The first step in being able to do this is to understand what our processes actually

TEACHER WISDOM

GRAHAM DEVEBER AND MODELLING

What is the greatest piece of advice you could give to a new language arts teacher (or the greatest piece of advice you've been given and you want to pass along)?

Over the last two years we [in the school district] have been looking at [language arts instruction] very carefully, and I think what I've discovered is the importance of one word said three times: model, model, model. If it's reading, whether it's Shared Reading or Read-Aloud, I talk a lot to the students about the processes. What am I doing in my head? So that it's not just reading. We're talking about the process, and modelling. What is an effective reader? What does an effective reader do? It's akin to dealing with your own children. I firmly believe that my own children don't necessarily listen to what I say, but they are keenly aware of what [I] do. The children in the classroom sit there for 5 hours a day and they watch us in the minutest detail, and they follow more what we do, I think then what we say. Model, model, model. Sometimes you feel a little silly. I find it hard if there is a grownup in my class, because I feel like I'm talking to myself all the time: "Oh, look at this, these words all start with the same letter. P-p-p-p. Well, isn't that interesting? That sounds like the engine." So you're talking to yourself all the time. And just out loud, so they can hear the processes involved in reading and writing. On my wall over there, there is a sticker, "Sing like no one is listening" and I enjoy singing like no one is listening. But I think we also have to write like no one is listening, so I'll write on the board as if nobody's there, I'm talking to myself. I'll read, and I'll interrupt myself as if nobody's listening. So it's sing like nobody is listening, read like nobody is listening, write like nobody's listening.

are. Take a moment to ask yourself some questions that you might pose to your own students about their metacognition and reading, such as:

- How do you know when you come across an idea in reading that you can't understand? What do you do about it?
- How do you decide what the most important ideas are to remember from reading?
- Where and when do you read easily?
- What types of texts are easiest/most difficult for you?
- What do you do when you come to a word you don't know in reading? (Rhodes & Shanklin, 1993.)

How many of these strategies did you think of? Don't worry if you're unsure of your own reading process. Bringing your awareness to the tacit strategies that you use in your reading is the first step to supporting others in developing their own.

Guided Reading

Guided reading is a prime reading instruction component for intensively working with children on reading strategies for making meaning. Drawing on the work of New Zealand educators such as Marie Clay (1993), educators Irene Fountas & Gay Su Pinnell (1996) developed guided reading to help children become strategic, independent, and self-extending readers. At the same time, other educators have developed their own ways of conducting guided reading. Figure 5.2, for instance, shows our interpretation of how Taberski (1996) uses guided reading within the context of her whole reading program and how these components relate to some of Cambourne's (1988) conditions.

Regardless of the exact form guided reading may take, its goals remain the same:

- to reinforce skills and strategies
- to engage children in questioning and discussion
- to allow the teacher to be a guide (e.g., selects texts and strategies to target)
- to allow the child to do the reading with the teacher as supporter

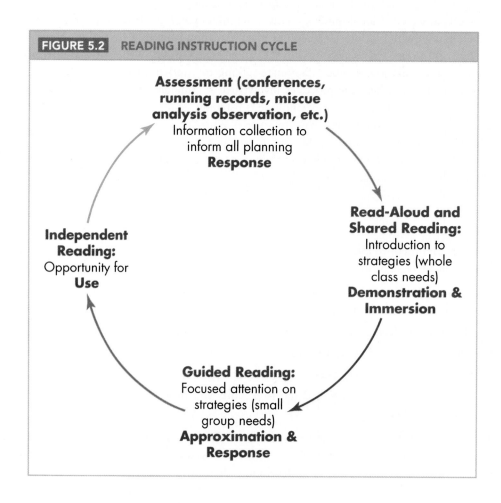

FIGURE 5.2 **READING INSTRUCTION CYCLE**

Assessment (conferences, running records, miscue analysis observation, etc.)
Information collection to inform all planning
Response

Read-Aloud and Shared Reading:
Introduction to strategies (whole class needs)
Demonstration & Immersion

Guided Reading:
Focused attention on strategies (small group needs)
Approximation & Response

Independent Reading:
Opportunity for **Use**

- to build independence in reading that can cross over into independent reading time (Rigby, n.d.).

The main questions you will need to answer to decide how you would like to conduct guided reading within the context of your own teaching situation include the following:

- How can guided reading sessions be run (e.g., What are the procedures teachers can use?)?
- How may groups be formed?
- How may texts be selected?

Running Guided Reading Sessions

At both the primary and upper elementary levels, guided reading usually involves intensive work with a small group of students using materials at a moderate degree of difficulty. By assessing students' reading, teachers identify what their students should be working on. Then teachers can follow steps like these:

- *Introduce the text to students.* The introduction is intended to create interest, raise questions, prompt expectations, and highlight or foreshadow information, concepts and strategies.
- *Read the text.* At the primary level, children read quietly or silently, while at the upper elementary level they read silently. While the children read, the teacher confers with individual children. A child is asked to read aloud, and the teacher observes and notes how the child is processing text, occasionally providing guidance in use of reading strategies. At the upper elementary level, the teacher might ask children to make notes on their reading in lieu of individual conferences.
- *Discuss and revisit the text.* Following the reading of the text, the children discuss what they read and the problem-solving strategies they used. They might reread a portion of the text to provide evidence for their thinking.
- *Teach for processing strategies.* The teacher selects a strategy that the students need further help with, and explains and demonstrates the strategy.
- *Extend understanding* (optional): The children might extend their understanding through reading response activities and drama.

Forming Guided Reading Groups

Many educators today conduct a reading assessment such as a DRA with their students and then place them into guided reading groups this way. Teachers might also use less formal assessment measures such as **running records** (with or without **miscue** analysis). Taberski (1996) combines running records, information from reading conferences, and her observations of students during all the reading instruction components in her literacy program to decide which students might need to work on similar strategies. When grouping students this way, teachers are able to put children together not just according to a level from a test but also by analyzing qualitative data about what children are (or aren't) actually doing in their reading and what they might need to work on next. Accordingly, you might decide that five students should go together because they all need help using text features to improve their comprehension of reading information texts. These students might, however, all score differently on the DRA (Beaver, 2001). If you do group students in ways that aren't just about levels, during the reading portion of the guided reading session you can do as Taberski (1996) has, having some students read independently, and reading along with others to support them.

No matter how you put readers together, remember that guided reading groups are not like the old "round robin" reading groups of yesteryear. Groups today should be flexible and short-term, and always capitalize on children's funds of knowledge (i.e., all the "low" children shouldn't always be lumped together).

Selecting Texts

Teachers should select texts that go hand-in-hand with the types of strategies that they want children to work on. For instance, Taberski (1996) selects series books and mysteries to help children understand how using the structure of various genres can boost comprehension. When selecting texts for guided reading, teachers will want to ask themselves:

- Is the text within the student's zone of proximal development?
- Is the text something the child would find engaging?
- Does the text tie in with what's being studied in other parts of the curriculum?
- Does the child have the background knowledge to access the text?
- What genre is the text?
- How long is the text?
- What is the text's layout like?
- Does the text contain supportive visuals?
- Is the text's use of language appropriate (e.g., vocabulary)?

Additional Considerations

Recently Rachel participated in a professional development day with elementary teachers who came from variety of school districts. She asked the teachers to identify what they felt they did well in their balanced literacy program. A number of teachers said they felt guided reading was something that they had come to feel confident about. When the teachers started to talk about what they did with guided reading, a heated discussion ensued, with teachers disagreeing about what they felt "really" counted as such. One group felt guided reading had to be done with levelled texts; another said no, it could be done with any literature that addressed the group's specific needs. So who was right? In our estimation, both were. Effective guided reading instruction depends less on "doing guided reading the one right way" and more on reflecting on the purposes of the instruction, most particularly which strategies you feel your students need to work on. We recommend that teachers critically examine all instructional components in relation to both the needs of the children in their classrooms and the curriculum guidelines for their jurisdictions. Also, teachers need to communicate to their students before, during, and after guided reading what the goals of the instruction are. For example, no reading program will be effective unless both teachers and students understand what a strategy involves as well as why, how, and when to use the strategy. Strategy instruction will not reach its potential of developing active, strategic readers unless it is taught in a thoughtful, responsive way (Villaume & Brabham, 2002).

Independent Reading

Independent reading (i.e., in which children select their own texts and read on their own) provides opportunities for children to practise or "use" (Cambourne, 1988) what they have been learning in the other components of the balanced reading program. This time for use is critical to children's reading achievement, as Allington (2006) has found that time spent reading is positively correlated with reading achievement. Allowing time for children to read also indicates to them that reading is a valuable activity (Rigby, n.d.), and it helps to provide for reading practice that children might not get outside of school. Another noteworthy opportunity created by independent reading is the benefit of helping foster students' engagement with reading and in turn, with school in general (Clausen-Grace & Kelley, 2007). The notion of engagement is of prime concern as children progress through elementary school, because the "proportion of students who are not engaged or motivated by their school experiences grows at every grade level and reaches epidemic proportions in high school" (Biancarosa & Snow, 2004, p. 9).

Materials for Independent Reading

One of the first considerations for setting up independent reading is ensuring that there are ample texts available from which children may select. Generally, children should be encouraged to read texts that they can handle independently, that is, read with about 96 to 100 percent accuracy (Rog, 2003). However, there may be times when it is appropriate for children to select texts that might seem to us to be more advanced than we might initially think the children can handle. These times include when children are intensely interested in a subject, know the content well, or are supported through visuals. What's important is that children have guided choice and that a large variety of texts are highly accessible to them (Allington, 2006). When you're building your classroom library of texts, think of including:

- multilevel books
- books from a variety of genres (e.g., information and fictional texts)
- series books
- books that draw on a variety of modes (e.g., graphic novels and hypertexts that can be read on the computer)
- reference material (e.g., dictionaries, thesauruses, online encyclopedias)
- student publications (e.g., Language Experience Approach stories, class books, newsletters, etc.)
- magazines (print and online)
- comics

Classroom library

Accessibility can mean that there are texts at arm's length, titles and covers are clearly visible and inviting, texts are well organized so that students can find what they want, there are ample opportunities to browse and borrow texts, there is a high volume of texts, and generally texts are embedded in the entire structure of the classroom.

To further make texts and text selection accessible, consider:

- Storing texts in tubs or on shelves and have them organized by theme, authors, series, favourite characters, or some other organizational structure that makes sense to you and that you have introduced to the class.

- Showcasing a selection of texts with their covers showing by placing them in plastic rain gutters that are affixed to the wall. Rachel found that running the gutters under the chalkboard worked really well (for installation directions, see Cunningham, Hall & Gambrell, 2002, p. 36).

- Creating book crates or baskets that can rotate through groups of desks or students that contain a selection of material that goes with a theme, topic, or reading level and that can literally be kept at arm's length to the students.

- Creating a classroom library that is well stocked and contains space for browsing and relaxed reading. The photo here shows the classroom library that Kathy Gillies has built over the years. In Chapter 13 we give some tips for building your own library, which can be a daunting (but exciting) task when you're starting out.

To match books to readers, a number of educators first conduct an assessment like a DRA (Beaver, 2001), and then have students pick from a selection of books that come with a level from the publishers or that have been levelled by the teacher using a guide such as Fountas and Pinnell's (2006). While we have mentioned that it is certainly important for children to have time every day to read books that are at their independent reading level, we do not advise text selection that is solely or even primarily based on level only, because of a number of factors related to the nature of reading and what is required for children to be proficient, independent readers. Readers' funds of knowledge, culture, identity, language, interests, and the like all have an effect on how easy or difficult it is for readers to access specific texts. Readers' profiles, however, are not part of levelling. Levelling occurs in a variety of fashions, but is most commonly related to readability levels, which are calculated through "a formula that measures sentence difficulty and word difficulty"; levelling can also be the result of applying "multiple criteria related to language predictability, text formatting, and content" (Dzaldov & Peterson, 2005, p. 222). Either of these forms of levelling seems to be premised on and promotes the belief that "the diversity of students' social, cultural, and experiential backgrounds can be whitewashed when matching readers to books" (p. 222).

Also problematic with levelling is that today there seems to be a widespread "levelling mania," in which levels are placed on "every text that students encounter during their school day" (Dzaldov & Peterson, 2005, p. 222), including library books (Hedrick, 2006). This reduces children's exposure to the variety of texts that are necessary for a balanced literacy program, and it can lead some students to resist reading because they are embarrassed to be reading within "their" level only (Hedrick, 2006). Levelling can also restrict the amount of high quality children's literature and authentic texts that make it into the hands of readers, even though we know that such texts are necessary for attracting and sustaining readers (Bowen, 2006). Lastly, by restricting or even eradicating readers' choices in text selection, Cambourne's (1988) condition of responsibility is not likely to be fulfilled and readers are not supported to learn how to make good decisions for themselves. So what's a teacher to do?

First, we need to acknowledge that levelling texts can be a useful practice, but it's how we use these texts that can make the difference between balanced and unbalanced reading instruction. Teachers, for instance, can combine levelling with interest inventories to help capitalize on readers' background knowledge and interests when facilitating text selections (Clausen-Grace & Kelley, 2007). Next, teachers can reserve levelled texts that are combined with interest inventories for only some parts of their balanced reading program. Guided reading might be the most appropriate component for these types of texts (Dzaldov & Peterson, 2005). Perhaps most importantly, teachers can implement a variety of strategies to help readers select texts during independent reading time that are appropriate for them. Box 5.3 shows two versions of similar strategies for text selection to share with your students. The first requires that readers spend some time with a book before deciding on its suitability. The second provides more of a quick scan of the book for suitability.

Running Independent Reading Time

There are many ways to run independent reading time. You can make this time more or less structured depending on your goals. Essentially, independent reading is an opportunity for

---

BOX 5.3   STRATEGIES FOR TEXT SELECTION

Routman's (2003) Goldilocks Strategy
Easy Books

Ask yourself these questions. If you answer yes, this book is probably an easy book for you. EASY books help you to read more smoothly and are fun to read aloud and silently.

▷ Is it a favourite book you have read before?

▷ Do you understand the story (text) well?

▷ Do you know (can you understand and read) just about every word?

▷ Can you read it easily and smoothly?

(Continued)

Just-Right Books

Ask yourself these questions. If you answer yes, this book is probably a "JUST-RIGHT" book for you. "Just-right" books help you learn the most, because you can figure out most of the words and you understand what's going on in the text.

▷ Is this an interesting book that you want to read?

▷ Are you familiar with the content, author, series, genre?

▷ Can you tell another person what is happening in the story and/or what you're learning?

▷ Do you sometimes need to reread a part to understand it?

▷ Are there just a few words per page you don't know?

▷ When you read are most places smooth and some choppy?

Hard Books

Ask yourself these questions. If you answer yes, this book is probably a HARD book for you. Spend a little time with it now and learn what you can. Perhaps someone can read the book to you. Give it another try on your own later (perhaps in several months).

▷ Are you interested in reading this book?

▷ Are you confused about what is happening in most of this book?

▷ Is it hard to understand even when you reread?

▷ Do you need lots of help to read this book?

Selecting a Book While Browsing: The Five Finger Test

▷ Take a look at the books on display.

▷ Pull out a few that attract you.

▷ While you're considering whether the books are interesting to you, examine text features such as the title, illustrations, genre, and size of the type, as well as the length of each book.

▷ Now, pick a book and read the first page, if it's a novel, or the first couple of pages, if it's a picture book.

▷ Put up a finger for each word you don't know or that you really struggle with.

▷ If you get to the end of the section and have five or fewer fingers up, then this is likely a book that you can read independently.

▷ If you have more than five fingers raised, consider coming back to this book another time.

readers to put into practice the strategies they've been taught in other parts of the balanced reading program and to engage with texts in meaningful ways. What we mean by meaningful is that the reading isn't done simply to practise a skill, but that readers have their own purposes for reading, such as pleasure, to learn more about a topic, or to find out how to do something (this again highlights the importance of giving children quality choices in their reading material). When running this component of your program, consider the following:

- Select a predictable, daily reading time.

- If your students are not used to independent reading, you might have to start with a short amount of time and gradually work up to a longer period.

- Some teachers espouse the rule that teachers must model the importance of independent reading by themselves always reading during this time. Others, like Taberski (2000), use this time to conduct reading conferences with students.

- Readers usually need to debrief or at least reflect on what they are reading to help with comprehension. You can do this through reading response activities. For instance, long-time teacher Deb DeBenedictis (2007) structures her independent reading time so that students have the option to sketch what they are reading.

- Allow students to get comfortable when they read.

- To cut down on students who spend all of independent reading time browsing for books that they never read, consider having students put together their own close-at-hand reading material that is made up of
  1. *My now text.* The text I'm reading right now.
  2. *My next text(s).* The text(s) I want to read next.
  3. *My quick-and-easy reads.* Some things that are good, quick, easy reading—such as a book of poetry, or magazines with short articles (*Highlights*, *Guinness Book of World Records*, etc.) (Cunningham, Hall, & Gambrell, 2002, pp. 68–69).

  Having these materials at the ready means that students don't need to be wandering around the classroom or visiting the library when they could be reading.

- Consider using reader response journals or logs for students to document their reading.

Scheduling the Components

A foundational principal of *Constructing Meaning* is that teachers, as professionals, must be responsive to the needs of their students. Balanced reading instruction, therefore, doesn't mean that teachers must spend x amount of time on this component and then, when the bell rings, switch to the next component. It means that teachers must assess where their students are, what the context demands, and plan accordingly. You, therefore, must decide on the amount of time that you should spend with your class and your individual students on each of the reading instruction components that we list in this and other chapters. There are, however, some guidelines that might be helpful:

▨ In his exhaustive literature review of studies regarding reading achievement and reading volume, Richard Allington (2006) concluded that one of the keys to reading achievement is that children need lots of time to actually read. Allington tells us that every child is different, but the more time we can create for students to read, the better. He, for example, reports that students in the 90th percentile for reading achievement read 40.4 minutes per day compared with students in the 10th percentile for reading achievement, who read for only 1.6 minutes per day. Thus, regardless of what instructional strategies you select, it is wise to include as much actual reading time as possible. Allington recommends a full 90 minutes a day of in-school reading time. This might seem like an impossible amount, but remember that reading can and should happen across the curriculum.

▨ A number of educators advocate that Read-Aloud and shared reading happen daily (Brown & Fisher, 2006), and Routman (2003) has found that teachers can often combine these two instructional strategies if they feel the need. While Routman finds that about 20 to 30 minutes daily is optimum for Read-Aloud, librarian Candy Blessing (2005) finds that her students usually get antsy after about 15 to 20 minutes.

▨ Students in the early stages of their reading will need more guided reading than upper elementary students. Guided reading can be scheduled at the same time as independent reading, with teachers meeting with a few groups a day for about 10 to 15 minutes per group (Routman, 2003, p. 158).

SUMMARY

This chapter has highlighted some of the major components of a balanced reading program: Read-Aloud, shared reading, guided reading, and independent reading. Each of these components offers students differing levels of teacher support, with the ultimate goal of creating independent readers who have purposes for reading, and who have a variety of strategies at their disposal to make sense of text. Within our discussion of the components, we have offered information to help new teachers make decisions regarding critical instructional issues such as the amount of time to spend on each component, the grouping of students, the selection of texts, and the running of the components. This chapter must be combined with the other chapters in this book to help teachers put together a comprehensive reading program. Chapter 6 is a particularly important companion to Chapter 5, as it offers specific ways to teach comprehension strategies, word study, phonics, and fluency within the context of the major balanced reading instruction components.

TALKING POINTS

1. Select early, middle, or late elementary. Create a **semantic web** that shows your emerging understanding of what you as a classroom teacher could do to help children in this division learn to read. Following the creation of this web, highlight the aspects of your web that you feel most comfortable implementing and the parts of putting together reading instruction about which you feel most nervous or unsure. You might want to structure this last part as a series of questions.

2. Reflecting on your semantic web, think about the various circumstances that might alter your plans. For instance, how would your web need to change if you were teaching children of a different age?

3. Share your semantic web with a colleague. What is the same? What is different? How do these webs deal with differentiation? How do they capitalize on funds of knowledge? What view of reading do they promote? What roles do they set out for the teacher and the students? What now might you change or keep the same?

SELECTED PROFESSIONAL RESOURCES

Librarian, teacher, and educational researcher Roz Stooke recommends ...

The International Children's Digital Library Foundation. (n.d.). *The International Children's Digital Library: A library for the world's children.* Available at: http://www.childrenslibrary.org.

The International Children's Digital Library is an online resource whose mission is to

> Excite and inspire the world's children to become members of the global community—children who understand the value of tolerance and respect for diverse cultures, languages and ideas—by making the best in children's literature available online.

Use this site to augment your classroom resources and to engage students with a diverse range of texts. Also wonderful about this site is that readers can access texts in a number of different languages.

Bureau of Education and Research. (2002). *Instructional strategies for guided reading that enhance students' reading comprehension: Grades 3–6* [videorecording]. Bellevue, WA: Author.

This video allows you to witness a range of teachers running guided reading groups to teach a variety of reading strategies. It also comes with a viewing guide that runs you step by step through the strategies and ways to teach them.

Taberski, S. (2000). *On solid ground: Strategies for teaching reading K–3*. Portsmouth, NH: Heinemann.

Not necessarily the newest, but definitely one of the best comprehensive looks at how to set up the major components of a reading program. This book takes you through Sharon Taberski's routine, which supports readers of all types and does so with respect for who they are, what they can accomplish, and the diverse purposes of reading.

Reading Strategy Development

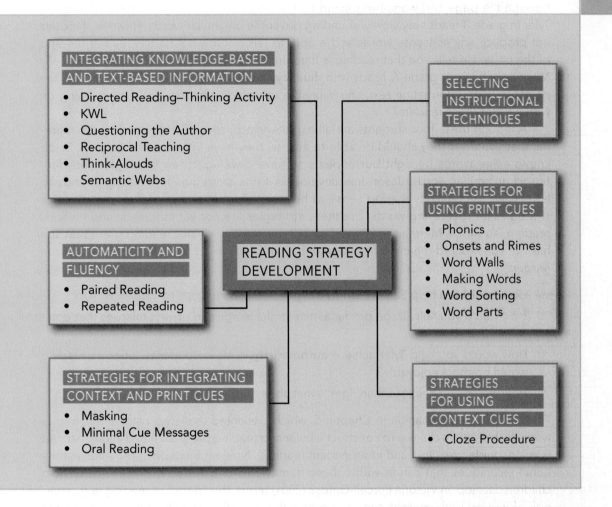

INTEGRATING KNOWLEDGE-BASED AND TEXT-BASED INFORMATION
- Directed Reading–Thinking Activity
- KWL
- Questioning the Author
- Reciprocal Teaching
- Think-Alouds
- Semantic Webs

SELECTING INSTRUCTIONAL TECHNIQUES

AUTOMATICITY AND FLUENCY
- Paired Reading
- Repeated Reading

READING STRATEGY DEVELOPMENT

STRATEGIES FOR USING PRINT CUES
- Phonics
- Onsets and Rimes
- Word Walls
- Making Words
- Word Sorting
- Word Parts

STRATEGIES FOR INTEGRATING CONTEXT AND PRINT CUES
- Masking
- Minimal Cue Messages
- Oral Reading

STRATEGIES FOR USING CONTEXT CUES
- Cloze Procedure

PLANNING FOR INSTRUCTION

Consider this scenario: Throughout your practice teaching assignments, you have encountered a number of different kinds of readers. Whenever you want to get to know new readers, you start by having them read aloud to you from narrative and expository material that has been designed for the students' approximate grade level. Sarah, who is in grade 4, begins to read her narrative text quite smoothly, but before she gets to the end of the first line of print she stops and looks to you for help. "I don't know that word," she says. This happens several times before she completes the first page. From grade 2, you work with Jason, whose reading is very different. He reads in a laboured manner, slowly sounding out words letter by letter, sometimes producing nonsense words rather than words that make sense in the sentence he is reading. He makes few corrections, plowing through the page and wondering aloud by the end what the story is about. Like Jason, Tyler in grade 3 reads very slowly, sounding out some unfamiliar words. However, he does not produce any nonsense words and is able to talk about what he has read at the end of the page. He tells you that reading is hard and that he doesn't read very much. Finally Meghan, who is in grade 7, reads with **fluency**, but when you ask her to retell the key points from an information text, she is unable to do so. *What do you think is going on with each of these readers?*

Although these four students are all experiencing some difficulty reading the material that you think they should be able to access, they have little else in common. Sarah knows some words by sight but appears to have developed few **strategies** for identifying unfamiliar words. Jason has developed some strategies for relating sounds to letters but has difficulty making sense as he reads. Tyler has developed some effective strategies for identifying words, but these strategies are not yet automatic and he finds reading laborious. Meghan can "word call," but is essentially not reading given that she has not constructed meaning from the text. *Now what would you do with each of these readers?*

- How would you help Sarah learn to use print and sound cues to identify words?
- How would you help Jason produce meaningful words and correct **miscues** that don't make sense?
- How would you help Tyler achieve **automaticity** in his word identification so reading would be more enjoyable?
- How would you help Meghan "get" what she's reading?

This chapter is a companion to Chapter 5, which presented the large instructional frameworks that teachers can use to construct a balanced reading program (Read-Aloud, shared reading, guided reading, and independent reading). Now we focus on the smaller instructional techniques that can fit within these frameworks or be used on their own to help children develop, in Victoria Purcell-Gates's (2001) terms, the "parts" of reading (e.g., strategies for using both **context cues** and cues within words). In this chapter we also present a variety of instructional strategies that you can use to support readers with their fluency and automaticity as well as comprehension. ☐

OVERVIEW OF WORD IDENTIFICATION INSTRUCTION

Readers can be taught to develop strategies for word identification within four major categories: sight vocabulary, phonics, structural analysis, and contextual analysis.

- *Sight vocabulary* refers to words that occur frequently and that readers are able to identify automatically. Skilled readers, recognize 99 percent of the words they read by sight.
- *Phonics* is the identification of words through the relationships between speech sounds and letters.

▪ *Structural analysis* involves identifying words by larger and more meaningful units such as prefixes and suffixes. Some people include syllabication as an aspect of structural analysis, while others consider it to be a component of phonics.

▪ *Contextual analysis* involves using the context of sentences or of passages to predict unfamiliar words. Most educators include both grammatical cues (Does it sound right?) and meaning cues (Does it make sense?) under the rubric of contextual analysis.

Strategies are essential for all readers, even those who we think of as proficient. Eventually every reader will encounter a text where the going gets rough. In the opening vignette, we see Sarah as a very dependent reader. She gets stuck right away and immediately turns to

TABLE 6.1 Instructional Techniques for Word Identification

Instructional Technique	Cue(s)	Helps Children Develop Strategies To
Names and other concrete words	Print	• hear sounds at the beginning of words • hear rhyming words • relate sounds with letters • differentiate upper- and lowercase letters
Hearing sounds in words	Print	• hear sounds in all word positions • relate letters with sounds
Word walls	Print	• identify common words as sight words • hear rhyming words • relate sounds with letters • use knowledge of letter sounds to identify words
Onsets and rimes	Print	• relate sounds with letters • identify new words through analogy to familiar words
Making words	Print	• relate sounds with letters • use knowledge of letter sounds to identify words
Word sorting	Print	• form generalizations about the sound and visual features of words
Word parts	Print	• use roots, affixes, and syllabication to identify words
Predictable books	Context	• use meaning and language cues to predict words
Cloze procedure	Context	• use meaning and language cues to predict words • use meaning and language cues to monitor predictions
Masking	Print and context	• use context cues to identify words • use letter sounds to identify words • use word parts to identify words
Minimal cue messages	Print and context	• use context cues to identify words • use knowledge of letter sounds and word parts to spell and identify words
Oral reading	Print and context	• use context and print cues to identify words • use context and print cues to correct miscues

her teacher for guidance. By contrast, independent readers can self-monitor and know when they are having trouble, and they can troubleshoot, having at the ready a bag of strategies they can implement to try to help them on the road to constructing meaning. We must always remember that with all strategies, but particularly those around word identification, the end goal needs to be constructing meaning. Strategy development is never an end in itself.

The strategies we describe in the following sections are organized in relation to cues that readers use for word identification—those within words, and those within sentence and passage contexts. In another section, we present instructional techniques to help children integrate both types of cues. Table 6.1 gives you an overview of these techniques.

STRATEGIES FOR USING PRINT CUES

In this section we describe instructional techniques to help children use letters and word parts to identify words as they read, but first we discuss of some of the considerations teachers face when planning their teaching of phonics.

Phonics

Considerations for Teaching Phonics

In Chapter 1 we told the story of Rachel, who, in her first year of teaching, used a commercial phonics program with her students, who were all Cree–first language. The program consisted of worksheets that moved students in a sequential fashion through various letters and their corresponding sounds. The sheets mainly consisted of pictures with accompanying parts of words, where students had to fill in the missing letters (e.g., a picture of a cat labelled with the word _at). Rachel used this program because she was nervous about "covering her bases" when she was teaching reading. She'll never forget the day she watched a frustrated student try to make sense of why a picture of what he interpreted as a donkey was on the worksheet for the [*m*] sound. Indeed the intent of the picture was to convey a "mule," not a donkey. Rachel realized, however, that her student's interpretation of donkey made good sense: she herself first saw a donkey too. It was only because she knew how such sheets worked and not because of her reading proficiency that Rachel was able to figure out the donkey/mule situation. Thus, in her witnessing of this scene, Rachel understood that these sheets, with their decontextualized images and shaky connection to reading itself, made no sense to most of her students and were a one-size-fits-few approach to creating learning opportunities about **graphophonetic** cues. Moreover, Rachel saw that using mules in the sub-Artic to teach reading was probably not the most culturally appropriate way to go! Importantly, however, within a balanced framework, the question is not *whether* to teach phonics, but *how* to teach phonics, and to do so in a way that allows readers to use their phonics knowledge in a strategic way that helps them in their construction of meaning from text.

Terminology   How important is it for teachers to use the "technical" language of phonics with their students? Box 6.1 presents definitions of some of the more common terms in phonics programs. Rather than inundating children with all these terms, you might prefer to think about

---

BOX 6.1   PHONICS TERMINOLOGY

▷ *Consonants.* All the letters of the alphabet except the vowels. There is one sound for most consonants, with the exception of *c* and *g* which have both hard (e.g., *car, go*) and soft (e.g., *city, gem*) sounds.

▷ *Consonant blends.* A combination of two or three consonants in which the sound of each of the consonants is retained and blended (e.g., *blue, free, smoke, street*).

▷ *Consonant digraphs.* A combination of two or more consonants that produce a new sound (e.g., *shoe, this, chick, phone*).

▷ *Vowels.* The letters *a, e, i, o, u* and sometimes *y* (when it is not the initial letter of a word, e.g., *my*) and *w* (when it follows a vowel, e.g., *how*).

▷ *Long vowel sounds.* The letter name of a vowel (e.g., *made, bead, kite, mope, flute*).

▷ *Short vowel sounds.* Another sound associated with single vowels (e.g., *had, bed, hit, mop, cup*).

▷ *Vowel digraphs.* Combinations of two vowels that have one sound (e.g., *coat, meat, wait*).

▷ *Vowel diphthongs.* A combination of two vowels in which the sound of each of the vowels is retained and blended (e.g., *join, boy, how, out*).

▷ *Controlled vowels.* Vowels that are followed by the letters *r* and *l* and which alter the sound of the vowel (e.g., vowels influenced by *r* as in *far, her, fir, for, purr*; and *a* influenced by *l* as in *fall*).

▷ *Onset.* The initial consonant or consonants in a syllable (e.g., *b* in *bat*, *br* as in *brake*).

▷ *Rime.* (Also known as *phonogram* or *word family*.) The vowel and remaining consonants in a syllable following the onset (e.g., *at* in *bat*, *ake* as in *brake*).

▷ *Syllable.* A group of letters that forms a unit and has only one vowel sound.

▷ *Closed syllable.* A unit in which one vowel appears between consonants (e.g., *cat, shop, back*). The vowel sound is usually short.

▷ *Open syllable.* A unit with a vowel at the end of it (e.g., *go, she, try, to* in *total*). The vowel sound is usually long.

---

what is key for your students to know and be able to do with their phonics knowledge. These terms serve primarily to facilitate communication between and among children and teachers when talking about letters and sounds in words. Because of this limited utility, it is more helpful to have children learn the possible sounds that are associated with a letter (e.g., for the letter *a* the possibilities are the sounds in *can, cane, car, and call*) rather than learn that these sounds are called "short, long, *r*-controlled, and *l*-controlled."

Phonics Rules   Should you teach phonics by teaching rules like "When two vowels go walking, the first one does the talking"? Back in the 1960s, Clymer (1963) showed that many phonics rules do not work very often: for example, in Clymer's study, the "two vowels go walking" rule only worked 45 percent of the time for words in four primary basal reading series. There are many exceptions to the rule, including all the vowel diphthongs (e.g., *join*, *about*). Consider as well the final *e* rule. Clymer found that this rule worked only 63 percent of the time. Many common words, such as *give*, *love*, *some*, *come*, and *live*, do not follow the rule. The most reliable rules are those involving consonants, for example, that *c* and *g* are soft following the vowels *e* and *i*.

Another major problem with phonics rules is that children are often able to recite them but are unable to use them to identify unfamiliar words. For example, a child may be able to describe in detail how the *e* at the end of the word jumps over the letter in front of it and kicks the vowel to make it say its own name, but that same child then identifies the word *mate* as *mat*. We don't recommend rule memorization as an effective way to help children learn to map sounds onto letters. This doesn't mean that children shouldn't be taught the common sounds associated with vowels. In a recent reconsideration of the utility of phonic generalizations, Johnston (2001) found that some vowel pairs are more consistent with the "two vowels go walking" generalization than others. For example, the most reliable pair is *ay* at 96.4 percent. She recommends teaching vowel pairs in groupings: five vowel pairs (*ai*, *ay*, *oa*, *ee*, and *ey*) that are highly regular where the first vowel does the talking; and four vowel pairs (*aw*, *oy*, *oi*, and *au*) that are also highly regular but do not have long vowel sounds. Other vowel pairs have two or more sounds (e.g., *boot*, *book*; *snow*, *how*; *seat*, *head*) and cannot be taught so easily. Johnston indicates that students need a flexible strategy with these pairs: they need to try more than one sound and check the results with their oral language and context.

Synthetic or Analytic Phonics
Another consideration in the teaching of phonics concerns whether instruction should be **synthetic**, in which children are taught letter sounds and then how to blend them to pronounce a word, or **analytic**, in which children examine known words to discover patterns and regularities to use when identifying unknown words. Synthetic phonics is what most people mean when they talk about children "sounding out" words.

An advantage of synthetic phonics is that children can use letter sounds to identify new words even when these words are visually dissimilar to words they know. However, it is important to keep in mind (as we indicated in Chapter 3), that it is very difficult to isolate sounds for many letters without distorting them. Another problem involves using this approach with words of more than one syllable. It is not uncommon to hear young children attempting to identify words such as *hammer* by saying, "huh, a, muh, muh, eh, er," and then having no idea what the word is. These children need to learn how to organize words into syllables in order to use their knowledge of letter sounds.

In analytic phonics, teachers often have children identify words by mapping sounds to larger chunks of letters. The chunks, generally labeled phonograms or **rimes**, consist of a vowel sound plus a consonant sound (e.g., *-ack*, *-ake*, *-eat*). These phonograms are used to create word families such as *back*, *pack*, *quack*, and *sack*. There are several advantages to this approach. Children find it easier to identify words using phonograms than rules, phonograms are fairly consistent, and a relatively small number of phonograms are found in many of the words in primary reading material (Vacca, Vacca, & Gove, 2006). Still, children do come across words in which they do not recognize a phonogram and therefore need to map sounds onto smaller units of words some of the time.

The National Reading Panel (2000) did not find that one approach to teaching phonics was better than another. As in any other aspect of reading instruction, one size does not fit all. The National Reading Panel cautioned teachers to be flexible in the phonics instruction they provide in order to adapt it to individual needs. Also, whenever teaching phonics, teachers should ensure that skills are used in "authentic contexts" and that reading materials are "engaging and meaningful" for readers (Ministry of Education, 2003, p. 23).

Separate or Integrated Instruction   Another consideration in the teaching of phonics involves the extent to which it should be taught as a separate entity. Sometimes educators schedule phonics instruction in its own time slot and phonics is taught in virtual isolation from the rest of the language arts program. The concern with this way of teaching phonics is that children may be able to associate sounds with isolated consonants and vowels and to recite phonics rules, but they may have difficulty using this knowledge when they read. The National Reading Panel (2000) cautions that "programs that focus too much on the teaching of letter–sound relations and not enough on putting them to use are unlikely to be very effective" (p. 10). Instead, the National Reading Panel recommends integration of phonics instruction into "complete and balanced programs of reading instruction" (p. 11). In our notion of a balanced reading program, we recommend instruction that focuses on helping children use their knowledge of letter sounds to identify words in the context of real reading: just as Purcell-Gates (2001) recommends with her whole-part-whole structure.

Incidental or Systematic Instruction   A related consideration involves whether phonics should be taught through explicit instruction in systematic lessons or incidentally when children experience difficulty as they are reading or writing. During the 1980s and early 1990s, phonics was frequently taught in mini-lessons as teachers identified specific needs while children were reading or writing. The National Reading Panel (2000) found support for systematic teaching of phonics. It may be that the power of systematic phonics instruction lies in organizing lessons so they logically reveal the nature of the alphabetic system, so instruction moves from less to more complex understandings (Adams, 2002).

We believe that some children need systematic phonics instruction but that others do not. Children develop phonics knowledge two ways: through instruction and from experiences with print (Johnston, 2001). Some children are better at implicit learning than others, and some aspects of phonics knowledge are easier to learn than others. Thus,

> a little phonics instruction may go a long way with some children, while others may need long-term systematic instruction to become independent readers. Teachers will need to carefully observe their students as they read and as they write to determine who needs what. (Johnston, 2001, p. 141)

This need for flexibility, responsiveness to children's needs, and teacher professionalism in the teaching of reading is something that elementary teacher Tara-Lynn Scheffel talks about in the Teacher Wisdom box here.

Phonics Instruction

Some children require specific instruction on the nature of the relationship between sounds and letters before they can develop strategies for using cues within words to identify them.

TEACHER WISDOM

TARA-LYNN SCHEFFEL AND PHONICS TEACHING

We asked primary teacher Tara-Lynn Scheffel about how she first started teaching phonics and how she matured in her understanding and instruction of phonics. Here's how she responded.

During my teacher preparation year, I distinctly remember learning about phonetic approaches, including phonemic awareness, but also whole story approaches to lessons with themes as well as more open-ended reading and writing activities. Similarly, I experienced both of these approaches in my practicum placements, as I taught specific phonics lessons in a workbook but also created my own lessons for stories without a prescribed manual that connected meaning with the opportunity to work on related phonics patterns. It was with these experiences in hand that I left my Faculty of Education program with a strong conviction that I wanted to have a language arts classroom that represented a "balance" between phonics and what was then considered "whole language."

Yet, it took another seven years for me to realize that the "balance" I thought I had taken with me into the classroom actually swayed very heavily in favour of a phonetic approach. In effect, I had done exactly what I was told not to do in my teacher preparation year: teach phonics rules in isolation. What happened? Looking back I realize it was a combination of things.

First, I was unaware of the strength of my previous experiences on my beliefs about teaching literacy. As a good student, often working one-to-one with students in volunteer experiences, I saw success in helping students learn the skills of sounding out words. What I did not consider at the time was that the act of providing individual assistance contributed to the success I perceived.

Second, I attributed success to the program I used rather than the context of my classroom and my beliefs as a teacher. As a new teacher, I was looking for an outline to tell me what to do to teach literacy and I fell into following a specific program that matched my beliefs in the way it suggested balance, but was actually very prescribed in that the phonics component consisted of isolated tasks that took place before the reading of the story. Yet, what I have come to learn is that students benefit most when these phonetic components are connected within the context of a story. A great way to think of this is from a whole-part-whole perspective. The overall lesson begins with a whole (e.g., a piece of literature) and then the phonics enters in as an opportunity to focus on a specific part (e.g. verbs or rhymes). The lesson is then brought back to the whole at the end as a way of allowing students to put into practice what they are learning (e.g., writing stories using verbs or rhymes).

Finally, my last piece of advice that I found contributed most to my growth as a teacher in relation to phonics is to speak with other teachers whenever you get the chance. The opportunity to see what is similar and different in your teaching reveals multiple ways of teaching and learning literacy that will enrich what you are learning now in your readings. While an approach to teaching language arts and literacy is necessary, much of teaching language arts and literacy is working out what you believe with what you are able to accomplish in the classroom.

As we discussed in Chapter 3, there is relationship between **phonemic awareness** and the ability to decode at word level. Interestingly, longtime educator Isabel Beck (2006), in her survey of the literature regarding this relationship, found that educators generally hold one of three main positions: (1) phonemic awareness is a prerequisite for instruction in decoding (such as phonics), (2) decoding instruction can result in phonemic awareness even if phonemic awareness is not explicitly taught, (3) there is a reciprocal relationship between phonemic awareness and decoding. What is a teacher to do when there are three different perspectives? In relation to when to begin phonics instruction as one part of word identification, teachers in a balanced reading framework will need to ascertain what their specific students require. In general, Beck suggests that phonics instruction may be taught at the same time as phonemic awareness, particularly once children are beyond preschool. In fact, some researchers have found that phonemic awareness instruction is more effective when letters are included (Ball & Blachman, 1991; Byrne & Fielding-Barnsley, 1993; National Reading Panel, 2000). As such, we next provide two sample strategies that create phonemic awareness and phonics learning opportunities: Names and Other Concrete Words and Elkonin Boxes. Both strategies involve looking at written letters as well as listening for sounds.

Sample Instructional Strategy 1: Names and Other Concrete Words

When we asked Tara-Lynn to share one of her favourite instructional strategies for this section, she told us that it was the Names and Other Concrete Words strategy from Cunningham & Allington (2007). Tara-Lynn likes this strategy because it begins, not with arbitrary words and sounds that are so often the focus of commercial phonics programs, but rather with the meaningful "whole" or context of children's names and words that they can easily identify with concrete objects. Here is how the strategy works:

Tara-Lynn writes the children's first names on sentence strips and cuts the names apart, with long names on long strips and short ones on short strips. Every day she draws a name, and the child selected becomes "king" or "queen" for the day. His or her name becomes the focus of several language and literacy activities.

■ The children interview the child, finding out what he or she likes to eat, play, and do after school, as well as how many brothers, sisters, dogs, and cats he or she has. Tara-Lynn writes this information on a chart and compiles a class book.

■ Tara-Lynn focuses the children's attention on the child's name (e.g., *David*), pointing out that this word is David's name. Tara-Lynn indicates that it takes many letters to write the word *David*, and the children count the letters. Tara-Lynn then says the letter names, *D-a-v-i-d*, and has the children say them with her. Tara-Lynn notes that the word begins and ends with the same letter and helps the children label one uppercase and the other lowercase.

■ Tara-Lynn writes the child's name on another strip as the children watch and chant the spelling of letters with the teacher. Tara-Lynn cuts the letters apart, mixes them up, and has children come up and arrange the letters in the right order to spell the child's name, using the original sentence strip as a model.

■ Tara-Lynn writes the child's name on a large sheet of drawing paper and draws a picture of the child on the other side. The featured child takes these drawings home.

■ As each name is added, the children compare them, talking about which names are longer or shorter and whether the names contain any of the same letters. When two names begin with the same letter, Tara-Lynn helps the children hear that they also begin with the same sound (e.g., *Luke* and *Linda*).

■ When a single-syllable name such as *Sam* is selected, Tara-Lynn has the children listen for rhyming words. For example, Tara-Lynn says pairs of words (Sam—ham, Sam—big), and the children indicate whether the two words rhyme.

■ When two names that begin with the same letter but different sounds are selected (e.g., *Caroline* and *Cynthia*), Tara-Lynn uses the opportunity to help children understand that some letters have more than one sound. Tara-Lynn writes the two names on the board and has the children say the two words several times, drawing out the first sound. Tara-Lynn then says several words beginning with the letter *c* but having different sounds (e.g., *cat, celery, candy, cookies, city, cereal, cut*). For each word, the children point to either *Caroline* or *Cynthia* to show which sound they hear, and the teacher writes the word under the name on the board.

Cunningham and Allington (2007) recommend using a similar technique with other concrete words, such as the names of colours or animals. The major focus is on hearing sounds at the beginning of words and associating these sounds with letters. The following instructional strategy can help children hear sounds in all word positions.

Sample Instructional Strategy 2: The Modified Elkonin Technique   To help children hear sounds in words, make the connection between letters and sounds, and figure out how to map letters onto sounds when spelling, and sounds onto letters when identifying unfamiliar words, Tara-Lynn also likes to use Marie Clay's (1993b) modified "Elkonin technique" (Elkonin, 1973) strategy. Teachers use this technique by first having children listen to figure out how many sounds there are in words and eventually by having children link the sounds they hear with letters. This technique, originated by Daniil Elkonin (1973), is designed to help children make the connection between letters and sounds and to figure out how to map letters onto sounds when spelling, and sounds onto letters when identifying unfamiliar words. To use this technique, Tara-Lynn first decides which words she wants to work with. For early-years students, you might use their names or concrete words associated with the sound you want to emphasize and connect this strategy to the one above; you might also use this strategy with a word that students themselves generate within the context of writing (including shared and independent writing); or, as in the example, you could select words from a shared reading text. Then, Tara-Lynn follows the following pattern we present in Box 6.2. Note that this technique can be used with whole class, small-group, or individual teaching.

Order of Sounds in Phonics Instruction

A big question that many teacher candidates have is in what order to teach the letters and sounds. A number of commercial programs have their own scope and sequence for this. As always, it is important for teachers to know where their students are at and begin from there. Consequently, you will have to decide when it is most beneficial to teach in a whole group,

BOX 6.2   ELKONIN TECHNIQUE

1. Teacher Tara-Lynn Scheffel prepares cards on which squares are drawn for each sound unit in words of two, three, and four sounds. For example:

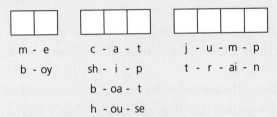

m - e	c - a - t	j - u - m - p
b - oy	sh - i - p	t - r - ai - n
	b - oa - t	
	h - ou - se	

2. Tara-Lynn provides a selection of counters for the children.

3. Tara-Lynn articulates a word slowly. The children watch the teacher's lips and copy the teacher.

4. The children articulate the word slowly. (A mirror can be used if it helps children become more aware of what their lips are doing.)

5. Tara-Lynn articulates the word slowly, putting one counter in each box, sound by sound.

6. The children put the counters in the boxes as Tara-Lynn says the word slowly, or she puts the counters in boxes as the children say the word.

7. The children put counters into boxes as they say the word.

8. Once the children are able to hear sounds in words, this strategy is applied to spelling words as the children write (within the context of, for example, guided or independent writing).

   a. Tara-Lynn encourages the children to articulate slowly the word they want to spell.

   b. Tara-Lynn draws a box for each sound segment and asks, "What can you hear? How would you write it? Where will you put it?"

   c. Initially the children write the letters they are able to associate with sounds heard and Tara-Lynn the others. For example:

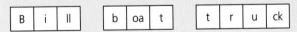

9. After the children are able to hear and record most consonants and some vowels correctly, Tara-Lynn draws them a box for each letter. Clay suggests using broken lines initially when two letters do not represent distinct sounds. For example:

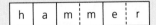

small-group, or one-on-one setting. Whatever you decide, there are some guidelines for the order in which letters and sounds are most typically acquired; but keep in mind that when a word or letter is important to a child (e.g., when it is in their own name or the name of someone they feel is important), this order is apt to go somewhat astray. Educator Bonnie

Burns (2006) suggests that teachers consider the following "general progression" in teaching phonics:

1. the letter names

2. a few consonants and one or two vowels "so that children can start learning the letter-sound correspondence and blend them together into simple words"

3. consonants that are "continuous or can be stretched," such as *m, s, n, f, z, v, l,* and *r*

4. consonants *b, d, k, t, p,* and *g,* which are harder to work with without vowels than the consonants that precede them

5. consonants *c, g,* which are tricky as their sound relies on the "letters around them"

6. short vowels, which are more consistent, though harder to hear, than long vowels

7. consonant clusters and blends (e.g., *bl, cl, fl*)

8. long vowels with silent *e* (though Burns suggests that speakers of Spanish and Chinese may have difficulty with long *e*; thus, teachers might start them instead with long *o*)

9. inflectional endings (e.g., *-ed, -ing*)

10. consonant digraphs (i.e., letter pairs that create a new sound rather than a blend of sounds, such as *ch, sh,* etc.)

11. two letter-one sound pairs (e.g., *-ck, kn, qu*)

After moving through the above progression, teachers may often see students processing larger chunks such as *-and, -ame, -ine, -ing,* and *-ed.* Teachers may then move on to lower-frequency vowel combinations such as:

12. *r*-controlled vowels, where the *r* changes the vowel sound so that it is neither long nor short (e.g., *ar, er*).

13. vowel dipthongs (e.g., *aw, ew, ow, ou*).

14. vowel teams (e.g., *ai, ea, oa, ee, eigh*) (p. 55)

Onsets and Rimes

As we have mentioned, there are several advantages to teaching children how to use word families (variously called *phonograms* or *rimes*) to identify words, particularly at the primary level. Perhaps one of the greatest advantages to this strategy is that children learn how to connect a known word and its pattern (e.g., *ball*) to an unknown word that has the same pattern (e.g., *tall*). In this way, children figure out unknown words through analogy, and they build their decoding from what they already know. In keeping with a balanced approach to reading instruction, some educators suggest that word family instruction is a good companion to letter-sound blending strategies (as we have described above) (Wanzek & Haager, 2003).

Instruction in word families begins with **onsets**, which are the consonants that precede vowels in syllables. The sounds associated with onsets are fairly consistent, and traditional phonics instruction for onsets works well (Rasinski & Padak, 2001). Rather than isolating letters and sounds, teachers can teach beginning consonant sounds by associating them with concrete words that begin with these letters. Teachers may have children listen to words that begin with the sound (e.g., *bicycle, ball*), ask children to brainstorm other words that begin with the sound, read words beginning with the letter, and read texts in which many of the words begin with the targeted letter.

After the children have mastered several consonant sounds, the teacher begins concurrently teaching rimes and helping the children to use knowledge of onsets and rimes to identify words. Teachers choose rimes that are the most productive. Almost 500 primary grade words can be made from just 37 rimes! These rimes are: *-ack, -ail, -ain, -ake, -ale, -ame, -an, -ank, -ap, -ash, -at, -ate, -aw, -y, -eat, -ell, -est, -ice, -ick, -ide, -ight, -ill, -in, -ine, -ing, -ink, -ip, -ir, -ock, -oke, -op, -or, -ore, -uck, -ug, -ump, -unk* (Starrett, 2007).

Here is one way that Tara-Lynn and other teachers have structured teaching rimes. This method has been adapted from Rasinski and Padak (2001):

▪ Print a rime on the board (e.g., *at*) and say the sound it represents several times, asking the children to do the same.

▪ Brainstorm a list of words that contain the *at* rime and print them on chart paper.

▪ Read the words with the students, and have them read the words in groups and individually.

▪ Have children respond to riddles for which the answer is two or more words containing the rime (e.g., "What do you get when you feed a pet too much food?").

▪ Introduce two or three poems, read the poems to the children pointing to the words as you read, and have the children join in when they feel comfortable. Children then read the poem chorally, read it in small groups, and finally read it individually throughout the day. Once the poem has been read many times, children are asked to find individual words and word parts in the poem. The poems can be selected from collections and anthologies (see Chapter 10 for poetry resources) or written by the teacher.

▪ Students are given a sheet of words containing the rime as well as the poems used for the rime. They take these home to practise reading and are also asked to write a poem of their own, using words containing the rime.

▪ The next day the students share their poems, read each others' poems, read the poems from the previous day, and identify individual words in the poems. You might consider introducing two rimes each week, with a review at the end of the week. You might also have children read and write books containing the rimes, use words containing the rimes for word sorts, complete cloze passages with words containing the targeted rimes, and use words containing the rimes in their daily writing. The teacher can also place some of the words on a word wall for further activities.

Word Walls

Through Cambourne (1988), we have seen the importance of immersing readers in print. Word walls are an important way of doing this. A word wall as a systematically organized collection of words displayed in large letters on a wall; the word wall is interactive, as it is a tool and not a display (Pinnell & Fountas, 1998). Word walls can be the core of systematic phonics and spelling programs, as well as documenting what has been taught (Brabham & Villaume, 2001). When "doing a word wall," Cunningham and Allington (2007) recommend that teachers

- be very selective about the words on the wall, including only the most common words in children's reading and writing (e.g., *was, saw, of, for, from, they, that, what, with, will*)
- add words gradually—no more than five each week
- make the word wall accessible to everyone, writing words in large clear letters
- have children practise words by chanting or writing them, because many children can't just look at words and remember them
- provide a variety of review activities so that children are able to identify and write words automatically
- make sure children spell word-wall words correctly in their writing

Cunningham and Allington (2007) also suggest teachers can arrange the words alphabetically on the word wall, giving children an immediately accessible dictionary for the most troublesome words when they are reading or writing. Children can also complete several activities with words on the wall. For example:

- Children can find words on the wall that rhyme with a word given by the teacher (e.g., "Find a word that begins with a *r* and rhymes with *sock*").
- The teacher writes a letter on the board and then says a sentence, leaving out a word that begins with that letter (e.g., "Write the word that begins with a *f* and fits into the sentence *Sandro wants to catch* _____ ").
- The teacher thinks of a word on the wall and gives five clues, some related to visual features ("It has four letters"), some to sounds ("It begins with the sound *r*"), and others to meaning ("It fits into the sentence 'I want to climb that big _____ '"). The children write the word they think the teacher has selected after each clue.

In addition to the ABC word wall described above, teachers can also create word walls containing

- theme words that change as units of study are completed
- words that are examples of the different sounds each letter can represent
- commonly misspelled words
- high-frequency words that lack predictable patterns
- words organized by the common spelling patterns of vowels (Brabham & Villaume, 2001)

Some of the most powerful instruction occurs during conversations about word solving that comes up as children are reading and writing (Brabham & Villaume, 2001). For example, when a child asks how to spell the word *feet*, they suggest pointing to *need* on the word wall and asking how it can help. In this way, teachers scaffold the development of strategies used by skilled readers.

Making Words

Making words (Cunningham & Cunningham, 1992) is a great teaching technique where teachers give children letters on cards, which they use to make words. During a period of about 15 minutes, children make 12 to 15 words, beginning with two-letter words and working up to longer words until they make a target word. Teachers prepare a set of small letter cards for each child and one set of large cards to be used in a pocket chart or on the ledge of the board. Each card has the lowercase letter on one side and the uppercase letter on the other. Teachers begin planning a lesson with a target word (e.g., *winter*) that ties in with some aspect of the curriculum and contains letter–sound patterns the children need to learn. Teachers then generate a list of shorter words that can be made with the letters in *winter* (e.g., *in, tin, ten, net, wet, win, twin, went, rent, tire, wire, twine*). They write these words on index cards and order the cards from shortest to longest and according to patterns. Once these materials are prepared, teachers may follow the steps outlined in Classroom Activity 6.1 (Cunningham & Allington, 2007). Note that making words is a terrific activity for upper elementary students too, and teachers might want to consult *Making Big Words* (Cunningham & Hall, 2001) to up the challenge for these students.

CLASSROOM ACTIVITY **6.1**

Steps in a Making-Words Activity

1. The teacher places the large letter cards in a pocket chart or on the board ledge.

2. Each child has corresponding small letter cards. The teacher holds up the large letter cards, names each, and asks children to hold up their matching cards.

3. The teacher writes the number 2 or 3 on the board and says a word with this number of letters in a sentence. He or she asks the children to make the word using the small letter cards (e.g., "Take two letters and make the word *in*"). The children all say the word *in*.

4. A child who has made the word correctly using the small letter cards forms the word using the large cards in the pocket chart or on the ledge, and the other children check their word.

5. This continues for other words, with the teacher giving cues such as the following: "Add a letter to make the three-letter word *tin*. Many cans are made of tin." "Now change one letter and the word *tin* becomes *ten*." "Move the letters around in the word *ten* and make the word *net*." Before telling them the last word, the teacher asks if anyone has figured out what word can be made with all the letters. If they don't know, the teacher tells them the word, and they make it.

6. Once all the words have been made, the teacher places the word cards one at a time in the pocket chart or on the board ledge, and the children say and spell them. The teacher then picks a word and asks the children to find other words with the same pattern.

7. To maximize learning, the children use the patterns they have found to identify new words written by the teacher and to spell new words dictated by the teacher.

Source: Based on P. M. Cunningham & R. L. Allington, *Classrooms that work: They can all read and write* (4th ed.) (New York: Longman, 2007).

Word Sorting

As children become more knowledgeable about letters and words, word sorting can be used as part of the making-words technique or separately for older children. This technique is designed to focus children's attention on particular cues in words. Children compare, contrast, and sort words according to specific print or sound features. Word sorts help children form generalizations about properties of words, and also help them link new words to ones they already know how to identify and spell. Teachers and/or children begin by developing a word bank of known words for word sorting.

There are two types of word-sorting activities. In a closed sort, the teacher specifies the feature the children are to use to find words (e.g., all words with the same vowel sound, all words with two syllables, all words with a soft *g*). In an open sort, the teacher does not specify how words are to be grouped—the teacher asks the children to group words so that they are all the same in some way. In both types of sorts, it is important that children talk about words as they sort them, because this helps them better understand generalizations. It is also important that the teacher model the process several times so that the children understand what to do and why they are doing it.

Here are some basic approaches to sorting words:

- *Sort words by how they sound.* Students begin with initial sounds and move to ending and middle sounds.
- *Sort words by how they look.* Students sort words that have double letters, double vowels, double consonants, and other common patterns.
- *Sort words by connections between meaning units.* Students sort words in relation to root words, inflected endings, prefixes, suffixes, compound words, synonyms, antonyms, and so on. (Pinnell & Fountas, 1998)

Word Parts

Structural analysis is the term traditionally used to refer to the identification of words using larger, more meaningful units than letters. It generally includes compounds, roots, affixes (e.g., *ly*), and syllabication. One way teachers can help children learn to use structural units to identify words is by demonstrating how the children can organize difficult polysyllabic words into units. The teacher writes such a word in parts on the board (e.g., *but ter fly*), pronounces each part, blends the parts, and checks to ensure that the word makes sense in its context. The teacher then encourages children to employ a similar strategy when they encounter other unknown words as they are reading. For many children, this is sufficient to help them develop an understanding of how structural analysis works and intuitive strategies for organizing unfamiliar words into parts. Precise syllabication is generally not necessary, since context is available to check possible pronunciations. For those children who require more explicit instruction, we recommend activities such as the following:

Compound Words

A common starting point to help children who have difficulty analyzing units larger than letters is compound words. Analyzing these words into two known real words is a concrete task. It also takes advantage of words that children already know how to identify. After a brief discussion of compound words, the teacher gives students a passage containing several compound words, with the compounds underlined. He or she asks the students to read the passage silently and be prepared to talk about what they have read. When students encounter difficult compound words, they or the teacher can write them in units on the board and discuss them.

Syllabication

The goal of this instruction is to have children identify syllables by hearing and seeing places in words where structural breaks occur. This is a means toward identifying longer unknown words independently. Exact division in accordance with the dictionary is unnecessary until students reach the point where they begin to hyphenate words at the end of lines in their writing. Old, but solid advice for teachers to give to readers is "Break the word down to the point where you can see how to say it, say it and move on" (Gallant, 1970, p. 93). Classroom Activity 6.2 presents steps for teaching syllabication.

Affixes and Inflectional Endings

We do not recommend systematically working through all affixes or inflectional endings, but rather recommend focusing on specific inflectional endings (e.g., -ed, -es) or affixes (e.g., pre-, -ness, -tion) when they cause difficulty in reading and writing. What works best is beginning with familiar words and then moving on to unfamiliar ones. Another approach to affixes and inflectional endings is the *Nifty-Thrifty-Fifty list* (Cunningham & Allington, 2007)—a list of 50 words that contain examples for all the common prefixes and suffixes as well as common spelling changes. It is advisable to introduce the words gradually, with students chanting and practising them until their spelling and decoding become automatic. The Nifty-Thrifty-Fifty list can be found online at http://www.teachers.net/4blocks/goodies.html.

This section has focused on helping children develop strategies for using cues within words to identify them. It is important that children know why they are learning these strategies. With the media's current heavy focus on phonics, you might feel considerable pressure to teach phonics for its own sake. Phonics is important, but it is best used in conjunction with other strategies for helping children identify unfamiliar words when they are constructing meaning. The next section focuses on helping children develop strategies for using cues beyond individual words.

STRATEGIES FOR USING CONTEXT CUES

We have explored the variety of cuing systems that readers can use to construct meaning from text. Context cues are one of several sources of information children have available to identify unfamiliar words. This section provides examples of instructional strategies to help teachers create learning opportunities for readers to develop their ability to use context cues, so that they will be able to use them *along with*, not instead of, print-based information.

CLASSROOM ACTIVITY 6.2

Steps for Teaching Syllabication

1. The teacher begins by helping children develop a concept of what syllables are in the words they hear. The teacher pronounces a polysyllabic word, accentuating the syllable breaks (*in for ma tion*). The teacher and children repeat the word together in syllables. Children who have difficulty hearing syllables in words often benefit from

   ▷ clapping every time they hear or pronounce a syllable, or
   ▷ putting their hand under their chin and feeling it move down for each syllable
   ▷ The children then repeat the words in syllables without the teacher's aid. It is not important for the children to show how many syllables are in a word; rather, they need to be able to pronounce words in syllables.

2. To relate the concept of oral syllable to written language, the teacher presents familiar polysyllabic words to the children with syllable boundaries shown (e.g., *re port, fun ny*). Since the children already know how to identify these words, the focus is on syllables and how spoken syllables relate to the visual units. The children then learn the following visual clues that can be used to analyze words into syllables:

   ▷ prefixes and suffixes form separate syllables
   ▷ double consonants or two consonants together are divided, except in the case of blends and digraphs
   ▷ a single consonant between two vowels often goes with the second vowel, and
   ▷ the consonant before *-le* usually goes with it

   The teacher selects one or two words to provide a visual reminder of each clue as they are introduced. He or she prints these on a chart (with syllable divisions shown) and places them where children can refer to them when a difficult word occurs in context. Eventually the children have models for all four visual clues.

3. The teacher has the children silently read texts containing polysyllabic words, reminding them to organize words into syllables if they have difficulty identifying them. They might lightly underline words that cause them difficulty, and these can be discussed after they finish reading. The teachers or students write selected words on the board in syllables for identification and discussion.

4. Finally, children use this strategy to identify polysyllabic words when reading independently. It is important that flexibility be stressed. If the word identified does not make sense, the children are encouraged to try it another way until they get a meaningful word.

Cloze Procedure

In the cloze procedure, words are deleted from a written passage and readers fill in the blanks using their knowledge of language and the world, along with clues available from the context. Material at a wide range of reading levels, including both narrative and informational texts, can be used to make cloze passages. For early readers or those experiencing difficulty, the teacher initially deletes only a few words, selecting those that are highly predictable from the context. As readers begin to make more effective use of meaning and language cues to predict words, the teacher deletes more words, including those that are less predictable. An easy way to make cloze activities is to cut up pieces of self-adhesive notes to cover selected words in texts. An example of a cloze passage created from a story in *Ranger Rick* (October 1994) is shown in Box 6.3.

Two children identifying words in context

When introducing cloze activities, the teacher might begin with a whole class activity focused on material presented on an overhead projector. The teacher models the process by reading through the entire passage with the students before they try to fill in the blanks. Once all students have read through the passage, a student volunteer reads the first sentence and supplies the missing word. Other students who responded differently read the sentence and provide their responses. You can focus class discussion on questions such as:

- Why did you choose this word?
- What do you know about the topic in this passage that helped you predict this word?
- What in the passage helped you to make this prediction?
- Is there a difference in the meaning when we choose your word rather than X's?
- Why did different students predict different words?

Later, the teacher gives students cloze passages to complete individually. The teacher asks children to explain, in small group discussions, why they used particular words, again focusing

---

BOX 6.3 **SAMPLE CLOZE PASSAGE**

The first paragraph (not shown here) is left intact so children will already have begun to make meaning by the time they get to the first blank. In that paragraph, Scarlett Fox and Ranger Rick Raccoon are in a picnic area near the ocean when they see a white shapeless form in the fog.

"Look, it's coming back!" Rick whispered in horror as the Thing came right toward them. Suddenly it _____ over their picnic basket and fell in a heap. Now Rick and Scarlett could see that the white thing was a _____ and out from under it crawled their friend Boomer Badger. He laughed gleefully between gulps of _____ as he tried to catch his breath.

Source: Reading passage excerpted from N. Steiner Mealy, "Adventures of Ranger Rick," *Ranger Rick*, October 1994, p. 40.

on knowledge and text cues. The small group discussions might then lead to large-group discussion of some of the more interesting or controversial items.

It is not important in cloze activities for children to predict the author's exact word. As long as the predictions make sense and sound right in relation to the rest of the passage, they are accepted. By insisting on exact replacements, the teacher sends the children the message that text cues are more important than knowledge when making meaning, and the task is reduced to a "guess what word the author used" activity.

As with instructional techniques for using cues within words, it is important that children understand why they are doing cloze activities. Otherwise they may not realize that they should use similar strategies to predict words when they come to unfamiliar words as they read both language arts and other materials across the curriculum.

STRATEGIES FOR INTEGRATING CONTEXT AND PRINT CUES

We believe that in a balanced literacy program most word identification techniques should help children use *both* context and print cues rather than one or the other. This section begins with a description of how one teacher provides this type of instruction. The remainder of the section presents instructional techniques designed to help children integrate strategies for using context and print cues as they read.

Maureen Kelly's Grade 2 Classroom

In Maureen Kelly's grade 2 classroom, the first thing children do in the morning is read the morning message to find out what they will be doing that day. Maureen omits letters from some of the words, which encourages the children to predict what words will make sense and sound right and to associate letters with sounds in those words. When she notes that several children in the class are having difficulty with marking long vowel sounds in their writing, her minimal cues message includes several words containing the final *e* (e.g., "Today we will mak_ puppets and writ_ a story about something we lik_"). As the children predict the words, they discuss what letter needs to go on the end of each word and notice that in all the words, the sound of the vowel in the middle is the same as the name of the letter.

After the morning message has been completed and the children are working on group projects, Maureen calls together the six children whose writing reflects difficulty with final *e* and provides direct instruction. She tells them what she has noticed in their writing, beginning by noting what final-*e* words they spelled correctly and then focusing on those spelled incorrectly. She gives the children word cards containing words with long vowel sounds, and they sort the words according to whether they contain the final *e* or not. Before they leave the group, the children revisit their writing and correct words containing the final *e*. When the children begin another writing activity later that morning, Maureen reminds them to think about the final *e* spelling pattern. The message the next morning again includes final-*e* words for review, but introduces two vowels together as well.

The instruction in Maureen's classroom is explicit, systematic, and at the same time integrated. In the remainder of this section, we describe instructional techniques that teachers can integrate into their language arts program to help children use both print and context cues as they read.

Masking

Masking can be used by teachers to help children use context cues, structural units, and letter sounds to identify words (Holdaway, 1979). Working with either a transparency or a big book, the teacher uses a strip of paper to mask text lines and slides it aside to gradually expose parts of words, complete words, and phrases. Children read to the point where the next word is covered and predict what will come next. Then the teacher uncovers the word so the children can use print cues to check their predictions. The class discussion focuses on how predictions are made and where cues come from.

Minimal Cue Messages

The morning message in Maureen Kelly's classroom described above was presented in a "minimal cue" format. Such messages, a modification of the cloze procedure, are set up to encourage integration of print and meaning cues and to aid spelling and word identification. Teachers can develop minimal cue messages to focus on specific types of print cues (e.g., endings, vowel digraphs) when the teacher identifies this need.

   The teacher writes a message to the children with some of the letters missing. Dashes are generally used to show how many letters are required. For example:

   Tod_ _ is a _ery sp_cial d_ _. W_ are go_ _ _ to th_ m_seu_.

   These messages work best when they are relevant to the children and the language is natural and predictable. It is important that teachers discuss with the children what cues they used in unlocking the minimal cue message. Discussion focuses on both meaning and print cues, such as "I knew the word had to be *museum* because you told us yesterday that we were going to the museum today. I also saw that the word began with the letter *m*."

   Initially the teacher fills in the children's predictions, but gradually the children take over the writing. Children who have been exposed to this technique often begin to write minimal cue messages to other students or the teacher.

Oral Reading

When children are reading orally, the way the teacher responds to their reading communicates a great deal about what cues and strategies the teacher thinks are important. If a teacher constantly says, "Sound it out" when the child has difficulty, the child may come to believe that reading equals sounding out. We recommend the following guidelines:

- If a child pauses during reading, wait to give the child time to use both context and print cues to identify the word. Encourage her or him to predict a word that makes sense, sounds right, and checks out.

- If a child makes a substitution while reading that is consistent with the author's meaning, ignore the miscue. Research shows that even good readers do not read with 100 percent accuracy; instead, they make some meaningful slips because of the constructive nature of reading. Ignoring such miscues communicates to children that making meaning is the essence of reading.

▪ If a child corrects a mistake, reinforce this by commenting on the appropriateness of the correction, rather than focusing on the error.

▪ If a child makes miscues that do not make sense, leave time for self-correction. If the child does not self-correct, ask whether what he or she read sounded right and made sense. Focus discussion on the meaning the child constructed from the reading.

For each instructional technique included in this chapter, we recommend having children talk about the strategies they use. Through discussion, they develop both metacognitive awareness of strategies and control of their reading. However, the ultimate goal is automatic application of word identification strategies most of the time so children are able to focus their attention on meaning. The next section deals with helping children achieve automaticity and fluency.

AUTOMATICITY AND FLUENCY

The amount of effort we need to invest in a task lies along a continuum with automatic processing at one end and controlled processing at the other end (Adams, 2002). We are able to complete tasks that are overlearned automatically. In contrast, we depend upon controlled processing for tasks that are not overlearned, and our mind can only focus on one controlled process at a time. During reading, the tasks of constructing and monitoring meaning place a continual demand on active attention. Hence, if we need to attend to word identification as we read, our comprehension will be negatively affected. It is clear that a crucial factor in skilled reading is the ability to recognize words effortlessly and automatically. In order to achieve automaticity, children need to read, read, and read some more (Allington, 2006). Rossman (1987) estimates that children need to read for a minimum of three-and-a-half hours every week to achieve automaticity when reading material at their independent reading level.

The National Reading Panel (2000) states there is ample evidence that one of the major differences between good and poor readers is in the quantity of time they spend reading. Research has revealed that children in high-level reading groups tend to spend more time reading than children in lower-level reading groups (Bloome & Green, 1984). The difference between good and poor readers in the amount of time they spend reading increases during their years in school. Good readers read more both at home and at school, while poor readers read very little in either context. Reading researcher Keith Stanovich (1986) refers to this as a "Matthew effect"—the rich get richer and the poor get poorer. Since good readers are more likely than poor ones to read outside the classroom, it is imperative that time be set aside in school for all children to read.

In many ways fluency can be seen as the companion to automaticity. It is "the ability to read connected text rapidly, smoothly, effortlessly and automatically with little conscious attention to decoding" (Meyer, 2002). Fluent reading is described as reading where there is "correct prosody and where attention can be allocated to comprehension" (Wolf & Katzir-Cohen, 2001, p. 219), because the reader is not having to consciously attend to decoding individual words. This is why educators have found there to be a significant, positive relationship between oral reading fluency and reading comprehension. Indeed, fluency can form a bridge to reading comprehension from decoding skills (Pikulski & Chard, 2005), and it is just as crucial for older readers to work on fluency as younger readers (Rasinski & Padak, 2005).

Readers can develop their fluency and automaticity through a variety of classroom reading activities, including one of our favourites, Reader's Theatre (Kinniburgh & Shaw, 2007), which is described in the chapter on drama. For readers who require more intensive support with their development of fluency and automaticity, in an examination of research on the efficacy of repeated oral reading, the National Reading Panel (2000) concluded that "guided repeated oral reading that included guidance from teachers, peers, or parents had a significant and positive impact on word recognition, fluency, and comprehension across a range of grade levels" (p. 12). As such, we include two oral reading techniques in this section, both of which involve considerable guidance and feedback.

Paired Reading

Paired reading (Topping, 1987) is a technique that involves a child reading with another reader from a book the child has selected. The other reader may be the child's parent, a volunteer, a teacher, or another child. The activity is done for 10 to 15 minutes on at least five days per week for eight to twelve weeks.

We present the steps in paired reading in Classroom Activity 6.3. Tutors praise children for appropriate signalling, self-correcting, and fluent reading. They also encourage children to talk about the meaning they have constructed both during and after reading.

CLASSROOM ACTIVITY **6.3**

Steps in Paired Reading

1. The child chooses a book to read.
2. Beginning with a prearranged signal, the child and another reader read aloud together.
3. It is important for the child to read each word correctly. If he or she doesn't, the other reader reads the word correctly, the child repeats it, and they continue reading together.
4. Using another prearranged signal (e.g., a nudge or tap), the child indicates that he or she is ready to read alone. The other reader praises the child.
5. The child reads alone until an error is made or a word is encountered that he or she cannot read in five seconds.
6. The reader immediately rejoins the child by saying the difficult word and having the child repeat it, and then they continue reading together until the child gives the signal again and the procedure is repeated or the session ends.

Source: Based on A. Brailsford, *Paired reading: Positive reading practice* (Edmonton: Northern Alberta Reading Specialists Council, 1991), pp. 3–4.

Repeated Reading

Repeated reading has been found to improve word identification skills, comprehension, and reading fluency (Mandlebaum, Hodges, & Messenheimer, 2007). The technique involves having the student read a short, meaningful passage several times until a satisfactory level of fluency is attained (Samuels, 1979). Either the teacher or students selects the material to be read, but it should be material the students are able to read independently or that they find engaging. If longer stories are chosen, short selections of 50 to 200 words are marked off for rereading.

To conduct a repeated reading, the student reads the selection to the teacher, who records reading speed and number of word recognition errors on a graph. The teacher and student set a goal for both reading speed (e.g., 90 words per minute) and accuracy (no more than five errors in a 100-word passage). The student practises reading the selection until he or she reads at or above the goal set. Then the teacher and student select another passage, and the procedure is repeated. The graph provides a visual display of the student's increasing fluency. Samuels found that both the initial speed of reading passages and the number of rereadings required to reach the goal decreased over time.

You can also modify repeated reading so that two children work together rather than with the teacher, making the technique more practical for the classroom (Koskinen & Blum, 1986). In paired, repeated reading, children read together for 10 to 15 minutes. Each child reads a short passage at his or her independent reading level three times and then evaluates his or her own reading, as well as that of a partner. Paired repeated reading involves the following steps:

1. Children choose partners or are assigned partners by their teacher.
2. Children select their own passages of approximately 50 words to read. Some children need guidance to select material at their independent level.
3. The children read their passages silently and then decide who will be the first reader.
4. The first reader reads his or her passage to a partner three times, asking for help with words if needed. After each oral reading, the reader fills in a "How well did I read?" self-evaluation sheet. This sheet consists of a Likert-type scale ranging from Fantastic to Needs Much More Practice (Fantastic, Good, Fair, Not So Good, Needs Much More Practice). For young children, teachers use pictures to represent the points on the scale. The partner listens to the child read, and after the second and third reading, tells the reader how his or her reading improved. The listener never makes negative comments.
5. The children switch roles.

Teachers introduce and model the technique for children, helping them understand (1) the procedures involved, (2) how to listen and make positive comments (e.g., "I noticed you self-corrected," "read in phrases," "read more smoothly," "knew more words"), and (3) how to select material for reading. After teachers provide supervised practice, children are able to use the technique independently.

INTEGRATING KNOWLEDGE-BASED AND TEXT-BASED INFORMATION

The focus of the techniques we describe in this section is on helping readers use what they know and what is on the page together as they read. We present an overview of the techniques and specific objectives for each technique in Table 6.2. We recommend that the reading strategies we describe in this chapter be applied across the curriculum as well as during language arts classes.

Directed Reading–Thinking Activity

The directed reading–thinking activity (or DRTA) (Stauffer, 1975) is a long-used instructional technique for use with narrative or expository material and for helping students develop critical thinking (Fischer, Brozo, Frey, & Ivey, 2007). Students first predict what they will

TABLE 6.2 Instructional Techniques for Integrating Knowledge-Based and Text-Based Information

Technique	Material	Helps Children:
Directed reading–thinking activity	Narrative texts with strong plot lines	• Set purposes for reading narrative texts. • Make and evaluate predictions during reading.
KWL	Informational texts	• Set purposes for reading informational texts. • Ask and answer questions during reading.
Questioning the author	Narrative and informational texts	• Construct meaning during reading. • Monitor meaning during reading. • Understand character and plot. • Fill in gaps in text. • Summarize text information.
Question–answer relationship	Narrative and informational texts	• Determine which information sources are required to answer specific questions. • Answer text-based and knowledge-based questions.
Reciprocal teaching	Informational texts	• Summarize text information. • Ask questions. • Clarify parts of texts that are confusing. • Make predictions.
Think-aloud	Narrative and informational texts	• Make predictions. • Form visual images as they read. • Link prior knowledge with text information. • Monitor ongoing comprehension. • Correct comprehension confusions.
Semantic webs	Narrative and informational texts	• Activate knowledge before reading. • Construct relationships among ideas. • Relate text information to prior knowledge.

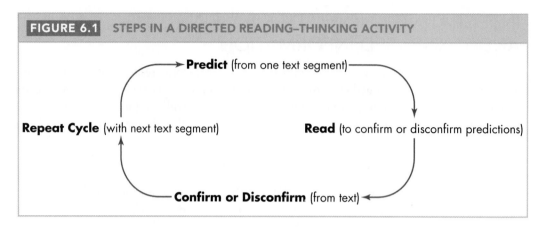

FIGURE 6.1   STEPS IN A DIRECTED READING–THINKING ACTIVITY

Predict (from one text segment)

Repeat Cycle (with next text segment)

Read (to confirm or disconfirm predictions)

Confirm or Disconfirm (from text)

read, and then they check their predictions through subsequent reading. The technique helps students actively seek information from the material they read. The teacher acts as a catalyst to thought by asking such questions as

■ What do you think?

■ Why do you think so?

■ How can you support it?

As readers predict what they will read, they rely on their knowledge, and as they check their predictions, they use cues in the text.

The DRTA is most appropriate for narrative material with a clearly defined plot that can easily be read in one sitting. Short mystery stories are ideal for this activity. The basic steps in the technique are outlined here and summarized in Figure 6.1.

1. On the basis of the title and illustration or first paragraph of a story, the teacher asks students to predict what will happen by asking questions such as:
   ❑ What do you think this story will be about?
   ❑ What do you think will happen in this story?
   ❑ Why do you think so?
   This last question is particularly important, because it gives children an opportunity to refer to both their knowledge and the cues in the title, picture, or first paragraph.

   During the prediction process, the teacher's role is not to evaluate predictions, but rather to activate thought by asking students to defend their hypotheses. In grade 1 classrooms, some teachers have the children whisper their predictions to a partner to ensure that all are engaging in the predicting process. The children then share their predictions in the group context, and the teacher writes them on the board for later reference. Once children are able to read and write independently, they can fill in prediction charts and share them with partners.

2. Students are then asked to read silently to a certain point in the material to confirm or disprove their hypotheses. It is particularly effective to have children stop at suspenseful points in the story.

3. After the students have read to the designated point, they discuss which of their hypotheses were confirmed. The teacher asks for evidence from the text to support the plausibility and accuracy of the hypotheses.

❑ What do you think now?

❑ Find the part in the text to confirm or disconfirm your prediction.

Students might read aloud a sentence or paragraph to provide this evidence. Again, this helps to focus attention on both text-based and knowledge-based information.

4. After students have completed the three-step process (predict, read, prove) with one segment of the material, they go on to the next segment. The process continues until they have read the entire text. Throughout, the teacher serves as a mentor to refine and deepen the reading–thinking process, but takes care not to evaluate the students' predictions. It is also useful to emphasize the importance of evaluating and finding proof in the text rather than deciding who is right or wrong. The DRTA is not a contest; it is a technique to make sure individuals start thinking before they begin to read.

It may be best to make no more than five stops in one story in one sitting so as not to interrupt the students' reading too frequently (Gillet & Temple, 1994). The DRTA is particularly helpful for those children who take a passive approach to reading and who appear to believe that the message is in the book. However, the technique will help these children become active, purposeful readers only if they know why they are doing it and how they can use a similar strategy when they read independently.

The KWL Technique

The KWL technique helps children "deepen reading comprehension and encourage active learning" when reading expository texts (Gammill, 2006). Modelling the active thinking involved in reading for information (Ogle, 1986), the technique involves children using the following three basic steps:

1. accessing what they *know*

2. deciding what they *want* to learn

3. recalling what they did *learn* as a result of reading

The children use a group or individual chart like the one in Box 6.4 to guide them through these steps.

1. *K: What I know.* The children brainstorm information they know about the topic or a key concept in the material (e.g., wolves). The teacher records what the students brainstorm on the board or an overhead. The goal of this brainstorming is to activate whatever

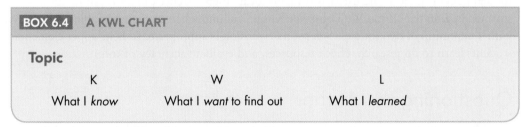

BOX 6.4 **A KWL CHART**

Topic

K	W	L
What I *know*	What I *want* to find out	What I *learned*

Source: Adapted from D. M. Ogle, "KWL: A teaching model that develops active reading of expository text," *Reading Teacher*, 39 (6) (1986), 565.

knowledge the readers have that will help them construct meaning as they read. Ogle (1986) suggests deepening students' thinking by asking questions such as:

- ❑ Where did you learn that?
- ❑ How can you prove that?

To avoid implying a transmission model of knowledge, some teachers have children differentiate between ideas they are sure about (everyone agrees) and those they are not so sure about (some agree).

Some teachers also ask children to complete a second, optional part of this step—thinking about what general categories of information they are likely to encounter when they read. The children consider the information they have brainstormed and group it into more general categories (e.g., what wolves eat, where they live).

2. *W: What I want to learn.* As the children think about what they know on a topic and what categories of information might be included in what they read, questions emerge. After the group discussion, each child records his or her own questions in the W column to focus attention during reading. The children then read the material.

3. *L: What I learned.* After the children finish reading, they write down in the L column what they learned from reading. The role of the teacher is to have them locate cues in the text that they used to construct this information.

If not all of the children's questions are answered in the material, the children generate a list of "Questions I Would Like Answered," and the teacher suggests further reading on the topic. This ensures that the children's desire to learn takes precedence over what the author has chosen to include.

Rachel has been stumped a number of times by her students including information that is incorrect in the K component of the technique. To deal with this, Sampson (2002) has extended the KWL technique by adding a confirmation component to deal with instances of children providing incorrect information in the "What I Know" column, for example, "a whale is a really big fish," and the proliferation of questionable information on the Internet. Sampson suggests changing the heading of the K column to "What We Think We Know." This provides support for brainstorming without giving the impression that the items listed are all accurate. After the students brainstorm what they think they know and what they want to know, they search for sources to either confirm information in the "What We Think We Know" column or answer questions in the "What We Want to Know" column. Columns labelled "Source" are inserted beside both the "What We Think We Know" and the "What We Learned" column, and sources (books, Internet addresses, magazines, electronic media) related to each item or question are listed as students locate them. A check mark is put beside a brain-stormed item in the "What We Think We Know" column when students are able to confirm it with a minimum of two sources. Sampson's extension is appropriate to help upper elementary students learn to do research, check resources, and evaluate accuracy of information.

Questioning the Author

The QtA technique can help upper elementary and middle-school children construct meaning during reading of both expository and narrative texts. The technique brings the author to the foreground, and students learn to question the author with a "reviser's eye" (Beck, McKeown,

Hamilton, & Kucan, 1997). It also allows opportunities for constructive conversation, where readers can negotiate meaning with each other and with the text (Nichols, 2006).

Planning

You can begin planning a QtA by conducting a careful reading of the text the students are going to read. As they read, teachers identify the major ideas students are to construct and potential problems they might encounter. They then segment the text so they can have students stop reading where the major ideas are or where the students might have problems. Finally, they develop queries, which are different from questions in that they are not used to assess comprehension after reading but rather to help students construct meaning *during* reading. There are three different types of queries: initiating, follow-up, and narrative.

1. *Initiating queries.* Draw attention to major ideas and the fact that ideas are written by the author.
   - ❑ What is the author trying to say here?
   - ❑ What is the author's message?

2. *Follow-up queries.* Help students construct the meaning behind the actual words of the author, connect ideas previously learned with the text, and figure out why the author included certain information.
   - ❑ What does the author mean here?
   - ❑ Does the author explain this clearly?
   - ❑ Does this make sense with what the author told us before?
   - ❑ Why do you think the author tells us this now?

3. *Narrative queries.* Deal with characters and plot.
   - ❑ From what the author has told us, what do you think this character is up to?
   - ❑ How does the author let you know that something has changed?

Implementation

1. *Introduction of QtA.* It is ideal that the classroom be arranged in a U shape to facilitate discussion, and, the first time QtA is used, that teachers tell students they will be discussing a text in a new way. The teacher talks about author fallibility, indicating that sometimes ideas are not as clear as they might be. The job of the student is to try to discern by the evidence in the text what the author might have been trying to convey. The teacher then demonstrates through a think-aloud the kind of thinking involved in constructing meaning from a text and that characterizes a QtA discussion. Following the demonstration, students are given the opportunity to ask questions about what the teacher was doing, and they can discuss the meaning that each constructed from the text.

2. *QtA process.*
   - ❑ As students read a text, the teacher asks them to stop at the end of each segment and poses queries to initiate discussion.
   - ❑ The students contribute ideas that can be refined, challenged, or developed by the students and the teacher. The students and teacher work collaboratively to grapple with ideas and construct understanding.

❏ The teacher serves as an initiator, facilitator, guide, and responder. In addition to queries, teachers use the first three "moves" listed below to make ideas students have offered in the discussion more productive and the next three to bring themselves into the interaction with students more directly:

◆ *Marking.* Paraphrasing or explicitly acknowledging an idea's importance.

◆ *Turning back.* Turning students' attention back to the text or turning responsibility back to the students for figuring out ideas.

◆ *Revoicing.* Rephrasing ideas students are struggling with.

◆ *Modelling.* Showing the students strategic processes they can use to grapple with text.

◆ *Annotating.* Providing information to fill in gaps or add information.

◆ *Recapping.* Pulling information together or summarizing the major ideas students have constructed to that point in the discussion. Students assume greater responsibility for recapping over time.

Question–Answer Relationship

The question–answer relationship (or QAR) was developed for enhancing children's ability to answer questions (Raphael, 1986) and can be particularly helpful in reading expository text (Jones & Leahy, 2006). The technique is based on a taxonomy of questions:

▨ textually explicit (answer in the text)

▨ textually implicit (answer involves use of both the reader's knowledge and text)

▨ scriptally implicit (answer is in the reader's knowledge) (Pearson & Johnson, 1978)

A QAR focuses on two major categories of information used for answering questions:

▨ *in the book* (text-based information)

▨ *in my head* (knowledge-based information)

Each of these two categories is subdivided into two question types, as shown in Table 6.3.

TABLE 6.3 **Question–Answer Relationships**

In the Book	In My Head
Right There	Author and You
The words in the question and in the answer are "right there" in one sentence. Find the words used to make up the question and look at the other words in that sentence to find the answer.	The answer is not in the story alone. You need to think about what you know and what the author tells you and fit it together.
Think and Search (Putting It Together)	On My Own
The answer is in the story but you need to find it in more than one sentence or paragraph. The answer comes from more than one part of the text.	The answer is not in the story. You need to use what you already know.

Source: Adapted from T. Raphael, "Teaching question-answer relationships," *Reading Teacher, 39* (6) (1986), 519.

When using this technique, teachers introduce students to the two major categories—*in the book* and *in my head*—before having them deal with the four question types (Raphael, 1986). In the initial stages of instruction, the students' answers to questions are less important than their being able to indicate which source of information is required. You might find the following suggested steps in teaching QARs helpful:

1. The teacher begins by explaining to the children that they are going to talk about questions and the best way to answer them. Some questions ask for information that the children can easily find in the book. Other times, they won't find it there and will need to use what they know to answer the questions. Each question can be answered by figuring out where to get the information needed for the answer.

2. The teacher asks specific questions, and discussion focuses on where the children get information to answer each question.

3. The teacher gives the children short passages and questions for which both answers and QARs are provided for further discussion.

4. The teacher gives the children short passages with questions and answers, and the children indicate which QAR each belongs to.

5. The teacher gives the children passages and questions, and they identify both the QARs and the answers to the questions.

6. The children then move to the two questions for in-the-book and in-my-head categories and eventually to longer passages.

7. The teacher provides regular review and extends the use of QARs to content area texts. (Raphael, 1986.)

The terms "in the book" and "in my head" can be confusing for primary children. Some teachers have found that substituting the terms "on the page" and "off the page" helps primary children gain a better understanding of the QARs involved in this instructional strategy.

Reciprocal Teaching

Reciprocal teaching (Palincsar, 1986) is a dialogue between a teacher and children to jointly construct meaning as they read. It is designed to promote four comprehension strategies:

1. summarizing a passage in a sentence
2. asking one or two good questions about the passage
3. clarifying parts that are confusing
4. predicting what the next part will be about

The teacher models these strategies using expository passages, and then the students assume the role of teacher, using segments of the text. There are four critical foundations necessary for capitalizing on this technique: **scaffolding**, thinking aloud, **metacognition**, and learning cooperatively (Oczkus, 2003). Here are some steps in using the technique:

1. *Modelling the strategy.* The teacher meets with a small group of students, each of whom has a copy of the same content area material, and models the four comprehension strategies while reading a paragraph from the material.

a. The teacher summarizes the paragraph, and the students decide whether the summary is accurate.

b. The teacher asks questions about the paragraph, and the students tell whether the questions involve important information in the passage and then answer the questions.

c. The teacher identifies parts of the paragraph that could be confusing and, with the students' help, clarifies these parts.

d. Finally, the teacher predicts what the next passage will be about, and the students judge whether the prediction is logical.

2. *Students assume role of teacher.* After the teacher has modelled the procedure with several segments of text, he or she asks a student to be the teacher. As the student teacher summarizes, asks questions, identifies confusing parts, and predicts what will come next, the adult teacher provides feedback and coaches him or her through the strategies. The other students are asked to judge the adequacy of the summary, importance of the questions, and logic of the predictions, as well as to help clarify points and support the student teacher. The following steps indicate how reciprocal teaching is used when students assume the role of the teacher:

a. The teacher presents the children with the title of the material they will be reading and asks them to use background knowledge they have about the topic to predict what they will learn in the material. A student teacher is then appointed for the first part of the material, and the group reads it.

b. The student teacher asks a question that the other students answer, and then summarizes what has been read. The students judge the accuracy of the summary and the importance of the questions.

c. A discussion follows about clarifications that the student teacher and other students made while reading, or about points that they think still need to be made.

d. Finally, the student teacher and other students make predictions about the next segment of the material, and a new student teacher is appointed.

Throughout the period where the student assumes the role of the teacher, the adult teacher provides the students with feedback and instruction on how to use the four strategies more effectively. For example, the teacher might help the students to produce shorter summaries or to ask questions about main ideas as well as details.

At the end of a half-hour reciprocal teaching session, the teacher sometimes gives the children a passage they have not read before and asks them to summarize it or answer a few substantial questions about it. Reciprocal teaching is more appropriate for students at the upper elementary level than for primary children.

Think-Alouds

Think-alouds as we describe them here are used to help readers clarify their views of reading and their use of strategies. The technique has also been found to promote self-efficacy, engagement, and comprehension in reading (Walker, 2005). You might consider structuring your think-alouds by using the following four steps (Davey, 1983):

1. *Teacher modelling.* The teacher verbalizes his or her own thoughts while reading orally to provide a "model." The teacher selects a short passage that contains points of difficulty, contradictions, ambiguity, or unknown words. As the teacher reads the passage aloud, students follow silently, listening to how the teacher thinks through the reading. The following are examples of points that can be made during reading to help children develop metacognitive awareness and control:

   ❏ Make predictions. (The teacher shows the children how to make predictions during reading.)

   > From the title, I predict that this story will be about a boy who wanted to fly.
   > In this next part, I think we'll find out why the boys got into a fight.

   ❏ Describe the picture you're forming in your head from the information. (The teacher demonstrates how to develop images during reading.)

   > I have a picture of this scene in my mind. The boy is walking through a dark alley and there are no other people around.

   ❏ Share an analogy. (The teacher links prior knowledge with new information in text. Davey calls this the "like-a" step.)

   > This is like a time we went to West Edmonton Mall and Sean got lost.

   ❏ Verbalize a confusing point. (The teacher shows children how to monitor their ongoing comprehension.)

   > This just doesn't make sense.
   > This is not what I thought would happen.

   ❏ Demonstrate fix-up strategies. (The teacher shows children how to correct their comprehension confusions.)

   > I'd better reread.
   > Maybe I'll read ahead to see if it gets clearer.
   > I'd better change my picture of the story.
   > This is a new word to me—I'd better check context to figure it out.

2. *Practise with student partners.* After several modelling experiences, children work together with partners to practise think-alouds. The partners take turns reading and thinking aloud with short passages.

3. *Independent practice.* Children practise independently with the use of checklists such as the one in Box 6.5.

4. *Use in other subject areas.* Teachers both model and provide opportunities for children to practise using think-alouds with content area materials. This helps children learn when and why to use certain strategies.

Semantic Webs

A **semantic web** is a visual representation of relationships among ideas. These graphic arrangements (sometimes also referred to as *semantic maps*) show the major ideas and relationships in texts (Sinatra, Stahl-Gemake, & Berg, 1984) or among word meanings. Webs can also

BOX 6.5	CHECKLIST FOR THINK-ALOUDS			
	Not Very Much	A Little Bit	Much of the Time	All of the Time
Predicting				
Picturing				
"Like-a"				
Identifying problems				
Using fix-ups				

Source: Adapted from B. Davey, "Think aloud—Modeling the cognitive processes of reading comprehension," *Journal of Reading*, *27* (1) (1983), 46.

help to create a visual representation of a reader's prior knowledge and the knowledge that is generated from transacting with a text (Irvin, Buehl, & Radcliffe, 2007). A web consists of nodes containing key words, with connecting lines between nodes.

Elementary teacher Joyce Bodell uses prior- and post-knowledge webs to achieve a number of significant purposes. Before beginning a new unit or theme, she has her students individually web everything that they already know about the topic. She writes the topic or idea on the board, reads it aloud, and then asks the children to take a minute or two to think of everything that they know about it and to record their ideas on a piece of paper.

Joyce asks the students to complete this activity individually for two reasons:

- First, she wants to know what level of understanding each child is bringing to the unit of study. This informs her teaching and enables her to plan for content and lessons that will meet the children's needs most effectively.

- Second, it enables children to recognize for themselves how much they already know and to raise questions about particular ideas, facts, or aspects that they are not sure about.

After the webs are finished, Joyce collects and reads them, and then stores them away until the students have finished their unit.

At this point, Joyce usually does a whole-class brainstorming activity and records it on chart paper. This provides a written record of the children's combined knowledge, which Joyce leaves posted in the classroom. The children often refer back to it during whole-class lessons and discussions when they learn something that validates (or invalidates) what they thought they knew, or when they find an answer to a question that someone raised.

Roz Stooke retelling a story with a flannel board

FIGURE 6.2 A SEMANTIC WEB OF CANADA

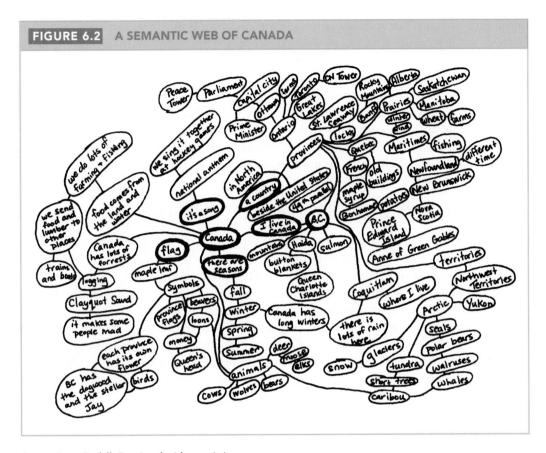

Source: Joyce Bodell. Reprinted with permission.

At the end of the unit, Joyce gives individual webs back to the children and asks them to use a coloured pencil to add their new knowledge to their webs and to cross out ideas that didn't really belong. The result is a two-colour web that provides the children with a powerful visual representation of all the learning they accomplished. Often, children ask for a second, larger piece of paper so that they can fit in all of their new ideas. They glue the original web in the centre and branch out onto the larger sheet. If a whole-class web was done, Joyce revisits this with the entire group, and together they build on their combined prior knowledge, adding all of the new information and understandings that they acquired. In the semantic web shown in Figure 6.2, the ideas within thick lines indicate the children's prior knowledge about Canada. The rest of the ideas indicate what they learned.

This second round of webbing offers the teacher a valuable **assessment/evaluation** tool. It demonstrates the breadth and depth of understanding that each student acquired. It can also be used to note what has not been learned, either by individuals or by most of the class. For example, if an important concept seems to be missing from most of the post-knowledge webs, it might indicate to the teacher that some additional instruction time needs to be spent on that area before the unit is drawn to a close.

Of note is that there are many ways in which teachers can help readers view and represent ideas from text. The photo on the previous page shows educator Roz Stooke using a flannel board with flannel pieces that she's created to retell a story. Besides making it a whole- or small-group activity, Roz also likes to set up the flannel boards in centres and have the students recreate and expand upon the stories they have learned. Upper elementary teachers might also consider how they and their students might employ Smartboards and other digital technology to view and represent what they have read.

All of the instructional techniques included in this section have the potential to help children develop awareness and control over their reading. This potential will only be achieved, however, if the teacher models strategy use and the children have opportunities to talk about and use the strategies being demonstrated. We also recommend having children evaluate which strategies work best for them in different contexts and for different purposes.

SELECTING INSTRUCTIONAL TECHNIQUES

The major focus of Chapter 6 has been on techniques to foster the development of effective reading strategies. You may choose to teach these strategies to the whole class, small group, or even with individual children when the resources allow. The strategies and techniques are all to be used within the larger balanced literacy framework. Your professional discernment, which begins with you assessing your students, will guide you as to which strategies, at what time, and in what way should be taught. Importantly, the strategies and techniques are appropriate for readers at all levels of reading proficiency. The key is to maintain the principles of balanced literacy while matching instructional techniques to the needs of specific readers. Table 6.4 summarizes common patterns of reading processing and identifies techniques that are appropriate to use with children who display each pattern.

TABLE 6.4 Matching Reading Patterns and Instructional Techniques

Type of Pattern	Recommended Techniques
• Child is a word caller and needs to make more effective use of background knowledge along with text to construct meaning.	• Select techniques from "Integrating Knowledge-Based and Text-Based Information."
• Child relies too heavily on phonics knowledge to decode words and produces nonsense words when he or she reads orally.	• Begin with techniques from "Strategies for Using Context Cues" and move quickly to those for "Strategies for Integrating Context and Print Cues."
• Child has few strategies for using cues within words and constructs a different meaning from text information or little meaning at all.	• Begin with techniques from "Print Cues," and as soon as the child develops some of these strategies, move to those for "Strategies for Integrating Context and Print Cues."
• Child can decode short words but has difficulty with longer ones.	• Select "Word Sorting" or "Word Parts" techniques.
• Child uses strategies for processing cues within words but constructs a different meaning from text information.	• Select techniques from "Integrating Knowledge-Based and Text-Based Information," emphasizing text-based information initially, and from "Strategies for Integrating Context and Print Cues."
• Child reads slowly and laboriously, giving so much attention to word identification that little is left for comprehension.	• Select techniques from "Automaticity and Fluency."
• Child appears to think the meaning is in the text and can deal only with factual questions.	• Select techniques from "Integrating Knowledge-Based and Text-Based Information."

SUMMARY

Teachers are routinely bombarded with claims that there is one answer to reading instruction, in particular, to instruction for children who struggle with their reading achievement. It may be a diet, it may be exercises, it may be a specific commercial program, it may be listening or visual devices. But whenever someone presents one answer for all children, alarm bells should sound. Reading is a complex process. Consequently, children's reading achievement arises from a complex interaction of factors within the child, the school, and the broader community. The job of teachers is therefore an equally complex one. Just as we saw with Tara-Lynn Scheffel and her struggle to learn how phonics could fit within her program, teachers must use their professional decision making to learn about their students, and what research has to say about learning to read and larger language processes, about the context(s) in which they are teaching, and about the various forms of instruction that fit their own teaching style.

The balanced reading framework we present in Chapters 5 and 6 is designed to align with the greater balanced literacy framework that we introduced in Chapter 1. The purpose of the reading framework is to help children acquire the skills and dispositions of "good readers," which we list in Chapter 4 (e.g., establish a purpose for reading, concentrate more on constructing meaning from texts than on identifying all the words in a text correctly, consistently orchestrate semantic, syntactic, pragmatic, and graphophonic cues, and have at hand a variety of strategies for when the text gets rough and know which strategies to use, depending on the situation). Chapter 6 focuses on smaller instructional techniques to foster strategy development and implementation related to word identification (e.g., phonics), context cues (e.g., cloze passages), integrating context and print cues (e.g., masking), automaticity and fluency (e.g., paired reading), and integrating knowledge-based and text-based information (e.g., directed reading–thinking activity).

With regard to using phonics in aid of teaching word identification, teachers are faced with several issues when planning phonics instruction, including how much terminology to use, how to deal with phonics rules, whether to use an analytic or a synthetic phonics approach, whether to provide separate or integrated phonics instruction, and, finally, whether to teach phonics incidentally or systematically. Techniques to help children develop strategies for using cues within words and for identifying words using phonics knowledge include word walls, onsets and rimes, making words, word sorting, and word parts.

Context cues provide a way for children to use their language and world knowledge to predict words as they read. In the cloze procedure, words are omitted from passages and children use their language and world knowledge to predict words and monitor their predictions.

The most effective instructional techniques for word identification involve developing strategies for using both print and context cues. Teachers can integrate techniques such as masking and minimal cue messages into daily reading activities and are thoughtful as they respond to children's oral reading, reinforcing use of print, language, and meaning cues.

The ultimate goal of word identification instruction is to help children develop automaticity and fluency in using both print and context cues so that they are able to focus most of their attention on constructing meaning. Paired reading and repeated reading are activities that can enable children to reach this goal.

No single set of instructional techniques will meet the needs of all children. Teachers must assess each child's reading needs and match the program as closely as possible with these needs. This is particularly critical for children who have difficulty learning to read. Ultimately, it is through reflective practice that teachers can best gauge how to achieve a balance in their reading instruction.

TALKING POINTS

First-year teacher Frank Emanuele has this to say about what it means to be a reflective practitioner:

Frank Emanuele

> Before any lesson in language arts, I have to ask myself: "What are my students going to get out of this lesson?" "Is it engaging enough?" "Will they enjoy it?" "What are my goals?". After each lesson, I try to reevaluate how the lesson went and if my goals were achieved. Although sometimes it's hard to keep updated, an ongoing journal about my lessons helps me to reflect on how well I'm doing as an instructor.

Think to yourself and share with your colleagues: When practice teaching and teaching reading, what kind of a journal might be helpful to you? What observations might you make about the intention of your lesson, the way the lesson actually went, and what would you do differently? What observations might you also make about your cooperating teacher's reading lessons and what might s/he have to say about her/his own process of reflection?

In the quest to begin reflecting on your own journey through this text and its application to your practice, consider completing one or more of the following activities, then discussing how they relate to the responses of your colleagues.

Option 1: Semantic Webs

Create a semantic web that shows your emerging understanding of what you can do in a classroom to help a child learn to read. Following the creation of this web, highlight the aspects of your web that you feel most comfortable implementing and the parts of putting together reading instruction about which you feel most nervous or unsure. You might want to structure this last part as a series of questions.

Option 2: Planning for Comprehension

Select a grade, a children's text, and a comprehension strategy to go along with them. Complete the comprehension strategy for the text (e.g., complete a story map; explain what you would say for a think-aloud). Explain why this comprehension strategy is a good match for the text and how you would initially teach this strategy to your students.

Option 3: Considering Phonics Instruction

Create a graphic organizer of your choice of the main issues related to phonics instruction. Indicate how these relate to the ways in which you were taught and to what you may have seen happening in classrooms more recently. Present what questions you have about the place of phonics in your own practice and in balanced literacy as a whole.

SELECTED PROFESSIONAL RESOURCES

Tara-Lynn Scheffel recommends ...

Cunningham, P. & Hall, D. P. (2001). *Making words: Multilevel, hands-on, developmentally appropriate spelling and phonics activities*. Columbus: Frank Schaffer Publications.

Cunningham, P. & Hall, D. P. (2001). *Making big words: Multilevel, hands-on spelling and phonics activities*. Columbus: Frank Schaffer Publications.

Both of these books give step-by-step instructions for making words activities. *Making Words* is great for earlier readers and *Making Big Words* for children who are ready for a greater challenge. Select words as part of a theme and/or as an accompaniment to a book you're reading. Maybe one of the best parts of this kind of word study is that it helps with both reading and writing.

Cunningham, P. M. (2005). *Phonics they use: Words for reading and writing (4th ed.)*. Boston: Allyn & Bacon.

This book includes terrific techniques and activities to teach a range of phonics-related strategies. What's different about this book from many other phonics-type publications is that *Phonics They Use* promotes the teaching of phonics within meaningful contexts and in purposeful ways.

Tovani, C. (2000). *I read it, but I don't get it: Comprehension strategies for adolescent readers*. Portland, ME: Stenhouse Publishers.

Chris Tovani is a long-time teacher of adolescents, and this book comes directly from her attempts to help her students who could say the words in a text but who couldn't make meaning from what they were "reading." Full of techniques that are about as classroom-ready as you can get, *I Read It, But I Don't Get It* caters specifically to the adolescent reader, but with modifications many of the strategies can equally be applied to younger readers.

Beers, G. Kylene. (2003). *When kids can't read, what teachers can do: A guide for teachers, 6–12.* Portsmouth, NH: Heinemann.

It seems that everyone these days is in love with this book. Like the others in my list, this is a practical guide to teaching reading strategies, but it is especially directed toward children who are experiencing difficulty with their reading achievement.

Literacy Across the Curriculum

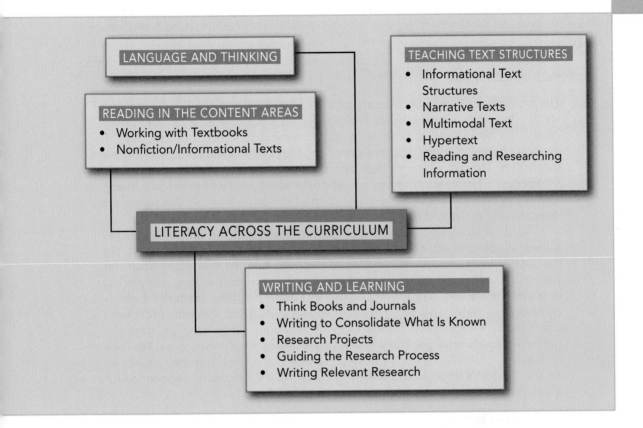

LANGUAGE AND THINKING

TEACHING TEXT STRUCTURES
- Informational Text Structures
- Narrative Texts
- Multimodal Text
- Hypertext
- Reading and Researching Information

READING IN THE CONTENT AREAS
- Working with Textbooks
- Nonfiction/Informational Texts

LITERACY ACROSS THE CURRICULUM

WRITING AND LEARNING
- Think Books and Journals
- Writing to Consolidate What Is Known
- Research Projects
- Guiding the Research Process
- Writing Relevant Research

JANET MCCONAGHY'S "LIFE-CYCLE" PROJECT

Grade 3 teacher Janet McConaghy has a wealth of experience in teaching literacy across the curriculum. In a recent conversation, Janet reminded us that "Every teacher is a teacher of literacy; across the curriculum and across modes. It's about knowing the language of the discipline (in mathematics, science, social studies, and all the other elementary subject areas), as well as about how to use language and literacy to make sense of what we're learning. Literacy across the curriculum includes terms (vocabulary), concepts,

Janet McConaghy

and content. It's about reading critically; thinking about what we are reading. It's knowing the difference between fact and opinion, and understanding how we are influenced by what we read, see, and hear, and how we make choices based on that information." Janet, with co-author Amy von Heyking, has used her teaching experience and insights to create materials for teachers, especially in the social studies (Von Heyking & McConaghy, 2001, 2003).

Every spring Janet embarks on a science project on life cycles, in this case metamorphosis. In Janet's words,

> The students each receive one caterpillar in a small, lidded cup (also containing food). The students are always excited by this project and they watch their caterpillars hour-by-hour, using every spare moment to check on them. They're intrigued by the changes that take place, and they become very attached to their caterpillars. They usually name their caterpillar and take a very personal interest in its progress. They need to know their caterpillar is safe and well cared for. Usually, one or two caterpillars don't thrive, so I keep a few "on reserve" so that no child is disappointed at the end of the project.
>
> The children watch in awe over a two-week period, as the caterpillar creates a hook shape and attaches itself to the lid of the container. By the next day the caterpillar is inside the chrysalis. It happens fast. At that point I transfer each chrysalis, very carefully, to a shoebox the children prepare. They bring in leaves, grass and twigs to make a good home for their butterfly. I add a small cup of water and sugar mixture to the bottom of the box and then I cover the box securely in plastic wrap. After about seven or eight days the butterflies finally emerge. The whole process takes about three weeks. We then release the butterflies into the bushes outside the school, but they usually sit on the children's fingers before they fly away. It's a very special experience for these youngsters.

The students keep a journal and record the caterpillars' changes. They draw what the caterpillar and chrysalis look like, the colouring and movement. They keep a time log, and they pay special attention to the sequence of events that take place. They also write expressively about the entire experience of metamorphosis from the perspective of their caterpillar. One entry is shown in Box 7.1. The children spend a lot of time talking with me and with each other as they interpret what is happening and check the books they are reading so they can hypothesize what will happen next. I have lots of books in a basket available for them to read at any time—both nonfiction and fiction. We read *Butterfly House* by Eve Bunting (1999), and nonfiction books such as *Butterflies & Moths* by Bobbie Kalman and Tammy Everts (1994); *Animal World: Butterflies* by Donna Bailey (1990); and *Animal Ways: Butterflies* by Gloria Schlaepfer (2006). I read aloud *The Trumpet of the Swan* (White, 1973) a chapter at a time every day before lunch. We use Sam's (a character in the story) journal entries as examples of journal writing. Many of the children end their entries with a question, just like Sam does.

A telecollaborative project on the same elementary science unit involving a different teacher and school district can be viewed at http://www.newlife.ecsd.net/Butterflies%20AA.htm. □

BOX 7.1 JOURNAL WRITING: A NEW ARRIVAL

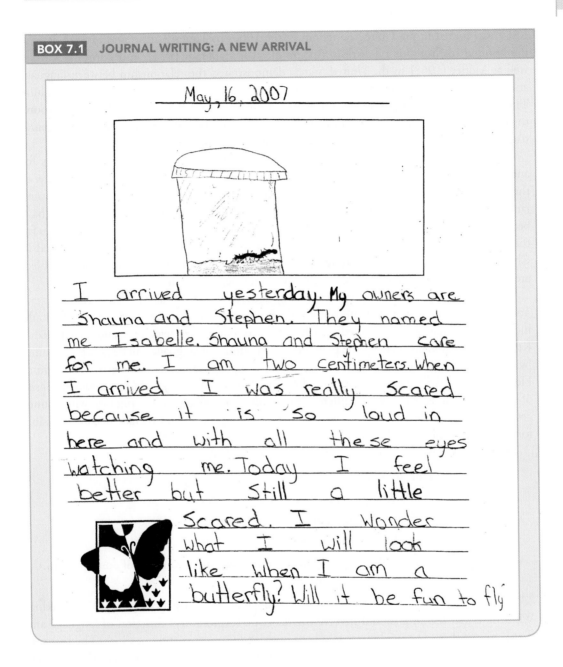

May, 16, 2007

I arrived yesterday. My owners are Shauna and Stephen. They named me Isabelle. Shauna and Stephen care for me. I am two centimeters. When I arrived I was really scared because it is so loud in here and with all these eyes watching me. Today I feel better but still a little scared. I wonder what I will look like when I am a butterfly? Will it be fun to fly

LANGUAGE AND THINKING

Throughout this book we emphasize the important role language plays in learning and thinking. When children write in a journal or talk with each other, as they do in Janet's classroom, about what they have observed and learned, what they have read and what they know, they are reflecting upon their knowledge and understandings. Through this use of language, students grapple with new ideas and often come to new realizations. The term "language across the curriculum," or

LAC, was coined in the United Kingdom in the 1960s by James Britton and his associates at the London Institute for Education. Britton (1970), Halliday (1975), and Barnes (1976), as well as Moffet (1968) in the United States, demonstrated the relationship between language and learning, and spoke to the role of language in learning across all areas of the curriculum. They highlighted the importance of students working together, as they do in Janet's classroom, to collaboratively explore new knowledge, and the importance of the individual expression of students' ideas and understandings in both written and spoken words.

Halliday, Moffett, Britton, and Barnes provided teachers with valuable structures for analyzing, understanding, and creating language learning opportunities in diverse areas of the school curriculum. Using Halliday's Functions of Language as a guide for developing language learning tasks (see Chapter 2 and Julie's work with *Hana's Suitcase*) teachers have been able to develop integrated, meaningful, purposeful, and cohesive learning experiences for their students. The guiding principles outlined in this chapter, as well as those presented in Chapter 2, can be applied to learning activities not only in language arts, but also in subject areas such as social studies, science, mathematics, music, and health.

Froese (1997) points out that the term "language arts" is often replaced by the term "literacy." Today, researchers suggest that literacy should be considered in its broader sense and should include text in many forms and media, such as fine arts, film, video, television, and digital media. Kress (2003) maintains that at some point very soon our use of language will be governed mainly by the screen, and students will need to understand language use within an electronic medium. He says language will not consist of printed texts with incidental images, but instead will consist of texts of all kinds with colour, different fonts, on monitors or mobile phones, with sound, gesture, and movement (Pahl & Rowsell, 2005). This broader view of literacy makes it possible for students to make meaning through a variety of representational modes.

Crowhurst (1994) outlined the following tenets of LAC:

- Language plays a central role in learning.
- Students are actively engaged in meaning-making processes.
- Teachers work as facilitators and guides.
- All six language arts strands are involved in active learning.
- Students are encouraged to express and explore their understanding of concepts and the curriculum using their own language.

LAC requires teaching strategies that encourage active, constructivist meaning-making. We believe that learning should involve the heuristic (exploratory) function of language and that language should be used purposefully to investigate concepts and questions. The best way for students to learn language is to engage in its purposeful use. Students are then actively engaged in meaning-making and are not expected to be passive recipients of the teacher's knowledge. When students are engaged in active learning experiences, they predict, observe, discuss, read, problem solve, and write about their learning.

Julie Gellner's "Hana Project" (see Chapter 2) and Janet McConaghy's "Life-Cycles" project both provide examples of teaching that fit the criteria listed above. The learning activities Julie and Janet designed were authentic and relevant to the students' lives, and they met the objectives of the mandated curriculum. Later in this chapter we provide samples of children's writing from a "Restaurant Project," which Julie's students initiated and which Julie supported and guided. It too is an example of an integrated, cross-curriculum project. In Julie's school, teachers use the Project Approach (Chard, 1998) to motivate students' learning by encouraging them to explore issues of relevance to their own lives and interests, as well as which fulfill the requirements of the mandated curricula. Vivian Vasquez (2003, 2004) supports the importance of student initiated research projects when she writes, "I found that issues raised by the children led to conversations that moved well beyond the traditional topics of study often associated with primary school curriculum" (2004, p. 2).

In a classroom that "balances" literacy instruction, information is not simply processed in isolation, but is shared, built on with peers, and discussed as it relates to real people and real contexts, especially to the students' own lived worlds. This aspect of learning is one of the strongest reasons for students to engage in group projects, where they can study and work together, pooling information and helping one another to clarify and test out specific learnings. Through reading, writing, group interaction, and exploratory talk, students question, make meanings more precise, and reinterpret past experience (which is why a personal story is often told to make a point). Interaction becomes crucially important as learners stretch their limits and move into areas in which they are uncertain, going beyond personal experience and specific situations. Recognizing the role of language in learning has caused educators to focus on processes such as collaboration, cooperation, and group work, and to value the many roles of language and literacy in the classroom.

Sometimes we read our way into understanding, sometime we talk ourselves into understanding, and sometimes we write ourselves into understanding. Reading and writing can create new worlds for the writer (and reader), but it may be that writing, even more than speech, "not only reflects our knowing … but … also causes our knowing" (Dillon, 1985, p. 9). We write letters, lists, papers, reports, and notes, and we also write for ourselves (poetry, stories, notes, diaries, logs). Journal writing is one of the ways in which we write for ourselves, as we attempt to recall and understand. Writing and then rereading our thoughts, pondering them, and revisiting them kindles personal and cognitive growth that we often cannot complete with other people. It is a task we have to accomplish alone. Writing encourages us to make our ideas separate from ourselves—putting our thoughts out there so we can examine them and hold on to them for future reference and ongoing reflection.

LAC is about all three levels of integration addressed in Chapter 1. In the first level of integration, we spoke about the importance of integrating the six language arts. In the second level of integration, we discussed what is known as language across the curriculum (LAC). The third level of integration moves learning from the classroom into the community and the world beyond it. In this chapter we provide examples of all three levels of integration, and we provide teaching scenarios that show how teachers can include the community in their students' learning.

In the chapters on reading in this book, we highlighted the importance of children writing and talking about what they are reading. In this chapter, we begin by addressing reading in the content areas.

READING IN THE CONTENT AREAS

If we want the students in our classrooms to be critically aware, discuss ideas, and get excited about what they are learning, they need to read material that will both interest them and engage them in reading and writing for real life purposes. Reading nonfiction or information texts can do just that. These texts connect language learning to content in specific subject areas such as science, mathematics, and social studies, and they activate the students' interests and curiosity.

Over the last number of years, ideas have shifted about how readers approach nonfiction texts. Initially it was believed that students learn by simply reading and memorizing information presented in a text. Today we no longer regard textual information in such simplistic terms. We believe that readers bring a reservoir of both linguistic and life experiences to the reading event. Readers "transact" with the text (see Chapter 11) in order to make meaning and construct individual knowledge. In content area reading, the teacher plays an important role in assisting students to construct meaning through carefully scaffolding students' background knowledge and language in order for them to successfully access and navigate the text.

Calkins (2001) argues that our schools have, in the past, provided little time for nonfiction reading. She argues that many classrooms still privilege fiction over nonfiction text, and thereby fail to acknowledge the importance of informational texts in students' daily lives. She points out that most reading conducted in adults' and students' lives is nonfiction. We read phone books, recipes, letters, bills, lists, directions, web pages, e-mails, blogs, and advertisements. Because many nonfiction books and grade-level textbooks can pose problems for young readers, it is even more important that teachers provide and read aloud to their students many different forms of nonfiction text. They can thus help their students become familiar with the structure of nonfiction writing and the textual features relevant to information text.

Working with Textbooks

Nonfiction texts are written in a number of forms, such as, biographies, brochures, directions, manuals, letters, newspapers, websites, encyclopedias and textbooks (see the section in Chapter 10 on informational texts). One of the most commonly used nonfiction texts in schools today is the grade-level subject area textbook. A good textbook is written at the students' reading level, but even a good textbook can be inappropriate for some of the children in our culturally and linguistically diverse classrooms, where not all children can read at the level presented in the text. Teachers who use textbooks need to consider how the textbook supports the individual needs of their students. We recommend that teachers who use a textbook in a given subject area go through the book carefully with the children, reading some of the book to them, and leaving parts for the students to read individually. Here are some other pointers for working with a textbook:

- Always scaffold the students' reading so they know how to use the text.
- Talk with the students about what they have read in the book.
- Teach the students how to pick out the main idea and the details in any paragraph.
- Teach students how to use the table of contents, the index, and the glossary.
- Engage the students in as many hands-on activities as possible, to make the contents of the textbook real to the children.
- With younger children (grades 2 and 3), guide the children to the appropriate page and paragraph when they are involved in a research project.
- Supplement the textbook with many other resources, including fiction and nonfiction books (e.g., in math, use *The Doorbell Rang*; Hutchins, 1986).

■ If there are questions in the book, take some time to work through the meaning of the questions with the students. Many math questions, for example, have more than one part, and young children can find this confusing.

■ Draw the students' attention to key words and phrases (e.g., *how many more, altogether, how many left*).

Nonfiction/Information Texts

Today there is a plethora of good quality nonfiction texts available for teachers and children. Nonfiction books have undergone a huge change in recent years, and they no longer convey information in an arcane and pedantic manner. There are many well-written and beautifully illustrated nonfiction books that address many topics, concepts, and practices in all subject areas. These nonfiction texts are also written at many different levels and more readily meet the diverse needs of students in today's classrooms. (See this book's Appendix for specific titles of information texts suitable for students at each grade level.)

Both Calkins (2001) and Allington (2006) recommend that, during independent reading time, students be encouraged to choose books that are interesting to them and which are at an appropriate reading level. Both these researchers see student interest as a vital aspect of developing a reader's ability to comprehend text, especially nonfiction text. Allington (2006) states that the diverse interests of students can only be met if a wide range of books is available to them. He recommends that every classroom should have at least 500 books available to the children, with these books split evenly between fiction and nonfiction. He does, however, state that no "specific quantity can serve all classrooms equally well" (p. 71). Some classrooms may need even more books than this. Calkins (2001) suggests that we invite students to talk about their inquiries and hobbies in order to cultivate their interest in reading nonfiction books, but teachers also need to share nonfiction texts with their students in order to help students understand an author's point of view and approach to the topic of the book.

Many school districts and universities provide lists of nonfiction texts that support specific areas of the curriculum. The Centre for Mathematics Science Technology Education (CMASTE) at the University of Alberta, for example, has developed bibliographies of outstanding quality children's literature that support Programs of Study for both mathematics and science. *Concepts and Practices in Science* (2007), is one bibliography available through CMASTE (Centre for Mathematics Science and Technology Education, http://www.ioncmaste.ca/homepage/index.html). Such resources help teachers and pre-service teachers to plan learning opportunities that connect their presentation of information on a specific topic to nonfiction literature that will support and extend students' engagement with the learning.

In recent years, a large number of biographies have been written specifically for children, providing a glimpse into the lives of celebrated individuals. In Box 7.2, we provide a sample of biographies of people connected with aviation. These books highlight some of the important contributions made to the history of flight, and they provide a stepping-off point for a cross-curricular approach to teaching.

Information texts can be used in elementary classrooms for a variety of purposes including:

■ to provide a context out of which inquiry might grow (Julie Gellner's use of *Hana's Suitcase* in Chapter 2 is a good example of this)

BOX 7.2   **NARRATIVE NONFICTION TEXTS: BIOGRAPHIES ON THE THEME OF FLIGHT**

Burleigh, R. (2003). *Amelia Earhart free in the skies.* (B. Wylie, illus.). Orlando, FL: Silver Whistle Harcourt. This biography of the pioneering aviator is presented in a full-color, comic-book format.

Boren, L. & Marx, T. (2003). *Touching the sky* (P. Fiore, illus.). New York, NY: Margaret K. McElderry Books. Lyrical text provides a glimpse into the extraordinary lives and achievements of Wilbur and Orville Wright.

Busby, P. (2002). *First to fly: How Wilbur and Orville Wright invented the airplane.* Markham, ON: Scholastic Canada. This biography is complemented by the original paintings of David Craig, and by period photographs, as well as by detailed diagrams and easy-to-follow features that explain how Wilbur and Orville mastered the challenges of flight.

Grimes, N. (2002). *Talkin' about Bessie: The story of aviator Elizabeth Coleman* (E. B. Lewis, illus.). New York: Orchard Books, an Imprint of Scholastic Inc. This biography is told as a series of richly imagined monologues that are fictional in form but based on fact.

Moss, M. (2001). *Brave Harriet: The first woman to fly the English Channel* (C. F. Payne, illus). New York, NY: Silver Whistle, Harcourt Inc. The book is written in the first person as though by Harriet Quimby, the first American woman to receive a pilot's licence and the first woman to fly solo across the English Channel.

- to stimulate discussion (Anne Gordon's activity with "heart maps" in Chapter 2 demonstrates this)
- to provide information (in Chapter 2 Julie Gellner's students used a nonfiction text to provide information about the Holocaust)
- to provide examples of quality informational (expository) writing
- to teach children about the textual features of information books in general, for example, graphs, indexes, diagrams (Janet McConaghy uses information texts in her guided reading sessions)
- to teach children specific strategies for reading information text, for example, cause and effect
- to retrieve information pertinent to their exploration, for example, clicking on hyperlinks and navigating the Internet, or skimming through headings in a book
- to increase children's interest and appreciation of information texts, for example, Janet McConaghy's classroom basket of books on "life cycles"

TEACHING TEXT STRUCTURES

It is easier for children to construct meaning when reading texts if they know how authors organize and relate ideas in various forms of text.

Informational Text Structures

Since parents generally don't select informational texts to read aloud to their children, few children come to school with an awareness of the structure of such texts. Informational **text structures** are the consistent features, such as subheadings and italics that cue the reader during reading. Writers use these text structures so that readers can make meaning of a text more effectively. Teachers know that if students don't understand and make use of text structures, they will likely not be able to focus their reading, monitor their understandings, and effectively retrieve text for study purposes (Allen, 2004). Two major types of text structures are "text organization" and "conventions of print." Text organization includes such things as titles, subheadings, paragraphs and sentences, diagrams, keys or legends, and photographs and illustrations. Conventions of print include bold type, italics, white space, and punctuation.

When teachers introduce a new text structure to their students, they often point out the new feature. Sometimes, they will provide a chart in which students can identify the specific structures used in the text (see Table 7.1). Students are also asked to consider the writer's purpose in using these structures. Janet McConaghy often teaches informational text structures in grade 3 during her guided reading sessions, when she has a small group of four or five students. She can then introduce various aspects of text to the children in an effective way. She begins by talking about the cover, asking the students to predict the content, and she poses a question for the children to consider while they are reading. Janet sometimes asks the children to begin by reading together chorally, and at other times they take turns. Then they continue reading quietly to themselves. Janet sits next to one student at a time and listens to them read. She works with the students individually, providing a follow-up task for each of them. Janet's students enjoy reading aloud—and will vie for first spot. In guided reading, the texts are at the students' instructional reading level and are therefore not too difficult for them. In addition, the children feel safe with each other in the small group. They enjoy both the small-group environment and the interaction they have with Janet.

The three most common types of organizational patterns for informational material are: sequence, cause–effect, and compare–contrast. The sequence pattern, which presents information in time order, is commonly found in historical texts, recipes, directions for assembling furniture, and scientific experiments. Cause–effect and compare–contrast patterns appear in a wide range of content areas. We used the Cause–effect pattern in Chapter 2 when we explained that children's language development can be suppressed in school if they are not engaged in authentic conversations. We used the comparison–contrast pattern in Chapter 3 when we contrasted concepts of emergent literacy with early literacy. An overview of these three organizational patterns for informational texts, including characteristics, signal words, and examples, is presented in Table 7.2.

TABLE 7.1 Informational Text Structures

Title of Book	
Heading	Example
Subheading	Example
Photograph	Page number
Illustration	Page number
Boldfaced words	Example & page number
Italics	Example & page number
Caption	Page number
Diagram	Page number
Focus question	Page number
Glossary/key words	Example

TABLE 7.2 Organizational Patterns for Informational Texts

Pattern	Signal Words	Example Passage
Sequence		
Lists events or items in order	*first, next, last, finally, then, how to, directions*	Here are the directions for making a peanut butter and jelly sandwich. First, take two pieces of bread. Then, put some peanut butter on one piece of bread. Next spread some jelly on the other piece of bread. Finally, put the two pieces of bread together. Make sure you put the jelly next to the peanut butter!
Compare—Contrast		
Tells how people, places, things, and ideas are the same and/or different	*different, like, however, same, both, but*	Jordan and Kate got new running shoes. Kate's runners are different from Jordan's. They have a Velcro fastener and Jordan's have laces. However, both pairs of runners are the same colour.
Cause—Effect		
Links one or more causes with one or more effects	*because, why, so, reasons, therefore, as a result*	Mary got mad at Jenny because Jenny let go of the balloon. It floated away and got stuck in the tree branches. As a result, Ahmed had to climb the tree to retrieve it. They were therefore late for the big celebration.

Narrative Texts

Children often read nonfiction or informational material for pure pleasure as well as to gain specific information. Many informational books for young readers today are especially appealing because they are written in the form of **narrative** (e.g., Anholt's *Stone Girl, Bone Girl: The Story of Mary Anning*, 1998; and Biesty's *Gold Quest*, 2002). Through narrative nonfiction, readers are presented with information that is embedded into the story. Chapter 10 of this book provides more information on narrative nonfiction, and the titles of many high-quality nonfiction materials are located in this book's Appendix.

As noted in Chapter 3, young children who have heard stories read or told to them on a regular basis learn what stories are like. It becomes relatively easy for them to construct meaning from narrative, because it is the form with which they are most familiar. They learn to connect ideas as they read and to anticipate what comes next. Teachers often find it helpful to create story maps collaboratively with their students. In the early grades, the maps might consist of a simple "Beginning," "Middle," and "End," with the students adding their own drawings to each of the three sections of the map. As we describe in Chapter 11, the map might literally be an invented map of where the story takes place, or the route a character in the story may have travelled. More often, in a story map, the students, or students and teacher together, plot the

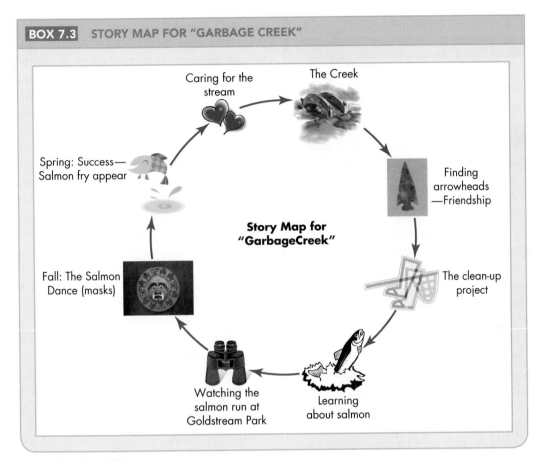

BOX 7.3   STORY MAP FOR "GARBAGE CREEK"

Caring for the stream

The Creek

Spring: Success— Salmon fry appear

Story Map for "GarbageCreek"

Finding arrowheads —Friendship

Fall: The Salmon Dance (masks)

The clean-up project

Watching the salmon run at Goldstream Park

Learning about salmon

Source: Valgardson, 1997.

main events, the key points in the narrative. Students can draw scenes/objects/characters from the story on their maps. A story map can serve as a useful summary of the story as well as a means of focusing attention on the main events—the turning points on which the story rests. A basic story map for Valgardson's short story "Garbage Creek" (1997) is shown in Box 7.3.

Story structures are attempts to delineate the basic elements of a well-formed story. Nearly all stories written in the Western tradition contain a plot, a setting, characters, a point of view, and a theme. The *plot* is the sequence of events that characters go through in order to achieve a set of goals or resolve a problem. It is the tension or conflict in the plot that makes readers want to continue reading. The most basic plot structure is that of beginning, middle, and end (or introduction, development, and resolution). The *characters* are frequently the most important element of a story. Well-rounded, strong characters make the story come alive. The *setting* tells where and when the story takes place, and can vary from a general "Once upon a time" backdrop, to a very specific location, time and climate. *Points of view* are first-person (I), omniscient (seeing and knowing everything), limited omniscient (focused on the thoughts and view of one character, but told in the third person), and objective (confined to recounting events with no insight into any character's thoughts or actions). The *theme* is the underlying meaning of a story, such as friendship, acceptance of self, or overcoming fear.

TABLE 7.3 **Story Structure Chart**

Setting
• Where did the story take place?
• When did the story take place?
• Who is the main character?

Events
Problem/Internal Conflict
• What is the problem faced by the main character?
• What does this character need?
• Why is this character in trouble?
• What conflict does the main character have?
• What does the character decide to do?
• How does the character feel about the problem?
Attempt(s) and Outcome(s)
• What did the character do about the problem?
• What happened to the character?
• What will the character do now?
Resolution/Reaction
• How did the character solve the problem?
• How did the character feel at the end?
• What would you do to solve the character's problem?

Story structures and specific terms should never be taught for their own sake, but only to help children construct meaning. Rather than imposing this terminology on children, it is more useful for them to generate their own terms, such as *who, where, what, why, and how*. The best way to build knowledge of story structure is to provide children with experiences with stories on a regular basis. However, some explicit attention to story structure will benefit children with limited story experience and those who do not appear to reflect this knowledge in their storytelling or writing.

Teachers sometimes prepare a chart or web, something like the one presented in Table 7.3, reflecting the structure of a typical story. Usually, the best type of story for charting a story is a problem-centred one. The teacher can read the story to the children, and as a group they analyze the story, completing a large copy of the chart. This can be followed by a range of activities, such as filling in a missing story element.

It is crucial that children understand why they are being asked these questions and how the information they are asked to locate relates to the overall structure of the story. Unless children are clear on the purpose for this activity, it will test their comprehension but not teach them how to construct meaning.

In narrative nonfiction, the specific setting, characters, and problem are usually essential to the presentation of information. In the biography *Stone Girl, Bone Girl: The Story of Mary Anning* (Anholt, 1998), the characters and setting of the story in Lyme Regis, England, are crucial in presenting information about the first discovery of fossils. In *Gold Quest* (Biesty, 2002), much of the story is based on real places and real events, but some of the characters are invented to aid the story along. The historical facts and events are all accurate, however, and like all nonfiction authors, Biesty conducted extensive research while developing the book. In *Thunderstorm* (Tripp, 1994), the specific characters are fictional, but the generalized location and the scientific descriptions of the storm are accurate. Criteria for evaluating the quality of nonfiction books are presented in Chapter 10.

In addition to accessing information books, students and adults increasingly search and retrieve information from the Internet and from other digital resources. These resources call upon particular skills if readers are to navigate and read electronic information successfully. In the next section, we address the use of multimodal forms of text in today's classrooms.

Multimodal Text

The term **multimodal text** refers to the integration of media such as sound, text, graphics, animation, and full-motion video into a single computerized system. It is a method of presenting information in an interactive mode. Children in school today belong to a "video generation" and are often referred to as "digital natives." Multimedia applications and artificial speech technology make writing more appealing to students, enabling them to incorporate sound, drawing, video, and pictures in their compositions. In particular, synthetic speech can be a very stimulating way of adding dialogue between writer and audience and can serve to reduce inhibitions about beginning to write. As well, by composing with media other than text, students can learn to become more critical users of media in their everyday lives.

With multimedia resources and the publication of students' work, young authors can now engage their readers through all the senses. Because this allows for presenting information in a nonlinear, interactive way, students are able to develop a greater sense of the interconnectedness of different kinds of information. This helps them organize complex information in many media forms from different sources, according to a particular theme. Many of the cross-curricular projects elementary students complete are supported by print text and by multimodal forms of text. Teachers are teaching and integrating technology at the same time the children are learning and using it. Information Communication Technology learner outcomes are therefore addressed as they are integrated into subjects and activities across the curriculum.

What is now often called **digital storytelling** is an appealing and appropriate way for students in the elementary grades to present their research reports or represent their learning. Quite often, teachers and students learn the strategies and skills alongside each other, as this form of representation is frequently new for teachers. Teachers are discovering that students have an affinity for these multimodal projects, and are facilitating their use in social studies and science in particular. Telling the stories of their newly found knowledge with photographs, clip art, video segments, maps and drawings, along with sound effects, music, and narration, is a satisfying and enjoyable learning experience for youngsters in elementary classrooms. This is one area in which the students can frequently take the lead and teach their teacher. For excellent resources and classroom suggestions, see Carol Vaage's website at http://www.k-3learningpages.net.

One particular blogging/multimodal project, facilitated by Sandra Gluth and Pete Mackay in Edmonton, can be found at http://buffalojump.resco.ca. This was a telecollaborative initiative between students at one elementary school and at a local high school. The students worked together to produce animated drawings of Head-Smashed-In Buffalo Jump in southern Alberta. The elementary students had been studying this World Heritage Site and wrote about "A Day in the Life of a Child at Head-Smashed-In Buffalo Jump." They then created drawings on their computers reflecting their research. The high school students animated the drawings with the help of a blog that enabled the two groups to discuss plans for the animation. The high school group used the opportunity not only to practise their animation skills but also to simulate an animator-artist process of creation toward a common goal.

In another project, Kevin, a grade 6 student, created and presented a futuristic creation myth using PowerPoint presentation software. He downloaded background music from the web (theme music from *Star Wars* and *2001: A Space Odyssey*), as well as animated cartoon characters, clip art, and graphics, which he incorporated into his presentation. As he presented

BOX 7.4   A GRADE 6 CHILD'S POWERPOINT PRESENTATION

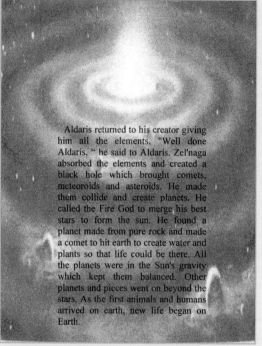

Aldaris returned to his creator giving him all the elements. "Well done Aldaris," he said to Aldaris. Zel'naga absorbed the elements and created a black hole which brought comets, meteorites and asteroids. He made them collide and create planets. He called the Fire God to merge his best stars to form the sun. He found a planet made from pure rock and made a comet to hit earth to create water and plants so that life could be there. All the planets were in the Sun's gravity which kept them balanced. Other planets and pieces went on beyond the stars. As the first animals and humans arrived on earth, new life began on Earth.

his story to the class, the text flew in from various sides of the screen, and the text was superimposed against a background of space scenes that he had downloaded from the NASA website. His classmates were able to view his presentation on the large-screen monitor mounted at the front of the classroom. Two slides from Kevin's presentation are shown in Box 7.4.

Hypertext

Hypertext is the form of text used in websites. It has become so common in our daily lives that we barely notice the special knowledge and skills it demands of readers. Unlike conventional printed text, which is linear and read from beginning to end, hypertext includes images, sound, and actions that are linked in non-sequential associations, allowing the reader to go through a topic in any order. As Jonassen (1996, p. 188) says, "Hypertext is super-text because the reader has much greater control of what is read and the sequence in which it is read. It is based on the assumption that the organization the reader imposes on a text is more personally meaningful than that imposed by the author." The organization of hypertext is usually achieved through links on which the reader clicks and is thereby connected to yet another chunk of text. Hypertext allows the reader to control not only the sequence in which information is accessed but also the speed with which it is accessed.

Reading and Researching Information

Social Construction of Meaning

The Internet is an ideal environment for the social construction of meaning. As children navigate through a wide variety of information sources, they discriminate between important and unimportant information, respond to e-mail, blog, and engage with other students in electronic chat sessions. In this process, what counts as knowledge is under constant construction, as the "knowledge base on the Internet becomes a function of social interaction among its users" (El-Hindi, 1999).

Learning on and with the Internet promotes the active construction of meaning for several reasons:

- *Currency.* Learners have immediate access to current information. Nearly all major newspapers publish online versions, and research findings in most fields are now available. Many websites are continuously upgraded.
- *Relevancy.* Learners can choose lines of inquiry and pursue personal interests. Topics are linked and cross-referenced to enable web surfers to navigate their own inquiry pathways.
- *Immediacy.* Students can learn about events almost as they happen.
- *Multiple perspectives.* Learners using web links can view and appraise the same information from a number of viewpoints.
- *Multiple dimensions.* The same event, concept, or topic is often available in multiple formats—text, chart, video, and sound.

It is the very currency and immediacy of the Internet, however, that causes both students and teachers their greatest frustration as sites appear and disappear overnight. By the time this book is published, several of the websites we reference will likely no longer be available or their web addresses will have changed.

In addition, teachers must be responsible for the material children encounter on the Internet during school time. Students need to know which sites are reputable and useful. Teachers must first do their "homework" to check the best sites children can use for any particular project.

Reading Hypertext on the Web

Teachers need to reflect on the extent to which reading on the web is the same as or different from reading conventional print materials. Sutherland-Smith (2002) uses the term *web literacy* to refer to finding, scanning, digesting, and storing Internet information. While these skills appear to be similar to those used with print, Sutherland-Smith believes that web literacy involves expanding critical reading skills to incorporate the evaluation of visual and nontext features of a hypertext document. According to her, reading web-based text:

- permits nonlinear strategies of thinking
- allows nonhierarchical strategies
- offers non-sequential strategies
- requires visual literacy skills to understand multimedia components
- is interactive, with the reader able to add, change, or move text
- enables a blurring of the relationship between reader and writer (Sutherland-Smith, 2002, pp. 664–665)

The volume of information, the speed of information access, and the structure of the web (as a series of interlinked points) differentiates web reading from the reading of printed texts.

Strategies for Web Reading

Sutherland-Smith (2002) recommends the following strategies for teaching web reading.

1. *Use the "snatch-and-grab" reading technique.* Children do not need to read every web text from beginning to end. Teachers help students understand how to skim text to identify a key word or phrase, and copy the required material to another document. Once they have compiled these texts, students read them in a more detailed manner and cull unwanted material. This technique emphasizes the broad nature of searching and helps students obtain a great deal of material in a limited time.

2. *Focus on refining keyword searches.* Teachers explicitly teach students to narrow the scope of their keyword search to find information more efficiently. For example, narrowing a search from the phrase *printing press* to *invention of* or *history of the printing press* will result in a more manageable and focused list of usable sites.

3. *Use the "chunking technique."* Sutherland-Smith coined this term to show students ways to break down a complex topic into manageable sections or chunks. For example, when researching the creation of a national airline such as Qantas, the teacher can explain how students can think about the topic in chunks—such as when and why the airline was created, and its effects on remote communities. Students then brainstorm words to use as a search focus.

4. *Provide shortcut lists to sites or search engines.* Teachers can provide shortcuts or bookmarks to reliable sites and hints for students to effectively organize their lists of web addresses.

5. *Limit links.* One strategy to assist students is to limit the number of links they follow. This helps them refocus on key words or questions and keep on track.

6. *Evaluate non-textual features (images, graphics).* Students need to learn how to decode visual images and not regard them merely as illustrations. They also need to learn to evaluate visual images and to discern discrepancies between visual images and text information.

BEN HAZZARD TALKS ABOUT NEW MEDIA

What does it mean to use new media in your language arts teaching? (I.e., what is new media and, in your estimation, why is it important?)

Using **new media** within a language arts classroom provides the context for instruction, while the content and reflective focus of teaching remains the same. New media, often referred to as information that is created, consumed, or distributed through the use of computing power, allows the distribution of information in the classroom through relatively new tools. Since the context of digital technologies permeates everyday interaction, I believe students need critical thinking skills in order to understand, evaluate, and make judgments about the messages embedded within the media. The new media of today will quickly become the old media of tomorrow.

In what ways have you used new media in your teaching?

In my classroom I use new media for engagement, collaboration, and community. When I teach inferencing in shared reading lessons, students are engaged through using video clips from user-generated video websites such as YouTube. Students also write, plan, film, and edit digital video segments based on song lyrics, commercials, and creative holiday segments. Students are writing for a true purpose and audience. Instead of asking about the minimum length of a writing assignment, they focus on the content.

New media has also provided opportunities to collaborate with other teachers and to connect students between classrooms. Tools such as blogging software allow students to easily publish their writing on the web for another classroom of students to read and comment on. Reading and writing are linked together through the creation of blog posts and then making connections to the posts of others. Moderated forums between students also allow students to interact with each other about science concepts using a style of interaction which they are very comfortable communicating with, i.e. informal digital communication. The key to each of these examples of collaboration using new media is the ability to interact socially with other students, teachers, and classrooms. The response and feedback is timely, relevant, and connected to classroom instructional content.

Through new media students become part of a larger community. The audience for their work extends beyond the classroom to their parents, school, and local community. A class website for showcasing student work, a current classroom task blog, and school website were all avenues to engage students, their parents, and the community in the learning process. Parents were able to have more meaningful discussions with their children about their studies; students often downloaded photos of classroom activities; and community

(Continued)

members were aware of work being done within the school. New media is not the answer to any or every educational dilemma; however the benefits in my classroom go beyond using cool new toys. The new media engage students in the learning process, enable collaboration with others, and facilitate sharing our learning with the community.

What's the best piece of advice you can give new teachers who aren't sure where to begin with new media?

The best place to start in your classroom is with a form of new media that you are familiar with, such as e-mail, and then encourage the students to expand on the ideas and context. The teacher provides the instruction and facilitates the interaction, while students may be able to extend their understanding through the context of new media.

The next section of this chapter moves from reading in the content areas (across curriculum) into writing across the curriculum. In the old days, students spent hours of their school day copying notes from the board into their scribblers so they could take the scribblers home and study the material later, usually for a written test. Writing was viewed as a way to capture information for use at a later time. Today's understanding of writing is much different. Today children take field notes, write in learning logs or journals, make lists of the steps they must take in a project, diagram their observations and understandings, and write about their thoughts and opinions on a wide range of topics. They do this to capture their thinking, to reflect on their learning and to make new meaning from the material and ideas they are encountering in their lives.

WRITING AND LEARNING

In many classrooms, students and teachers write to explore topics, ideas, and subject area content, as well as to demonstrate their understandings. Writing not only demonstrates what we have learned but it also provides a powerful tool that can help us to make sense of our learning as we engage in it. As Donald Murray points out, "when we write we discover what we know" (1984, p. 7).

Toby Fulwiler (1987) drew our attention to three basic assumptions that are particularly important to teachers with regard to writing across the curriculum:

1. When people articulate connections between new information and what they already know, they learn and understand that new information more effectively (Bruner, 1966).

2. When people write about new information and ideas—in addition to reading, talking, and listening—they learn and understand them better (Britton et al., 1975).

3. When people care about what they write and see connections to their own lives, they both learn and write with greater efficacy (Moffett, 1968).

In *Writing and Primary Science*, MacAlister, Kydd, and Jones (1988) suggest that the pieces of writing children complete in science, and the drawings and charts that accompany them, can provide a rich source of evaluative and diagnostic information for teachers. "Reading an explanation written in a child's words tells the teacher more about their level of concept development than any multiple choice test" (p. 27).

These findings have led teachers to become acutely aware of how they can help their students to make their thinking visible, to develop confidence in their ability to think, and to value their own thoughts. Thus, writing for learning is not restricted to particular forms or genres. Journals, notes, letters, diaries, scripts, commercials, brochures, invitations, reports, presentations, and posters all provide opportunities for students to demonstrate the meanings that they have constructed. In addition, journals, think books, notebooks, and learning logs allow children to share their thinking with their teacher or peers in a supportive environment that encourages students to expand and explore their ideas further.

Newkirk (1987) maintains that young children learn most effectively when they write in their own voice in ways that are meaningful to them. He also suggests that young children develop organizational skills *as they write*. He believes that children learn and organize their ideas through writing about the world they know. Once they are comfortable with doing that, they can begin to represent their understandings of the world more abstractly. What they need is opportunity. Tanya's writing about seasons, Box 7.5, was prompted by her winter vacation in the Caribbean. While on vacation, she began to think about seasons across the world, and the similarities and differences that exist between her own experiences in Canada and the experiences of people elsewhere. The piece suggests that although Tanya usually experiences winter as being very cold, she now understands that in some parts of the world even winter is warm. Thus the teacher encourages students to record and examine their immediate experiential world before they move on to more formal and abstract writing.

As illustrated in the writing done for the "Restaurant Project" in Julie Gellner's classroom (exhibited in Boxes 7.10 through 7.14) students demonstrate their capacity for writing in a variety of genres to meet a range of purposes. Their writing demonstrates, in particular, their abilities to organize their thinking and record it on paper. Overall, it is clear that children can write in many genres, and for many purposes, from the very beginning of schooling.

Think Books and Journals

In the past, educators have frequently thought of writing as something that is done when the ideas are fully formed. But writing for learning is an intrinsic part of the total learning process. It makes learning personally meaningful and creates what we might call "action knowledge" rather than "book knowledge" (Barnes, 1976). When children write in journals, they reflect, reshape, and redraft as they engage in learning—what D'Arcy calls the "three Rs of learning"—a cycle of learning that people repeat throughout their lives. She quotes the Children's Learning in Science Group in the United Kingdom when she says, "If a pupil's own picture of how the world works is ignored, her ability to make sense of someone else's picture, the teacher's or the textbook writer's, is seriously impeded" (D'Arcy, 1989, p. 3).

The writing learners do as they learn—writing about emerging ideas, insights, thoughts, and reflections—is part of their own picture of how the world works. Because that picture is constantly changing, the writing is not moving toward a finished product, but is part of the process of helping learners clarify their thinking and develop new understandings. Journal

BOX 7.5 TANYA'S WRITING ABOUT SEASONS

About Seasons

It is almost spring. The weather changes to be
warmer because the season is changing to be spring.
After spring is summer which is very hot.
In some countries are even very hot during winter
because they are closer to the equator, especially
Africa. Some of Africa is on the equator. That's
why giraffes live there.
After summer comes fall again. In the fall the leaves
start to fall off the trees and get ready for winter.
Winter has a lot of snowstorms and people wear a lot
of clothes because the weather is very cold and people
think that if they wear a little more clothing
they will keep warmer.
Each season is different every year.

writing acts as a platform on which other ideas can be built. Students can go back to the writing and reexamine the ideas captured there, reflect upon them, refine them, and build on them as they integrate new knowledge with the old.

Barnes (1976, p. 76) says that "As pupils write they can—under certain circumstances—reshape their view of the world, and extend their ability to think rationally about it." James Britton (1982) refers to this same process as "shaping at the point of utterance." The advantage of students writing about their ideas as they are processing them is that they are forced to focus on them to a far greater degree than when they simply talk about them. Talked-over ideas are often lost; we may be distracted and lose the thread of our thoughts. But writing provides a record of where we have journeyed in our thinking, and points to where we might travel next.

While academic prose tends to be logical, formal, conventional, organized, assertive, and objective, the writing in a journal is conversational in tone and reads much like talk. Journal writers begin with what they know and build their understandings as they write. The journal entry in Box 7.6, written by Sarah in grade 3, provides an example of what is meant by writing to understand. Sarah clearly explains the concept of multiplication as repeated addition, demonstrating her learning by drawing six bookshelves each with seven shelves. Here, Sarah is actively making meaning from new learning.

In 2000, the National Council of Teachers of Mathematics' in the US published *Principles and Standards for School Mathematics* (NCTM, 2000), in which, "learning to communicate

---

BOX 7.6   SARAH'S MATH JOURNAL ENTRY

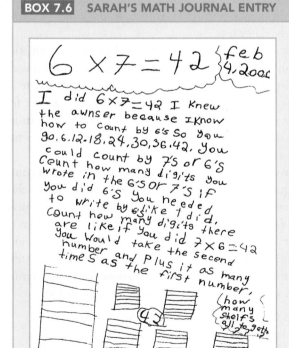

I did 6 × 7 = 42. I knew the answer because I know how to count by 6's. So you go 6, 12, 18, 24, 30, 36, 42. You could count by 7's or 6's. Count how many digits you wrote in the 6's or 7's. If you did 6's you needed to write it like I did. Count how many digits there are. Like if you did 7 × 6 = 42, you would take the second number and plus it as many times as the first number. How many shelfs all together????

mathematically" was listed as a primary learning outcome for all students. This publication has strongly influenced Canadian provincial programs of study in mathematics. The publication suggests that instructional programs from pre-kindergarten through grade 12 should enable all students to

- organize and consolidate their mathematical thinking through communication
- communicate their mathematical thinking coherently and clearly to peers, teachers, and others
- use the language of mathematics to express mathematical ideas precisely

Communication and the exploration of ideas both orally and in writing have thus taken on a more prominent role in mathematics education; a significant move away from the transmission model of mathematics teaching prevalent for many years. Students are now urged to explore, problem solve, and link learning to their own lives. They are increasingly challenged to validate their own mathematical ideas and abilities and to learn to communicate their mathematical thinking clearly, especially in writing.

Many high-quality resource materials are available to help teachers understand and implement writing in mathematics. *Math Is Language Too: Talking and Writing in the Mathematics Classroom* (Whitin & Whitin, 2000) is a joint publication of the National Council of Teachers of Mathematics and the National Council of Teachers of English. Marilyn Burns' many publications are also highly recommended: *About Teaching Mathematics: A K–8 Resource*, 2nd Edition (2000); *Math and Literature (K–1)* (2004); and *Writing in Math Class* (1995). Burns writes, "Although the final representation of a mathematical pursuit looks very different from the final product of a writing effort, the mental journey is, at its base, the same—making sense of an idea and presenting it effectively" (1995, p. 3).

Research by Edwards (1992) on the use of learning journals or think books in mathematics in grades 2, 4, and 6 showed that journals can provide a safe and challenging environment where students can display what they know (as Sarah did in Box 7.6), and they can come to terms with what they do *not* know. Sometimes students will express confusion and ask for help, and at that point peers or the teacher can provide support. Edwards found that learning journals took the focus away from marks and correct answers, and focused instead on what individual children understood and could clearly articulate.

In grade 2, the students would often leave spaces in their math journals so their teacher could provide feedback or answer a question. Frequently, the children drew a line on which the teacher was expected to respond. For example, Julia wrote, "I get up at 7:30. What time do you come to school? _____." A further journal entry from this class is shown in Box 7.7. The children in this classroom made connections with their prior learning and were consolidating it into a more holistic understanding of the world. For example, children noticed that words used in one context could be used in a completely different context. Billy related his new knowledge of temperature and thermometers with prior knowledge in science, and observed a rule of capitalization:

Today we learned about temperature and Celsius and Mr. Celsius. A thermometer is something that tells the temperature. Do you know what the grey stuff is in a thermometer? It is called mercury. There is a planet named Mercury. The grey stuff in a thermometer is spelled with a smaller m and the planet is spelled with a big M. Mr. Celsius is now dead. He was called Mr. Celsius! He invented the thermometer! He named the thermometer after him.

GRADE 2 MATH JOURNAL PAGE

We learned about time. It was fun. We learned 60 minutes is 1 hour and 30 minutes is a half hour. 24 hours is 1 day. I like time very much. Math is fun. Did you know time is math?

Gradually, communication skills improve, especially in the area of **expressive writing**, which in turn leads to greater facility with **expository writing**. Children need to feel their way through the concrete world of the known before they can begin to represent their understandings abstractly. Learning journals provide one vehicle through which children can do this.

Learning journals are not only beneficial learning experiences for students, but are powerful vehicles that encourage teachers to examine their teaching and knowledge base. As teachers read the student journals, they learn much about how they can improve their own practice. They might reflect on

- the complex and sophisticated questions children ask
- their own knowledge and understandings of various subject areas and how these can be improved
- the need for extremely clear and explicit teaching
- the effectiveness of journals as informal assessment tools
- the clues the students' writing provides as to what they understand and what they do not understand
- how all of this information can be used to adjust and adapt specific teaching content, methodology, and student groupings in the classroom
- When teachers use learning logs or journals in their classrooms, they
- read the student journals regularly to see how they might adapt their instruction and further facilitate their students' learning
- teach children what constitutes an appropriate entry
- model entries on the overhead projector to help children become comfortable with a journal (not to tell children what to say, but to demonstrate a variety of ways in which they might write about their learning)

Writing to Consolidate What Is Known

Many forms of writing serve to consolidate what a person knows, including journal writing and writing in notebooks. As we drafted the manuscript for this book, we rethought our understandings, worked through difficult ideas, consolidated what we knew about teaching and learning in language arts, and raised more questions. The writing of this book is part of our own continuing search for understanding.

Writing that consolidates what a person knows meets the representational function of language that Halliday (1975) identified, and it uses what Britton (1970) has termed the expository or transactional voice. Writing that consolidates knowledge is a reflection of what the writer knows *at the time of writing*, and it acts as a kind of summary of the learning journey. Box 7.6 demonstrates Sarah's consolidated knowledge of multiplication, and Box 7.8 demonstrates how Alida, in grade 3, consolidated her knowledge of homesteading on the Prairies.

Understanding can be consolidated at key junctures in the learning process, not only as a final activity. Students record what they have learned, with specific reference to content and processes (such as measuring or estimating in mathematics). After teaching a grade 6 unit on scale and its uses, Ms. Redfern asked her students to write a consolidating entry about scale in their math journals. Here is a selection of the class's entries:

Scale is used for maps, to tell you how far it is from one place to another. Scale tells you the distance and how many kilometers or miles it takes to get from one place to another.

Scale is anything that you can measure in linear instead of drawing the real size of whatever it is! You have to do this because if you don't it could take the rest of your life to draw it the real size!

I know scale a little better now because I know some questions I didn't know before like who does scaling? People who build houses and cartographers. Now I know that you can measure scale with anything. What do you measure money and time with?

In science, teachers often encourage students to write and share anticipatory questions and predictions in their journals (exploratory writing) before they engage in a science activity. Students are later encouraged to write their observations in their notebooks as the activity proceeds. The specialized vocabulary of science (or of any discipline) becomes much more important and relevant to children when they understand the concept embedded in the language. The talk that takes place when learners write in a learning log or journal, as well as the actual writing, provides a forum for sharing and clarifying ideas that leads to understanding the concept and internalizing the specialized vocabulary. Box 7.9 presents a science notebook entry from Thomas in grade 1 (Ozdoba, 1992). Here, Thomas is consolidating his learning.

This writing reveals the range of meanings children create from their learning, and the ways in which they are able to apply that knowledge to the world. The writing provided excellent feedback for their teachers and also enabled the children to discover for themselves what they knew and how well they knew it.

Research Projects

In adult life, research reports are frequently written in engineering, law, medicine, social services, business, and academia, to name just a few professions. Reports in these contexts are always predicated on a question or line of inquiry. Researchers essentially gather data to help them answer questions. When children are required to complete research reports in school contexts, the purpose is often unclear. Children are asked, for example, to write reports on a Canadian province, an animal, or a community. But the first step in any research endeavour is to formulate questions to guide the study. The most interesting and most motivating questions are those developed by the students themselves. When students conduct research in school, it is essential that they formulate the questions, have a genuine interest in the topic, and be motivated to discover answers to their

BOX 7.8 HOMESTEADING

GETTING A HOMESTEAD

Many people came to ALBERTA to get a homestead. A homestead is peace of land you can farm on. To make the homestead yours you had to live on it six month of three years.

You got the peace of land free but you had to pay $10.00 for the registration fee. After you pay while you live on the peace of land you had to get thirty acres planted into crops. You also had to build a house worth at least $300.00 dollars.

By the way the people looking for homesteads look for water near by. They also look for people near by too. THAT'S HOW THEY GOT HOMESTEADS 100 YEARS AGO.

BOX 7.9 THOMAS'S WRITING IN SCIENCE

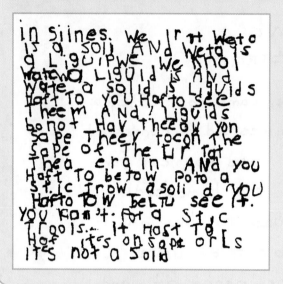

In science we learned what is a solid and what is a liquid. We know what a liquid is and what a solid is. Liquids have to, you have to see them and liquids do not have their own shape. They take on the shape of the jar that they are in and you have to be able to put a stick through. A solid you have to be able to see it. You can't put a stick through it. It has to have its own shape or it's not a solid.

Source: A. Ozdoba, "Writing to learn: Science journals in year one," M.Ed. thesis (Edmonton: University of Alberta, 1992), p. 100.

questions. Teachers play a key role in establishing interest and motivation, in guiding students to formulate their questions, and in helping students learn relevant research strategies.

Vivian Vasquez (2004) describes how she accessed issues in the social lives of her kindergarten students to sustain a critical curriculum in her classroom. In the process of the study, Vasquez and her students created an "audit trail," which consisted of the artifacts gathered by the children and which represented their thinking. These photographs, book covers, posters, newspaper cuttings, magazine advertisements, and printouts from the web were displayed on a "Learning Wall" in the classroom. The display of artifacts allowed the children to revisit their learning and rethink their ideas over the course of the school year. Their discussions included issues such as the environment, fairness, gender, and the media.

Teacher Julie Gellner, who uses the Project Approach in her grade 4/5 classroom, supported her students as they designed a Restaurant Project in Health Education. In Chapter 2, we described how she supported her students' research into World War II and the Holocaust in preparation for a Remembrance Day assembly. The Restaurant Project grew out of the students' interest in media reports of unsanitary conditions in some city restaurants. The students conducted extensive research into restaurants and organized a "restaurant evening" at their school as a culminating experience (not all research must end with a formal written report). The total project lasted for about three months. Julie strove to maintain an atmosphere in which the children's interests were piqued and their thinking and writing were challenged. She created a community of learners that supported one another in asking and answering questions, and in which the children and teacher respected one another's ideas.

In preparation for the event, the students visited a number of restaurants and markets, and they invited guest speakers to visit their classroom (including a local health inspector). They made

BOX 7.10 KENNEDY'S FIELD NOTES

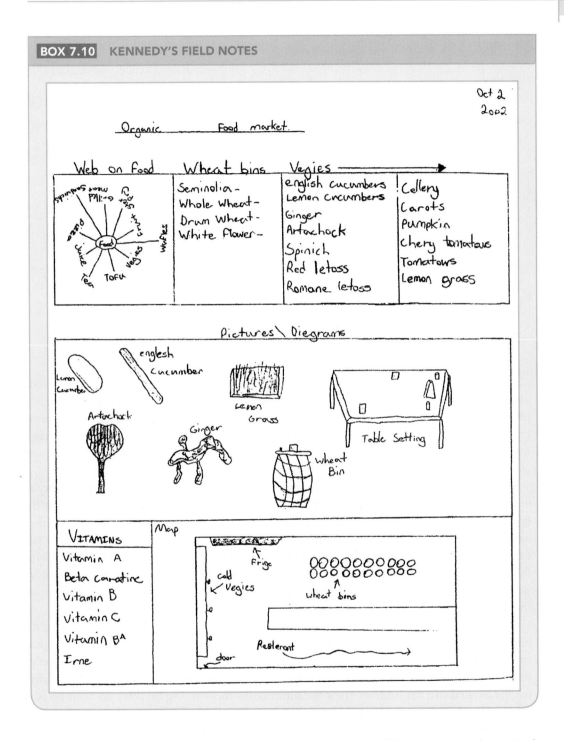

field notes about how the restaurants were run, wrote reviews of the restaurants they visited, explored the jobs people hold in restaurants, and how restaurants plan and organize for their patrons. Box 7.10 shows how Kennedy organized his field notes after he visited a local organic market and café. Box 7.11 displays Marina's review of a restaurant she visited with her mother.

BOX 7.11 **MARINA'S RESTAURANT REVIEW**

Harold's Veggie House

This restaurant makes the best food in the whole world. Maybe the whole galaxy. By now you are probably wondering what does this restaurant make that is so good? Five words 'sweet and sour veggie pork'. I am a vegetarian. You, I am guessing, are wondering if she is a vegetarian how can she eat pork? Simple, fake meat like tofu. My mom would agree the sweet and sour veggie pork, but she prefers the lamb curry. We both like to share the veggie hot pot. The service at this restaurant is fabulous as soon as you come to your seated. They leave you to take your coats off and get comfy.

Then they come and take your drink order. Your drink comes quickly you have to read the menu and decide what your ordering. Your food comes quickly. They check on you enough times that you know your being taken care of, but not so many times that you feel as if you don't have any privacy. I would recommend this restaurant to people who like to try new things. Stop by your local veggie house today.

Each student in the class applied for a job in the restaurant. They created letters of application and personal résumés, which they sent to the manager (Julie). Allisa's letter of application and résumé are presented in Box 7.12. The students decided on what dishes would be on the menu, created and wrote menus for the evening (shown in Box 7.13), designed invitations for parents and friends, made placemats, and organized the various jobs, timetables, cooking schedules, and cleanup. Will's job description for the position of waitress is presented in Box 7.14.

To write about their research in a school context, students need to develop the ability to write exposition. As Newkirk demonstrated (1987), children's early writing is usually in the expressive voice, but as they pursue questions that are of interest and relevance to them, they learn to organize their ideas and begin to write in a variety of forms and voices. This was evident in Tanya's piece, "About Seasons," in Box 7.5, and also in the writing completed during Julie's "Restaurant Project." However, children still benefit from instruction in expository writing, as well as in the research process. The challenge for teachers is to help students make the transition from expressive to expository writing in an interesting and enjoyable way.

For many children, the only audience for expository prose is the teacher (and that means the teacher as evaluator). But children learn by doing—they learn as they write, and through their writing they can acquire the transactional or expository voice. Box 7.15 demonstrates Kelly's transactional voice in an excerpt from her report on the solar system completed in grade 5. Kelly's teacher ensured that her students knew the audience for their writing (in this case, their peers in the classroom), and she encouraged her students to write specifically for that audience on a topic of their own choice. Kelly's writing is well organized and includes information that she found to be personally intriguing as well as challenging. Kelly was fascinated by the notion that stars are born and die. Her illustration for this section of the report shows her playfulness with the idea, and, at the beginning of each page, Kelly posed the question to her classmates, "Is this fact or fiction?" Kelly's research not only started with a question, but posed the question throughout the text.

BOX 7.12	ALLISA'S LETTER OF APPLICATION AND RÉSUMÉ

Allisa Garden
306 Dalrymple Road
Winnipeg, MB
M9X 5P2
325-4709

Ms. Gellner, Manager
Trail End Café
Dalrymple Community School
Winnipeg, MB

Dear Ms. Gellner:

My name is Allisa Garden and I am a very talented chef. I always do my best and try really hard. So right now I am trying to get a job at the Trail End Café. I would love to be a dessert chef, a salad chef, or a bar tender.

I think I would be the best person for the dessert chef job, because I went to a mini-chef camp this summer for two weeks. There I made lots of good treats. My family and friends really enjoyed the pleasant treats that I made.

I hope you will consider me for the dessert chef position. I have lots of enthusiasm and you will not regret hiring me. I hope to meet you soon and I think it would be a great pleasure to work for you.

Sincerely yours,

Allisa Garden

Allisa Garden

RÉSUMÉ

Allisa Garden
306 Dalrymple Road
Winnipeg, Manitoba
M9X 5P2
325-4709

Education

September 2003
Dalrymple Community School
Winnipeg, Manitoba
Grade 5

Experience and Extracurricular Activities

I cook with grandmother often
I help my mother make supper
I took a cooking camp at Maple College for two weeks this summer
I like swimming, rock climbing, dancing, and skiing

Special Skills

I have good people skills
I am very creative
I love to cook
I like to experiment with recipes
I wash my hands frequently

Name of References

Nora Garden
Mom
Phone: 325-4709 or 562-3798

Malcolm Garden
Dad
Phone: 325-4709 or 562-5103

Alison Sung
Best friend
Phone: 896-3568

Children have a much greater chance of successfully completing a research project if their teacher provides specific guidance for them. Effective teachers teach their students how to

- use library resources
- use the table of contents and index of a book

BOX 7.13   MENU FOR THE TRAIL END CAFÉ

Trail End Café

Appealing appetizers		Delicious desserts	
Veggies and dip	$2.50	Variety of squares, cookies, tarts, and cakes	$2.00
Chips and salsa	$3.00	**Desirable drinks**	
Hummus and pita bread	$3.00		
		Italian soda	$2.25
Scrumptious salads		Shirley temple	$2.25
Caesar salad	$3.00	Fruit punch	$2.25
Tossed salad with vinaigrette dressing	$3.00	Cherry cola	$2.25
Exotic entrée		**Complimentary**	
Veggie bagel melt	$4.00	Coffee and tea	

BOX 7.14   "WHAT CAN I GET YOU?"

A waitress is someone who serves people and asks for their orders. They use a notepad and a pen. Now the waitress brings their order to the kitchen. When they are done ordering the people have to wait for a little bit before they get their food. Finally, the waitress comes back with the food on the tray. She gives people their food. After the people are done eating the waitress takes the dirty dishes, and then goes and gets the bill. After that the waitress gets the change if necessary. So that's what the waitress does.

- locate information in books, encyclopedias, and magazines
- interpret information from pictures, charts, graphs, videotapes, and audiotapes
- use the Internet effectively
- paraphrase what they read, make notes, and put what they read into their own words
- translate information into visual form on charts, graphs, and diagrams
- conduct interviews
- search archives
- organize their findings into a report

These strategies are best taught in the context of the research process, presenting the various strategies at times when the students need them. Teachers may begin by helping students to develop a report or multimodal presentation collaboratively. Young children learn to conduct library research and write exposition or develop presentations more effectively when teacher and students find information together, working as a class, than if they work independently. The more children are shown *how* to do research and the more they are actively *involved* in doing it, the more effectively they will learn.

BOX 7.15   FACT OR FICTION? THE SOLAR SYSTEM

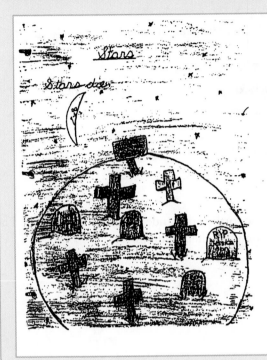

True. Stars are born in clouds of gas and dust called nebulas. Millions of years later the dust particles and gas are pulled together so they can heat up. When the gas is hot enough, a nuclear reation, like a bomb, sets off and it is born. Changes occur as the star gets older. Some keep growing and then shrink. Other stars project gas into space. When the stars are quite old they start to shrink and they are called white drawf stars. When they start to cool off they become black drawf stars and then the star is dead.

Guiding the Research Process

Teachers in grades 1 to 4 sometimes provide students with an outline, matrix, or web to help them organize information once they have located it. These devices help students make decisions about what information is relevant and what is not. Some devices have room for children to make their own notes in the spaces provided. These outlines, matrices, or webs are not like the typical outlines we used to see in high schools. Rather, they are graphic organizers that help children make sense of their research. Not all children will need such a device; however, graphic organizers do provide a sense of direction for those children who need some structure and guidance in putting together a report. An example of one graphic organizer—a data collection chart—is shown in Figure 7.1. Another form of graphic organizer is that used at the beginning of each chapter in this textbook to help the reader see the "big picture" as well as how the sections of the chapter relate to one another. Kennedy's graphic organizer (shown in Box 7.10) was self-designed as he sought to make sense of the field notes he made at the market.

When one grade 3 class was learning about animals, they focused on the concept of adaptation. The guiding question was "How do animals survive?" A class case study was created around the polar bear. Once the children began locating resources for the study, they zeroed in on the research question and found relevant information that helped them answer it. Thus, their reading was conducted from a specific perspective. Information was noted

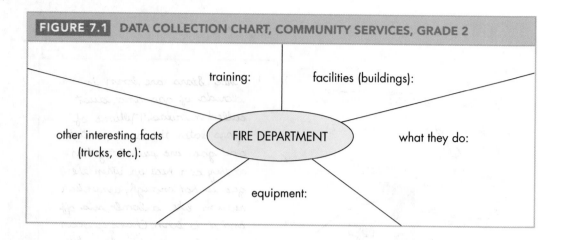

FIGURE 7.1 DATA COLLECTION CHART, COMMUNITY SERVICES, GRADE 2

through words, phrases, charts, diagrams, and so forth as the students collected their data. The following headings emerged as the students compiled their findings:

- physical appearance
- habitat
- food
- enemies
- migratory patterns
- conclusions (how the research answered the question)

These headings were not meant to dictate how the research report was to be written. Instead, they provided structures that guided the children's developing sense of organization.

Today, traditional report formats often give way to more interactive, visual, or imaginative presentations of research. Multimodal presentations, as noted earlier in this chapter, provide opportunities for students to represent their learning using a range of formats and media. Children also develop new ideas for research reports from reading nonfiction books. Many current nonfiction materials available for children, such as Peter Sis's book *Starry Messenger* (1996), employ formats and strategies that are compelling and exciting. Expository prose can be full of the enthusiasm and excitement we feel when we discover something new and want to share it with a wider audience, as demonstrated in the excerpt from Kelly's report shown in Box 7.15.

Writing Relevant Research

A fascinating research project completed for many years by grade 4 children at Petite Rivière Elementary School in Lunenburg County, Nova Scotia, was a series of books about the local area. Each year the children, who were bussed to the school from a wide area, selected a community within the county and pursued the questions "What makes this community unique?" and "What makes this community such a special place to live?" The project involved more than library research. The students went into the community to interview residents and businesspeople, complete correspondence, and search archives in order to answer their

BOX 7.16 STORES IN CROUSETOWN

The first store in Crousetown was owned by Beechum Crouse. It used to be attached to the house that Robert Crouse is living in today. Beechum Crouse's Store sold pipes, tobacco and many different things.

Robert Crouse's father (Merle Crouse) opened a store in 1936.

Later Arthur Bolivar ran Merle Crouse's store. Merle sold the business, but he wouldn't sell the building. Arthur Bolivar then retired from the store in the early 1970s.

Johnny Himmelman had a store and a post office in Crousetown at the same time as Merle Crouse's store. John Himmelman's store is still standing across from the Community Cemetery.

Source: Petite Rivière Elementary School, *History of Crousetown* (Lunenburg County, NS: Petite Rivière Publishing, 1993), p. 24.

guiding questions. Once the research was completed, they wrote and presented the material in a final bound form that was accessible and interesting to the general public. The books were printed (complete with ISBN number) and bound by a local company and sold by the school. Stories, drawings, biographies, history, lists, poems, recipes, directions for games, minutes from meetings, maps, and posters were all included. One excerpt from *History of Crousetown* (1993) is shown in Box 7.16, and a further excerpt is presented in Box 8.2.

Before researchers begin the process of writing a research report, they try to understand their subject as much as possible so that they can communicate their findings clearly and interestingly. Mrs. Haché, the grade 4 teacher at Petite Rivière Elementary School, writes:

> Each student chose several topics that would become part of the history book. They researched their topics in the following ways: I took a group of students to the Public Archives in Halifax to research the old newspapers of that community. People from the community brought in artifacts and information to our classroom museum (a collection of old items from the community). I took the students, four at a time, after school to interview older citizens in the community (the students were prepared for the interview with questions from the whole class and a release form for each person interviewed). These interviews were videotaped and used for reference in the classroom by the students as they wrote their reports. The students checked these reports for grammar, spelling, and punctuation. The students then discussed their finished report with the teacher and proceeded to put their information and artwork together in the format for the history book.

The final stage of the project was an evening presentation in the community hall for everyone in the community. The children sent special invitations to the people they interviewed and they presented their finished books to them that evening. They prepared an evening of entertainment based on the project (readings, drama, and an old-fashioned singsong) and then served food prepared by their parents. The importance of this celebration for the community, and its impact on all the people gathered together for this special evening, cannot be overemphasized.

Mrs. Haché integrated many aspects of the language arts into this project each year. The children interviewed, discussed, listened, made notes, read, and wrote as part of the project. They worked collaboratively in some areas and individually in others. Mrs. Haché provided guidance and structure, while at the same time giving the children the opportunity to make the book truly their own. All the students had parts of their work included in the book, and the purpose of the project was clear to the children from the very beginning (as it was to the community and to the celebratory audience in the community hall). It was through their involvement in this personally and socially relevant project that the students were able to develop their ability to write effective exposition. In addition, the students learned to write for a more general audience than the immediate one they were familiar with in their classroom and homes.

The grade 4 oral history project at Petite Rivière became a tradition. Each year's class looked forward to it, and as the children moved into grade 5, they took care of marketing and promoting the book and handling the accounting required for publication and sales. Mrs. Haché and the children selected a different local community to study each year, so the books and the project remained unique and interesting for both the children and their teacher, as well as for community members.

Children frequently find visual depictions of their learning, such as designing and drawing posters, satisfying vehicles for representing what they have learned about a topic. Children at the beginning of the 21st century are particularly visual in their learning. They watch television and movies, play video games, and use the Internet more than any children in the past. When children combine their artwork and writing, they provide striking demonstrations of what they know. Frequently, these integrated presentation formats are more appealing to children than more traditional forms. Similarly, charts, graphs, maps, and diagrams often provide children with opportunities to share their understandings more fully. The importance of report writing lies in the fact that it remains a major format for organizing and presenting information to others. In addition, research reports provide opportunities for children to organize their thinking and learning about the world.

SUMMARY

Integrating literacy across the curriculum provides an opportunity for learners to read and write as they are learning, and to think about their learning, making greater sense of what they know. It provides opportunities to question, hypothesize, predict, and consolidate knowledge. Reading and writing across the curriculum can be done from grade 1 onward, as shown by the samples of young children's writing presented in this chapter. Reading and writing for learning is best taught when it is modelled by teachers or developed in collaborative efforts with students and teacher working together. In addition, research and study skills are taught with the aim of helping children to become independent learners who feel confident in locating and using library resources and in accessing primary sources through such means as interviews and archival searches. Many of the skills needed to conduct research involve organizing information. This important ability can be taught collaboratively in the early grades as children become familiar with the use of webs, grids, and charts to facilitate their learning.

Children can have difficulty in reading textbooks and information books if their teachers have not specifically taught them how to attend to the organization of information material and how to use the features of an information text. The successful reading of information material calls on different skills than those required for reading narrative. Children must be shown how to read content materials through the use of such features as subheadings, glossary, index, and table of contents. It is important that teachers model these skills for their students, not just talk about them (an interactive whiteboard is excellent for use in this kind of situation).

Being able to write thoughts on paper is one way people remind themselves of what they know and think. It is also a way to communicate those thoughts to others. As students develop their abilities to read and write for multiple purposes and for varied audiences, they take greater control of their own learning. The ability to recount and reflect on their experiences and emerging understandings is a critical life skill. Most importantly, through the skills students develop as they write in journals, conduct research inquiries, and complete reports, they are provided with a repertoire of powerful learning strategies. Through employing these strategies, students can make personal sense of their learning and connect their learning to the world at large.

This chapter opened with Janet McConaghy telling us about her "Life Cycles" project in grade 3 science. Her students read, listened to stories, and wrote their own observations in their learning journals. They were invited to ask questions when they were unsure of something, and they each had a personal record of what they had learned. Janet had evidence of what her students were learning—and her students had experienced a strong personal connection to the science curriculum. We end this chapter with Janet's insights about planning and integrating language and literacy across the curriculum.

JANET MCCONAGHY

What would you suggest is the most important thing beginning teachers can do in regard to language and literacy across the curriculum?

At the elementary level we have to think about how subjects are connected, not about subject areas in isolation. And the main connection is literacy. Even if you see yourself as a music specialist or a science specialist, you are still teaching literacy in every subject you teach. We know that by the junior high grades many students have difficulty in reading textbooks, so we need to attend to that all the way through schooling. We can help students to avoid those problems by working on it directly in the elementary grades; by teaching students how to read texts of different kinds and in different subjects; and by talking about what they are learning. Through asking questions, talking, reading, and writing, we become clearer about what we understand and know.

What strategy is the most important to you as you integrate literacy across the curriculum?

Without doubt the most important thing for me is modelling. Children need to see how to do something and they need to be shown how. So it's really important that I model strategies for children, and show them what is expected. For example, the kinds of discussion I have with my students sets the tone and climate for the kind of learning that I expect in my classroom. I like to get children thinking, so recently, I asked my students, "What surprised you in what we just read about Peru?" One student said that because Peru is near the coast, he didn't expect that people might be short of water to drink. We then talked about the difference between seawater and fresh water. It wasn't part of the intended learning, but it turned out to be a really important discussion.

How do you balance this kind of exploratory learning with the requirements in the program of studies?

There definitely has to be a balance between direct teaching and open-ended responses and activities. When we are reading a textbook, I take my students through it carefully, scaffolding their learning along the way. I check frequently for their understanding, and I provide lots of examples. I ask them to raise questions when they don't understand something, and I try to help them make connections with their own lives. I develop routines in the classroom, so the students know what is going to happen and there are no surprises. It has to be predictable and safe.

What final piece of advice do you have for beginning teachers?

Start to develop your own professional library and build a set of good books to use with the children in your classrooms. Knowing the right book for the right time is not something you begin teaching with. But it is a skill you develop through reading lots of children's books, both fiction and nonfiction, and by listening to students' interests. It's amazing how many children read information books for pleasure. In my classroom most of the boys prefer nonfiction to fiction, so I make sure I have lots of good nonfiction books available—and I balance fiction and nonfiction books in my guided reading sessions as well.

TALKING POINTS

1. How can you integrate language and literacy across the curriculum at the start of your teaching career? Think about what you have come to know about the broader notion of literacy presented throughout this text. Consider the purposes for reading and writing in the world at large. How can your students speak, listen, read, write, view and represent in order to stimulate their curiosity, answer their questions, and demonstrate their learning?

2. How can you access resources such as children's literature in your school district? How can you find out what materials and funding are available? In order to provide appropriate resources for your classroom, you may need to find answers to the following questions: Who are the language and literacy consultants in the school district? Does the school have a teacher/librarian? Is there a curriculum resource person in the school? Does the community have a Children's Literature Roundtable you can join? Does the community have a local reading teachers' association (e.g., the IRA)? Does the school provide each teacher with a budget for books for the classroom?

3. How can you teach your students to retrieve information from the Internet that is accurate and not misleading? When you set a task for students to accomplish, consider your role as a facilitator of children's learning. What is your first responsibility? Is it helpful for children to randomly search the Internet for information? How can you ensure children access reliable sites? How familiar are you with organizations such as "2learn.ca" that have created materials for use in classrooms or that list reputable educational websites? How critical are you in your own use of material accessed from Internet sites? How does critical literacy, mentioned earlier in this text, relate to your use of the Internet?

RECOMMENDED PROFESSIONAL RESOURCES

Janet McConaghy recommends ...

McLaughlin, M. & Allen, M. B. (2002). *Guided comprehension: A teaching model for Grades 3–8*. Newark, DE: International Reading Association.

This is a book I refer to almost every day. It has provided me with helpful suggestions for effective ways of engaging children in comprehension strategies, multiple roles of assessment and many other teaching ideas. It includes blackline masters to use right across the curriculum.

Harvey, S. & Goudvis, A. (2000). *Strategies that work: Teaching comprehension to enhance understanding*. York, ME: Stenhouse Publishers.

This useful book is full of information and practical ideas that I have used over the years to help my grade 3 students become more reflective, critical and thoughtful readers. I have found the section on inferential thinking particularly helpful in teaching children how to "read between the lines"—a powerful strategy for deepening their understanding of what they are reading.

The 2Learn.ca Education Society. (2007). Retrieved June 1, 2007 from: http://www.2learn.ca.

The 2learn.ca resource has provided me with some high quality curriculum materials, tools, and support for the integration of information communication technology outcomes into subject areas across the curriculum. The site includes materials for grades 1 to 12.

Ben Hazzard recommends ...

The Speed of Creativity Blog & Podcast. http://www.speedofcreativity.org.

This podcast (Internet radio show) provides creative ideas and reflection about using new media in education. It has helped to bring me up to date on many current issues and thoughts about how to create an engaging and interactive classroom that uses technology effectively as a tool for learning and teaching.

SMART Board Software. http://www2.smarttech.com/st/en-US/Support/Downloads/default.htm.

This software is a free download with an amazing gallery. It accompanies this particular brand of interactive whiteboard. The software can be used to help students understand the power of moving beyond simply "viewing" to interacting with and deconstructing the content of new media. I've found it extremely helpful as I work with multimodal literacies in my classrooms.

Friedman, T. L. (2006). *The world is flat: A brief history of the twenty-first century.* New York: Farrar, Straus & Giroux.

This book isn't so much about education as about how technology has changed our world. Friedman shows how the "flattening" of the world is actually strengthening local and regional identities rather than homogenizing them. He says that we are experiencing a fundamental shift in the world, much like the shift that happened on the invention of the printing press, the rise of the nation-state, or the Industrial Revolution. The book made me see things in a new way, and it allowed me to understand some of the possibilities available in our connected world.

University of Western Ontario. Education Library. (2003). Lesson plans and additional resources. Retrieved June 1, 2007, from http://www.lib.uwo.ca/education/lessonplans.shtml.

This Canadian site connects teachers to a wide range of web-based resources for use across the curriculum. It includes lesson plans, library resources, drama ideas, science, social studies, art, and more—and most of it involves writing.

The Process of Writing

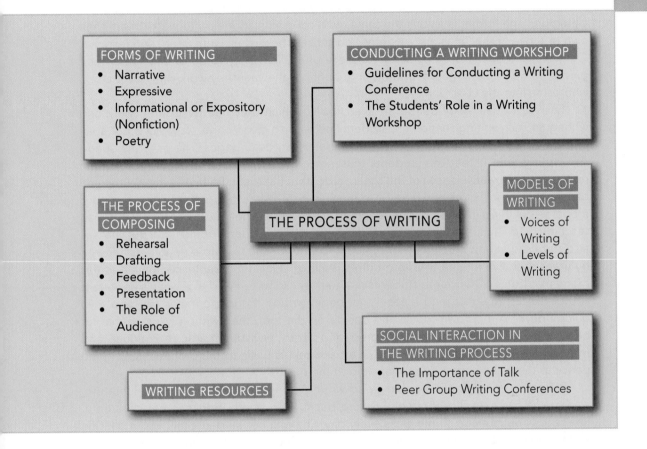

FORMS OF WRITING
- Narrative
- Expressive
- Informational or Expository (Nonfiction)
- Poetry

CONDUCTING A WRITING WORKSHOP
- Guidelines for Conducting a Writing Conference
- The Students' Role in a Writing Workshop

THE PROCESS OF WRITING

THE PROCESS OF COMPOSING
- Rehearsal
- Drafting
- Feedback
- Presentation
- The Role of Audience

MODELS OF WRITING
- Voices of Writing
- Levels of Writing

SOCIAL INTERACTION IN THE WRITING PROCESS
- The Importance of Talk
- Peer Group Writing Conferences

WRITING RESOURCES

My Brother

My brother is like the weather
You have to prepare for him
If you don't, it will be a big mess
When crying, it's raining
When smiling, it's sunny
A tantrum is a tornado
I wish I knew the forecast better.

—Peter (Grade Five)

Raffaella Montemurro

WRITING IN RAFFAELLA MONTEMURRO'S GRADE 4 CLASSROOM

The Artists'/Writers' Workshop takes place every week in Raffaella Montemurro's grade 4 classroom. The format is always the same, with children responding to works of art (their own or those of the "masters"), poetry, and prose. They listen, write, read, and respond. Other times they make art or discuss a piece of art first. They listen to each other read pieces, as well as to Raffaella, and often throughout the year they work with guest artists who come into the classroom.

Each child has a coil-bound art sketchbook, which they use for both artwork and writing. In each writing session the students begin on a clean page. Raffaella is not at all prescriptive, never setting an expected number of words or pages. The only rule during this writing time is that the students must write *something*, and they must be quiet, respecting the creative space of the other students in the room. Raffaella writes alongside her students. The writing can be a list, a menu, a note, a few thoughts on a topic, a story, a poem—anything inspired by the readings or artwork of the day. When she first began teaching grade 4, Raffaella was surprised at how well her students could read. But she was also surprised at how much they struggled with writing. She therefore now starts her year by using daily five-minute writing prompts, such as "Finish this sentence: My life at this moment is like … ." Once the students realize they can write—and that what is important is their voice, thoughts, and ideas—they begin writing more spontaneously, and they quickly develop their own topics and decide on the form their writing will take, having been introduced to a wide variety of prose and poetry, newspaper articles, critiques, and memoir. The connection between visual art and text is basic to the process. Putting the pencil to the blank page is of primary importance.

Raffaella strongly believes that good writing comes from reading good literature, and so she has a wealth of novels, picture books, and poetry books in her classroom. She reads poetry aloud to her class every day. She and her students talk about specific words and phrases, and they delight in the creativity of the writers whose work they are enjoying. Raffaella also has a collection of beautiful art books and prints in her studio-classroom. She is an artist herself, and teaches art regularly and frequently to her class. The classroom walls and bulletin boards are covered with artwork created by her students. Often the students will look at works of art in the books or on the walls, discuss them and talk about their titles. They might try to figure out why an artist has given a specific title to a specific work. Raffaella points out that a title is always there for a reason, even if we do not always understand why. She feels titles are important in comprehending and appreciating a work of art.

Sometimes Raffaella suggests her students write a piece with the same title as an artwork or some other artifact. As a "warmup" activity, Raffaella prints titles on small strips of paper. They might be the titles of pieces of art ("On Sundays We Ride the Swans," "Dogs Dancing"), or of stories, magazine articles, or headlines from a newspaper. The students enjoy selecting a title and "playing" with the piece of writing or art they develop from it.

Everything the children write in their sketchbook is dated and kept. At least once a month, the students leaf through their books, deciding if a piece is worth revising and working on some more. When they need an editor, or a conference with Raffaella about any aspect of their writing, they set an appointment with her. If the child does not have time to type the piece into the computer, Raffaella quickly types it for them so they can see the words on the screen in large font. Together, they work on voice, content, phrases, wording, and punctuation. They also work on the visual appeal of the piece, whether it is a story, a poem, or any other form. They decide how it should be set out and presented on the page. They look at the ways in which other authors set out their work, and they often invite other children to make suggestions during the conferences.

The children in Raffaella's classroom look forward to sharing their work with each other voluntarily, and do so several times a year in a "Poetry Café" where they read a written work of their own choice and display their works of art. Raffaella's students have, over the years, had numerous exhibitions of their art and writing at local galleries, downtown cafés, as well as in the school—and yearly, in the city transit system in the collaborative project "Take the Poetry Route."

The Living Room

There are many special places in my house but I think the one I like best is the living room. The living room is not that big, but it has hiding places and interesting books and even a little box with musical instruments. There is one window which looks out onto a forest and you can hear the birds in the trees. Late in the day we sit on a cushion and find images in the flickering firelight. We close our eyes and try to guess the names of the birds who are singing. Once a year we each get one marshmallow to roast upon the fire. I always look forward to those happy days—in the living room.

—Skye (from Raffaella's grade 4 class)

Writing instruction in elementary schools has changed dramatically over the last 20 years. The new digital technologies are challenging the way we think about writing, and changing the ways in which we *do* writing. The mouse, the touch screen, and the keypad on a cell phone are all writing technologies. We are no longer tied to the technologies of paper, pens, pencils, crayons, scissors, staples, tape, and so on. Children in elementary classrooms today draw on their funds of knowledge about digital literacy from their lives outside school, from their home and social environments and their parents' work environments, as well as from their school contexts. A good place for beginning teachers to start is to reflect on their own experiences as writers and to think about what students need in order to develop their abilities to create and express their ideas in writing. We suggest they consider the following questions as useful entry points:

- What do children need to know and be able to do in order to develop as writers?
- What role does the teacher play in helping young writers to grow?
- How can the teacher structure writing instruction to promote growth in both fluency of ideas and control of writing skills?

- How can the teacher balance the need for creative expression with the need for clear communication?
- What forms of writing are appropriate for elementary students? □

MODELS OF WRITING

Over the years, the field of education has experienced a number of different models or approaches to writing instruction. In the 1960s and early 1970s, writing was seen as a process of encoding speech into print. The focus was on handwriting, spelling, grammar, and other conventions of the language, and these elements were taught in isolation. It was believed that children needed to learn these elements of writing before they could engage in "real" writing. Later, writing was seen as a form of self-expression and the term "creative writing" was used.

In the 1980s, teachers and researchers began to observe young writers in the act of composing (Graves, 1983; Calkins, 1986). They began to ask questions about the processes that children use when writing: How do writers craft a piece of writing? How do they work on their ideas? How do they learn to shape the writing so that it is interesting and piques the interest of the audience? How do writers ensure that the piece says what they want it to say and that they have communicated the information and feelings they want to communicate? Teachers such as Graves and Calkins concluded that writing is a complex set of processes and skills that requires a command of the print code (*graphophonics*), grammar (*syntax*), and meaning-making devices (*semantics*), as well as of the physical act of creating print (handwriting or word processing). It is a generative rather than a receptive process. Pat D'Arcy (1989), in her work as a language arts consultant, identified four elements of students' writing: processes (the thinking involved), products (the pieces of formatted writing), codes (spelling, punctuation, grammar, letters, words), and media (handwriting, word processing, notes, jottings, and so on).

In the 1990s, the systematic and explicit teaching of specific genres of writing was seen as necessary, and today, there is an emphasis on the setting and culture of the writer and the writing pieces they create. Teachers are aware that writing is always carried out with a specific purpose and for a distinct audience. We use different voices, styles, genres, formats, and media, depending on the purpose and audience the writing is to serve. When student writers develop a sense of purpose and audience, they recognize that different genres help them to achieve their communication goals: letters, memos, poems, reports, editorials, invitations, journal entries, logs, diaries, essays, plays, film scripts, multimedia stories, textbooks, novels, short stories, lists, recipes, instruction manuals, and so on. As writers, we can never separate a piece of writing from its form, function, or audience. Each one affects the others and shapes the piece of writing and the presentation of the writing. It is important that students encounter many different real-world purposes, situations, and genres in their classroom writing. The goal of writing instruction is for students to communicate and express their ideas, questions, knowledge, and opinions to others who they may wish to influence or inform.

Today, there is a focus on balance in a writing program. Like all writers, the creators of "My Brother" and "The Living Room" generated meaning using all the cuing systems of their language and culture. And today, we also attend to the "new literacies," to ensure that students become "cognitively and socially literate with paper, live, and electronic texts" (Anstey & Bull, 2006, p.23). Anstey and Bull remind teachers that the increasing rate of technological innovation has produced new forms of text. With the increase in film, video, gaming, and the Internet, and the increased visual content in books and magazines, a whole range of texts has developed that are not print-based. Print knowledge is now seen as necessary but not sufficient in today's "knowledge economy." With the advent of new technologies and new forms of media, print text is no longer the only basic.

Today's elementary school students are creating text that is mediated through popular culture. Many children come to kindergarten and grade one with sophisticated levels of technological literacy (Merchant, 2005). Film, video, television, magazines, the Internet, and gaming are part of the culture of childhood like never before. When children are creating stories in school, they draw on their experiences with these media, and expect to use the new media in their classrooms. Teachers and students together are learning to work with the new media and are learning how to talk about these new forms of texts (including still and moving images) and their meanings as they create and respond to these multimodal texts. Here print information blends with visual, audio, spoken, nonverbal, and other forms of expression produced through a range of technologies. Visual literacy plays a more critical role in literacy education than ever before. At the same time, teachers still need to be aware of the role of text (of all kinds) in our lives and of the models and approaches that can help them be effective teachers of both written and multimodal forms of text. In the next section we present some of the traditional models of writing.

Voices of Writing

James Britton (1970) proposed a model of writing based on the **voice** of the writer. Voice refers to the combined effects of the writer's purpose, style, tone, and other intangibles, such as commitment, energy, conviction, and personality. Britton identified three voices of writing: expressive, poetic, and transactional.

The **expressive voice** is used when we write in a journal, write a personal e-mail to a friend, or write a greeting card. It expresses who we are and what we think and feel. In expressive writing, which usually tends to be informal, we articulate ideas that are close to us, that may not yet be fully shaped. Below is an excerpt from a piece of expressive writing by a student in grade 4, written as he thought about the novel *On My Honor* by Marion Dane Bauer (1986):

> I hate it when my friends try to convince me to do things they want to do. I think Tony is being quite mean to Joel. I think that Tony just wants Joel to do what he wants to do. I can swim but not too good. But even if I was a professional swimmer I'd never swim in a river. I think it's a bad idea because the water is pushing you. It would just suck you up. A few minutes later you'd be dead.

Poetic writing is more literary and is used in stories as well as poems. Usually created for an audience other than the self, poetic writing often contains an aesthetic element not usually present in either expressive or transactional writing. "The Living Room" is an example of poetic writing, and so is the following poem, completed by a student in grade 3:

Cowboys
Brave and dirty,
Hazing,

> Roping,
> Digging their spurs into the horses.
> Riding,
> Racing,
> Branding the cattle
> Cowpunchers.

Transactional writing is used when the writer wants to convey information to others in a report, list, essay, recipe, movie review or textbook. It is usually more formal than personal, focusing principally on the effective communication of content. Many examples of transactional writing were presented in Chapter 7, including the writing Julie Gellner's students completed during their "Restaurant Project."

Britton noticed that young writers frequently move from one voice to another as they write. When writing a report on an animal, for example, they might add a personal anecdote about their pet, and hence combine the expressive and transactional voices. Similarly, they may shift from the poetic to the expressive voice when writing a story, adding themselves as a character and writing in the first person. Britton terms this the *transitional voice*. In the poem "About Seasons" presented in Chapter 7 (Box 7.5), although it did not alter the voice of her writing, Tanya could not resist adding her address and phone number to the bottom of the page, ensuring her own personal stamp was placed on her piece. Usually, as writers mature, they are able to select an appropriate voice for their writing and remain consistently within that voice.

Levels of Writing

James Moffett (1979) proposed a model of writing development that suggests a hierarchy, according to the skills the writer needs and the purpose the writing is to serve. The levels are

- drawing or handwriting, in which children struggle to make sense of the written language system and try to replicate it
- copying, in which children can copy from a model provided by someone else; the focus is on learning the correct form of letters and sentences rather than generating ideas
- transcribing or paraphrasing, in which writers take someone else's ideas and write them in their own language and own words
- crafting, in which children generate meaning through writing in a conventional form; the focus is on the structure of the piece and on communicating meaning to the reader in the most effective way (e.g., the poem "Cowboys")
- "the revision of inner speech," which Moffett claims is the only true form of writing, because it involves expressing and shaping one's own thoughts; Moffett also claims that it is rarely found in classrooms

An example of the final level is shown below. The piece was written just after the writer, in grade 4, had read *On My Honor* (Bauer, 1986).

> Chapter eight confused me at the beginning. It didn't exactly say that Joel had gone home. When he was at home, I think I understood why and how he lied. Telling the truth in tough

situations is very difficult. I would never lie at all, even in a problem like that. My friend's mom just moved here a little while ago and the apartment they lived in was allowed no children. Quite absurd! She only got to live there because she said she was a doctor. Stuff like that makes me very untrusting of the world. Taking a person by how much money they have etc. When I read that chapter I felt Joel's insecurity. He seems to be not acting normal with the problems he's having. A kid dealing with something like that is real scary!

In this piece, the writer is thinking through her feelings about lying. As she writes about the character in the book, she reflects on her own experiences with telling the truth and how, at times, people are moved to lie in order to survive. The writer struggles with the ambivalence she feels, knowing that lying is wrong, but understanding a little of why at times even good people might be dishonest.

Moffett (1979) maintains that children are more likely to be successful, thoughtful, articulate, and skilful writers when they engage in all five levels of writing in the classroom. He also maintains that all levels of writing should be taught. Moffett expresses concern that if instruction is confined to working from an organizer or "prompt," children will be less likely to develop the skills necessary for writing their own compositions. Likewise, if children are restricted to crafting polished pieces of writing with the aim of making them public in a writing workshop, or in an exhibition, they will be denied the opportunity of learning how to use writing as a way of exploring thought. Moffett's chief concern, in 1979, was that too much of the writing children were required to do in school was for the purpose of evaluating what they had learned. This remains a concern to many educators today.

FORMS OF WRITING

Narrative

Narrative writing links a series of events together either through a sequence in time or through cause and effect. The purpose of most narrative writing is to entertain. Much of the narrative writing completed by students in elementary classrooms is fictional, but narrative can also be used for nonfiction texts. Narrative seems to be an almost natural way for human beings to make sense of the world. Barbara Hardy (1975) says that narrative is a "primary act of mind." We seem to think in narrative, retelling events to ourselves to see how the pieces fit together, or telling ourselves how something works as we try to figure out a problem.

A distinction must be noted between a recount and a narrative story. A *recount* is simply a retelling of events with no particular attention to setting, plot, problem or conflict resolution, climax, and so on. When writers develop a *story*, however, they craft the narrative in a certain way. In Western cultures a story is usually structured around an introduction, a middle section with a problem or conflict (sometimes a series of conflicts), and then an ending, which achieves some resolution of the problem. Applebee's 1978 study of the development of children's concept of story suggests that children have to learn to do two things simultaneously to successfully write or tell a story: chain events together and focus on a theme, problem, or character. Applebee's research demonstrated that children begin to form stories from the age of two onward, but they learn to apply these two essential elements over time, mastering the story form (or "story grammar," as it is sometimes called) over a period of years.

As children mature, their stories become more complex and cohesive. Children become aware of an audience for their writing, and strive for clarity and an engaging text. An excerpt from a story written jointly by Sharon and Erica in grade 5 is shown in Box 8.1. Unfinished at the end of the school year, the story was put "on hold" by the girls because they were not sure what to do with it next and they had another piece of writing they wanted to start. This story will be referred to again later in the chapter, in the section about the importance of talking about writing; at that point, the girls' struggle with crafting and ending the piece becomes more apparent.

**BOX 8.1   AN EXCERPT FROM "THE WELLINGTON STORY"
(WRITTEN COOPERATIVELY BY SHARON AND ERICA, GRADE 5)**

When the story begins, Mr. Wellington, a well-known artist, and his wife are hosting a dinner party.

After [the guests] arrived they all sat down for dinner. "Cheers to Mrs. Wellington for having this party," said Miss Murphy in a loud voice. Then they all lifted their glasses and clinked them together. "I'll go get my husband for dinner," said Mrs. Wellington and left. A few minutes later, Mrs. Wellington came back into the dining room. "My husband will be coming shortly," she said as Yvette started carving the turkey. After about ten minutes had passed Mrs. Wellington asked Yvette to go see where her husband was.

Yvette left the dining room and went to the paint house. There was a moment of silence and then Miss Murphy spoke. "The strangest thing happened to me yesterday," she said. "I I … Ahhhhhh." Miss Murphy was interrupted by a loud scream. Mrs. Wellington dropped her fork.

"It's coming from the paint house," said Mr. McGregor. They all rushed out to the paint house and saw Yvette shaking, with a knife in her hand. Mrs. Wellington gasped and walked into the paint house. She saw her husband lying dead on the floor. "Yvette," she screamed.

"How could you?" Mrs. Landenburg walked into the room, looked at the body and fainted. "Somebody call the police," said Mrs. Hunt. Mrs. Wellington started to cry. Mr. McGregor called the police. About 5 minutes later they arrived. "We were in the neighborhood," they said. "Now what happened?" Mrs. Wellington explained the whole thing. "Then we walked in and saw her," she said pointing to Yvette, "standing there with a knife in her hand. She did it officer, I know she did."

"Why don't you go into the house and rest while we look around and take the body away," said the police officer. Mrs. Wellington went into the lounge with the other guests. "It's all right Margaret. It had to happen sooner or later being a famous painter and all," said Miss Murphy. "He was such a kind husband to me," said Mrs. Wellington and then started to cry. Meanwhile in the paint house officer McCarther was searching around the floor when he spotted a loose floorboard.

He pulled back the floor board and saw a white dress with a red wine stain on it. "Hmm," he said. Then he put on a pair of rubber gloves, picked up the dress and placed it in a plastic bag. Then he took a second look, and saw the top of a broken wine bottle.

He picked up the wine bottle and put it into a plastic bag. Then he walked over to where Mr. Wellington was lying and picked up the knife that Yvette dropped and went into the lounge. "I'll have to take finger prints," said officer McCarther and pulled out a stamp pad in front of Mrs. Wellington. "Are you accusing me of killing my own husband? Why would I kill him?" asked Mrs. Wellington. "You might kill him for his money and besides everyone in the room is a suspect," said officer McCarther. "Why didn't I wait until he dies?" asked Mrs. Wellington.

The girls ended the story with the following note to themselves:

tired of story change some parts

Stop story for now

want to start cat bylaw not doing a play

yet at least!

Source: C. Lewis, "Partnership writing: Ten-year-olds talking and writing together," M.Ed. thesis (Edmonton: University of Alberta, 1989).

Expressive

Expressive writing, found in blogs, diaries, and journals, is the kind of personal writing we do informally as thoughts form in our mind. We rarely revise or craft expressive writing. (Britton's use of the word "expressive" to describe one of the three voices of writing differs from this use, though there is some overlap in meaning.) Expressive writing is generally done for an audience who knows the writer, and sometimes the audience is the self. Expressive writing is a means through which we present our ideas, thoughts, feelings, and interpretations of events. It may include responses to books we have read, movies we have seen, or events that have taken place. The two written responses to *On My Honor* (Bauer, 1986) quoted earlier in this chapter are examples of expressive writing. Expressive writing is essentially exploratory. In expressive writing, just as in expressive speech, we speculate, hypothesize, predict, and generally articulate our thoughts.

Informational or Expository (Nonfiction)

Intended to explain, persuade, or instruct, **expository writing** requires the writer to be well organized, clear, and coherent. This writing is not meant to convey feelings or to be primarily entertaining, but to pass on information to an audience. Reports, textbooks, memos, flyers, editorials, and the writing from Julie Gellner"s "Restaurant Project' presented in Chapter 7 are examples of expository writing. Lewis and Wray (1995) identified six nonfiction genres used regularly in our society: persuasion, recount, explanation, report, procedural, and discussion. They maintain that children in the elementary grades should be taught the basic elements of each of these genres, and should have many opportunities for using them in the classroom. An example of a grade 4 child's report writing is shown in Box 8.2.

    Persuasive writing is used more often in our society than we realize. Advertising, editorials, political campaign literature, religious tracts, and much of the unsolicited junk mail

BOX 8.2	GRADE 4 REPORT WRITING: MUSIC IN CROUSETOWN

The Anglican Church in Crousetown, has the oldest pipe organ in Nova Scotia. It is still used in 1993. Every Sunday music was a big entertainment in those days and it still is today.

Most of the music of long ago was made up for fun. Some children might take some spoons and clack them against their knees, or a little boy might put some beans in a can and shake the can.

At night some people might gather together in someone's house and listen to each other play fiddles and accordians.

In those days there were no heavy rock bands or electric guitars. In the old days some homes had pianos or pump organs and if there was someone who could play the piano or organ they would play for sing along songs. Instead of electric guitars some people would play wooden guitars.

They had just about the same fun the old fashioned way as we do with rock bands.

Source: Petite Rivière Elementary School, *History of Crousetown* (Lunenburg County, NS: Petite Rivière Publishing, 1993), p. 4.

that arrives in mailboxes consists of persuasive writing. Someone wants to persuade others to do something, buy something, or believe something. Children use persuasive writing when they create a poster presentation about a book or advertise an event that is to take place in their school. They write persuasively when they want something and have to convince an adult to allow them to have it. At school, for example, this can be channelled into writing to government agencies to request a change of some kind. The writing might be part of a social studies or science project, and may involve a letter-writing campaign. An excerpt from a piece of persuasive writing by a grade 6 child follows:

> I think instead of having a curfew we should have police patrolling the streets at night as a pair. I think we shouldn't have a curfew at night because there are a lot of people out that are not vandalizing the streets.

I would like to talk about why there should be two policemen in each community and how they should work the streets. In my area we have different sorts of gangs. One kid that I know was riding his bike down the street and one of the gangs called Devil's Knights, one kid threw a knife and almost hit the kid. I think the police should talk to different people and ask questions about the gangs and where they meet. I hope we can get the perfect president to run a place like this.

The writing of a **recount or anecdote** can form the foundation for a highly descriptive verbal picture of a scene or event. Such writing invites the reader to participate in the experience through rich sensory detail. Careful crafting can make a descriptive recount particularly dramatic. Below is an excerpt from a recount written by a student in grade 5.

We'd been flying for almost an hour when a grotesque aroma floated from the back of the plane and filled the air. From experience, I knew that the meal was salmon and spinach. My stomach turned inside out at the thought of it. The old woman who I was sitting beside didn't help my stomach because she stank of Super Polly Grip, Efferdent and cheap perfume. The clickety-clack of her knitting needles was driving me insane as I tried to write a letter to my best friend, Brooke. I knew that she was going to be knitting for a long time because she had a pattern for a large sweater taped to the back of her tray and she was still on the first cuff!

Explanatory writing is frequently required in social studies, science, and mathematics. Students must think carefully and logically when writing an explanation, and teachers need to scaffold such writing assignments so that students will be successful. Dr. Perry Klein at the University of Western Ontario studied students' writing of explanations in science. He found that, overall, students who were taught about writing explanations were better able to use writing as a tool for learning about science. The grade 5 students in his study participated in guided reading of several explanations with their teacher. They learned that the purpose of an explanation is to tell how or why something happens; that an explanation often includes several steps, and it tells why each step happens. The students also learned that when writing an explanation, it is important to make good use of sources of information, whether these are science observations, written texts, or other kinds of media.

The students were asked to complete a piece of explanatory writing with a partner. Their goal was to explain what had happened to the young fish that were missing from the Stony River. They received a small portfolio that contained a variety of documents: a newspaper clipping, a map of the town, "fast facts" about acid (see below), a "backgrounder" on what causes acid rain and snow, a line graph of acidity in the river throughout the year, and a table on the effects of acidity on water animals. The documents did not tell what had happened to the missing fish, but they provided a host of clues.

Fast Facts: What Is Acid?

- An acid is a substance
- Acids are usually found dissolved in water
- Mild acids taste sour
- Vinegar, lemon juice and orange juice are mild acids
- Strong acids rust metal and burn skin
- Acidity is measured in "ph"
- Pure water has a ph of 7.0
- *Lower* ph means *more* acidic

BOX 8.3	THE MYSTERY OF THE MISSING FISH

Missing Young Fish

We think that the young fish in Stoney River are missing because the water in stoney River is very acidic & most young fishies will not survive. Since there is high acidity in the spring & most fish lay there eggs then, the eggs may not hatch. If they do hatch, they have a very little chance of surviving. Since the water is frozen in the winter months, there is very little chance that acid would get into the water. When it melts in the spring all the acid that has gathered in the ice will melt & go staight into the river. Since the fish are usually babies during the spring months then their babies cannot hold the acid. as well as adults, they will die if they stay in the acidic water for too long. If the fish had their babies in Juin-August then they will have a better chance of surviving.

So thats why we think that there are so many young fish missing from the Stoney River!! Thank you for reading our papers!

The partners worked together through oral discussion and writing to interpret the documents and build an explanation. One example is provided in Box 8.3.

Poetry

Although poetry is a genre of writing rather than a specific form such as narrative, explanatory, or persuasive writing, we are including a section on writing poetry here because beginning teachers frequently ask for advice on how to teach poetry writing in elementary classrooms. Poetry is a genre that attempts to capture feelings, events, places, and people in an aesthetically pleasing way. A few

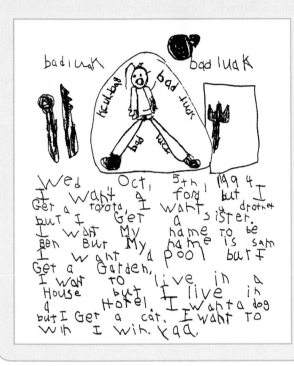

Bad Luck

I want a Ford but I get a Toyota.
I want a brother but I get a sister.
I want my name to be Ben but my name is Sam.
I want a pool but I get a garden.
I want to live in a house but I live in a hotel.
I want a dog but I get a cat.
I want to win. I win. Yaa!

poetic words or phrases can convey a whole set of meanings in a particularly striking manner. Poetry is not defined by a rhyme scheme or rhythm, but is uniquely artistic, although sometimes disconcerting. "My Brother," "Cowboys," "Soccer," and "Bad Luck" (presented in Box 8.4) are examples of poetry written by children in the elementary grades. The children who wrote these poems found the genre to be most effective for the meanings they wanted to convey. Children at all the elementary grade levels seem to find poetry a singularly appealing genre for their writing.

Elementary grade students write much excellent poetry when they are encouraged to make each word do its "most effective job." We stress here that it is not helpful to provide children with a pattern for their poetry writing (such as haiku, cinquain, limerick, or diamante). When children are faced with fitting their words into an already established pattern, they frequently encounter difficulties because the constraints of the form are too limiting. Writing a good limerick or haiku, for example, is extremely difficult and takes a great deal of hard work, even for an experienced writer. Children can end up with a poorly written poem that has been created simply to fit the assigned form. Teaching children various forms of poetry is appropriate only insofar as students are being introduced to the form and are aware of its structure and its name.

Teachers can prepare their students for writing poetry by encouraging them to use strong and colourful verbs and specific nouns in all of their writing, rather than decorating their writing with adjectives and adverbs. In addition, students can be encouraged to experiment with syntactical patterns to create particular effects. Poems can be changed radically if the last line becomes the first (do that with "Soccer" and note the impact), or if the poem is given a different (often more simple) title. Sometimes, teachers may challenge their student writers to capture an event, scene, or idea by "saying the most with the fewest words possible." Anne Gordon, in Chapter 2, explained how she engaged and motivated her student writers by encouraging them to create "heart maps." Raffaella Montemurro uses discussions about art (that of both the students and the "masters") to inspire her students to think about the words and phrases they use in their writing. Grade 5 teacher Diana Dixon reads at least one poem aloud to her students every day, and she has books of poetry available for free reading in her classroom. Diana frequently talks about poetry with her students, and together they compile lists of their favourite poems. Writing poetry helps Anne's, Raffaella's, and Diana's students to focus their writing and to realize just how flexible and powerful written language can be.

Soccer

A soccer ball
Is like
An eraser
It erases away my thoughts.
When I kick it
I do not think.
My mind is lost
In the game.
The ball flies
Towards the net.
The ball bends
In mid air
The goalie jumps one way
The ball flies the other.
We win the game!

—Jarico (from Diana Dixon's grade 5 class)

Diana Dixon and reading group

A number of recent "verse novels" have fostered children's interest in writing poetry. Sharon Creech's book *Love That Dog* (2001) is a series of found poems written by the protagonist, Jack, on the urging of his teacher. Although Jack doesn't consider himself a poet, he writes about the poems and the poets his teacher introduces to the class. His "found poems" reveal his thoughts and feelings about himself as a writer and about the things that are most important to him. Steven Herrick's two Australian titles *The Spangled Drongo* (1999) and *Tom Jones Saves the World* (2002) recount the humorous and heart-warming adventures of two boys as they come to terms with the opposite sex and with their parents. The books make superb "Read-Alouds," and they demonstrate to children how "saying the most with the fewest words possible" can create lasting images and tell intriguing stories.

INSIDE CLASSROOMS

Diana Dixon and "Love That Dog"

Diana Dixon so enjoyed *Love That Dog* **that she decided to introduce the book to her grade 5 students. She says:**

I didn't really know what to do with the book. I knew I didn't want to ruin it by "teaching" it, so I decided that we would just enjoy the book as a class. It took us just over a week to read. We read together, discussed, and responded to the book. At the beginning of the book the students were obsessed with the yellow cover and the blue print (interestingly, I didn't notice the blue print the first time that I read the book—yikes!). The students were comfortable saying that they didn't understand the poems or the story line. As a teacher I have (finally!) stopped trying to explain everything to them. I underscored the idea that we don't all understand everything in the same way, or at the same time, and that's okay. So my students felt free to question and ponder. I was impressed that they did not hesitate to share their ideas.

In their written responses, students were given various options—they could write a response journal entry, write a detail/response chart, draw, cartoon, or respond in any way they desired. At the beginning of the book many students didn't know how to respond. They ended up copying print directly from the text, just as early readers copy environmental print from the classroom. I was shocked, as this class had never done anything like this before. However, as the book progressed, they started getting more comfortable with using different types of responses to get their ideas down.

One student said, "the pages are so short I can read this easily in a week." Another student said, halfway through the book, "I don't know why this is such a special book." But most students enjoyed the book and many responded in poetic form—they enjoyed creating shape poems but struggled if they tried to make a poem rhyme. At times they just shared their thoughts in free verse or drew in their notebooks. One student drew Walter Dean Myers and described him as, "a soft man and is not too old but has white hair already. He also has a peachy smile on his face."

One student asked, "Why does Jack take stuff from poems? I think I know the answer … but what is your opinion?" This same student also said at the end of the book, "I can't tell if Love That Dog is a book or a boy saying stuff like someone would in a diary. What is your opinion?"

Our final activity with the book was a group activity where the students listed the poetry lessons that Jack learned throughout the story. Here are a few of the things they came up with:

▷ poems include repetition

▷ poems don't always rhyme

▷ writers get inspiration from other poems

▷ lines can be as long as you want

▷ both boys and girls can write poems

▷ write about what you know lots about

(Continued)

▷ start small

▷ don't be scared to let your ideas flow

▷ poems should be read over and over again

▷ any words can be poems

▷ any poem can be powerful

▷ you don't have to understand poems to enjoy them

▷ don't be afraid to let poems out of your heart

▷ poetry is not just words put into sentences, it is feelings

▷ poems can be funny, sad, happy, exciting, serious, rhyming, or nonsense

▷ in some poems you make up words

▷ some poems relate to you and some don't

▷ poems have to sound and look good

I enjoyed reading the book and I felt that it engaged many of my enthusiastic readers. My reluctant readers were happy with the length of the book, the time we took to read a whole book, and the shared reading that we used throughout. I know the book is still in my students' thoughts as a boy suggested yesterday, during oral recitation of a poem, "Well, girls are better at 'singing' poems than boys," and one of his classmates responded, "No, they aren't! Didn't you learn anything in *Love That Dog*?"

Children can have a great deal of fun with **found poetry**. Found poems are created by culling words from other sources, such as newspapers, magazines, advertisements, songs, and stories. They can be authored by individual children or by groups of students working together. As a reader response activity, students may collect their favourite words and phrases from a story and reorganize them to express their responses to the book. After reading *Looking for X* by Deborah Ellis (1999), one group of students created the following poem, entitled "Khyber":

Nobody looked happy
Even though it was the end of the work week
And they were heading home.
"Happy," said David.
Autism, group home, clothes and toys in boxes.
I cried until I fell asleep.
A van pulled up beside me
And Elvis stepped out.
"Winsome—You know,
You win some, you lose some."
Blue suitcase, great backpack.
Keep it simple and keep it dignified.

Now, everyone who meets me
Will go away thinking they've met
Someone very interesting indeed.

THE PROCESS OF COMPOSING

In the 1970s, Donald Graves (1983) conducted research that led to a major shift in the teaching of writing in elementary schools, secondary schools, and colleges. His work, along with that of Lucy Calkins (1986 and 1991), Nancie Atwell (1998), and others, focused on the process of writing and promoted a workshop approach to the teaching of writing. This means that children work with one another and their teachers, composing, drafting, revising, editing, and publishing their works. Graves' work enabled teachers to reconceptualize writing as a series of processes that a writer goes through. The danger with this approach is that teachers can become locked into a linear, step-by-step approach that is not reflective of the process most writers go through. The writing process is cyclical and most of us write, read, revise, reread, revise some more, etc., especially when working on a word processor.

When teachers take a workshop approach, they engage in writing themselves and so develop a fuller understanding of what a writer goes through to create a composition, making it clear and conventionally appropriate for an audience. Not every piece of writing will be shared with others. Much of our writing will stay in our writing folder, with only a few pieces making it through to the "sharing with a public" stage. The process requires time, thought, and the reworking of multiple drafts. The focus is on the process of composing and the thinking that must take place to develop a successful piece of writing. Graves' work has fundamentally changed the way educators think about the writing process and the teaching of writing in schools.

Most of what is known about composing comes from observations of real writers and authors and the insights they provide to educators. These writers often say there is no such thing as a finished piece of writing. As they write they think, and as they think and receive feedback, they revise, develop new ideas, begin new pieces, share old ones, and continue their development. Raffaella Montemurro invites local authors into her grade 4 classroom because they can explain to her students the processes and struggles they engage in as they write. Their modelling is a powerful teaching strategy for young writers. As one aspect of thinking, writing both reflects and facilitates the exploration of ideas. The composition process is more spiral than linear, for writers do not stay in the same place for long when they write. They constantly anticipate what is needed and, in the process, develop new writing strategies, techniques, and ideas.

Rehearsal

The first stage of composing is often called collecting, rehearsing, or prewriting. At this point, writers collect ideas, memories, and experiences that help them to decide on a topic. They decide on what should be included in the composition, and what memories and recollections they can use to develop it. Writers use mixtures of people they have known, places they have visited, and their own experiences, whether real or vicarious. Writers of published works tell us that all their stories are about themselves in some way. We retain our memories and emotions, and these become the raw material of our writing. Children are just as capable as adults of choosing a topic and working with their experiences. They need help and encouragement, but the more they have ownership of their writing (i.e., assume responsibility for key decisions about topic choice, format, audience, and production time lines) and write about topics that interest them, the more they are likely to work at their writing and improve it. We learn to write by writing.

At this stage, writers think about the form or media they will use for the composition. Is this piece going to be created on the word processor? Will it have artwork or illustrations along with it? Will it use multimedia technology? Will still or moving images be incorporated? Will it have a print form, or will it be entirely a digital presentation?

Drafting

Once a topic has been determined, the writer begins to draft a text, putting onto paper the intentions developed in the rehearsing stage. The text may go through many drafts, and be modified and reworked, with the original intentions in mind. During the drafting stage, the writer becomes clearer about what can actually be done and what needs to be changed. The writer may play with the drafts, changing words here and there, adding to it, deleting parts that are not effective, and rewriting parts that simply don't work. It is during this stage that the writer asks, "Am I meaning what I say and saying what I mean?" Writers strive for clarity and try to maintain the interest and attention of the audience. Sometimes thoughts do not fall into place until the writer starts writing; the actual process of writing enables the ideas to flow. In a sense, writing seems to slow down thinking. As writers write, they have time and opportunity to capture their thoughts, reflect on them, and connect them to previous thoughts in a generative process. Published writers go through dozens of drafts of a text before it is ready for an audience. Elementary school children might complete three drafts in total, especially if they are just beginning to work with the writing process.

Editing and revision skills can be taught in mini-lessons before or after a writers' workshop, or in group and individual conferences like the ones Raffaella conducts with her students. When children are writing on paper, they can prepare for revision by writing on one side of the paper only and on every other line. These practices enable them to cross out, write over top, use carets to insert text, and make other changes without having to copy a whole piece over. When writing with a word processor, drafting and editing are much easier, which is one reason why most teachers today ensure that a number of computers are available for the students within the classroom. Going to a computer lab is not helpful for students on a day-to-day basis.

The writing shown in Boxes 8.5 and 8.6 demonstrates the changes that Wendy, in grade 2, made to her report on whales as she worked through the writing process. The two pieces presented here are excerpts from the first draft and the final draft of the report. The children in Wendy's classroom were used to working through the writing process with both their poetic and transactional/expository writing.

BOX 8.5   EXCERPT FROM FIRST DRAFT OF WENDY'S REPORT ON WHALES

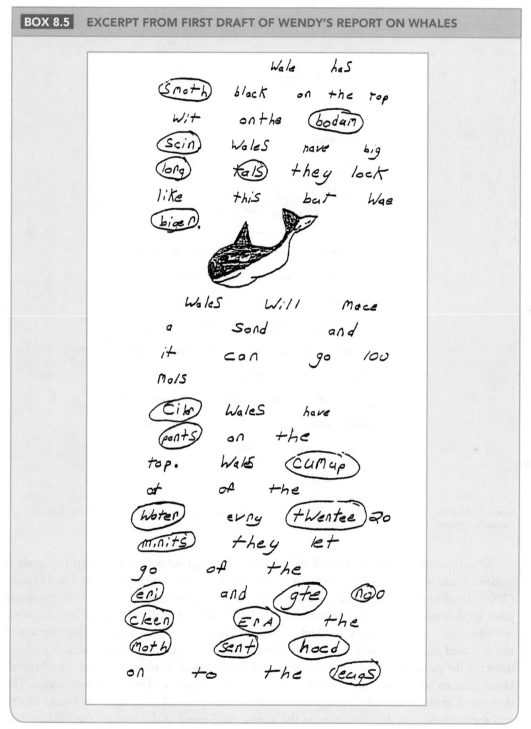

Source: F. Maaskant, "Children's perceptions of writing in a Grade One/Two classroom" (Appendix), M.Ed. thesis (Edmonton: University of Alberta, 1989).

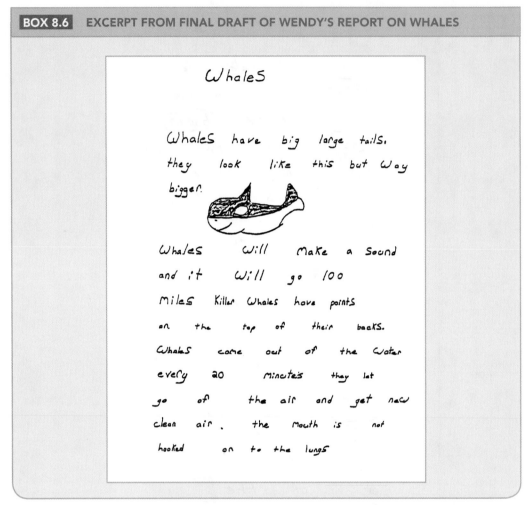

| BOX 8.6 | EXCERPT FROM FINAL DRAFT OF WENDY'S REPORT ON WHALES |

Source: F. Maaskant, "Children's perceptions of writing in a Grade One/Two classroom" (Appendix), M.Ed. thesis (Edmonton: University of Alberta, 1989).

One elementary teacher enlisted the support of a high school class to help her grade 6 students create **digital stories** in response to Gordon Kormans' *Dive. Book One: The Discovery* (2003). In addition to several reading and writing responses, the students used a basic computer paint application to paint their favourite scenes from the book. Labelling this a "telecollaborative adventure," the elementary and high school students wrote a blog in which they negotiated the animated story that would be developed from each child's picture. The high school students dissected the paintings and animated them using Macromedia's Flash application. The "stories" lasted between 30 seconds and one minute. Sound effects, music, and narration were added. The elementary students drafted the story, and collaboratively planned the visuals, the sound effects, and the movement of the characters on the screen. At the end of the project, the students had a face-to-face meeting in which the animations were unveiled and screened to the combined classes. The children, their parents, and other relatives enjoyed the digital stories that were eventually posted on the school website. A distinct advantage of posting children's work online is that relatives (especially grandparents) can participate in the children's school life even if they are separated by geography. Although some teachers express concern at posting children's work on the web, there are ways of maintaining security, and a school district technology consultant will provide the necessary information.

Many software tools are available to help youngsters with their writing and presentation. One is IntelliTools Classroom Suite, which contains templates for writing, and also includes graphics and animation. This is a program children very much enjoy working with. Comic Creator (Marcopolo), endorsed by NCTE and IRA, and Comic Book Creator (CNET) are software programs that are either free or inexpensive and that facilitate children's comic-book-making. Photographs can be imported or clip art from the program can be used to create a story or to write an imaginative report in science or other subject area. One class of students created comic books on various types of clouds; it provided an interesting and creative alternative to the research report. Other students use the software to tell family or classroom stories, or to create their own comic book character and adventures.

As an additional aid to storytelling, many teachers access websites belonging to children's authors. In particular, Jan Brett and Dav Pilkey's sites are worth a visit, as they are instructive and interesting to young writers.

Feedback

While creating a composition, student writers need feedback, both from peers and from their teacher. Peer conferences *and* group or one-on-one conferences with the teacher are necessary so that children can obtain this feedback when they need it, and not when it is too late to make changes. It is during these conferences that children have the best opportunity to learn about writing. This is where Raffaella does most of her teaching of writing. Some guidelines for conducting writing conferences are presented later in this chapter.

Presentation

The very last phase of the writing process is presentation, publication, or celebration. When a piece of writing is finished to an author's satisfaction, the piece can be shared with a wider audience. It might be sent home to family, read aloud to a whole class or group, displayed to the class on-screen or posted on the school website or the class blog. It might be made into a book and placed in the classroom library, or shared with residents of a seniors' home. This is a time for celebrating the accomplishments of the writer. It is no longer a work-in-progress, and it is no longer appropriate for the audience to make critical comments or suggestions for change. The work will stand alone, ready for public scrutiny and the future enjoyment of reading audiences. Such is Skye's prose piece "The Living Room" and Peter's poem "My Brother."

The Role of Audience

Establishing an authentic audience for children's writing makes a difference in how children go about the process of composition and revision. Awareness that a real audience is going to hear or see their written pieces makes all the difference in the world. Raffaella

Montemurro talks about the importance of "writing in community." When children write together, talk about their writing, read their writing to each other, and listen to published authors talk about their work, they have a different purpose and motivation in learning to become good writers. Writing is not simply a functional skill to be learned in order to send e-mails, write wish lists, and complete school assignments. It becomes an art that can entertain and delight, and it can produce great pride in young writers who know it is a valuable accomplishment.

CONDUCTING A WRITING WORKSHOP

One teacher/researcher who has influenced the teaching of writing and the development of writing workshops is Nancie Atwell. In 1987, Atwell published her first book, *In the Middle*, and in 1998 she developed a second edition of the book, modifying her ideas after many more years of classroom teaching. In the second edition, Atwell lays out the expectations she has for writers' workshops and the guidelines she uses for her students' writing sessions. Although Atwell's suggestions are made largely with students in grades 5 to 9 in mind, many of the ideas are modifiable for teachers and children in grades 2 to 4. Box 8.7 lists some of Atwell's suggestions for conducting writing workshops in the classroom.

Guidelines for Conducting a Writing Conference

Lucy Calkins (1991) and Nancie Atwell (1998) point out that young writers want to be listened to and want honest responses to their work. Sharing a piece of writing with an informed audience can be a most effective means of obtaining feedback. In the process, writers learn new ways of making meaning, building on their already existing writing skills. Teachers can teach or model feedback strategies that are productive and sensitive to the fact that every piece of writing is very special to its author. The writing is essentially a part of the writer, and as such it must be respected by the audience. Students can learn how to receive the work of others gently, how to give constructive feedback and positive comments, and how to make suggestions for future drafts and new pieces of writing. Teachers who model and promote a constructive and respectful process help to ensure that, when children share their pieces of writing with a group, they will feel safe and will be able to accept the feedback.

In a writing conference, the writer usually reads the piece to the teacher or to the group. This enables the listener (or listeners) to focus on the ideas, wording, and flow of the piece of writing. At the elementary school level, a three-part response system works well. First, children or teacher provide a positive comment about the piece—what works well or sounds good. Next, they ask questions about anything that is not clear in the piece. Finally, they make suggestions about what can be done to make the piece better.

A conference might be very brief—just a few minutes of conversation with the teacher—or it can be a more formal and lengthy affair with a small group of students. In a conference, the teacher's goal is to provide feedback designed to improve the students' writing. The conference is effective when the teacher's responses provide strategic information that the writer can act

BOX 8.7 CONDUCTING A WRITING WORKSHOP

1. A writing workshop has a predictable format, so that students know when it is to occur, what is expected of them, and what they can expect from the teacher and the situation. Teachers work out for themselves what feels comfortable and what seems to work in their classrooms. Time is provided for children to write, as well as respond to each other's writing, and time is also provided for teachers to respond to individual students' work. Teachers also try to build into their schedules time for their own writing, so that children can see them modelling the writing process.

2. A writers' workshop, as Raffaella noted, is something like an artist's studio and has all the necessary resources. Young children need different colours and sizes of paper, scissors, tape, felt pens, pencils, pens, and staplers so they can create their own booklets for writing and drawing. Older children need dictionaries, a thesaurus, reference books, rulers, whiteout, and staples. If computers are available, the students need easy and regular access to them, printing facilities, a safe place to store disks, and some degree of privacy while they type.

3. A writers' workshop can be noisy, because children need to talk about their writing. However, teachers like Raffaella plan quiet times when all the students are writing. These times are agreed upon by the students. Many children say that they cannot do any real writing or reading at school because it is too noisy. Teachers try to respect this need as well as the need for interaction. The quiet time is used for writing only, and at that time any conversation must be in a whisper. There is also open time, when students can write or meet together in a response group. In addition, some teachers schedule group conferences where they interact with the children in a more traditional way.

4. A writing folder or large notebook (Raffaella's students use an art sketchbook) is essential for each person in the classroom, including the teacher. Rather than have children keep these folders or notebooks in their desks, it is usually easier if they are kept in a filing cabinet that is accessible to the children at all times.

5. All pieces of writing are dated with a draft number printed at the top. Students save all writings, even those that "don't work." This allows them to see how their work is changing. Sometimes a writer will go back to an earlier draft of a piece because it is better than a later one.

6. Students can generate a list of possible writing topics and keep them at the front of the folder, or in the front of their notebook. They can add to the list on a regular basis as they discover new topics and experiences that will make good stories. Teachers often encourage children to take a few minutes every few weeks to update their list of possibilities, and discuss topics students have chosen to put on their lists.

7. Writers are encouraged not to erase their work, but instead put a line through changes and insert new material above. Writing on every other line and on only one side of the paper facilitates this process and encourages children to make changes and insertions

(Continued)

without having to rewrite the whole piece. When children compose on a word processor it is more difficult to separate drafts, as changes are made to a text on a continuing basis. However, it is helpful if children can print drafts at various stages of development, label them, and keep them in their folder. Alternatively, drafts can be saved on the computer, numbered in the same way.

8. Writing conferences might focus on the content of a piece, the topic, or the organization, clarifying the ideas and focusing the writing toward a more cohesive whole. A writing conference generally deals with only one of these elements at a time, because young writers cannot revise everything at once. The information given in a writing conference should be in small enough chunks that the writer can think about it and act on it.

9. Lessons are taught as a result of specific points that arise in a writers' workshop, usually in the context of the children's writing. These lessons can be a vehicle for teaching many writing skills, such as capitalization, the use of commas and periods, particular spelling that is difficult for a large number of children, and clarification of ideas. Raffaella Montemurro does not teach lessons during a writing workshop. She teaches lessons the following day so that she can teach directly to the needs the children have demonstrated during the workshop. She will often use a piece of her own writing to demonstrate an idea to her students, and she will ask them to make suggestions about how the piece can be improved. The aim is always to improve the piece of writing, making it more interesting, effective, and enjoyable.

10. In writing conferences, teachers invite the writer to read the work aloud. The teacher is then free to listen and to encourage the writer to lead the conference as much as possible. This way, the writer can remain in charge of the piece. The role of the teacher and the other students is to make suggestions and share responses as interested listeners and co-writers. The conventions of writing can be attended to later in the process, when the ideas and organization are firmly in place.

11. In order to be authentic and to model the writing process, teachers write themselves, either with the children or at some other time if they are too busy during the writers' workshop. In addition, teachers share their writing with their students. Children need to see that even adults struggle with creating good writing.

Source: This material is based loosely on N. Atwell, *In the middle: Writing, reading, and learning with adolescents* (Portsmouth, NH: Heinemann, 1987), pp. 83–84, 94.

on. Conferences can be conducted at a table in a quiet part of the room, or if the conference is one-on-one with teacher and student, it can be at the student's desk.

One of the key elements of a writing conference between student and teacher is response time. Most teachers find "wait time" difficult and frequently jump in with a suggestion before the student has had a chance to think and respond thoughtfully. One of the greatest challenges facing teachers in a writing conference is allowing the student time to think, not rushing in with a ready-made solution for the student writer. The writing belongs to the writer, and the teacher's role is to help the student become a better writer. Box 8.8 contains suggestions (from Atwell, 1998) for conducting writing conferences.

Writing conferences are not restricted to poetic writing, nor is poetic writing the only kind of writing that benefits from having an audience. Transactional writing also benefits from peer and teacher responses as it is created. In fact, any piece of writing we wish to do well may require input from others along the way. Letters to a business or government agency, reports, and play scripts can all benefit from feedback from others. Writers may work on their ideas and original drafts alone, but at some point they require feedback to clarify and present those ideas to a reading public.

Teacher with child engaged in a writing conference

BOX 8.8 GUIDELINES FOR WRITING CONFERENCE

1. Keep an eye on the time, and do not spend too long with one student.
2. Meet with as many writers as possible each day.
3. Circulate from one area of the room to another. Go to students' desks whenever possible.
4. Make a conference personal. It is a conversation. Kneel or sit next to the student.
5. Whisper and ask students to whisper when they confer with you. Do not distract other writers.
6. Build on what writers know and have done rather than telling them what they have not done.
7. Avoid generalized praise and moral evaluation, such as saying "good." Attending to the writer in a serious manner is more effective than giving a few words of praise.
8. Focus on one aspect of the writing in the conference, and don't try to "fix" everything or clarify all the "fuzzy" thinking.
9. Focus on meaning, and ask the questions you genuinely want to know about.
10. Invite students to note their intended actions at the end of the conference. You can add this to the conference record sheet.
11. At the end of the conference, ask the student to summarize the points discussed.
12. Be prepared to take notes of your questions and observations.
13. Don't take over the piece of writing, making it your own. Ask for permission (e.g., "May I show you a way to do this?").

Source: Some of this material is based loosely on N. Atwell, *In the middle: Writing, reading, and learning with adolescents* (Portsmouth, NH: Heinemann, 1987), pp. 94–95.

BOX 8.9	GUIDELINES FOR STUDENTS IN A WRITING WORKSHOP

1. Save everything. You never know when you might want to refer to a piece of writing again.

2. Use a writing notebook or sketchbook instead of loose sheets of paper.

3. Date and label everything so you can keep track of what you have done. This is especially important when working on a word processor.

4. When a piece of writing is finished, clip all the drafts, notes, and brainstormings together with a copy of the final draft on the top.

5. Write on one side of the paper only, and always double-space (write on every other line only).

6. Format your writing as you go (in paragraphs, lines, stanzas).

7. Try to attend to conventions as you write. Check spelling as soon as possible. Attend to punctuation as you write. Ask for help when you need it.

8. When working on a word processor, print every couple of days or every few pages of text. Read the piece through with pen in hand, so you can attend to the flow of the whole piece and not just chunks of the text as they appear on the screen.

9. Begin each writing session by reading over what you have already written. This allows you to establish where you are in the piece and creates momentum for the day's writing.

10. Writing is thinking. Don't interrupt other students while they are writing. Don't attempt to tell other people what to write.

11. If you need to talk to the teacher, speak in a whisper.

12. When you need to receive feedback from a student or teacher, move to the conference area and write down the comments as they are made. This way you will have a record of suggestions to take back to your writing.

13. Edit your work in a different colour from the text.

14. Always write as well, and as much, as you can.

Source: Adapted from N. Atwell, *In the middle: New understandings about writing, reading, and learning,* 2nd ed. (Portsmouth, NH: Heinemann, 1998), pp. 115–116.

The Students' Role in a Writing Workshop

Atwell (1998) and others (e.g., Calkins, 1986, 1991) have provided guidelines that will help students in working through drafts of their writing, eventually leading to pieces they feel proud of sharing with an audience. These guidelines (see Box 8.9) are appropriate for students engaged in poetic and transactional or informational writing, where a finished draft is important. Students who are engaged in journal writing or other forms of expressive writing may not need this structure. They do, however, need quiet time to write, assistance with the conventions of written language, and an opportunity to discuss their writing and their ideas with others.

WRITING RESOURCES

Over the years, many writing programs and resources have been available for teachers to use in their classrooms. It is worth mentioning some of the better-known models or programs here. If teachers need to supplement their own open-ended or balanced model of writing, they need to know which programs or models to explore. Teachers such as Raffaella Montemurro, Diana Dixon, and Julie Gellner have taken university courses and workshops on teaching writing. We might call them "master" teachers. Raffaella reminds us (see the Teacher Wisdom box near the end of this chapter) that teaching writing, and writing itself, is about taking risks. If teachers are willing to take a few risks, write with their students, and value real writing for authentic purposes in their classrooms, they will have little need for imported programs. Teachers who use programs usually outgrow them quickly and develop their own integrated process for teaching writing. However, some programs are worth noting because they can be extremely helpful and informative for beginning teachers.

6 + 1 Trait Writing, developed by the Northwest Regional Educational Laboratory in the United States, is probably the most widely used program or model in Canada. Many schools and school districts across the country have adopted the model. It is important to note that the producers of "6 + 1 Trait" maintain that the model is intended to *support*, not supplant, rich instruction, and that it aims to help teachers to prioritize, focus, and individualize writing instruction. It is intended to complement reading-writing workshops and writing across the curriculum, not to *dictate* a writing curriculum. The developers believe the model creates a consistent vocabulary for the teaching of writing, and facilitates teachers' provision of feedback on student writing and the assessment of that writing. "6 + 1 Trait Writing" describes the qualities of writing (traits) as: ideas, organization, voice, word choice, sentence fluency, conventions, and presentation. You will note that these traits are very similar to the criteria Canadian provincial ministries of education use to assess children's writing at various grade levels (see Chapter 9).

The "6 + 1 Trait" model aims to make explicit the use of the traits in various genres of writing, the features of good writing, and some of the techniques writers can use to craft their writing for particular audiences and purposes (Culham, 2003). In this model,

- Ideas make up the content of the message.
- Organization refers to the internal structure of the piece—the pattern of ideas.
- Voice is what makes the writer's style unique; the writer's feelings and beliefs come through the writing.
- Word choice is the specific selection of rich and appropriate words.
- Sentence fluency is the flow and "sound" of the language.
- Conventions are the accepted, or "correct," ways to use grammar, punctuation, capitalization, and so on.
- Presentation refers to the form and the layout of the piece—the visual aesthetics.

In her book, Culham (2003) quotes and accesses the work of many leading scholars and teachers in the field of writing instruction (e.g., Mem Fox, Donald Murray, William Zinsser). She provides well-organized and well-researched suggestions for teaching the 6 + 1 traits, and she writes for the thoughtful teacher. Her ideas and suggestions fit perfectly into a writing process model and can only strengthen a teacher's classroom writing program.

Over the years since the Northwest Regional Educational Laboratory developed "6+1 Trait Writing," various publishing companies have created spinoff products. These products are sometimes of dubious quality, and beginning teachers need to examine the materials carefully before enthusiastically embracing them for their own classroom use. *Write Traits*, published by Houghton Mifflin (Spandel, 2004) and presented in a colourful box, takes us back to the days in the 1960s and 1970s when basal readers, with their blackline masters (pages to photocopy) and teachers' guides, were used almost exclusively in North America. It provides step-by-step instructions for lessons, along with the words teachers can say at each step of the way. These materials are designed to be "teacher-proof." Any person, with or without a teacher education, can go into the classroom and conduct these activities. There are many good ideas and good points in the materials, but you have to dig for them. Teachers don't need the box or the books to be able to teach writing effectively in their own classrooms. *Books, Lessons, Ideas* (Spandel, 2001), from the same series, contains a list of some excellent works of children's literature from around the globe, but many of the lesson ideas are weak. Again, teachers beware. Good reader-response strategies and a true appreciation of children's literature are the essentials here, and you do not get that from a teacher resource.

We highly recommend the use of *First Steps: Second Edition* (2006), a literacy program developed at Edith Cowan University in Perth, Australia, and produced by the Department of Education and Training in Western Australia. The program is represented in Canada by Pearson Professional Learning. *First Steps Writing Resource Book* (2006) draws on contemporary research and developments and focuses on the explicit teaching of different forms of text and on writing processes, forms, and conventions. The program suggests a daily block of time for writing, which includes time for explicit instruction and time for students to engage in independent writing and feedback. The recommended procedures for teaching writing are based on the gradual movement of responsibility for the writing flowing from the teacher to the students. They include:

- modelled writing
- language experience
- shared and interactive writing
- guided writing
- independent writing
- author's chair

The *First Steps Writing Resource Book* provides specific and detailed examples of each of these procedures and ideas for implementation. The program also contains a Writing Map of Development, which is designed to help teachers record and monitor student progress. The Map is organized according to seven phases of development: Role Play, Experimental, Early, Transitional, Conventional, Proficient, and Accomplished. In these "labels" we can see the influence of earlier researchers such as James Britton and James Moffett and the models of writing development they proposed. The Writing Map of Development resource will be referred to in greater detail in Chapter 9. *First Steps* provides a strong foundation for a classroom or school-based writing program, with excellent assessment procedures built in.

Lucy Calkins' series of books, *Units of Study For Teaching Writing, Grades 3–5* (2006) is a high-quality resource based on many years of research and implementation in elementary classrooms. *Launching the Writing Workshop* contains information on establishing the writing workshop approach, qualities of good writing, holding writing conferences, choosing ideas for writing, the revision process, drafting, editing, timelines for the process, and celebrating finished work. Other books in the series are*: Raising the Quality of Narrative Writing*; *Breathing Life into Essays*; *Writing Fiction: Big Dreams, Tall Ambitions*; *Memoir: The Art of Writing Well*; *and Literary Essays: Writing About Reading* (particularly helpful in reader response). All the books contain numerous examples of children's writing, teaching ideas, tips on assessment, and additional resources. We highly recommend this series for beginning teachers.

A set of materials published in Canada by *JoAnne Moore* (1995) is popular in some areas of the country. This material is seductive to beginning teachers because it consists of specific ideas for specific lessons, and there are many blackline masters teachers can simply copy and use. The material is neither a program nor an approach, and is presented as "a manual that covers a year's writing curriculum for grades one to six." The author of the series offers it as an alternative to teaching the process of writing and it consists mainly of techniques for working with a range of writing structures, grammar, and conventions of the language. It is a series of classroom activities rather than a program based on children's ideas, voice, and authentic purpose. We do not recommend use of this material unless it is a small occasional supplement to your own open-ended process writing program.

The International Society for Technology in Education (http://www.iste.org) produces some quality materials that can assist teachers in their writing instruction in elementary classrooms. These include *Structured Writing Volumes I and II* (2001). *Structured Writing: Using Inspiration Software to Teach Paragraph Development* and *Structured Writing II: Using Inspiration Software to Teach Essay Development* are designed for students who experience special challenges in reading and writing. If students have difficulties in planning or organizing their writing, the templates provided on the CDs in these resources can help. The guidebook provides lesson plans and assists teachers in breaking writing into manageable steps for students. *Inspiration* and *Write: Outloud* software is used with these resources. Many digital resources have been mentioned earlier in this chapter. Intellitools, Comic Book Writer, and many other software packages are available at low cost.

SOCIAL INTERACTION IN THE WRITING PROCESS

Although educators have long realized that learning to talk is a social process, it is only recently that we have acknowledged the importance of social interaction when writing. If, as Moffett (1979) maintains, true writing occurs only when we revise inner speech, then children need to become aware of what the revision of inner speech entails. Teachers like Raffaella Montemurro and Diana Dixon encourage children to make their inner speech explicit and to wrestle with the ideas they are attempting to articulate. They encourage the notion of "writing in community," and their students learn from each other by talking about their writing and by sharing their writing with each other. Moffett says that teachers "have no choice but to work in the gap between thought and speech" (1979, p. 278). He also suggests that, "writing cannot be realistically perceived and taught so long as we try to work from the outside in" (p. 279). In other words, true writing comes from within the writer, who must learn to articulate thought and put it into print. When children work collaboratively in the writing process (or in creating multimedia projects), they have opportunities to explore the gap between thought and speech. When teachers listen to them, they can find out how children negotiate meaning and how they come to understand the structural elements of writing. Through their talk, as Michael Halliday (1969) has said, children learn "how to mean."

The Importance of Talk

As children talk together or with a teacher, continual scaffolding is evident. Through constant interaction, the students become teachers and learners interchangeably. The following excerpt is a planning session where Erica and Sharon, in a grade 5 classroom, considered each other's opinions and incorporated them into a written discussion of the city cat bylaws (Lewis, 1989).

SHARON: Want to do a debate?

ERICA: Yes, then we can each have our own opinion.

SHARON: What's yours about?

ERICA: My what?

SHARON: Your issue you want to debate. I want to do the cat bylaw. OK?

ERICA: OK. I'll just put "Cat Bylaw" at the top of the page.

SHARON: OK. If I was in charge of the world I'd change the cat bylaw.

ERICA: Do you want to do this one [pause] together? I don't have a cat, you do, so it makes a difference, doesn't it?

SHARON: Cats should be able to walk around.

ERICA: And I'm going to write against that! Cats go to the bathroom everywhere and …

SHARON: Good, we disagree then we agree on that. [Laughter.]

ERICA: And it smells! Write on the top of the page "Cat Bylaw" again.

SHARON: Why?

ERICA: Because we're going to do it together. … We'll put my opinions and your opinions so we know whose is what.

SHARON: I want to ask you a question. If you don't have a cat, would you still not like the rule as much? I still think it's dumb.

ERICA: Ya, but you wouldn't like it as much, like it wouldn't be. … Even if you had a cat would you still hate it more?

SHARON: No, exactly the same.

ERICA: What! I'm writing against you, right?

SHARON: Well, cats … I agree that cats do that, go to the bathroom, I mean.

ERICA: I agree in a way. [Writes this down slowly.]

SHARON: Don't write this next part down till I figure it out.

In their continuing negotiation of meaning, the two girls found that they became very much aware of writing for an audience. They began to negotiate meaning and work out details, where each sentence, and at times each word, was important. Disagreements were common, and they questioned the logic of each other's ideas. The following excerpt, from a discussion Sharon and Erica held while co-writing "The Wellington Story," concerns the phrases looked closer and looked again.

ERICA: "He looked closer into the hole …"

SHARON: "He looked again" sounds better.

ERICA: Well, Sharon, if you looked closer, would you stick your head right into the hole?

SHARON: It doesn't mean that.

ERICA: Well it does to me!

SHARON: Closer isn't sticking your face into the hole, but "looked again" just sounds better.

ERICA: Sharon, you don't listen!

SHARON: So, we don't use "closer" or "again." We say "he looked into the hole and saw the top of the wine bottle."

ERICA: No, "he looked closer." A bit closer, know what I mean?

SHARON: Why would he look closer to see the wine bottle?

ERICA: 'Cause the dress might have covered it up, you know. Then "he looked again" doesn't mean "he looked closer."

SHARON: Yes it does!

ERICA: Sharon, I don't know. It's the way the sentence, the way …

SHARON: The way you put it sounds dumb.

ERICA: Well, where did he actually look?

SHARON: Under the floorboards.

ERICA: Well, I don't think he needs to get closer to see under the floorboards that's what I really mean.

SHARON: When you say "looked closer," it doesn't necessarily mean you looked closely right in the hole, it means you sort of took a second look.

ERICA: Ya, that's it, he took a second look!

SHARON: Oh, wow, we got it!

ERICA: Phew!

Peer Group Writing Conferences

The following group conference was initiated and conducted by four students who relied on strategies their classroom teacher had taught them. The transcript, taken from Lewis (1989), shows how the students used these conferences to further their own writing development. Erica began by reading the unfinished "Wellington" story quoted in Box 8.1 earlier in this chapter.

ERICA: "'It's coming from the paint house,' said Mr. McGregor. They all rushed out to the paint house and saw Yvette shaking, with a knife in her hand."

SHARON:	That's as far as we've got.
CRAIG:	I have a question. Who's Yvette?
ERICA:	The maid.
CRAIG:	What's her husband's name?
ERICA:	The maid? She doesn't have one.
DANA:	No, Craig. Mr. and Mrs. Wellington.
CRAIG:	Oh, right.
DANA:	All of a sudden you brought in that Mr. McGregor. Who's he supposed to be?
SHARON:	One of the guests. When it says well, we didn't want to just list them all.
DANA:	You could say, "Mr. McGregor, one of the guests …"
ERICA:	Good idea.
DANA:	Where do you guys go from here?
SHARON:	Well, we're not sure. We have to have the loose floorboards so the police can find the …
ERICA:	We also think we want it to be a play and we talked about highlighting the speaking parts, except Sharon wants to write it all out so …
DANA:	Hey, you guys, we forgot to say our favourite parts. The part about the paint house really catches my eye. Is this guy a painter, a famous one?
ERICA:	Ya, and that's why Yvette kills him because he painted a picture of her and she is afraid that Mrs. Wellington will find out.
DANA:	Wouldn't it just be easier to destroy the painting than to kill the guy?
SHARON:	Well, another idea we had is that it's not Yvette. It's the wife and she kills him for his money. We aren't exactly sure about that part yet.
CRAIG:	I like the part where they find her holding the bloody knife.
ERICA:	We didn't say it was bloody.
CRAIG:	Well, it would be, you know.

Because of the importance of talk and the amount of learning that takes place in group conferences, it is important to encourage and facilitate this kind of dialogue as part of writers' workshop. Through interaction, students become more aware of their covert writing processes and of the conventions necessary for effective communication with an audience. Sharon said,

I like to talk about all my ideas and I like to figure it all out with someone else. It got kind of hard, you know, because I get really excited and I yelled at Erica, she's so picky, though, you know. [Smiles.]

The following statements illustrate the students' thoughts on writing conferences:

DANA:	Some days it's easy all goes well, and some days it's bad it's really hard.
ERICA:	Well … it's both actually easy and hard. Maybe at different times it's harder …
CRAIG:	It helps me, I love talking to someone.
SHARON:	She helps me about quotations and … other things, too.

TEACHER WISDOM

RAFFAELLA MONTEMURRO

What advice can you give to beginning teachers in regard to teaching writing? What do they need to know?

First of all, writing is about risk-taking. We often ask students to do things in our classrooms that we wouldn't want to do ourselves. We must take the same risks we ask our students to take, so that we understand what we are asking them to do. We need to write *with* our students and share our writing with them so they can see that we all work hard to create a good piece of writing. We all have to think carefully and get advice from others when we write. We have to reread and revise. Teachers must model that.

Secondly, don't get caught up with the end result. Focus on the process and the product will emerge. It may not always be fantastic, but the students will learn more about writing on each attempt. The more experience they have with writing, and the more they can talk about their writing, the better they will become.

Third, I think we need to show that we value writing and be faithful to it in our classrooms. We shouldn't skip it for the sake of something else. If we value writing, we will honour the space for it in our schedules, and we'll create a routine or ritual for the way we go about our writing. We have to ensure our students get lots of quiet, thoughtful time for writing.

The fourth thing is that we should use only the very best literature and poetry in our classrooms, the same way we want to use only the very best quality of art supplies and materials. We can't do a good job with shoddy supplies. There is no shortage of pop culture and things that are "cool." In the classroom we have an opportunity to provide high-quality experiences for our students. We want them to be writers and readers, with a passion for it. I think teaching is like working with an upside-down funnel. Teachers put in a small bit at the narrow end and the children create all kinds of good things from it that come out at the wide end. That's why we've got to put high-quality materials in at the narrow end.

There is a myth in the arts that you are born with talent—a gift—this is not so. There are gifted people in all areas, but everyone has potential. Very few of my students would be considered gifted or talented, yet I am amazed and thrilled at what they produce in art and in writing.

I suggest beginning teachers start by looking at some of Georgia Heard's books. They'll get lots of excellent ideas there.

The extensive use of expressive language enables students to clarify and extend their thoughts as they write. Children benefit from talking through their understanding at every stage of the process. Some days, there is more talk than writing, but it is through this talk that children make explicit their understandings of what writing is and what writing can do. They also articulate their understandings of literary structures and what makes a piece of writing work. In "The Wellington Story" (see Box 8.1), Sharon and Erica demonstrated a command of the mystery story genre and of the conventions of story writing. Carefully crafted with an audience in mind, their story undoubtedly reflects some of their recreational reading.

SUMMARY

Writing is both an art and a skill, an activity that can give enormous pleasure to the writer as well as to the reader. Most people need to write on a daily basis, either in their jobs (a phone message, a technical report) or in their personal lives (a letter to their child's school, a grocery list, a diary, a poem). With the advent of the process approach to the teaching of writing, teachers help their students to develop both composition and presentation skills. Writing instruction, as a process, stresses the purpose for writing, the audience for the writing, and the relationship of these to form and function.

As they compose, students are encouraged to write for a variety of audiences and for particular purposes. James Britton (1970) pointed out that expressive writing is written either for the self or for an audience close to the writer. It records or captures personal thoughts, feelings, and intentions. Transactional writing takes place when the writer wants to convey information to others in a formal report, list, essay, or textbook. Poetic writing is usually created for an audience other than the self. It contains aesthetic or literary elements and is the voice used in stories as well as poems. Teachers teach skills that range from drawing the letters and words (handwriting), to transcribing, paraphrasing, crafting, and revising inner speech (Moffett, 1979). In a balanced program of writing instruction, all of these voices, levels, and genres of writing are taught. Students can then learn to write effectively for a range of audiences and purposes.

When composing and crafting a piece of writing or a multimedia project, young writers need a structure in the classroom that will allow them large chunks of quiet writing time, conferences that provide feedback from an interested and informed audience, and the opportunity to share finished pieces with "the public." Writing conferences help writers to draft and revise their thoughts until they are sure they are saying exactly what they want to say. It is in the writing conference that most teaching occurs, and it is the entire process of drafting, revising, editing, and sharing that helps children to become better writers.

Teachers now recognize the important role that children's talk plays in their development as writers. When children are on-task and are engaged fully in a shared writing experience, they learn a great deal from one another through exchanging and negotiating ideas. The quest for clarity and appropriateness of language, the response of the readers, and the power of words to evoke images and feelings are the elements young writers learn about as they write together in the classroom.

TALKING POINTS

1. What kinds of writing have you engaged in recently on a daily or weekly basis? Have you written in a journal or blog recently? When was the last time you attempted to write poetry? Have you ever shared your poetry or creative writing with a friend or colleague? How much of a risk are you willing to take in writing with your students in the classroom? These are questions to think about now, because we know that when teachers write with their students and talk about their writing with their students, it provides one of the most powerful motivators and models for students' own writing.

2. How comfortable are you with using the computer to make comic books or for painting pictures? Have you taken a good look at the Elementary Information Communications Technology outcomes for your province? Would you be surprised or do you know what to expect? Have you intentionally put time aside to "play" with some of the writing programs and comic book programs that are available as free downloads from the Internet? How can you get to know the programs your students enjoy using at home so that you can help them make the home–school connections that are so important for their growth as learners?

3. How might you value and celebrate the multimodal texts children produce? How might you showcase students' work? Knowing that the interplay of the visual and the verbal is a critical piece of children's imaginative creations, are you ready to embrace them in your classroom and to facilitate the celebration of them in your school community?

RECOMMENDED PROFESSIONAL RESOURCES

Diana Dixon recommends ...

Atwell, N. (2002). *Lessons that change writers: A yearlong writing workshop curriculum.* Portsmouth, NH: Heinemann.

In this most recent publication, Nancie Atwell presents over a hundred mini-lessons and samples of writing in order to focus teachers on the mini-lesson as a vehicle for helping students improve their writing. Although the intended audience is middle-years teachers, I have found this resource incredibly helpful in grades 4 and upwards. In looseleaf binder format, the resource includes many samples of Nancie's own writing, and of writing done by students, which beginning teachers could easily use for mini-lessons. The binder includes numerous bibliographic references. For me, Nancie Atwell, through her book (*In the Middle*) and the binder (*Lessons That Change Writers*), epitomizes the idea of "learning alongside students."

Atwell, N. (1998). *In the middle: New understandings about writing, reading, and learning* (2nd ed.). Portsmouth, NH: Boynton/Cook.

This book is a superb resource to help in organizing writing workshops in the classroom. Atwell establishes guidelines for conducting workshops and describes how to prepare for a writing workshop, how to get started, how to respond to writers and their writing, and how to conduct mini-lessons.

Raffaella Montemurro suggests …

Booth, D. & Swartz, L. (2004). *Literacy techniques for building successful readers and writers* (2nd ed.) Markham, ON: Pembroke Publishers.

I have found this book particularly valuable, because it helped me to explore the very best techniques for teaching reading and writing. It's virtually an encyclopedia of approaches to literacy. I think it will help beginning teachers to reflect on their teaching style and select the best approaches for meeting the needs of every student in their classroom. It has lots of checklists and guidelines, which makes it a really useful tool for substitute teachers, parents, study buddies, and other volunteer partners.

Julie Gellner recommends …

Livingston, M. C. (1991). *Poem-making: Ways to begin writing poetry.* New York, NY : HarperCollins Publishers.

Over the years, I've found this book to be very helpful, because it introduces different kinds of poetry and provides opportunities for children to experience the joy of making a poem. Myra Cohn Livingston is a well-known author, anthologist, poet, and teacher. In the book, she explores what a poem is, and moves students away from the notion that it is simply a matter of taking words, writing them out in verse form, and making them rhyme. Livingston shows how rules about meter, form, and rhyme are used to create a framework for the expression of special observations and ideas. *Poem-Making* introduces children to types of rhyme and other elements of sound, rhythm, and metrics, and some of the most common forms of poetry.

Janeczko, P. (2002). *Seeing the blue between: Advice and inspiration for young poets.* Cambridge, MA: Candlewick Press.

Like the previous title, this book is also written by a children's poet. Janeczko's book has been inspirational for me, as it contains letters and poems from 32 internationally renowned poets. These writers provide words of wisdom and examples of their own work. Contributors include Kalli Dakos, Rob Farnsworth, Bobbi Katz, Naomi Shihab Nye, Jack Prelutsky, and Jane Yolen. The letters are personal, friendly, and supportive. The contributors encourage young writers to read, and the importance of revision is emphasized. There's lots of humour in the book, and the selected poems cover a wide range of styles, moods, and subjects.

Assessment and Conventions of Writing

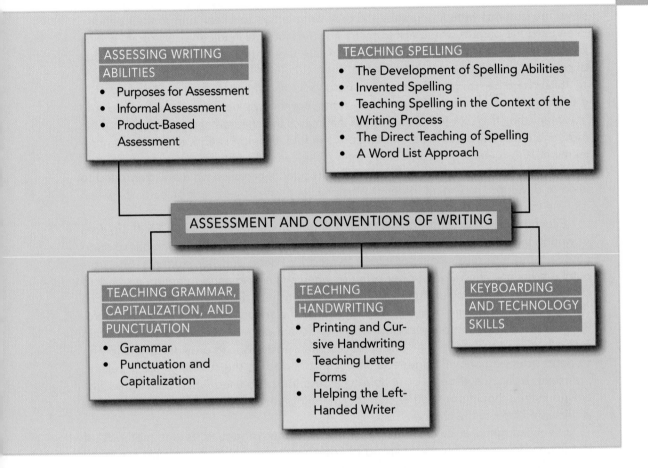

ASSESSING WRITING ABILITIES
- Purposes for Assessment
- Informal Assessment
- Product-Based Assessment

TEACHING SPELLING
- The Development of Spelling Abilities
- Invented Spelling
- Teaching Spelling in the Context of the Writing Process
- The Direct Teaching of Spelling
- A Word List Approach

ASSESSMENT AND CONVENTIONS OF WRITING

TEACHING GRAMMAR, CAPITALIZATION, AND PUNCTUATION
- Grammar
- Punctuation and Capitalization

TEACHING HANDWRITING
- Printing and Cursive Handwriting
- Teaching Letter Forms
- Helping the Left-Handed Writer

KEYBOARDING AND TECHNOLOGY SKILLS

ASSESSING WRITING IN EILEEN LOUGHLIN'S GRADE 2 CLASSROOM

As often as possible when her students are writing, Eileen writes alongside them. Before each writing session, she and the students talk about ideas for their writing, and every few days they share their writing together. She and the students have a clear sense of audience; they write for each other. Eileen and her students sometimes write stories or poems, but quite often they write descriptive pieces about a person, a place they have visited, or an event that had has happened to them—an anecdote of something they remembered. They have even written their biographies. Eileen reminds her students that interesting writing doesn't always have to be a story, and in fact, a good story can be very hard to write.

Eileen Loughlin

Eileen uses the writing process in her classroom, but she has the students take only two narrative pieces each year through to the publishing stage. In grade 2, revision and redrafting is hard work, and at that stage in their schooling, the students have a lot to learn about writing. Many are still struggling with manuscript printing, and spelling is often slow. The students write in journals, and they write letters to Eileen and to their parents. Eileen and the parents write back to them. For the students in Eileen's classroom, writing is purposeful and is clearly a way to communicate thoughts and ideas with a wide range of people.

Eileen and her students keep writing notebooks and they also keep writing folders. It is therefore clear what the students have written, how many pieces they have finished, and how many they have started. She can tell what topics the children enjoy writing about the most and what they do their best writing on. The folders help Eileen with "assessment *for* learning." From reading the students' writing, she can tell what she needs to teach, and she often gathers a group of students for a particular mini-lesson on a skill they need to learn or develop. The writing folder also helps Eileen with assessment *of* learning—when it's time to do report cards.

Eileen is not expected to give a mark or letter grade to her students for the pieces of writing they do, but she does provide detailed feedback to the students based upon criteria listed in a rubric collaboratively created by Eileen and her students. She uses numbers when scoring work for her own use when she is preparing to assign a standard on the report card. For example, she uses the numbers designated in the Provincial Achievement Test writing rubric to help her devise a standard for the child's report card. She uses the grade 2 rubric developed by her school district to assess students within grade level, and the grade 3 Provincial Achievement Test rubric to provide criteria for the students achieving above grade level. In her school district, the standards are excellent, proficient, basic, insufficient, or unable to assess (perhaps used when a child has just arrived in the school from another country). More information about Eileen's report cards is presented later in the chapter.

Eileen Loughlin is aware that individual students require different methods of instruction depending on their varying needs. Sometimes children learn best in small groups, sharing their writing, receiving feedback, and receiving instruction through their teacher's comments and advice. At other times, students learn more effectively in individual writing conferences, and on occasion they need direct lessons in specific areas. Assessing students' writing abilities is a crucial part of the planning and instruction cycle. Ongoing, formative assessment in the classroom provides teachers with the information they need to make instructional decisions that will enhance their students' learning, and it provides students with information so they can see how well they are doing and what they need to work on.

Summative assessment at the end of the school term or year provides the school district with a measure of the success of their programs and provides individual children with a regular statement of their progress in school. To become well-rounded writers over their years in school, children need assistance in learning the transcription skills of spelling, punctuation, and grammar, as well as involvement in writing and reading workshops. This chapter addresses the areas of assessment of writing and the direct instruction of transcription skills, often referred to as the conventions, or tools, of writing. ☐

ASSESSING WRITING ABILITIES

Purposes for Assessment

There are ways in which the teaching of writing and the assessment of writing are so closely interconnected that teachers cannot do one without doing the other. Teachers like Eileen conduct ongoing assessment in order to provide their students with appropriate feedback on their writing. This does not mean *grading* student work but *assessing* student work using appropriate criteria. Cooper and Odell (1999) remind us that one set of criteria is no longer sufficient for assessing writing, although some general concerns such as "organization" or "quality of ideas" may be valid across genres. However, as students are now encouraged to write in a range of genres, teachers need criteria appropriate to the genres, and they also need to *show* children how they can improve their writing. Many teachers find it helpful to develop assessment criteria and rubrics with their students. It becomes part of the teaching. If students know what good writing looks like, and what constitutes good writing, they are more likely to be able to compose good pieces.

In their classroom practice, teachers use a variety of strategies for assessing children's writing depending on the purpose for the assessment. Writing assessment is always focused, in some way, on improving the writing abilities of the children in our classrooms. Most often, assessment is conducted informally to guide a teacher's planning and instruction. The more information teachers possess about their students, the more effectively they can understand and meet their individual students' learning needs. A second purpose for assessment is to provide feedback to students so they know what they do well and what they can focus on in order to become better writers. A third purpose is to provide information to parents and caregivers about student progress. A fourth purpose is to provide information to school districts and provincial governments about the writing abilities of the children in their schools. Successful teachers strive to maintain a balanced approach to assessment, developing a broad picture of their students' learning. They do this through using a wide range of assessment techniques, including observation, anecdotal records, checklists and profiles, portfolios or writing folders, student self-evaluation, writing conferences, analyses of samples of student writing, and provincial or local district achievement tests.

In order to describe and assess children's writing effectively, teachers attend not only to the surface features of the writing (transcription skills such as handwriting, spelling, and punctuation) but also to the content or message of what is written, which is, of course, the purpose for the writing. Rather than "marking," "correcting," or "grading" student writing, teachers usually respond to the writing or provide feedback to the student. Like Eileen, they offer comments, either orally or in writing, on the form of the writing (the extent to which the writing meets the purpose or genre) or on the content of the piece, and only later do they attend to transcription errors. They look not only at samples of writing but also observe the students at work, listening to the running commentaries children engage in as they write, listening to student conversations and conferences with peers, watching the way they form letters or attempt to spell unknown words. In their instruction and evaluation of student writing, teachers show respect for the idiosyncratic nature of the writing process and value both the written products and the writing processes of individual students.

Teachers and researchers now know that it is not possible to objectively assess any single piece of writing. Every reading of a text is affected by the values and cultural expectations of the reader (most often the teacher). We also know there is no *one* way to evaluate children's writing,

TABLE 9.1 **Writing Assessment Strategies**

Purpose	Informal/Formative	Product-Based/Summative
To inform instruction	• writing conferences (group and one-on-one) • observations of performance (including checking for spelling and other transcription skills) • anecdotal notes • journals/learning logs • student self-assessment • checklists • review of writing folders	• teacher-developed whole-class tests (e.g., spelling, word usage) • whole-class writing tasks with teacher/school developed rubric • analytical reviews of writing samples • portfolio assessment • student writing profiles
To inform students	• writing conferences (group and one-on-one) • responses to journals/learning logs • responses to writing folder/portfolio • checklists • review of writing folders	• whole-class writing tasks • tests • parent/child/teacher conferences • portfolio review
To inform parents	• portfolios of written work • learning logs/journals • student self-assessment • checklists	• whole-class writing tasks • tests • parent/child/teacher conferences • student writing profiles
To inform school administration, school district, provincial Department of Education	• writing samples with analysis	• norm-referenced achievement tests (e.g., provincial achievement tests) • teacher-developed tests and writing scales

no way to generate one mark or grade that represents the child's level of development in writing as a whole. The primary focus of assessment is on helping children to enhance their learning and on helping teachers to plan for instruction. As a result, a range of assessment strategies is necessary depending on the purpose for the assessment. Table 9.1 summarizes some of the methods teachers find useful in assessing student progress in writing in relation to the purpose for the assessment.

Informal Assessment of Writing

Teachers need to keep track of student progress in their classrooms every day. No other area of the curriculum is as complex to assess and monitor as that of writing, but teachers have found a number of informal strategies valuable when they use them regularly. These are observations, anecdotal records, conferences, student self-assessments, writing folders and portfolios, checklists, and profiles.

Observations

Focused observations (and keeping relevant notes) of children as they write, participate in writing groups and conferences, revise and proofread their writing, and share their finished pieces with an audience can provide much useful information for teachers. Children's attitudes to writing, their writing strategies, how they interact with other children, and how they seek out other children for assistance or in sharing their writing can be revealed through observation. While making observations, teachers can ask the students questions to clarify what they have observed, for example, "Would you like to share that with a partner?" "Do you have a title for this piece?" Tompkins (2007) suggests that, while making observations, the teacher sit next to, or across from the student, and simply say, "I'm going to watch you as you write so I can help you become a better writer."

Anecdotal Records

Notes taken by teachers informally in the classroom can be much more useful than a simple grade or mark recorded in a grade book. Anecdotal notes provide detailed information about a child's writing and knowledge of written language. These notes describe specific events and observations *without evaluation or interpretation*. They can be collected in a binder, notebook, or set of cards, and they can be entered into a database on the computer. A collection of notes taken over a period of months can provide a powerful tool for ongoing literacy assessment. Teachers usually approach their note-taking systematically, concentrating on a small number of children each day (three or four). Time is set aside for reviewing the notes periodically, rereading them, analyzing them, identifying each child's strengths and weaknesses, and making inferences about children's writing development.

Checklists

Many published and teacher-made checklists have been developed to aid teachers in their informal assessment of student progress in writing. Canadian teacher Stephen Leppard (1991) developed a reading–writing continuum designed to record the developing writing abilities of children as they pass from kindergarten to grade 3. A copy of the continuum for each child is passed along from the teacher of one grade to the next throughout the primary years. The list of descriptors is read by the teacher, and those pertaining to the child being assessed are highlighted. Each assessment period (three to four months) is noted in a different-coloured highlighting pen. Thus, over a period of time, the child's progress is revealed as the different colours flow through the continuum. An excerpt from the continuum is presented in Box 9.1. The continuum is easy to use and convenient for teachers, since the observations have only to be recorded by highlighting specific characteristics.

Conferences

One-on-one or small-group conferences (two or three students) might focus on a particular topic or principle, or they can be general in scope. These conferences provide opportunities for joint assessment of student writing as teachers and children discuss student progress. Unlike the instruction or process-oriented conferences listed in Chapter 7 (such as prewriting

---

BOX 9.1 **WRITING CONTINUUM: INDIVIDUAL WRITING STAGES**

1. Take-Off Stage

▷ Can write name.

▷ Excited about writing.

▷ Wants to write (stories, lists, letters, or ideas).

▷ Does not rely on patterning.

▷ Invented (temporary) spelling becomes closer to standard.

▷ Writing is more meaning-centred.

▷ Can pick out words that are spelled incorrectly.

▷ Understands that each letter or combination of letters is a representation of a sound (phonetic understanding).

▷ Use of characters is moving closer to standard form.

▷ Sound correspondence more complete.

▷ Sound features of words are represented according to the child's hearing and articulation (leads to omission of preconsonant nasal, e.g., *NUBRS—numbers*).

▷ Realizes that print can conserve a thought statement permanently.

2. Independent Writing

▷ Writes stories with some sense of story structure.

▷ Awareness of grammar and language conventions.

▷ Spelling is near standard *or* spelling deteriorates because more complex words are being used.

▷ Understands that vowels are included in every word.

▷ Understands that vowels are included in every syllable.

▷ Vowels may be used inappropriately (e.g., *MEAK—make*).

▷ Developing a sense of punctuation.

▷ Developing an ability and desire to self-edit some corrections (spelling, simple sentence structure).

▷ Written work can be carried over, or continued, the next day.

▷ May begin to understand the inconsistencies within the English language.

Source: S. Leppard, "A reading–writing continuum," *Program continuity: The positive link.* © Access: The Education Station, 1991. Reprinted with permission.

---

conferences, drafting conferences, and editing conferences), assessment conferences are usually held on completion of a composition. Teachers invite children to reflect on their piece of writing, their writing competencies, and their growth as writers. Teachers also ask students to set goals for future work. In a portfolio conference, teachers meet with students individually, review the writing samples and discuss the writing with the students. Teachers may also use this occasion to decide on a grade for the project in collaboration with the student.

Student Self-Assessment

It is generally agreed that effective assessment must begin with the learner. If students are to improve their writing, they must be able to see the need for that improvement—hence the need for student self-assessment. In self-assessments, "children pause to consider what they have learned and what has been important from their own perspectives" (Pappas, Kiefer, & Levstik, 1995, p. 317). Opportunities for children to assess their progress are provided when they select writing for a portfolio or when they are at the end of a unit or writing project (Farr & Tone, 1998). Pappas, Kiefer, and Levstik (1995) point out that what students may think is significant in their learning may not seem important to a teacher or parent. Asking children to assess their own work (and providing a rationale for the assessment) is important, therefore, because it gives children the opportunity to be responsible, confident, independent, and autonomous learners. Children are required to be self-evaluative throughout the writing process when they decide on ideas for a piece of writing, make decisions about what to revise and redraft, and decide when a piece is finished or when it needs more work. These decisions and evaluations are made explicit in a student's self-assessment. Teachers often provide prompts or guidelines (questions) for student self-assessments. Children who are too young to write a self-assessment may provide an oral self-assessment to the teacher and the teacher makes notes.

Teachers frequently use these self-assessment conferences as an opportunity to prepare for student-led conferences with parents (see Box 9.2). Children select the piece of writing they want to share, and they think about and write notes about why they want to share this particular piece with their parents and teacher. They might also be asked to select one piece of writing they plan to work on, and they explain why they want to work on it and what they might do. In other words, what can improve this piece of writing?

BOX 9.2   STUDENT-LED CONFERENCES

School principal, Joanne Bergos, encourages her staff members to hold student-led conferences twice each year, usually in November and March. Student-led conferences are highly effective ways to communicate authentically and directly with parents, and they put responsibility for the process in the hands of the students. Reviewing a portfolio of the student's work during the conference becomes a learning experience for all involved (Guskey & Bailey, 2001), and the emphasis is squarely placed on assessment *for* learning rather than as assessment *of* learning.

In order for student-led conferences to be effective, teachers begin planning well ahead of time, and lead their students through both the process of selecting the material they wish to talk about, and the process of the conference itself (Benson & Barnett, 2005). Children write invitation letters to their parents, and are responsible for confirming whether their parent/caregiver will attend. The students take time to go through their writing folders and talk with their teacher about their selection of one piece of writing to discuss during the conference. Children put

(Continued)

stickies on their pieces ahead of time, with a few notes about what is important to them about this piece. These notes will help the conference to flow more easily. The students also talk with their teacher and a small group of their peers about the goals they are setting for themselves for the remainder of the school year. The teacher and students might role-play parts of the conference ahead of the event so children are comfortable introducing their parents to the teacher and their teacher to the parents, and in leading their parents through the conference.

Joanne makes sure her teachers prepare the students well for the student-led conferences. Each child prepares a written agenda for the conference that is designed by the teacher in a format that allows for individual student success. Parents are asked to follow the agenda and encourage the student to lead the discussion. When parents enter the classroom, the children make the introductions and may offer juice and cookies to the parents. Once everyone is seated, the students will likely begin by talking about something they have learned in language arts that is important to them. This may be followed by a demonstration of how well the child can read a passage from a book they are currently enjoying, and a brief verbal explanation of a theme from the book that has been explored in class. Then the student will show a piece of writing, and explain why this piece has been selected. They may have a second piece to discuss—this time to explain what they are working on to improve this piece. Student-led conferences will likely also include agenda items that demonstrate learning in mathematics, social studies, science, and often in selected curriculum areas such as art, physical education, and music. The students may end the conference by talking about their goals, by answering any questions their parents might have, and by engaging their parents in some kind of activity—a tour of the school, tour of the library, or browsing through some of their favourite books in the classroom library.

Joanne has discovered that the children must be well prepared; otherwise parents tend to take over the conference and may begin a conversation with the teacher *about* the student, and that is not helpful at this time. Joanne ensures that parents know they can request one-on-one time with the teacher at a later date if they still have questions about their child's progress in school. She recommends starting by holding three of four conferences in the room at the same time (but no more than this). The teacher circulates around the room, joining one conference for five or ten minutes and offering students support and guidance before moving on to another conference.

Joanne makes sure that each classroom displays work created by the students and that it is accompanied by quality assessment criteria, which may include the school district's assessment criteria for writing at that grade level. These criteria are accompanied by samples of writing (from the school district) to demonstrate the criteria. In this way, parents can see which piece of writing most closely approximates their own child's work and they have a sense of the expectations for that age/grade level.

For parents uncomfortable with parent/teacher conferences, the student-led conference is much less intimidating. Most parents want to be present to support their child. In cases where a parent cannot attend, Joanne arranges for the child to conduct the conference at home, *and* plans an opportunity during the school day for the child to conduct their conference with an available staff member. That person might be the principal, assistant principal, the custodian, or the library aide. What is important is that each student has an opportunity to talk about their learning with someone who is interested in listening to them. Through that articulation, students become clearer about their learning, and about what they need to work on in order to grow.

Portfolios

Portfolios and **performance assessment** have become popular in the last decade because they promote and assess the *application* of the language arts. Keeping a portfolio, and selecting pieces to include in the portfolio, enables students to become active learners and allows students to take control of their own development as readers and writers (Farr & Tone, 1998). Portfolios and writing folders are used for quite different purposes. A writing folder is a "working file," containing work in progress, some finished work, and topics that might be the basis for future pieces, whereas a portfolio is a collection of one student's completed work, carefully selected to demonstrate what that student can do. As described in Chapter 7, a writing folder may contain stories, reports, poems, recipes, movie reviews, résumés, letters, and other informal material the student is working on (including notes for a forthcoming piece). Children are encouraged to keep all their drafts and finished compositions dated and clipped together, and students' self-assessments of finished work may be attached to the written pieces. If students take a piece of writing home permanently, teachers usually photocopy it for the writing folder. From time to time, children are invited to select their best pieces of writing for review, and these are placed in a portfolio. It is important that a range of genres be included in the portfolio, as the aim is to showcase the student's abilities.

The portfolio itself might be a concertina folder that expands to accommodate objects other than sheets of paper. Published books and reports might go into the portfolio, as well as comments from peers who have read or heard pieces written by the student. Students usually create a list of contents to go at the front of the portfolio and older students might add a letter stating why each piece of writing has been selected. Teachers can use the portfolios to document and illustrate a child's writing progress, and they can be used to great effect during parent–teacher conferences. When reviewing portfolios, teachers emphasize what students know and can do, rather than what students are learning to do or cannot do. Many teachers find it helpful to review portfolios with a colleague. The practice helps to inform teachers' assessment criteria and helps them develop a greater range of strategies for supporting individual children's learning.

Portfolio assessment is a form of process or performance evaluation. The aim is not to take one piece of writing in isolation, but to look at a collection of children's writings in many genres and voices. A portfolio might include stories, poems, letters, journal entries, lists, semantic maps, responses to literature, book reviews, artwork associated with the language arts, puppets, and writing from across the curriculum. In this way, children can see their writing as more than separate, isolated pieces. Portfolios also give children the opportunity to self-evaluate their work in choosing what they wish to put into the portfolio.

Farr and Tone (1998) provide many suggestions for developing and assessing portfolios. Among them is that teachers look at the volume of work in the portfolio, the interest and attitudes of the writers, and, of course, the development and growth of the writing. Farr and Tone also suggest how teachers can use portfolios to aid them in their instruction. Through discussion, writing, and reflection, portfolio assessment helps children become better thinkers and communicators. Portfolio assessment is not something teachers do *to* children but rather *with* them. Portfolio assessment is a reflection of holistic, constructive language learning and teaching in action. A sample of one teacher's comments on children's portfolios is presented in Box 9.3.

BOX 9.3   ASSESSING THE CONTENTS OF A PORTFOLIO

What the Teacher Notices in the Portfolio	What That Suggests
There is little fluency and connection within pieces of writing in Keith's portfolio.	There is very little evidence in Keith's writing that he thinks much about a topic before he begins writing. The teacher needs to get him to think and plan more about what he will say.
This fifth-grade boy reads one comic book after another and does not record all of them on his logs. Most are humorous types; many are about Garfield the cat.	The teacher should look for some humorous stories about cats for him to read—perhaps with a character as ornery as Garfield.
Anders has a note attached to two mysteries he has written, saying that they are his favourites. He also has indicated on his log that an adventure story he wrote is his best because "it is exciting." There is not a large amount of writing in the portfolio, however.	The teacher could develop more opportunities for Anders to write. The adventure is a good story. Perhaps if Anders shared it with some fellow students and saw how they enjoyed it, he would be encouraged to write more.
Tad doesn't write a lot, but he draws well and is considered the best artist in the class by his classmates. His journal, which is spotty, is mainly about sports heroes. He also seems to write kinds of reviews about scary movies he has seen somewhere.	The teacher might ask Tad to be the sports editor on the next issue of the class newspaper. He could also illustrate one of his friend Adam's stories and perhaps write a sequel to it. The teacher decides to see if Tad might like to read *Joe Montana and Jerry Rice* by Richard J. Brenner and the mystery *Is Anybody There?* by Eve Bunting. Another book she could recommend to him is *Scary Stories to Chill Your Bones* by Alvin Schwartz. He could review the ones he reads for the paper and/or for the bulletin board and do illustrations for them.
Heriyadi's story "A Pizzaman's Adventure" is a kind of string of things that happen to a delivery person. It is the same character name as the "Gary" in his story "The City Street." Both of these stories have stringy plots but are very rich in details that build and build until offering the reader a rather complete picture of the character.	There is keen evidence that Heriyadi is thinking about what he writes and its impact on his reader. It's as if he keeps wanting to ensure that the picture is really complete enough for his readers to see it as he does. He should be encouraged to write some detailed descriptive pieces.

Source: From *Portfolio and Performance Assessment: Helping Students Evaluate their Progress as Readers and Writers*, 2nd edition by FARR, ET AL. 1998. Reprinted with the permission of Wadsworth, a division of Cengage Learning: www.cengage.com/permissions. Fax 800 730-2215.

A general assessment of the portfolio can also be made using the organizational outline adopted by the Department of School Education in Victoria, Australia, in their *English Profiles Handbook* (1991). An example of how this might be done is demonstrated below (p. 73):

> *What the writer does.* Shaun edits work to a point where others can read it. He corrects common spelling errors, punctuation, and grammatical errors, especially when he reads his pieces aloud to peers. He develops ideas into paragraphs and uses a dictionary or thesaurus to extend and check his writing vocabulary.
>
> *What the writing shows.* Sentences have ideas that flow. Paragraphs have a cohesive structure. Shaun shows the ability to argue and persuade. The messages in his expository and persuasive writing can be identified by others, but sometimes information is omitted. Brief passages are written with clear meaning, accurate spelling, and appropriate punctuation. Shaun can shift appropriately from first to third person in his writing. He consistently uses the correct tense in his writing. He uses compound sentences with conjunctions. His vocabulary is appropriate for a familiar audience such as peers, younger children, or adults, but he occasionally chooses an inappropriate word. Shaun has a consistent handwriting style, and when using the word processor, he uses a variety of fonts and print styles appropriate for the task.
>
> *Use of writing.* Shaun creates characters from his imagination and makes appropriate use of narrative and other forms of writing. He writes properly sequenced narratives with convincing settings.

Further examples and ideas for portfolios can be found in Easley and Mitchell's book, *Portfolios Matter: What, Where, When, Why and How to Use Them* (2003). This book is a quick reference for information about both portfolios and student-led conferencing.

Profiles

Once data has been collected through writing conferences, observations, checklists, samples collected in writing folders, written conversations, note-taking, published writing, and discussion with parents, teachers can create writing profiles of their students. One reliable and much-used resource for describing what children can actually do and how they can do it is the First Steps (Second Edition) Map of Development (2006), developed by the Education Department of Western Australia. First Steps "acknowledges the importance of sociocultural perspectives to the teaching of writing" (p. 3) and takes a multidimensional view of writing instruction. The Map of Development is based on seven phases of development: role-play, experimental, early, transitional, conventional, proficient, and accomplished. For each phase of writing development, a global statement summarizes the general characteristics of the phase and describes the types of text students in that phase might create. A list of key indicators is then presented for each phase, and major teaching emphases are suggested. The indicators listed are not meant to provide evaluative criteria; rather, "the purpose is to link assessment, teaching and learning in a way that best addresses the strengths and needs of all students" (p.11). First Steps pays particular attention to children who speak English as a second language. The Map of Development is a useful tool for deciding on teaching strategies for individual children, for small groups, or for whole-class instruction. An overview of the first phase, Role-Play, is presented in Box 9.4.

BOX 9.4 FIRST STEPS WRITING MAP OF DEVELOPMENT: OVERVIEW OF ROLE-PLAY PHASE (1ST PHASE)

In this phase, writers emulate adult writing by experimenting with marks to represent written language. Role-Play writers are beginning to understand that writing is used to convey meaning or messages; however, as understandings about sound–symbol relationships are yet to be developed, their messages are not readable by others. Role-Play writers rely heavily on topic knowledge to generate text.

Key Indicators

Use of Texts

▷ Assigns a message to own written and drawn symbols.

▷ Demonstrates awareness that writing and drawing are different.

▷ Knows that print carries a message but may "read" writing differently each time.

Contextual Understanding

▷ States purposes or audience for own writing—for example, "This is a card for Dad."

▷ Identifies and talks about characters from literary texts.

▷ Identifies and talks about people and ideas in informational texts.

Conventions

▷ Begins to demonstrate an awareness of directionality—for example, points to where print begins.

▷ Uses known letters or approximations of letters to represent writing.

Processes and Strategies

▷ Relies upon personal experiences as a stimulus for writing

Major Teaching Emphases

Environment and Attitude

▷ Create a supportive classroom environment that nurtures a community of writers.

▷ Foster students' enjoyment of writing.

▷ Encourage students to experiment with different facets of writing—for example, using known letters, composing messages.

▷ Encourage students to value writing as a social practice.

Use of Texts

▷ Expose students to a range of text forms pointing out purpose—for example, recipes tell how to make something.

▷ Provide opportunities for students to "write" a range of texts for authentic purposes and audiences.

▷ Model the connection between oral and written language—for example, what is said can be written down.

▷ Demonstrate that written messages remain constant.

▷ Foster students' sense of "personal voice" and individual writing style.

▷ Teach students the metalanguage associated with writing, and encourage its use.

Contextual Understanding

▷ Discuss that writing has a purpose and an intended audience.

▷ Draw students' attention to decisions writers make when composing texts.

▷ Draw student's attention to the way characters are represented in literary texts.

▷ Draw students' attention to the way people and ideas are represented in informational texts.

Conventions

▷ Provide opportunities for students to develop and use new vocabulary.

▷ Begin to build the bank of words students can automatically spell and use—for example, personally significant words.

▷ Build phonological awareness and graphophonic knowledge, such as:
  ▷ recognizing, matching, and generating rhymes
  ▷ listening for sounds in words
  ▷ linking letter names with their sounds, focusing on the regular sound

▷ Teach students the conventions of print.

▷ Model one-to-one correspondence between written and spoken words.

▷ Model the composition of simple sentences, including the use of punctuation—for example, capital letters, full stops.

Processes and Strategies

▷ Build students' semantic, graphophonic, and syntactic knowledge—for example, topic knowledge, sound–symbol relationships.

▷ Teach strategies used throughout the writing process—for example, connecting.

▷ Teach spelling strategies—for example, sounding out.

▷ Model simple publishing alternatives—for example, text and illustration.

▷ Model how to find required information in texts.

▷ Model how to reflect on the writing process and products, and encourage students to do the same.

Source: From *First Steps (Second Edition): Writing Map of Development: Overview (2005)*, by permission of STEPS Professional Development on behalf of Education and Training, Western Australia.

PRODUCT-BASED ASSESSMENT

From time to time, teachers must complete more formal assessments of children's progress in writing. These assessments may be part of the ongoing formative or diagnostic assessments that contribute to effective classroom instruction, or they may be summative assessments used for report cards or end-of-year school district testing. This type of assessment is usually conducted through a review of written products rather than assessing the processes students engage in when writing. Assessment of a portfolio and/or writing folder, and the creation of student writing profiles can also be useful summative assessment tools; however, it is frequently the finished product or the test score that parents, school administration, school districts, provincial departments of education, and employers use to judge writing abilities.

Unfortunately, the assessment requirements of some school districts and provincial governments are frequently at odds with the needs of students and teachers. Where students want to know how they can improve their writing, and teachers want to inform their planning in order to meet their students' learning requirements, school districts and provincial governments (and sometimes parents) want to know how their students' abilities compare with the abilities of students in other jurisdictions. They also want a measure of how much their students know and can do—and the more objective, the better. As a result, teachers need a broad repertoire of assessment procedures, including formal ones that demonstrate accountability to the general public as well as informal procedures designed to provide feedback to individual students and input to instructional planning.

Student performance on product-based tasks cannot be "machine-scored," but must instead be judged according to well-defined criteria. The vehicle containing these criteria is commonly known as a *scoring rubric*—a fixed scale and a list of characteristics describing performance for each of the points on the scale (see Marzana, Pickering, & McTighe, 1993). A rubric differs from a scoring key in that a scoring key does not contain descriptive characteristics, just a list of how points are to be assigned. Various provincial ministries of education and school districts in Canada have developed their own rubrics for the assessment of student writing. Samples of these are presented later in this chapter in Boxes 9.5, 9.6, 9.7, and 9.8. Teachers are trained to mark these writing tests as objectively as possible, minimizing reader bias and ensuring that scoring is consistent. Reliability checks are conducted regularly throughout the marking sessions.

Analysis of Writing Samples

When reading samples of students' writing, teachers are mindful that writing is not a single skill. Writing is a complex and sophisticated process that involves the effective utilization of syntax, organizational strategies, vocabulary, transcription tools, and ideas. Each of these varies according to the purpose and audience for the writing. The purpose and intended audience for a piece of writing shape the composition. Expressive writing is writer-oriented: its purpose is to reveal feelings, attitudes, and perceptions. Expository writing is subject-oriented: it is meant to explain or present information on a subject. Persuasive writing is audience-oriented: the writer takes a position on a topic and tries to convince others about it. The stimulus, or prompt, for a writing task also frames the piece of writing and influences the piece considerably. Therefore, when teachers read and score student writing samples, they take all of these factors into consideration, varying their reading of the piece according to the purpose for the writing and the stimulus provided.

Many teachers and language arts consultants develop rubrics and scoring guides for assessing and marking writing in their own classrooms. Frequently, these guides are developed in collaboration with the students themselves. Teacher Eileen Loughlin reminds us that the collaborative process facilitates three things:

1. As the students and teacher together develop the guide, they explore what constitutes a good piece of writing.

2. The students become aware of the criteria on which they will be evaluated.

3. Students remain in control of all aspects of their writing from onset to completion.

Eileen firmly believes that the collaborative nature of the process demonstrates her respect for her students and recognizes their contributions in the classroom.

Holistic Scoring

In **holistic scoring** students are evaluated on what they do *well* rather than on what they fail to do. This method encourages teachers to focus on the specifics they have in mind for rating essays and other pieces of writing before reading them. These specifics may include

- the students' attention to purpose and audience, and the ability to organize ideas according to the needs of communicating with that audience, whether through poetic, persuasive, expressive, or informative modes

- the students' attention to the visual and verbal cues of the assignment (e.g., "Give at least one reason . . .")

- the students' developmental capabilities, allowing for the general language characteristics of children of a similar age (e.g., the invented spelling of children in the primary grades)

- constraints of the evaluation situation—that is, the context or setting where the writing takes place (in many evaluative situations, for example, children do not have time to revise, edit, or ask for peer or teacher assistance)

A number of different methods for conducting holistic assessments have been established, and many rubrics have been developed over the years. The rubric displayed in Box 9.5 was developed by the Regina Board of Education. It is used for scoring writing at the grade 4, 8, and 10 levels.

An alternative method of holistic assessment, and probably the simplest, is *general impression marking*. The rater scores the paper by deciding where it fits in the range of papers produced for that assignment on that occasion. Although there is no analysis of specific features and no summary of scores, this method has high reliability, because experienced raters use an implicit list of features in much the same way as classroom teachers. If teachers were to spread out in front of them a set of writing from all the children in their class, written on the same day and on the same topic, it would be fairly clear which were the "best" pieces of writing and which were the least well developed. The middle-ranked pieces would be more difficult to arrange in some kind of order, but eventually a teacher would be able to make the decision on the basis of an implicit or internalized set of criteria. The use of this method for scoring or assessing writing can be facilitated in a school setting by a second teacher working collaboratively on the assessment. On such occasions, the teachers' implicit criteria are made explicit as problematic pieces of writing are discussed and a grade is decided upon.

| BOX 9.5 | HOLISTIC RUBRIC FOR WRITING ASSESSMENT |

Upper-half papers are characterized by well-supported, original ideas, clear evidence of an organizational plan, and general mastery of the conventions of standard English, although even the strongest papers may contain some developmentally appropriate errors in spelling or sentence structure.

▷ The "6" paper contains original, sophisticated ideas, well supported by relevant details. Organization is clear and logical, with a strong lead and effective conclusion. Vivid and precise word choice, varied sentences, and a clear, well-developed writer's voice combine to create a coherent and original and piece of writing. Any errors in conventions are usually the result of risk-taking.

▷ The "5" paper contains original ideas with relevant and appropriate details. It is well organized and usually has a strong lead and adequate conclusion. Clear and descriptive word choice and a developing writer's voice are evident. There may be some variation in sentence length and complexity. Minor errors in conventions do not interfere with the meaning of the piece.

▷ The "4" paper is likely to have somewhat mundane, but adequate ideas that are somewhat supported by details. A hint of writer's voice may be apparent. There is evidence of a good organizational plan with an adequate lead, though the conclusion may be weak. Word choice is generally appropriate, though lacking in precision and originality, and sentences may lack variety. Some errors in conventions are common.

Lower-half papers lack originality or effective support for ideas. Vocabulary may be immature and control of conventions of standard English is inadequate.

▷ The "3" paper is likely to contain unoriginal ideas with marginal support, or irrelevant details that do not support the main idea. The organization is limited, with a weak and/or missing conclusion. A writer's voice may not be evident. Word choice may be correct, but lacking maturity, and sentences tend to be simple in structure. Frequent errors in conventions are common, but the piece should be readable.

▷ The "2" paper contains trivial ideas without supporting details. It is characterized by an inadequate organizational plan, immature vocabulary, short, simple sentences, and frequent errors in conventions that may, at times, interfere with understanding of the piece.

▷ The "1" piece is characterized by such inadequate mastery of conventions of standard English that the piece may be barely comprehensible. Ideas are incomplete or confusing, organization appears haphazard, and vocabulary choice is very limited.

▷ An asterisk code, "*", is used for papers that are blank, illegible, or written on a topic other than the one assigned.

Source: Based on the Regina Board of Education Scoring Guide. Originally adapted from the Northwest Regional Educational Laboratories 6 + 1 Traits Writing Program by Sandra Pace, Lori Rog, Trudy Loftsgard, Myra Froc, and Greg Smith.

Analytic Scales

Analytic scales break the writing performance down into component parts, such as organization, wording, and ideas. It takes longer to accomplish than holistic scoring, but provides more specific information and is usually regarded as being more objective. The list of features assessed may range from four to twelve, with each feature described in some detail and with high-, mid-, and low points identified and described along a scoring line for each feature.

Analytic assessment of writing is used by many school districts, including Edmonton Public Schools. Their Highest Level of Achievement Tests (HLATs) are administered in the spring of each school year and are intended to provide grade level achievement and growth data at the student, school, and district levels. Each student's writing is assessed as "excellent," "proficient," "adequate," or "limited" at each grade level. Box 9.6 presents the performance and achievement criteria for writing judged to be of "excellent" quality at the grade 3 level.

BOX 9.6   CRITERIA FOR "EXCELLENT" WRITING AT GRADE 3

Performance Criteria: EXCELLENT

The writer fulfils the task and purposefully controls details and language to *shape the writing*.

The paper shows *overall unity* and artistry of communication.

The writing is focused, sustains the reader's interest, and *engages audience*.

The content is imaginative, memorable and the topic is *skillfully* developed.

Vocabulary and usage are often clever, and *well chosen* for the form and purpose.

The organization and style of the paper create a sense of voice *unique* to the writer.

Spelling and grammar, capitalization, and punctuation applications are *controlled* to enhance the impact of the writing; errors are hardly noticeable.

Achievement Criteria: GRADE THREE

▷ Audience appeal
  ▷ choose words and language patterns to create desired effects
  ▷ hold reader's interest in presentation of ideas

▷ Content and planning
  ▷ support the piece of writing with some specific details
  ▷ elaborate on ideas in plan and/or writing

▷ Vocabulary and usage
  ▷ choose words appropriate to the context of their writing
  ▷ use a variety of applicable words to add interest and detail

▷ Organization and clarity
  ▷ use sentence variety to link ideas
  ▷ order information in a connected sequence
  ▷ provide an introduction
  ▷ provide closure

(Continued)

▷ Style and voice
  ▷ express thoughts and ideas using an authentic personal voice
  ▷ choose words and language patterns to convey personal feelings
▷ Sentence structure and grammar
  ▷ vary sentence beginnings by using different words
  ▷ show general control of subject and verb agreement
  ▷ construct complete sentences correctly
▷ Mechanics: spelling, capitalization, punctuation
  ▷ use conventional spelling for most common words
  ▷ use capitalization for sentence beginnings, proper names, *I*, acronyms, and titles
  ▷ use end punctuation correctly (.?!)
▷ Editing and revising
  ▷ make changes in word choices and spelling
  ▷ *Key*
    ▷ Sample shows evidence of this criterion.
    ▷ No evidence of this criterion in sample.

Observations—Applying Criteria to the Sample, "The Fox Family"

Dear Anty

You wouldent beleve what we saw on the way up to Didsbury on Sunday. It was an amazing sight. We were driving along lisening to my music when suddenly a fox poped out of the tall grass my mom slamed on the bracks. The fox was a light gray. My mom started going again but we stoped again traling behind the mother was two baby foxes. There so adorable me and Scott said. But there was only one problem a big semy truck was coming. Hurry up little foxes you'r going to get ran over my mom mutered but luckily the little baby foxes got across in time hufe that was close me Scott and mom said in re leaf those are some realy lucy foxes.

Love your sunshine girl Annie

This sample was judged excellent because the choices of words and descriptive images add to the reader's enjoyment of the piece. Most criteria at the grade three level were met. This piece contains several expressions of ideas that reflect the writer's voice and style and contribute to the original and well crafted memory, e.g. "... *suddenly a fox poped out of the tall grass,*" "*Hurry up little foxes you'r going to get ran over my mom mutered*" and "... *hufe that was close ... .*"

Students like this writer may benefit from sharing this piece in a student writing publication. The teacher could prepare this student by working on editing techniques that focus on spelling and punctuation errors.

Source: Reproduced from Edmonton Public Schools, Resource Development Services, *Teacher Resource for Highest Level of Achievement Test: HLAT writing, 2006 Edition* (Edmonton, AB: Edmonton Public Schools, 2006), p. 30. Reproduced with permission.

The task in 2006 was to describe to a friend or relative a memorable day, and show why it was memorable. The topic might be personal, realistic, or imaginative. The criteria have proven useful to teachers in developing a vocabulary for discussing and conducting formal writing assessment, and in developing an explicit sense of what constitutes good writing.

Alberta Education also uses analytic assessment in the grades 3, 6, and 9 provincial tests of written language. The students are required to produce two writing samples: one a narrative piece prompted by a story starter, and the other a functional piece prompted by a stated specific purpose for a specific audience. The test provides for some choice of topic and includes time for planning and discussion with peers. The functional piece may be a business letter or a news article, for example, and is assessed according to "content" (development and organization, fulfilling the purpose, tone of the piece, and awareness of audience) and "content management" (accuracy and effectiveness of words and expressions, control of sentence structure, usage, mechanics, and format). The reporting category of content for the grade 6 functional writing task (2007) is shown in Box 9.7. Box 9.8 presents the descriptors for content management. In this example, the functional writing task is a news article. Each category is scored from INS (Insufficient) through 1 to 5.

Narrative writing is assessed in the Provincial Achievement Tests in Alberta according to five criteria: content (context, plausibility, details, awareness of audience), organization (introduction, sequencing, cohesion, and closure), sentence structure (type, length), vocabulary (specific, image-creating, accurate, and effective), and language conventions (capitalization, spelling, punctuation, format, usage, clarity, flow).

Below are the grade 6 descriptors for a narrative text that "approaches the standard of excellence":

Content

- The context is clearly established and sustained.
- The events and/or actions are consistently appropriate for the established context.
- Supporting details are specific and consistently effective.
- The writing captivates and holds the reader's interest and is creative and/or original.

Organization (or Development)

- The introduction is purposeful; interesting; clearly establishes events, characters, and/or setting; and provides direction for the writing.
- Events and/or details are arranged in paragraphs in a purposeful and effective order, and coherence is maintained.
- Connections and/or relationships among events, actions, details, and/or characters are consistently maintained.
- The ending ties events and/or actions together.

Sentence Structure

- Sentence structure is effectively and consistently controlled.
- Sentence type and length are consistently effective and varied.
- Sentence beginnings are varied.

BOX 9.7   ALBERTA EDUCATION GRADE 6 DESCRIPTORS FOR CONTENT (FUNCTIONAL WRITING—NEWS ARTICLE)

Focus	
When marking CONTENT appropriate for grade 6 functional writing, the marker should consider • effectiveness of development and organization of the news article • whether the purpose of the assignment is fulfilled with complete and appropriate information • appropriateness of tone for the assignment and awareness of audience	
5 Meets the standard of excellence	• The ideas are well developed and organization of the news article is clear and effective. • Complete information is presented, and this information is enhanced by precise and appropriate details that effectively fulfil the purpose of the assignment. • A tone appropriate for the assignment is clearly and effectively maintained.
4 Approaches the standard of excellence	• The ideas are generally well developed and organization of the news article is generally effective. • Complete information is presented, and this information is substantiated by appropriate details that fulfil the purpose of the assignment. • A tone appropriate for the assignment is clearly maintained.
3 Clearly meets the acceptable standard	• The ideas are adequately developed and organization of the news article is adequate. • Some sufficient information is given, and this information is supported by enough details to fulfil the purpose of the assignment. • A tone appropriate for the assignment is generally maintained.
2 Does not clearly meet the acceptable standard	• The ideas are poorly developed and organization of the news article is ineffective. • Essential information may be missing. Supporting details are scant, insignificant, and/or irrelevant. The purpose of the assignment is only partially fulfilled. • A tone appropriate for the assignment is evident but not maintained.
1 Clearly below the acceptable standard	• The ideas are not developed and organization of the news article is inadequate. • Essential information and supporting details are inappropriate or lacking. The purpose of the assignment is not fulfilled. • Little awareness of tone appropriate for the assignment is evident.
INS Insufficient	• The marker can discern no evidence of an attempt to fulfil the assignment, or the writing is so deficient in length that it is not possible to assess content.

Note: Content and Content Management are equally weighted.

Please advise students that their work must be related to the assignment. Those assignments that are completely "off topic" will be awarded a mark of Insufficient.

Source: Alberta Education, *English language arts grade six provincial testing bulletin,* 2007. Retrieved June 22, 2007, from: http://www.education.gov.ab.ca/k_12/testing/achievement/bulletins/default.asp. Reproduced with permission of the Minister of Education, Province of Alberta, Canada, 2007.

BOX 9.8	ALBERTA EDUCATION GRADE 6 DESCRIPTORS FOR CONTENT MANAGEMENT (FUNCTIONAL WRITING—NEWS ARTICLE)

Focus	
When marking CONTENT MANAGEMENT appropriate for grade 6 functional writing, the marker should consider • accuracy and effectiveness of words and expressions • control of sentence structure, usage, and mechanics (spelling, punctuation, etc.) • clarity and flow of the communication Proportion of error to length and complexity of response must be considered.	
5 Meets the standard of excellence	• Words and expressions used are consistently accurate and effective. • The writing demonstrates confident and consistent control of sentence structure, usage, and mechanics. • Errors, if present, do not reduce the clarity or interrupt the flow of the communication.
4 Approaches the standard of excellence	• Words and expressions used are usually accurate and effective. • The writing demonstrates competent and generally consistent control of sentence structure, usage, and mechanics. • Errors that are present rarely reduce the clarity or interrupt the flow of the communication.
3 Clearly meets the accept-able standard	• Words and expressions used are generally accurate and occasionally effective. • The writing demonstrates basic control of sentence structure, usage, and mechanics. • Errors that are present occasionally reduce the clarity or interrupt the flow of the communication.
2 Does not clearly meet the accept-able standard	• Words and expressions used are frequently vague and/or imprecise. • The writing demonstrates faltering control of sentence structure, usage, and mechanics. • Errors reduce the clarity and interrupt the flow of the communication.
1 Clearly below the accept-able standard	• Words and expressions used are inaccurate and/or misused. • The writing demonstrates lack of control of sentence structure, usage, and mechanics. • Errors severely reduce the clarity and interrupt the flow of the communication
INS Insufficient	• The writing has been awarded an INS for *Content*.

Source: Alberta Education, *English language arts grade six provincial testing bulletin*, 2007. Retrieved June 22, 2007, from: http://www.education.gov.ab.ca/k_12/testing/achievement/bulletins/default.asp. Reproduced with permission of the Minister of Education, Province of Alberta, Canada, 2007.

Vocabulary

- Words and expressions are used accurately and effectively.

- Specific words and expressions are used to create vivid images and/or to enrich details.

Conventions

▪ The quality of the writing is enhanced because it is essentially error-free.

▪ Errors, if present, do not reduce the clarity or interrupt the flow of the communication.

As a demonstration, Box 9.9 presents an excerpt from a composition, "Zulu," written by a grade 6 student, together with an evaluation of the piece based on the above criteria.

Assessing Student Progress for Report Cards

Each school district has its own method of reporting student progress to parents through report cards, and sometimes there are differences in report cards from one school to another within

---

BOX 9.9   ZULU

They came over to me talking in soft mumbling sounds that I couldn't understand. I backed into the corner of the stall and watched as they brought out a small harness. The creature reached out a hand and stroked my neck.

"He's a big one Alana, are ya still sure you want 'im?" One asked, obviously refering to me.

"Yes, the bigger they are the higher they jump."

The first speaker stepped forward and held out the soft leather thing, which they called a halter, for me to smell. It had no scent but I drew my head back and turned away. I looked for my mother, she was watching, but did nothing. The one they called Alana took the halter and slipped it over my head. I shook my head, not liking this thing tight on my face. I ran around the stall and rubbed my face on the rough wood of the wall.

"He's a spirited one alright." Henry said (The first one)

"Yeah, I don't intend to break that." Alana commented

"What are you going to call him?"

"Well his sire is Zulu Royaal and then his mother is Gotoit, so his name is Go to it Zulu. A pretty good name I think."

Henry came over, took hold of the halter and rubbed my ears. His hands were strong and gentle, I now knew why my mother was kind to these creatures.

A week passed. I got used to the halter and lead rope. I saw Henry and Alana each day. I asked my mother about them. She told me that Alana was her master and mine too. She said that I was to do what Henry and Alana wished me do and never to kick or bite. They have big plans for you, she would say, you will become great one day, till then you must do as they say.

When they came into the stall I could tell that there was something different about them. Not as happy. Alana came over to me right away and rubbed my nose and ears. I sniffed at her pockets as I had seen my mother do. She patted my side and slipped the halter over my head. I had grown much stronger over the last few days and loved to play tug'a'war with the shank. I looked at my mother, who I still would not move far from, Henry had put a halter on her too. I knew something was different today.

Analysis

Content. The piece of writing demonstrates a strong voice. Written as a first-person narrative, its details and description create an immediate engagement with the central character, a horse. The vivid description is enhanced by the use of dialogue. Rather than telling the reader that Zulu is a large horse, the writer demonstrates it in Henry's comment: "*He's a big one Alana, are ya still sure you want 'im?*" The reader is also forewarned of coming events through Alana's response: "*Yes, the bigger they are the higher they jump.*" The entire excerpt from the story is focused on the events in the stall, the early breaking of the young horse and his introduction to the harness. There are no extraneous details, no irrelevant content. The reader's interest is captivated and sustained.

Organization. The introduction is interesting and clearly establishes a setting and a point of view. The events of the story are arranged in paragraphs in a coherent sequence and are clearly connected, creating a cohesive piece of writing. The unfolding of events reveals the horse's character and situation, and the ending ties events together, as well as foreshadowing the events of the next chapter.

Sentence structure. The sentence structure is effectively controlled, with a variety of sentence lengths and types from coordination ("*I backed into the corner of the stall and watched as they brought out a small harness*") to subordination ("*The first speaker stepped forward and held out the soft leather thing, which they called a halter, for me to smell*"). There are no sentence fragments or run-on sentences. The sentence beginnings are varied ("*When they came into the stall, …*"

Vocabulary. Words and expressions such as *halter*, *shank*, and *lead rope* are used accurately. The vocabulary is varied and colourful. Words such as *mumbling*, *creative*, *scent*, and *spirited* create vivid images and add to the rich detail presented in the piece.

Conventions. The conventions of written language are of a high standard and the piece is enhanced because it is virtually error-free. Quotation marks are used appropriately, as are question marks and periods. Paragraphs are well formed, and the indentation of paragraphs and direct speech is formatted correctly. Occasionally dialect is used, and appropriate punctuation is used to mark this (as in *'im*). There are numerous commas where periods or semicolons would have been more appropriate, but this does not reduce the clarity or break up the flow of the text ("*I looked for my mother, she was watching, but did nothing*"). This usage is likely connected to the reading the student has done. The writer's favourite book was *Black Beauty* by Anna Sewell, originally published in 1877. *Black Beauty* uses a more old-fashioned style, with the frequent use of commas to break up the text, rather than periods or semicolons.

a district. However, there are similarities among them. Very few districts ask for percentages or numeric marks. Some districts require a letter grade, but most districts today require a descriptor to be used instead. These descriptors are generally tied to the criteria set out in the provincial or school district writing assessments. Some school districts use the learner outcomes listed in the provincial language arts program of studies when developing their assessment criteria. Since there are hundreds of learner outcomes, consultants carefully reduce

> **BOX 9.10** **SAMPLE REPORT CARD COMMENTS, GRADE 2**
>
> Key learner outcomes for writing for this period were
>
> ▷ Generates and organizes ideas during pre-writing.
>
> ▷ Writes and illustrates original texts based on formats explored in class.
>
> ▷ Revises written and illustrated work to clarify and enhance the text message.
>
> ▷ Edits for missing words, spelling, capitals, and end punctuation.
>
> ### Constantin
>
> One focus this term has been upon narrative writing. Constantin is an imaginative author, creating delightful stories that express his developing style. His story beginnings are well developed, with clear characters and settings. This clarity of organization is not as evident throughout the middle and end of his stories. Although it is not yet consistent, his developing use of lively verbs and phrases when a character is experiencing a strong emotion add energy and create visual images in the reader's mind. Once Constantin is finished a story, he must take more time to revise the middle and end of his stories to be sure that the events written on the page clearly describe those in his imagination. More careful editing of punctuation and legibility will also assist in this area. Constantin needs to take more care with his manuscript printing.
>
> ### Paisley
>
> One focus this term has been upon narrative writing. Paisley is able to write delightful stories that draw the reader into the plot. Her beginnings are well developed, clearly introducing the character, events, and setting. The organization of the middle and end are not consistently maintained, causing the reader to pause and reread for clarification. Paisley uses vocabulary to create a picture in the reader's mind, with phrases like "the sweet green pine tree smell" and "her hands shot up like fireworks." Well done! Paisley must take more responsibility for editing all of her work, in all subjects. Her lack of attention to this area, despite direct instruction and assistance, impedes her written communication. Paisley has a wealth of wonderful ideas that need to be shared in a manner that more closely reflects her ability.

the list to a manageable number. Eileen Loughlin's district uses a total of 60 outcomes, and each teacher can select 10 to 12 outcomes per term as a focus for their teaching and assessment during the term. These are the criteria listed on the report card for that term, and teachers assess each child according to one of the following standards: excellent, proficient, basic, insufficient, and unable to assess. Box 9.10 contains a sample of report card remarks Eileen has put together to demonstrate what her report cards look like. The attention to detail included in the comments is a reflection of the time Eileen has taken over the years to familiarize herself with the provincial program of studies and the school district's assessment practices. Eileen is a master teacher, and beginning teachers can learn much from working with colleagues like Eileen once they begin teaching.

The assessment strategies we have discussed in this chapter provide teachers with information about all major aspects of children's writing. The strategies are designed to meet the many

TEACHER WISDOM

EILEEN LOUGHLIN

What's the best piece of advice you would give to beginning teachers about teaching and assessing writing?

Try not to feel overwhelmed. There's one feeling about teaching that's common across most teachers—you never feel to be doing enough for the children, or doing well enough in terms of all the new things you have to learn. There's always more you can do for a child. As a teacher, you don't often get to see other teachers teach. It's an isolated profession, in that sense, so you always wonder what other teachers are doing. It's one thing to hear teachers talk about what they're doing, but it's quite different to observe in a classroom. We can learn so much by observing in another teacher's classroom. So whenever you have an opportunity, go into a colleague's classroom and just watch. Then you can take just one thing you have seen and try it in your own room. You have to try one thing at a time.

How can beginning teachers gain confidence in their ability to assess children's writing?

The hardest thing for beginning teachers—and for teachers starting to teach in a new grade—is knowing what is "normal" for that grade level. I strongly suggest that teachers "buddy up" with a colleague or group of colleagues and talk about specific pieces of writing and how they can be assessed. The best guide is to use the criteria and the exemplars provided by provincial ministries of education, or those provided by the local school district. Alternatively, use the rubrics provided in the "6+1 Trait Writing" guide. Beginning teachers need to examine these rubrics so they have a standard to work with. The teachers in my school engage in collaborative planning, and they do it by division (Division 1 is K–3, Division 2 is grades 4–6). They need to see what children across the grades can do, not just the children at the grade level they teach. This provides them with a broader view of students' competencies and the ways in which children grow across the grades.

I would also say you have to work with a master teacher, a teacher who has not only been teaching for a few years but has continued their own professional education—taken workshops and training sessions and kept up with new developments—someone who is involved with district initiatives. That might sound a bit scary, but once you start teaching, you will discover teachers you really trust; people you can talk to, question, and learn from. These are the people you need to work alongside, so you can do things together. Not just showing you how to do assessments but working through some together so you become really familiar with the criteria and how to apply them to pieces of writing. I'm not talking here about a formal mentorship, but a teacher you feel safe with and who will give you the time and walk you through the procedures.

What about developing a writing program?

If you don't feel comfortable developing your own program at first, use a published program or a reputable resource. Go back to your university textbook and look at the

(Continued)

suggestions there. You're not without ideas, you just need to start with one thing at a time, and if you need a language arts series to get you started, then go with it. There are lots of good ideas in those books. Start wherever you feel comfortable. Once you become really familiar with the program of studies, you realize you don't need those series, and you can manage your own writing program. I am always amazed at the strengths of our beginning teachers. They are well prepared, but we often assume they begin their careers with the skills of a master teacher and that's not possible. So stay focused and if you need a language arts series, use one.

purposes for which teachers are required to make assessments. In classrooms such as Eileen Loughlin's, instructional decisions are based primarily on the students' needs. Information about those needs is gained through appropriate assessment strategies. Whether assessments are informal or formal, completed through observation, anecdotal records, checklists and profiles, portfolios or writing folders, student self-evaluation, writing conferences, analyses of samples of student writing, or provincial or local district achievement tests, the aim is always to effectively teach to the needs of students.

TEACHING SPELLING

The Development of Spelling Abilities

No aspect of the school curriculum is more researched than the teaching of spelling. Some of the very first educational research was conducted in spelling about a hundred years ago. Researchers wanted to know whether children could spell specific words correctly, and which method of instruction was most effective. During the 1970s, researchers began to explore how children develop the ability to spell correctly and the factors that affect their development. Is correct spelling tied to reading ability? Do word lists and frequent spelling tests help children become better spellers? Do children learn correct spelling as they read and write?

Invented Spelling

Children's very early writing attempts demonstrate what is known as **invented spelling**. A lot of research was conducted in the area of invented spelling during the 1970s (e.g., Beers & Henderson, 1977; Gentry, 1978, 1981), particularly on how children move from invented to more conventional spelling. Invented spelling is part of the developmental progression children make as they journey toward mastering orthodox spelling, and it occurs as a result of them listening acutely to the spoken language they hear around them and attending to the meaning of words. Young children are particularly sensitive to the sounds of words, and as they attempt to encode words into print, they try to put the sounds they hear into symbol form (Read, 1975). Students' early spellings can be thought of as approximations or experimentations with the sounds, patterns, and meanings of words.

Researchers have learned that there are three layers to the orthographic structure of spelling (Bear, Invernizzi, Templeton, & Johnston, 2004). The *alphabet layer* represents the relationship between letters and sounds in English. In a left-to-right sequence, the word "can" is represented by three different letters for the three different sounds heard in the word. Sometimes two letters represent one sound, like the *sh* in "push." The *pattern layer* overlays the alphabet layer. English has evolved over time and is an amalgam of many languages. One letter does not represent only one sound. Instead, in English there are patterns of spelling to guide us through groupings of letters. These patterns give rise to some of the rules of spelling—even though they can be very inconsistent. For example, the silent *e* that makes a vowel long, as in "cake." The third layer is the *meaning layer*, and this is where prefixes and suffixes, root words, and words borrowed from other languages come in. If we know the root word, we can build the correct spelling of other forms of the word from it; for example, *connect, reconnect, disconnect,* and *connection*.

During the process of acquiring orthodox spelling abilities, children generally move through five or six major stages of invented spelling (depending on which researcher's work you use). The process can last from age 3 or 4 through to age 11 or 12 (the grade 6 or 7 level). Before the age of 3, most children draw and make letter shapes, but their attempts are not usually referred to as spelling, though it is recognized that these young learners are indeed "writing."

The five stages of invented spelling we find most useful to know are:

1. *Prereading or emergent spelling.* This stage of invented spelling consists of the random orderings of whatever letters children can draw. There is no awareness of sound–symbol relationship, and so strings of letters such as Beth's writing (in Box 9.11) of *REaEoEfa aogrt NOCe baEONOEOLE* might appear on the page. Children may have their own "meaning" to go along with the letters, and may tell a coherent story to accompany them.

BOX 9.11   BETH'S PREREADING SPELLING

BOX 9.12   IAN'S PREPHONETIC SPELLING

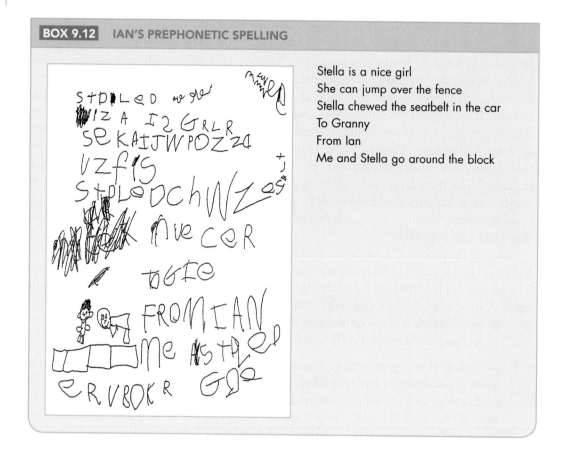

Stella is a nice girl
She can jump over the fence
Stella chewed the seatbelt in the car
To Granny
From Ian
Me and Stella go around the block

An adult might transcribe this story onto the same page as the child's print. In Beth's case, her mother transcribed the message "I like Santa's mustache. I got my Christmas tree up last night." At this stage, Beth has no knowledge that specific configurations of letters and words are needed to create meaningful print. However, she does have a firm grasp of the message concept—that what is written on a page signifies a particular meaning.

2. *Prephonetic or semiphonetic spelling.* In this stage, children have a primitive concept of the alphabet and of letter names, and so letter names are used as clues in spelling. Children in this stage might write *NHR* for "nature," or represent a whole word with one letter, usually an initial consonant. Rarely are vowels used; a child's spelling in this stage consists almost entirely of consonants. Ian's writing, shown in Box 9.12, is moving into the **phonetic** stage, but much of his spelling still reflects semiphonetic elements, as in his spelling of *GRL* for "girl" and *JWP* for "jump."

3. *Phonetic spelling.* This is the stage most commonly seen in students from kindergarten through grade 3. Children have an understanding of sound–symbol correspondence, but they represent the features of words according to how they themselves hear and articulate the words. This often leads to the omission of preconsonant nasals, such as the *M* in *NUBERS* or the *N* in *SWIMIG*. Boxes 9.13, 9.14, and 9.15 illustrate children's spelling during this stage.

BOX 9.13   **OMAR'S PHONETIC SPELLING**

The one with the spider and the turtle.

BOX 9.14   **HANNAH'S PHONETIC SPELLING**

On the weekend I got a new pair of shoes.

---

4. *Transitional spelling.* In grades 2 through 4, children generally include a vowel in every syllable and use familiar spelling patterns, though they are frequently used incorrectly. The word "make" may be spelled as *maek*, or "was" as *whas*. Rules are overgeneralized, and the aspects of spelling a child is currently learning become obvious through error patterns in the writing. In Box 9.16, the writer spells "witch" as *wich*, and in Box 9.17, "came" is spelled *caem*. Bear, Invernizzi, Templeton, and Johnston (2004) draw similarities between children's spelling development and the development of spelling across time in the English language. They recall the phonetic spelling of the Anglo-Saxons, which shifted to the introduction of French spelling and the use of the silent *e*. It is remarkable that some spelling at the transitional stage looks very similar to spelling used in Chaucer's time. The feature is certainly evident in the children's writing presented here.

As we have mentioned, children also use the meanings of words to help them spell. One child wrote a note to his mother who was attending university at the time: "I hope you have a good time at youknowvursdy." There is no doubt that he understood that

BOX 9.15	GILLIAN'S PHONETIC SPELLING

I can write letters to my mom.

BOX 9.16	APRIL'S TRANSITIONAL SPELLING

My favourite part was when the witch kissed Thistle.

university is a place where people come "to know." Boxes 9.16, 9.17, and 9.18 show the transitional spelling of writers in grade 2. These students are exploring the nature of spelling conventions such as the use of *ch*, the *-ed* suffix, *ck*, and silent vowels (*caem* for "came") and are developing a core vocabulary of standard spellings (*I*, *my*, *the*, *on*).

BOX 9.17 ZAK'S TRANSITIONAL SPELLING

When pig blew up and the family came out of pig's stomach.

BOX 9.18 MICHAEL'S TRANSITIONAL SPELLING

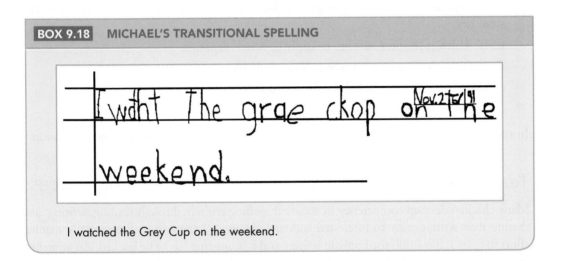

I watched the Grey Cup on the weekend.

5. *Standard spelling.* Generally, at about grade 5 or later, children demonstrate a more sophisticated understanding of spelling. They understand the constraints of syntax and morphology on their spelling (i.e., the conventions of spelling), and they use dictionaries to assist in correct spelling. Children at this age have learned that correct spelling is a courtesy to the reader, as well as necessary for expressing meaning clearly to an audience.

Although these stages appear to be a natural progression for most children, the question remains as to how and when conventional spelling should be encouraged or required in classrooms. The answer is that spelling always counts, and conventional spelling can always be encouraged—but young children must first of all be helped to compose their own texts before they are *required* to adhere to the conventions of written language. In addition, it is important that teachers and caregivers focus on the words children use in their writing most frequently—words such as *I, was, and,* and *but.*

Much standard spelling can be taught during editing conferences, but some children need a more structured approach to learning conventional spelling. When adults write in journals or write letters to friends, even their spelling may not be 100 percent correct. What is important in these cases is that they make an effort to spell correctly so they can communicate with themselves (through the journal) or friends (through letters). When focusing on spelling in children's writing, it is helpful for teachers and parents to keep in mind the audience and the purpose for the writing. There are many occasions when the message to be conveyed is more important than correct spelling, especially if the piece is to be read by a limited audience.

Teachers and parents can, however, help students to become better spellers by being mindful of the things that *good* spellers do, emphasizing these behaviours in their children. Most of the time good spellers do the following:

- recall spelling patterns and generalizations they have learned through their reading and writing
- know about words and how to use them
- have a repertoire of spelling strategies to choose from and do not rely only on one or two strategies
- know which is the best strategy to apply in which situation
- do not rely on sounding out words (too unreliable)
- do not rely on spelling "rules" (again, too unreliable)
- use visual memory in conjunction with other strategies

In summary, good spellers *think* about their spelling and do not rely on rote memorization.

Teaching Spelling in the Context of the Writing Process

Many children develop competency in standard spelling entirely through reading, writing, and sharing their writing with an interested audience. However, standard spelling usually requires effort to master; it is a skill used only in writing and it is one that has to be learned. An awareness of the need for correct spelling can be taught from grade 2 onward. It is easy for any writer to become lazy about spelling, but it is essential for a committed writer to adhere to conventional forms. Habits formed in childhood often persist into adulthood, though usually adults have only one or two major error patterns in their spelling. For some, the error pattern will be confusion over double consonants (words such as *embarrass*); for others it will be problems with reversing letters, or omitting letters in a word (e.g., *contain* spelled as *contian* or *cotain*). Once adult writers become aware of the nature of their error patterns, they can make efforts to learn the specific words they have difficulty with, usually words such as *embarrassment* or *containment*.

Teachers can help their students learn conventional spelling by conducting regular brief lessons using the overhead projector, focusing attention on common misspellings, and encouraging children to watch for these specific words in their spelling that particular week. More idiosyncratic misspellings can be addressed in writing conferences, but usually not until a piece is ready for a final draft, unless the word is an unusual one for the child to write (e.g., *cornucopia* and *satellite*). This also applies to errors in capitalization, punctuation, and grammar. In elementary school, teachers rarely focus lengthy language arts lessons on these

INSIDE CLASSROOMS

Teaching the Conventions of Writing in Wayne McNamara's Grade 4 Classroom

Wayne McNamara has been teaching for three years, and he believes strongly that elementary students should take responsibility for their learning. Students need to understand what they are expected to learn and why they are expected to learn it. In other words, their learning goals must be clear and purposeful to them. He understands that children cannot do this without help and guidance from their teachers. Wayne takes various rubrics, especially those in 6 + 1 Trait Writing, and he modifies them to meet his students' needs, often reducing the number of items on the rubric. These are then a form of self-assessment for the students. The rubrics contain statements such as

> My piece of writing has capital letters in the correct places.
> My piece has correct spelling.
> My piece has periods in the right places.
> My piece is legible and easy for others to read.

Wayne focuses on a few criteria at a time, depending on what he is teaching in mini-lessons and what he sees in the children's writing. Sometimes he may focus on organization or content (ideas), and at other times on sentence structure, word usage, or voice.

Wayne tracks children's spelling growth in two ways: through weekly spelling lists with a test and through their everyday writing. He uses a spelling textbook, but he carefully selects the activities he asks his students to complete. He does not mark these activities or keep a record of the students' results, but he does have the children check their own work, or check a partner's work (and he frequently double-checks the work later, to make sure the students have marked the work correctly). Many of the activities he selects not only raise an awareness of correct spelling, but they also teach vocabulary or word usage. Some of the activities teach grammar and punctuation.

Wayne talks with the students about the spelling activities, and he emphasizes that spelling is important because throughout their lives they will need to communicate with other people in writing. He talks with them about the writing they need to do in school, and the writing their parents do, be it a greeting card, a note to the teacher, an invoice they have to write for their business, or a lengthy report. He says that children have to "buy in" to the importance of correct spelling and grammar and legible handwriting if they are to deal with it seriously in school—and teachers have to value those things as well.

Generally, Wayne teaches the conventions of writing in the context of the revising and editing processes. His students write on every other line of their paper so they can make revisions to their work without having to rewrite the entire piece. Grade 4 students' editing skills are not strong, so he tries to encourage editing whenever he can without turning writing into an onerous task. Interestingly, Wayne found that when he taught his students

(Continued)

to use a thesaurus, they thoroughly enjoyed it and made use of one regularly—though on occasions he has had to negotiate with some students about just how many "thesaurus words" they should use in one sentence!

Wayne makes sure the creative writing his students do is enjoyable as well as imaginative, and he often sets short assignments for them with prompts such as, "Tell me about a time when you *had* to take a bath" or "Tell me how you got your name." Students love it, and want to write well because they want to share their stories with the class. Wayne gives them lots of time to organize their ideas ahead of time. Although his students have previously learned how to create a web, he finds that does not help them in organizing their writing. Consequently, he has created a three-part "grid" for them to use as an organizer—basically around the beginning, middle, and end of the piece.

In Wayne's school district, the students move from manuscript printing to cursive handwriting in grade 4. Many of the children are very eager and excited to learn (and some have already been developing their cursive handwriting on their own). But some of the students are anxious and nervous, and they begin to hold their pencils too tightly, or they labour over every letter in an attempt to create perfect copy. Wayne first of all teaches how to form each letter correctly, and later he talks to the students about developing a personal style. Legibility is the criterion that matters the most, closely followed by size and spacing. Slant and consistency of style are other criteria Wayne demonstrates to his students. He has found that his students are very critical of their peers' handwriting if they cannot read the words on a spelling test. At a certain point in the year, the students are required to do all their writing in cursive hand rather than in manuscript printing.

The school district uses a keyboarding program called All the Right Type, and Wayne believes the sooner children learn to keyboard the better. The program is on all the computers in the labs across the district, and he and his students have learned to keyboard together. One thing Wayne notes is that his students are much faster at learning keyboarding than he is. Today, it is a crucial skill for everyone, and the students are keen to learn—and they have a lot of fun with it. They enjoy knowing that this is a skill at which they can outperform their teacher!

aspects of writing, nor do they provide worksheet exercises for the students to complete. The skills are more likely to be addressed in the context of their students' current writing, and through brief lessons interspersed with other activities.

Lessons of 10 minutes' duration are usually more effective than drills and worksheet pages of exercises. It is the context of the usage and the relevance to the child that make an impact on their learning. Skills learned out of context are rarely transferred to writing completed in workshops or to writing done across curricular areas. If a number of children in the class have problems in one specific area, a group can be formed so that the teacher can give direct instruction to those who need it. There is no point in teaching to a whole class if only a few children really need to learn that skill. Through reading children's writing, and through listening to the talk children engage in while they write, teachers can gain much useful knowledge about who needs to be taught certain skills and who has already mastered them.

The presence of *spell-check tools* on computer word processing programs provides both advantages and disadvantages for students. Before working with the tools, students need guidance in using them effectively and appropriately. Students can be encouraged to use the tool as a first step in eliminating typographical errors and in identifying misspelled words. Following this, students must check for homonyms and homophones. Which word did they actually intend to use? The computer does not make distinctions of this nature and will not catch such misspellings. Here, the spell-check tool provides an interesting focus for instruction, teaching students an awareness of homonyms and homophones as spelling items *and* teaching young writers not to rely on computer spell-checkers completely. The program will also not make up for the misspelling of an intended word that is another, different word, for example "fog" instead of "frog." It's up to the writer to proofread the piece for these kinds of errors. Many spell-check tools have an "auto-correct" feature that individual children (or the class as a collaborative whole) might want to program with their own frequent misspellings. Again, this process provides a vehicle for instruction as students identify their common misspellings and focus their attention on them.

Following are some specific strategies for aiding students in their spelling development:

- Ask students to write on every other line of a paper so that they can make changes without rewriting or erasing.

- Encourage writers to leave blank spaces for words they do not know how to spell. It is important that thoughts continue to flow; omitted words can be inserted later. Students can be encouraged to write the first few letters of the omitted word so they will have a greater chance of remembering which word they had intended to use.

- Note spelling errors by putting an asterisk in the margin of students' writing. Ask the students to find the errors themselves. Children can frequently recognize incorrect spelling, and in doing so they are reminded of the words they have difficulty in spelling.

- Encourage children to have paper at their desks so that words they are unsure of can be written down for them.

- Refrain from providing only an oral spelling of a word; always accompany it with a written model. Spelling is essentially a visual memory activity that is only conducted in writing. It is therefore important that students *see* the word they need help in spelling.

- Teach students how to use a dictionary, thesaurus, and other word books effectively, and encourage their use. A spelling dictionary is usually more effective for elementary school students than a conventional dictionary. A student who needs to spell *rein* will usually look under *ra* in a conventional dictionary, thus meeting with little success.

- Alphabet games help students to understand how dictionaries and encyclopedias are organized. Activities such as lining up in alphabetical order according to last name or first name also help children understand how to use telephone books and other reference aids.

The Direct Teaching of Spelling

Research studies have demonstrated that new and different words enter the language on an ongoing basis. Dictionaries are updated regularly, but many of the new words they contain will appear in children's writing first. Ves Thomas' landmark Canadian study (1979) showed that *more* words were used in children's writing in the late 1970s than were used 40 years before that time. Since 1979, language has changed enormously, largely through advances in science and technology that have brought new words and phrases into everyday use; words such as *mouse*, *windows*, *Internet*, *microchip*, and *browser*. At the same time these words have entered the lexicon, there has been a shift in the way writing is taught in elementary schools. Children are encouraged to write about what they do and what they think, bringing more of the child's personal world into the classroom. Characters from video games and movies now appear in children's stories, increasing the number of words children must learn to spell correctly. Children are using more words, are writing more, and are attempting to spell a greater range of words than in the past.

Spelling competence is relatively easy to test; a word list can be dictated to a student, and the examiner can check to see whether the words are spelled correctly. However, words spelled correctly on a word list do not necessarily transfer to a piece of writing created in a different context. Unless the words have been internalized and become part of the stored knowledge a writer possesses, the spelling remains in doubt. Spelling a word correctly on a test list is no guarantee that the same word will be spelled correctly in a shopping list, a journal entry, a letter, or an essay.

Adding to the problem is the fact that spelling textbooks generally do not present the teaching of spelling in ways that are consistent with research findings about learning to spell. Activities in spelling textbooks generally do not encourage risk-taking, which is a critical component of learning, and they encourage students to rely on rote memorization. Many of the activities in textbooks are repetitive and rarely help poor spellers become strong spellers. The books often contain "busy" pages with mixtures of cartoon graphics, bold colours, and many different fonts. There are frequently so many different activities on one page that it is difficult to tell what is being taught. Activities range from crossword puzzles to "Alphaspell," "Noun Hunt," "Syllable Count," "Letter Ladders," and "Word Chains." Research has shown many times that the only real way to become an effective speller is to do lots of writing for audiences other than oneself, read widely, and check spelling in a dictionary or word book whenever there is doubt. Even the most recent spelling textbooks do not focus on *teaching* spelling, but focus instead on children's word games. Teachers must ask, "What am I teaching by doing these activities, and what else could I do with this time that would be more beneficial to my students in learning how to be good spellers?"

A number of good resources are available to assist teachers in helping their students become strong and independent spellers. These include *Spelling: Sharing the Secrets* (Scott, 1993), *The Spelling Teacher's Handbook* (Phenix, 2001), and *Words Their Way* (3rd ed.) (Bear, Invernizzi, Templeton & Johnston, 2004).

Children are more likely to become effective spellers if their motives for using correct spelling stem from communicative needs rather than a desire to please the teacher. If children have something important to say, and they have an audience they wish to address, correct spelling will help them convey their message clearly to the reader. Correct spelling is a courtesy to the reader, and is also important in transmitting a clear message. Correct spelling adds to the writer's credibility. This is especially important for teachers, who are generally perceived as role models. Teachers are expected to spell every word correctly (if a word is spelled incorrectly on a wall chart or on the chalkboard, one can almost guarantee that a visiting teacher or parent will notice it!), and certainly teachers should not send to parents or the public any of their writing that has not been carefully checked for correct spelling.

A Word List Approach

When employing a word list approach in the direct teaching of spelling, teachers ensure that they use

- a reliable word list created from either the words children in the classroom have difficulty spelling or from a reliable resource book such as Thomas (1979)
- a self-corrected pretest of 10 to 12 words
- a study procedure to ensure that children learn effective strategies for memorizing words
- "check tests" with a buddy throughout the week
- a mastery test of the entire list of words originally provided on day one
- a record of spelling achievement (on a chart at the back of the spelling scribbler)

Word Lists

When a teacher has observed children's writing and has identified those students needing direct spelling instruction (which would rarely be more than half the class), a word list approach is usually effective. The word list compiled by Ves Thomas, found in his book *Teaching Spelling: Canadian Word Lists and Instructional Techniques* (1979), remains one of the most reliable and thorough resources for teachers today. The word lists in the book are based on the frequency of usage of words in children's writing in Canada, so that the most frequently used words are on the word list for the youngest children (grade 2), and so on up through the grades. It is suggested that word lists and study procedures *not* be used with children before grade 2.

If teachers choose to create their own word lists, they may base them on the spelling errors they notice in the students' writing in their classroom. The use of either a preexisting list or a teacher-compiled list should provide an effective vehicle for students to study the correct spelling of words. It is not suggested that children learn spelling from lists of words compiled from current units of study across the curriculum. Words on such lists are usually used for only a short period of time, when the unit is being studied, and the words are not usually the most frequently used words in the students' writing in general. The most important factors in creating a word list are that the words be relevant to children's lives and be used regularly in their writing.

Many studies have been conducted on the most frequently used words in both adult and children's writing. It has been found that the most common 100 words used by elementary school children in their writing make up about 60 percent of all the words children write. The most common 500 words make up 70 percent of all words written, and the most common 2000 words make up 83 percent of all words written (Simpson, 1980). The average elementary school program teaches between 3500 and 4500 words over a five-year period. It is therefore essential that the words taught on those lists form part of a child's *core* spelling vocabulary. The remainder of the words children use in their writing have to be learned by memory from the simple experience of writing them and checking for correct spelling in dictionaries and other word books. Thomas' research finding (1979) that Canadian children

TABLE 9.2 The 100 Most Frequently Used Words in Children's Writing

a	find	like	over	up
about	first	little	people	use
after	for	long	said	very
all	from	made	see	was
an	has	make	she	water
and	have	many	so	way
are	he	may	some	we
as	her	more	than	were
at	him	most	that	what
be	his	my	the	when
been	how	no	their	where
but	I	not	them	which
by	if	now	then	who
called	in	of	there	why
can	into	on	they	will
could	is	one	this	with
did	it	only	through	words
do	its	or	time	would
down	just	other	to	you
each	know	out	two	your

Source: Copyright © 1971 by Houghton Mifflin Company. Adapted and reproduced by permission from *The American Heritage Word Frequency Book*.

are using an increasing number of words in their writing has implications for the teaching of spelling, since it is not possible to teach all these words by memory in the five years of an elementary school spelling program. Table 9.2 displays one well-known list of the 100 words most frequently written by children in elementary school (Carroll, Davies, and Richman, 1971).

Self-Corrected Pretest

A word list is most effectively used when it is preceded by a self-corrected pretest. All the children in a spelling group are given a test *before* the words are presented to them in list form for study. This procedure allows children to identify which words they actually have difficulty spelling correctly. As children self-correct the pretest, they become aware of the spelling errors they have made, and this feature alone allows most children to correctly spell the word the next time they use it. The self-corrected pretest is probably the single most effective strategy for improving spelling ability. It provides each child with an individualized list of words that need to be studied, because the words spelled correctly can be put aside until the end of the week. At that time, a mastery test will be given that includes all the words on the original list.

It is very important that children correct their own pretest, for much learning occurs while they check their spelling. Sometimes only two or three words might be incorrectly spelled, and at other times there may be as many as five or six. If a child is presented with more than five or six words to study in one week, it is usually too many to be learned effectively. Children who experience difficulty in spelling need to work with small amounts of material and short lists of manageable words. In the early grades, a pretest of 10 words is usually sufficient. In upper elementary school, the list may include from 10 to 12 words.

Study Procedure

Words spelled incorrectly on the pretest are written out correctly and are used as a model for the study procedure (see Box 9.19). On the day following completion of the study procedure, students can work in pairs, giving each other buddy tests of their own personal spelling words. All students can benefit from learning a study procedure for spelling. There are many variations of study procedures, and if children do not have success with one version, they can try a modified version. For most children, the study procedure is a "key to the door" where successful spelling is concerned. Spelling is a visual memory task, and a good study procedure provides weak spellers with a concrete structure for their learning. A suggested study procedure is outlined in Box 9.19.

A sound study procedure eliminates the irrelevant and time-consuming activities sometimes found in spelling textbooks. It focuses the energies of the students on the direct learning of specific words that the individual finds difficult. There are likely to be occasions in the classroom when other methods of teaching spelling are necessary. For example, children with special needs may require alternative strategies that more specifically meet their learning requirements.

BOX 9.19   **SPELLING STUDY PROCEDURE**

1. Look at the word, pronounce it, and say the letters (auditory and visual stimulation).
2. Listen to the sounds and notice how they are represented (sound–symbol relationship).
3. Close your eyes and try to see the word as you pronounce it (recall–visualization).
4. Keep your eyes closed and say the letters in order.
5. Open your eyes and check.
6. Write the word without looking at the model. Check writing (kinesthetic recall).
7. Write the word a second time and check it.
8. Write the word a third time. If it's correct, consider it learned.

Mastery Test

A final mastery test given at the end of the week consists of the complete pretest list originally provided to the students at the beginning of the week. Spelling scores can be recorded on a chart at the back of a spelling scribbler so that children can track their own progress.

Spelling Practices to Avoid

Over the years, educators have become aware that some teaching strategies have not proven helpful in assisting children with improving their spelling:

- Pointing out the "hard spots" in words may be helpful only to a small number of children, and the hard spots are likely to be different from one child to another.

- Teaching spelling rules is not effective, since very few spelling rules can be applied regularly. Sayings such as "*i* before *e* except after *c*" may be very useful to most writers, but if they are taught as rules, then words that do not follow the rules must also be pointed out (such as *weigh* and *neighbour*). It is more effective to teach how to add suffixes (e.g., *baby* becomes *babies*) than it is to teach specific spelling rules. Most rules have almost as many exceptions as adherents (Clymer, 1963).

- Avoid having students copy spelling lists as a punishment, which establishes a negative attitude toward spelling that is not helpful to children's feelings about writing in general. Educators strive to promote enthusiasm for writing and try not to detract from the joys of writing by making writing, or any other school activity, abhorrent to children.

TEACHING GRAMMAR, PUNCTUATION, AND CAPITALIZATION

Grammar

As discussed in Chapter 2, educators often use the terms "grammar" and "syntax" interchangeably. *Syntax* is the term linguists use to describe the organization of language structures. **Grammar** is a term teachers usually use to define a prescriptive set of rules to be followed. Syntax is derived from the spoken language, but when it is taught in schools, it usually pertains to writing and is labelled "grammar." Educators and researchers have long believed that grammar should not be taught in elementary schools in a formal manner. However, children need to know the difference between what is acceptable or appropriate and what is considered poor grammar. They also need a vocabulary to be able to talk about language if they are to engage in writing conferences and develop an awareness of the writing techniques good writers use. Three basic perspectives on grammar are presented in Box 9.20.

The teaching of grammar, usually based on the traditional, prescriptive model, was once perceived as a core feature of the elementary school curriculum. Today it is relegated to a somewhat minor role. Only a few decades ago, memorizing grammar rules, as well as memorizing poetry and quotations from plays, was believed to be good for the mind. The mind was conceptualized as a muscle, and memorization as good exercise for that muscle. Today, however,

---

BOX 9.20   THREE PERSPECTIVES ON GRAMMAR

Linguists describe the structure of language in three ways, and all three ways influence the way grammar is taught.

1. The best known is *traditional* or *prescriptive grammar,* which provides rules for socially correct usage. This perspective dates back to the Middle Ages and has its roots in the study of Latin. The major contribution of traditional grammar is in the terminology it provides for students and teachers to talk about language. Because this form of grammar is based on Latin, it is not entirely appropriate for use with the English language, as it cannot adequately explain how language works. However, the three elements of grammar continue to be taught and prove useful to writers as they work their craft—types of sentences (declarative, interrogative, imperative, exclamatory); parts of sentences (simple, compound, complex, compound–complex); and parts of speech (nouns, pronouns, verbs, adverbs, adjectives, prepositions, conjunctions, and interjections).

2. *Structural grammar* attempts to describe how language is used. Structural grammar is not prescriptive, but descriptive, and it highlights the differences between written and spoken language patterns. The study of structural linguistics has provided detailed information about language in use, but it focuses on form and does not attempt to relate meaning to usage. Seven basic sentence patterns are identified, and it is the variations and combinations of these seven patterns that make up all the sentences people speak or write.

3. *Transformational grammar* is the most recent approach to the study of grammar. Transformational linguists attempt to describe both the way language works *and* the cognitive processes used to produce language. They refer to two levels or structures of language (the surface structure and the deep structure) to describe how meaning in the brain is transformed into the actual sentences people speak. Much research and development work was conducted during the 1960s and 1970s to make this approach viable for use in classrooms.

A thorough exploration of grammar and its teaching can be found in C. Weaver's *Teaching Grammar in Context* (Portsmouth, NH: Boynton/Cook, 1996).

---

grammar is not taught as an end in itself, but as one of the tools to be used in the process of writing. Knowledge and control of grammar enables writers to strengthen their writing and clarify meaning, facilitating effective and precise communication. Correct and appropriate grammar also enables people to speak in a manner approaching "standard English," the form of English that conforms to established educated usage and is generally considered correct.

Studies in language development have shown that many concerns voiced by teachers about "grammar" are mostly concerns about usage, and usage depends on the dialect learned when children are young. A person's dialect can change when he or she moves from one area to another, or works among people speaking a closer approximation of standard English. However, the basic rules of grammar learned in childhood usually persist throughout life, and the majority of those rules are correct. By the age of six, when most children enter school, they have already mastered most of the grammar of the language.

Controversy has arisen in the past about whether dialect is part of a child's cultural heritage, and therefore to be protected and respected, or whether educators have the responsibility to teach children standard English so that all children will have a greater opportunity for success in higher education, business, and the professions. It is generally agreed, however, that grammar should be taught in school so that children learn to become effective writers and have the opportunity to move between dialect and standard English in speech.

It has been acknowledged for many years that teaching grammar in isolation from a child's actual writing is ineffective. Creating teaching units and providing worksheets on grammar have little effect on children's writing and speaking. More effective learning occurs when grammar is taught as part of the editing process of composition, and in brief lessons when necessary. Children can sometimes detect grammatical errors in their compositions, especially if the flow of the language or the meaning is disturbed by the error. However, much of the time, children cannot detect their own grammatical errors because the writing makes sense to them.

As members of language communities, we accept certain phrases and incorrect usage as the norm, and it is difficult to teach children to change that usage. This is where a direct lesson is useful, because the whole group can focus on that particular item of usage and there is more likelihood that children will retain an awareness of it. One caution: students should at no time be embarrassed by their language usage. Language is an idiosyncratic part of every human being, and children (as well as adults) feel belittled if their language is criticized or faulted. Effective teachers handle this issue sensitively, aware that one dialect is not better than another, but different. Children can be taught that when playing with friends it may be acceptable to say "I should've went," but when they are in school their writing and oral language is expected to more closely adhere to standard English, and "I should've gone" is correct and appropriate. Likewise, students need to know that writing "should of" instead of "should have" is neither acceptable nor correct.

A lesson on the differences in usage between *taught* and *learned*, *lent* and *borrowed*, or *seed* and *saw* might, for example, be necessary in some classrooms. A lesson on misplaced participles can be fun for children in the elementary years, as they can see the humour in sentences such as "I saw the lady walking down the hill with purple hair," and they enjoy figuring out why the sentence is ambiguous as well as how to fix it. It is through meaning that grammar can be taught most effectively, not through parsing sentences or learning definitions of parts of speech.

Knowledge of labels and definitions of parts of speech allows writers and speakers to talk about the language they are using. It is in this context that these items can be taught in school. In writing conferences and during the editing process, labels such as noun, adverb, and clause can be used. Through direct lessons they can be taught to the entire class. A brief 10-minute presentation, using examples on an overhead projector and involving the children in discussion, can be effective in reminding children about grammar and usage and in introducing certain concepts to children for the first time. Lengthy lessons with exercises on worksheets are generally not necessary. It *is* necessary, though, for children to learn these labels and their meanings so they can talk about their writing and hence improve it.

Punctuation and Capitalization

Punctuation and capitalization are the "mechanics" of written language. Writing conferences and short lessons are the most effective and appropriate vehicles for teaching the skills of

CLASSROOM ACTIVITY

Quotation Marks

Farha is writing a story and wants to use dialogue for two of the characters. She stops in her writing at "Who's going to run for help and who's going to stay here she asked." Farha does not know where to place the quotation marks. The teacher can make an overhead transparency of a comic strip to demonstrate how quotation marks are used. Whenever the actual words spoken by a character are shown in a comic strip, they are inside a "balloon." In a story, quotation marks are used instead of a balloon. Only the actual words spoken belong inside the quotation marks. The teacher can demonstrate this with an overhead transparency of a section of a familiar story that includes dialogue. Working through Farha's original piece of writing, the class can work with the teacher, putting in the quotation marks where they belong. As in many other learning situations, a collaborative approach is helpful, since students can engage with the problem as a group rather than in isolation. Instead of a follow-up exercise to see if the children have understood, it is more effective to observe the children's writing and remind them, when necessary, about the lesson. Lessons can be repeated, using different examples, whenever appropriate.

punctuation and capitalization. As with grammar and word usage, worksheets of drill and skill exercises are not effective. During instruction, it is useful to refer children to the literature they are currently reading. Novels provide a quick reference for checking how direct speech, paragraphing, and the capitalization of names and places are addressed. Children often remember rules of capitalization and punctuation for a short time after they have been taught, but then forget to use them when they are composing and focusing on ideas. Lessons are enhanced when teachers make them directly relevant to situations that affect the students—for example, through using samples of children's writing or questions children have raised themselves. It is a good idea to refer to these questions and honour their intent. Children who ask questions are the ones who want to learn.

TEACHING HANDWRITING

It might appear, in the early years of the 21st century, that handwriting is a lost art. Certainly, the fine penmanship recognized in our grandparents is not evident in the handwriting of most students in today's classrooms. In fact, the focus of instruction has shifted from penmanship to composition, and without a doubt, the use of the keyboard has changed the amount of handwriting we do. Yet most of the writing done by elementary students in classrooms today is still done by hand, and not on a keyboard. For adults as well as children, notes, jottings, journal entries, memos, and greeting cards are usually handwritten. The need to teach handwriting in elementary school still exists so that children can produce legible script with a minimum of *time*, *effort*, and *concentration* (the three criteria that are key to teaching handwriting). Students need to be able to read their own handwriting, and we all need to be able to read the handwriting of others.

Some points for teachers to remember:

- Students are greatly helped if they are taught to write in a way that is fluent, easy, routine, and comfortable.

- A teacher who pays little attention to handwriting is suggesting to students that handwriting is not important.

- The true test of handwriting is in situations where it is used on a day-to-day basis, doing such regular jobs as making lists, writing notes, leaving messages, and writing letters.

- In handwriting instruction, good teaching and modelling are essential, not just in the early grades but throughout elementary school.

- A teacher's handwriting on the chalkboard, on wall charts, and on student work is a model for students of how letters are formed and what good writing looks like.

Printing and Cursive Handwriting

Two styles of handwriting are taught in elementary school: **printing** (also called **manuscript** writing) and **cursive** writing. Children generally begin with printing, and toward the end of grade 2 or the beginning of grade 3 they move into a cursive hand. The specific styles of each vary according to region and country. In North America there are a number of popular cursive styles, including D'Nealian (described below). Box 9.21 presents a comparison between traditional script (manuscript and cursive) and D'Nealian script. While some Canadian curricula have a model of handwriting to be followed, increasingly provincial departments of education are not providing a model script. Curriculum guides and programs of study should be consulted before any handwriting style is taught, as it is important that students have a consistent style across the grades.

Children generally learn manuscript printing in the primary grades because it is easier to learn, and simpler to copy than cursive or "connected" handwriting. The clear circles and horizontal and vertical lines are easier for children to control. Printing is also easy to read and is close in form to the print children see in their reading materials. Toward the end of grade 2 many children are eager to begin cursive handwriting and some will begin to make the transition on their own. Other children will not be comfortable with cursive script until well into grade 3. Many children today are expressing a preference for continuing to print, some reverting to manuscript printing in the later grades. There is no particular reason why they should move into cursive handwriting other than that it is an accepted adult convention.

One of the advantages of D'Nealian script is that it was developed specifically to make the transition from printing to handwriting easier for children. A simplified form that flows from manuscript to cursive with little change in letter form, this script is extremely legible and easy to use. Most other styles of cursive handwriting are more difficult for children, and specific lessons on individual letters have to be taught. Children working with D'Nealian or similar scripts usually move into cursive writing toward the middle of grade 2. With D'Nealian script, the formation, size, slant, and rhythm learned in kindergarten and grade 1 are continued and built upon in grades 2 and 3. As a result, grade 2 and 3 students don't have to "start over" when they begin learning cursive forms.

BOX 9.21 **D'NEALIAN SCRIPT**

Traditional		D'Nealian		Traditional		D'Nealian	
a	_a_	_a_	_a_	n	_n_	_n_	_n_
b	_b_	_b_	_b_	o	_o_	_o_	_o_
c	_c_	_c_	_c_	p	_p_	_p_	_p_
d	_d_	_d_	_d_	q	_q_	_q_	_q_
e	_e_	_e_	_e_	r	_r_	_r_	_r_
f	_f_	_f_	_f_	s	_s_	_s_	_s_
g	_g_	_g_	_g_	t	_t_	_t_	_t_
h	_h_	_h_	_h_	u	_u_	_u_	_u_
i	_i_	_i_	_i_	v	_v_	_v_	_v_
j	_j_	_j_	_j_	w	_w_	_w_	_w_
k	_k_	_k_	_k_	x	_x_	_x_	_x_
l	_l_	_l_	_l_	y	_y_	_y_	_y_
m	_m_	_m_	_m_	z	_z_	_z_	_z_

Source: D'Nealian® alphabet. © 1993, 1999 by Scott, Foresman. Reprinted by permission of Addison-Wesley Educational Publishers Inc.

Teaching Letter Forms

Handwriting is more than simply a motor skill, fine muscle coordination, and practice. Children have to remember letter forms, somehow internalizing them. Each child has to build a mental image of each letter. It is a thinking process as well as a fine motor process. In the early years of schooling, children must have a clear concept of how each letter appears, saying out loud how each letter is formed, while at the same time drawing it. The same process is used in teaching both manuscript printing and cursive writing. Steps in the instructional process are described in Box 9.22.

A guided practice of the manuscript letter *d* might go as follows: Pencil on the midline, go counterclockwise, round to the baseline, back up through the midline, up to the headline,

> **BOX 9.22** **STEPS IN TEACHING HANDWRITING**

▷ The teacher models handwriting instruction on the board (or an overhead projector). Clear lines are drawn on the board so that children can see the spacing of letters and the lines on which they are positioned.

▷ The teacher uses a consistent writing vocabulary such as *baseline, midline, headline,* and *tail-line.*

▷ As the teacher draws a letter on the board, he or she describes where the letter begins, the direction in which the hand moves, and the place where the letter ends.

▷ The children describe aloud the strokes the teacher is using as the teacher draws the letter again.

▷ The children draw the letter, saying aloud the description as they write, while being guided by the teacher.

▷ After the letter is completed, the children compare the letter they have drawn with a model already on paper at their desks.

retrace down to the baseline. Stop. This would be repeated a number of times until the children begin to master the letter.

A model of the letter on each child's desk provides immediate feedback as the child compares the written letter with the model. An example of one model is presented in Box 9.23. The teacher attends to the number of strokes, the starting and stopping points, the direction of the strokes, and the size of the letters. The process should not be repeated more than five times during each practice session, or handwriting will lose quality—one good reason for not having children write lines or copy tedious work as a punishment.

The approach can be used for teaching cursive writing in much the same way as with printing. However, a new vocabulary has to be used to describe the strokes necessary. Children beginning cursive writing become familiar with terms such as *undercurve, overcurve, downcurve,* and *horizontal curve.* These are the strokes necessary for linking letters to create a fluid handwriting style. The most difficult aspect of learning cursive handwriting for most children is forming capital letters. This is the area in which children generally need most guidance and practice. It is not unusual for adults to use a simplified version of cursive capital letters (and often they print them).

In the intermediate grades, children may not need handwriting lessons every week, but they do need them from time to time, when the teacher can see that some children are having difficulty with a certain letter or letter combination. A lesson on the overhead projector can result in improvements in children's awareness of their handwriting and in penmanship legibility. These lessons are sometimes referred to as "maintenance lessons."

Evaluation of handwriting considers

- the form and size of the letters
- the spacing of letters and words
- alignment according to headline and baseline
- uniformity of slant

BOX 9.23 **MODEL OF WRITING: *S* FOR SNOOPY**

Many handwriting scales are available for evaluating handwriting, but most do not allow for individuality in writing style. The criteria listed above are usually sufficient for providing feedback to a student and for talking about ways in which handwriting can be improved.

Helping the Left-Handed Writer

Approximately 10 percent of children in North America are left-handed. Although educators no longer insist that children write with their right hand (as was once the case), learning to write can still pose challenges for children who are left-handed. These children have unique instructional needs because of the nature of writing in the English language. English is written from left to right, thus creating a movement of the arm away from the body for right-handed children. Left-handed children physically move their arm toward their body as they write. In addition, as left-handed writers move their arm, they cover up what they have just written. Not only do they have no clear visual image of what they have written, but in covering up their writing they are also more likely to smudge their work and have further difficulty in rereading their script. Since their writing is covered by their hand, left-handed children cannot read their writing as they go, but have to stop and move their arm to reread their script.

Teachers can help left-handed children to write clearly and legibly without discomfort, developing a hand that requires a minimum of time, effort, and concentration. This is particularly important because, in order to produce clean copy and be able to read their work as they write, left-handed children frequently develop a "hooked" motion, curling their wrist over the top of the page and distorting the motions necessary to form letters. Left-handed writers may therefore require more one-on-one instruction from the teacher than right-handed writers, but sensitive teachers understand that this is necessary if the students are to be given the opportunity to develop handwriting that is legible, well-formed, evenly spaced, and with a uniform slant.

Here are some suggestions to help left-handed children at school and at home:

- Make sure the child is holding the pencil correctly—about three to four centimetres from the point and with the correct grasp by the fingers (i.e., further away from the point than right-handed writers).

- Position the paper so that it is tilted downward at the right-hand side. This allows for an even slant and lets the child see what he or she has already written. Some teachers have found it helpful to place a piece of masking tape on the student's desk to indicate an appropriate tilt.

- Try to prevent the development of a "hooked" wrist—the habit of hooking the wrist around the writing—so as not to cover up what has been written.

- Seat the child so that light comes over the *right* shoulder and therefore the shadow of the hand does not fall on the writing.

- Provide children who need it with a lower desk surface to write on, or a cushion so that they can be higher in their seat and have a clearer view of their work.

- Do not insist on a slant to the right in letter formation. Many left-handed children write more effectively with a vertical formation.

KEYBOARDING AND TECHNOLOGY SKILLS

Merchant (2005) writes that young children explore computers, cell phones, and video games with great interest, and need little assistance from adults in figuring out how they work. Sometimes, they demonstrate an impressive sophistication in their knowledge of digital technology. They appear to be familiar with the basic operational concepts of these devices well before they are of school age. Merchant observed children in a preschool setting (ages three and four) in the United Kingdom, and noted how the children were willing to explore and experiment and had no fear of technology. They would frequently play at text messaging on a phone or at using a mouse and clicking on an Internet site.

Merchant discovered that Clay's principles of writing (e.g., the recurring principle and the flexibility principle) are just as evident on the computer as they are when children use paper and pencil. In addition, Merchant added some new principles for writing on screen. These include the "gaze principle"—children have to know where to look on the screen, where to focus their gaze—and the selection and pressure principles. The latter two refer to the keyboarding skills required; where to apply pressure and for how long.

Researchers have shown that children who use a word processor for writing are more motivated to write, write more, and incur fewer spelling errors (D'Odorico & Zammuner, 1993;

Hetzroni & Shrieber, 2004). Other research (Preminger, Weiss & Weintraub, 2004) shows that handwriting and keyboarding entail different skills, but that keyboarding may be an alternative for students with handwriting difficulties. Some adults still express concerns about what technologies are appropriate for young children, but when the emphasis is moved away from technology and placed on meaning making and communication, it makes much more sense to integrate digital and media literacies with paper and pencil literacy. They exist side by side in the world young children inhabit outside of school. School literacy should be no different.

At school, at work, and at home, word processing programs provide an alternative transcription tool to handwriting. Much more writing is done on word processing programs now than is done by hand. Over the years, there has been debate about when it is appropriate to teach children basic keyboarding skills. Most Canadian provincial ministries of education have mandated ICT programs of study. The Alberta ICT Program of Studies (2000) is not meant to be a "standalone" document. ICT skills are to be infused across the curriculum, and learned by children through their use in purposeful situations. The document lists the following outcomes relevant to writing on the screen for Division 1 (grades K–3):

- perform basic computer operations including moving the cursor, clicking on an icon, using pull-down menus, saving files, retrieving files, printing, and closing down

- use proper keyboarding techniques for the home row, enter, spacebar, tab, backspace, delete, and insertion point arrow keys

- create original text, using word processing software, to communicate and demonstrate understanding of forms and techniques

- edit complete sentences, using such features as cut, copy, and paste

In Division 2 (grades 4–6) the outcomes include:

- use appropriate keyboarding techniques for the alphabetic and punctuation keys

- create and revise original text to communicate and demonstrate understanding of forms and techniques

- edit and format text to clarify and enhance meaning, using such word processing features as thesaurus, find/change, text alignment, font size, and font style

Teaching basic keyboarding skills is no longer an option for teachers. Many children will learn these skills at home, but many will not. It is especially important that ICT skills are taught to children who come from homes where computers may not be available for children to play and work on. Computer access remains an issue for children from lower-income families, and as such, ICT can privilege some children over others.

Keyboarding programs for children are numerous and information about programs and why such programs are valuable can be found on websites such as Typing for Kids Software Review (http://typing-for-kids-software-review.toptenreviews.com). Wayne McNamara uses the program All the Right Type 3.6 (2007) by Ingenuity Works in his school. The students love it because it incorporates games and a futuristic campus into the lessons that teach sequential keyboarding skills, realistic posture, correct fingering, and speed. Sunburst's Typing to Learn 3 is designed for grades 3 to 12, and includes 25 lessons in an animated program. The free online program Dance Mat Typing on the BBC Schools website (http://www.bbc.co.uk/schools/typing), is an introduction to touch typing for children aged 7 to 11 accessible to children at home as well as in school.

Keyboarding and handwriting habits formed in the early years of schooling frequently persist into adulthood. It is therefore essential that these skills be taught effectively in the elementary school, with emphasis placed on legibility and comfort in writing. The example teachers set in their own handwriting and keyboarding has an impact on children. Teachers' writing on the chalkboard should therefore be clear and legible, for, as with spelling and computer use, teachers are the primary models.

TEACHER WISDOM

WAYNE McNAMARA

As a "fourth year teacher," you are still close to those early experiences of having a classroom of your own. What is the most important piece of advice you would give to pre-service teachers?

I know you can't do this as a pre-service teacher but once you have your own classroom, know the curriculum; know the Program of Studies; know the learning outcomes for your grade level. Make yourself familiar with them over the first couple of years you are in a classroom. When you begin teaching you cannot know all the outcomes in the Language Arts Program of Studies. Accept this and then make sure that you learn them. They're key to everything you do with your students and they're key to what you comment on in the report cards.

Can you tell us what you have found to be the biggest challenge in teaching writing?

When I started teaching I was really apprehensive about assessing students' writing. I didn't consider myself to be a particularly good writer, and so I didn't think I'd be able to provide the instructional support the children needed. I just decided the best way to get going was to jump right in. I often wrote alongside the kids and before every writing session, we'd talk about ideas for the writing. We shared our writing together, talking about what had come easily to us, and what we needed to work hard at. Over the months, I started to see which students excelled at writing and which students needed a lot of support. I kept notes for myself in a logbook. I had a page for each student and wrote notes as a reminder of what each student was writing about and how they were progressing. They were just anecdotal observations of their writing and writing processes, or notes about a conversation I'd had with the child. I'd try to find time to sit with some students while they wrote so that I could see what they did, and what challenged them the most. That really helped me when it came time to do reports, but it also helped me to understand what kind of support the students needed from me.

Do you have any advice on organizing your classroom for instruction?

At first it was hard for me to know how to group students. I saw pretty quickly that they could be very dependent on me and I didn't have the time to be able to help every single student at all times of the day. What I found out was that sometimes it worked best to have the students select their own group to work in, but at other times, I selected the groups. It depends on the kind of work they're doing. If they're doing a novel study, they can select the group they want to be in according to the novel, and generally they support each other really well. But if I want a group to help each other with writing and conduct conferences with each other, then I select the group so that there is leadership within the group and I don't have to be there all the time. I have to be careful to provide support to the good writers, though, so that they are also well supported and so that they are not always the ones called upon to help the more dependent writers.

Any final words?

Yes. Be well prepared! Know what you want to teach and why. I was constantly pressed for time the first couple of years I was teaching. I felt as though I could never fit everything in. Now I'm much better organized and I see how things fit together, how you can actually do two things at once in your writing or reading program. I've learned what books the kids really like and I've learned about some of the resources that are out there to help me as a teacher. I've also learned how valuable my colleagues are and I've found one or two teachers that are superb and who are willing to spend time with me and help me when I need advice or help with anything at all.

SUMMARY

Assessments of student writing abilities are undertaken for four purposes: to inform teachers' instructional practices, to inform students of their progress and the areas on which they need to focus future learning, to inform parents of their children's progress, and to inform school administration and school districts about the competencies of the children in their schools. Although formal measures provide accountability for teachers, assessment is most valuable for the ways in which it helps teachers to meet the needs of individual learners. As teachers assess their students' writing abilities, they gain direct information as to what they need to teach and reteach and how they might conduct that instruction. Appropriate assessment of student writing provides invaluable feedback to teachers on what students need to learn and what teachers need to teach.

Composing a written text is a complex process. The criteria for determining *good* writing varies according to gender, personality, social group, and culture. In their instruction and assessment of student writing, teachers show respect for the idiosyncratic nature of the writing process and value both the written products and the writing processes of individual students. In constructivist classrooms, teachers focus on a wide range of writing abilities and recognize that there is no one way to evaluate children's writing, nor one mark or grade that adequately represents a student's writing development or abilities.

Writing assessments can be informal or formal, formative or summative. Informal assessment usually consists of process strategies that attempt to record the writing behaviours and attitudes of the students as well as the written product itself. Data is collected through observations, anecdotal notes, conferences, conversations with parents, portfolios of written work, checklists, and writing profiles, as well as through careful reading of writing samples. Teachers make informal assessments on the basis of their reviews of collections of student writing samples in different genres—poetry, stories, learning log entries, reports, letters, persuasive pieces, explanations, response journal entries, and more.

More formal assessments of student abilities are undertaken through holistic analysis of writing samples or through the more analytic criteria-based scales. Holistic scoring is a guided procedure for sorting and ranking pieces according to general criteria or by matching them with other pieces of writing from the same class of students. Criteria-based scoring assesses writing according to component parts such as voice, vocabulary, sentence structure, conventions of written language, development, and organization.

Many students learn to use the conventional transcription tools (including spelling, punctuation, capitalization, and usage) as they engage in the writing process or as teachers provide feedback during editing or writing conferences. Alternatively, these skills can be taught through direct instruction based on the children's own writing and their questions and challenges. Many students will require multiple lessons using direct instruction: demonstration, guided practice, individual application, and assessment. Teachers use a range of strategies to reteach a concept or skill until they are reasonably certain the students have successfully learned it. Children in kindergarten through grade 2 continue to use invented spelling as they explore the written symbol system and the graphophonic system. Sound–symbol relationships are complex in the English language, and most children take a number of years to move entirely into standard spelling. Direct instruction in spelling is advised for children who experience particular difficulties in the area, but only in grade 2 or later. Word lists with a study procedure and mastery test remain the most effective means of direct instruction.

Handwriting is taught regularly and often in the primary grades, but students in the intermediate grades also require maintenance lessons occasionally. An instructional approach can be used throughout the grades that requires students to verbalize letter descriptions or say them silently as they draw the letters. A handwriting model at each student's desk is invaluable. Teachers' own handwriting, particularly their writing on the chalkboard, has a major influence on how students value handwriting and strive to achieve a legible hand. The aim of handwriting lessons is for each student to achieve legible handwriting with a minimum of time, effort, and concentration. An alternative transcription tool is the computer word processing program. Because so much of our writing is now done on the screen, children need to be taught basic keyboarding and other computer skills from the primary grades onwards. Teachers are responsible for teaching the provincial ICT Programs of Studies, and for infusing digital technologies across the curriculum, including in the language arts.

Young children bring to school a vast store of knowledge about language and how it is used. Teachers plan programs that allow children to use this knowledge to communicate with a wide range of audiences for a variety of purposes. An integral component of that writing program is teaching the conventions of written language. Without a working knowledge of these conventions, compositions cannot be as effective as their writers would wish. Much of the empowerment of writing comes from its precision, clarity, and imagery, whether in a novel, journal, poem, or report.

TALKING POINTS

1. What are the "essentials" of writing? Are you ready to teach these essentials in your classroom? What do you think children need to learn about becoming good writers? Are these the things you will assess in their writing and provide feedback on? How will you conduct that assessment and provide that feedback?

2. How might you keep a portfolio of student literacy work right from the beginning of the school year? How can you plan for this and keep writing samples in a systematic way? How many samples would you want to have in the folder before the first report cards are due?

3. How can you ensure that your students have access to computers on a regular basis in the classroom and learn basic keyboarding skills as they write? Are you prepared to provide some direct lessons in keyboarding for them?

4. Are you well informed about teaching handwriting? Have you assumed that someone else will have taught your students how to have a legible and comfortable handwriting style? Are you ready to provide direct lessons in handwriting? Have you practiced your own handwriting so that children can read it? Have you practised writing on the chalkboard *and* the whiteboard so that your printing is legible in both chalk and felt pen? Can you keep a straight line of writing as you move across the board?

5. Are you prepared to admit that your spelling might not be perfect? Who can you ask to check your spelling before you send notes home to parents? Who can you ask to proofread wall charts? Are you aware of how incorrect spelling is socially unacceptable in a teacher and is often used as an indication, in society as a whole, that a person is not well educated?

RECOMMENDED PROFESSIONAL RESOURCES

Eileen Loughlin suggests ...

Fountas, I. & Pinnell, G. S. (2001). *Guiding readers and writers, grades 3 to 6: Teaching comprehension, genre and content literacy.* Portsmouth, NH: Heinemann.

Even though this book is designed for grades 3 to 6, I find it very useful in grade 2. It really shows you how to organize your classroom; for example, what to do in the first 20 days of a writing workshop. It provides a good scaffold for teachers because it provides the theoretical framework and the practical application. It uses children's literature and authors' lives as a way of getting to know children's books. It prepares children for tests and shows teachers how to do assessments. It became my "bible" when I became a literacy coordinator, and I started keeping a writer's notebook on account of the recommendations in the book. It's an excellent resource.

> Kendall, J. & Khuon, O. (2006). *Writing sense: Integrated reading and writing lessons for English language learners, K–8*. Portland, ME: Stenhouse Publishers.

Because the book is intended primarily for students learning English as a second language, it is applicable across all the grades. It gives a big picture of the conditions necessary for successful writing instruction, including how all the parts fit together and how specific strategies can be used. It includes lesson plans as examples, and focuses on best practices. The book presents a three-day writing assessment that I found extremely useful—what to assess over a three-day period. It's applicable to students at all levels of language learning, so it's a very handy book to have.

Wayne McNamara recommends …

> Culham, R. (2003). *Theory and practice: 6 + 1 Traits of Writing, the complete guide grades 3 and up*. New York: Scholastic.

I've found this resource especially helpful in my first few years of teaching, because it breaks writing into traits and allows teachers and students to think about one trait at a time as they are teaching/learning. These traits are very similar to the criteria the provincial achievement tests use. Even though grade 4 is not involved in the PATs, it was helpful for me to look at one trait at a time and see not only how I could teach that trait in my grade 4 class, but how I could assess it. It was through reading about each trait individually that I came to a better understanding of what I was trying to teach and what I meant by good writing. The book contains samples of student writing at different grades and levels, and then presents descriptive assessments of each piece. There's a scoring guide for each trait, and instead of using letter scores you can use a number score, which helps when you're doing report cards.

> Alberta Assessment Consortium. Available: http://www.aac.ab.ca.

This website has been really useful to me, mainly in informing me of just how many different assessment processes and resources are available to teachers. I can trust the material presented on this website—and the links to other sites are excellent—because it is a nonprofit collaboration across a large number of school boards and the Alberta Trustees Association. The site connects teachers to a range of assessment materials, professional development opportunities, and networks with other agencies. The site also has on it principles of fair assessment and how to communicate evaluations.

Children's Literature for the Classroom

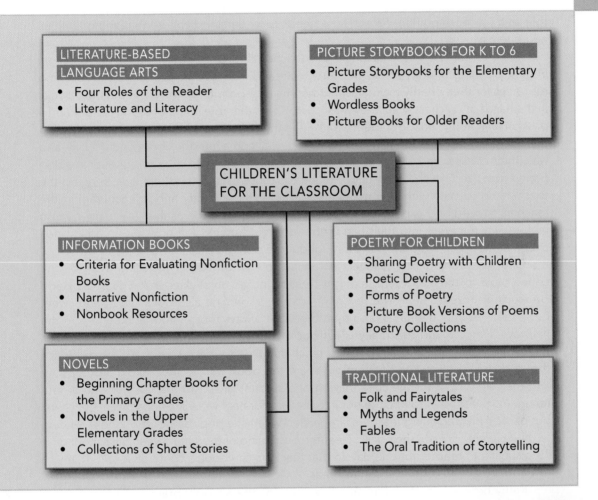

CHAPTER 10

LITERATURE-BASED LANGUAGE ARTS
- Four Roles of the Reader
- Literature and Literacy

PICTURE STORYBOOKS FOR K TO 6
- Picture Storybooks for the Elementary Grades
- Wordless Books
- Picture Books for Older Readers

CHILDREN'S LITERATURE FOR THE CLASSROOM

INFORMATION BOOKS
- Criteria for Evaluating Nonfiction Books
- Narrative Nonfiction
- Nonbook Resources

POETRY FOR CHILDREN
- Sharing Poetry with Children
- Poetic Devices
- Forms of Poetry
- Picture Book Versions of Poems
- Poetry Collections

NOVELS
- Beginning Chapter Books for the Primary Grades
- Novels in the Upper Elementary Grades
- Collections of Short Stories

TRADITIONAL LITERATURE
- Folk and Fairytales
- Myths and Legends
- Fables
- The Oral Tradition of Storytelling

TEACHER/LIBRARIAN KATHY OSTER

Kathy Oster is quite convinced that when elementary school students are learning complex and sophisticated concepts and ideas, whether in mathematics, social studies, or music, they need stories to make those ideas real and relevant to them. Kathy is a rich source of information on books and stories that connect to the program of studies in every one of the content areas taught in the elementary grades. She has lists of books relevant to a wide range of subjects and themes, and she can access them at a few moments' notice. Kathy also knows her school library well, and can take teachers and students directly to the books they are searching for. She is the person responsible for

Kathy Oster

selecting books to order, both on the recommendation of teachers and from her own browsing of catalogues and websites for the latest high-quality materials (e.g., United Library Services, http://www.uls.com/ULS/index2.jsp, and National Book Service, http://www.nbs.com/choiceawd.htm). Knowing the K–6 curriculum is crucial in her role as a teacher/librarian. As well, she needs to understand children's reading abilities and interests.

Kathy has three major roles to fulfil as a teacher/librarian. One is in supporting teachers in their planning of units across the curriculum and in locating and assembling teaching resources for them. Kathy maintains that her main responsibility is "to put the right books in the hands of teachers when they need them." Another role is in promoting literacy and a passion for reading among students. Kathy is in the unique position of meeting and getting to know every single student in her school. They all come into the library, individually, and with their classes, and she is able to get to know their ways of reading, their reading preferences, and which books might pique their interests. A third role is in bringing the teachers up to date with new materials available in the library and in encouraging the teachers to read and experience more children's literature themselves—actually getting high-quality materials into their hands (interestingly, Kathy's staff now has an adult book club that meets on a regular basis throughout the school year).

One way Kathy directs teachers' attention to new books is by placing them on the coffee table in the staff room, along with short notes on stickies that indicate a good curricular fit or reason why she recommends the book. She also does "short and sweet book talks" at staff meetings, and then there are always those informal meetings in the hallway: "Hey, I found this really great book that will complement your social studies topic." Physically handing the book to teachers helps to make sure the book will reach the students. Alternatively, Kathy might share the book with a class during literacy time and then sign it out for the class, having one student give it to the teacher with a note reminding the teacher to add the book to their list for next year. She finds that all teachers, but particularly beginning teachers, are thrilled when she pops a bucket of books relating to their current topic on their desk. Near the beginning of the school year, the school pays for a substitute teacher for one day so that teachers can book a conference with Kathy to talk about their needs for the coming year.

Kathy orders lots of children's magazines for the school library, including *Ranger Rick, Owl, Chirp, Chickadee, Your Big Backyard* (National Wildlife Federation, ages 3–7), *Sports Illustrated for Kids, Zoobooks,* and *Highlights.* She orders multiple copies, as these magazines go through many small hands. When asked about children's favourite books, Kathy commented that picture books are enjoyed right across the grades, and she noted *The Stranger* by Chris Van Allsburg (1986) and *The Giving Tree* by Shel Silverstein (1964). One of her own favourites for reading aloud to children is *Dawn* (Bang, 1983) based on a Japanese folktale. The younger children love the "Stella" series of books by Marie Louise Gay. The most requested novels these days are *The Tale of Despereaux* (DiCamillo, 2004), and all of Cornelia Funke's books (especially by the boys). At the present time, the boys are also enjoying graphic novels and the girls increasingly request historical fiction. Favourite books of historical fiction are those by Kit Pearson, Patricia Reilly Giff (e.g., *Lily's Crossing,* 1997), *Number the Stars* (Lowry, 1989), *Sadako and the Thousand Paper Cranes* (1977), and *Hana's Suitcase* (Levine, 2002).

Kathy's own favourite picture books include *My Lucky Day* (Kasza, 2003) and *Wolves* (Gravett, 2005). Some other personal favourites are *The Moccasins* (Einarson, 2004), a very short paperback book about an Aboriginal boy who is in a foster home, and *The Family Book* (2003) and *The Peace Book* (2004) by Todd Parr, both with bright, colourful cartoon illustrations. □

Take a few moments to think about your own reading history. Do you remember learning how to read? Some of your early reading experiences might have been in school, others at home. Some might have involved teachers and librarians, while other memories may be of grandparents, older siblings, and parents sharing stories and books with you. Many people can remember the exact moment when they knew they could read by themselves. Others feel they could always read and have very few specific memories. Some people, including teachers, struggled to learn to read and have some powerful memories of those difficult times. What are some of the earliest stories and books you can recall? Where did you read? Did you visit a library? Did your family subscribe to book clubs or to magazines? These are important questions to keep in mind when designing a literacy program for a classroom, because we know that literacy learning is complex and multifaceted, and children do not learn to read only through classroom instruction.

In this textbook, we use the term **children's literature** to refer to those books, both fiction and nonfiction, that are acknowledged by critics to be of high quality and well written, and which provide children with pleasurable and challenging reading experiences. The term **trade books** has a broader definition, including all books that are published for preschoolers, young readers, and young adults, but *not* as part of a basal reading series or as textbooks for use in schools. Trade books encompass many genres of literature, including comics, series books such as those by Lemony Snicket (e.g., *The Bad Beginning (A Series of Unfortunate Events)*, 1999), and magazines. The term **reading series** refers to a set of materials specifically designed for teaching reading and language arts, and they frequently form the basis for an instructional program in reading. Many current reading series are anthologies of materials taken directly from published works of literature by well-known authors. These series generally consist of teacher guides, student anthologies, workbooks, and supplemental materials such as assessment materials, big books, correlated trade books, audiovisual aids, and computer software.

Genre, a word borrowed from French, means "literary form." The epic, tragedy, comedy, essay, biography, novel, and poetry are traditional genres. New forms have been added to this list over the years, and now the term is used as a convenient (and somewhat arbitrary) way of classifying literary works. Today, genre refers to a body of literature that has certain common elements. The genres usually referred to in children's literature are picture books, wordless books, concept books, biographies, classics, legends, myths, folk tales, fairytales, fables, historical fiction, contemporary realistic fiction, fantasies, science fiction, poetry, and nonfiction—and each of these may in turn be subdivided into a number of different categories or subgenres.

Competent and avid adult readers often recollect with fondness their visits to the bookmobile in the city, the arrival of the *Star Weekly* in the mailbox, comics, their first library card, favourite books, and endless series books, from Nancy Drew to the Babysitter's Club. Learning from this, and from all that has been written about teaching reading and

Teacher and students at book display

the language arts, educators have embraced the concept of literature-based reading instruction, and many have created language arts programs based on trade books of many genres. Teachers understand the power of children's literature and have high regard for the authors and illustrators who create literary works for children. The locally organized Children's Literature Round Table groups that meet across Canada are well attended, and children's literature conferences are met with great enthusiasm by teachers and teacher/librarians alike. One example is the Kaleidoscope Conference, held every four years in Calgary (sponsored by the Alberta School Library Council of the Alberta Teachers' Association).

Reading good books, or hearing stories read to them, is one of the great pleasures in the lives of most children. Students often remember well into adulthood specific books their teachers read to them in the elementary grades. These stories engage the imagination and connect us with people and places that are both like us and different from us. Books help us to be aware of the larger world and provide a context within which we can better understand who we are and the lives we can lead.

LITERATURE-BASED LANGUAGE ARTS

With a careful choice of books and appropriate instruction, children learn to read from interesting and well-written, well-illustrated trade books as well as from reading series. Literature-based language arts instruction calls upon certain knowledge and skills on the part of teachers. Not only must teachers know children's books (including their titles, authors, themes, plots, characters, and structures), but they also must understand how books work and how books teach young readers about reading and being a reader. Literature-based instruction is important because it incorporates all of the language arts and may involve such activities as novel studies, shared reading, drama (see Chapter 12), art activities, puppetry, journals and other kinds of writing, and book talks by children. It thus requires a good deal of organization and knowledge of strategies (e.g., literature circles and response groups). It also demands that teachers read the books their students are reading and be prepared to participate with children as they generate shared meanings from the books they read.

Four Roles of the Reader

What is the advantage of working with literature in the classroom? Reading is more than matching written symbols with sounds, more than acquiring a reading vocabulary, more than understanding word meanings. Reading ability is more than being able to answer someone else's questions about a text. Freebody and Luke (1990) describe four roles of a reader (sometimes called the Four Resources Model): code breaker, text participant, text user, and text analyst. They maintain that successful reading means being able to accomplish all four of these roles simultaneously.

- Being a *code breaker* involves understanding the sound–symbol relationship and the alphabetic principle.

- Being a *text participant* means developing the resources to engage the meaning systems of discourse (i.e., the processes of comprehension, drawing inferences, connecting textual elements and background knowledge, and so on).

- Being a *text user* means knowing how to use a variety of texts in real social contexts throughout daily life (i.e., knowing how to read and access different forms of text in given social contexts—e.g., newspapers, poetry, websites, blogs).

- Being a *text analyst* means reading critically, or having "conscious awareness of the language and idea systems that are brought into play when a text is used" (p. 13) (i.e., being able to recognize the ideological perspective of a text and to stand outside that perspective and critique it).

Well before they enter school, many children learn to read from the reading materials they have in their homes, usually magazines and books. Scholars, researchers, and teachers have learned that children's literature has a greater likelihood of encouraging children to take on the four roles of the reader than most school-based reading materials do. The more contrived or artificial stories sometimes found in reading series are generally designed to encourage code breaking rather than any of the other three roles. Works of children's literature are more likely to challenge readers not only to be code breakers, but also to make inferences, to analyze the text, and to predict events and outcomes.

In *Come Away from the Water, Shirley* (Burningham, 1977), for example, the reader is encouraged not only to decode the text and read the words, but also to read the pictures that, at first glance, appear to have nothing at all to do with the words on the page. In order to construct a meaningful story, the reader has to engage with the book as a text participant, text user, and text analyst. There is more than one story being told in these pages. Participating only as a code breaker would create a limited story with little appeal to children. *Rosie's Walk* (Hutchins, 1969) provides a further example of this phenomenon.

There are times today when a reading series can be very useful to teachers. If a large and varied collection of children's reading material is not available, or when a student has a particular learning need, then a reading series may provide the resources necessary for instruction. In general, however, most children will learn more about reading from children's literature than from a reading series. Children clearly need to learn code-breaking skills early in their lives, but they also deserve to learn how to be text users, text analysts, and text participants if they are to become independent readers capable of constructing meaning from the texts they read. From children's literature, children are provided with the opportunity to learn both how to read and how to appreciate how texts work. The combination of the two creates rich possibilities for reading for pleasure and for information throughout life.

Literature and Literacy

Research in language learning and literacy development has consistently shown that one of the most important factors in a child's early literacy development is the amount a child is read to (and with) in the preschool years. Wells's (1986) longitudinal study of language development, conducted in Britain during the 1970s, showed that the single most important factor in reading development is the amount a child is read to during the preschool years. The study also demonstrated that

- Children who are read to from infancy onwards have an enormous advantage when they begin formal schooling (this finding has significant implications for teaching those children who come from situations where reading is not common and is not regarded as a pleasurable or satisfying endeavour).
- Early reading experiences affect writing as well as reading abilities, and are also influential in developing children's listening and comprehension skills.
- The more children read and are read to, and the more children talk about what they are reading and writing, the more successful they are likely to be in school and in their literacy endeavours.

Many preschool children love books. They are fascinated by the pictures on the page and by the shared experience of reading on a caregiver's lap. This pleasurable anticipation of books provides parents and educators with the opportunity to provide quality works of literature for the young. *Each Peach Pear Plum* by the Ahlbergs (1978) is a contemporary extension of traditional literature that has become a classic. *Each Peach Pear Plum* contains illustrations rich in the detail of the nursery rhymes, folklore, legends, and fairytales of western Europe. It is a book that can be read on a range of levels. The very young child, who is still unable to follow the plots of traditional stories, can enjoy the repetition of "each peach pear plum" and the rhyming patterns, as well as the predictability of the language. Older children enjoy the humour derived from their prior knowledge of the fairytales and nursery rhymes alluded to in the book.

Children learn from books such as this that reading is an active experience. In addition to what children learn about values, culture, and life, they learn about handling and "reading" books—much of what Holdaway (1979) refers to as "literacy set." Children learn directionality: the front and back of a book, which way is the right way up, and which way the story moves through the book—in the case of *Each Peach Pear Plum*, with text on the left, pictures on the right, and a "cuing" picture above the text. Children learn that books can be actively responded to, and that books are a way into a pleasurable experience.

Children's early experiences with books such as *Each Peach Pear Plum*, and the experiences they have with reading in school, affect how they perceive themselves as readers and how they perceive reading: whether it is a relevant activity, whether it is a pleasurable activity, and whether books are worth the time and effort needed to have a truly *satisfying* reading experience. Teachers who use literature as a basis for their reading instruction demonstrate to children that books *are* worth the time and effort required of a reader, and thus children are more likely to become readers as adults. Teachers who clearly enjoy reading—and who demonstrate this joy in their daily life in classrooms—invite children into the world of books with enthusiasm and excitement.

PICTURE STORYBOOKS FOR K TO 6

Every genre of literature is represented in **picture books**. The label "picture book" refers to a general category of books having the same basic format and way of communicating a message. Some books may more appropriately be called "illustrated books." True picture books involve a partnership between text and pictures, with the pictures and text together telling the story or presenting information. The most common genres of picture books are wordless books, concept books (such as counting and alphabet books), predictable books, easy-to-read books, and picture storybooks. There is often overlap among the genres within picture books. This section of the chapter focuses on picture storybooks rather than on the other picture book genres, such as alphabet or counting books.

Picture Storybooks for the Elementary Grades

Picture storybooks are a powerful vehicle for teaching children both how to read and how to become readers. It is understood that reading should be taught in the context of real texts, but it is not until we look in detail at books such as *Come Away from the Water, Shirley* (Burningham, 1977), *Tuesday* (Wiesner, 1991), and *Zoom Upstream* (Wynne-Jones, 1992), that we fully understand the reading lessons children are receiving from picture books. Meek (1988) refers to these as "private lessons," the lessons good readers learn about reading without formal instruction. *Come Away from the Water, Shirley* tells one version of the story through the pictures (and through Shirley's eyes) and another version of the story through the text (and through the parents' eyes). In *Zoom Upstream*, Wynne-Jones' simple adventure story about a cat is remarkably extended by Eric Beddows's detailed and imaginative illustrations of the "catacombs" of ancient Egypt.

An example of a picture book that can be read on many levels is *Rosie's Walk* (Hutchins, 1969). It contains 1 sentence, 32 words, and 27 pages of pictures. *Rosie's Walk* is a story that, if told in words alone, would take many paragraphs and lose much of its allure. *Rosie's Walk* contains at least two stories: the story of Rosie the hen and her barnyard walk, and the story of the fox who silently follows her but is not even mentioned in the text (though he is prominent in the illustrations). The reading lesson, which transfers directly to adult books such as *Divisadero* by Michael Ondaatje (2007), is an important one—there is more than one story in any book, and there is more in any book than is written on the page.

Young readers understand the way picture books work because they attend to multiple cues, not only to text. They focus on visual cues much more significantly than adults do. Today's young readers are engaging in completely different reading experiences than previous generations of children because they have access to picture storybooks that are more challenging and interactional than before, and they engage in video games, television, movies, and websites that are animated, fast-paced, and extremely visual. While critics might say that children are using their imaginations less than ever before, many observers of young children would say they are more imaginatively involved in various forms of "storytelling" than ever.

In literary terms, books such as *Rosie's Walk* and *Tuesday* are often called "writerly" texts, because readers must use their imaginations to fill in the textual gaps and thus "complete" the writing of the story. "Readerly" texts are those in which the writer has provided most of the information for the reader, and the writer's meanings tend to be clear and direct. The reader has to do less work.

Early readers need experiences with both writerly and readerly texts, and teachers provide the instructional support children need to be able to move from one to the other. As a result of their early reading experiences with writerly texts such as *Rosie's Walk* and *Come Away from the Water, Shirley,* more children are likely to enjoy novels such as Ondaatje's *Divisadero* when they grow up. They are also more likely to continue reading for pleasure as well as for information as adults.

Box 10.1 lists some picture books that are appropriate for children in the elementary grades, and Box 10.2 lists specifically Canadian picture books.

BOX 10.1   A SELECTION OF PICTURE STORYBOOKS

Ahlberg, J. and Ahlberg, A. (1986). *The jolly postman.* London, UK: Heinemann.

Ahlberg, A. and Briggs, R. (2001). *The adventures of Bert.* London: Penguin.

Base, G. (2001). *The waterhole.* New York: Penguin Putnam.

Brett, J. (1989). *The mitten.* New York: Scholastic.

Briggs, R. (1975). *Father Christmas goes on holiday.* Harmondsworth, UK: Puffin Books.

Browne, A. (1983). *Gorilla.* New York: Alfred A. Knopf.

Carle, E. (1974). *The very hungry caterpillar.* Harmondsworth, UK: Puffin Books.

Curtis, J. L. (2000). *Where do balloons go?* An uplifting mystery. New York: Harper Collins.

Fox, M. (1990). *Possum magic.* New York: Harcourt Brace & Company.

Fox, M. (2006). *A particular cow.* New York: Harcourt Books.

Graham, B. (2000). *Max.* Cambridge, MA: Candlewick Press.

Kent, J. (1971). *The fat cat.* Harmondsworth, UK: Puffin Books.

Rathmann, P. (1995). *Officer Buckle and Gloria.* New York: Putnam.

Ross, T. (1993). *The three pigs.* London: Arrow Books.

Steer, D. (1999). *Just one more story.* New York: Dutton Children's Books.

Van Allsburg, C. (1985). *The polar express.* Boston: Houghton Mifflin.

Waddell, M. (1988). *Can't you sleep, Little Bear?* Cambridge, MA: Candlewick Press.

Waddell, M. (1991). *Farmer Duck.* London: Walker Books.

Wild, M. (1990). *The very best of friends.* New York: Harcourt Brace & Company.

Yolen, J. (1987). *Owl moon.* New York: Philomel Books.

BOX 10.2	CANADIAN PICTURE BOOKS

Andrews, J. (1985). *Very last first time*. Vancouver: Douglas & McIntyre.

Eyvindson, P. (1996). *Red parka* Mary. Winnipeg: Pemmican.

Gay, M. L. (1999). *Stella, star of the sea*. Toronto, ON: Groundwood Books.

Gilman, P. (1992). *Something from nothing*. Richmond Hill, ON: North Winds Press.

Gregory, N. (2001). *Wild Girl and Gran*. Red Deer, AB: Red Deer Press.

Harty, N. (1997). *Hold on, McGinty*. Toronto: Doubleday Canada.

Jam, T. (1997). *The fishing summer*. Toronto: Groundwood Books.

Khalsa, D. K. (1986). *Tales of a gambling grandma*. Montreal: Tundra Books.

Lawson, J. (1999). *Bear on the train*. Toronto: Kids Can Press.

Lee, D. (2001). *The cat and the wizard*. Toronto: Key Porter Books.

Major, K. (2000). *Eh? To zed*. Red Deer, AB: Red Deer Press.

McFarlane, S. (1991). *Waiting for the whales*. Victoria, BC: Orca Book Publishers.

McGugan, J. (1994). *Josepha: A prairie boy's story*. Red Deer, AB: Red Deer College Press.

Morck, I. (1996). *Tiger's new cowboy boots*. Red Deer, AB: Red Deer College Press.

Morin, P. (1998). *Animal dreaming*. New York: Silver Whistle Harcourt Brace & Company.

Munsch, R. (1980). *The paper bag princess*. Toronto: Annick Press.

Oberman, S. (2000). *The wisdom bird*. Honesdale, PA: Boyds Mills Press, Inc.

Oppel, K. (2000). *Peg and the whale*. Toronto: HarperCollins.

Ruurs, M. (1999). *Emma's eggs*. Markham, ON: Fitzhenry & Whiteside.

Simmie, L. (1995). *Mr. Got to Go*. Red Deer, AB: Red Deer College Press.

Vaage, C. (1995). *Bibi and the bull*. Edmonton: Dragon Hill Press.

Wilson, B. (2001). *A Fiddle for Angus*. Toronto: Tundra Books.

Wynne-Jones, T. and Nutt, K. (1985). *Zoom away*. Toronto: Groundwood Books.

Wordless Books

Children in preschool and kindergarten enjoy sitting alone or in small groups reading wordless books. In actively encouraging emerging readers to engage with books, it is appropriate for teachers to share such books with the class, especially "big-book" versions that enable all the children to see the pictures. It is also important that teachers take a close look at the pictures before the book is shared with children (part of the preparation required in these circumstances), for children will ask many questions and make observations about the illustrations. Children focus heavily on the illustrations in books and can be particularly insightful about

BOX 10.3	WORDLESS BOOKS

Aliki. (1995). *Tabby: A story told in pictures.* New York: HarperCollins.

Anno, M. (2004). *Anno's Spain.* New York: Philomel Books.

Baker, J. (2004). *Home.* New York: Greenwillow Books

Banyai, I. (1995). *Zoom.* New York: Viking.

Briggs, R. (1978). *The snowman.* New York: Random House/Scholastic.

Collington, P. (1997). *A small miracle.* New York: Knopf.

Dematons, C. (2003). *The yellow balloon.* Asheville, NC: Front Street/Lemniscaat.

Dupasquier, P. (1988). *The great escape.* Boston: Houghton Mifflin.

Fleischman, P. (2004). *Sidewalk circus.* Cambridge, MA: Candlewick Press.

Goodall, J. (1988). *Little Red Riding Hood.* New York: M. K. McElderry Books.

Karlin, B. (1991). *Meow.* New York: Simon & Schuster.

Keats, E. J. (1974). *Kitten for a day.* New York: Four Winds Press.

Lehman, B. (2004). *The red book.* Boston: Houghton Mifflin.

McCully, E. (1988). *New baby.* New York: Harper & Row.

Popov, N. (1996). *Why?* New York: North-South Books Inc.

Rogers, G. (2004). *The boy, the bear, the baron, the bard.* Crows Nest, NSW: Allen & Unwin; Brookfield, CT: Roaring Brook.

Romann, E. (1994). *Time flies.* New York: Random House.

Schories, P. (2004). *Breakfast for Jack.* Asheville, NC: Front Street.

Sis, P. (2000). *Dinosaur.* New York: Greenwillow Books.

Weisner, D. (1992). *Tuesday.* Boston: Clarion/Houghton Mifflin.

the details. In their early reading experiences, children rely heavily on pictures in order to create meaning from the page. As teachers acknowledge the observations children make and the questions they ask, they enhance the children's response to the book and help expand their understanding through discussion and interaction. Box 10.3 lists wordless books that are appropriate for children from preschool to grade 3.

Picture Books for Older Readers

Picture books are not only for pre- and beginning readers, just as wordless books, such as *Sunshine* (1981) and *Moonlight* (1982) by Jan Ormerod, are not only for children who cannot yet read. Similar to *Each Peach Pear Plum* in its intertextual references (to *Red Riding Hood* and many other folk tales and fairytales) is *The Tunnel* by Anthony Browne (1989). Intended for children in the upper elementary grades, this book requires many readings to unravel its multilayered (polysemic) text and illustrations. There is a great deal of reading to be done in the gaps in the turn of a page, or between text and picture. It is in these gaps that readers are invited to take an "inferential walk" (Eco, 1978) or, in other words, to read between the lines. Thus, readers learn the key role that inference plays in reading and in constructing meaning. Some readers may encounter difficulty in following the story depicted in *The Tunnel* and feel that Browne has omitted too much, has left too many inferential gaps, and in general has created too writerly a text. These readers want the story to be laid out for them more explicitly, so that they receive a direct message from the author and don't have to create the meaning themselves. (Many adults also struggle with the story in the book and with the nature of the illustrations, because Browne manages to create allusions to several of the more disturbing aspects of relationships and growing up, leaving readers to relate their own experiences to the story and perhaps respond at deeply personal levels.) In such books, then, teachers play an important role, through dialogue and discussion groups, in helping children take inferential walks, draw inferences, make educated guesses, and understand overall that there is no correct answer when "gap filling" in texts.

Many picture books are aimed at an audience of older children, children who can already read well and who have a rich experience in working with text. Sixth-grade children respond powerfully to books such as *Black and White* (Macaulay, 1990) and *June 29, 1999* (Wiesner, 1992). *Black and White* is an adventure in metafiction, a constant and deliberate reminder that a book is something an author and reader create together—something that is not real and is open to many interpretations and structures. The book consists of four narrative strands, each making use of different narrative and pictorial techniques. Each double-page spread is divided into four sections so that the four narratives unfold at the same time. On the title page of the book there is a warning from the author: "This book appears to contain a number of stories that do not necessarily occur at the same time. Then again, it may contain only one story. In any event, careful inspection of both words and pictures is recommended."

In *June 29, 1999*, a very different story, student Holly Evans develops an ambitious and innovative project for her science assignment. While her classmates are sprouting seeds in paper cups, Holly launches seedlings into the sky on tiny air balloons. Although her teacher and fellow students are skeptical, only five weeks later giant vegetables begin to fall from the sky, landing in various parts of the United States. The book displays Wiesner's unconventional artwork and the same dry humour he uses in *Free Fall* (1988) and *Tuesday* (1991).

These picture books, and others created for older readers, are not necessarily easy-reading books. Many of them deal with mature themes and contain illustrations that provide powerful messages supporting and adding to the text. Two books set in Europe during World War II are *Rose Blanche* (Innocenti, 1985) and *Let the Celebrations Begin!* (Wild, 1991). Where *Rose Blanche* is a story about the darkness of war, *Let the Celebrations Begin!* is a story of hope. It is a tribute to the human spirit and to the survival of so many innocent people who lived for years in horrific conditions in concentration camps. In addition to these books about Europe during World War II, there are a number of powerful picture books about the dropping of the atomic bomb on Hiroshima on August 6, 1945. These include *Hiroshima No Pika* (Maruki, 1980), *My Hiroshima* (Morimoto, 1987), *Sadako* (Coerr, 1993), and *Shin's Tricycle* (Kodama, 1995).

Although many of the books noted above are of a serious nature, many others for older readers are entertaining, playful, and clever, stimulating the imagination and stretching our notions of reading. Picture storybooks aimed at older readers include *Night in the Country* (Rylant, 1986), *Piggybook* (Browne, 1986), *The Widow's Broom* (Van Allsburg, 1992), and *The Mummer's Song* (Davidge and Wallace, 1993). Each of these books creates a sense of wonder and provides challenging perspectives on the reading event and on the nature of the picture book. Additional titles of picture books suitable for older readers are presented in Box 10.4.

Picture books, then, have the potential to teach important concepts about reading that can come only from working with real texts, and they are important in forming the attitudes of young children toward books in general. There is a wealth of high-quality picture books

---

BOX 10.4 **PICTURE BOOKS FOR OLDER READERS**

Barbalet, M. and Tanner, J. (1992). *The wolf.* Toronto: Doubleday.

Base, G. (1997). *The eleventh hour, A curious mystery.* New York: Puffin.

Blake, W. (1993). *The tyger.* (Neil Waldman, illustrator). New York: Harcourt Brace Jovanovich.

Briggs, R. (1982). *When the wind blows.* New York: Schocken.

Browne, A. (1998). *Voices in the park.* New York: DK Publishing Inc.

Carrier, R. (1985). *The hockey sweater.* Montreal: Tundra Books.

Heffernan, J. and McLean, A. (2001). *My Dog.* Hunters Hill, NSW: Margaret Hamilton Books.

Hunt, E. (1989). *The tale of three trees.* Colorado Springs, CO: Lion Publishing.

Lemieux, M. (1999). *Stormy night.* Toronto: Kids Can Press.

Macaulay, D. (1995). *Shortcut.* Boston, MA: Houghton Mifflin.

Major, K. (1997). *The house of wooden Santas.* Red Deer, AB: Red Deer Press.

Marsden, J. (1998). *The rabbits.* Port Melbourne, VC: Thomas Lothian.

Oberman, S. (1993). *The always prayer shawl.* Honesdale, PA: Boyd Mills Press.

Scieszka, J. (1995). *Math curse.* New York: Viking.

Scieszka, J. and Smith, L. (1998). *Squids will be squids.* New York: Scholastic Inc.

Spiegelman, A. (2000). *Little lit: Strange stories for strange kids.* New York: Harper Collins Publishers.

Valgardson, W. D. (1996). *Sarah and the people of Sand River.* Toronto: Groundwood Books.

Van Allsburg, C. (1984). *The mysteries of Harris Burdick.* Boston: Houghton Mifflin.

Wild. M. (2000). *Fox.* La Jolla, CA: Kane/Miller Book Publishers.

Yee, P. (1996). *Ghost train.* Toronto: Groundwood Books.

Zhang, A. (2004). *Red land, yellow river: A story from the cultural revolution.* Toronto: Douglas & McIntyre.

---

available for children in the elementary grades today, books containing artistry, excellent writing, and vivid imagery.

Take the time to locate one of the books mentioned in this section of the chapter, and see if the comments made here match the meanings you create from the book. Did the comments in this chapter help you see the book or the experience of reading in a new light? What does this experience demonstrate to you about your role in teaching reading and in mediating texts with children?

NOVELS

Beginning Chapter Books for the Primary Grades

As children become more familiar with picture books and with story structures, and as their reading abilities become more sophisticated, they move from using pictures as a primary means of creating meaning to an increased reliance on text. Many beginning novels are available for young readers (which children in grades 2 and 3 frequently refer to as *chapter books*), and they fall into all of the major genres. It seems that the movement from reading picture books to reading books with chapters denotes a transition in an individual's growth as a reader. This is not to suggest that children are no longer interested in reading picture books or that picture books cannot continue to capture their interest and imagination.

The reading levels of many beginning chapter books range from grades 2 to 4 (i.e., a level calculated by the application of a readability formula). Readability does not depend on the complexity of language alone, however, but has much to do with the structure of the book and the background experience the reader is required to bring to it. Often, beginning chapter books contain illustrations, and these assist readers in the transition from picture books to novels. The content and writing style of numerous beginning chapter books are equally appropriate for older elementary students whose reading level is below grade level, and for those who simply wish to read a "good" (albeit easier) book.

There are many well-known "entry-level" novels, among them Mordecai Richler's three titles about Jacob Two-Two: *Jacob Two-Two Meets the Hooded Fang* (1975), *Jacob Two-Two and the Dinosaur* (1987), and *Jacob Two-Two's First Spy Case* (1995). These books are a combination of fantasy and realistic fiction, and are suitable for reading aloud to the class as well as for independent reading. There are also many recommended beginning novels of realistic fiction, including novels written by Canadian authors Ken Roberts, Budge Wilson, Jean Little, and Sylvia McNicoll.

Budge Wilson's story *Harold and Harold* (1995) is about a young boy named Harold whose friendship with a beautiful blue heron also named Harold assists him in being accepted by his new coastal community. In the novel *The Big Race* (1996), McNicoll tells the story of a grade 3 boy's constant competition with a female classmate who excels at everything she does. Various events, including a broken nose, eventually bring the characters together in friendship.

Denslow's book *Georgie Lee* (2002) is a gentle tale of the close relationship between JD and his grandmother (and her cow). A summer visit to the farm includes a trip to a haunted house, the rescue of an elderly neighbour who has fallen and spent the night outside, a storm, and the day his grandmother gets stuck in a tree. Through all of these events is Georgie Lee, a cow with a mind of her own, who always wants to be in on the action. The book is episodic in nature and so it makes a good read-aloud for lower-elementary students or an enjoyable choice for beginning chapter-book readers.

A selection of beginning novels is presented in Box 10.5.

As children begin to move from picture books to chapter books, their book selection will be determined largely by the encouragement of their teacher, their peers, and their own interests. Teachers help children to grow by making book suggestions on the basis of each child's

---

BOX 10.5   BEGINNING NOVELS

Choyce, L. (1998). *Famous at last.* East Lawrencetown, NS: Pottersfield Press.

Cleary, B. (1984). *Ramona forever.* New York: Bantam Doubleday Dell.

Dadey, D. (1990–2006). *Adventures of the Bailey School Kids—Series.* Boston: Little Apple.

Dahl, R. (1970). *Fantastic Mr. Fox.* New York: Knopf.

Dahl, R. (1980). *The twits.* New York: Bantam Skylark Books.

Elste, J. (1996). *True blue.* New York: Grosset & Dunlap.

Fleischman, S. (1986). *The whipping boy.* New York: Greenwillow.

Gardiner, J. R. (1980). *Stone fox.* New York: Crowell.

Gauthier, G. (1995). *Mooch forever.* Translated by S. Cummins. Halifax: Formac.

Gravel, F. (1992). *Mr. Zamboni's dream machine.* Translated by S. Cummins. Toronto: James Lorimer & Company.

Gutman, D. (2004). *Mr. Klutz is nuts.* New York: HarperTrophy.

Jinkins, Jim. (2005). *Pinky Dinky Doo. Shrinky Pinky.* New York: Random House.

Korman, G. (1997). *Liar, liar, pants on fire.* Richmond Hill, ON: Scholastic Canada.

Lowry, L. (2001). *Zooman Sam.* New York: Dell Yearling.

MacLachlan, P. (1985). *Sarah, plain and tall.* New York: Harper & Row.

MacLachlan, P. (1994). *Skylark.* New York: Harper Trophy.

McDonald, M. (2003). *Judy Moody predicts the future.* Cambridge, MA: Candlewick Press, 2003.

Park, B. (1982). *Skinnybones.* New York: Alfred A. Knopf.

Paterson, K. (1992). *The king's equal.* New York: HarperCollins (originally published in picture book format).

Pilkey, D. (1997). *The adventures of Captain Underpants.* Boston: Little Apple.

Richardson, G. (1997). *A friend for Mr. Granville.* Edmonton: Hodgepog Books.

Roberts, K. (1994). *Past tense.* Vancouver: Douglas & McIntyre.

Sachar, L. (1991). *The boy who lost his face.* New York: Alfred A. Knopf.

Smucker, B. (1987). *Jacob's little giant.* Toronto: Puffin Books.

Steele, M. (1993). *Featherbys.* Victoria, BC: Hyland House.

Wishinsky, F. (1998). *Crazy for chocolate.* Richmond Hill, ON: Scholastic Canada.

interests and reading ability. Children benefit because a novel requires a greater investment of time and effort than a picture storybook. At the same time, children need to know that a book they select has the potential to engage their interests as well as being at an appropriate reading level. In general, reading materials of high personal interest are more fully comprehended than materials of low interest. A reader's strong interest in a topic can transcend his or her reading abilities (Hunt, 1970). Research also shows the importance of teachers reading the books their students are reading, so they can discuss the books with their students (Pantaleo, 1994). Through these discussions, teachers may challenge students to extend their interpretations and to add new dimensions to the meanings they create.

Novels in the Upper Elementary Grades

Many children begin their foray into novels with **contemporary realistic fiction**, perhaps because it is one of the avenues through which they can, on the one hand, come to know the world in which they live and, on the other, explore issues of which they have little personal experience. This genre continues to be the most widely read of them all in the upper elementary grades. Deborah Ellis's novels *Looking for X* (1999) and *The Breadwinner* (2000) are rapidly becoming Canadian classics.

Looking for X (a Governor General's Award winner) is set in inner-city Toronto. The protagonist, 11-year-old Khyber, finds herself in a tough situation. With a single mom and twin autistic brothers, Khyber has to take care of the boys more than she would like, and she finds it hard to make friends. Besides, she prefers her own company—except for her friend X. But when her mom decides the boys must go into a group home, and X disappears, Khyber's life becomes confusing, complicated, and dangerous.

The Breadwinner (2000) is the first of a trilogy of books set in Afghanistan under the Taliban regime. Because her father is imprisoned and her mother is not allowed to work, Parvana reluctantly takes on the role of the family's breadwinner. Disguising herself as a boy, Parvana finds herself involved in numerous occupations—including collecting bones for pay.

Finders Keepers (Spalding, 1995) tells the story of two boys in Fort McLeod, Alberta, who become unlikely friends. Danny, a child of Ukrainian decent, and Joshua, a Peigan boy, find ways to help each other after Danny discovers an 8000-year-old arrowhead. Together they uncover the origin of the arrowhead and in doing so become great friends, learning how to deal with their respective difficulties and differences (including a learning disability).

In *Barry, Boyhound* (Spearman, 2005), Barry wakes up one morning no longer a boy, at least on the inside. He may look the same, but he is beginning to act and feel like a dog—the result of a flea bite the day before, perhaps. Barry tries to come to terms with the situation, but cannot control his dog urges. As a result, he gets into lots of trouble and has some amazing escapades. In this humorous and unusual book, the narrator talks to the reader, and includes sidebars, appendices, and footnotes to add information and detail to the story.

Other recommended titles of contemporary realistic fiction are

- *The Daring Game* (Pearson, 1986)
- *Afternoon of the Elves* (Lisle, 1989)

- *Maniac Magee* (Spinelli, 1990)
- *Walk Two Moons* (Creech, 1994)
- *Because of Winn-Dixie* (DiCamillo, 2000)
- *Up on Cloud Nine* (Fine, 2002)
- *The Crazy Man* (Porter, 2005)

Novels such as these encourage students to explore personal and social issues that may help them attain an increased understanding of themselves and others.

Mystery is a genre much enjoyed by children in the upper elementary grades. These stories challenge children to become actively engaged in problem solving. Young readers enjoy putting the pieces of the puzzle together, hypothesizing, and making inferences as they act as detectives in solving the mystery. There are now numerous well-written mystery stories available for readers, but many children discover the genre through series books such as the Hardy Boys, Nancy Drew, or Encyclopedia Brown. They will frequently read all the books in the series in their desire to remain engaged with the genre. As they become familiar with a particular series, they also become increasingly better at predicting solutions and fitting clues together. The result is that children tend to grow out of these rather predictable plots and patterns, becoming ready for something more demanding and more sophisticated. In the 1990s, children turned to the genre of horror stories in addition to mysteries. The Goosebumps series by R. L. Stine was extremely popular for a number of years, and many parents and educators expressed concern over children reading these books. Not unexpectedly, however, readers soon outgrew the books, wanting a greater challenge and a new thrill in reading.

There are many excellent mystery stories to recommend. *The Thief Lord* by Cornelia Funke (2001) is about orphaned brothers, Prosper and Bo. After running away from their guardian aunt and uncle in Germany, the boys find themselves in Venice, where they decide to hide out. There they meet the Thief Lord, the young leader of a ring of street urchins and petty thieves, who claims to steal from the wealthy to help the poor. A mysterious man hires the Thief Lord to steal a particularly significant item, and the boys' lives suddenly become full of adventure, colourful characters, and deep secrets.

In *Silent to the Bone* (Konigsburg, 2002), Branwell is unable to utter a word after the horrible crime that put his little sister, Nikki, into a coma. While Branwell is retained in a juvenile behavioural centre, accused of perpetrating the crime, his best friend attempts to discover what really happened to Nikki and clear Branwell's name.

Betsy Byars has authored a series of mystery books about a character named Herculeah Jones. Two titles in the series are *Dead Letter* (1996) and *Death's Door* (1997). Other recommended mystery titles are

- *The Dragon Children* (Buchan, 1975)
- *Secrets in the Attic* (York, 1986)
- *Lucy Forever & Miss Rosetree, Shrinks* (Shreve, 1987)
- *Megan's Island* (Roberts, 1988)
- *The Westing Game* (Raskin, 1990)
- *Bunnicula: A Rabbit Tale of Mystery* (Howe, 1996)

- *Sammy Keyes and the Hotel Thief* (Van Draanen, 1998)
- *The Boy in the Burning House* (Wynne-Jones, 2000)
- *Crispin: The Cross of Lead* (Avi, 2002)
- *Bernie Magruder and the Bats in the Belfry* (Naylor, 2003)
- *Chasing Vermeer* (Balliett, 2004)
- *Nate the Great Talks Turkey* (Sharmat, 2006)

Historical fiction is a genre that presents new challenges for many young readers, for it typically presents fictional characters in a historically accurate context. The genre often requires that the reader have some prior knowledge of the time period in which the story is set. Historical fiction is a particularly suitable genre for teachers to share with their classes as a read-aloud. It also helps in creating a context and a deeper understanding of many social studies topics, and can inspire themes for work across the curriculum.

The Watsons Go to Birmingham, 1963 (Curtis, 1995) begins as a humorous romp through family life in Flint, Michigan. Kenny has to put up with his teenage brother, Byron, who is an "official juvenile delinquent." Momma decides the only remedy is to take Byron to stay with his grandmother in Birmingham, Alabama, for the summer. The family piles into the car and heads off to what turns out to be a life-changing experience for the whole family. The book is a warm and wonderful read, but the emotional impact of the events in Birmingham make the book unforgettable. This is a perfect book for book clubs and response groups.

Hitler's Daughter (French, 1999) is an intriguing Australian novel about Anna, who tells stories to her friends as they wait for the school bus. What if Hitler had a daughter, a child who would have been their age during the war? Anna invents Heidi, a girl who could have lived in Germany and could have been Hitler's daughter. The story causes Anna's friend Mark to ask questions about his own family and about what it means to trust someone. How would you know if your parents were doing something wrong? Would you confront them, or would you go along with it? The book has a disturbing and fast-paced plot that raises questions about relationships, belief systems, and questions of right and wrong. This is a perfect book for literature circles.

Al Capone Does My Shirts (Choldenko, 2004) is set on the island of Alcatraz in 1935. Twelve-year-old Moose Flanagan has recently moved to the Rock because his father is an electrician and guard at the prison. The family hopes that Moose's older sister, Natalie, who is autistic, can go to a special school on the mainland in San Francisco. Moose is very protective of Natalie, and distinctly nervous at being so close to such notorious criminals. The warden's daughter, Piper, hatches a scheme to make money from the children at their school on the mainland, and she forces Moose to be her accomplice, using her knowledge of Natalie's condition as "leverage." Although family dilemmas and relationships are central to the story, Choldenko weaves a compelling novel around the history and setting of Alcatraz, and of course, around one of the most famous inmates, Al Capone.

Books of historical fiction about Canada and by Canadian authors include *Underground to Canada* by Barbara Smucker (1977), dealing with slavery; *A Very Small Rebellion* by Jan Truss (1977), about the Riel rebellion; *The Sky Is Falling* by Kit Pearson (1989), about World War II; *Rebellion: A Novel of Upper Canada* by Marianne Brandis (1996), about the 1837 rebellion; and *Chasing the Moon* by Penny Chamberlain (2006), about smuggling on Vancouver Island during the prohibition years. Two series, *Our Canadian Girl* (Penguin), and *Dear Canada* (Scholastic), have created considerable interest in Canadian history and have won a solid readership in the elementary grades. Both series present events through the eyes of female protagonists, and both series use the talents of well-known Canadian authors, including Cora Taylor, Julie Lawson, Deborah Ellis, Sharon McKay, Sarah Ellis, Carol Matas, and Kathy Stinson.

Our Canadian Girl covers topics such as the Halifax explosion, the Frank Slide, and Montreal's smallpox epidemic of the 1880s. The *Dear Canada* series aims to provide a springboard for exploring different periods of Canadian history, and topics include the battle on the Plains of Abraham, building the Canadian Pacific railway, the Red River settlers, and the War of 1812. Two teacher resource packages, *Teaching with Dear Canada, Volumes 1 and 2*, have been prepared by teacher educator Amy Von Heyking (2002 and 2004).

A list of historical fiction is provided in Box 10.6.

BOX 10.6   **HISTORICAL FICTION**

Canadian

Attema, M. (1996). *A time to choose*. Victoria, BC: Orca (young adult).

Bellingham, B. (1985). *Storm child*. Toronto: James Lorimer & Company.

Berton, P. and Van Der Linde, H. (1996). *The Klondike stampede*. Toronto: McClelland & Stewart.

Clark, J. (2002). *The word for home*. New York: Penguin.

Ellis, S. (2001). *Prairie as wide as the sea: The immigrant diary of Ivy Weatherall* (Dear Canada Series). Markham, ON: Scholastic.

Greenwood, B. and Collins, H. (1998). *The daily life of a pioneer family*. Boston: Houghton Mifflin.

Haworth-Attard, B. (2001). *Flying geese*. Toronto: Harper Collins Publishers.

Lawson, J. (2001). *Across the James Bay Bridge: Emily* (Our Canadian Girl Series). Toronto: Penguin Books Canada Ltd.

Lottridge, B. (1995). *The wind wagon*. Toronto: Groundwood.

Lunn, J. (1986). *Shadow in Hawthorn Bay*. Toronto: Lester and Orpen Denys.

Schwartz, V. (2002). *If I just had two wings*. Toronto: Stoddart Kids.

Walters, E. (1998). *War of the eagles*. Victoria, BC: Orca Book Publishers.

Walters, E. (1997). *Trapped in ice*. Toronto: Penguin Books.

Yee, P. (1989). *Tales from Gold Mountain*. Toronto: Groundwood Books.

Non-Canadian

Filipovic, Z. (1994). *Zlata's diary: A child's life in Sarajevo*. New York: Putnam.

Fox, P. (1973). *The slave dancer*. New York: Bradbury.

Greene, B. (1973). *The summer of my German soldier*. New York: Bantam.

Lowry, L. (1989). *Number the stars*. New York: Houghton Mifflin.

McSwigan, M. (1942). *Snow treasure*. New York: E. P. Dutton.

O'Dell, S. (1970). *Sing down the moon*. New York: Bantam Doubleday Dell.

O'Dell, S. and Hall, E. (1992). *Thunder rolling in the mountains*. New York: Bantam Doubleday Dell.

Reiss, J. (1972). *The upstairs room*. New York: Scholastic.

Speare, E. G. (1958). *The witch of Blackbird Pond*. New York: Dell Publishing.

Speare, E. G. (1983). *The sign of the beaver*. New York: Bantam Doubleday Dell.

Uchida, Y. (1978). *Journey home*. New York: Aladdin Paperbacks.

Time-slip fantasy is a genre that has its roots in *Tom's Midnight Garden* by Philippa Pearce (1958). Time-slip stories usually begin in the present, and then, through some artifact from the past, the protagonist is transported into a different time, typically a specific period in history. *The Castle in the Attic* by Elizabeth Winthrop (1985) fits into this category of novel, and so does Janet Lunn's book *The Root Cellar* (1981), which is about the American Civil War. A well-known Australian time-slip fantasy is *Playing Beatie Bow* (1980) by Ruth Parks. Three Canadian time-slip fantasy books were published in 1987: *The Doll* by Cora Taylor, *Who Is Frances Rain?* by Margaret Buffie, and *A Handful of Time* by Kit Pearson. In *Who Is Frances Rain?* a pair of spectacles takes Lizzie back into the isolated pioneer times of rural Manitoba in the early part of the 20th century. Through her experiences in a different time, Lizzie is able to deal with her life in the present in a more effective and positive manner.

Fantasy literature engages the reader's imagination and gives free rein to endless possibilities. The reader is taken to worlds where animals and toys can speak, and where people can travel across time and into completely fictional worlds. The genre is popular in all the elementary grades. Young children, for example, enjoy *Charlotte's Web* (White, 1952) and *James and the Giant Peach* (Dahl, 1961). Older children enjoy *The Dark Is Rising* (Cooper, 1969) and *Harry Potter and the Sorcerer's Stone* (Rowling, 1998). Although fantasy literature has a devoted following in grades 5 and 6, it can be a challenging genre for children and teachers alike because of the complexity and sophistication of the ideas embedded within it.

Many books of **high fantasy** (usually quest stories), such as *The Hobbit* (Tolkien, 1937) and *The Golden Compass* (Pullman, 1996), are read by both children and adults. Much modern fantasy has its roots in ancient myths and legends, especially in the *Tales from the Mabinogian*, which is a collection of Welsh myths dating back many hundreds of years. Both Susan Cooper and Alan Garner (*The Owl Service*, 1967) refer to the *Mabinogian* in their writing, and it is useful if readers have at least a nodding acquaintance with this material when reading these authors' books. A modern children's version by Gwynn Thomas and Kevin Crossley-Holland (1985) is a wonderful addition to any classroom library.

Skellig (Almond, 1998) is an award-winning book that is distinctive in its theme and plot. Ten-year-old Michael has moved into a new house with his parents and new baby sister. The house is being renovated and in the back yard stands an old garage, waiting to be torn down. The garage is full of junk and Michael finds it a fascinating place to explore. One day, when moving an old tea chest, Michael sees a dark figure beneath the spiderwebs and dead flies. The figure speaks—he needs food, and his name is Skellig. The only person Michael can confide in is his new friend, Mina. Through Mina and Skellig, Michael learns about love, trust, poetry, and art—and about William Blake. *Skellig* is as much contemporary realistic fiction as it is fantasy, and a better description of the book might be "magical realism."

Additional examples of fantasy literature for children are

- *The Wind in the Willows* (Graham, 1908)
- *The Lion, the Witch and the Wardrobe* (Lewis, 1950)
- *The Borrowers* (Norton, 1952)
- *A Wrinkle in Time* (L'Engle, 1962)
- *Tuck Everlasting* (Babbit, 1975)
- *The Keeper of the Isis Light* (Hughes, 1980)
- *Redwall* (Jacques, 1987)
- *The Giver* (Lowry, 1993)
- *Silverwing* (Oppel, 1997)
- *The Tale of Despereaux* (DiCamillo, 2003)

Box 10.7 lists a selection of Canadian novels suitable for students in grades 4 to 6.

BOX 10.7 **CANADIAN FICTION FOR UPPER ELEMENTARY READERS**

Alexis, A. (2005). *Ingrid and the wolf.* Toronto: Tundra Books.

Burtinshaw, J. (2005). *The freedom of Jenny.* Vancouver: Raincoast Books.

Clark, J. (1995). *The dream carvers.* Toronto: Viking.

Cumyn, A. (2002). *The secret life of Owen Skye.* Toronto: Douglas & McIntyre.

Doyle, B. (1984). *Angel Square.* Toronto: Douglas & McIntyre.

Friesen, G. (2005). *The Isabel factor.* Toronto: Kids Can Press.

Guest, J. (2004). *Belle of Batoche.* Victoria, BC: Orca.

Heneghan, J. (2002). *Flood.* Toronto: Groundwood Books/Douglas & McIntyre.

Horrocks, A. (1996). *Breath of a ghost.* Toronto: Stoddart Kids.

Horvath, P. (2001). *Everything on a waffle.* Toronto: Groundwood Books.

Hutchins, H. (1997). *The prince of Tarn.* Toronto: Annick Press.

Johansen, K. V. (2006). *The Cassandra virus.* Victoria, BC: Orca.

Pearson, K. (1996). *Awake and dreaming.* Markham, ON: Viking.

Sherman, G. T. (1997). *Grave danger.* Richmond Hill, ON: Scholastic.

Smith, L. (2004). *The minstrel's daughter.* Regina, SK: Coteau Books.

Trembath, D. (2002). *The bachelors.* Victoria, BC: Orca Book Publishers.

Wilson, E. (1997). *Escape from Big Muddy.* Toronto: HarperCollins.

Collections of Short Stories

The short story, as a literary form, has existed only since the middle of the 19th century. A short story is a brief fictional narrative (though it can be anything from 500 to 15 000 words) that consists of more than just a mere record of an incident. It has a formal structure with unity of time, place, and action. Generally, a short story reveals the true nature of a character.

Today, there are a growing number of high-quality collections of short stories for children in grades 4 to 6 (see Box 10.8). These are delightful and frequently thought-provoking

---

BOX 10.8   COLLECTIONS OF SHORT STORIES FOR CHILDREN IN GRADES 4 TO 6

Asher, S. (Ed.). (1996). *But that's another story: Famous authors introduce popular genres.* New York: Walker and Co.

Coville, B. (1994). *Oddly enough: Stories.* San Diego: Harcourt Brace & Co.

Datlow, E. & Windling, T. (Ed.). (2003). *Swan sister: Fairy tales retold.* New York: Simon & Schuster Books for Young Readers.

French, J. (2002). *Ride the wild wind: The golden pony and other stories.* Sydney: Angus & Robertson.

Hancock, P. (1995). *Strange and eerie stories.* Richmond Hill, ON: Scholastic Canada.

Hughes, S. (1993). *Stories by firelight.* New York: Lothrop, Lee & Shepard.

Jennings, P. (1985). *Unreal! Eight surprising stories.* Ringwood, Victoria, Australia: Puffin.

King-Smith, D. (1999). *Hogsel and Gruntel and other animal stories.* New York: Orchard Books.

Little, J. (1998). *What will the robin do then? Winter tales.* Toronto: Viking.

Lunn, J. (Ed.). (1994). *The unseen: Scary stories.* Toronto: Stoddart.

Mackay, C. (Ed.). (1997). *Laughs: Funny stories.* Plattsburgh, NY: Tundra Books.

Mahy, M. (1994). *Tick tock tales: Stories to read around the clock.* New York: Margaret K. McElderry Books.

Mark, J. (1981). *Nothing to be afraid of.* New York: Harper & Row Publishers.

Matthews, A. (Ed.). (1995). *The Kingfisher treasury of funny stories.* Boston: Houghton Mifflin.

Pearce, P. (2002). *Familiar and haunting collected stories.* New York: Greenwillow Books.

Potok, C. (1998). *Zebra and other stories.* New York: Alfred Knopf.

Rylant, C. (2000). *Thimbleberry stories.* San Diego: Harcourt Brace.

San Souci, R. (1998). *A terrifying taste of short and shivery: Thirty creepy tales.* New York: Delacorte.

Soto, G. (1990). *Baseball in April, and other stories.* New York: Harcourt.

Tulloch, R. (1989). *Stories from our street.* New York: Cambridge University Press.

Turner, M. W. (1995). *Instead of three wishes.* New York: Greenwillow.

Vande Velde, V. (2000). *The Rumpelstiltskin problem.* Boston: Houghton Mifflin Company.

Yolen, J. (1998). *Here there be ghosts.* San Diego, CA: Harcourt Brace & Co.

---

stories that are well-crafted pieces of writing. Readers familiar with Tim Wynne-Jones's picture books will be especially appreciative of his three books of short stories: *Some of the Kinder Planets* (1993), which won the Governor General's Award and the Boston Globe–Horn Book Award for Children's Literature, *The Book of Changes* (1994), and *Lord of the Fries* (1999). Kit Pearson has edited an anthology of short stories and excerpts from works of Canadian children's literature titled *This Land* (1998). *Back of Beyond* (Ellis, 1998) and *Garbage Creek* (Valgardson, 1997) are also excellent collections of short stories suitable for the upper elementary grades.

TRADITIONAL LITERATURE

Traditional literature remains a staple of the elementary language arts curriculum from kindergarten to grade 6. Today there are many beautifully illustrated retellings of traditional stories, originating from around the world. This section presents a sampling of these books.

The genre of traditional literature, which is sometimes referred to as "folk literature," includes fairytales, folk tales, Mother Goose rhymes, legends, myths, proverbs, epics, fables, and more. These are mostly short stories that reflect the values and dreams of a society, and through which societies and their cultures come alive. Traditional literature is, in general, a body of work that was originally passed from generation to generation orally. Scholars and educators agree that traditional literature is a most important genre for children, and it is frequently the first genre with which children become truly familiar. "Once upon a time" is a phrase that young children all over the Western world associate with the telling of a story. It signals the beginning of a narrative designed to take the child into the world of imagination. The classic fairytale has a structure that has become ingrained in the Western psyche. Jean Little's *Once upon a Golden Apple* (1991) plays with children's internalization of the structure of fairytales, and the humour in the book is based on children understanding these "rules" and knowing those rules are being manipulated.

Folk and Fairytales

Many traditional versions of folk and fairytales are available today. Some author/illustrators have become well-known for their renditions of these stories, people such as Laszlo Gal, Leo and Diane Dillon, Jan Brett, Trina Schart Hyman, Jane Yolen, Paul Galdone, Robert San Souci, and John Steptoe. Galdone's version of *Little Red Riding Hood* (1974) is particularly appropriate for young children, while Hyman's rendition of *Little Red Riding Hood* (1983) is more appropriate for older readers. *The Twelve Dancing Princesses* has been retold by Janet Lunn (1979, illustrated by Laszlo Gal), Ruth Sanderson (1990), and Marianna Mayer (1989, illustrated by Kinuko Craft). Jan Ormerod has retold *The Frog Prince* (1990 illustrated by David Lloyd), and Glen Rounds has produced a version of *The Three Billy Goats Gruff* (1993).

There are also parodies of well-known tales in books such as *The Three Little Wolves and the Big Bad Pig* (Trivizas, 1993) and *The True Story of the Three Little Pigs* (Scieszka, 1989). Both of these books are based on the traditional story *The Three Little Pigs* and depend on intertextual connections for their humour and impact.

In a number of clever retellings of fairytales, the texts deviate little from the original version, but the illustrations create a powerfully different meaning to the story. *Hansel and Gretel*, retold by Anthony Browne (1981), is one such book, in which the traditional story is retold in a modern setting. Ian Wallace's (1994) rendition of *Hansel and Gretel* also places the story in a contemporary setting, this time in Atlantic Canada.

Modern fairytales such as *The Tough Princess* by Martin Waddell (1986, illustrated by Patrick Benson) and *The King's Equal* by Katherine Paterson (1992, illustrated by Vladimir Vagin) play with readers' expectations and knowledge of the fairytale genre. These books raise questions about traditional gender roles and the messages implicit in most fairytales (e.g., that a woman must be rescued by a man and is then dependent on him for living happily ever after). *The Tough Princess* does this in a humorous way that questions traditional expectations from the first page. Paterson's book, *The King's Equal*, raises the same questions as *The Tough Princess*, but in a different manner, and the book accomplishes much more than a reversal of traditional gender roles. Paterson has created a story in which all the participants learn from their actions, and the presence of the mysterious wolf adds a mystical element. As teachers and students read and interact with these modern versions of fairytales, readers may discover deeper meanings in the traditional tales. They may also be moved to question them, given the context of current societal beliefs and values.

Myths and Legends

Many novels for children and adults are based on the patterns, characters, and plots of the best-known myths and legends, and certain recurring themes in literature can be traced back to myths. As a result, it is helpful for young readers to be introduced to myths and legends as part of the repertoire of elementary school reading. Greek, Roman, Celtic, and Norse myths are the better-known of these stories, though many books now available are devoted to Aboriginal American, Chinese, and South American myths. Joseph Campbell (1988) argues that myths are powerful literature that should be read by everyone to help us understand ourselves as human beings and as social and spiritual creatures.

One such recent retelling of a Chinese myth, *The Dragon's Pearl* by Julie Lawson (1992), is beautifully illustrated by Paul Morin. The book won the Amelia Frances Howard-Gibbon Award for illustrations in 1993. Also illustrated by Paul Morin is Tololwa Mollel's Tanzanian myth *The Orphan Boy* (1990), which won the 1990 Governor General's Literary Award for illustration. Priscilla Galloway has retold a number of Greek myths, including *Aleta and the Queen: A Tale of Ancient Greece* (1995), *Atalanta: The Fastest Runner in the World* (1995), and *Daedalus and the Minotaur* (1997). All are illustrated by Normand Cousin. It is interesting to note that myths and legends have spawned many phrases in the English language. Greek myths in particular have generated phrases such as "the Midas touch," "Pandora's box," "Herculean effort," and "a Trojan horse."

Legends are stories told about real people and their feats or accomplishments. Usually the narratives are mixed with superstition, and they expand and enhance the actual exploits of their heroes. Legends are closely related to myths, but they do not contain supernatural deities as myths do. The stories of Beowulf, King Arthur, Robin Hood, William Tell, Davy

Crockett, and Johnny Appleseed are legends. From reading myths and legends, children are encouraged to seek explanations for the phenomena in their lives—to ask questions about modern "legendary" figures and heroes and perhaps relate them to the possibilities inherent in their own lives.

Fables

The origin of the fable is thought to reside with a Greek slave named Aesop, who lived in the 6th century BC. Experts, however, believe there were many sources of the fable, since it is found worldwide. Fables are fictional tales that are meant to entertain though they also contain a moral. They usually have only two or three characters, frequently talking animals who possess humanlike characteristics. Fables are popular with young children today largely because of the presence of the talking animals and the humour the stories contain. Fables such as "The Town Mouse and the Country Mouse" and "The Tortoise and the Hare" remain particular favourites with children. There are also many variations of "The Lion and the Mouse" and "The Raven and the Fox."

The Oral Tradition of Storytelling

True storytelling calls upon stories that are part of the tradition of oral literature, stories that have many versions and can be modified to suit audience and purpose. These are the stories that are handed down within families or within cultural groups. The Aboriginal peoples of Canada, the United States, Australia, and New Zealand have a rich fund of stories, some of which are ritual stories that may not be shared with the general public. Families also have their stories and storytellers—stories of early settlement in homesteads on the prairie, stories of great-grandfathers who worked on the trans-Canada railway, stories of great hardship, illnesses, long journeys at sea, family treasures, and great adventures. These are the stories that cannot easily be written down and neatly illustrated. They are stories that have a special significance to the listener and frequently appeal to a small audience. This is the difference between storytelling and "performing" a text.

Children in the elementary grades generally enjoy a good storyteller. They enjoy hearing a senior citizen speak of times past in a small community, and they enjoy collecting the stories of community members. True storytelling demands discipline, so that a story is captured and shaped to suit the audience and the purpose for its telling. A rambling recollection of an event that occurred a number of years ago is not the same thing as a story. Thus, teachers who wish to engage in storytelling, or to have their students tell stories in the classroom, should hone their storytelling skills. This includes perfecting the nuances of chosen vocabulary, intonation, facial expressions, and hand gestures, as well as ensuring that stories have cohesion, development, and appropriate closure, just as a good written tale does. Storytelling must also be rehearsed, just like any other performance, before it is shared with an audience.

Teachers can make full use of storytelling in their classrooms and help children develop as storytellers by having them read many different versions of a traditional story and then retell it in their own way. In this way children can invest the oral story with their own thoughts and feelings, story and storyteller becoming one. Two excellent resource books for teachers are *And None of It Was Nonsense: The Power of Storytelling in the Classroom* by Betty Rosen (1988) and *Stories to Tell* by Bob Barton (1992). Rosen describes her thinking, preparation, follow-up work, and lessons. The book also includes selections of her students' work. Barton has put together a set of resource materials for storytelling, and draws on his experiences as a Canadian storyteller/teacher/writer. He encourages teachers to tell their own stories, including the songs, rhymes, jingles, chants, and sayings they remember. Barton connects the worlds of storytelling, drama, games, movement, and role-play in the creation of new stories, reminding us that stories can be revisited and remade again and again. In *Stories in the Classroom*, Bob Barton and David Booth (1990) collaborated in furthering their work on storytelling, drama, and response to literature. It provides another valuable resource for teachers.

POETRY FOR CHILDREN

The nursery rhymes, songs, and jingles of their infancy constitute a core of literature for most children. Poetry has a major role to play in the language arts curriculum. This section of the chapter presents selections of poems, poetic forms, and poetic devices appropriate for the elementary grades.

Many adults remember clearly the nursery rhymes, jingles, skipping songs, and playground chants they heard when they were preschoolers. Opie and Opie (1963) refer to these oral rhymes as "the true waifs of our literature in that their original wordings, as well as their authors, are usually unknown" (p. 7). Many of these rhymes, now considered suitable only for the nursery, were not originally intended for children. They stem from old ballads, political lampoons, and "worldly songs." The Opies spent more than 20 years collecting and researching nursery rhymes, and the section of incidental notes at the back of their collection, *The Puffin Book of Nursery Rhymes*, provides fascinating insights into the history of many rhymes in the book. Young children continue to enjoy nursery rhymes, with their unusual words, frequent nonsense, and compelling rhythms.

As adults we also remember the deeply meaningful and emotive poems read to us by family members and teachers, poems such as "The Highwayman" by Alfred Noyes. Refrains and particularly humorous stanzas from poems such as "The Adventures of Isabel" by Ogden Nash also remain fixed in our memories. We may remember writing poems in school or responding to poems in response journals or through drama activities. Huck, Hepler, Hickman, and Kiefer (2004, p. 350) write that

> Poetry can both broaden and intensify experience, or it might present a range of experiences beyond the realm of personal possibility for the individual listener. It can also illuminate, clarify, and deepen an everyday occurrence in a way the reader never considered, making the reader see more and feel more than ever before. For poetry does more than mirror life; it reveals life in new dimensions.

Poetry communicates experience by appealing to both the thoughts and feelings of the reader. Every word is carefully chosen by the poet for the nuances and emotive meanings it conveys. Children usually need to experience poetry as being pleasurable and often amusing before they can experience its more beautiful and philosophical aspects. Poetry should be as much a part of the literary world of children as contemporary realistic fiction or picture books are. Learning to understand and appreciate poetry is an ongoing process, as it is with other forms of literature. Children are more likely to enjoy poetry if they have experienced it from their earliest days, through nursery rhymes, jingles, and songs. Nursery rhymes and skipping rhymes cannot be considered poetry, but they do lay the foundation for later journeys into poetic language.

Defining poetry is a challenge, for many contemporary poets are breaking the traditional expectations of poetry, both in content and form. Words are placed across the page, at angles, and in bunches. Contemporary poetry is written about subjects not previously dealt with (taking the garbage out, watching father eat mashed potatoes at dinner time, listening to a fight between parents). However, poems continue to make children laugh, ponder, imagine, remember, and see the world in new ways. Indeed, poetry helps to develop insights and new understandings.

As Booth and Moore (1988) write, "Children's poetry has a special appeal: the form and language of poetry speaks directly to the child, to their senses, their imaginations, their emotions, their feelings, their experiences of childhood" (p. 22). Experience tells us that children are not interested in static poems that describe the seasons, weather, or events in nature. Rather, they are interested in poems of action, rhythm, rhyme, and energy that invite them to participate and relate to their everyday experiences. Children are naturally rhythmical. From the earliest nursery rhymes to the poems of Dennis Lee, a musical rhythm pervades the text. Children are generally intrigued by the sound of language as they play with it and learn its melody.

Sharing Poetry with Children

Children become readers and appreciators of poetry by experiencing poetry with adults who enjoy, read, and share poetry with them. Hearing the skilfully crafted arrangement of the sounds of a poem read aloud is one of the primary pleasures of poetry. Although enunciation is a fundamental component of any kind of oral sharing of poetry, it is also vital that poetry be read interpretively. This means that a reader must learn to focus on the emotive meanings conveyed by a poem, whether those meanings are playful or wistful. When children hear Sheree Fitch read her poems aloud, they are entranced by her sheer energy and engagement with the words:

> I've a yearning
> That is burning
> A desire for Higher learning
> I would like
> To go to college
> To improve upon
> My knowledge. ...

(From *If You Could Wear My Sneakers* by Sheree Fitch [poetry] and Darcia Labrosse [illustrations]. © 1997 Sheree Fitch and Darcia Labrosse. Reprinted with the permission of Sheree Fitch.)

Readers of poetry, whether adults or children, consider the mood they wish to set when reading a poem aloud. The interpretation of a poem is greatly influenced by how a reader varies its tempo, volume, rhythm, pitch, and juncture. Briefly,

- *Tempo* refers to how slowly or quickly words or lines are read.
- *Volume* refers to loudness.
- *Rhythm* describes emphasis or stress.
- *Pitch* refers to the lowering or raising of the voice.
- *Juncture* describes the location and length of pauses.

Teachers and students may vary these elements when reading poetry and then discuss whether and how the changes affected their interpretations of the poems.

Choral reading and the implementation of drama strategies enhance children's understanding and awareness of poetry. Sound effects, mime, puppets, shadow plays, and role-playing are dramatic techniques that can be used when working with poetry in the classroom.

Poetic Devices

Rhyme is a very common element of poetry. Indeed, some children believe rhyme to be the sole determining feature of poetry. The poems of Michael Rosen, Dennis Lee, Jack Prelutsky, and Shel Silverstein are contemporary works whose use of rhyme, rhythm, and playfulness forms part of their appeal. Although rhyme is a popular device of poets, children may need to expand their definition of poetry if they are to enjoy more sophisticated poems in later years.

Comparison is another device used by poets. The use of similes, explicitly comparing one thing with another using the words "like" or "as," and the use of *metaphors*, comparing two things by implying that one is like the other, are two common comparison techniques used by poets. A beautifully illustrated picture book of similes is *As Quick as a Cricket* (Woods, 1982). A tongue-in-cheek collection of similes for older readers is *As: A Surfeit of Similes* (Juster, 1989). A further poetic device used by writers is *alliteration*—the repeated use of the same initial consonants in consecutive words or the use of words that are in proximity and produce a pattern of the same or similar sounds. Chris Van Allsburg used alliteration in his alphabet book *The Z Was Zapped* (1987). *Some Smug Slug* (Edwards, 1996) is another example of the use of alliteration to tell a tale.

Onomatopoeia is a device wherein writers use sound words (e.g., *splash, slurp, boing*) to make the writing more vivid and sensory. The elements of tempo, volume, stress, and pitch can be manipulated in ways to assist in conveying the meaning and imagery of sound words. *Machine Poems* (Bennett, 1993) and *Click, Rumble, Roar: Poems About Machines* (Hopkins, 1987) are collections of poems that contain many examples of onomatopoeia. The repetition of words and phrases is another device used by many poets. For example, in the book *A Dark Dark Tale* (Brown, 1981), the author repeats the words "dark, dark." As the poem continues, each location described in the text as "dark, dark" progressively decreases in size. The poem begins, "Once upon a time there was a dark, dark moor" and the next dark, dark location is a wood, and the next one a house, and then a door, and so on.

Imagery and *figurative language* are other important poetic elements that play a role in poetry for children. Langston Hughes's poem "City" (1950) creates the image of the city as a bird, and Carl Sandburg (1944) likens the fog descending on a city to a cat in his poem "Fog." The language, imagery, and rhythm of poetry interact in creating the emotional force of a poem. Langston Hughes's poem entitled "Poem" (1960) evokes a powerful emotional response in most readers, as does "Listening to Grownups Quarrelling" by Ruth Whitman (1968).

Forms of Poetry

One of the most popular forms of poetry with children is *narrative poetry*, poetry that tells a story. One narrative poem that has been reproduced in picture book format is *The Cremation of Sam McGee*, written by Robert Service and illustrated by Ted Harrison (1987). Lyric and free verse are two other forms of poetry enjoyed by children. Lyric poetry frequently describes a mood or feeling and elicits strong emotions about the subject of the poem. Although free verse poetry generally lacks rhyme, this type of poetry allows poets great freedom in creating their own rules of rhythm. Emotional language and imagery are important elements of free verse. The topics of free verse poetry are often abstract or philosophical.

Haiku and *cinquain* are forms of poetry that have prescribed structures. Haiku is a form of poetry originating in Japan; a haiku is a three-line poem with the first and last lines each having five syllables and the middle line having seven syllables. Traditionally, haiku dealt with topics associated with nature or the seasons, but modern haiku are written about a much broader range of subjects. A cinquain, a five-line stanza, is structured around 22 syllables in a 2-4-6-8-2 syllable pattern.

Rhyme, rhythm, and sound are important poetic elements that influence students' opinions of poems, and children love to chant and move with the words, whether it's *Dirty Dog Boogie* (Lesynski, 1999) or a limerick. Edward Lear popularized limericks, now a favourite form of poetry among children and adults alike, in his book, *The Complete Book of Nonsense* (1846, 1946). Limericks are usually humorous or silly five-lined verses, with the first and second lines rhyming with the fifth line and the shorter third and fourth lines rhyming with each other. Often the fifth line is a repetition of the first line. Two books of limericks are *The Book of Pigericks* (Lobel, 1983) and *The Hopeful Trout and Other Limericks* (Ciardi, 1989).

Concrete poems are arranged in a particular manner on a page in order to create an image or visual shape of the poem's subject. For example, in the poetry collection *A Hippopotamusn't* (Lewis, 1990), Lewis has written a concrete poem about the flamingo, cleverly arranging the words in a flamingo shape. Concrete poetry is meant to be seen even more than heard. This form of poetry often lacks a rhythm or rhyming pattern. *Seeing Things: A Book of Poems* (Froman, 1974) and *Concrete Is Not Always Hard* (Pilon, 1972) are two collections of concrete poetry.

Picture Book Versions of Poems

There are many picture book versions of single poems, including Robert Frost's "Stopping by Woods on a Snowy Evening," illustrated by Susan Jeffers (1976), and Eugene Field's "Wynken, Blynken and Nod," also illustrated by Susan Jeffers (1982). Jan Brett (1991) has illustrated a picture book version of "The Owl and the Pussy Cat" by Edward Lear, and Ed Young (1988) has illustrated Robert Frost's poem "Birches." Ted Rand has illustrated two poems: "My Shadow" (1990) by Robert Louis Stevenson and "Arithmetic" (1993) by Carl Sandburg.

Diane Siebert has created two picture poetry books: *Train Song* (1990) and *Motorcycle Song* (2002), written for children in grades 3 to 7. In *Motorcycle Song*, readers follow a motorcyclist on an exhilarating journey through towns, narrow lanes, highways, and open country, with a poetic rhythm that matches the vehicle's movement. Illustrated by Leonard Jenkins, the mixed-media paintings are rich in colour, energy, and movement, capturing the freedom of the open road.

In the picture book *In Flanders Fields: The Story of the Poem* by John McCrae (1995), Linda Granfield not only presents "In Flanders Fields" but also shares information about the poet and his experiences working in a field hospital. She describes the living conditions and daily routines of the soldiers and provides information about World War I. She also explains the origin of the symbolic gesture of wearing a poppy. The illustrator, Janet Wilson, travelled to Flanders to do research for her paintings, because she wanted them to be as accurate as possible.

Poetry Collections

Many books of poetry are collections of one individual's works. Examples include:

- *A Light in the Attic* (Silverstein, 1981)
- *The New Kid on the Block* (Prelutsky, 1984)
- *Roomrimes* (Cassedy, 1987)
- *Day Songs, Night Songs* (Priest, 1993)
- *Beast Feast* (Florian, 1994)
- *If You Could Wear My Sneakers* (Fitch, 1997)
- *Daft as a Doughnut* (Mitchell, 2004)
- *Something's Drastic* (Rosen, 2007)
- *Collected Poems for Children* (Hughes, 2007)
- *Shout: Little Poems That Roar* (Bagert, 2007)

David McCord, John Ciardi, Dennis Lee, Loris Lesynski, and Myra Cohn Livingston are also known for collections of their poetry.

Many poetry books are specialized collections of poems related to a single theme or topic—for example, snow, dinosaurs, monsters, dragons, magic, festivals, machines, Halloween, and nightmares. General anthologies of poetry are useful for teachers to have on hand. Notable anthologies include *The Oxford Book of Poetry for Children*, compiled by Edward Blishen (1963); *The Random House Book of Poetry* by Jack Prelutsky (1983); *Til All the Stars Have Fallen* by David Booth (1989); and *Images of Nature: Canadian Poets and the Group of Seven* by David Booth (1995). A number of poetry anthologies suitable for use in elementary school classrooms are listed in Box 10.9.

BOX 10.9 **POETRY RESOURCES**

Balaam, J. and Merrick, B. (1989). *Exploring poetry: 5–8.* Sheffield, UK: National Association for the Teaching of English.

Fleischman, P. (1985). *Joyful noise: Poems for two voices.* New York: Harper and Row.

Foster, J. and Paul, K. (2000). *Pet poems.* Oxford: Oxford University Press.

Harrison, M. and Stuart-Clark, C. (Comp.). (1995). *The new Oxford treasury of children's poems.* Toronto: Oxford University Press.

Janeczko, P. (2001). *A poke in the I.* Cambridge, MA: Candlewick Press.

Larrick, N. (Ed.). (1991). *To the moon and back.* New York: Delacorte.

Lee, D. (1974). *Alligator pie.* Toronto: Macmillan Canada.

Lesynski, L. (2004). *Zigzag: Zoems for zindergarten.* Toronto: Annick.

Mayo, M. (2000). *Wiggle waggle fun: Stories and rhymes for the very very young.* Toronto: Random House.

Merrick, B. (1991). *Exploring poetry: 8–13.* Sheffield, UK: National Association for the Teaching of English.

Numeroff, L. (2002). *Sometimes I wonder if poodles like noodles.* New York: Aladdin Paperbacks.

Prelutsky, J. (1996). *A pizza the size of the sun.* New York: Greenwillow Books.

Priest, R. (2002). *The secret invasion of bananas.* Victoria, BC: Cherubim Books.

Rosen, M. (1984). *Quick, let's get out of here.* New York: Dutton.

Silverstein, S. (1974). *Where the sidewalk ends: Poems and drawings.* New York: Harper.

Stepanek, M. (2002). *Celebrate through heart songs.* New York: Hyperion.

INFORMATION BOOKS

Nonfiction or information books are an important learning resource for use across the curriculum as well as for recreational reading. Nonfiction books must be current, accurate, and appealing to children. This section of the chapter presents various types of nonfiction books, as well as criteria for evaluating nonfiction materials.

Information books (also known as nonfiction literature) play a major role in every elementary classroom. It is this genre that provides the resource material for most teaching across the entire curriculum. Through reading about a topic from many sources and from a number of different perspectives, students are able to construct a fuller understanding of the topic. Each piece of information and each point of view helps to create a broader picture in the mind of the student and provides the fertile ground for new meanings to develop. Meaning, after all, resides in the individual learner. Many children in the primary grades (and earlier) thoroughly enjoy reading nonfiction materials, and it is this genre that caters to the special interests of students and provides them with the resources they need for pursuing their avocation.

However, it is only recently that educators have recognized children's interests and pleasure in reading nonfiction materials and have begun to teach children how to read expository texts as well as narrative texts (see Chapter 7).

Children need both narrative and non-narrative reading and writing experiences. Now, with children in the primary grades encouraged to work on cross-curricular projects using nonfiction materials for information, educators are teaching youngsters how to use the index of a book, the glossary, and the table of contents, as well as how to browse through a book quickly to see from the pictures and the headings if the book is going to be helpful or interesting.

There are at least eight major types of nonfiction books for children:

- photo-documentaries
- "how-to" books
- question-and-answer formats
- experiment and activity books
- sequential explanation (survey) books
- field guides
- biographies
- narrative nonfiction

Some of these nonfiction books are designed to be used as reference materials and have a typical expository format. Others are to be read from beginning to end, more like a work of fiction, and consist of narrative text.

Nonfiction material has improved a great deal in quality and presentation over the last 10 years. Nonfiction materials still on library shelves from the 1980s look dull and uninviting compared with more recent publications. The advances in technology, allowing for the superb reproduction of photographs, maps, and other graphics and a more interesting and accessible page layout, has created a splendid new age of nonfiction, especially for young readers.

Many awards have been specifically created for nonfiction books. These include the Information Book Award sponsored by the Children's Literature Round Tables of Canada, the Orbis Pictus Award for Outstanding Nonfiction for Children established by the National Council of Teachers of English (in the United States), the Boston Globe–Horn Book Award established jointly by the *Boston Globe* and *The Horn Book Magazine* (United States), and the Times Educational Supplement Information Book Awards (United Kingdom). The designation of these awards is a mark of the increasing recognition accorded nonfiction books, as well as a recognition of children's strong interest in

Two readers share nonfiction book

informational materials. It is also an indication that the quality of nonfiction materials has improved sufficiently to merit awards specifically for the genre.

Criteria for Evaluating Nonfiction Books

The information available in any subject area grows rapidly over time. Keeping a nonfiction collection up to date is a major challenge and a major expense for any school or library. Books published on a topic 10 or 15 years ago are likely to be out of date today. It is therefore important that nonfiction books be purchased for the school or classroom library with discrimination, and with the aid of library selection tools such as *CM: Canadian Materials*, *The Horn Book Magazine*, *School Library Journal*, *Teacher Librarian*, or *Booklist*. It is also important that the books made available to children be current, and that they not be allowed to remain on the shelves for many years without being reviewed. A list of evaluation criteria for nonfiction books is presented in Box 10.10.

The *accuracy* and *authenticity* of material is probably the most difficult criterion for educators to assess. The first thing to look for in any nonfiction book is an indication from the author(s) that either they have the expertise themselves (as with Nic Bishop, 2004, *Forest Explorer*), or they have consulted with experts in the creation of the book (as in *The Shortest Day*, Pfeffer, 2003). The latter book contains excellent illustrations, clear explanations, and interesting activities for readers to complete either at home or at school. It contains a list of further reading on the topic and a list of related websites. The book contains an acknowledgment of the assistance provided by a professor of physics at Rhodes College and a history professor at the College of New Jersey. This last piece of information tells the reader that the information contained in the book has come from a reliable source. Whatever is provided for the reader, however, the main criterion for selecting a book must be compatibility with the reader's own background knowledge of the subject. Teachers play a crucial role in assisting their students to select books that are appropriate in content—books that are neither too simple nor conceptually overloaded.

The *format* of nonfiction books is an especially important area to evaluate. Some nonfiction books are too "busy" in their layout for young readers. The visual effect is one of overload, as the reader has to attend to too much input at one time. An aesthetically appealing and effective book in terms of content and format is *Forest Explorer: A Life-Size Field Guide* (Bishop, 2004), which presents the wilds of the forest in a unique photographic style. Seven double-page life-size habitat scenes capture more than 130 animals from beetles to squirrels. With a superb picture index, the book can be used as a field guide, but it is also a book readers enjoy perusing and reading in depth. This book is highly suitable for a classroom collection.

Unfortunately, many nonfiction books are still printed without colour photographs and diagrams. They may contain lots of interesting information and ideas for children, but they are not appealing to today's visually oriented generation of students. As a result they appear inaccessible for young readers. Too much information is often presented in a black-and-white format, so that readers cannot easily pick out the chunks of information they are seeking. Children can become overwhelmed by the amount of information, even if it is in the form of a diagram or drawing, and they may close the book and move on to something else. Colour photographs and drawings help young readers move their eyes and their attention around the page from one unit of meaning to another more easily.

BOX 10.10   CRITERIA FOR EVALUATING NONFICTION BOOKS

Format

▷ Is the book well made so that it will stand up to wear?

▷ Is the page design uncluttered?

▷ Is the book visually appealing? Does it invite the reader to browse through it?

▷ Does it pique the reader's interest?

▷ Are there enough visuals and enough colour to make the book appealing?

Organization and Style

▷ Is the material presented in a clear and unambiguous way?

▷ Does the book create a feeling of reader involvement and convey a positive tone?

▷ Does the author use vivid and interesting language?

▷ Is the content structured clearly and logically, with appropriate subheadings?

▷ Are there reference aids, such as a table of contents, index, bibliography, glossary, and appendix?

Content

▷ Is the content presented in a manner that allows children to connect it with their own experiences?

▷ Where content has been simplified, does it retain accuracy?

▷ Does the book include the author's sources as well as additional information for keen readers who want to learn more?

▷ Does the book provide Internet links?

▷ Is the book current and does it reflect (and mention) current research activity in the field?

▷ Are the qualifications and experiences of the authors presented?

▷ Does the book avoid stereotypes and present differing viewpoints?

▷ Is a distinction made among fact, theory, and opinion?

▷ Does the book foster a scientific method of inquiry?

▷ Are there appropriate and sufficient maps, charts, and diagrams to add to the reader's understanding of the text?

▷ Are the graphics and illustrations an appropriate size?

▷ Are the graphics and illustrations clearly understandable and well labelled?

▷ Do the maps, charts, and diagrams contain appropriate detail?

Source: Based on F. Smardo Dowd, "Trends and evaluative criteria of informational books for children," in E. Freeman and D. Person (eds.), *Using nonfiction trade books in the classroom: From ants to zeppelins* (Urbana, IL: National Council of Teachers of English, 1992), pp. 34–43.

Hugh Brewster's *At Vimy Ridge* (2006) is a well organized and well formatted account of the Battle of Vimy Ridge in France during World War I. The book allows the reader's focus to move smoothly from text to diagram to photograph and back to text. The format helps the reader take in the information and make sense of it. Clear maps, period photographs, excerpts from soldiers' letters home, and excellent text make this book an engaging reading experience for adults as well as children. The story of the battle is grim, but is told in such a way that readers are helped to understand the nature of gas attacks, and life in the trenches. Brewster's careful explanation of a "creeping barrage" is well illustrated, and the double-page photograph of the battle at Hill 145 is more eloquent than any text could be on the nature of war and the resulting deaths. The description of Armistice Day and the end photographs and description of the newly restored and stunning memorial at Vimy add a deeper layer of meaning to this "war story."

Narrative Nonfiction

Some of the most fascinating nonfiction materials are narrative texts that incorporate details and explanations into a story. One of the best-known books of narrative nonfiction for young children is the award-winning Australian book *Where the Forest Meets the Sea* by Jeanie Baker (1987). It is an innovative picture book that chronicles the reflections of a young boy exploring the rainforest of northern Queensland with his father. The illustrations (also done by Baker) consist of relief collage constructed from a mix of natural materials, including lamb's wool, fabric, and leaves. The result is a rich, three-dimensional perspective on the rainforest that invites the reader to explore the secrets of the forest and the majesty of nature. The boy plays, imagines, wonders, and questions: "Will the rainforest still be here when we come back?" No answers are provided, no didacticism. It is left to the reader to ponder the question.

Thunderstorm! (Tripp, 1994) is a book that describes the large and small changes that take place in the atmosphere when weather fronts move. Such changes warn animals and humans to seek shelter from the explosive forces of a storm. The book, illustrated by Juan Wijngaard, tells in narrative style how a thunderstorm develops over one farm, building in intensity and transforming quiet farmland into nature's most spectacular sound and light show.

Snowflake Bentley (Martin, 1998) is a book of narrative nonfiction that won the Caldecott Medal in the United States in 1999. William Bentley, a Vermont farmer/photographer, had a special interest in exploring and photographing natural phenomena. During the early part of the 20th century, Bentley created photographs that demonstrated that no two snowflakes are alike and that each one is startlingly beautiful. At the time, Bentley's work with snow was often misunderstood. His book *Snow Crystals* and his "lantern slides" were, however, well respected and were used by many colleges and universities. Author Jacqueline Briggs Martin accompanies the gentle story with sidebars containing snippets of information and explanations of Bentley's work. The woodcuts created by illustrator Mary Azarian bring the story beautifully to life.

Bat Loves the Night (Davies, 2001) offers vivid descriptions of the pipistrelle bat's nocturnal hunting, flying, and squealing. The book explores the bat's navigational skills and explains how the bat wraps her baby inside her leather wings to keep it safe and to suckle it. Bat facts are presented unobtrusively in a different typeface at some distance from the story itself. The facts can be read along with the story or left for a future reading. The book is beautifully illustrated, and the tone created is tranquil and reflective. Where many information books "shout" at the reader, this book creates an appreciative space for the reader to meet the pipistrelle bat and understand why "bat loves the night."

BOX 10.11   A SELECTION OF HIGH-QUALITY NONFICTION BOOKS

Anholt, L. (1998). *Stone girl, bone girl: The story of Mary Anning*. New York: Orchard Books.

Arnold, C. (2006). *A penguin's world*. Minneapolis: Picture Window Books.

Brenner, B. (2004). *One small place in a tree*. New York: Harper Collins.

Burleigh, R. (2003). *Into the woods: John James Audubon lives his dream*. New York: Atheneum books for Young Readers.

Davies, N. (2001). *Ice bear: In the steps of the polar bear*. Cambridge, MA: Candlewick Press.

Godkin, C. (1995). *Ladybug garden*. Markham, ON: Fitzhenry & Whiteside.

Heller, R. (1999). *Color, color, color*. New York: Puffin.

Hutts Aston, D. (2007). *A seed is sleepy*. Vancouver: Raincoast Books.

Mann, E. (1996). *The Brooklyn Bridge*. New York: Mikaya Press.

Markle, S. (2005). *A mother's journey*. Watertown, MA: Charlesbridge.

Prager, E. (2000). *Sand*. Washington, DC: National Geographic Society.

Schlein, M. (1996). *The puzzle of the dinosaur bird*. New York: Dial Books for Young Readers.

Sis, P. (1996). *Starry messenger*. New York: Farrar, Straus & Giroux.

Tomacek, S. (2007). *Dirt*. Washington, DC: National Geographic Society.

These and other well-written, well-illustrated nonfiction books for children have moved the genre into a new era. A few exemplary nonfiction books are listed in Box 10.11. They truly are books to be read purely for pleasure, and not only for the information they offer. And ultimately, though written for children, they make compelling reading for all ages.

Nonbook Resources

Sometimes we give the impression to young readers that books are the only legitimate source of reading materials. Yet, when we think about the different items we read each day, books are only one of many reading sources. Some of the other items we read each day include newspapers, magazines, TV guides, phone books, brochures, advertisements, signs, labels, and a range of texts on the Internet. If we want children to become literate and read widely for both information and pleasure, we need to ensure they read a wide variety of materials in school as well as outside of school.

Newspapers are a source of print that many of us read nearly every day. We read newspapers for both entertainment and information about current news and events in our area. We read them to decide where to shop for groceries and which movies to go to. Many local newspapers employ education specialists and provide newspapers and suggestions for their use to classroom teachers upon request. There are also many newspapers and magazines designed specifically for children. They focus on a variety of areas, including outdoor life, science, and popular culture. Some of those available are listed in Box 10.12. These materials can be useful in a number of instructional activities, particularly in relation to content-area reading. They provide up-to-date information on a range of topics related both to curriculum and children's interests. Morrow and Lesnick (2001) provide research to support the positive contributions that magazines make to classroom and literacy experiences of children. They also provide enjoyable recreational reading for children.

Children are increasingly reading material on the Internet or in software programs. All of the children's magazines listed in Box 10.12 have websites that provide further literacy experiences and activities. Like all other materials, those on the computer are only appropriate if they meet the needs of specific children in your classrooms.

BOX 10.12   CHILDREN'S PERIODICALS

Let's Find Out and *Storyworks*

▷ *Let's Find Out* (kindergarten): Mini-books, news stories, classroom photo stories, activity pages

▷ *Storyworks* (grades 3 to 5): Fiction, nonfiction, poetry and classroom plays, interviews with authors, hands-on activities, student-written book reviews

Scholastic Canada Limited

http://www.scholastic.ca

Your Big Backyard and *Ranger Rick*

▷ *Your Big Backyard* (ages 3 to 7): Photo stories, activities

▷ *Ranger Rick* (ages 7 and up): Nonfiction, fiction, photo stories, activities, environmental tips about wildlife around the world

National Wildlife Federation

http://www.nwf.org/kids

National Geographic Explorer

▷ Grades 3 to 6: Nonfiction, photo stories, activities for junior members of the National Geographic Society

National Geographic Society

http://www.nationalgeographic.com

Ladybug, Spider, and *Cricket*

▷ *Ladybug* (ages 2 to 6): Stories, poems, activities, games, songs, crafts, some nonfiction

▷ *Spider* (ages 6 to 9): Stories, articles, games, activities, jokes

▷ *Cricket* (ages 9 to 14): Stories, folk tales, biographies, science fiction, cartoons, poems, activities, crafts, crossword puzzles, nonfiction

Cricket Magazine Group

http://www.cricketmag.com/home.asp

Weekly Reader

▷ Children's newspapers at a variety of age and grade levels

Weekly Reader Corporation

http://www.weeklyreader.com

Chirp, Chickadee, and Owl

▷ *Chirp* (ages 3 to 6): Read-out-loud stories, puzzles, games, crafts

▷ *Chickadee* (ages 6 to 9): Stories, nonfiction, activities, games

▷ *Owl* (ages 9 to 12): Nonfiction, activities, puzzles, news stories, contests

Chirp, Chickadee, and Owl Magazines

▷ These magazines are Canadian.
http://www.owlkids.com

Sesame Street

▷ Ages 2 to 6: Stories, poems, activities, posters, children's drawing and writing

Children's Television Workshop

http://www.sesameworkshop.org

Highlights for Children

▷ Ages 2 to 12: Stories, puzzles, games, activities, jokes, riddles
http://www.highlights.com/magazine

TEACHER WISDOM

KATHY OSTER, TEACHER/LIBRARIAN

I always suggest that our student teachers start as many lessons as they can with a book or an oral story. So many of the wonderful picture books we have in the library relate directly to the topics and concepts they are teaching, right across the curriculum. I think of all the books that are suitable for math—books like *The Doorbell Rang* (Hutchins, 1986), which is a huge favourite in the early grades. And for social studies topics there's *Josepha: A Prairie Boy's Story* (McGugan, 1994) and *The Red Sash* (Pendziwol, 2005). Then there's *Boy of the Deeps* (Wallace, 2005), set in Cape Breton. Starting with a story focuses the students' attention and creates a context for the lessons they are learning. Stories make things more real to the children. Stories help them to visualize events and settings.

(Continued)

I also suggest that beginning teachers don't start buying books for use in their prospective classrooms but instead start a list—and keep it somewhere really safe. The best place is in a binder. You can add to the list every time you see a book you think will be helpful in your teaching, and you should add the bibliographic information as well, and if possible, some ideas for how you would use the book with students. Before you start buying you need to know which grade level you will be teaching, and you need to have an idea of which books are good books. You also have to remember that you will be able to draw on the school library once you are teaching. If the library doesn't have the book, you will be able to order it through the library. That doesn't mean that you don't need your own personal book collection—just be sure that the books you buy are really good books that you will use over and over again.

I mentioned some of my favorite books at the beginning of this chapter, but other books I have used a lot with students across a range of grades are *The Important Book* (Wise Brown, 1977) and *A House Is a House for Me* (Hoberman, 1978) because there are so many writing and oral language activities you can do with these books right across grades 1 to 6. I've linked the patterning in *The Important Book* to social studies and we've done our own books, for example *The Most Important Thing About Nunavut*. The music teacher did it on the instruments of the orchestra. It's lots of fun to work across the curriculum this way.

SUMMARY

Scholars such as Meek (1988) and Wells (1986) have demonstrated how children who are read to in their preschool years and who learn to appreciate good stories and interesting books are much more likely to experience success in their literacy development and in their learning in school. They are also more likely to read for pleasure when they are adults. Learning from this, educators have embraced the concept of literature-based reading instruction, and many have created language arts programs based on the many genres of trade books available. Consequently, children's literature is incorporated into most language arts programs in Canada, whether it is used to balance a basal reading series or used as the foundation for the literacy program. It is also widely used across the curriculum.

A wide range of top-quality literature is available for children in the elementary grades. The picture book genre is growing most rapidly in terms of scope and quality. Many picture books are produced for students in upper elementary and junior high schools. Likewise, most novels for children are available in paperback and include fantasy, contemporary realistic fiction, historical fiction, time-slip fantasy, and mystery. Modern classics—books such as *Charlotte's Web* (White, 1952) and *The Dark Is Rising* (1973)—are part of the cultural heritage of youngsters. Traditional stories, poetry, and storytelling all play a role in the repertoire of literary materials and activities with which children engage. Books of all genres continue to create opportunities for children to take on the four roles of the reader as described by Freebody and Luke (1990): code breaker, text participant, text user, and text analyst. Mastering these four roles not only enhances a child's reading ability, it also contributes to the lifelong pleasures he or she will have from reading.

The quality and number of nonfiction books available for the classroom have increased markedly over the last 15 years. Current technology has assisted in reproducing colourful, interesting, and understandable diagrams, charts, and maps. Graphics are generally appealing, and photographs are reproduced with greater clarity than ever before. Authors of nonfiction material for children must write intelligently for an audience that has access to more information than was ever previously available. Such materials must therefore be current, accurate, well designed, and interesting, for they are competing with the Internet, television, and movies as sources of information for students. However, good nonfiction literature for children must also be aesthetically appealing to a wide audience, including adults. This is especially the case in books of narrative nonfiction, where information is embedded in a contextualized narrative.

As language arts programs increasingly incorporate works of children's literature as instructional resources, teachers are finding they must be knowledgeable about books, authors, and illustrators, and must be able to talk with children about the books they are reading. Teachers regularly recommend books of all genres to children. This means that teachers increasingly read books written for children and are familiar with the reading interests of their students. If teachers enjoy books and welcome children into the world of literature, their students are also likely to enjoy books and become lifelong readers.

TALKING POINTS

1. Do you consider yourself to be a reader? What kinds of reading materials are you drawn to most often? Do you talk about books, magazines, or websites with friends? Do you find yourself recommending books to your friends and colleagues? These are important questions to consider, because if a teacher is interested in books and reads for pleasure, the students in that teacher's classroom are more likely to read, talk about books and magazines, and value reading.

2. Have you read any children's books recently? Go to a local bookstore or library and get some recommendations from the staff. Check out a few books and become familiar with the books that are popular with children in elementary classrooms today, both fiction and nonfiction. You need to be ready to recommend good books to the students in your classroom.

3. Visit the local library and watch children making book selections. Talk to them about their favourite books while they have books in front of them. You can learn a lot about children's interests and reading preferences from listening to them talk about the books they read and why they make the specific selections.

SELECTED PROFESSIONAL RESOURCES

Kathy Oster suggests …

Huck, C., Hepler, S., Hickman, J. and Kiefer, B. Z. (2004). *Children's literature in the elementary school* (8th ed.). Dubuque, IA: McGraw-Hill.

This American text remains one of the most encompassing of resources on children's literature that I know of. It is an excellent source of information on the different genres of literature, the history of children's literature, author and illustrator profiles, and planning for instruction in the elementary school. The book provides a wealth of background information, and is a useful reference tool for classroom teachers and teacher/librarians. A database on CD-ROM accompanies the text. Over 4000 books can be accessed by author, title, genre, and more. Full bibliographic information, plus the approximate interest level (by grade) is provided for each book. Unfortunately, very few Canadian books are listed.

Vandergrift, K. *Kay Vandergrift's special interest page.* Available at: http://www.scils.rutgers.edu/~kvander.

This noncommercial site was developed by Kay Vandergrift, then Director of the Information, Technology and Informatics Program in the School of Communication, Information and Library Studies at Rutgers University, New Jersey. The site contains lists of picture books, juvenile novels and young adult literature, as well as lists of multicultural and multiethnic books, many of them Canadian. The lists include Aboriginal, Islamic, traditional, and feminist literature. The site also has videos about children's authors and illustrators, as well as articles on featured authors and books. Sections of the site are devoted to a history of children's literature, literature applicable to teaching topics across the curriculum, and resources to support teaching. It's a really good reference site.

CM: Canadian Review of Materials. Available at: www.umanitoba.ca/cm.

This is the site I use the most. *CM* has been published by the Manitoba Library Association since 1995. It's an electronic reviewing journal issued biweekly from September to June every year. Reviews of materials of interest to children and young adults are provided, with a maple leaf symbol denoting Canadian materials, and a globe symbol indicating non-Canadian materials (but that have a Canadian distributor). Also included are author and illustrator profiles, interviews, and publishing news. Back issues are online from 1995 onward and access is completely free of charge. The journal provides an archived collection of items from the years 1971 to 1994, when the journal was published by the Canadian Library Association (in print form) under the title *CM: A Reviewing Journal of Canadian Material for Young People.*

Responding to Literature

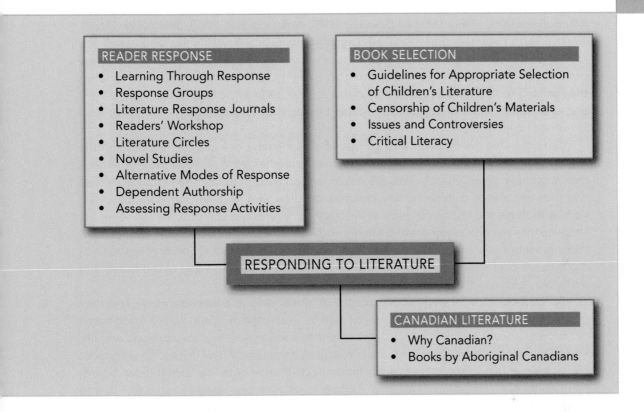

READER RESPONSE
- Learning Through Response
- Response Groups
- Literature Response Journals
- Readers' Workshop
- Literature Circles
- Novel Studies
- Alternative Modes of Response
- Dependent Authorship
- Assessing Response Activities

BOOK SELECTION
- Guidelines for Appropriate Selection of Children's Literature
- Censorship of Children's Materials
- Issues and Controversies
- Critical Literacy

RESPONDING TO LITERATURE

CANADIAN LITERATURE
- Why Canadian?
- Books by Aboriginal Canadians

LITERATURE RESPONSE IN JAN SMITH'S GRADE 6 CLASSROOM

Jan Smith reads aloud to her students almost every day; fiction and nonfiction, poetry and magazine articles. In the past, her students' favourite "read-aloud" novels were *Gregor the Overlander* (Collins, 2003) and *Camp X* (Walters, 2002). Jan sees series books as being comforting to some children because they provide continuity and familiarity to students. Through knowing the characters, students can develop confidence, especially if they are not strong readers. By reading one of a series to the entire class, Jan feels she hooks some of the more reluctant readers into reading additional books in the same series.

Jan Smith

Jan organizes part of her reading program around book clubs, which she conducts three or four times a year. At the beginning of the year, she orders multiple copies of a range of novels from the district's learning resources centre: historical fiction, fantasy, and realistic fiction. In the past, her students have read *The Amazing Journey of Adolphus Tips* (Murpurgo, 2006), *Maniac Magee* (Spinelli, 1990), *Holes* (Sachar, 1998), *Silverwing* (Oppel, 1997), *Chasing Vermeer* (Balliett, 2004), *Escaping the Giant Wave* (Kehret, 2003), and *The City of Ember* (DuPrau, 2003). When the books arrive in the classroom, the students are provided with an extended period of time to browse through them and decide which ones they would like to read. Jan asks her students to scan six to eight books, reading the front and end matter, and making notes about the books. They then rate the books from 1 to 3 in terms of their interest.

Jan organizes the students into groups of six for each book club on the basis of the students' interest in each of the books. She makes sure her reluctant readers get their first choice of book, and the book clubs are not organized according to reading ability. Instead Jan tries to balance talkers and shy children, children who tend to dominate conversations with those she knows can work well together. Sometimes she puts friends together, because they need to enjoy this experience and look forward to it. Jan says you must know your students if you are to make successful groupings for book clubs. Sometimes she finds a group will consist entirely of boys or of girls, depending on the topic of the book, and that's okay because these groupings are not long-term.

At the beginning of each book club the students receive a calendar page and they decide which sections of the book they will read for each meeting date. The children agree not to read ahead, and they sign an agreement that will make the club work successfully. This agreement is student created and is rewritten each time a new book club is formed. The agreements become more specific (and effective) over time. For example, an agreement might say, "I will read as far as … I agree to let everyone speak. I agree to listen to other people's opinions and ideas. I will come to each meeting with a passage to share." The children each sign the agreement.

Jan gives each student a package of post-it notes so they can write on them instead of in the book if they wish to, or they write in their notebooks. They come to each meeting with a passage to share and talk about. They take it in turns to share their passage and they explain why this passage is important or memorable to them. They may make connections to personal experiences (text to self), to another book or movie (text to text), or to events in the local community or globally (text to world). Sometimes the students illustrate their passage, and write a caption below it. Through these activities, the students explore the content of the book, the characters, the setting, their predictions, and their questions.

Jan says her students have no problem staying on task in their book clubs. First, they look forward to them and they don't want to waste any time, so they keep each other focused. Second, they trust each other and they trust her as a teacher to guide them and create a safe space for sharing thoughts and questions. Third, she does some teaching and practising beforehand so her students know what is expected of them. Part of the response process consists of commenting on how well the book club worked. This tells Jan what she needs to teach or reinforce. Jan believes strongly that children need to be taught some skills before they begin book club and so she does a lot of scaffolding. Sometimes she gives out cards with a topic or question written on it (it may be a favourite holiday or favourite gift, a question about pets, or something about family members). The students are asked to talk for three minutes on the topic, and the others listen and must not interrupt. At the end of the three minutes, they can ask questions and have a friendly discussion. This serves as a good reminder to the students about how they need to conduct themselves during book club.

The book club usually lasts about three to four weeks. The discussion groups meet twice a week for an hour, and Jan meets with each group for about 15 to 20 minutes during that time. Jan has found that meeting with one group at a time works best for her, as she gets so much information from the students about their engagement with the text. Not all the children are engaged in book club at the same time, however. Two groups might meet while the rest of the students work on responses, read assigned book sections, or write poems, journal entries, or conduct other response activities described later in this chapter. Students decide whether to write a journal response before a book club discussion or after it. The choice is theirs—as is their mode of response, most of the time.

Jan has learned that not all children need to talk during book club. Often, a shy child might enjoy a book and the book club discussion, while saying little and thinking a lot. Jan keep notes about the type of comments the students make and the passages they choose to share. This is valuable information that directs her teaching in mini-lessons, which she conducts during other blocks of time. Jan generally circulates around book clubs, sitting on the edge and listening. Later she gives feedback to the group. Sometimes she gets more involved in the discussion—but she is very conscious about not taking over. In book club, the students' voices are more important than hers. ☐

This chapter addresses questions about how teachers facilitate literary response in their classrooms and how they go about selecting literature for the classroom. Jan Smith and Carol Walters from the Comox Valley, BC (whom we will meet later in this chapter), will share their insights and teaching practices to help to demonstrate some of the basic principles of reader response. Before we embark on this journey, think about your own reading history and reading habits. When you were in elementary school, did your classroom have its own collection of books? Were you allowed to read some books and not others? Who decided what you could and could not read? Did you participate in response activities such as group discussions, puppet shows, or journal writing about the books and stories you were reading? Did your teacher read books aloud to the whole class regularly, and talk with the class about well-known authors and illustrators and their work? The decisions teachers make about these issues deeply affect the literacy programs they develop and implement with their students. Jan and Carol read children's books widely, and they plan reader response activities and response groups thoughtfully, always with the aim of enhancing children's reading abilities and their pleasure in reading and thinking about books.

READER RESPONSE

Reader response refers to the events that occur within a reader when a piece of text is read. Rosenblatt (1978) maintained that text is simply squiggles on a page until a reader reads it. When a reader reads the print, *something* happens within the reader. That "something" is often labelled "response." The response might be boredom, confusion, interest, sadness, empathy, irritation, or joy, but a reading event is never undertaken without a variety of responses. People respond to all kinds of events in their everyday lives—a menu read in a restaurant, a movie seen at the cinema, an e-mail note from a friend, a television show, international news on the radio, a song, a play, an editorial in the newspaper. Response is part of the human condition, part of our interactions with the people and the world around us. It is part of the meaning-making process, and as such, response to literature is an important component of a language arts program.

Rosenblatt (1978) referred to the reading experience as a transaction between *text* and *reader*, a transaction that creates what she called the *poem*, or the "lived-through experience with the text." Readers respond to the "poem" (a term used broadly by Rosenblatt to mean the **transactional reading** experience) as they read, after they read, and when they reflect on or recapture their reading experience. Rosenblatt maintained that a response is dictated to a considerable extent by the purpose for reading or, in other words, by the *stance* from which the reader approaches the text.

A reading stance can be anywhere on a continuum from **efferent** at one end, where the reader seeks information of some kind, to **aesthetic** at the other, where the reader focuses on appreciating what is read. Response fluctuates along this continuum as we read. At one moment a reader may be reading for the pure pleasure and appreciation of a work, and the next moment might be noticing something interesting and memorable in the text, or something that relates to a piece of information received from a different source in the recent past. For example, when reading *The Doll* (Taylor, 1987), a reader may first appreciate the artistry of the language and the tantalizing nature of time-slip fantasy. Then, suddenly, his or her attention might shift to a focus on prairie fires and the devastation they can cause to farmland and livestock—a thought that can be connected with a newspaper article he or she read the previous day. The reading experience thus moves from an aesthetic stance to a more efferent stance.

The extremes of response on this continuum can be demonstrated by two quite different reading events. When someone reads a first-aid manual to treat an injury, the reading has a very pragmatic purpose—to allow the reader to gain essential information that will directly affect his or her behaviour in the immediate future. The reading of a first-aid manual is *efferent reading*, at the far end of the continuum. When that same person reads a novel, however, the purpose is likely to be for pleasure, or to allow the reader to gain a deeper understanding of human experience. As readers engage with a novel, they enter into the space of the novel and disconnect themselves from the time of their own existence as well as their own ongoing or chronological time. This is where Rosenblatt (1978) used the term "lived-through experience with the text" to describe an *aesthetic reading* (Cooper, 1985, p. xiv). A good book is almost certain to evoke a deep personal engagement, whether that turns out to be one involving angst or one involving pleasure.

Teachers can provide opportunities for children to respond aesthetically to a text, whether that text is in a reading series or in a trade book. Rosenblatt maintained that, "once the work has been evoked, it can become the object of reflection and analysis, according to the various critical and scholarly approaches" (Farrell and Squire, 1990, p. 106). In other words, a text first evokes an aesthetic or "lived-through" response and then evokes a more efferent response as the reader consciously thinks about the text and the reading experience. For example, a short story such as "Tashkent" (in *Some of the Kinder Planets*, by Tim Wynne-Jones, 1993) may be read in such a way that the reader enters the story's time, identifying with the protagonist's illness and recuperation, and leaving behind the more immediate concerns of the world. When reflecting on the story, however, the reader constructs meaning (on the basis of the text) that may relate to other stories or poems, to geographical facts, to information the reader already possesses, or to the reader's own life or that of a friend. When readers reflect in this way, they reenter ongoing chronological time and engage in a more efferent response. A *totally* efferent response to "Tashkent" might include summarizing the story as we retell it to a friend, locating in an atlas the place names mentioned in the story, or comparing the story with a poem that has a similar theme. These transactions form the cornerstone for the creation of possible meanings, as well as for coming to understand how texts work.

What is seen of response to literature in a classroom is like the tip of an iceberg: much of it remains out of sight (Purves & Rippere, 1968). Teachers like Jan and Carol keep the following points in mind as they engage students with literature:

- The extent to which students show their responses in a classroom context depends on the reading abilities of the individual children.
- The depth of response students demonstrate depends on the level of trust they feel in the classroom environment.
- People in general do not share feelings and thoughts if they don't feel safe.
- If children are taught that there is one "right" response to a piece of literature (usually the teacher's response or interpretation), they are less likely to express their own responses.
- Through sharing and discussing responses, students discover that meaning can be negotiated and constructed in a multitude of equally valid ways.
- When students are encouraged to respond to texts and to engage in dialogue among themselves, their peers, and teachers about books, they are more likely to see that meaning is created by the learner, and that multiple ways of knowing and responding to literature are valid and necessary.
- Students who share their responses to literature and have their responses accepted respectfully are likely to become more thoughtful and critical readers than those students who do not experience a fair exchange of responses.

Learning Through Response

Children learn a great deal through responding to literature. They discover how texts work, what constitutes a good book, how language can be used in different ways to create different meanings and effects—in short, how to become readers, not just people able to read. As a result of active responding, children are likely to take ownership of the reading process and come to understand that literature can be interpreted in many varied ways. However, as Rosenblatt (1978) wrote, some responses are more legitimate or appropriate than others, because a response must be based in the text read. Through learning to respect and honour their own interpretations of what they have read, students gain the confidence to become more critical in their thinking about texts, more creative in their own writing, and much more capable in their ability as language users and language learners. In effect, they take on the four roles of the reader (Freebody & Luke, 1990) described in Chapter 10: code breaker, text participant, text user, and text analyst.

Literature can form the basis for an entire language arts program in elementary classrooms, for the nature of reading and response encourages children to integrate their knowledge, make personal sense of it, and express it through movement, the visual arts, music, drama, writing, and dialogue. Thomson (1987) reminds us that, "the development of a mature response to literature involves a progressive movement from close emotional involvement to more distanced reflective detachment, and from an interest in self to an interest in other people and the human condition" (p. 153). This means that the process of response almost always begins with an aesthetic, personal experience of the text—the very experience that a response activity in the classroom aims to encourage and facilitate.

Response Groups

One important vehicle for exploring a text is the response group, or what Jan Smith calls a book club. Adult readers have also discovered the pleasures of reading clubs or book clubs, where members read a book in their own time and then come together as a group to discuss the book and explore interpretations of it. Such groups can play a valuable role in elementary language arts classrooms, as Jan has described.

Teachers and researchers have discovered that children benefit from *orally* sharing and shaping their responses to books. As they share their own responses and listen to the ways in which other readers have responded to a book, children become aware that no two readers read in the same way or create meaning in the same way. In the process of discussion, their attention is drawn to details they might have missed, and they are called to think about things that, as individual readers, they might not have thought about.

Taking part in a response group can be a fascinating experience. It can also be a frustrating experience if readers want everyone in the group to respond to a book in the way in which *they* have responded to it. Research conducted by Eeds and Wells (1989) formed the foundation for *Grand Conversations* (Peterson & Eeds, 1990), a book that underscores the importance of dialogue in constructing meaning from a text. Peterson and Eeds (1990, p. 21) write: "The lecture model places knowledge outside the students for them to passively receive; dialogue recognizes that knowledge is something students actively construct." The authors provide many suggestions and insights for teachers who work with response groups, including ideas for selecting books, facilitating literature study, and evaluating responses to literature. They also reiterate that children need time in class just for reading, and that children should not be expected to do all of their reading outside class time.

Critical to the success of response groups is the respect teachers afford each child's ideas, not imposing their own ideas on the class. There are many occasions when teachers have to put their own feelings and opinions aside to listen to the students' voices. Classroom discussions can be extremely enlightening for a teacher and can provide a springboard for choosing and creating alternative ways of responding to books. The role of the teacher in literature response groups is that of sensitive guide, helping to create links from the text to actual life experiences and to other texts, and inserting literary insights at appropriate moments. Peterson and Eeds (1990) maintain that asking direct questions such as "What was your favourite part of the story, and why?" can close down real conversation for students. The question is artificial and requires a fabricated response. Carol Walters makes comments such as "Let's think more about that," because open-ended "wondering" comments help children reflect on their reading and deepen their responses to the reading. Talking with students about a book can be an effective teaching strategy, because it immediately creates possible connections to the child's own life and demands a personal engagement with the text.

Stanley Fish (1980) says, "Not only does one believe what one believes, but one teaches what one believes, even if it would be easier and safer and more satisfying to teach something else" (p. 364). If we believe that teaching reading means asking children questions, requiring them to provide a retelling of almost every story they read, or picking out the main ideas from a chapter in a book, then our teaching of reading will betray those beliefs. Langer (1994) writes: "The thought-provoking literature class is an environment where students [and teachers] are encouraged to negotiate their own meanings by exploring possibilities, considering understandings from multiple perspectives, sharpening their own interpretations, and learning through the insights of their own responses" (p. 207). She goes on to remind us that response is based as much on the reader's own personal and cultural experiences as it is on the particular text and its author. Langer also believes that with instructional support "even the most 'at-risk' students can engage in thoughtful discussions about literature, develop rich and deep understandings, and enjoy it too" (p. 210).

Literature Response Journals

Literature response journals provide children with opportunities for reflection on what they are currently reading. They are not the same as personal journals or learning logs, but, as Parsons (2001) explains, they usually consist of a notebook, folder, section of a binder, or an electronic file "in which students record their personal reactions to, questions about, and reflections on what they read, view, write, represent, observe, listen to, discuss, do, and think and how they go about reading, viewing, writing, representing, observing, listening, discussing or doing" (p. 9). Response journals are usually intensely private and personal, for they depict exactly how a reader interprets a text and responds to it. When teachers read students' response journals, they try to be sensitive to the nature of the writing and aware of the privileged position they hold in accessing this material. They do not correct grammar or spelling errors, but try to respond to the content, reading in the role of "fellow reader," not as an "authority" on the text. The grade 2 children who wrote the following entries in response to *Miss Rumphius* (Cooney, 1982) certainly were not focusing on correct spelling as they completed their entries. In these peer-dialogue journals, they wrote an entry, exchanged journals with a partner, and then wrote a response to their partner's entry. The teacher did not draw attention to their invented spelling, but instead complimented the pair on their interesting exchange and added a comment about her own dislike of some aspects of gardening.

MELISSA: This story reminds me of me becos I alwiys wanted to plant a garden over in they emtey lot acros from us but my mom sade it wood be to mush work, but I'm saving my alowince for some plants and flowers so I can plant some ther.

STUART: I like planting flowers and vegebals but I hate it when I have to take a slug off a flower there so slimy and ugly but I kind of have a indoor green house that I got from Scholastic books.

In response to *Two Bad Ants* by Chris Van Ahlsburg (1988), the two wrote:

MELISSA: This reaminds me of wen I went to the mountins and I fownd a wered object it looked like a melted tin but it was verry hard to bend. at ferst I thot I wood end up richer than my parentes but I endied out not beaing rich atole. Do you think the ants were beaing gready or wanted to try their musteyris cristels that we know is sugar. It also reaminds me of the time my brother fownd a white rock and thot it was a cristel and he came in yelling mom—mom I fownd a white crustel.

STUART: The rock your brother found probely had shiny minirels in it but doase your brother still have the rock.

MELISSA: he still thinkes ther cristeles so he heas got tuns.

Literature response journals work most effectively when they are open-ended and unstructured. However, students need to know the expectations, requirements, and routines associated with them. For example, students need to know how often they are expected to write in their journal, how their journal writing will be assessed, how often the teacher will read the journal, and how they are expected to record the titles and other pertinent information about the books they read. Parsons's book *Response Journals Revisited* (2001) suggests a number of organizational strategies teachers can use in the upper elementary/middle-years grades. Parsons also emphasizes that teachers must make time in the classroom for reading as well as for responding, and that students can respond to read-aloud sessions as well as to their silent reading.

Directing children to focus their responses on some specific aspect of the text such as plot, setting, characters, or theme does *not* appear to be as effective as leaving the response options open to the students, providing suggestions only where necessary. However, cueing questions can be very effective in getting students started on writing a response. These are not a prescribed set of questions provided by the teacher, but may include such questions as: "After reading this far, what more do you hope to learn about what these characters plan to do, what they think, feel and believe, or what happens to them?" (Parsons, 2001, p. 37). Response writing, like any other type of writing, is learned. Children who are not used to writing in the expressive voice (see Chapter 7) may need some time to get used to the idea that this is an acceptable form of writing. It is not a matter of learning *what* to write, but rather of learning what to focus on and *how* to write a response.

Teachers keep in mind that a student's written responses to a text are part of the student's meaning-making. Written responses rely heavily on the child's ability to comprehend what has been encountered through the reading. For this reason, teachers engage their students in strategies that will help them to comprehend the text as well as shape a reflective response to it. Successful response

Carol Walters

INSIDE CLASSROOMS

Children's Literature in Carol Walters' Grade 4 Classroom

Carol Walters believes there's nothing like children's literature to get children hooked into reading—and into writing. Good books engage children like nothing else. Through good literature teachers create motivation for learning and they provide models of excellent writing. When Carol reads aloud to her grade 4 students, which she does frequently, she uses a think-aloud procedure and she pauses as she reads, talking about what is going through her mind as a reader. "Oh, I wasn't expecting that. I wonder what he's going to do now." "Why do you think she did that?" "Do you notice how the author said that? What does it make you think about?" "What a wonderful description. It's worth reading a second time."

Carol has also learned the power of series books, and, like Jan Smith, she sometimes reads aloud a Nancy Drew or other series book, especially near the beginning of the school year. Her students' favourite read-alouds include *Escaping the Giant Wave* (Kehret, 2003), *Holes* (Sachar, 1998), both of which Jan Smith accesses in grade 6 for book club reading, *The Vicar of Nibbleswicke* (Dahl. 1991), and *My Name Is Seepeetza* (Sterling, 1992) which connects well with the social studies curriculum and the United Nations Rights of the Child (1990). Grade 4 children relate easily to the issues raised in *My Name Is Seepeetza*, and can connect them to their own family and personal lives. Carol says many of these books demonstrate what is meant by a writer's voice, and she often talks about this and about how the students can develop their own voice in their writing. The main criteria Carol uses for choosing a book to read aloud to the class are that the children will enjoy it and that they will look forward to hearing it.

Carol notes the very wide range of reading abilities in most grade 4 classrooms, with some children reading at a grade 6/7 level and others at grade 2. She maintains that a wide selection of reading materials, picture books, novels, and lots of good nonfiction books and magazines help to ensure that every one of her students will engage with reading. Open-ended activities allow all the children to be included successfully in reader response, and they ensure that all the students' reading needs are met and supported. Working with peers in writing, reading, discussion, and other modes of response is essential, in Carol's view. Less-able readers are then supported by their peers, and they can participate fully, even if they are not reading at grade level. Working with a buddy or with a small group enables these children to develop trust and confidence and encourages them to take some risks, which is necessary if they are to become capable independent readers. Carol knows the importance of developing a safe classroom climate in which children can take the necessary risks with support and not ridicule.

Carol carefully selects reading buddies for some of the students in her classroom. Having a partner to read and discuss the book with is immeasurably important to struggling readers. The system acknowledges that not all students read at the same rate or level of competency and it balances their contributions to the act of reading. Sometimes the pairs take turns reading a paragraph at a time, or they might read a whole page. They help each other with the reading and they talk about what they're reading as they go along. The buddies can find any comfortable spot in the classroom for their reading and they often go outside of the classroom into an open area close by, where they can feel cosy and relaxed as they read.

Buddy-reading

writing is partly about making the invisible "visible." As a first strategy in helping students to write a response, teachers assist them in identifying some of the invisible processes of reading.

Teachers like Carol Walters explain to their students that successful readers use two types of voices while they are reading. The first can be referred to as the *reciting voice*, which is the voice in the reader's head that says the words found on the page. The second voice can be referred to as the *conversation voice*, which is the voice in the reader's head that responds to what the reader is reading. Many students are unaware that their conversation voice needs to be present for good reading to take place. As a result, they use only the reciting voice, and they need to be taught how to develop their conversation voice. One way to aid in this development is to have students pay attention to their thoughts while watching a television show or a movie. Students initially seem to find it easier to recognize their conversation voices in this context rather than trying to "hear" it while reading.

Carol models this process by sharing her thoughts (think-aloud) while she is reading aloud to her class. Students can join the discussion with Carol by sharing what their conversation voices were saying. Responses in the conversation voice might vary from predicting to questioning or sharing an opinion about something that happened in the story. The think-aloud strategy shows students how an expert reader makes sense of text. "By sharing your thinking out loud, you make the elusive process of comprehension more concrete" (Tovani, 2000, p. 26). If students are aware of the tools needed to make text meaningful they will be more able to respond with greater depth in their response journals. The think-aloud strategy is straightforward and requires little planning.

Using the picture book *Thank You, Mr. Falker* (Polacco, 1988), for example, a teacher might make the following comments during the first two pages of the book: "I wonder why the grandpa is pouring honey on the book; I remember when I learned to read in grade 1; I loved it when my grandma would read to me, because she always read to me in a rocking chair; why is Trisha not able to read? I think Trisha is going to have trouble learning to read."

After the teacher models the process, the students can practise their conversation voices while reading instructional level text. They may record their thoughts on a separate piece of paper or on a post-it note. With the post-it they can mark the pages in the book that evoked the response. Alternatively, they might write responses in the margin of a photocopied page from the book. The teacher can then provide opportunities for the students to share their conversation voices with a partner, the teacher, and perhaps the entire class. The teacher and students together can begin to identify and record on a class chart the types of conversation voices used during reading. Below are of some of the conversation voices successful readers use while reading.

- predicting
- visualizing
- disagreeing
- agreeing
- questioning
- clarifying

- reminding
- summarizing

- inferring
- relating

Teachers can also model journal writing for their students using the think-aloud strategy, recording their responses on an overhead acetate or on chart paper. Once students become comfortable writing in their response journals, teachers may continue to model written responses but without thinking aloud. Teachers write their own responses while the students are writing theirs. Because writing in a response journal involves the complex processes of reading and writing, some students may struggle with the task. Here are some suggestions for providing support to such students:

- Encourage the students to work at "listening" for one of the conversation voices identified on the class chart and write their response in that voice.

- Encourage struggling writers to record their responses in picture or point form rather than sentences.

- Encourage them to read the teacher's modelled responses as a springboard for getting started themselves. Perhaps the teacher's response reminds them of something they thought about when they read the text, or that they were confused about and might now write about.

- Before students begin writing in their response journals, encourage them to share past entries or thoughts they might include in their latest entry.

Any response to literature that students might write is shaped by the text itself. Some texts, such as *Gorilla* by Anthony Browne (1983) or *The Breadwinner* by Deborah Ellis (2000) invite immediate responses, though the responses will differ significantly from one reader to another. Most readers readily identify with the protagonists of these two stories and can empathize with the situations in which the characters find themselves. Other texts, such as *The Golden Compass* by Philip Pullman (1995), may at first appear strange, complex, or even baffling. The text may generate many questions before a reader can shape a response to it, and the response is likely to change as the reading progresses.

Whether the reader's response to a book is tentative and questioning, or confident and fully engaged, teachers and researchers have found that the written responses of children to books demonstrate what the children know, what and how they think, and how they have comprehended a text. Thus, there is little need for having a child retell the story to ascertain whether he or she has understood a book or not. It is clear, for example, that Ron, in grade 5, not only enjoyed *The Dragon Children* (Buchan, 1975), but also understood the complex plot:

> I really liked this book because there were two mysteries in the whole book. One of the mysteries was if the crook would make it out of town in time, and if John, Scott, Cathy and Steven would get the crook or not. The other mystery was to find out who or what Steven really was. I figured out what Steven was by putting all the clues together. At the end of the book I found out who Steven was. At first I thought that Steven was a ghost (even though he was) that the crook had drowned in the river. I was half right about that.
>
> It was a surprise to me when John, Scott, and Cathy found out that the crook wasn't who they thought he was. It surprised me because when Steven told John that the crook was driving a green car with a license plate number 5K-206 it wasn't the crook driving it. Instead it was the

man who had come with his family for their vacation. The man did seem like a crook though because when he was walking through the woods with his son, it looked like he had kidnapped the child.

My favorite part, though, was when Scott sneaked up behind the real crook and poked the needle in his back-end. I liked it because it really made me laugh.

Ron wrote this response about how he played detective as a reader in order to fit all the pieces of the story together, making meaning and unravelling the two mysteries. The response demonstrates how Ron engaged with the text, and how he experienced a more distanced response to the book rather than a personal identification with the characters and their actions.

Mitch, in grade 5, wrote the following dialogue journal entry in response to Chapter 3 of *The Iron Man* (Hughes, 1968), which the teacher had read aloud to the class:

I think the Iron Man will be like the machine in the scrap metal yard that gets rid of the metal. The Iron Man will be happy, the farmers will be happy and Hogarth can visit the Iron Man all the time. Who were the people that had the picnic on the hill and will they show up again? If the Iron Man is controlled by something, who or what is it and what will it think of the Iron Man being so happy? If there is more Iron Men does the Iron Man we know about keep in touch with them? If he does, maybe our Iron Man will tell the others and they will come too. I like how the author called all the metal delicacies. I can see how the chain is spaghetti and maybe the knobs on the bed were chocolate covered candy. Brass covered iron. I don't understand how different kinds of metals have different kinds of tastes. What do you think the Iron Man's favorite kind of metal is? … What will happen when the Iron Man runs out of food at the metal scrap yard? Will they bring him food from other towns? Do you think the Iron Man will ever go back to the sea? Maybe if he leaves the scrap yard all the townsfolk will look for him at the sea. Do you know if the farmers filled up the hole? I sure hope so. It would be disastrous if somebody fell down the hole. If somebody did fall down the hole, maybe the Iron Man will help them out and then he might not be hated so much. Is the Iron Man hated? I think it starts out in the story that the Iron Man was hated but now I think maybe he is more liked.

Mitch's response is like "stream of consciousness" writing. He has put onto paper the many questions raised for him as he listened to this chapter of the story, and has highlighted some of the images in Hughes's writing. The response demonstrates the engagement Mitch experienced as he listened to the story, processing the thoughts that went through his mind about this chapter. Mitch moved quickly from one idea to another, not stopping long to reflect on any one aspect of the chapter, but trying to capture the excitement and wonder evoked by this modern fairy-tale. Mitch makes predictions about the fate of the Iron Man, accurately foretelling the Iron Man's role in the community and the shift in the populace's perceptions as the Iron Man becomes an ally of the people instead of an enemy to be defeated.

Children sharing a literature response journal

Literature response journals provide opportunities for teachers to deliver instruction and feedback to students that is student-oriented as well as text-oriented. Response journals do not replace discussion, they reinforce and support discussion. Response journals provide a place for children to slow down their thinking and reflect on their reading (and on their group discussions), asking questions, wondering, predicting, and synthesizing. Here children can genuinely work at seeking to understand how literature weaves its magic, how reading is accomplished, and how books work.

Readers' Workshop

Readers' workshop was a term made popular by Nancie Atwell in the 1980s. The second edition of her book *In the Middle: New Understandings About Writing, Reading and Learning* (1998) continues her exploration of children's reading and response. A complaint frequently voiced by children is that they are given very little time in school to actually *read*. Instead, they are required to devote most of their time to activities *about* reading. Like Peterson and Eeds (1990), Atwell suggests that if children are to truly enjoy the reading experience, time for reading as well as for learning about reading must be established in school. She maintains that because children read magazines, TV guides, and other such material out of school, teachers play an important role in encouraging students to broaden their reading repertoire by selecting novels, poetry, plays, biography, and works of nonfiction when they are in school. The books, however, should be of interest to the students and, where appropriate, self-selected.

Atwell proposes a readers' workshop format where most of the in-class time is spent reading, and mini-lessons are used for what Purves (1993) suggests is "schooling in the teaching of reading and literature." Atwell offers the following guidelines for conducting a readers' workshop:

- Have children come to the workshop prepared with a book in their possession that they are ready to read or are already in the process of reading. The book should be self-selected from either the classroom or the school library. Readers' workshop is not a time for making book selections.

- Regardless of grade level, ensure that students have a sustained and uninterrupted time for reading. Suitable time lines for readers' workshops vary from grade level to grade level. Grades 5 to 7 require 20–30 minutes for reading. Younger students require much less, depending on their ability to sustain silent reading. Thus in grades 1 and 2, the reading time might be only ten minutes.

- Encourage children not to talk or disturb others during reading time, though they may sit or recline anywhere, depending on the physical constraints of the classroom.

- Help students understand that quiet time is important when reading. Most readers cannot read fluently if there is noise around them, or if they are trying to attend to more than one activity at once.

Mini-lessons, whether planned or spontaneous, should usually be brief (say, between five and fifteen minutes), and designed in response to the students' needs. A mini-lesson may be

- a discussion of a topic (e.g., the need for quiet time during reading, the procedures and agendas for response groups, how the classroom library is organized, classroom literary resources, organizing a reading folder and keeping a record of books read, self-assessment procedures, and goal setting)

- a book-share by the teacher (reading part of a book to the class), a book talk by the teacher or a group of students, or some other presentation of activities completed by students *in response* to a book they have read

- a presentation on a particular author, where the teacher shows the class a number of books by that author; information about authors is available in libraries in publications such as *Meet Canadian Authors and Illustrators* (Gertridge, 2002) or the book series *Something About the Author* (ed. Commaire, annual)

- a further exploration of a book in response groups, journal writing, or alternative response activities

The key role of the teacher in a readers' workshop is to facilitate students' learning as they progress from personal interpretations and understandings ("My question is …" "It reminds me of …" "I don't understand why …") to shared meanings ("This story is about …") and on to negotiated meanings ("We think the writer wanted us to understand that …"). The readers' workshop is a place where students can read, take ownership of their reading, and respond in their own language to the material they have selected to read. They discuss their ideas about a text with other readers and come to shared and negotiated understandings of the meanings of the stories, poems, and plays they are reading.

Purves (1993) has emphasized that reading in school can never be like reading out of school, because in school it is the teacher's job to facilitate children's growth in book selection, reading skill, confidence, fluency, and ability to express thoughts and opinions and to engage in critical and creative thought. As Purves writes: "I urge us to see our task in schools as helping students read literature and understand the culture, to speculate on the ideas and the imaginative vision, and to speculate on the nature and the use of the language that is the medium of the artistic expression" (p. 360). Much of this can be achieved, we believe, in well-handled readers' workshops.

Literature Circles

In his book *Literature Circles: Voice and Choice in Book Clubs and Reading Groups*, Daniels (2002) writes, "Literature circles are small, temporary discussion groups whose members have chosen to read the same story, poem, article or book. While reading each group-assigned portion of the text (either in or outside of class), members make notes to help them contribute to the upcoming discussion, and everyone comes to the group with ideas to share" (p. 2). In other words, literature circles are student-led discussion groups. Each literature circle in a classroom is likely to be reading a different book, but the groups meet regularly according to a schedule. The teacher acts as a facilitator for the groups. Role sheets, which give a different role to each group member, are often used at first, as they help to guide the students in the roles they agree to take on. Daniels emphasizes that the aim is to make the role sheets obsolete. After using role sheets once or twice, students usually opt to work without them as they learn how to tailor the group processes to meet their own needs. Roles might include:

- *Questioner.* Develops a list of questions the group might like to discuss—generally helps the group to talk over the big ideas.

- *Connector.* Finds connections between the book and the world outside (the school, the community, events at other times and places).

- *Literary luminary.* Locates a few special sections of the text the group might like to hear read aloud—emphasis is on interesting, funny, powerful, or puzzling sections.

- *Illustrator.* Draws some kind of picture or representation related to the text.

- *Summarizer.* Prepares a brief summary of the day's reading—the essence of it.

- *Researcher.* Digs up background information on any topic related to the book or the author/illustrator.

- *Word wizard.* Looks out for a few especially important words—new, interesting, strange, or puzzling.

Daniels's system is highly organized, and can be both interesting and enjoyable for students. Most teachers find that literature circles provide an excellent structure for beginning group work in response to literature. Many teachers report that students no longer need the role sheets after they have participated in the system two or three times. The students learn how to organize the groups themselves and understand the possibilities response groups can offer for discussion of innumerable topics and ideas related to their reading. Teachers need to be aware that literature circles can become mechanistic and, if due care is not taken, can function from an efferent stance. The greatest learning is likely to take place when students write in response journals in addition to discussing their reading in a response group, and engage in the unstructured "grand conversations" described by Eeds and Wells (1989).

Novel Studies

The term *novel study* is used to describe a range of group activities that encourage and facilitate students' reading and responding to novels. At the elementary school level, novel studies provide a vehicle for children to experience a novel in a small group setting, much like a book club or response group. Novel studies can be conducted with a whole class of children, though they can usually be separated into small groups for many of the discussions and activities. Novel studies can also be conducted in small groups of four to six students, as in a literature circle.

Multiple copies of novels are necessary for a novel study, so it is most economical to involve no more than five or six children with one novel at any one time. Prepared novel study sets are usually packaged in groups of six books. Many teachers complete one whole-class novel study at the beginning of the year to set out the expectations for novel studies and to establish guidelines and procedures for novel study activities. After the initial whole-class study, teachers usually work with small groups, as in literature circles or the book clubs Jan Smith runs.

Successful novel study requires a classroom community where reading is important and students and teachers behave like "real readers." As highlighted by both Atwell (1998) and Daniels (2002), children benefit from opportunities to self-select reading material and from having substantial time to read independently. Students can be assigned to groups on the basis of their approximate reading speeds, or they can self-select a reading group on the basis of their interest in the novel. The group chooses a book to read, and the group members meet regularly to discuss the book and complete response activities. The activities can be designed by the students or suggested by the teacher.

In preparation for the group activity, the students agree to achieve specific goals for each meeting. The goals may include reading a certain number of pages before the meeting, or accomplishing certain tasks such as answering questions raised in the previous meeting. This is a way of "thinking back and thinking ahead." It provides students with a means of synthesizing their reading, making predictions, asking questions, and negotiating meaning with the group. During the discussion time, the teacher circulates about the room, listening to the ongoing conversations and participating where appropriate. Once the discussions are complete, each group sets a new reading goal that can be recorded on a small chart posted at the front of the classroom. The teacher can monitor the reading goals to ensure they are appropriate for the various groups. The students spend the rest of the period reading their novels, writing in their response journals, or engaging in alternative response activities. The teacher can either read silently during this time or assist individual students with their responses.

Journal responses can be written at any time during the reading of a novel: the midpoint, on completion of the texts, or (as more frequently happens) during the reading. The students can decide on the content of their responses (there is no particular structure or format for the entries), but they are encouraged to select and write in depth about one or two ideas, images, feelings, memories, or thoughts they experienced during or after their reading. This helps the students to explore, extend, or develop their reading experiences. Some students relate the story to other books, movies, or experiences in their lives; some evaluate a situation or a character, or put themselves in a character's position in the book and discuss what they would feel or do and why; and others discuss the author's writing purpose, style, or techniques.

Reading instruction also occurs in a novel study when individual students or groups of students require assistance in dealing with comprehension difficulties, selecting novels, or organizing themselves to meet their goals. Because students in this activity are largely inde-pendent in their work, they need to be aware of the expectations for novel studies, such as when it is appropriate to write in their response journals and when to hand responses in to the teacher. It is also important that children know where to find the novels they are interested in reading, the procedures for signing out books, and any other classroom routines related to this study activity.

As mentioned above, a number of packaged novel studies are available for use in classrooms. A word of caution: many commercial novel studies are not of high quality and include exercises more like the ones found in old-fashioned reading series (formerly called "basal readers"). This approach has been referred to as the **basalization** of children's literature—turning the work of literature into skill-building exercises (or "dummy runs" as Britton, 1970, called them). Teachers use their professional judgment when assessing the value of such resources for their own classrooms. They keep in mind their own objectives in working with literature in the classroom, and the needs of the students they teach.

Alternative Modes of Response

As children begin to read, continue reading, and finish reading a novel, they can engage in many interesting activities that will help them explore, interpret, and more fully understand the text. Many of the drama strategies suggested in Chapter 12 could be included as part of a novel study. Benton and Fox (1985) also provide a rich source of activities for promoting children's explorations and meaning-making from books. Their suggestions for working with *Tuck Everlasting* (Babbitt, 1975) include

- creating a timeline
- drawing portraits of the characters
- "hot-seating" the characters
- writing character sketches
- interviewing characters for a talk show
- making wanted posters for Mae Tuck (a character in the book)
- creating a map of the story's setting
- writing an imaginary diary entry as the character Winnie

These activities encompass the full spectrum of response, from aesthetic to efferent. Halliday's (1969) functions of language (discussed in Chapter 2 of this text) also provide a solid foundation for creating a diverse range of purposeful language activities for children as they respond to and explore novels. In the rest of this section, more than a dozen examples of response activities are described, using the novel *The Miraculous Journey of Edward Tulane* by Kate DiCamillo (2006). This novel is unusual in that it has a wide appeal across the grades, and is enjoyed by children from grades 3 to 6.

In *The Miraculous Journey of Edward Tulane*, a vain, cold-hearted, and proud toy rabbit loves only himself—and resents being referred to as a toy. Edward Tulane is made of china and has wire joints at his knees and elbows. He has the most beautiful and elegant clothes, and even a little pocket watch that actually works. Abilene, his 10-year-old owner, loves and adores Edward. But one night, Abilene's grandmother tells them a bedtime story about a princess who doesn't know how to love. She whispers to Edward, "You disappoint me." When Edward is separated from Abilene, he is forced into a journey that is long and dangerous, and which takes him on a path that teaches him about love, and eventually brings him great joy.

Here are a number of drama strategies that could be used to facilitate responses to the story:

- *Hot-seating.* One of the characters Edward Tulane meets on his journey is Nellie, an old woman whose husband is a fisherman and away from home for most of every day. He has rescued Edward from his fishing net, and now Edward will live with them in their cottage. Nellie adores Edward, but calls him Susanna and makes dresses for him. She talks to Edward and sits him on a cupboard in the kitchen each day as she cooks and bakes and sews. In groups of three, students take turns "being" Nellie. What questions do the other students have for Nellie? What do they want to know about her? Alternatively, at this point in the story, students might want to hot-seat Edward and find out what he is thinking and what he hopes will happen next. The student in role as Nellie or Edward draws on personal experiences and prior knowledge to answer the questions in the context of the story. This is a strategy teachers will likely need to model first, using one of the other characters in the book as an example.

Tableaux. Bryce is a boy who has had a hard and sad life. He has had to work for a living because his family is very poor. Now Bryce's mother and little sister are dead, and his father is hardly ever at home. Bryce hits the road with Edward and makes money as a street performer, attaching strings to Edward's arms and legs so that Edward can dance like a marionette. At the end of the day, with enough money to buy a good meal, they go to Neal's Diner and Bryce orders the meal of his dreams, pancakes, steak, and eggs. But when the bill comes, Bryce does not have enough money to pay. Neal grabs Edward in anger and cracks Edward's head against the counter. In groups of four to six, students can create tableaux—still pictures of the scenes in the diner. Each group first decides what it wants to include in its tableau, and plans who will take the role of each character. Once this is determined, the students take up their positions, perhaps by acting out a brief portion of the story and freezing the action at a given moment. The children then orchestrate the tableau so that it becomes an artistic and aesthetically pleasing portrayal of the scene. Students can imagine this as either a photograph or as a diorama exhibit in a museum. Each group is given the opportunity to show its tableau to the rest of the class.

Thoughts-in-the-head. While engaged in their tableaux, the teacher touches each character gently on the shoulder. At the touch, the students, in role, say what thoughts are going through their minds at that moment. If any students do not wish to speak, they may remain silent and the teacher moves on to the next character.

Puppets. Many different kinds of puppets can be created to put on a play of some part of the story. From paper-lunch-bag, sock, or paper-plate puppets to more elaborate creations, students generally enjoy this activity. Some groups of students may want to script the play first; others may simply create the dialogue as they go. Either way, all groups should have the opportunity to rehearse before sharing their work.

Readers' theatre. Readers' theatre is a form of oral presentation in which scripts are read aloud rather than memorized. Participants read their parts expressively and use their voices, gestures, and facial expressions to communicate images, events, and actions in the minds of audience members. In readers' theatre, the characters may sit on stools or a high bench to read their parts. Often, to identify themselves, the participants wear an item of clothing typical of the character they are "reading." Thus, Bull, the hobo, might wear a tattered hat and a scarf around his neck. Edward might wear a bow tie. For this dramatic activity, the teacher may need to rewrite or script portions of the original text or provide students with instructional assistance as they create the readers' theatre script themselves. The chapters are short in *The Miraculous Journey of Edward Tulane*, and so they lend themselves nicely to this means of interpretation.

Character profile. Students select a character from the book and dress as that character. Each student enters the classroom donned in appropriate attire and tells the other students about him or herself. Drawing on the novel, the student describes the character and the significant events that happened to him or her (as the character). Classmates may ask the character questions.

These activities represent only a few of the many drama strategies that can be used in a literature or language arts program. More drama strategies for use in reader response are presented in Chapter 12. Drama activities frequently take longer than might be expected and they should not be rushed. Throughout their drama work, students are encouraged to talk with one another about their interpretations, opinions, likes, and dislikes, and personal "pictures" of the characters and setting. This oral processing enhances the students' personal engagement with the text, and can help them have a more satisfying and memorable experience with a book. Only one or two of the above activities should be selected for use with any one text. A common option is to have groups of children in a classroom work on different activities, which makes sharing the sessions with one another all the more interesting. Readers are usually curious about other readers' interpretations of the work under consideration.

Visual art activities have the same appeal as the drama strategies suggested above, allowing children to become actively involved in creating an artifact representative of their responses. Drawing, painting, and making models, dioramas, wall charts, and portraits are just a few of the activities that give children the opportunity to display their responses to a text. For the book, *The Miraculous Journey of Edward Tulane*, the following activities could be considered:

- *Photograph album.* Students create a "photograph album" of Edward's journey and the people he met along the way. "Photographs" can consist of pictures taken from magazines, or the children can create them themselves, either with a camera or with art supplies. A caption can be added beneath each image. The students can explain why they chose to include their specific image in their album.

- *Scrapbook.* In a similar manner to the photograph album, students make a scrapbook of the mementos of Edward's adventures. Students can make notes, menus, paw prints, sketches of dresses, and other such memorabilia from Edward's journeys and his encounters with the various characters along the way.

- *Mapping.* Students create large and colourful maps of the routes Edward may have taken from his first home on Egypt Road in Memphis, to his travel on the *Queen Mary*, the fishing village in which he found himself and so on. The map is not necessarily intended to be a realistic depiction, but can be created from the descriptions provided in the text. If students wish to locate a real map of the United States and base their renditions on it, this will also extend their learning and responses to the story.

- *Silhouettes.* Individually or in small groups, students draw on overhead transparencies a silhouette of a character from the story. The finished drawings can be displayed using the overhead projector. What features have the artists given the various characters? Why are these features important?

- *Drawings.* After reading parts of the book or the entire book, students draw scenes, characters, or various aspects of their own interpretation of the story. Drawing can elicit some insightful responses from students that might not otherwise be captured. Students may also want to write about their drawings. An opportunity is presented here to use a paint program on the computer and later perhaps have students in an older grade animate the painting into short movies (as described in Chapter 8).

- *Book covers.* Students usually have very definite ideas about the appropriateness of a book cover. Some students may want to design an alternative cover for *The Miraculous Journey of Edward Tulane.* The cover by Bagram Ibatoulline, and his illustrations throughout the book, are striking, but what do students think? What might they create as a cover for this book? The graphics used, the positioning of the title and author's name, and the colours are important elements in creating a book's initial appeal. A book cover can invite readers into the text or be a factor in dissuading them from reading the book. An important facet of a student's response to a book can be found in the alternative cover he or she might design. Covers created by students can be displayed along with other items profiling the novel.

▨ *Dioramas.* Any setting from a book can be used as the starting point in creating a diorama. A number of settings in *The Miraculous Journey of Edward Tulane* lend themselves to this kind of interpretation (e.g., the ocean, the garbage dump, Neal's Diner). Dioramas are frequently made from large shoeboxes, and many odds and ends of materials can be carefully put together to create an effective representation of the setting and atmosphere of the novel as a whole. Dioramas can provide an enticement for other students to read the book.

▨ *Advertisements.* If a reader had to create a poster advertising *The Miraculous Journey of Edward Tulane*, what would it be like? Most students are familiar with movie posters, but what would a publishing company look for in a poster designed to promote a book? What would a prospective reader want to know about the book? What ambiance could be created through a poster? What colours would be most effective in portraying this story? After students have read a novel, an advertising poster can be an exciting way to share their responses to the book with the rest of the class.

▨ *Wall charts.* There are many kinds of wall charts students can develop to help themselves understand a book. For *The Miraculous Journey of Edward Tulane*, students might consider creating a timeline that tracks the story's events, the characters that enter the adventures, or the settings of each period of Edward's journey.

Benton and Fox (1985) suggest that teachers, when considering various oral, dramatic, visual, and written response activities, ask themselves two fundamental questions: "Will this activity enable the reader to look back on the text and to develop the meanings he has already made?" and "Does what I plan to do bring reader and text closer together, or does it come between them?" (p. 108). Activities that meet the criteria set by Benton and Fox will extend students' reading transactions, enhance students' meaning-making from the text, and avoid any unnecessarily lengthy examination of the text that may detract from the reading experience.

Dependent Authorship

Adams (1987) coined the phrase "dependent authorship" to describe activities that invite students to write from within the world of the literary text. The writing depends on the original text, since it is based on knowledge and understanding of that text. Meyers (1997) suggests a number of dependent authorship activities, including writing

▨ a dream that a character in the book may have

▨ a flashback that illuminates a character and some aspect of the character's personality

▨ a flashforward that extends the story

▨ a continuation of the work, picking up where the author left off

▓ an interior monologue that captures the unspoken thoughts of a character

▓ a poem or song that might appear in the work

▓ a diary entry for one of the characters

▓ a new passage that incorporates a character from another story into this work

▓ letters a character might have written

Children reading *The Miraculous Journey of Edward Tulane* have written diary entries in role as Abilene or Nellie; they have written a letter from Maggie to Bryce, 10 years after the story ended; a poem written by Abilene after her visit to Lucius Clarke's shop; a dream that Bull, the hobo, had; a biography about Bryce; and a new passage incorporating Meg from Cora Taylor's story *The Doll* (1987), in which Meg helps Nellie adjust to her life without Susanna.

Dependent authorship activities can be generated by teachers when they have a thorough knowledge and understanding of Halliday's seven functions of language (1969). Keeping in mind the primacy of the purposes of language enables teachers to develop learning activities that are authentic language acts. Dependent authoring is conducted from "inside" the literary work, and always takes the student into a deeper understanding of it. It also underscores the intertextual elements of any piece of writing, "recognising that every literary work is a well-spring for others" (Meyers, 1997).

Assessing Response Activities

Response activities are usually conducted in small groups or as individual writing activities. Teachers assess student growth during these activities on an ongoing basis and the assessment practices are usually formative—they help the teacher to monitor children's development and they provide input into instructional planning. When students are engaged in group activities, assessment is usually completed through teacher observations: listening to and talking with students as they discuss books and engage in various response activities—artistic, dramatic and written. The listening and speaking assessment practices suggested in Chapter 2 are particularly applicable here. Teachers also carefully read or examine the products of group work and engage in conversations with their students about such artifacts and the production of them.

Teachers who work with literature circles and discussion groups have to do a lot of listening in their classrooms. They try to discover how children interpret their reading; how they apply their ideas to the world around them, both in and out of school; how they attend to the language of a book; what they learn as a result of their reading; how they dialogue with other students in their group; how they listen and acknowledge the ideas of others; what questions they raise; and how they express their own ideas and responses. If teachers are to effectively monitor and assess children's growth as readers through literature circles or novel studies, they need to

▓ read the books the children are reading

▓ sit in on the circles or group discussions (some teachers take an active role in them)

▓ keep anecdotal/observational notes on each child's progress

▓ use checklists where appropriate

▓ conference with the students and keep notes

▓ monitor the work samples and portfolios

Because well-planned and -implemented response activities encourage children to use high-level critical and creative thinking skills, teachers listen for such things as how children interpret their reading; how they apply their ideas to the world around them, both in and out of school; how they attend to the language of a book; what they are learning as a result of their reading; how they dialogue with other students in their group; how they listen and acknowledge the ideas of others; what questions they raise; and how they express their own ideas and responses.

One group of teachers identified the following criteria for guiding their assessment of students' responses to literature (Bainbridge, Coleman & Gellner, 2004):

1. growth in responding to literature
   ❑ responsibility and ownership
   ❑ personal connections with the book
   ❑ appreciation of multiple interpretations of a text
   ❑ critical reading and critical literacy
   ❑ increase in repertoire of responses to literature

2. growth as a strategic reader
   ❑ Views self as a successful reader.
   ❑ Demonstrates metacognitive awareness of the process of reading.
   ❑ Development of knowledge, strategies and skills.

For each of these areas, the teachers developed checklists for use in their classrooms. Box 11.1 presents their checklist for the area of "Critical reading and critical literacy."

BOX 11.1 **ASSESSMENT CRITERIA FOR CRITICAL READING AND CRITICAL LITERACY**

Date: _____

Student's name: _____

In discussions and/or written responses,* the student:	Rarely	Sometimes	Usually	Frequently	Always
Questions or wonders about points in the text					
Understands that texts reflect a particular historical, cultural, and social context					
Can detect stereotypes, hidden agendas, etc. (no text is neutral)					
Shows increased awareness of social or ethical issues arising from text					
Analyzes the author's intent or purpose for writing text (persuasion, ideology, explanation, etc.)					
Comments:					

*Indicate on the checklist whether you've seen the characteristic in D (discussion) or in W (written response).

The assessment of response journals is most effective when teachers read their students' journals frequently, and take the time to respond to the entries, either in brief notes in the journal itself, or on post-it notes on the relevant pages. Teachers usually take in four or five journals every few days so that they can respond to their students' ideas regularly, and students receive feedback on their entries in a timely fashion. They engage in a brief written conversation with students, noting interesting comments, applauding thoughtful ideas and asking questions that encourage deeper thinking about an issue. Teachers often write notes to themselves about a students' work immediately after reading the journals, and they also provide feedback to the student regarding how they're functioning and how they can improve their work.

Teachers like Jan Smith and Carol Walters try to refrain from making summative judgments about journal work, and they do not give grades. Instead they devise simple rubrics based on performance criteria and divided into levels. These rubrics include information that will help students understand what they do well plus how they can improve their work. In his book *Response Journals Revisited*, Parsons (2001) presents a number of checklists for teachers and students and some basic rubrics for assessing response journals. These are based on teacher expectations and routines agreed upon in the classroom in regard to working with response journals. Box 11.2 presents an assessment guide based on Parson's suggestions.

BOX 11.2 **ASSESSMENT GUIDE FOR RESPONSE JOURNALS**

Level	Criteria
Noncompliant	Insufficient reading Insufficient number and/or length of responses Content superficial or perfunctory Student-teacher conference required
Functional	Sufficient reading accomplished Sufficient number and length of responses Responses characterized by: frequent retelling, likes and dislikes, occasional relating to personal experience, some prediction
Extended	All routines established plus some additional reading and responding Responses additionally characterized by: brief retelling when necessary, frequent relating to personal experience, prediction, offering reasons for opinions and conclusions
Independent	All routines established plus considerable additional reading and responding Responses additionally characterized by: recognition of characters' motivations, linking cause and effect, opinions usually supported by evidence from the text, awareness of author/illustrator's purposes

BOOK SELECTION

This section of the chapter explores the definition of good literature and who has the right to make that determination. Which awards are devoted to children's literature? Which books should be selected for use in the classroom, and how are decisions made? The confounding question facing most elementary school teachers is: Who decides what constitutes a "quality" book for children?

Over the years, it has generally been accepted that children, parents, teachers, and librarians are all involved in making decisions about purchasing or selecting books for school and home. When it comes to prestigious awards for children's literature, however, it is mainly adults on library association and other committees who make the decisions. Examples include the Amelia Francis Howard-Gibbon Award and Governor General's Award in Canada, the Caldecott and Newbery Awards in the United States, and the Kate Greenaway and Carnegie Medals in the United Kingdom. We know that children's choices of "good" literature frequently vary from adult choices. Children enjoy books that involve mystery, excitement, humour, and adventure. Teachers, on the other hand, often think it is more important that the reader be interested in, and able to identify with, the characters in a story (elements, not surprisingly, ranked much lower by children). Thus teachers and librarians sometimes recommend books to children that may be good for the adult reader but hold little appeal for children. The result is that children often learn to ignore these book suggestions.

A number of "Children's Choice" awards do exist at the regional level in Canada and at the state level in the United States, however. Voting for the awards is often conducted through the schools in collaboration with local public libraries. In order to vote, students must have read a certain number of titles from a list created by teachers and librarians. The list consists of recent books but not necessarily those published in the last year. The Silver Birch Award in Ontario, the Manitoba Young Reader's Choice Award, the Rocky Mountain Book Award in Alberta, and the Red Cedar Award in British Columbia are examples of children's choice awards in Canada. The awards are highly regarded by authors and illustrators and they provide children with a chance to show their support for the books they like. Unfortunately, these awards are not generally highly acknowledged by libraries and book sellers. This has prompted many observers to question the perceived significance of children's interests and opinions about books, and the intended purpose of the more prestigious awards.

We have to ask: If a book is good, what is it good *for*? Is it a challenging reading experience that will delight readers and help them become *better* readers by showing them something new? Is it a good book for taking on vacation and reading on the beach? Is it a good book for teaching more about language arts skills, or for helping readers learn how to do something of special interest to them, such as keeping a healthy tropical aquarium? Is it a good book because it enables the reader to escape from real life and see life differently? In trying to answer questions such as these, teachers, librarians, and even scholars of children's literature are coming to realize how difficult it is to describe the specific characteristics or features of "quality" literature. A book that demonstrates how to create a healthy tropical aquarium will differ enormously from a book of short stories. A book that a person finds so notable that he or she wants to keep a copy for a long time may be very different from the pocket book picked up as reading material for a long plane trip. Clearly then, describing quality in each of these cases must vary according to the format of the book, the purpose of the author, and the purpose, interests, and reading experiences of the reader.

Guidelines for Appropriate Selection of Children's Literature

When selecting materials to include in a classroom or school library, teachers and teacher/librarians make every effort to choose books that meet the needs of both children and the curriculum. Knowledge of child development and the literary quality of books, as well as knowledge of the provincial programs of study and of curriculum expectations, help teachers make appropriate selections. Critics might say that "book selection" is simply a code for a librarian's own brand of censorship, but as Roberts (1996, p. 19) asserts, there are distinct differences between selection and censorship:

> Selection is a positive process that supports intellectual freedom when the selector considers resources in a holistic manner with the intent of including as many as possible in the library collection. Resources are selected objectively, according to set criteria, without regard for a selector's personal biases. Conversely, censorship is a negative process in which the censor searches for reasons, either internal or external, to exclude a resource.

Sound selection decisions are guided by the quality of reading and learning, even when, as Booth (1992, p. 9) says, "reading reveals unpleasant truths or viewpoints opposed to those of a particular parent or child, as long as the child is deemed capable of dealing with such ideas."

The selection of print materials for use in schools is a complex issue, for it is difficult to say in a public education system who should decide what children should and should not read. There is also a difference between making book selections for a school library and selecting material that will be used for teaching purposes in a classroom. The debate involves freedom of expression and beliefs about what is appropriate for children, what is moral and what is immoral, and what is acceptable and not acceptable in society. It is highly likely that most children will confront difficult and disturbing ideas as they grow up. Reading and discussing a broad range of literature can help children become critical thinkers and thoughtful human beings capable of making sound judgments, both as individuals and as members of society.

The selection debate relates directly to emancipatory or critical literacy presented in Chapter 1 of this textbook. It is a compelling and difficult issue, and one that teachers are frequently required to address.

In 1974, the Canadian Library Association issued a statement on intellectual freedom that was subsequently adopted by the Canadian School Library Association. Two parts of that statement are of particular relevance for educators. The first asserts that it is a person's fundamental right to have access to all expressions of knowledge, creativity, and intellectual activity and to be able to express one's thoughts publicly. The second states that libraries must guarantee and provide access to all expressions of knowledge and intellectual activity, including those elements that conventional society might deem unacceptable or unpopular (Canadian Library Association, 1974). Thus, anyone who endorses this statement, and who thereby advocates selection as opposed to censorship of materials, still has the right to object to certain books if he or she so chooses, but not to insist on their removal from library shelves so that others are denied access to them. Advocates of book selection also respect the child's intellectual freedom (and innate common sense) and believe that adults have an obligation to be honest with children. This approach to selection does not argue that all books for children are of equal quality and equal value, or that they are even appropriate for children of all ages, but it does assert that children have the right of access to the best literature and learning resources available.

The most important things teachers can do when engaged in selecting reading materials are to be aware of their own biases and values; to stay current with issues, themes, and book publications and reviews; and to maintain files of policy statements, useful resources, procedures for dealing with challenges to materials, and guidelines from recognized authorities. ("Challenges" are those occasions where books or other materials are considered by an individual or group to be inappropriate for the audience, and a request is made for the material to be removed from the classroom or library.) Many professional resources and tools are available to aid teachers and librarians in selecting books. By far the best resources are professional journals. As Kathy Oster mentioned in Chapter 10, *CM: Canadian Review of Materials* provides book reviews and profiles of Canadian authors and illustrators. *Canadian Children's Literature*, published by the University of Winnipeg, provides reviews of Canadian publications as well as articles about Canadian children's literature. *School Libraries in Canada* (**http://www.cla.ca/casl/slic/slicindex.html**), the journal of the Canadian Association for School Libraries (published by the Canadian Library Association), contains book reviews, author/illustrator profiles, and well-informed articles on school librarianship in Canada. *Teacher Librarian*, published jointly in Canada and the United States (out of Toronto and Maryland), presents articles that reflect literature-related concerns common to both countries. Other worthy professional journals include *Language Arts*, *The Reading Teacher*, and *The Horn Book*.

In addition to journals, a variety of other resources are available to help teachers with book selection. One of these is the *Our Choice* catalogue, issued annually by the Canadian Children's Book Centre in Toronto. It lists recommended materials published every year in Canada, including fiction and nonfiction books, videos, CD-ROMs, and audio-ocassettes. Also helpful is the *Canadian Book Review Annual*, an evaluative guide to Canadian-authored, English-language publications. It reviews the year's scholarly publications, reference materials, and publications for children. The emphasis is on analyzing and evaluating materials, with brief descriptions of the books reviewed.

As this section has shown, many book selection tools are available in Canada for students, beginning teachers and teacher/librarians who want to engage their students with the very best of children's literature. Information about book censorship is also available. Since censorship and challenges to books and periodicals in school libraries are unpredictable and usually emotional, it is critical that teachers try to remain up to date and well informed about processes for dealing with book challenges. We discuss these issues in the next section.

Children making book selections in library

Censorship of Children's Materials

As already noted, there is a clear difference between selecting materials for use in schools and censoring these materials. Where book selection uses positive criteria to determine which books to place in a collection—what Nodelman (1992) calls the "books we approve of"—censorship seeks to remove, suppress, or restrict books *already present* in a collection. Censorship is generally ineffective in ensuring that only the most "appropriate" of books are read by students, yet it can be extremely disruptive to the life of a school. Occasionally, a **challenged book**, removed from library shelves, will become a bestseller and read more widely than if it had not been challenged.

School libraries and classrooms encounter far more challenges to books than do public libraries in North America (Schrader, 1996). This makes it imperative that teachers and librarians be informed on the issues and prepared to debate the relative merits of the materials selected for use in their schools. Educators have a responsibility to fulfil their professional obligations to learners by providing students with the very best in children's literature, meaning material that challenges children to think critically and explore new ideas and perspectives. Teachers have a further role, however, which is to help their students become more thoughtful and critical about their own choices of reading materials, and to help them develop their abilities to think for themselves and make sound judgments.

Teachers are often surprised to see which children's books are commonly challenged. *Bridge to Terabithia* (Paterson, 1977), *The Paper Bag Princess* (Munsch, 1980), *Thomas's Snowsuit* (Munsch, 1985), *Who Is Frances Rain?* (Buffie, 1987), and *Harry Potter and the Sorcerer's Stone* (Rowling, 1998) have all had censorship threats in recent years. Jenkinson (1994) found that challenges to books increased in Manitoba in the 10-year period between 1983 and 1993. The authors challenged most often in Jenkinson's study were Robert Munsch (*Giant: Or, Waiting for the Thursday Boat*, 1989, and *A Promise Is a Promise*, 1988), Roald Dahl (*Revolting Rhymes*, 1982, and *The Witches*, 1983), Alvin Schwartz (*Scary Stories to Tell in the Dark*, 1981), and William Steig (*The Amazing Bone*, 1976). The top ten reasons Jenkinson identified for challenges were

1. concerned witchcraft or the supernatural (24 percent)
2. contained or concerned violence (18 percent)
3. contained material inappropriate for an immature audience (12 percent)
4. described or showed explicit sex (10 percent)
5. contained questionable morality (9 percent)
6. described or showed nudity (9 percent)
7. contained obscenities (8 percent)
8. contained profanities (7 percent)
9. contained sexism or role stereotypes (6 percent)
10. contained beliefs contrary to those of a particular religious ideology (5 percent)

In addition to challenges are the indirect instances of censorship, in which books simply go missing, have pages removed, or are ripped up or defaced. Censorship can also be an attempt by special-interest groups to protect themselves against ideas or beliefs that may threaten their status. *Maxine's Tree* by Diane Leger-Haskell (1990), for example, was challenged in 1992 by members of the IWA-Canada on British Columbia's Sunshine Coast as being "emotional and an insult to loggers" (Nodelman, 1992, p. 132). The religious right is particularly noted for making censorship demands in schools, because many members of such religious groups often have problems with public schools and with the whole notion of secular education.

Explicit procedures detailing how book complaints will be received and reviewed can be set up by school boards or by individual schools. Information about past legal rulings, groups behind challenges, and approaches to resisting challenges is available from organizations such as the Book and Periodical Council (Toronto), the Canadian Library Association (Toronto), the National Council of Teachers of English (Urbana, Illinois), and the International Reading Association (Newark, Delaware). An extremely useful publication is *The Students' Right to Read*, published by the National Council of Teachers of English (1982). The book includes sample forms for collecting a statement of concern from a complainant, a sample letter to a complainant, instructions for establishing an evaluating committee, and suggestions for evaluating the complaint.

The National Council of Teachers of English and the International Reading Association developed a CD-ROM resource, *Rationales for Challenged Books* (National Council of Teachers of English, 1998), which includes more than 200 rationales for over 170 commonly challenged materials for kindergarten through grade 12 (though the emphasis is on publications for grades 7 to 12). Publications are listed both by title and author on this web-type resource, and information is provided about book challenges and on what schools and libraries can do to counter challenges.

TEACHER WISDOM

JAN SMITH AND CAROL WALTERS

How do you make the best use of children's trade books (literature) in your classroom?

Jan: I integrate as much as possible, and it seems that no matter what I'm teaching in the various subject areas, there'll be a good children's book or two that add to the understandings the children develop. I don't mean pure nonfiction. We do use encyclopedias ("Just the facts, ma'am"), and we use nonfiction books, but I've also used the poem *The Shark* by E. J. Pratt (1923) and magazine articles, when we're looking at "life under the sea." The visualization from a poem can be amazing and the children's writing becomes much more interesting and detailed when I make those connections. I also use Linda Granfield's book *Where Poppies Grow* (2002) in connection with Remembrance Day and I bring in photos from the National Archives so we can look at them and make inferences. How would you feel if you were that soldier or that nurse, or that carrier pigeon? Good examples of good writing lead to good writing.

What do you do about books that might be controversial or offensive to some parents?

Carol: I guess *The Vicar of Nibbleswicke* would be a good example in grade 4. It's vintage Roald Dahl and it's pretty much bathroom humour in places, but the kids love it. A dyslexic vicar is reafflicted with his childhood problem when he becomes nervous in front of his congregation. He pronounces key words backwards, so they end up worshipping dog, and even the simplest of things he tries to say, as in referring to the lady who "knits" and the issue of where to "park" cars become shocking to his congregation. I explain to the children that parts might be quite rude (it's mostly in their heads as they have to do most of the reversals), but we giggle about it, and I have never had a parent complain. But you do have to be sensitive about what is appropriate in the community, especially with the younger children. It's a good idea to send book lists home every once in a while, so the parents can see which books we are reading in response groups and which books I am reading aloud. If any of the parents want to borrow the books to read themselves, I am always delighted to put a copy in their hands.

How do you stay on top of the numerous children's books that are published each year?

Jan: I check on the web for the various award winners and I especially pay attention to the books that are nominated for the "Tree" awards across Canada. My students usually participate in the Red Cedar Awards, and so we make sure we have all those books on hand in the library, and copies in classrooms as well. The children love to talk about the various books and then vote on them at the provincial level. It's a lot of fun and it keeps me reading. But I don't find it hard to read children's books. There are so many excellent books out there. I listen to what other teachers are reading and talking about and I pick up copies from the local bookstores for myself—or I borrow them from the public library. I almost always have a children's book on hand to read. It's so important to be able to talk to students in detail about books and make recommendations when they ask you. And they need to see their teachers as readers too.

How do you manage to meet all the individual needs of your students and meet the outcomes in the language arts program of studies as well?

Carol: That can definitely be overwhelming to a beginning teacher. Language arts is a massive subject area, but if you keep literature at the centre of it, you can do a lot. I would advise beginning teachers to get to know their colleagues and talk about children's books with them. Ask which books are favourites. Get to know the person in charge of the school library and visit the public library as well. Get to know the latest and best information books, because a lot of readers choose those books for free reading, not only for information for a school project. Also, be aware of the technology tools that can help struggling readers and writers. There's Dragon Naturally Speaking (Nuance) that is speech recognition software, and Kurzweil systems that provide visual and auditory feedback. You can scan a document and the program reads it back to the student in synthetic speech. And it helps them to do note-taking and to create study guides. There's a lot to stay on top of, but you can do it if you network with colleagues and ask questions when you need to.

Issues and Controversies

The most recent flurry of challenges and censorship activities has involved picture books depicting same-sex family relationships (gay and lesbian couples). The 1998 court case in Surrey, BC, regarding *Asha's Mums* by Rosamund Elwin (1990), *Belinda's Bouquet* by Leslea Newman (1998), and *One Dad, Two Dads, Brown Dad, Blue Dad* by Johnny Valentine (1994) was not about whether children should have access to these books in the school library but whether the books should be used in classrooms for teaching purposes. The debate under-scores the complex nature of censorship and reminds teachers how difficult it can be to ensure that all children have access to books about a range of social and family contexts, while not insisting that all children read the same books.

No less controversial has been the issue of racial discrimination in literature. In the middle-to-late 20th century, it was not uncommon to find books for children that were explicitly racist in their treatment of blacks or Native North Americans. When many of these books were originally published, however, society in general was not sensitive to the discrimination portrayed in them. Since the 1948 Universal Declaration of Human Rights by the United Nations General Assembly, book publishers and educators have fought hard to prevent the publication of books that are clearly discriminatory.

In the first edition of *The Bobbsey Twins* (Hope, 1904), for example, the reader was told what a good mother Flossie was to her dolls, for she protected them from a black doll given to her by one of the servants. Flossie told her friends that the doll didn't really belong in the family. However, since Flossie's mother explained that there were "no asylums for black orphans," the doll was allowed to stay with the others—separated from them by a piece of cardboard. Given the nature of American society at that time, it was hardly surprising to see such blatant racial discrimination in a book for children. What is surprising is that the piece was not removed from the book until the 1950s.

One of the earliest "multicultural" books in North America was *The Story of Little Black Sambo* (Bannerman, 1899), set in India but with illustrations depicting black characters. Although Bannerman's book has received much criticism for its racial stereotyping, the story has remained hugely popular. It has been retold numerous times, and has been published in two newer editions. *The Story of Little Babaji* (Bannerman and Marcellino, 1996) contains the original text, except that the characters are given authentic Indian names. Fred Marcellino's illustrations place the story clearly in India. *Sam and the Tigers: A New Retelling of Little Black Sambo*, written by Julius Lester and illustrated by Jerry Pinkney (1996), depicts black characters but the fantasy setting (Sam-sam-sa-mara) removes it from any specific geographic location.

Stereotypical images abound in literature, from the works of Shakespeare to *Anne of Green Gables* (Montgomery, 1908) and *The Adventures of Huckleberry Finn* (Twain, 1885, 1963). The central feature of many of the American classics containing racist stereotypes was the presence of "indolent, happy-go-lucky slaves" (Miller-Lachmann, 1992). Other books, such as *The Five Chinese Brothers* (Bishop, 1938), seemed to promote the stereotype that all Chinese people look alike. Such books now provide a springboard for discussing issues such as racism, slavery, social class, and stereotyping in general.

Literature portrays all aspects of human nature, and children's literature is no exception. Through the library collections that teachers make available in schools, students can learn to appreciate the human condition, to discriminate good from bad and just from unjust, and to make sense of the world and their feelings toward it in a new and deeply personal way. As they select literature for children, teachers face the challenge of putting their own feelings and biases aside and presenting a balanced and equitable view of our diverse global community.

Critical Literacy

How can teachers help students to become aware of the biases built into texts—of whose interests are being served and whose are not? How can children become critical users of texts? The term **critical literacy** is used to describe one of the goals of literacy instruction—to help children learn to critically interrogate all texts, whether in books, in the media, or on the Internet, so that their understandings reflect the social, political, and power relations embedded in those texts. Only from this perspective are children able to gain control over printed texts, media and other technologies, and make use of their understandings of all texts for personal and social transformation. The purpose of critical literacy instruction, then, is to empower teachers and students to actively participate in a democracy and move literacy beyond text to social action (Cadiero-Kaplan, 2002).

Critical literacy reflects a fundamentally different view of knowledge and learning than has been seen in traditional views of literacy. Essentially, critical literacy approaches textual meaning as a process of construction. One constructs meaning, "imbuing a text with meaning rather than extracting meaning from it" (Cervetti, Pardales, & Damico, 2001, p. 5). Textual meaning is understood in the context of social, historic, and power relations. Reading is an act of "coming to know the world as well as the word," and is seen as a means to social change. The ultimate goal of social action is the creation of a fairer and more just society for all people regardless of race, culture, class, or gender.

Critical literacy has been defined in several different ways by literacy educators and theorists. Lewison, Flint, and Sluys (2002) reviewed definitions presented over the past 30 years and synthesized them into the following four dimensions:

- disrupting the commonplace (seeing the everyday through new lenses to consider new frames from which to understand experience)
- interrogating multiple viewpoints (standing in the shoes of others to understand experience and text from our own perspectives and the viewpoints of others)
- focusing on sociopolitical issues (stepping outside the personal to interrogate how sociopolitical systems and power relationships shape perceptions, responses, and actions)
- taking action and promoting social justice

Although these dimensions are not sequential, Lewison, Flint, and Sluys found that teachers generally focus more on the first two or three dimensions than on the last one.

In their four resources model, Luke and Freebody (1997) remind teachers that analyzing and critiquing texts is one of four necessary reading and writing practices: text analyzer, code breaker (word identification and spelling), text participant (constructing meaning), and text user (using texts for pragmatic purposes). These cannot be taught as four discrete practices, but are critical elements of reading and writing at all stages and levels. As Cadiero-Kaplan (2002, pp. 378–379) notes, "Even children as young as four and five years old can engage in critical dialogue on issues of race and skin colour."

Planning for Instruction in Critical Literacy

The development and implementation of critical literacy instruction is not easy because of the complexity of the issues involved (Green, 2001). In addition, many beginning teachers are nervous about approaching what could be perceived as difficult topics in elementary classrooms (Johnston, Bainbridge, Mangat, & Skogen, 2006). As a beginning point, Wilson (2002, p. 129) suggests nurturing children in "classroom societies where they each feel valued, regardless of class, culture, race, or gender, and where the curriculum they live helps them better know and understand one another."

Although all Canadian curriculum documents value critical reading and/or critical literacy, they provide little information to help teachers plan critical literacy lessons for the classroom. Box 11.3 presents some questions teachers can use when discussing texts with students. These

---

BOX 11.3   QUESTIONS TO INTERROGATE TEXTS

▷ Who wrote this text?

▷ Why did the author write this text?

▷ What is the author's experience and expertise on this topic?

▷ What does the author have to gain from writing this text?

▷ What evidence supports what the author wrote?

▷ What do other authors write about this topic?

▷ Who benefits from this text?

▷ What voices are being heard?

▷ Whose voices are left out?

▷ Is there another point of view?

▷ How are the (girls, boys, women, men, mothers, fathers, grandmothers, grandfathers, etc.) portrayed in this text?

▷ What is this text saying about (boys and girls, men and women, the elderly, people from different cultures, people with a disability, people living in poverty)? Is this true for all members of this group?

▷ What difference would it have made if the main character were a (boy, girl, man, woman, person from a different culture, person with a disability)?

▷ What is the world like for people in the text?

▷ Which people have power in this text?

▷ Is this fair?

▷ What is the author's underlying message?

▷ If violence was used to deal with a problem in this text, in what other ways could the problem have been solved?

▷ How has the author used language to position the reader?

▷ What are the design features of this text? Why were they included?

questions are designed to invite children to interrogate the assumptions embedded in texts, as well as their own assumptions and beliefs about the world. The questions can help students to identify issues of fairness and social justice in the materials they encounter. Initially, teachers can guide children in their thinking by presenting these questions during discussions. The goal is that children will eventually ask themselves these types of questions as they read and write.

Some of the questions in Box 11.3 are appropriate for children at all ages, while others are more appropriate for children in the upper elementary grades. In addition, some questions are appropriate for both stories and informational texts while others are appropriate for only one of these types of texts.

Although most narrative material can be used for critical literacy lessons, some educators have identified specific texts that are particularly appropriate for this use. Wason-Ellam (2002) calls these critically conscious stories; Lewison, Flint, and Sluys (2002) refer to them as social issues books; and Leland, Harste, Ociepka, Lewison, and Vasquez (1999) use the term *critical books.*

Leland, Harste, Ociepka, Lewison, and Vasquez (1999) developed the following criteria to identify critical books:

- They don't make difference invisible, but rather explore which differences *make a difference.*
- They enrich our understanding of history and life by giving voice to those who traditionally have been silenced or marginalized.
- They show how people can begin to take action on important social issues.
- They explore dominant systems of meaning that operate in our society to position people and groups of people.
- They don't provide "happily ever after" endings for complex social problems.

They (1999) believe that a diversity-and-difference model of education serves multilingual and multicultural societies (such as those in the United States and Canada) better than the conformity-and-consensus model that has traditionally permeated education systems. In Box 11.4 we present titles of some critical books written by authors from different cultures for use with children in elementary classrooms. Many of these books are Canadian in origin.

Beyond Examples

The major goal of the examples provided in this section of the chapter is to transform both the curriculum and children's thinking. According to Freire (1970), the development of critical awareness of inequities and injustice is the first step in social change. Much of this change will be situated at the classroom and school levels, with both teachers and children taking responsibility for change. For example, in relation to gender equity the following actions can be taken at the classroom level:

- Teachers ensure that learning materials are appropriate, representing both genders fairly and equally so both boys and girls have appropriate role models.
- Learners of both genders are encouraged to be actively involved in the learning process.
- Teachers and children agree that stereotypical language referring to males and females is not acceptable in the classroom, and they are vigilant in their reading of other authors' work and in their own classroom interactions and writing to detect and exclude this type of language.

BOX 11.4   **BOOKS FOR DEVELOPING CRITICAL LITERACY**

Bedard, M. (1999). *Clay ladies*. Toronto: Tundra Books.

Browne, A. (1998). *Voices in the park*. New York: DK Publishing.

Bunting, E. (1991). *Fly away home*. New York: Clarion Books.

Butler, G. (1998). *The Hangashore*. Toronto: Tundra Books.

Cowen-Fleetcher, J. (1994). *It takes a village*. New York: Scholastic Press.

Cheng, A. (2000). *Grandfather counts*. New York: Lee & Low Books.

Davis, A. (2003). *Bagels from Benny*. Toronto: Kids Can Press.

Fletcher, R. (1998). *Flying solo*. New York: Clarion Books.

Hesse, K. (1998). *Just juice*. New York: Scholastic Press.

Highway, T. (2001). *Caribou song*. Toronto: HarperCollins Publishers.

Isadora, R. (1991). *At the crossroads*. New York: Greenwillow.

Kaplan, W. (1998). *One more border: The true story of one family's escape from war-torn Europe*. Toronto: Groundwood Books.

Littlechild, G. (1993). *This land is my land*. San Francisco: Children's Book Press.

McKee, D. (1987). *Tusk tusk*. London: Beaver Books.

Myers, C. (2000). *Wings*. New York: Scholastic.

Setterington, K. (2004). *Mom and Mum are getting married*. Toronto: Second Story Press.

Spalding, A. (1999). *Me and Mr. Mah*. Victoria, BC: Orca Book Publishers.

Van Camp, R. (1998). *What's the most beautiful thing you know about horses?* San Francisco: Children's Book Press.

Woodson, J. (2001). *The other side*. New York: Putnam's Sons.

Yee, P. (1996). *Ghost Train*. Toronto: Douglas & McIntyre/Groundwood.

Overall, teachers and children create classroom contexts and school communities in which all children are valued regardless of gender, age, race, exceptionality, or class.

One issue in critical literacy instruction relates to the wide range of diversity portrayed in children's literature, including differences in family structure, ethnicity, gender, age, exceptionalities, values, socioeconomic status, and ways of communicating. Although this literature provides opportunities for children to see both themselves and their families portrayed by authors, some parents feel uncomfortable when children are exposed to family structures and values different from their own. As indicated earlier in this chapter, parents and community groups challenge the use of some books in schools and even challenge their availability in school libraries.

In addition to the question of censorship, a major challenge teachers face is what to do when the meaning a child constructs from a story is quite different from the meaning they have constructed (or the meaning most of the students in the class have constructed). How can the teacher (and the other students) accept the child's interpretation as a valid and valued point of view in the classroom? Teachers have also reported difficulty knowing how to respond when they overhear disparaging remarks made by students to peers, such as "Chinese people are weird." Lewison, Flint, and Sluys (2002) suggest that the most appropriate response is to plan and conduct critical literacy lessons focused on racism.

Teachers also have difficulty during critical literacy lessons when students respond in ways that are biased against those with less power. In one example presented by Lewison, Flint, and Sluys, a novice fifth-grade teacher read aloud the book *Randall's Wall* (Fenner, 1991) about a boy who is ostracized by his classmates because he is unclean due to not having running water in his house. When asked what might happen if Randall joined their classroom, the students' responses were similar to those of the children in the story; they discussed not befriending Randall for fear of jeopardizing their status with peers. It took considerable discussion to help children begin to "understand how they are constructed by larger power structures" (Lewison, Flint, & Sluys, 2002, p. 387).

We are just beginning to figure out how to help children develop critical literacy abilities in elementary classrooms. We know that children need to work in groups rather than individually, and that interrogating text is at the heart of this type of instruction. While critical thinking is important, however, the ultimate goal is taking action for social justice.

CANADIAN LITERATURE

In this section, we address the reasons why it is important for Canadian children to read Canadian literature in addition to international literature, and we suggest many book titles that are specifically Canadian in context.

Over the years, Canadians have become accustomed to receiving media largely from the United States and Britain. Children's print materials are no exception. Most professional books currently available for teachers, especially those about multicultural literature, are from the United States, and they largely (and sometimes entirely) refer to American children's books. However, the stories and experiences of Hispanic Americans, African Americans, Chinese Americans, and other ethnic and cultural groups are not necessarily parallel to those of Canadians.

It is well accepted that children need to see their own culture represented in the books they read. In the 1980s, Canadian publishing companies increased their publication of Canadian trade books for children and young adults. Today, many excellent children's books are written and produced in Canada. The Canadian Children's Book Centre in Toronto (CCBC) publishes lists of books, and information about authors. More information about CCBC is presented in Box 11.5.

Why Canadian?

Literature can be a powerful vehicle for the transmission of national culture anywhere in the world. Texts written for children both mirror cultural attitudes and play a part in acculturating young readers. Canada prides itself on its official multiculturalism and its "cultural pluralism": the importance of accepting different races, ethnicities, languages, and cultures. The rights and privileges of Canada's diverse population are entrenched in law, but for those citizens outside the white mainstream, Canada remains a country where much of the power resides in the hands of those of European descent. Bissoondath (1998) warns that Canada's

> **BOX 11.5** THE CANADIAN CHILDREN'S BOOK CENTRE
>
> The Canadian Children's Book Centre (commonly referred to as the CCBC), located in Toronto, was established in 1976. The organization provides information to members on current Canadian books, and their authors and illustrators. The Centre contains a collection of Canadian children's materials available for browsing by members of the society, and extensive files on Canadian authors, illustrators, and the Canadian book publishing industry. The newsletter *The Children's Book News* highlights what's new and exciting in the Canadian children's book world, including information about Canadian Children's Book Week. *Our Choice*, published annually, is a guide to the year's best books, audio recordings, videos, and CD-ROMs. Online resources include industry news, a calendar of events, a guide to Canadian Children's Book Awards, and a listing of Children's Literature Roundtables across the country. Reference services are available to members by phone, fax, or e-mail. Online resources include links to publishers' sites and a complete list of Canadian Children's Book Awards. For information contact: CCBC, 40 Orchard View Boulevard, Suite 101; Toronto, ON M4R 1B9. Online at: http://www.bookcentre.ca. Phone: (416) 975-0010. Fax: (416) 975-8970. For inquiries e-mail: info@bookcentre.ca.

policy of multiculturalism could lead to a reinforcement of stereotypes and a "gentle marginalization" of those who accept and display their ethnic heritage. He maintains that Canadian multiculturalism has emphasized difference and has retarded the integration of immigrants into the Canadian mainstream. Bissoondath writes that "we need to focus on programs that seek out and emphasize the experiences, values and dreams we all share as Canadians, whatever our colour, language, religion, ethnicity or historical grievance. And pursue acceptance of others—not merely tolerance of them" (1998, p. 22).

If children are to know themselves and Canada, they need frequent opportunities to access resources that are Canadian and that depict Canadian culture and identity. Although it is essential that Canadian children have opportunities to read about Canadian people and places in the literature they encounter, until the last 25 years or so there was very little Canadian children's literature available and there was little Canadian readers could identify with. Most Canadian children grew up with a canon of British literature.

Today, a wide range of high-quality children's literature is published across Canada, and some of that literature is published by school districts and by relatively small publishing houses. This has had an impact on children's reading across the country, for now students can read about Canadian people and places from Peggy's Cove and Saskatoon to Ungava Bay and Yellowknife. When they read Canadian materials, children can imagine the prairie, mountains, or seacoast, and they learn more about Canada and who they are as Canadians. Many scholars and writers have suggested that the land, the actual environment or physical landscape of Canada, characterizes Canadian literature. *The Doll* by Cora Taylor (1987) is a time-slip novel set in Fort Carlton, Saskatchewan, *Rebellion* by Marianne Brandis (1996) is a novel set in historical Toronto, *The Fishing Summer* (Jam, 1997) is a picture storybook set on Canada's east coast. Each of these books provides different insights into Canada and what it means to be Canadian, and each is profoundly reliant upon the landscape in which it is set. Perhaps through reading Canadian literature, children can develop an appreciation and understanding of Canada's role in the global community. Defining

---

BOX 11.6 **A SELECTION OF CANADIAN LITERATURE FOR GRADES 4 TO 7**

Bedard, M. (1990). *Redwork*. Toronto: Lester & Orpen Denys.

Bishop, M. (2001). *Tunnels of time*. Regina: Coteau Books.

Bly, D. (1993). *The McIntyre liar*. Edmonton: Tree Frog Press.

Brouwer, S. (1993). *The accidental detectives: Shortcuts*. Wheaton, IL: Victor Books.

Buffie, M. (1987). *Who is Frances Rain?* Toronto: Kids Can Press.

Buchholz, K. (1999). *How Lone Crow became Magpie*. Winnipeg: Pemmican.

Doyle, B. (1984). *Angel square*. Toronto: Groundwood Books/Douglas& McIntyre.

Ellis, D. (1999). *Looking for X*. Toronto: Groundwood Books.

Ellis, S. (1997). *Back of beyond*. Toronto: Groundwood.

Godfrey, M. (1988). *Send in Miss Teeny Wonderful*. Richmond Hill, ON: Scholastic TAB.

Horvath, P. (2001). *Everything on a waffle*. New York: Farrar Strauss Giroux.

Hughes, M. (1980. *The keeper of the Isis light*. London: Mammoth.

Lunn, J. (1997). *The hollow tree*. Toronto: Alfred A. Knopf Canada.

Oppel, K. (1997). *Silverwing*. Scarborough, ON: HarperCollins.

Scrimger, R. (1998). *The nose from Jupiter*. Toronto: Tundra Books.

Spalding, A. (1995). *Finders keepers*. Victoria, BC: Beach Holme Publishing.

Smucker, B. (1989). *Jacob's little giant*. Toronto: Puffin Books.

Taylor, C. (1985). *Julie*. Saskatoon: Western Producer Prairie Books.

Wilson, E. (2001). *The Emily Carr mystery*. Toronto: HarperCollins.

---

our identity as Canadians is a continuing process and one in which our students have a role. Box 11.6 presents a list of Canadian fiction suitable for children in grades 4 to 7.

From Canadian books such as those noted above, children not only learn about Canada and what it means to be Canadian, they also learn that Canadians are authors and illustrators, and that authors and illustrators live in places where the students might also live. Authors become real people, and writing and illustrating become possible professions. Well-known authors and illustrators now visit schools on a regular basis, and some of the hard work and the craft of writing and illustrating are demonstrated to children as they listen to artists speak about and read their published work. Several organizations across Canada, such as the Young Alberta Book Society, exist for the sole purpose of enhancing literacy development and introducing Canadian authors and illustrators to children in schools.

In addition to fiction materials, good nonfiction books about Canada have been written and published by Canadians. In *To the Top of Everest* (Skreslet & MacLeod, 2001) Laurie Skreslet relates his experiences in becoming the first Canadian to reach the summit of Mount Everest, a feat he accomplished in 1982. The book is filled with stunning photographs of the mountain and the climbers, as well as a first-person account of the perils encountered during the adventure. Skreslet recalls the long years of preparation, and recounts how he had to overcome fear and learn how to survive in the thin air and harsh weather conditions. The

BOX 11.7	A SELECTION OF CANADIAN NONFICTION FOR CHILDREN

Beatty, O. and Gieger, J. (1992). *Buried in ice: Unlocking the secrets of a doomed Arctic voyage.* Mississauga, ON: Random House.

Berkowitz, J. (2006). *Jurassic poop: What dinosaurs (and others) left behind.* Toronto: Kids Can Press.

Bowers, V. (2000). *Wow Canada! Exploring this land from coast to coast to coast.* Toronto: Owl Books.

Brewster, H. (2005). *On Juno Beach: Canada's D-Day heroes.* Toronto: Scholastic.

Dudley, K. (1997). *Wolves: The untamed world.* Calgary: Weigi Educational.

Granfield, L. (2001). *Where poppies grow: A World War I companion.* Toronto: Stoddart Kids.

Graydon, S. (2004). *Made you look: How advertising works and why you should know.* Toronto: Annick Press.

Hill, L. (1993). *Trials and triumphs: The story of African-Canadians.* Toronto: Umbrella Press.

Hodge, D. (2001). *The kids book of Canada's Railway and how the CPR was built.* Toronto: Kids Can Press.

Hodge, D. (2006). *The kids book of Canadian immigration.* Toronto: Kids Can Press.

Kenna, K. (1995). *A people apart.* Toronto: Somerville House.

Levine, K. (2003). *Hana's suitcase.* Toronto: Second Story.

Romanek, T. (2006). *Squirt! The most interesting book you'll ever read about blood.* Toronto: Kids Can Press.

Ross, V. (2006). *You can't read this: Forbidden books, lost writing, mistranslations and codes.* Toronto: Tundra Books.

Raskin, L. and Pearson, D. (1998). *52 days by camel.* Toronto: Annick Press.

Shoveller, H. (2006). *Ryan and Jimmy and the well in Africa that brought them together.* Toronto: Kids Can Press.

Swanson, D. (1994). *Safari beneath the sea.* Vancouver: Whitecap Books.

Tanaka, S. (1998). *The buried city of Pompeii: What it was like when Vesuvius exploded.* Richmond Hill, ON: Scholastic.

Thornhill, J. (2006). *I found a dead bird: The kids' guide to the cycle of life and death.* Toronto: Maple Tree Press.

Ulmer, M. (2001). *M is for maple.* Chelsea, MI: Sleeping Bear Press.

book is visually appealing and well laid out, with sidebars explaining various aspects of the expedition. The text is immensely readable and appeals to a wide range of readers, adults as well as children. A list of recent Canadian nonfiction books is presented in Box 11.7.

Books by Aboriginal Canadians

In recent years, Aboriginal Canadian authors and illustrators have created many excellent books for children. The works of George Littlechild, Michael Arvaarluk Kusugak, Thomas King, Richard Van Camp, and Tomson Highway have become particularly popular. George Littlechild's book *This Land Is My Land* (1993) is a particularly stunning introduction to Aboriginal literature, with personal stories about Littlechild's family members and ancestors. The short narratives are unforgettable in their intensity and poignancy. Littlechild writes and paints about his experiences in boarding school and recalls memories, many of them tragic, of family members. He speaks excitedly about his first visit to New York City, and describes the development of his artwork. The book ends optimistically, with Littlechild telling about the current revival of Aboriginal culture and traditions and emphasizing the pride he feels in his ancestry.

Tomson Highway's three books for young readers, *Caribou Song* (2001), *Dragonfly Kite* (2002), and *Fox on the Ice* (2003), make up a trilogy, *Songs of the North Wind*. The books are superbly illustrated by well-known Canadian artist Brian Deines, and the text is presented in Cree and English. The stories tell of the magical adventures of two brothers, Joe and Cody, as they play together, encountering wildlife and entertaining themselves through the seasons in northern Manitoba.

Two Pairs of Shoes by Esther Sanderson (1990) is a picture storybook about Maggie, and two special gifts she receives for her eighth birthday. Maggie's mother gives her a pair of shiny, black patent-leather shoes, and her *kokom* (grandmother) gives her a pair of hand-made beaded moccasins. Grandmother tells Maggie, "From now on you must remember when and how to wear each pair." The author has dedicated the book to "all children who walk in two pairs of shoes."

Michael Kusugak has produced many well-received picture books, most of them illustrated by Vladyana Krykorka. One of the best known is *Northern Lights: The Soccer Trails* (1993). The book embodies the life and spirit of the Inuit people of the North. Each double-page spread consists of a full-page illustration on one side and the text, adorned with a beadwork flower or motif set above or below, on the other. Krykorka depicts the children's toys, the dogs, and the landscapes in dazzling colours that capture the tones of the Arctic and the unique flavour of the Inuit culture. *Hide and Sneak* (1992) by the same author/illustrator team also captures the traditional culture and way of life in the Arctic. The book contains illustrations surrounded by Inuit script opposite each page of English text. It is a celebration of the mythology and traditional symbolism of Inuit culture.

Box 11.8 features a selection of books by Aboriginal Canadian authors and illustrators.

The valuable role played by literature in helping children to understand themselves and their world cannot be underestimated. By providing multiple ways for children to respond to literature, teachers clearly demonstrate the many options a reader has when constructing personal and shared meanings from a text. In a democratic society such as Canada's, a reader is free to make informed choices about reading material. As teachers guide children in their book selections, a key consideration must be a respect for multiple viewpoints and for lifestyles that might be different from our own.

BOX 11.8   **CHILDREN'S MATERIAL BY ABORIGINAL CANADIANS**

Ahenakew, F. (1999). *Wisahkecahk flies to the moon.* Winnipeg: Pemmican.

Ballantyne, E. (2001). *The Aboriginal alphabet for children.* Winnipeg: Pemmican.

Bouchard, D. and Vickers, R. H. (1990). *The elders are watching.* Tofino, BC: Eagle Dancer Enterprises.

Bruchac, J. (1993). *Fox song.* Toronto: Oxford University Press.

Bruchac, J. (2000). *Crazy Horse's vision.* New York: Lee & Low Books.

Campell, N. (2005). *Shi-shi-etko.* Toronto: Groundwood Books.

Condon, P. (2000). *Changes.* Saskatoon: Gabrial Dumont.

Einarson, E. (2004). *The moccasins.* Penticton, BC: Theytus Books.

Highway, T. (2003) *Fox on the ice.* Toronto: HarperCollins.

Highway, T. (2002). *Dragonfly kite.* Toronto: HarperCollins.

Highway, T. (2001). *Caribou song.* Toronto: HarperCollins.

King, T. (1992). *A coyote Columbus story.* Toronto: Groundwood Books.

Kusugak, M. (1990). *Baseball bats for Christmas.* Toronto: Annick Press.

Kusugak, M. (1993). *Northern lights: The soccer trails.* Toronto: Annick Press.

Littlechild, G. (1993). *This land is my land.* Emeryville, CA: Children's Book Press.

Loewen, I. (1993). *My kookum called today.* Winnipeg: Pemmican.

McLellan, J. (1989). *The birth of Nanabosho.* Winnipeg: Pemmican.

Oliviero, J. and Morrisseau, B. (1993). *The fish skin.* Winnipeg: Hyperion Press.

Paul-Dene, S. (1992). *I am the eagle free (sky song).* Penticton, BC: Theytus Books.

Sanderson, E. (1990). *Two pairs of shoes.* Winnipeg: Pemmican.

Van Camp, R. (1997). *A man called Raven.* San Francisco: Children's Book Press.

Van Camp, R. (1998). *What's the most beautiful thing you know about horses?* Markham, ON: Children's Book Press.

Yerxa, L. (1993). *Last leaf first snowflake to fall.* Toronto: Groundwood Books.

SUMMARY

"Reader response" refers to the events that occur within a reader when he or she reads a piece of text. That response is part of the meaning-making process, and as such it is an important component of a language arts program. Rosenblatt (1978) maintains that a response to literature is dictated to a considerable extent by the purpose for reading or the *stance* from which the reader approaches the text. A stance can be anywhere on a continuum from efferent at one end, where the reader seeks information of some kind, to aesthetic at the other, where the reader focuses on appreciating what is read. A text first evokes an aesthetic or "lived through" response, and then evokes a more efferent response as the reader consciously thinks about the text and the reading experience.

Through reading works of literature and responding to them, children come to understand how texts work, what constitutes a good book, how language can be used in different ways to create different meanings and effects—in short, how to become readers, not just people able to read. Children are more likely to take ownership of the reading process and to understand that there is no right "answer" to literature when they are invited to respond to a text (though, as Rosenblatt says, some responses are more legitimate or appropriate than others). Responses to literature can be captured and represented in written, oral, visual, or dramatic form.

An important vehicle for exploring a text is the response group or book club. Teachers and researchers have discovered that children benefit from orally sharing and shaping their responses to books, and successful group work can enhance the enjoyment children experience in their reading. Literature response journals provide children with opportunities for written reflection on what they are currently reading, as do literature circles, novel studies, readers' workshops, and drama and art activities. There are also many "dependent authoring" activities that enhance children's enjoyment and understanding of literature.

When selecting materials to include in a classroom or school library, teachers and teacher/librarians must make every effort to choose books that meet the needs of children as well as the needs of the curriculum. The selection of print materials for use in schools is a complex issue, for it is difficult to say in a public education system who should decide what children should and should not read. There is, however, a clear difference between selecting materials for use in schools and censoring these materials. Where book selection uses positive criteria to determine which books to place in a collection, censorship seeks instead to remove, suppress, or restrict books already present in a collection. Guidelines for handling complaints about books can be established by school boards or by individual schools, and many agencies provide guidelines for creating such processes.

Educators understand that when children read aesthetically, they may identify with the characters, setting, or events of a story. However, until the last 25 years or so, Canadian children had little they could identify with in the literature available to them. Today, a wide range of high-quality children's literature is published across Canada. Canadian literature for children is now noted and characterized by its multicultural nature, and there are many excellent Aboriginal Canadian authors and illustrators creating books for children. Perhaps through reading Canadian literature, children can develop an appreciation and understanding of what it means to be Canadian and Canada's role in the global community. Defining our identity as Canadians is a continuing process and one in which our students have a role.

TALKING POINTS

1. Have you thought about your own identity as a teacher and as a Canadian? How are you like the students you will probably teach, and how are you different? Where did you grow up? Was it in a large town or a small rural community? Were your parents or grandparents immigrants to Canada? Do you attend church, mosque, or temple? Do you think of yourself as a privileged Canadian (e.g., you have a good home, do not live in poverty, have had a good education)? Or do you take these things for granted? Have you lived in a number of different countries or locations in Canada? These are important issues to consider as you prepare to teach critical literacy in your classroom and to meet the learning needs of a diverse range of Canadian children.

2. As you visit schools and classrooms, talk to students and find out what kinds of materials they enjoy reading, where they like to read, and whether they visit the public library. Ask them about their reading online, the television shows and movies they watch, and the magazines or comics they have at home.

3. Have you thought about the "difficult topics" you will encounter in your teaching? How willing are you to put your own opinions on hold and listen to the thoughts and views of your students? How will you communicate with parents about the books and magazines available in your classroom? Are you willing to take risks and deal with the difficult topics of social justice, racism, and stereotyping that will emerge in your classroom?

RECOMMENDED PROFESSIONAL RESOURCES

Jan Smith suggests ...

Gear, A. (2006). *Reading power: Teaching students to think while they read*. Toronto: Pembroke Publishing.

I like this book because it's really very practical. It shows you how to teach children specific strategies to use while they're reading. The book's organized around five reading strategies: connecting, questioning, visualizing inferring, and transforming. Gear uses quality children's literature to demonstrate how you can model, encourage practice, and foster independent reading. She includes lists of children's books organized around grade levels, and includes tips for developing classroom book collections.

Rog, L. J. and Kropp, P. (2004). *The write genre*. Toronto: Pembroke Publishers.

This book is interesting because it shows how the insights that real writers (like Paul Kropp) develop can help students with their own writing. It's organized around six writing genres, and it presents numerous mini-lessons based on a workshop approach to writing. The book makes the reading–writing connection very strongly, and explores fiction and nonfiction genres.

Carol Walters recommends ...

Allington, R. (2006). *What really matters for struggling readers: Designing research-based programs* (2nd edition). Boston: Pearson/Allyn and Bacon.

In this book, Allington raises some really important issues, such as: How much time are children engaged with their reading in school, and how much time do they actually spend in reading at school? The time spent reading, both in and outside of school, is very important, and it's one thing we can stress with parents. In addition, we can encourage parents to read with their children, read to their children, and listen to their children reading. And most of all, they need to talk with their children about what the children are reading. The book deals with developing instruction for struggling readers, improving classroom instruction, and making support available for older struggling readers. Teaching reading doesn't stop in grade 6.

Calkins, L. and McEvoy, M. (2006). *Literary essays: Writing about reading*. Portsmouth, NH: Firsthand/Heinemann.

This book really helped me, because Lucy Calkins makes the connection between students' responses to literature and teaching. She shows teachers how to support children in reading well in addition to writing well, how to be active readers. The key is in demonstration. She models how to help children to "write inside the story," study characters, develop ideas, use stories as evidence, and write personal essays. She shows how to keep lists, favourite quotations, and other material, and she emphasizes the importance of rereading parts of a text, as well as rereading your own writing. She suggests mini-lessons and focuses on talking about books as well as writing about them. In sum, this book is about teaching students to become "literary essayists," and thoughtful, reflective readers and writers.

Drama in the Elementary Classroom

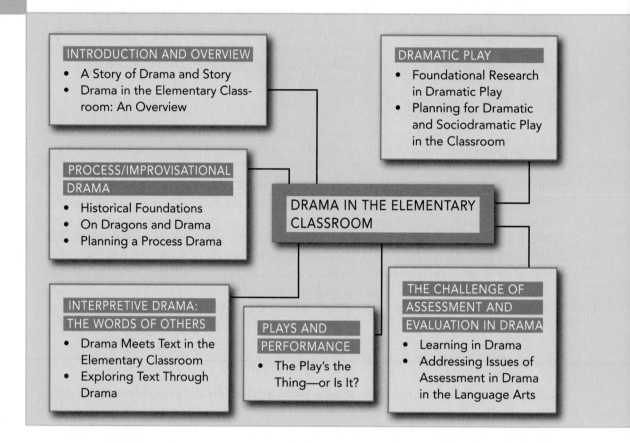

INTRODUCTION AND OVERVIEW
- A Story of Drama and Story
- Drama in the Elementary Classroom: An Overview

DRAMATIC PLAY
- Foundational Research in Dramatic Play
- Planning for Dramatic and Sociodramatic Play in the Classroom

PROCESS/IMPROVISATIONAL DRAMA
- Historical Foundations
- On Dragons and Drama
- Planning a Process Drama

DRAMA IN THE ELEMENTARY CLASSROOM

INTERPRETIVE DRAMA: THE WORDS OF OTHERS
- Drama Meets Text in the Elementary Classroom
- Exploring Text Through Drama

PLAYS AND PERFORMANCE
- The Play's the Thing—or Is It?

THE CHALLENGE OF ASSESSMENT AND EVALUATION IN DRAMA
- Learning in Drama
- Addressing Issues of Assessment in Drama in the Language Arts

INTRODUCTION AND OVERVIEW

A Story of Drama and Story

My doctoral research project gave me the opportunity to work with a multi-grade classroom of eighteen grade 4, 5, and 6 students in a small urban school in western Canada. In response to the classroom teacher's request that I show her how drama might be used to teach English language arts, I explored folk tales by engaging her students in process drama activities. The following excerpt from my research journal demonstrates the power of process drama to evoke students' engaged response and purposeful use of oral and written language. Our starting point was the story of the Pied Piper of Hamelin.

> The context was set for a discussion of the stealing of the children, and as the students conversed I took on the role of messenger and delivered the scrolled letters from the Pied Piper giving them the news about their children. Soon all the letters were delivered and the family

groups were reading them. They were given the chance to discuss how they felt and what to do next before we ended the episode.

Coming out of role, I asked them how they were feeling about the disappearance of the children. One student, Allison, mentioned that some people would be happy that there were no children to cause accidents and make troubles. Some felt guilty because they'd caused the problem by cheating the Pied Piper. A few were angry at the mayor. Some were lonely without the children.

At this point we were to have the town meeting and chart the plans each household had for getting the children back. The Pied Piper wasn't supposed to come until tomorrow, but I could see that they needed a writing activity rather than more discussion and also needed a conflict injected to deepen the engagement of the group. The messenger explained that the Pied Piper was angry and was going to need some real convincing. Each family would need to write a letter to convince him they deserved to have their children back.

The letters written by the students were passionate and convincing (see Box 12.1). The old Pied Piper story had a surprisingly emotional impact on students' written response. The experience of classroom drama and role-play can support a variety of English language arts purposes and learning, as this chapter will demonstrate.

BOX 12.1   **LETTER TO THE PIED PIPER**

To The Pied Piper,

The Pike Family misses our two loving children we are willing to pay what you ask, but please don't hurt them. We miss them very much and we need them home soon. We love them very much. Tell them that we love and miss them. We have found in our hearts we can't live without them. We know we have acted badly before but we are willing to change our ways. Their names are Emily (2) and Cathy (13). Please forgive us for our wrong doings

Sincerly,
Pike Family ☹

Drama in the Elementary Classroom: An Overview

This chapter will explore the place of educational drama in the K–8 English language arts classroom. We will discuss drama forms that occur on a continuum from unstructured dramatic play to more formal performance work. We will examine how children create and construct understandings through written and oral language as they participate in the magical worlds of drama.

Table 12.1 details categories of dramatic activity that may be found in the elementary classroom and describes how these activities are appropriate to different grade levels.

We will examine the foundations for each category of dramatic activity in terms of historical practice and/or pedagogy and explore how teachers may plan for and introduce each type of drama into the elementary English language arts classroom program. Children's books, stories, and poetry form the core sources for all dramatic work that is described here. The importance of inclusive education and addressing issues of diversity and culture through drama work is implicit in our exploration of drama in the English language arts classroom. The chapter concludes with a discussion of the challenges facing teachers in the evaluation and assessment of drama work.

TABLE 12.1 Categories of Classroom Drama

Dramatic Category	Description	Appropriate Grade
Dramatic play	Children engage in self-directed games of "let's pretend" determined by their own interests and choices. Teachers provide designated space, costume pieces, structures, and props according to the needs and interests of students.	Kindergarten–Year 1
Process or improvisational drama	Teacher-structured and -sequenced learning activities that invite students to assume roles and actively engage in fictional worlds of story in order to learn and understand rather than perform.	Year 1–Year 8
Interpretive drama	Denotes any classroom activity where students are engaged in bringing some type of predetermined text to life through voice and/or movement. Storytelling from books, choral reading of poetry, reader's theatre, and writing scripts and performing them are included in this category.	Year 2–Year 8
Performance or theatre	Approaches that support students if the expectation is that they will perform for an audience. Alternatives to scripted plays, such as collective creation and polishing interpretive work, are highlighted.	Appropriate grade level is dependent on the particular approach and how it is used.

DRAMATIC PLAY

Foundational Research in Dramatic Play

"Let's pretend …": these are words most of us remember as invitations we issued or accepted from our friends and playmates during our earliest preschool play experiences. For some of us, our kindergarten or primary-level teachers supported "let's pretend" in the classroom, and the magic of entering specially designed play spaces where we could use props, toys, and imitation to understand the adult world, extended beyond our early years into our school experience.

Educational researchers have been emphasizing the importance of supporting children's exploration of ideas and behaviours through "let's pretend" play for many decades. Piaget (1962) refers to this work of early childhood as *symbolic play* where children use language, toys, and props to make sense of social relationships. Vygotsky (1978) and Bruner (1986), perhaps two of the most influential researchers in child development and language learning, suggest that giving preschool and primary-level children unstructured opportunities to play "let's pretend"—alone or with others—create spaces in which adult roles and language can be imitated and integrated. Booth (1987) explains how language develops and vocabulary is extended when young children are encouraged to assume roles and create their own stories in a well-designed classroom dramatic play area.

Smilansky and Shefatya (1990) make a clear distinction between **dramatic play** and **sociodramatic play**. Toddlers as young as two years old may often be observed imitating the language and behaviour of parents or caregivers as they play alone with their dolls and toys. This solitary role-playing behaviour (**dramatic play**) allows the child to interpret what it means to live in and be a part of the social world of others and to explain the social world to himself or herself. **Sociodramatic play**, on the other hand, occurs when two or more children engage in negotiating the same make-believe context.

Early childhood teachers can be instrumental in supporting positive and productive sociodramatic play within the classroom. Calabrese (2003) suggests teachers designate a special area of the classroom for drama and stock it with durable materials, toys, and print materials. She suggests that teachers should rotate materials often and relate materials to stories or poems children enjoy, but cautions teachers not to interfere with the story lines the children create, except in circumstances in which safety is an issue (pp. 607–608). Balke (1997) states "teachers with vivid interests and awareness … can create an atmosphere that inspires children to be creative" (p. 356).

Planning for Dramatic and Sociodramatic Play in the Classroom

Building in time for sociodramatic play requires that there be periods of time during the school day when children are free to choose activities that interest them and participate in those activities with minimal teacher interference. Sustained periods of sociodramatic play outside the classroom context may extend to up to two hours if children are truly engaged in the world of "let's pretend" and are cooperative with each other. Most classroom teachers, however, suggest periods of approximately 30 minutes as appropriate to the needs of their students (Smilansky 1990, p. 38).

TABLE 12.2 Creating a Drama Play Space in the Classroom

Theme	Structures	Costumes and Props	Other Materials
Castles and dragons	cardboard "castle" created from a large appliance box; paint box grey and paint black lines to create stones; cut top of the box to resemble turrets plastic or wooden blocks in various sizes for building furniture	cloth swatches in shades of silver; gold and other fine fabrics costume jewellery paper or plastic crowns soft plastic swords (optional) helmets, "armour" half-masks* representing dragons and other mythical creatures	tape and/or glue blunt scissors paper markers cardboard or tag board (for making shields or other props) clips or clothespins to fasten "costumes" picture books about castles and dragons thematically related dolls, puppets, and stuffed animals
Space travel	cylindrical recycle bin rocket ship covered with tinfoil or painted silver; cut a hole for the door plastic or wooden blocks in various sizes for building furniture	space suits— (Halloween costume variety) alien half-masks soft plastic lasers (optional) swatches of varied fabrics	tape and/or glue blunt scissors paper markers cardboard or tag board clips or clothespins tinfoil thematically related books, dolls, puppets and toys
House and home	playhouse blocks in various sizes for building furniture toy stoves, fridges, table, and chairs	hats, ties, aprons, suit coats, shawls, dress-up shoes briefcases, brooms, telephones, toy dishes, telephones, toy appliances	as above, plus a variety of books about families and dolls of various sizes and shapes puppets

*Half-masks, which cover only the eyes or the top half of the face and allow full peripheral vision, are more appropriate than full masks for young children. They help the child assume a role in a concrete way but do not interfere with speech, breathing, or movement.

Teachers can support sociodramatic and dramatic play periods by planning for a rich, stimulating, and frequently changing environment in the classroom dramatic play centre. Table 12.2 describes how a classroom space might be designed and transformed to meet the changing interests of children.

A well-equipped drama play space will encourage dramatic play and sociodramatic play as an integral part of the young child's school experience. Oral and written language growth is encouraged in such an environment. Children experiment with levels and functions of language as they adopt powerful roles like the queen of the castle or the captain of the spaceship (since queens must use the language of royalty and captains must adopt the technical jargon used by astronauts and space explorers). Booth (1987) reminds us "language is not just a by-product: it grows from the play, because of the play and structures the play, all at once" (p. 22).

Literacy experiences also occur naturally and purposefully in the dramatic play area. The props children create to concretize their imagined contexts or situations will often involve pretend writing: grocery lists for the pretend family, posters warning the people of the kingdom that a dragon is on the loose, spaceship repair books to take along on the journey through the galaxy. Often picture books and informational books must be consulted to ensure that the details of the imagined world are accurate or to resolve conflicting opinions among the players. These are purposeful opportunities for reading and writing that emerge from children's involvement in voluntary play rather than literacy lessons imposed by the teacher.

The potential power of dramatic and sociodramatic play to bring children together across cultures and in spite of learning disabilities or special needs is great when the teacher is sensitive to the rich diversity of experiences, abilities, and cultural backgrounds present among the players. The drama play space allows students to learn from each other in a safe and nonthreatening environment as they work out roles and negotiate "how the world works" among themselves. Books, toys, structures, and other materials that celebrate the cultural backgrounds of all students should be available in the drama area. Children may be invited to bring materials from home or they may be consulted about how the teacher might include toys and props to enhance their episodes of "let's pretend." The sensitive teacher, although maintaining distance from the play, will be prepared to interrupt or join in the play when feelings are at risk or racist stereotypes are being perpetuated. Through careful teacher questioning and thoughtful reminders, children will expand their understandings of themselves and their peers when they engage in dramatic and sociodramatic play experience.

PROCESS/IMPROVISATIONAL DRAMA

Historical Foundations

During the past century, educational theorists and researchers have begun to explore how children's natural tendency to learn through games of "let's pretend" can be understood and transformed into a pedagogy of drama in the school classroom. Readers who are interested in tracing the development of drama in education pedagogy may wish to consult the work of pioneers such as Peter Slade (1954) and Brian Way (1967); theorists such as Gavin Bolton (1985; 1992), Cecily O'Neill (1995), and Jonothan Neelands (1984, 2000); and foundational practitioners such as Dorothy Heathcote (Heathcote & Bolton, 1995).

Canadian drama educators have contributed important practices and theories in the development of drama pedagogy, especially by exploring connections between drama education practice and English language arts. David Booth's (1987; 2005) **story drama** model explains how the conventions and strategies of process drama may be used to engage children's involvement and understanding of poetry, stories, and other forms of children's literature. Booth's research has also explored the impact of drama work on children's writing (Booth & Neelands 1998). Norah Morgan and Juliana Saxton (1987) provided a detailed and teacher-friendly resource for the classroom teacher to use in planning drama work. Patrick Verriour's and Carole Tarlington's (1991) *role drama* is a practical approach to working with drama and traditional stories in the elementary grades. Most currently, Carole Miller and Juliana Saxton (2004) provide classroom teachers with well-structured and organized drama units developed from popular and recently published children's books.

Although the teaching resources developed by these drama educators and others provide classroom teachers with an excellent selection of process drama lessons plans and units, teachers who know how to create their own dramas from stories and poems will be able to directly address the needs and interests of their particular group of students. The remainder of this section will address practical questions of planning process drama work for the elementary language arts classroom. We'll begin with the story of one process drama developed from the popular picture book *The Paper Bag Princess* by Canadian children's author Robert Munsch.

On Dragons and Drama

The children in Ms. Grey's third-grade class have been reading books about medieval times: knights in shining armour, jousting tournaments, castles with drawbridges and, of course, fire-breathing dragons. Ms. Grey invites her students to think about what it might have been like to live in a castle in the make-believe world where dragons flew through the air and knights and kings did battle with these creatures. A discussion about pretend creatures ensues, and children offer their experiences with books and movie creatures such as *Shrek* and his friends. Ms. Grey asks them to think about how people might warn each other about threatening dragons during a time when there were no phones or computers or cell phones. Since no one suggests a daily newspaper, Ms. Grey interjects that writing might be used to communicate warnings and other information. She then inquires if her students would like to do some drama with her, and explains that she will take on a role (pretend to be someone else), and help them take on roles as well by giving them information and asking them questions. Most students are eager to participate in "let's pretend."

Ms. Grey explains that she will briefly leave the room, and when she returns act as if she is someone else. Students are to listen carefully so they can learn who they will be in the drama. When Ms. Grey returns as the Assistant Editor of *The Castle Times,* she brings with her a special memo (see Box 12.2) from the Editor-in-Chief, Fester Grunhilde, which she reads to the class. (Students may also be given the "memo" and asked to read it for themselves.) A brief discussion about the memo follows and students in role are free to ask questions of the Assistant Editor.

The students are assigned to groups of three or four, and are asked to prepare for the meeting by recording what they know about fire-breathing dragons from books they've read, stories they've heard, or films they've viewed. Some groups decide to design their own "dragon-proofing kit" to show Mr. Grunhilde. Ms. Grey has a "*Castle Times* dragon file" of pictures of different kinds of dragons that students can borrow to help them generate ideas.

Ms. Grey circulates among the groups in her role as Assistant Editor and encourages the students to prepare carefully for the meeting with Fester Grunhilde. They are supplied with markers and chart paper so that they can record their ideas and diagrams. This work takes almost the entire lesson time, so Ms. Grey decides to hold the "staff meeting" on the following day. She makes sure to tell her students when she is coming out of role and responding to them as their teacher again. She asks them to come out of role and tell her a little bit about their group work or ask any questions they might have about the drama so far.

The following day, the class re-enters the drama world to share their group work in role. Just as the last group has finished showing their work to Fester Grunhilde (the teacher has taken on this role for the "staff meeting") and answering questions from the other *Castle Times* reporters and photographers, there is a knock on the classroom door. Ms. Grey has asked an older student

BOX 12.2 **MEMO TO THE NEWSPAPER STAFF**

The Castle Times

"What discriminating Royals Read"

MEMO

FROM: **Fester Grunhilde, Managing Editor**
TO: **Reporters and Photography Staff members**
RE: **Sightings of fire-breathing dragon**

As we all know by now, there is a fire-breathing dragon loose who has been targeting castles in neighbouring kingdoms for immolation purposes. According to your reports and photographs, this dragon has created much destruction and has so far eluded capture. My sources tell me that it is now heading for the Castle of the King, Queen, and Princess Elizabeth in our very own kingdom.

It is essential that the *Castle Times* cover this breaking story as quickly as possible. We need a concerted effort from reporter/photographer staff teams to prepare the readership for the probable arrival of the dragon in this kingdom.

Before our next staff meeting (to be held within the hour), I will ask you to meet in your 5–6 member reporter/photographer teams to outline any information you have gathered about this dragon and the havoc it has wrought in other kingdoms. Pictures and news stories will be much appreciated. We also want information on the newly available "dragon-proofing" kits that are becoming so popular. I understand that some of you have collected some information and pictures about several different kinds of kits. We will need to buy some for our staff, so we also would like some of this information brought to the staff meeting.

Thank you!

from another classroom to play a special role for her during the drama session. This person wears a large medieval hat and carries a scroll (see Box 12.3) that is unrolled and read to the students.

The reporters and photographers of the *Castle Times* ask the messenger questions about what happened, but unfortunately the messenger isn't very helpful, and explains that he must leave immediately, since there are others who must hear the news. Fester Grunhilde then announces that the meeting is adjourned because this new development creates a more pressing concern. "He" leaves and Ms. Grey comes back as herself. She asks the children if they are ready to hear the story of what really happened and gathers them together to hear *The Paper Bag Princess*.

BOX 12.3 THE MESSENGER'S SCROLL

Hear Ye, Hear Ye!

A news bulletin from the Royal Castle.

The Fire-Breathing Dragon has broken through all the Royal defenses and has burned down the Royal castle. It is known that the King and Queen were away on a hunt at the time of the burning. Princess Elizabeth is said to have escaped the fire. Royal informants assure us that no human remains have been found, so we are quite sure Prince Ronald also escaped.

Luckily the royal court and servants were down at the summer castle in the south cleaning it up, so no one else was injured.

Further information will be forthcoming as soon as it is available.

The drama continues for three more class periods following the reading of the story. During these sessions, Ms. Grey assumes a new role as the Royal Chancellor to Princess Elizabeth and her parents, the King and Queen. Students choose hats that confer upon them the roles of advisors to the royal family, ladies-in-waiting to the queen, palace guards, and friends of Princess Elizabeth. In these roles, they engage in tasks such as designing tests of skill to help the King find a successor for Prince Ronald, planning and designing a feast and royal ball to help the Queen entertain tournament participants and spectators, and acting as advocates who will convince the King to allow Elizabeth to rule the country by herself. Students work in small groups to prepare their plans and designs and then share their work in an audience with the royal family (volunteers from the classroom groups). This meeting begins with much pomp and ceremony and demands that the courtiers defend their decisions and choices. Spirited debate breaks out between the King, Princess Elizabeth, and the members of the court, and so the teacher comes out of role and asks the students to decide individually whether they think Elizabeth should be allowed to run the kingdom on her own. Students voice their opinions by standing along an imaginary line, with one end for people who agree with the King and the other end for those who agree with Elizabeth. Most of the students choose Elizabeth, and the out-of-role discussion that follows this activity demonstrates that most students believe girls like Elizabeth can run kingdoms on their own without any help from princes or kings. This discussion closes the drama.

Planning a Process Drama

It should be evident from the *Paper Bag Princess* drama that the purpose of process drama work is *not* to have children reenact or retell stories that someone else has already told. We will explore this type of work in the interpretive drama section of this chapter. In process work, children create, extend, and **improvise** their own story episodes from a source or idea.

Although the students are the creators, classroom process drama work requires careful planning and preparation on the part of the teacher. In addition to preparing the *Castle Times* memo, the scroll for the messenger to read, and collecting or creating hats for all the students in the classroom, Ms. Grey needed to think about the choices and possibilities she would offer to her students. She wanted her students to own their work, solve the problems, and use their imaginations throughout the drama; but she also realized that she would not maximize the language learning opportunities inherent in the source (storybook) if she sent the students off by themselves to "make a play" about *The Paper Bag Princess*. Her challenge was to balance opportunities for creative freedom and student ownership with the safety of a structured plan that would allow children to move forward along a purposeful and focused pathway of drama activity and experience.

There are many ways to approach the planning of a process drama for elementary students. The following planning approach evolved from ideas I collected and adapted from a variety of sources (O'Neill & Lambert, 1982; Morgan & Saxton, 1987; Booth, 1987; Heathcote & Bolton, 1995; Neelands & Goode, 2000). The steps in this approach are guidelines rather than prescriptive: every classroom group is different and every teacher has different strengths and talents that must be factored into the planning process. The steps are listed in Box 12.4, and then elaborated in reference to the planning of a process drama from the children's book *Silver Threads* by M. F. Skrypuch.

BOX 12.4   PLANNING STEPS FOR PROCESS DRAMA

Step 1: Select a source that is relevant to the needs and interests of your students. Possible sources include: picture storybooks, newspaper clippings, photographs or paintings, songs, short stories, poems, Internet resources, etc.

Step 2: Find a dramatic focus for your drama that is suggested by the source. Some questions that may help you identify the focus are:

▷ What problems, challenges, or conflicts are suggested by this source?

▷ Where might these problems, challenges, or conflicts be explored?

▷ Who might be involved in exploring the problems, challenges, or conflicts? You want to find a group of roles rather than specific roles.

▷ If you plan to use teacher-in-role, you will also need to think about specific roles for the teacher.

Step 3: Establish the dramatic context. Develop one or two context-building activities that will introduce students to the drama and allow them to think about their roles within the drama. These activities should:

▷ identify the initial group of roles and give each student time to think about what role he or she will play within this group

▷ identify the situation or location in which the drama begins and give students time to think about what this location is like

▷ identify and describe the problem, conflict, or challenge that the group will have to solve

(Continued)

Step 4: Begin to build the narrative thread or story line. Develop one or two narrative activities that move the drama along. These activities develop the initial context further and raise new issues and events for the group to face and consider. These activities should:

▷ supply information that will enable the students (in role) to solve problems, create new possibilities, and engage more deeply in the issues that emerge from the source

▷ allow the students to create the story inherent in the drama through their joint and individual contributions and suggestions

▷ offer the students the opportunity to take on different roles so that they can see the conflict, challenge, or problem from a different perspective

Step 5: Develop one or two poetic activities to help students' construct their understanding of issues at a higher level of meaning. These activities should:

▷ take the students out of an overconcern with the plot or "what will happen next" and get them thinking about the symbols or lessons in the drama

▷ deepen the students' emotional involvement in their work

Step 6: Include one or two reflective activities so students can consider the meaning of their work in role. These activities should:

▷ invite students to stop and consider the meaning of what has happened so far in the drama

▷ sometimes occur "out of role" so that students can step out of making the story and think about what the story means

▷ bring the drama to a successful conclusion and give students an opportunity to reveal their understandings about the dramatic work

Step 7: Review your plan to make sure you have:

▷ Whole-group activities in which all the students are involved. These activities should be used when everyone needs common information to proceed with the next episode of the drama.

▷ Small-group activities in which students work in groups of three to six. These activities develop cooperation and problem-solving skills.

▷ Pair activities involving two students. Sometimes pairs of students can take on problem-solving tasks more efficiently than a small group can.

▷ Individual activities where children work alone. Writing-in-role or drawing-in-role are activities that give students the chance to imagine possibilities for themselves before negotiating these possibilities with the group. These activities can be used throughout the drama to slow things down and to create a variety of possible directions for the next episode.

Step 8: Review your plan to ensure you have addressed the learning objectives you wanted to achieve.

Step 1: Selecting a Source

The story *Silver Threads* by Marsha F. Skrypuch (1996) might be an appropriate choice of book for fifth- or sixth-grade students who are exploring the cultural experiences of Canadians from various cultural traditions. Anna and Ivan, a young couple, emigrate from the Ukraine to avoid political persecution and homestead in western Canada. As they struggle to establish their farm with little money and little support, Ivan is conscripted into the army and shipped overseas to fight in the war. Anna tries to carry on without him, but life becomes increasingly difficult as the years pass and Ivan fails to return home. Then, one Christmas Eve, just as Anna is about to give up any hope, a spider spins a web in the Christmas tree that miraculously glows with the candlelight through the window and beckons Ivan as he returns through the cold December night to his home and his bride.

This book explores issues of persecution, prejudice, and courage in the face of overwhelming odds. It invites students to look at these issues from the safe distance provided by a historical setting.

Step 2: Finding the Focus

A careful reading of the story suggests that there are a variety of problems and challenges that might provide a focus for drama work:

- bureaucratic injustice toward cultural minority groups
- facing hardships alone far from home and family
- good-luck charms and beliefs—the subplot of the spider

The teacher considers setting the drama in an internment camp, but realizes that students who are totally unfamiliar with such an experience might be confused or might respond in a superficial way to this context. Instead, s/he chooses the rural community where Anna and Ivan live as the setting, as the classroom group is studying Canadian history. Since there are only two main characters in the book, the teacher needs to create a group of roles that could be implicated in Anna's and Ivan's story. The following possibilities are considered:

- neighbours in the farming community
- the spiders who spun the web
- the bureaucrats who conscripted immigrants from the Ukraine to fight in the war

As the teacher considers what role s/he might play within the drama, the following ideas come under scrutiny:

- a neighbour who has heard of Anna's plight (an **intermediary role** that confers the opportunity for leadership and decision making upon the students)
- the Captain of an international spider communication system that monitors how Ivan and Anna treat spiders and decides to show gratitude with the Christmas tree web (a **leadership role** that provides security if students aren't sure what to do next)
- a bureaucrat who is responsible for conscripting Ivan into the army (an opposer role that encourages children to confront and challenge authority)

The teacher considers all of these possibilities and decides on the following focus for the drama. The focus is most helpful when stated as a "what if" question:

Focus: What would happen if pioneer neighbours offered to help Anna and she was too proud or too frightened to accept their help?

Once the focus of the drama has been selected, the teacher decides she will introduce the pretext for the drama (O'Neill 1995, p. 38) by reading the story to the students up to the point where Ivan is conscripted and leaves Anna to run the farm alone.

Step 3: Establishing the Context

All of the conventions suggested in the following steps are described in Neelands and Goode's (2000) *Structuring Drama Work: A Handbook of Available Forms in Theatre and Drama*. Conventions are bolded and page numbers included to provide readers with easy reference within this helpful resource.

The teacher decides to help students establish their roles in the drama by using the **role-on-the-wall** convention (p. 22). Students will self-select into groups of three or four, and will be asked to create charts that describe the members of a farm family living in Anna's community. There will be as many people in the family as there are members of the group, since everyone in the class must have a role. Once these charts are completed, students will be asked to create a family portrait with their bodies using **still image** (p. 25). The images will be brought to life so that each member of the group can introduce him or herself to the rest of the class.

The next episode of the drama will see all the families in the community gathered at a town hall **meeting** (p. 35). The **teacher-in-role** (p. 40) as Anna's neighbour informs them that she found a letter in the field that must have blown away from Anna's house. The letter comes from Anna's mother (**unfinished materials**, p. 28) and advises Anna to go to her neighbours for help while Ivan is away, and not be so proud and determined to do everything for herself. The "neighbour" says she had no idea Anna was having so much trouble, and asks the members of the community for ideas about how they could help.

Step 4: Building the Narrative Thread

The teacher will then invite the students to come out of role and discuss how there might be different opinions among members of the community. She will suggest that there would probably be some people who would *not* want to help Anna. The out-of-role discussion that ensues should help to create tension, an ingredient that engages students more deeply in the dramatic situation and provides further problems for them to solve. Bolton (1992) reminds us that tension is essential to drama and may evolve from **conflict** between characters or from **constraint** where characters experience but do not act out the internal conflicts they feel (p. 53). If no tension exists, problems are solved too easily and the drama may lose its impetus.

The next episode of the drama utilizes the **overheard conversations** convention (Neelands & Goode, 2000, p. 37). The teacher will invite students to divide into two large groups. One group will represent the people of the community who do *not* want to help Anna, and the second will be those who do want to help her on the farm. Within each group, students will pair up and **interview** (p.33) each other about the reasons for their character's decision. Once the students have generated reasons for both perspectives, one group will conduct their conversations in an imagined venue, such as coming out of church or meeting at the general store, and the members of the other group will be the listeners. Then the groups will trade places and hear the opinions and ideas of the group that holds the opposite viewpoint. This strategy suggests how gossip and hearsay might operate to affect how people respond to someone in the community who is different or in difficult circumstances.

Step 5: Poetic Conventions to Look at Symbols

The teacher decides it would be a good idea to have students stop and consider all of the characters in the story and think about what motivations drive them to act as they do. She might invite the students to use fun foam or maché to create **half-masks** (p. 61) that reveal the emotions or feelings that drive the characters they've met in the story or created in the drama. As these masks are shared with the group, others may try to guess which character is being revealed (i.e., Anna's might be sad; the government official might be evil or angry; the spider might be concerned; etc.). This episode or activity takes the students away from the plot of the drama and presses them to think more deeply about why some people act as they do in certain situations.

Instead of masks, the students might design a gift they would give to Anna to help her with her struggles on the farm. This gift might be a real object, like a plow or a team of oxen, or it might be a symbolic gift such as friendship and kindness. Students need to find a way to represent their gift in a concrete way (possibly as a **picture or diagram**, p. 19, or as an **object of character**, p. 20) so that they can present it to Anna in a **ritual** (p. 69) gift-giving ceremony. The teacher will take on the role of Anna for this episode. Students' characters who do not want to help Anna may create still images to demonstrate their disagreement or displeasure during the gift-giving ceremony. Rituals are excellent ways to engage students at a deeper emotional level in the dramatic context.

Step 6: Reflecting and Concluding the Drama Work

The teacher wants the students to consider their work carefully and predict what will happen next in the story on the basis of the work they have done (since the drama has focused on a midpoint in the actual unfolding plot of the book). The teacher decides to use the **narration** convention (p. 85) to consider possibilities. Will Ivan come home or not? Will Anna accept help or not? How will the story of the spider enter into the ending of the story? Possible endings will be charted or listed on the board; then students select small groups according to which ending they believe will happen. Each group creates the ending and either tells it to the others as a group or has one or two narrators and the rest of the group acting out the ending (**mimed activity**, p. 63). Students try to decide which ending is the most plausible and consistent with the story as written so far.

When this activity is completed, students will be eager to find out which ending is the "right" one! The teacher will read the remainder of the story to her students.

Step 7: Reviewing the Plan

The episodes of this drama have been mapped, but the teacher needs to ensure that s/he has used a variety of groupings across the episodes of the drama. S/he creates the following list to demonstrate her attention to varying her grouping practices:

Whole Group

- the town hall meeting where the families hear about Anna's plight from the concerned neighbour
- the ceremony where Anna receives the gifts from those who wish to help her

Small Group

- the creation of the role-on-the-wall family groups
- the still-image episode, in which students create family portraits
- the narration episode, in which groups create their predicted ending for the story

Pairs

- interviews in which students decide if they want to help Anna or not
- overheard conversations, in which community members discuss why they do or do not want to help Anna on the farm
- creation of the masks to represent characters or the gifts to present to Anna

This teacher realizes s/he doesn't have enough individual activities to give balance to the drama, and so decides to have the students individually write the letters from Anna's mother at the beginning of the drama (Neelands & Goode, 2000, p. 16) rather than preparing this letter herself ahead of time. This episode will be added between the role-on-the wall activity and the town hall meeting, and the teacher will insert a shared reading time to choose the letter that will be read.

Step 8: Learning Objectives and Assessment

Because provincial English language arts curricula are specific to each province in Canada, the precise wording of learning objectives in these documents will vary. But there is general agreement among drama educators and researchers that process drama work creates a variety of opportunities for students to use language in purposeful and meaningful ways and to practise both oral and written language skills (Booth, 1987; Tarlington & Verriour, 1991; Wagner, 1998; Smith & Herring, 2001).

In this process drama unit, students have been immersed in language learning opportunities. They have used both oral and written language in purposeful ways to become more deeply involved and engaged with a children's storybook. Table 12.3 details the opportunities for purposeful language that have emerged in the two process dramas described here. Halliday's (1969) functions of language model (as described in Chapter 2) provides a framework to demonstrate the variety of oral language purposes that are addressed.

The process dramas we have explored in this section are constructed from a variety of teaching strategies or conventions. Although the following list (Table 12.4) summarizes the strategies that were used in both dramas, readers may wish to consult the work of Jonothan Neelands and Tony Goode (2000), Carole Miller and Juliana Saxton (2004), or David Booth (2005) for a more detailed description of ways of working in process drama.

Teachers may address issues of inclusive teaching practice and social justice in process drama through both the content of books they select as sources or **pre-texts**, and the kinds of questions they ask their students to consider during episodes of reflection that occur both within and outside the dramatic fiction. By framing dramatic work in fantasy or historical contexts, students are afforded the opportunity to explore positive and negative ways that people treat each other apart from their own lives and experience. It is safe to talk about ways that some

TABLE 12.3 Purposeful Language in Process Drama

Halliday's Language Functions	The Paper Bag Princess	Silver Threads
Instrumental (asking for help or assistance)	The teacher-in-role asks for help in meeting the requests of the royal family.	The teacher-in-role asks members of the community to help Anna.
Regulatory (language to control others' behaviour)	The King, Queen, and Elizabeth make demands on the members of the Royal Court for contests, a party, and a voting campaign.	Students in role as Anna's mother write the letter that will advise Anna to seek and accept help from others.
Interactional (language to establish and maintain relationships)	The members of the Royal Court present their work to the royal family in hopes of pleasing them.	The members of Anna's community ask for permission to give her the gifts they have made.
Personal (language to tell about ourselves and our feelings)	Elizabeth's friends tell about themselves as they explain to each other why they became friends with Elizabeth.	The members of the community participate in interviews to tell about their feelings about Anna and whether they want to help.
Heuristic (language used to find out why and ask questions)	Reporters and photographers of the *Castle Times* must research dragons and find out what they are like.	Students (out of role) must find out who the character behind the mask really is, and will need to ask questions to do this.
Imaginative (language used to create new ideas and stories)	The dragon-proofing kits are created and explained by the reporter, photographer groups.	Students create the gifts—real or symbolic—for Anna from their own imaginations.
Representational (language to communicate information)	The staff of the *Castle Times* reports their work to Fester Grunhilde.	The community members tell their reasons for wanting or not wanting to help Anna.

members of that community long ago may have been cruel to Anna even though she was alone and needed help. It is not safe to talk in class about the ways you have been isolated and bullied on the playground. You may play the role of a victim in a drama when you are, in reality, a perpetrator of injustice against your classmates, and thus you may learn how it feels to be on the receiving end of power abuse without any direct instruction or lectures from your teacher. Conversely, you may be given the opportunity to play the powerful role of king or queen in a drama, when biases engendered by disability, race, or gender interfere with your performance of powerful roles in real life. The sensitive teacher is alert to opportunities provided by process drama work to indirectly teach powerful lessons about the human condition and exemplify practices of fairness and kindness that can be applied to real-life situations.

Both dramatic/sociodramatic play and process drama focus on participants as **improvisers** and invite them to draw on their experiences, imaginations, opinions, and speculations to **improvise** and create their own stories and dramatic representations of the understandings they wish to communicate. But the art form of theatre also includes aspects of **interpretation**, and theatre artists, as readers of scripts, are invited to interpret the ideas or understandings of the playwright through their directing, acting, and technical theatre skills. Drama as **interpretation** will be the focus of the next section of this chapter.

TABLE 12.4 **Process Drama Strategies/Conventions**

Process Drama Source	Strategy/Convention	Description
Pied Piper of Hamelin	**Reading-in-role:** Students read prepared documents when they are playing roles within the dramatic fiction.	The families of Hamelin who have lost their children each receive a letter from the Pied Piper giving them information, making demands, and setting conditions for the children's return.
	Writing-in-role: Students are asked to write as if they are someone else within the dramatic fiction.	The families compose letters to persuade the Pied Piper that they really have reformed and will take better care of their children in the future.
The Paper Bag Princess	Reading-in-role	The students, in role as reporters and photographers, read the memo from Fester Grunhilde, Managing Editor of the *Castle Times*.
	Writing-in-role	Reporters from the *Castle Times* share charts and other forms of written information about dragons they have written.
	Teacher-in-role: The teacher takes on a particular type of role (leader, intermediary, opposer among others) so that s/he can guide students and provide information within the dramatic context.	The teacher takes on three different roles in three different episodes of this drama: • the **intermediary**, Assistant Editor of the *Castle Times* • the **leader**, Fester Grunhilde, who approves the work • the **intermediary**, Royal Chancellor to the royal family
	Mantle of the expert (Heathcote): Students may keep their own names and personas within the drama but they act *as if* they have specialized knowledge or expertise.	Students take on the expertise of photographers and reporters and do the research, draw the diagrams and pictures, and report their findings as if they were actually on the staff of the *Castle Times* newspaper.
	Drawing maps/diagrams: Students create visual representations within the drama to make it more concrete and establish shared understandings.	1. The "photographers" draw or reproduce pictures of dragons to accompany the dragon reports. 2. The ladies-in-waiting draw dress designs and make diagrams of decorations for the Queen's party.
	Meetings: This strategy pulls the whole group together to provide information and gather opinions within the drama.	The Royal Chancellor calls all the members of the royal court together to give them information about the wishes and requests of the King, the Queen, and Princess Elizabeth.

Process Drama Source	Strategy/Convention	Description
	Rituals: These are whole-group improvisations in which everyone in role repeats an agreed-upon phrase before performing an action. These deepen engagement in the dramatic focus.	The members of the royal court address the members of the Royal Family with a "By your leave, your Majesty" or "By your leave, your Royal Highness" before they can share their ideas and plans.
	Props/costumes: Simple costume pieces (such as hats, masks, or capes) and simple props (a magic wand for example) are used to make the drama more concrete for students.	All of the students receive hats (prepared ahead of time by the teacher) to identify them as belonging to a particular group within the royal court.
	Guest roles: Someone from outside the classroom group is asked to enter the drama in role to provide information or create tension.	The Messenger arrives at the door to tell the photographers and reporters of the *Castle Times* that the dragon has burned down the Castle and Prince Ronald has disappeared.
	Prepared documents: The teacher creates documents such as letters, memos, posters, or reports ahead of time that are used inside the drama.	The teacher creates the memo from Fester Grunhilde to the staff of the *Castle Times* and the news scroll read by the messenger that announces the deed done by the dastardly dragon.
	Spectrum of difference: Students demonstrate their agreement or disagreement with an opinion or decision by placing themselves along an imaginary line in relation to both extremes.	The students indicate whether they want to elect Elizabeth as sole ruler of the Kingdom by placing themselves on a continuum from Completely Agree to Completely Disagree.
Silver Threads	Writing-in-role	The students write the letters that might have come from Anna's mother.
	Teacher-in-role	The teacher is a concerned neighbour who wants to help Anna.
	Drawing maps and diagrams	Students represent their gifts to Anna as diagrams or pictures of what they want to give to help her on the farm.
	Meetings	The people of the community gather at a town meeting to talk about Anna's plight and if/how they should help her.
	Rituals	Anna's gift-giving ceremony requires each student to repeat a line such as "I give you this gift to help you _____ because _____" (or something similar).

(Continued)

Process Drama Source	Strategy/Convention	Description
	Props/costumes	Students create half-masks that represent the different attitudes of different people in the community where Anna and Ivan live.
	Role-on-the-wall: Students are supplied with chart paper and asked to describe the attributes of characters (imagined or from sources) they will play in the drama. These may be posted on the wall for later reference, to help them play characters consistently.	The "family" groups describe each member of their pretend family in a list of attributes. These lists will help them decide whether the person will decide to help Anna on the farm (depending on the attributes of the character they already created).
	Still image: Students use their bodies to create pictures or to freeze a moment of action in time.	Families in the pioneer community where Anna lives create family portraits with all the members of the family posed for the camera.
	Tapping in: The teacher can "unfreeze" people inside a still image one at a time to provide individual perspectives or information.	The teacher taps the shoulder of each member of the family portrait and this person is allowed to unfreeze and introduce him or herself to the whole group.
	Interviews: Students interview each other in role to help them make their roles more concrete and uncover their characters' motivations and opinions.	The members of the community interview each other to find out who supports and who does not support the plan to help Anna. Interviewees must explain why they hold this stance or opinion.
	Overheard conversations: Students "eavesdrop" on each other in role to find out information and to practise careful listening skills.	Members of the community listen to conversations conducted by people who hold the opposite point of view as a way of identifying the problems created by gossip.
	Narration: These are bridges of storytelling that replace dramatic action and help move the drama along. This strategy allows students to condense events in the drama if time is a concern. Teachers may also prepare bits of narration to introduce new ideas or information.	The students create the endings of Anna's and Ivan's story based on the information in the first part of the book and the work they have done in the drama. This episode becomes the summary or reflection on the work that has gone before in this drama.
	Pantomime: Actions without words are used to communicate information or ideas.	Some students mime the activity as others narrate the stories about how Anna's and Ivan's story will end.

INTERPRETIVE DRAMA: THE WORDS OF OTHERS

Drama Meets Text in the Elementary Classroom

The importance of story in promoting children's growth and development as creative language users is illuminated in the following passage:

> Children play out their lives through story. It tells them that life will go on, and gives form to what has happened, what is happening, and what may happen, ordering their experiences through gossip and anecdote and tale. They need stories from us to give reassurance to their inner stories, the ones that demonstrate their curiosities, fears, and concerns. (Barton & Booth, 1990, p. 18)

The "stories from us" are the orally told traditional stories, the films, the TV shows, the children's storybooks, the poetry, the plays, and the novels that we introduce to our children at home, in movie theatres, in libraries, but perhaps most often in school classrooms. Too often, we assume that if we teach children how to decode the written symbol system of their mother tongue and how to comprehend the structures of written language, we have given them all the tools they need to engage with recorded story; perhaps that assumption should be challenged.

The oral tradition of storytelling has been a part of teaching and socializing the next generation in every culture since humans came together in community groups. Cultural groups with written symbol systems inevitably recorded stories for the young as part of their legacy. When oral and written story traditions come together in the classroom, we harness powerful traditions to help our students order their experience and construct meaning in their lives. Although the play script may be the most easily recognized combination of oral and written storytelling traditions, there are other ways we can invite our students to bring the written word to life. This section explores forms of interpretive drama that may be more appropriate to the elementary classroom than the traditional play.

Lundy, in her very practical description of interpretive drama teaching strategies for the elementary classroom, reminds us of the importance of allowing children to make their own meanings from texts:

> As literacy teachers, we need to know how and when to use various teaching techniques to help our students grapple with complex texts that have multiple meanings. We need to make a shift in the kinds of literacy tasks we ask our students to undertake, the kinds of thinking we invite them to do, and the kinds of responses we prompt them to make: they can become literate by talking themselves into understanding and writing to understand as well as to be understood. (2007, p. 99)

When children use their bodies, their minds, and their voices to concretize and enliven written words, their own experiences, imaginations, and beliefs become a part of the story and something new is created that belongs only to them. Thus, Rosenblatt's (1978) reader response theory finds concrete representation in the work children create from this interaction of text and their own lives.

Teachers may draw upon several dramatic forms to engage their students in interpreting texts that have been written by others. Forms that are most familiar and/or appropriate in the elementary classroom context include:

- reenactment of stories
- storytelling

- story theatre
- reader's theatre
- choral poetry work

Teachers may also invite students to orally interpret student-written poetry, prose, and plays, thus including both writing and reading in the interpretive experience. The following section examines interpretive teaching strategies that support work with children's literature in the elementary classroom.

Exploring Text Through Drama

Reenactment of Stories

Many teachers equate educational drama with students making and performing plays from traditional or contemporary children's stories. Heinig (1993) details her approach to **story dramatization** by emphasizing the importance of selecting simple stories with plenty of action, so that children will not become confused by details of plot when they bring the story to life. She suggests teachers add crowd scenes or groups of roles to the original story so that everyone has a part to play in the final production. She also recommends that teachers double- or triple-cast the main roles so that more children have the opportunity to play these parts.

In spite of the popularity of reenactment or story dramatization as a classroom activity, many educational drama specialists caution against overuse of this form of drama in elementary classrooms. Booth (1987) suggests that asking children to retell stories they have heard or read does little to engage their imaginations (although this work may challenge children to remember sequences of events in a story). The work of Bolton, Heathcote, Neelands, O'Neill, and other drama education theorists discussed in the previous section is founded upon the belief that students should use story as a source or pre-text for improvising and building their own stories. The too-frequent retelling of stories as student-performed plays is often discouraged in circles that support and encourage process drama work.

Most young children do not possess the mastery of language needed to become polished and proficient actors who can make a dramatized story interesting to an outside audience. Frequently the memorization of lines, the blocking of movements, and the staging of plays become tedious and time-consuming for student actors and teacher directors. Ask any teacher who has been in charge of directing the annual Christmas pageant! Although we find it endearing when a grade 1 child breaks character and waves to Grandma in the middle of bringing gifts to a swaddled Cabbage Patch doll, audience laughter can be misinterpreted by that child as ridicule. Many people have become terrified of public speaking as a result of just such an incident.

However, some learning opportunities are afforded by involving children in the reenactment of well-known stories in the safety of the classroom rather than in front of parent-packed auditoriums. Students become acquainted with the power of dialogue to communicate information indirectly, and may integrate more dialogue into their writing as a result of turning stories into play-script form. The technical aspects of theatre may receive more focus when the story is known and children can turn their attention to creating costumes, sets, and props to help them bring their play to "the stage." Story structures and elements must also be carefully considered and addressed purposefully when children write plays from stories they have heard or read.

When children use **puppets** to reenact stories or perform student-written plays, teachers may avoid the pitfalls of putting children in front of audiences as actors too early in their development. The puppet is less likely to be self-conscious, wave to Grandma, or forget lines (since its operator can have a script to read out of sight behind the puppet stage). Students may create their own puppets or use the commercial or teacher-created variety. Puppet collections and puppet stages are valuable additions to the elementary classroom drama corner. Classroom resources that describe puppet construction and use are available and include the Walkers's (1989a, 1989b) teacher guides. These very practical resources are still available for purchase.

Storytelling

Since the oral tradition of storytelling has been explored in Chapter 10 in some depth, readers are invited to review this work. Drama strategies that can support storytelling and storytelling strategies that support drama in the classroom include:

- *Soundscapes.* The teacher as storyteller invites students to create the background sounds as they occur in the story to create mood and atmosphere (Neelands & Goode, 2000, p. 73).
- *Guided tours.* The teacher as storyteller retells or creates a story to provide students with background information and visual details about the dramatic context or setting for a process drama. Often students are given time to relax and close their eyes as they listen to the story that sets the stage for the drama work to come (p. 18).

When storytelling is supported by pantomimed action, it becomes the interpretive approach known as *story theatre,* which we will now discuss.

Story Theatre

Story theatre is similar to storytelling except that "all the actions and movements in the story are played out" (Lundy & Booth, 1983, p. 87). Story-theatre stories should include extensive dialogue, strongly defined characters, and many opportunities for simple action and movement. Lundy and Booth suggest the best choices for this work are myths, legends, folk tales, and other stories from the oral tradition.

Students and teachers can make choices about how they will interpret a story using story-theatre techniques. They may decide that the narrator(s) will read or tell the story, including the dialogue spoken by the characters. This might be the best approach to take with young children whose reading skills are emerging. Older students or the teacher will read or tell the entire story and the younger students will pantomime the action as it is described. This approach helps primary level children to develop listening skills, as they must attend closely to the words of the story in order to know what actions to perform.

Older students may choose the more complex and traditional approach to story theatre in which the characters who play out the action also speak the dialogue written in the text. Sometimes the narrator reads everything that is not actual dialogue, as in the following example:

NARRATOR:	Little Red Riding Hood skipped through the forest on her way to Grandma's house. Suddenly she stopped because she noticed something moving behind a tree.
LITTLE RED RIDING HOOD:	Oh my—is that wolf I see?
NARRATOR:	… she cried in terror. The wolf became very, very still.

The reading or telling of the story may be smoother, however, if characters speak not only the dialogue but the entire sentence that includes the dialogue:

NARRATOR:	Little Red Riding Hood skipped through the forest on her way to Grandma's house. Suddenly she stopped because she noticed something moving behind a tree.
LITTLE RED RIDING HOOD:	"Oh my—is that wolf I see?" she cried in terror.
NARRATOR:	The wolf became very, very still.

Story theatre requires that students engage more thoroughly with the text of a story in order to uncover approaches to staging the story as drama. They may have to edit or abbreviate parts of the text that do not work well with this form. They may need to insert direct dialogue where it does not exist in the original story. Adapting a book or story for story theatre requires students to practise both oral and written-language skills.

Again, teachers are reminded to consider carefully before producing story-theatre work for large audiences in venues such as the school auditorium or gymnasium. Often students will be eager to show their work, but small voices and fledgling performers operate best in the classroom or drama room context, performing for small and supportive audiences of parents, teachers, or fellow classmates.

Reader's Theatre

Because it requires little attention paid to staging or the other technical aspects of the traditional play, reader's theatre has become a popular strategy for working with play scripts in the classroom. Teachers may also create opportunities for students to write plays. Motivation to write may increase when students know their written work will lead to a reader's theatre performance. Finding stories that can be turned into play scripts may become a meaningful activity for students to help them analyze character, plot, and dialogue in short stories or storybooks.

The conventions of reader's theatre focus primarily on vocal interpretation. Players must consider how they will bring characters in the play to life using their voices and facial expressions. Elements of the spoken word, such as intonation, pitch, pace, volume, and juncture, can be discussed and explored in purposeful ways when students are discussing how to communicate mood and subtext with their voices. Lundy (2007) adapted to the needs of English-as-a-second-language learners in her classroom reader's theatre work by putting this group in charge of creating the sound effects or soundscape for the performance (p. 49). This important contribution created a brilliant theatrical effect.

Certain conventions define traditional reader's theatre performance:

- Players are seated on the stage or in front of the classroom on chairs or stools. When someone turns his/her back to the audience, it usually means that this character is no longer present in the action.
- Players may stand or gesture to emphasize their lines but characters do not face each other or play to each other during the performance: all lines are played to the audience.
- Often students use a music stand or podium to hold the script so that their hands are freed for gestures.
- Players wear black or some type of uniform costume so that the audience is not distracted from the oral interpretation of script.

Numerous collections of reader's theatre scripts are available for classroom work. Dixon, Davies, and Politano (1996) include preparation exercises, staging ideas, learning objectives, assessment suggestions, and cross-curricular connections in a very practical reader's theatre resource.

Choral Poetry Work

The power of poetry to engage children in drama is matched only by the power of drama to open up the delights of poetry for children. Drama and poetry both highlight the melodies and rhythms of oral language and both genres find their appeal in the actively spoken interpretation of words. Evocative poetry creates an excellent pre-text for process drama work, because good poems are usually both intense and condensed distillations of human emotions and story.

One of the most powerful process dramas I've developed to work with my pre-service drama education students was based on the pre-text of a Stan Rogers song, "The Northwest Passage." This song tells the story of the men who sailed into the Arctic Ocean with Sir John Franklin in search of the fabled sea passage to the Orient—a trading route sought by the early explorers to North America. The ships were lost and the men died in the frozen Arctic wasteland. The song compares this journey with the poet/songwriter's journey across the expanse of Canada to find his fortunes in the west. The process drama episodes that follow my sharing of this song with the students are characterized by their sincerity and eagerness to explore this place and time in Canadian history. Rogers's words communicate so powerfully a spirit of both adventure and loss that the work of building belief and creating context is almost accomplished before the drama even begins.

Although poems or songs that tell or suggest stories are most effective as sources for improvisational or process drama work (Fleming, 1994), poetic genres extending from the epic narrative to the lyric and the nonsense rhyme may be considered when teachers are searching for interpretive possibilities. When children interpret poetry with their voices and their bodies, they bring the words of the poet to life. Just as songs are meant to be sung, poems are meant to be read out loud. When the oral reading is enhanced by dramatic use of voice and gesture, the students' work becomes **choral reading**, **choral speech**, or

TABLE 12.5 Inviting Students to Interpret Poetry

Question	Vocal Element
How do we want the people who are listening to us say this poem to feel when we say it for them?	**mood**
What do you think is the most important thing the poet is trying to say in this poem? Can you say it in just one sentence?	**theme**
Where are the places in the poem where we should read more quickly? More slowly?	**pace**
Where are the places in the poem where we should pause or take a little rest before we continue reading?	**juncture**
Where are the places where we need to make our voices soft or very soft? Loud or very loud?	**volume**
Are there any places where we need high voices? Low voices?	**pitch**
Are there places in the poem where we want only one voice saying the line? Two voices? A few voices? The whole class?	**colour**
Are there important words in the poem that we should make stand out for the people who are listening?	**emphasis**

choric drama. Choral speech is the term that defines poetry that has been memorized by the children so they no longer depend on the printed page. Choric drama includes pantomimed action or gesture, so that the interpretation of the poem is relayed through movement as well as voice.

Some excellent resources are available to support teachers' work with choral poetry work. Lundy's (2007) book *Leap into Literacy: Teaching the Tough Stuff So It Sticks!* includes an extensive component of student-created poetry as well as suggestions for inviting students to interpret the poems of others. Lundy and Booth (1983) detail a variety of approaches to working with poems in the drama classroom. Fleming (1994) provides examples of poems that work well for process as well as interpretive work. The number of children's poetry anthologies that are available to teachers is growing rapidly. Interpretive drama work can make poems—and poetry as a genre—both memorable and magical for children.

It is most important to empower students to create their own interpretations of a poem rather than impose the teacher's interpretation as the "correct" way to say it. Some questions that teachers may ask to invite student interpretations are detailed in Table 12.5. Of course, the teacher will not ask all of these questions at once. Children should be given many run-throughs to experiment with what their voices can do to enhance or interpret the meaning of the poem before they "set" and practise their interpretation.

The following poem by Lewis Carroll provides one example of how a poem might be interpreted dramatically by a year 4 or 5 class.

My Fairy by Lewis Carroll (1845)

I have a fairy by my side
Which says I must not sleep,

When once in pain I loudly cried
It said "You must not weep"
If, full of mirth, I smile and grin,
It says "You must not laugh"
When once I wished to drink some gin
It said "You must not quaff."
When once a meal I wished to taste
It said "You must not bite"
When to the wars I went in haste
It said "You must not fight."
"What may I do?" at length I cried,
Tired of the painful task.
The fairy quietly replied,
And said "You must not ask." (1845)

Students have been reading *Alice in Wonderland* and are interested in Lewis Carroll's particular brand of humour. The teacher introduces this poem and asks them to think about how Carroll wanted people to feel when they read or heard it performed. The students decide that he was trying to make people laugh. One student offers the idea that this fairy sounds just like a parent who is always telling you not to do things you want to do. The others agree that this is just how it feels sometimes. There are few giggles about the poet wanting to drink gin, but the teacher suggests that Carroll was an adult when he wrote this poem and perhaps this is why he included this line. She asks if there are any words that the students are unsure about and students mention *mirth* and *quaff*, but are able to decide what these words mean by the context clues provided in the poem.

Students suggest that there should be a combination of groupings of voices to provide the vocal colour in the poem. They decide to have each of the fairy's first five lines read by five individual voices. The whole group will read "What may I do?" at a strong volume and the small group of five "fairy" voices will whisper in unison "You must not ask." The students decide this poem would benefit from some sound effects so they appoint a small group to inject snoring sounds, yelps of pain, laughter, "glug glugs" for the drinking line and "ouch" for the fighting lines. The rest of the students divide themselves into small groups to read the "When" lines in the poem. Someone suggests that they should start out slowly and then read faster and faster as the poem continues. They try this suggestion out and discover it does little to enhance the meaning or mood of the poem for them, so they elect to keep an even pace throughout the reading. Someone else believes that the word "must" should be strongly emphasized every time it occurs in the poem. A second student responds that the word "not" should receive even more emphasis than "must." When students experiment they all agree that this phrase should jump out at the listeners, with "not" receiving slightly more emphasis than "must."

Students read through the poem several times and are delighted with the way their voices bring out the humour and naughty mood of Carroll's work. Someone suggests that they should practise and perform this poem at the upcoming school assembly. The teacher is confronted with the classic dilemma of the classroom drama teacher: To perform or not to perform? This question leads us into the final section of this chapter.

PLAYS AND PERFORMANCE

The Play's the Thing—or Is It?

The high-school drama club is often recognized as an important venue for students with acting or other theatre talents to gain their first experiences of what it means to be a theatre artist. The question of how old children need to be to perform scripted plays for outside audiences has often been raised. Of course there are child prodigies for whom acting is as natural as breathing, but does this mean that all children should participate in theatrical performance as part of their elementary school experience? This question has evoked the concern of drama educators over several decades of research and writing in educational drama.

Slade (1954) and Way (1967) strongly advocated for the importance of dramatic *experience* as the primary purpose of drama in the elementary school context. They suggested that conscripting young children into memorizing lines and *performing* plays was antithetical to the goals of humane and progressive education and that it would result in "showing off" and "artificial" performances. Drama educators of the Slade and Way school of thought argued that children younger than 12 or 13 did not have the maturity or language skills necessary to rehearse and perform at a satisfactory level to hold the attention of an audience, and should be spared the experience of performing badly.

In the 1980s and 1990s, educational drama theorists who had initially agreed with the "anti-performance" approach to classroom drama began to more deeply examine their understandings of what is meant. Gavin Bolton (1992) explains that young children "need the foundation offered by the existential experiencing and, for them, too much early emphasis on credibility, repeatability and communicability to an audience can be damaging" (p. 23). But he also suggests that theatrical elements (such as tension, symbol, and contrast) and sharing of work with classmates are essential components of classroom drama. Morgan and Saxton (1987) address the students' requests to put on plays: "They see showing as a major part of drama. Of course, some just want to show off, but others have a genuine need to test out the validity of their work" (p. 129). These authors define this type of performance as **sharing** rather than as theatre.

Fleming demonstrates the evolution of Bolton's understanding of performance and distils the changing perspectives toward performance and classroom drama that characterize current thought:

> The distinction between "process" and "product" created false trails in thinking about drama teaching. The assumption that a performance in a theatre to an audience constituted a "product" and that improvised work in a drama studio amounted to a "process" does not stand up to scrutiny. As Bolton (1998:261) suggests, it is mistaken to give the impression that "process" is to be seen as an alternative to "product" for they are interdependent not polar concepts. (2001, p. 115)

If performance to an audience is considered a natural part of the process when senior elementary level students express the willingness and the need to "put on a play," how can teachers maximize the learning potential of this experience for their students? The literature suggests the most meaningful approach might be to have the students create their own play rather than memorize lines from a prewritten play script. **Play-building** or **collective creation** is an approach that may meet the developing need to perform that occurs most often for middle-years students.

Making a Play

The term "collective creation" (Goffin, 1995) identifies both a collaborative process undertaken by actors/students and their director/teacher and the creative product or "play" that results from that process. The collective creation differs from the traditional play in several ways: (1) it is "written" by a group of individuals rather than an individual playwright, (2) it usually encompasses a variety of viewpoints or "episodes" around a theme or idea rather than telling a plot-driven story, and (3) the collective participant assumes all theatre roles (set designer, director, actor, script writer, technical designer) at one time or another during the collaborative process.

Collective creation work supports students' understanding and skill development in the art form of theatre and in social interactions with peers (Horn, 1992). Using the collective creation model with adolescents may invite students to gain objectivity, break out of old patterns of thinking, and gain different perspectives (Berk & James, 1992). Collective play-building also provides an excellent forum for the exploration of social justice issues (Gallagher, 2000; Grady, 2000; Belliveau, 2004; Conrad, 2004).

The instructional process of engaging students in making a play on a topic of their own choice demands that teacher/directors be patient, willing to live with ambiguity, and possess at least a rudimentary knowledge of theatre and theatrical conventions (Lang, 2002). The teacher must allow a considerable amount of time for students to explore ideas dramatically, to discover how to present these ideas so they will be interesting to the audience, and to rehearse their work for performance. Often collective work is improvised rather than scripted, since young performers can lose momentum when the additional challenge of script-writing is added to the already demanding experience of creating and performing a piece of theatre.

The pedagogical implications of working in collective creation with elementary-level students have barely been considered in the drama education literature: most of the research and writing in this area has been with students in secondary- and postsecondary-level settings. Although students in seventh or eighth grades who have considerable experience with drama may become successfully engaged in the collective creation process, the elementary-level teacher may want to focus on providing students with a variety of process/improvisational and interpretive drama experiences, so that students are grounded in the "basics" of drama before they enter the world of theatre at the high-school level. Showing or sharing interpretive and process work with small audiences made up of parents or classmates may provide important beginnings for collective and theatre work in high school.

THE CHALLENGE OF ASSESSMENT AND EVALUATION IN DRAMA

Learning in Drama

Drama educators have been struggling for decades with the characteristics that make student assessment and evaluation in drama challenging for teachers. Some writers have approached this topic by exploring the kinds of learning that occur in classroom drama. Davies (1983) suggests that students learn in four different areas when they engage in classroom drama activity:

- *Improvisational skills used to seek meaning* (the ability to suspend disbelief, concentration, use of imagination, group process skills, imaginative action)
- *Understanding of themes and topics* (learning of concepts and information in other subjects through drama: includes adopting other points of view and problem-solving skills)
- *Theatre presentation skills* (voice, interpretation of script, characterization, technical skills)
- *Appreciation of theatre* (understanding of acting, play script, and the technical aspects of theatre from an audience point of view)

He maintains that the improvisational skills are the most difficult to assess in relation to student progress, and advises teachers to address theatre presentation and appreciation skills at the secondary-school level (pp. 96–104).

Morgan and Saxton (1987) state: "No systematic approach to evaluation in drama has evolved because the subject itself operates in a curriculum model which is heuristic (the pupil is trained to find out things for himself) rather than technological (the students are trained to assimilate a defined body of knowledge)" (p. 189). This statement, made in reference to process drama, prefaces their classification of learning objectives in the drama classroom. They suggest that summative evaluation in drama is possible only when you are addressing student progress in the measurable areas such as

- *Administrative behaviours* (attendance, punctuality, respect for space and equipment, completing assignments, following instructions)
- *Content knowledge* (knowing the rules of the game, the vocabulary, history, and literature of theatre)
- *Skills* (mime, memorization, improvisation, use of costume, mask and props, knowing when to speak and when to be silent, maintaining role) (pp. 191–193)

They suggest that the more *important* areas of learning and growth (self-discipline, willingness to trust, initiation and extension of ideas, sensitivity to the contributions of others, risk-taking, skills of cooperation, and personal engagement, to name but a few) are more difficult to measure, because growth in these areas is not readily apparent to the outside observer (pp. 195–197).

Bolton (1992) also emphasizes that the most important learning that occurs in process drama happens when students construct meanings for themselves from dramatic experiences. He suggests that teachers look for evidence of credible understandings, intellectual effort, coherence, and significance (p. 141). Evidence of this kind of learning is almost impossible to measure with any degree of objectivity. Wagner (1998) ties the challenges of assessment in drama to English language arts when she suggests "part of the problem in assessing the effects of drama on reading is the use of standardized tests. They are not sensitive to the kinds of language gain that facilitate deep understanding and empathy; in other words, they are not valid tests for measuring the effect of drama" (p. 177).

Another assessment/evaluation issue arises because drama is such an active and experiential approach to learning. When teachers are so deeply involved in participating in drama work with their students, they don't often have the opportunity to observe the evidence of growth that these drama theorists emphasize is important. We need to explore more accessible approaches to assessing the impact of drama activity so that we can make informed decisions about the progress of our students.

Addressing Issues of Assessment in Drama in the Language Arts

Because our context is drama in the English language arts classroom, we will focus specifically on language learning that may be enhanced by drama work. The following list of questions would be used informally to help teachers reflect on students' response to drama. Because drama is primarily a group activity that emphasizes cooperation rather than competition and individualistic achievement, I frame the questions to assist teachers in assessing the progress of the classroom group.

Reading

1. Are students expressing an interest in reading books that may have themes or authors in common with books introduced or used as pre-texts for drama work?

2. Are reluctant readers more willing to read "in role" than they are when they are engaged in daily reading routines?

3. Do books used in drama come up more frequently in "favourite book" lists, book talks, or other places where children reflect on their choices in literature?

4. Do students express more interest in reading poetry or plays?

Writing

1. Do students include more dialogue and action in their written work?

2. How does the writing-in-role work compare with out-of-role written work completed by the same student in terms of length and complexity?

3. Do students suggest that they would like to write plays or poetry in response to process or interpretive work with these genres?

4. Are students willing and motivated to keep drama journals or records of their work with drama?

Speaking

1. Do you notice new vocabulary (that was introduced in drama) being integrated into students' conversation inside and outside the classroom?

2. Is students' oral reading becoming more expressive outside the context of drama activity?

3. Are students moving more easily among formal and informal registers of oral language (e.g., sentence structure and complexity, use of vocabulary)?

Listening

1. Are students listening more attentively to directions and instructions since participating in drama activities?

2. Are students able to retain and sequence ideas that they have heard more easily since working with process drama?

This list of questions is both informal and limited in scope, but it may provide you with one approach to assessing the impact of drama work in your English language arts classroom.

SUMMARY

This chapter has explored the place of drama in the elementary English language arts classroom. We began with an examination of the role of unstructured dramatic and sociodramatic play in early childhood learning experiences. Secondly, a discussion of the purposes and foundations of process drama established a context for describing how to plan dramas from selections of children's literature. Instructional strategies and conventions for process drama were described.

Descriptions of interpretive drama strategies (including story theatre, reader's theatre, and choral poetry work) extended the discussion of drama work in the English language arts. Appropriate grade levels and purposes for working with plays and performance were explored (including a brief description of collective creation or play-building for senior elementary students). The chapter concludes with a discussion of the challenges inherent in assessing and evaluating drama and offers an informal list of questions that teachers may use to reflect on the impact drama has on students' language growth and development.

Although drama is an excellent support to English language arts teaching practice, it is also a valuable and important area of study in its own right. Readers are encouraged to read some of the resources listed in the following reference section to better acquaint themselves with the myriad of learning opportunities offered to students in drama work.

TALKING POINTS

1. Try to remember one experience of "let's pretend" (sociodramatic play) from your own childhood and write a short description addressing the following questions. Where did it happen? Who shared the "let's pretend" game with you? What role(s) did you assume in your shared play? Now share your description with a classmate and compare experiences: How are they similar? Different? What reasons can you construct to explain similarities and differences in your memories of dramatic play? What did you learn about social roles from this play? If memories of this kind of play are difficult or impossible to recapture, why do you think this is so?

2. Drama works well with a child's storybook when most of the following criteria are met:

   ▷ The text of the story includes or suggests groups of characters who interact with the protagonist in an active way.

   ▷ The supporting characters in the story may be flat or stereotypical so that children can use their imaginations to round out the characters themselves.

▷ Stories that are located in geographically distant or fantasy worlds allow children to discover "universal truths" while maintaining a safe distance from their own world.

▷ The theme of the story should be implicit rather than explicitly stated so that children can discover it for themselves through their work with drama.

▷ Stories that contain some element of magic or fantasy may ignite children's imaginations and invite them into the make-believe world of drama.

Select a favourite picture storybook that would be appropriate for a grade level you would like to teach, and assess it as a source for drama using these criteria.

3. When you have found a storybook that does meet the criteria outlined in point 2 above, draft a plan for a process drama using this book as a source and using the eight-step process that is outlined in this chapter. Compare plans in small groups of four or five. Which steps were the easiest to complete? Which were the most difficult? What would you need to know/do in order to make your plan work in a classroom situation?

4. Find a popular children's poet and choose a poem to interpret chorally in a small group of four of five. Use the questions in Table 12.5 to focus your choral interpretation.

PROFESSIONAL RESOURCES

Some practical resources that elementary teachers will find helpful for drama work are included below. All four resources may be ordered from Theatrebooks (http://www.theatrebooks.com) in Toronto.

Neelands, J. & Goode, T. (2000). *Structuring drama work: A handbook of available forms in theatre and drama* (2nd ed.). Cambridge: Cambridge University Press.

This coil-bound resource catalogues 71 different approaches or conventions that teachers may use to involve students in process drama. Each convention gets a one- or two-page treatment that includes: (1) a description of what to do, (2) cultural connections, (3) learning opportunities provided by the convention, and (4) examples of the convention as part of a specific process drama. The conventions are organized into four main classifications: context-building, narrative, poetic, and reflective. Since I have used Neelands's categories in the eight-step planning process outlined in this chapter, this text would be especially helpful as a complement to that process.

The following three resources are current, are written by Canadian drama educators, and include many practical drama activities and well- researched ideas for teaching.

Booth, D. (2005). *Story drama: Creating stories through role playing, improvising and reading aloud* (2nd ed.). Markham, ON: Pembroke Publishers.

This is the second edition of Booth's classic text that explains how drama work supports literacy learning and growth. The new edition includes excellent examples and suggestions for involving students in a variety of literacy experiences (including reading, story creation, and writing in and out of role). Booth addresses the entire spectrum of drama work—including performance—while retaining several stories about his own experiences working with children. His very practical chapter on assessing drama work includes checklists, criteria, and suggestions for assessing both drama programs and the progress of students in drama. This is an excellent resource from one of the leading scholars in both literacy and drama education.

Lundy, K. G. (2007). *Leap into literacy: Teaching the tough stuff so it sticks!* Markham, ON: Pembroke Publishers.

Although this brand-new resource includes many strategies that develop from current drama education pedagogy, students' literacy growth and development is the central focus. Lundy includes planning strategies, teaching ideas, and practical suggestions for working with poetry, reader's theatre, photographs, scripts, and objects as part of a "drama-rich" literacy program. The book includes checklists, assessment suggestions, and a variety of examples to support the integration of drama into the elementary language arts classroom.

Miller, C. & Saxton, J. (2004). *Into the story: Language in action through drama.* Portsmouth, NH: Heinemann.

Carole Miller and Juliana Saxton have created a resource that is incredibly supportive and clear for teachers who are just beginning to work with process drama approaches in the English language arts classroom. They offer 10 detailed, structured, and clearly explained process dramas based on current children's books that were published in the 1980s and 1990s. Each drama includes explanations of why the book was selected, key understandings and questions that will focus learning for students, and between 10 and 17 episodes per drama that ensure students explore the story in depth and over a period of several lessons. They also include an large extensions list for each process drama, a variety of grouping strategies, and lists of all materials and supplies that will be required. I highly recommend this book for beginning teachers.

Planning and Organizing Language Arts Programs

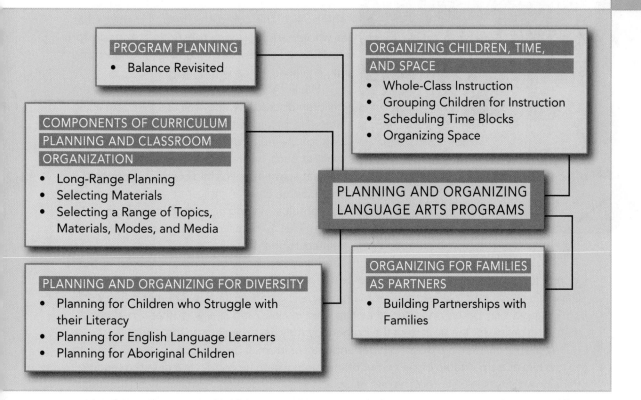

CHAPTER 13

PROGRAM PLANNING
- Balance Revisited

ORGANIZING CHILDREN, TIME, AND SPACE
- Whole-Class Instruction
- Grouping Children for Instruction
- Scheduling Time Blocks
- Organizing Space

COMPONENTS OF CURRICULUM PLANNING AND CLASSROOM ORGANIZATION
- Long-Range Planning
- Selecting Materials
- Selecting a Range of Topics, Materials, Modes, and Media

PLANNING AND ORGANIZING LANGUAGE ARTS PROGRAMS

PLANNING AND ORGANIZING FOR DIVERSITY
- Planning for Children who Struggle with their Literacy
- Planning for English Language Learners
- Planning for Aboriginal Children

ORGANIZING FOR FAMILIES AS PARTNERS
- Building Partnerships with Families

DAVID PAUL'S GRADE 2 CLASSROOM

Every day when the children enter David Paul's grade 2 classroom, they are greeted with a letter he has written to them on the chalkboard. In the letter, David tells about unusual class activities they will do that day, or comments on class events from the day before. Today, the children read the letter and David helps them use words on the classroom word wall as a resource when identifying unfamiliar words. On other days, David presents the letter as a minimal-cues message.

David then draws the children together on the floor in a group and reads them a poem about a dragon to set the theme for the group composition they will write later. As he reads, he stops at the end of some lines to give the children an opportunity to predict meaningful words.

Next, David tells the children that they are going to write a composition together about an imaginary pet dragon. He planned this instructional activity because he has noticed that many children in the class are having difficulty generating and organizing ideas in their compositions. As the children in the class brainstorm ideas, David writes them on the SMART Board. Then, with the assistance of his questions, the children organize the ideas into groups. As they do so, David uses text in various colours to circle ideas in

Children working collaboratively

each group—for example, how the pet dragon looks, what it does, and what it eats. The children discuss what they want to write and then dictate ideas while David records their ideas on the board. The completed text is then read as a whole, and some suggestions are made for revisions. The revised text, revision marks and all, is placed in the writing centre.

While the group is still intact, David and the children discuss how they will use their remaining time. He provides them with a sign-up chart to control the number of children who choose to work at each centre, as well as to keep a record of what activities each child completes during the week. Some children indicate that they are going to continue writing a composition from their writing files. Others are working on a graphic text related to the dragon theme. Others decide to read independently or write a response in their journal to a book they are reading. One group of children chooses to play a dragon game David has developed to reinforce a problematic spelling pattern (final *e*). Another group works on a puppet play based on a story they had read in class, and finally another group checks their blog online for the update of the dragon toy they have sent across the world.

While the children are working independently or in small groups, David asks six children to join him at a small table in the corner of the room where he conducts a directed reading–thinking activity (see Chapter 6) as part of a guided reading lesson. He has noticed that these children are making limited use of their own knowledge when they read. Their responses to what they are reading tend to focus on story details rather than on linking story events or characters to their own lives. He will provide guided reading for another small group tomorrow, but will continue to work with this group in subsequent lessons until they are able to make more effective use of both print and knowledge-based information.

With five minutes left before recess, David asks the class to come back together to share what they learned that morning. One child talks about a book she is reading, another child shares a piece of writing, and another discusses the images she is making on the computer to create her graphic text. The children working on the puppet play say they have completed their puppets and are ready to share their play with the class the next day, and the children who checked the blog report that the classroom dragon has just made it to Italy!

Issues Arising from the Vignette

In this vignette, we see the children in David's classroom involved in all the language arts: listening, speaking, reading, writing, viewing, and representing. The children worked with the teacher, with other children, and by themselves. They completed some assigned activities and were able to select others based on their interests and skills. The children moved from one activity to another with very little waiting, and they appeared to engage actively in the activities. This did not happen by accident, but rather reflects careful planning and organization of the program. Careful planning leads to meaningful learning for children, which in turn motivates them and reduces behaviour problems. Planning and organization are key to effective classroom management.

- How did David Paul plan the period described above?
- How can classrooms be organized to ensure that the literacy program children receive is balanced?
- How can children be grouped to meet individual needs?
- How do teachers decide the amount of time to schedule for different aspects of language arts?
- How can the physical space in classrooms be organized to maximize children's learning?
- How can a language arts program be organized to meet the range of individual differences found in any one classroom?

These are only a few of the questions you might ask yourself as you sit down to plan the language arts program in your classroom. In the previous chapters in this text, we focused heavily on instructional techniques for teaching the language arts. But that is only part of the story. In this chapter, we discuss how to put these pieces together in a classroom context to meet the needs of a diversity of children. ☐

PROGRAM PLANNING

We begin this chapter by revisiting the notion of balance in language arts programs that we set up in Chapter 1. We then identify some of the dimensions that teachers consider as they organize their classrooms to maximize learning.

Balance Revisited

When language arts educators write about balance, they sometimes refer to the need for work on word identification and comprehension in reading and on meaning and mechanics (e.g., spelling, punctuation, and handwriting) in writing. However, as indicated in Chapter 1, teachers who hold a **social constructive** perspective view "balance" from a broader perspective. They are interested in balancing *what* they teach and *how* they teach and interact with children. They are also keenly aware of the various contexts in which children are learning (e.g., home and school), and they try to balance the various language resources and perspectives that each of these contexts hold.

In terms of *what* to teach, balanced literacy teachers view literacy as encompassing more than just reading and writing. They recognize the evolving nature of literacy and the many ways that humans communicate and make sense of their world. They understand that literacy teaching in the 21st century must be based on all the language arts so that children have access to multiple modes and media for optimum communication opportunities. At the same time, balanced literacy teachers are cognizant that print literacy holds an elite place in society (Kress, 2003). Consequently, teachers have to balance which language arts to emphasize when and where.

In relation to the *how* of language arts, all teachers are faced with more difficult decisions. These include:

- how much time to allocate for teaching and to having children practise using **strategies** and skills
- when to provide explicit instruction and when to foster implicit learning
- how to **differentiate** expectations, materials, and activities to meet the language needs of all learners
- how to help children learn new strategies and develop **automaticity** in using the strategies they have learned
- when to provide assistance to **scaffold** children's learning and when to have them work independently
- how to balance control of children's learning with opportunities for them to control their own learning
- how to decide when children should work alone or with other children

The answers to questions such as these begin with the words "It depends." Several factors affect the decisions you will make. Some of these include the needs of individuals and groups of children, the stages children have reached in their learning, the resources available in your school, the program of studies mandated by provincial and territorial governments, your theoretical orientation to language arts and learning, and the philosophy of your school and school district. As indicated at several points throughout this text, no one answer will be appropriate for all children at any one time or for any one child all the time. Organizational patterns change as children grow and change, but, increasingly, as we discussed in Chapter 1, educators are recommending that balance is critical to effective language arts programs.

The planning process should also, as we discussed in Chapter 1, be seen as a "dialogue" (Routman, 2000, p. xxxviii) that is based in children's funds of knowledge and the teacher's appraisal of the context in which s/he's teaching. We described techniques earlier in this text for assessing children's oral language, **early literacy**, reading, and writing. Another crucial piece of information that guides planning involves the provincial and territorial curriculum documents for language arts education. (See Chapter 1 for a list of websites for these documents.) These documents delineate objectives or expectations to be reached in each strand of language learning. One of your tasks in planning is to determine which objectives each child has already achieved and what s/he needs to learn next. Other tasks involve selecting appropriate materials, scheduling language arts time, organizing the physical space in the classroom to facilitate children's learning, and planning whole-class, small-group, and individual instruction and activities.

We've included in Box 13.1 some issues you might ask yourself when you are considering the balance in your classroom language arts program (i.e., what and how you teach). We recognize that depending on the context in which you are teaching, you may have more or less "negotiation" room in your program. Knowing what you would like to work toward achieving "some day," however, is a step in the right direction. Also, at this moment you might have little idea of how to respond to the questions in the box, but as you go back through the text and move into teaching (e.g., practice teaching or new teaching job), you might choose to return to the questions to gauge your professional growth.

BOX 13.1	QUESTIONS TO EVALUATE BALANCE IN YOUR LANGUAGE ARTS PROGRAM

1. To what extent is communication and the creation and sharing of meaning at the centre of my program?

2. To what extent does my program expand or limit my students' identity options?

3. To what extent does my program treat all my students as "at-promise"?

4. To what extent is my program based on my students' funds of knowledge (including the language(s) they speak)?

5. To what extent does my program address all the language arts? To what extent does my program recognize that different language arts might need to be emphasized at different times depending on what my students need?

6. To what extent in my program have I considered and planned for all of Cambourne's conditions for learning as they apply to literacy?

7. To what extent do I understand how to plan for and implement the balanced literacy instructional components outlined in Figure 1.2?

8. To what extent do I recognize that my program is a work in progress, and am I pursuing the kinds of professional development experiences that are required to support my teaching (e.g., talking with a mentor, reading a range of professional and research articles, and/or taking courses)?

9. To what extent is my program patient with learning (both my own and that of my students)?

COMPONENTS OF CURRICULUM PLANNING AND CLASSROOM ORGANIZATION

Different classrooms reflect different views of language learning. When desks are arranged in rows and children face the front, the focus is generally on teacher talk, with the teacher making most decisions about what children do and when they do it. When teachers arrange children's desks in groups with the children facing one another, they encourage student talk and create some of the conditions for cooperative learning. Other decisions you will make about the use of space include:

- where to place the teacher's desk
- whether to set up reading and writing centres
- whether to have a classroom library in addition to the school library
- where to place computer and other equipment

Space is just one of the variables teachers consider as they plan and organize their classrooms to facilitate children's learning.

Time is also a crucial variable. Some jurisdictions recommend that a minimum amount of time be scheduled for language arts instruction at each grade level. However, teachers have flexibility within this time allocation to decide whether to organize language arts instruction in one or two large time blocks or to devote small time blocks to specific skills or activities. They also make decisions about how to allocate time to ensure that children receive a balanced language arts program.

A third variable teachers must take into account when planning a language arts program is materials and equipment. As with time, provincial and territorial governments recommend materials for use in language arts instruction at each grade level. A list of these materials is available at **http://www.curriculum.org/csc/resources/provincial.shtml**. Teachers make decisions such as the following:

- the extent to which language arts series are used as compared with **trade books**
- the range of levels of reading materials included in classrooms
- who selects materials or topics—children, teachers, or both
- whether materials are organized thematically or some other way

Finally, the most critical variable teachers take into account when planning language arts programs is the children themselves. How can children inform the curriculum, and thereby maximize their learning? Teachers make daily decisions about when, why, and how to organize whole-class, small-group, and individual activities. In the next sections, we describe ways teachers plan, organize materials, children, time, and space to meet the need of learners in their classrooms.

Long-Range Planning

As a teacher, you will be planning moment by moment, day by day, week by week, and also through long-range plans. Long-range plans provide an overview of the year and help establish a direction for you and your students. As with all areas of the curriculum, even though these plans are written down before the school year begins, they should be seen as a guide that can evolve and be negotiated as you learn more about your students. The Teacher Wisdom box below is an interview with teacher Linda Levely. In this interview Linda describes her planning.

Linda's interview highlights a number of important points about planning:

- Curricular planning is an ongoing cycle of planning, implementing, assessing, evaluating, and revising.
- Planning should be long-range and moment by moment.
- Planning is an individual and collective activity.
- Getting to know your students, the resources in your school and community, and curricular mandates are fundamental.
- While it is imperative to base your curriculum on your specific circumstances (e.g., your students' funds of knowledge), it is important to have a general sense of where you're going and what you need to accomplish.
- Planning is not just in the service of your students but is also a fundamental part of your own professional development.
- Curriculum, in so far as possible, should be meaningful and balanced between the "whole" and the "part."

One of the most common ways of accomplishing this last point is by planning according to themes. This organization is also evident in most of the language arts series developed in

TEACHER WISDOM

LINDA LEVELY AND PLANNING

In your first year you taught junior kindergarten. Tell us how you planned. Did you make long-range plans?

I definitely did. The long-range plans—plans that showed an overview of what I was going to do in the year—weren't as formal as for the senior kindergarten—they were more guidelines for junior kindergarten, but you definitely needed to have a defined direction of where you were going. We also had to submit the plans to our principal.

Tell us about the experience of drawing up those long-range plans for the first time.

The first time you do it, it's more just trial and error. You're putting together your own map, and it's going to be changing continually, because when you draw up the plans, you don't know the kids: you don't know their social skills; you don't know their academic background; how much support they've had at home; etc. So you can have your long-range plans all laid out, but honestly after that first week of school, you may be back at home rewriting your whole set of long-range plans if the students are either going beyond where you thought they would be or if you're having to really slow down and spending way more time on certain "basics."

You've now been teaching grade 2 for six years. Tell us about the planning process when you've had the same grade for a good amount of time.

Ah! It's fabulous! Not only do you have the background, but also when you've been in a school for a few years you know the students coming up. Now, I try to build a relationship and get to know the kids that are in grade 1 so that at the beginning of the next year I don't have such a brand new "getting to know you time." There's a foundation.

Working on my long-range plans has also gotten easier. I write my long-range plans and put them in a binder. Then, as I'm teaching through the year, I'll just jot down little notes on the plan. When you're teaching you're looking at the kids, seeing what works, what didn't work. Did you get time to cover everything? If not, how can you juggle them around and what can you combine to get two things covered at once. I've also been lucky enough to team teach with another grade 2 teacher, and we've done most of our planning together. My partner has a real science background, so we've pulled a lot of the materials and activities that she has created and we've taken the material that I did last year, and we've put that together to create a new unit to cover the same topic. We draw on the each other's expertise.

What are the timelines for when you're planning for September?

Usually in May of the previous school year we start meeting as a division. We start looking at the kids, figuring out who they are, including their academic needs and their social needs, and just start playing around without anything written in stone. We look at which groupings

(Continued)

we want together, and ask: Are there students that work well together? We also look at teaching styles, there are some teachers who are much more into centres and group work and students have more freedom in their activities and then there are teachers who are very structured, and you need to look at the children who will benefit from which teaching style—also just personalities. You need to see who will bring out the best in a child.

Then, we look at our long-range plans, which we build largely around the provincial curriculum. We just tear the curriculum apart and pick and choose what seems appropriate for which term. Of course with language arts we have the different areas which we break into smaller chunks. A lot of the chunks we visit each term, but within each chunk we'll break it down, so that in term one it's very general. In term two, we do more review and a lot of the building of the new skills. In term three, we'll review those new skills and start to develop a little bit further. At the same time, we also look at classroom resources and school resources. We also, of course, look at the kids in our May meeting and this ultimately guides all of the planning.

Does integrating curricular areas through themes enter your planning?

Yes! For example, we just did a big science unit on animals and we also wanted to work on our writing, so we've worked in riddle writing, where we have the kids forming questions and doing research skills and mind mapping, so we're covering their language aspect as well as reviewing what they've learned in science.

Is it a challenge working in themes as a way of integrating curriculum?

It's definitely a challenge in some areas. The unit we just finished on animals was very easy to do, because the children are interested in it. Also, there are tons of books in our libraries that our kids can read independently. Also, there are other resources that we have where the children can see the different setup of information books such as table of contents, index, and glossary, and they can become more familiar with that. I do find it more challenging when we start to get into topics like structures and mechanisms, which is a required topic in science. That's when I really rely on my teaching partner—to bounce ideas off of her.

Is there a reflective practice component to your planning of long-range plans?

When I'm planning, I also try to pick a focus on anything I want to improve on within my own teaching. For instance, I found that I wanted to try to improve my spelling program. I had questions: Should I use a speller? Do I use high-frequency words? The next year I decided not to use a speller, opting instead for high-frequency words and the words the students are using in their day-to-day activities. And so over the summer, I did some reading, I looked on the Internet, I talked to other teachers, and I started putting together my own program to implement. As a teacher, I like to pick one area to improve on. You can't focus on all the areas and you're not going to forget about the other areas, but something I've learned is that you take one step at a time. In my first classroom, I was trying to be perfect in all the areas and it did take a little bit to realize that no one can be perfect in all the areas, and even still, your students *are* going to learn, you're going to have a good year, they're going to benefit from you, and you will affect them, but you just have to take small steps yourself so that you can grow as a teacher.

Canada, which often come with suggestions for teachers to provide children with opportunities to talk, read, write about, as well as view and represent ideas related to each theme. Some teachers go beyond the language arts and develop interdisciplinary or cross-curricular thematic units, integrating social studies, science, mathematics, art, music and other subjects with the language arts. There may be several advantages to **thematic organization**, such as:

- Children transfer knowledge and skills from one context to another. In addition to integrating strategies across the language arts, they build upon their knowledge base and connect what they know with what they are learning.

- Children examine a topic more closely, going beyond the superficial to develop in-depth conceptual ways of thinking about information.

- By selecting books on a common topic at a variety of reading levels, the needs of learners at varying levels of reading proficiency can be met.

- Thematic organization also leads to opportunities for children to work cooperatively on a common topic or problem.

- Reading and writing tasks are relevant and contextualized, and children use a range of media to gather and represent information.

When considering whether to plan thematically, teachers also need to be aware of some potential disadvantages. One is that even when the teacher selects the theme in consultation with the children in the classroom, some children may be more interested in it and have a greater sense of ownership than others. Another potential problem is that the theme might take precedence over curriculum concerns, with the result that goals in a specific subject area become secondary in importance. The most sensible approach is to make links when appropriate, but not to force links that distort curriculum goals or fail to serve children's learning needs.

Thus, while there are many advantages to thematic organization, teachers must take several factors into account when they are planning thematic units. The most important of these is children's funds of knowledge, but other factors include mandated outcomes, available resources, and district initiatives. When you're planning through themes, select themes that are not only interesting to children but substantive enough to challenge them to seek information beyond what they already know. To facilitate planning, use a web to develop a teaching plan for the thematic unit. Such a web should show cross-curricular connections and include a variety of reading materials and contextually embedded activities (Vogt, 1997). You can find an example and other pointers on thematic planning at **http://www.eduplace.com/rdg/res/vogt.html**.

Selecting Materials

There are many different materials that teachers commonly use in language arts programs. Each one comes with its own considerations. Note that, traditionally, language arts materials have been print materials in book form, though, increasingly, language arts programs may be built around new media resources such as hypertexts. That said, even the basal reading series we present in this section and that contains print and image is multimodal, as modes are rarely ever found or used in isolation (Jewitt & Kress, 2003). Consequently, if the materials teachers use are not clearly identifiable as part of a **new literacies** vein (Knobel & Lankshear, 2007; Lankshear & Knobel, 2003), the way we *use* them and should therefore *teach* students how to access them to their fullest should be new.

Language Arts Series

Basal reading series have dominated the teaching of reading in North America since the early part of the 20th century. These series generally consist of teacher's guides, student anthologies, student workbooks, and other materials such as tests, worksheets, audiotapes, and computer software. Basal readers were developed in the first two decades of the 20th century to reflect the learning theories and research of that time and a concern about the quality of reading instruction (Goodman, Shannon, Freeman, & Murphy, 1988). The explicit instructions in teacher's guides and structured skill development for students were presented as a solution to this concern. The promoters of basal series believed that all teachers needed to do was follow the instructions in the guides and children would learn to read. Although this promise of basal readers has never been realized, more than 90 percent of elementary school teachers in the United States were still using basal reading series in the 1980s (Goodman, Shannon, Freeman, & Murphy, 1988).

Initially, basal reading series in Canada were essentially Canadianized versions of series from the United States (Murphy, 1991). However, over the past 25 years, Canadian series have been developed in this country, and they are quite different from those produced in the United States. One major difference is the attempt by Canadian publishers to produce integrated language arts series rather than focusing primarily on reading.

Another major difference involves the inclusion of more children's literature. In the past, basal reading series in the United States were criticized for including too much material written specifically to teach reading (e.g., with controlled vocabulary). Even when children's literature was included, it was often adapted to such an extent that it is almost unrecognizable (Goodman, Shannon, Freeman, & Murphy, 1988). In contrast, many Canadian series developed in the 1980s and 1990s made an effort to offer high-quality children's literature, and by the early 1990s, this was occurring in series produced in the United States as well (Hiebert, 1999).

Today, popular series include *Gage Cornerstones* (2001), Prentice Hall/Ginn's *Collections* (2001), and ThomsonNelson's *Nelson Language Arts* (1999 & 2000) and *Crossroads* (2000). These series feature Canadian content and are structured around many if not most of the instructional components of balanced literacy that we feature in this text. Another change in today's series is that they attempt to correlate teacher resource books with the learning outcomes identified in curriculum documents from different regions of the country, resulting in a different edition for each region. In addition to resource books, core teacher materials include assessment handbooks, blackline masters, and, for *Collections*, learning strategy cards. At the grades 1 and 2 levels, core children's materials include small anthologies or mini theme books, sets of levelled library or little books, and audiocassettes and/or CD-ROM audio sets. At grades 3 to 6, all three series provide anthologies with a variety of genres as well as media resources. *Collections* also includes genre books and novels. Supplementary materials vary by series and include such things as writing handbooks, chapter books, and alphabet flip charts.

Although language arts series have changed a lot since the early days, they still place considerable power and control in the hands of publishers rather than teachers and children (Ajayi, 2005; Shannon, 1989). Language arts series determine not only what children read, but also what teachers do with these materials. When using a series, teachers might ask themselves some important, critically oriented, reflective questions, such as:

- How can the students and I remain in charge of our language arts program?
- How can we select from and adapt the materials in the series rather than use them in a rigid, inflexible manner?
- How can the materials serve our interests, funds of knowledge, and needs, rather than us serving the materials?

Teachers are the experts about the interests and needs of the children in their classrooms, so they are in the best position to critically examine the materials in language arts series to determine whether, when, and how they can be used to meet their students' needs.

Trade Books

Those teachers who continue to use language arts series frequently supplement them with **trade books**. This is what David Paul does in his classroom, exposing the children to a wide range of materials, not just a Canadian language arts series.

The use of children's books either as the core of language arts programs or in addition to basal series has become so widespread that a special chapter of this textbook is devoted to describing children's literature and how to use it in elementary classrooms. In addition, a list of children's literature is presented by grade level in the Appendix. However, including children's literature in classrooms may not necessarily lead to balanced language arts instruction.

In the early 1990s, there was some concern about "the basalization of children's literature" (Jobe & Hart, 1991, p. 147). What this meant was that what many teachers were doing with children's books was very similar to what they did with stories in traditional basal reading materials. In novel studies, for example, many teachers still assigned a chapter to be read and 10 questions to be answered, developed fill-in-the-blank worksheet exercises about the stories, and asked children to define words on a list from the story and use them in a sentence. Such practices are problematic, because they confuse "remembering" with "comprehending"; that is, most of these activities ask readers to simply supply facts that they remember from reading a text rather than asking them to use their higher-order thinking skills and critical reading skills to construct meaning from text (Allington, 2006).

By the mid-1990s, another agenda was being imposed on children's books, namely guided reading. This agenda, grounded in New Zealand reading programs, was presented for widespread consumption in North America by Fountas and Pinnell in 1996. Fountas and Pinnell argue that guided reading is a significant component of instructional programs in language arts, and that to be effective, children need to be matched with "just-right" texts. To achieve this match, they use the following factors to place children's books at increasing levels of difficulty:

- length of the book
- appearance and placement of print on the page
- degree of support of pictures
- complexity and familiarity of concepts
- predictability to the text
- proportion of unique or repeated words to familiar words

As outlined in Chapter 5, Fountas and Pinnell (1999; Pinnell & Fountas, 2002) provide lists of books levelled from kindergarten through grade 6, including a variety of formats (picture books, short stories, chapter books) and both fiction and nonfiction.

Although guided reading has increased the focus on developing strategic readers (Fawson & Reutzel, 2000), some educators are becoming concerned about whether this type of text progression fits the instructional needs of all children at all points in their literacy development (Brabham & Villaume, 2002). For children above a beginning level of reading, "levels can actually be limiting factors, because they don't take into account students' varying interests, background knowledge, and motivation" (Routman, 2000, p. 84), and sometimes teachers concentrate on moving children to the next level of text rather than on helping them learn and use strategies they really need (Szymusiak & Sibberson, 2001). We also worry that the **aesthetic** aspect of reading will be lost in the emphasis on levels and strategies. Consider, for instance, this story from educator Kathy Hibbert (in press). Kathy was in a store one day when she overheard a conversation between the store owner and her son. The son was really excited, because he had been "moved up a level" in reading at school. The mother was also excited and wondered to the son if the latest Harry Potter novel (Rowling, 2005) was rated at her son's current level. The son said that, no, the new Harry Potter was in a higher level than he was in at school. He then remarked that he would just have to read the novel at home as he had done with all the other books in the series.

This story raises many questions about how levelling is used. For instance,

▪ What is the role of engagement (including interest and motivation) in reading achievement and to what extent does levelling take this into account?

▪ What is the role of background knowledge in reading achievement (including knowledge of particular characters, settings, etc.) and to what extent does levelling take this into account?

▪ In short, how might teachers use levelling in ways that expand children's engagement with text and their reading choices?

Educators also need to answer questions related to how beginning-reading texts should be levelled. Although **predictable books** are useful in helping children develop many understandings and concepts during the emergent stage of learning to read, some children have difficulty shifting attention to print and developing strategies for using letter–sound relationships. In this specific case, children might benefit from another form of text progression based on systematic phonics instruction (Brabham & Villaume, 2002). Progressions of decodable text support children as they develop and practise phonics knowledge in connected text. Be aware, however, they often involve contrived language that is difficult to comprehend, and may result in too heavy a reliance on knowledge of letter sounds. Indeed, selecting a just-right book for children is an art.

It is clear that no single type of text or levelling system will meet the needs of all children. One option is to use several different single-criterion progressions in order to provide a balanced view of reading to children. Another is to use current materials and sort them according to different criteria for different children in relation to their instructional needs. Yet a third option is to use materials that meet several criteria. Some Dr. Seuss books, such as *Green Eggs and Ham* (1960), do just this. When using such texts, watch your students closely. If any of them are having difficulty, consider if such a text is introducing too many different words too quickly (Hiebert, 1999). Too many new words too quickly might also affect comprehension if readers have limited or no meaning for these words (Nichols & Rupley, 2004). For these children, new

TEACHER WISDOM

LINDA LEVELY ON BUILDING A CLASSROOM LIBRARY

In terms of building your classroom library when you first started to teach, did you have many resources?

In my first classroom I had to put in most of the books. The classroom didn't have many books left in it, and kids have to have books! I had kept a lot of books from my childhood, so I brought them in. The kids quickly learned that you're not always going to have all these brand-new books and that if you have a book that's worn out, then that means that it's a good book, because its been read and enjoyed a zillion times. They then learn that they should give it a try. I also learned to share books with teachers, you can rotate them. ... Now I have a huge amount of books from garage sales, from schools that are cleaning out their libraries—just wherever you can get books bring them in, and then keep them organized for yourself. I keep a section aside where I have my seasonal and holiday and different subjects that I pull out when I need to. And it's always great to see the excitement of the kids when that cupboard opens, and they try to anticipate what books are going to be pulled out.

I also use the school and public library to put together books for themed units like author studies. Yes! Yes! Definitely use the school library, have your library call other schools if you're missing books. As well, the kids can be great for bringing you books. If you're doing an author study and kids in your class say, "Oh, I have this book at home" or "We have a book written by the same author," invite them to bring it in. It gives them a great opportunity to do a book talk, makes them interested in a book, and when other students see them sharing a book, they want to do it too. So it can just start the whole snowball.

texts need to be generated, incorporating the repetitive and rhythmic nature of predictable books with a low density of high-frequency words and multiple exemplars of one or more **rimes**.

One challenge for many teachers can be how to collect enough book resources for their classroom. In the Teacher Wisdom box concerning classroom libraries, Linda Levely describes how she has addressed this challenge. Recall too from Chapter 3 that some of the best resources are made by children themselves, as in the case of class books and Language Experience Approach stories.

Nonbook Resources

Sometimes we imply to children through what we do and say that books are the only legitimate source of reading materials. Yet, when we think about all the items we read each day, books are only one of many reading sources. Some of the other items we read in a normal day include newspapers, magazines, TV guides, brochures, advertisements, signs, labels, and a range of texts on the Internet. On this last point in the list, we indeed must provide students with opportunity to expand their viewing and representing knowledge and skills. If we want children to become literate and read widely for both information and pleasure, we need to ensure that they engage with a wide variety of materials in school.

In terms of print resources, most young children are aware of print in their environment before they go to school. They know the sign for fast food restaurants, and they can identify their favourite cereal by looking at the box. When they begin school, they encounter print in their classrooms, including their names; the names of their classmates; the days of the week and months of the year on the calendar; words on tape recorders, computers, and other equipment; words on charts; and labels in work centres. By making this print the focus of instruction, teachers build on children's experiences with printed language and help children make use of it.

For children beyond an early level of literacy, nonbook materials can include such items as:

- pamphlets and brochures from a variety of sources (e.g., travel agencies, tourism bureaus, flyers, and advertisements)
- instruction manuals (e.g., for video games)
- comic books
- trading cards
- newspapers
- magazines
- material on the Internet and computer software

There are also newspapers and magazines designed specifically for children. Materials are available at a range of reading levels and focus on a variety of areas, including outdoor life, science, and popular culture. Some of those available are listed in Box 13.2, and all of the children's magazines listed in the box have websites that provide further literacy experiences and activities. These materials can be used for several instructional activities, particularly in relation to content area reading. They provide up-to-date information on a range of topics related to both curriculum and children's interests.

BOX 13.2 CHILDREN'S PERIODICALS

Let's Find Out and Storyworks

Scholastic Canada Limited

http://teacher.scholastic.com/products/classmags.htm

▷ *Let's Find Out* (kindergarten): Mini-books, news stories, classroom photo stories, activity pages

▷ *Storyworks* (grades 3 to 5): Fiction, nonfiction, poetry and classroom plays, interviews with authors, hands-on activities, student-written book reviews

▷ *Action* (content targeted for grades 6–12, with a reading level of grade 3–5): Reader's theatre based on popular culture, "true" teen nonfiction, activity pages

Your Big Backyard and Ranger Rick

National Wildlife Federation

http://www.nwf.org/kids

▷ *Your Big Backyard* (ages 3 to 7): Photo stories, activities

---

▷ *Ranger Rick* (ages 7 and up): Nonfiction, fiction, photo stories, activities, environmental tips about wildlife around the world

National Geographic Explorer

National Geographic Society
http://www.nationalgeographic.com/magazines/magazines.html

▷ Grades 3 to 6: Nonfiction, photo stories, activities for junior members of the National Geographic Society

Ladybug, Spider, and Cricket

Cricket Magazine Group
http://www.cricketmag.com/home.asp

▷ *Ladybug* (ages 2 to 6): Stories, poems, activities, games, songs, crafts, some nonfiction

▷ *Spider* (ages 6 to 9): Stories, articles, games, activities, jokes

▷ *Cricket* (ages 9 to 14): Stories, folk tales, biographies, science fiction, cartoons, poems, activities, crafts, crossword puzzles, nonfiction

Chirp, Chickadee, and Owl

http://www.owlkids.com

▷ *Chirp* (ages 3 to 6): Read-out-loud stories, puzzles, games, crafts

▷ *Chickadee* (ages 6 to 9) and *Chirp* (ages 2 to 6): Stories, nonfiction, activities, games

▷ *Owl* (ages 9 to 12): Nonfiction, activities, puzzles, news stories, contests

Sesame Street

Children's Television Workshop
http://www.sesameworkshop.org

▷ (Ages 2 to 6): Stories, poems, activities, posters, children's drawing and writing

Highlights for Children

http://www.highlights.com/magazine

▷ (Ages 2 to 12): Stories, puzzles, games, activities, jokes, riddles

Yes Mag

▷ http://yesmag.bc.ca

▷ The Canadian science magazine for adventurous minds.

Stone Soup

http://www.stonesoup.com

▷ Includes stories and artwork from young authors and artists

Know: The Science Magazine for Curious Kids

http://www.umanitoba.ca/outreach/cm/vol12/no21/knowsciencemag.html

▷ A themed magazine focusing on science information and illustrations for kids, including hands-on investigations

With the explosion of technology in classrooms, children are increasingly engaging with material on the Internet or in language arts software programs or even in gaming programs. Box 13.3 provides a list of some online material that might be of interest to students.

As in all other areas of language arts, when engaging with materials such as those listed above, we as teachers have a responsibility to help our students read critically. For example, given that magazines are full of advertising, we might lead a grade 6 class in a discussion about representations of bodies in these advertisements. In addition, newspapers and other "factual" sources are never without bias. We can thus help our students understand this by, for instance, juxtaposing multiple news sources on the same topic. These sources can be from a variety of modes and media, including print, Internet, radio, and television.

BOX 13.3 ONLINE RESOURCES

WebQuest Resources

http://www.ldcsb.on.ca/schools/cfe/WebQuests/index.htm

▷ Resource list of WebQuests available, including information on WebQuest

Internet4Classrooms

http://www.internet4classrooms.com/using_quest.htm

▷ Provides information on the characteristics of a WebQuest, and outlines their use in the classroom.

InspireKidz

http://www.gigglepotz.com/inspirek_webq.htm

▷ WebQuests for children of all ages.

Read Write Think

http://www.readwritethink.org/index.asp

▷ Language Arts resources, lessons, student materials, and interactive programs

Literacy Resource Websites

http://www.literacy.uconn.edu/78sites.htm

▷ Literacy website resources for middle school

Teaching Today

http://www.glencoe.com/sec/teachingtoday/index.phtml

▷ Teaching tips, lesson plans, and educational articles

Educator's Reference Desk

http://www.eduref.org/cgi-bin/lessons.cgi/Language_Arts/Writing

▷ Language Arts lesson resources

CBC Kids

http://www.cbc.ca/kids

▷ For reviews, games, contests, and TV show information

News 4 Kids (Canadian)

http://www.news4kids.ca/issues/october06/reviewRm_games.asp

▷ Includes games, contests, book reviews, and special features

Cyberkids

http://www.cyberkids.com

▷ Stories, artwork, puzzles, and more, created mostly by other kids

A Kid's Life

http://www.kidslife.com

▷ Information for girls, boys and parents for creating crafts; includes lessons, fun stuff, and complete instructions

KidsReads

http://www.kidsreads.com

▷ Information about books, series, and authors; includes title reviews, author interviews, and special features; also find trivia games, word scrambles, and contests

Giggle Poetry

http://www.gigglepoetry.com

▷ This site is full of funny poems kids will love to read; includes links where you can write your own poems and read ones written by other kids

Storybooks Online

http://www.magickeys.com/books

▷ Choose from a selection of a dozen stories for primary, middle school, and older children

Weekly Reader

http://www.weeklyreader.com

▷ Online news stories for teachers, elementary and secondary school students; includes games, contests, and a forum for voicing your opinion

Scholastic News

http://teacher.scholastic.com/scholasticnews/news/index.asp

▷ Online news for students from *Junior Scholastic* and *Scholastic News* magazines

Selecting a Range of Topics, Materials, Modes, and Media

Whether or not teachers use a basal series as part of the language arts program, we recommend that you make wide range of materials available in your classroom. By including materials that cover various degrees of difficulty, all children have the opportunity to engage with both challenging and independent material every day. Having material on a range of topics and taking the viewpoints of multiple cultures provides at least some material related to each child's interests and knowledge.

From the available materials, we recommend that children be allowed to have as much choice as possible. When all materials are selected by someone else (the publisher or teacher), children do not gain a sense of ownership or control over their own communication. They often feel that they are reading, writing, or the like for someone else rather than for themselves. Note that David Paul in the opening vignette provides students with controlled choices which allows children to take responsibility for their literacy practices.

ORGANIZING CHILDREN, TIME, AND SPACE

In preparing to read this section, try to recall how your language arts classrooms were organized when you were in elementary school. Did you have your own desk or were you seated at a small table with other children? Did your teacher provide reading instruction to the whole class or were you in a small group? Did you have a separate time each day allocated for spelling, reading, and writing instruction? Now take a look at the photo of Kathy Gillies's classroom. How does this compare to your former classrooms? The decisions teachers make about how they organize children, time, and space for language arts instruction reflect the goals and philosophy of their program.

When organizing children for instruction, you might keep the following in mind:

- There is a wide range of experience, knowledge, and skills among any group of learners.
- Every child is different from every other child in some knowledge and skill.
- Children learn at different rates.

For these reasons, we recommend that children be organized in different ways throughout the school day, and that time and space be organized to facilitate whole-class, small-group, and individual instruction and practice. This is in keeping with the instructional components of balanced literacy that are part of the framework of *Constructing Meaning*, and that are listed in Figure 1.2. When considering these instructional components, consider how some components may be more conducive to a whole group situation (e.g., read-aloud and write-aloud), others more conducive to

Kathy Gillies's classroom

independent work (e.g., independent reading and independent writing), and still others more conducive to being conducted in a small group (e.g., guided reading and guided writing). Every form of grouping has its own considerations. The next sections highlight some of these.

Whole-Class Instruction

There are several advantages of whole-class instruction. Talking and working together as a whole class helps to develop a community of learners—a community in which children help and respect one another. Children learn a great deal from one another. This learning is enhanced when children are provided with the opportunity to interact with others of differing abilities rather than only with those at a similar level of language achievement. Whole-class instruction is also an efficient use of teacher time. When introducing children to a new theme or strategy, it is more efficient to work with all of them at the same time than to teach the same thing to each child individually. In the example at the beginning of this chapter, David Paul used a minimal-cues message to teach strategies for identifying words to all the children in his class. He also read a poem to the class and had the children brainstorm ideas for a writing project. The amount of time spent on large-group instruction varies with the day and needs of the children.

Additionally, sharing time in a whole-class situation near the end of the language arts time block gives children an opportunity to talk about what they have accomplished and to evaluate their learning. They may discuss books they have read, read aloud what they have written, or talk about what they have learned. When children talk about their language processes, they can learn about themselves as language users and develop their **metacognition** (Taberski, 2000). In turn, this provides the children and the teacher with an opportunity to evaluate the effective-ness of instruction and serves as the basis for planning the next day's objectives and activities.

Because of individual differences in language development and needs, however, whole-class instruction needs to be supplemented with other ways of organizing children. If all instruction is provided to the class as a whole, the more-able readers and writers will spend much of their time completing activities designed to teach them what they already know how to do. Conversely, the less-able readers and writers will often be involved in activities beyond their **zone of proximal development**.

Grouping Children for Instruction

Ability Grouping

The major purpose of ability grouping is to produce a more homogeneous group, making it easier for the teacher to plan and give appropriate instruction. Despite the long history of ability grouping, recent reviews of research about it have produced few conclusive findings to either support or refute its impact on achievement. As a result, many educators are now questioning the value of this grouping practice (Loveless, 1998; McCoach, O'Connell, & Levitt, 2006). Ability grouping may offer some advantage to academically gifted students (Huss, 2006), but results are far from clear even for this group and questionable for average- and low-ability groups. Even when teachers are very careful in the names they select for different groups, children know which group is high and which is low. This has negative implications for the self-esteem of children in the low group (Vaughn, Hughes, Moody, & Elbaum, 2001).

In terms of reading instruction specifically, researchers have also investigated whether children are taught reading differently in high-ability as compared with low-ability groups. Again the findings are inconsistent, although there does seem to be some cause for concern as some studies indicate that students who are placed in the "lower" ability groups do not engage in as many instructional activities as their "higher" group peers, are less likely to be asked critical comprehension questions, and receive less opportunities to select their own reading material (Chorzempa & Graham, 2006). In light of these findings, ability grouping has come under considerable criticism. The instructional components of balanced literacy thus take a more varied approach to grouping where varied, flexible groupings based on a variety of factors, not just ability, are used every day.

Other Ways to Group Children

David Paul organized children into interest groups, research groups, next-step groups, and pairs. All these groupings are far less permanent than ability groups. Interest groups in his classroom are sometimes set up for one day, for example, when children come together to play a game. Other groups, such as the one working on the puppet play, stay together for several days.

■ *Interest groups* are generally made up of children at different ability levels. They tend to exist for a relatively short time, disbanding when their purpose has been achieved.

Collaborative group work

■ *Research groups* are similar to interest groups in that they are temporary, although teachers are generally instrumental in a research group's formation. In addition, the focus of the research group is on a topic that the children research rather than on completing an activity or pursuing an interest. Often the teacher and students together set specific goals, and a written or oral presentation is produced at the end. Like interest groups, these groups are frequently composed of children of varying ability levels.

■ *Next-step groups* are set up for different reasons than interest or research groups. Through careful classroom observation, teachers identify the next step that children may need to take in an aspect of the language arts. For instance, David Paul identified several children who needed to make greater use of their own knowledge as they read. He brought these children together into a small group for a few lessons to help them understand the importance of their knowledge and develop strategies for using it as they read. Once the objectives for special-needs instruction have been met, these groups are disbanded.

In *collaborative pairs*, children work together on a common activity, helping one another at points of difficulty. David organized the children in his classroom into collaborative pairs for part of the language arts time. Each pair found a space and shared books. While one child read, the other listened. This gave each child much more reading practice than is the case when children read orally in groups or the whole class. Because the children chose the books themselves, the books interested them and were also at an appropriate level. Collaborative pairs can also easily be used for writing activities, and it has been found to help children make connections between oral and print language (Wilkinson & Silliman, 2000).

A more common way of organizing children into pairs involves *peer tutoring*, either with same-age or cross-age dyads. Generally, a more proficient reader or writer is paired with one who is less proficient, and they complete a specific activity designed to facilitate skill development. This type of pairing can also be used when children need to access information from a common text in social studies or science. The child who has developed sufficient skills and strategies to construct meaning from the text reads it to the child who has not yet reached this level of reading proficiency. Another type of activity that is appropriate for peer tutoring is paired reading (see Chapter 6). As with most types of grouping, research has yielded conflicting results on peer tutoring, although it seems that both the child being tutored and the one doing the tutoring benefit from the experience (Pugh, 2005), and it appears to work best when programs are structured, short in duration, and focused on specific skills (Indrisano & Paratore, 1991).

Cooperative Learning

Many of the groupings described above lend themselves well to cooperative learning. Cooperative learning is a technique in which "students work on learning activities in small groups and receive rewards or recognition based on their group's performance" (Slavin, 1980, p. 315). There are many ways in which cooperative groups can work in the language arts classroom:

In one scenario, two students work together to complete a writing task, discussing what they will say and how they will say it. When they finish writing, they hand in one paper with both names on it.

In another scenario, a group of students attempting to make sense of a poem first jots down questions about the poem and then discusses and shares different interpretations. The understanding the students come to as a group is different and often deeper than most children could have constructed individually.

Still another example involves different students completing different parts of the same project and meeting regularly to discuss what they are doing. Again, one paper is handed in as a result of this work (Golub, 1994).

Cooperative learning challenges the traditional authority structure of classrooms by placing more control in the hands of children. Another major difference is that, instead of each child being evaluated individually, children work together and are evaluated as a group. This encourages them to work cooperatively rather than competitively (which happens when teachers organize children into groups but still base rewards on individual achievement). Some of the additional benefits claimed for cooperative learning groups include:

- increased exchange of ideas
- development of social skills
- wider acceptance and respect for other children
- increased learning
- increased motivation
- development of a sense of group (Gillies & Boyle, 2006)

Individual Activities

There is little doubt that children need classroom time to actually work in the language arts in order to become proficient language users: that is, we learn to read by reading, view by viewing. It is not enough to allow children to select a book for reading or to write something of their own choice after they complete their other work or to suggest that they do these types of activities at home. Independent time to use the language arts must be scheduled into each school day. The added bonus to independent work is that it is inherently multilevel, with each child working at an appropriate level of difficulty.

Scheduling Time Blocks

In allocating time, teachers are faced with deciding whether to divide language arts into a series of separate time periods devoted to different aspects of language arts, or to designate large time blocks for language arts (or a cross-curricular thematic unit) and organize a range of activities within these blocks.

Short Time Blocks

A major advantage of short time blocks is accountability: it is relatively easy to account for how much time has been spent on each aspect of the language arts curriculum. For example, if families are concerned about writing, you can assure them that a certain number of minutes are devoted exclusively to writing instruction every week. This way of allocating time also provides a great deal of predictability for the children. They know what they will be doing at each point during the school day.

There are, however, also several disadvantages to organizing different aspects of language arts into separate time slots. First, it does little to foster links between or even within the language arts. For example, when phonics is taught in a separate 10-minute block each day, some children will not see its relevance for writing or reading. Second, separate time blocks make it difficult for the teacher to pursue children's needs and interests as they arise in the classroom. Instead of teaching children a strategy when they need it, the teaching is put on hold until the appropriate time in the school day. In addition, just when children get really interested in a topic they are discussing, it is often time to switch to another subject area. Third, short time blocks necessitate many changes in activity during the day, and a considerable amount of time may be lost during transitions between activities.

Long Time Blocks

An alternative to short time blocks is to organize one or two larger daily time blocks for language arts and to include language learning opportunities in other subject areas as well. The major disadvantage of this type of organization is the difficulty of balancing time spent on each area of the language arts. Careful planning and record keeping are necessary to ensure that each child receives a balanced language arts program. However, the advantages far outweigh the disadvantages. There is more flexibility to pursue children's interests and learning needs. Activities are not cut off while children are still engaged in meaningful learning, nor are activities prolonged to fill a predetermined time slot when children are no longer interested or learning.

Time Guidelines

Each teacher's actual daily timetable will depend on many factors, including the requirements of the school system or provincial department of education; the philosophy of the school; times allocated for recess, lunch break, gym, and library; the grade level involved; and children's learning needs. We have provided guidance regarding time guidelines for some aspects of the instructional components of balanced literacy throughout the book. To consolidate this information, we also offer some general guidelines for allocating time in Tables 13.1 and 13.2. Please note that within all the components in the tables, all of the language arts should be

TABLE 13.1 Guidelines for Allocating Time in Primary Language Arts

Activities	Kindergarten to Beginning Grade 1	Grades 1 to 3
Opening and closing routines (e.g., calendar)	10–15 minutes	15–25 minutes
Reading to children	10–15 minutes	10–20 minutes
Shared reading and writing	20–30 minutes	10–15 minutes
Reading and writing instruction (including guided reading and writing)	20–30 minutes	40–60 minutes
Independent reading	10–15 minutes	15–30 minutes
Independent writing	10–15 minutes	15–30 minutes

TABLE 13.2 Guidelines for Allocating Time in Upper Elementary Language Arts

Activities	Frequency	Time Allocation
Reading to children	daily	15–20 minutes
Independent reading	daily	20–30 minutes
Reading instruction (including guided reading)	2 or 3 times each week	20–30 minutes
Writing instruction (including guided writing)	2 or 3 times each week	30–40 minutes
Independent writing	2 or 3 times each week	20–30 minutes

integrated within these. For instance, reading can involve reading hypertext and writing can involve writing hypertext. These activities thus also promote learning opportunities for the development of viewing and representing.

Although the activities in Table 13.1 are completed every day in primary classrooms, some are completed less frequently with upper elementary students, because older children often require longer time blocks for activities. The following guidelines are adapted from those presented by Cunningham and Allington (2003):

- *Every day.* Teacher reads books and other types of materials (e.g., newspapers, magazines) aloud to students, children read something they choose, and children do a word wall activity or some form of word study.

- *Two or three times a week.* Children participate in guided reading activity and a focused writing lesson, the teacher models writing, children write on a topic of their own choice, and children work with words.

- *Once a week.* Children share something they have written and something that they have read, read to or with a younger child, and do research related to a topic. One-third of the class revises, edits, and publishes a piece of writing.

TEACHER WISDOM

LINDA LEVELY AND TIMETABLING

Tell us about your timetabling and how you fit in the various components of balanced literacy into your timetable. How does that all work?

Right off the bat I would say that we're always doing a shared reading story and that goes in everywhere. It doesn't matter what the subject is—science, math—so scheduling an actual shared reading time doesn't happen a lot as it's integrated. I do schedule literacy centres, which provide an opportunity to do guided reading lessons with the kids. Not every day, and some weeks it doesn't even happen! Instead, we go through cycles where we are often doing guided reading. Right now as I'm team teaching, we've created a great schedule to try to fit in guided reading. What we do is pair up our classes for calendar. One teacher does calendar with the majority of students while the other does guided reading with a small group. Then we alternate. This calendar time is also used for other things. It just allows my partner and I time to work independently with a child or a small group, and we're able to do shared reading, shared writing during that time, and to get on top of our reading assessment.

How would you say your timetabling changes throughout the year? For instance, is it possible that at the beginning of the year you don't do as much independent work?

Right. Once the children get on to a routine and are used to working in different groups or doing the different activities, then everything runs much smoother. It doesn't take long to build the kids up to that level. But it definitely takes some time to build their confidence and to give them strategies and the resources in the classroom to be able to work independently.

It is important to keep in mind when using the guidelines in either Table 13.1 or 13.2 that the times recommended extend across subject boundaries, since language use is involved in all areas of the curriculum. This is particularly true at the upper elementary level, where a considerable amount of children's language arts activities relate to social studies and science units. Take a look at the Teacher Wisdom box below where Linda Levely briefly describes how she timetables.

As with everything else in language arts, there is no one best time schedule for all classrooms. Just like Linda Levely's practice, we recommend that time schedules be used in a flexible way, extending the time for activities when children are obviously learning and discontinuing activities when they are not. The goal is to consistently provide optimum learning opportunities for your students without becoming a slave to your time schedule.

Organizing Space

When you are assigned your classroom you likely will not have much control over the amount of space or type of equipment or furniture in it, but you will have control over how that space and furniture are arranged. The physical arrangement of the classroom reflects the goals and philosophy of your language arts program.

Whole-Class, Small-Group, and Individual Activities

The children's desks in David Paul's classroom are organized in rows. He uses this physical arrangement at the beginning of the day for large-group instruction when children discuss the minimal-cues message on the chalkboard. On the day we described, he then asked the children to push aside the desks in the middle of the room to create a space for them to sit on the floor while he read them the poem. He preferred this arrangement so the children would be closer to the book and to one another.

In some classrooms, a rug in one corner provides a place for children to come together for whole-class discussions, to listen to their teacher read, and to share what they have accomplished. This setup can be used even in junior classrooms. Children can also be organized for whole-class activities by having their desks placed together in groups, as shown in Figure 13.1, so that everyone can view the board and screen. Tables can easily replace groups of desks in this arrangement.

In David Paul's classroom, children work together in groups in many different locations:

- They play learning games at a table placed at the perimeter of the room.
- They sit together in pairs on the floor or at adjacent desks to read books to one another.
- On the day recounted, a small group joined the teacher at a table for a lesson using the directed reading–thinking activity.

The classroom organization depicted in Figure 13.1 places a high value on children working together. In addition to organizing desks in groups, a table on one side provides a place for children to come together to work with the teacher or to work with one another on projects.

In David Paul's classroom, most independent activities are completed by children at their desks. Having desks arranged in rows facilitates independent work, although children are still able to consult with their neighbour if they need help. The children in David's classroom also often find a quiet space on the floor when they are working independently.

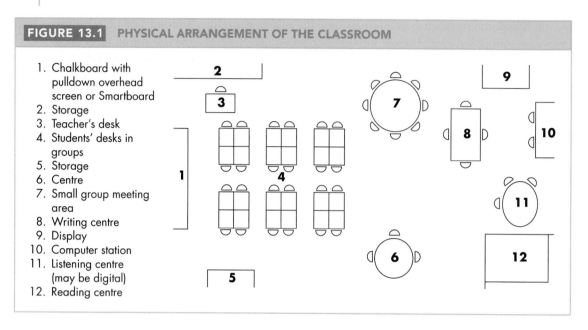

FIGURE 13.1 PHYSICAL ARRANGEMENT OF THE CLASSROOM

1. Chalkboard with pulldown overhead screen or Smartboard
2. Storage
3. Teacher's desk
4. Students' desks in groups
5. Storage
6. Centre
7. Small group meeting area
8. Writing centre
9. Display
10. Computer station
11. Listening centre (may be digital)
12. Reading centre

While the classroom depicted in Figure 13.1 is more conducive to small-group than individual work, children do have individual desks, and there are many spaces around the perimeter of the room where children can go to work alone. The reading centre, in particular, is appropriate for both group and individual reading.

Learning Centres

Many teachers set up learning centres in order to provide opportunities for children to work together in groups. Some centres, such as reading or writing centres, are permanent. Reading centres generally include a classroom library; comfortable rugs, chairs, or cushions; and often a listening centre with taped stories. When you're setting up reading centres, you might want to consider some classic advice, such as:

- Select materials that draw on a range of children's background knowledge and interests.
- Materials should be at a range of level of difficulty.
- Introduce new materials regularly to ensure continued interest.
- Involve children in planning and managing the centres, developing rules for their use, naming them, and keeping them neat (Morrow, 1989).

Writing centres often include a display area for children's writing, materials for writing, and computers and printers. Create centres that include materials for making books, and be sure to place books made by children in the reading centre to share with other children. Remember that books can also include e-books.

Other centres can be less permanent, often being set up on a thematic basis related to topics in social studies, science, and other subject areas (see, for example, the fairy tale centres in Chapter 3). While learning centres can be very useful in facilitating children's language development and cooperative learning, a couple of cautions are in order. Sometimes centres seem to be valued for their own sake rather than for how they contribute to learning and curricular goals. As with all instructional tools, learning centres need to be integrated into the curriculum to maximize their usefulness. Also, with centres, be sure to update them to address the nature of literacy in the 21st century. As such, be sure that insofar as possible **new media** is included in the centres. Add, for instance, a variety of software. To further augment the development of all the language arts, include opportunities for digital voice recordings, materials for making artwork, and other visual communication modes and media such as digital cameras. Often schools will allow classrooms to borrow this kind of equipment from a central bank of equipment. On the topic of where to procure resources for the classroom, see the Teacher Wisdom box below, where Linda Levely talks about setting up her first classroom and subsequent classrooms.

TEACHER WISDOM

LINDA LEVELY AND CLASSROOM SET-UP

Tell us about when you first found out that you had a teaching job.

I was very excited, very overwhelmed, but the overwhelmed part doesn't start sinking in until you're actually in the classroom and see what's there. My first classroom was a junior kindergarten classroom and JK had just been brought in to the province, so when I walked into the classroom there was pretty much nothing, because it had all been taken by the other teachers to use in their classrooms. This would have been in August, so at that point I just had to start talking to my principal and finding out what resources I had to draw on to find the basics—even furniture!

What was the first thing you did with your new classroom?

The first thing I wanted to do was create centres. I really wanted to have some definite kitchen areas, and craft area, definite reading area for the kids to use and other centres depending on where I could find the furniture to go back there. We pulled that together and I quickly learned that your first year of teaching you will spend a lot of your own money. I went out and bought lots of stuff that I knew I could use. That has definitely changed, which is a nice part of many years of teaching.

How do you now collect resources and supplies for your classroom?

I now have accumulated a lot of supplies, and I've learned that you don't have to always put out your own money. Today I scrounge around and talk to the principal and other teachers to see what funding and money is available to buy what I need. And I've also learned that I can make a lot of things and that it does not all have to be commercial products. The students can make things. For instance, when I first started teaching I used a lot of posters

(Continued)

and press-outs directly from books, whereas now, I make my own posters to really customize them to my own teaching style and needs. For example instead of buying a signal-type chart for the kids to know when I want them to look at me and to listen, I've made my own for "freeze threes": it simply says, "Freeze three. Stop, look, and listen." I also make name tags for the kids. I've also learned that when you're setting up the classroom, instead of having everything set up, I like to leave an area now for the kids to personalize and make their own, during that first week of school. So that's taken a lot of pressure off getting ready for September.

How do the students contribute to the classroom setup?

They make the border to go around the bulletin board. They bring in pictures of themselves, their drawings of themselves, work that they have done in the past, and as the year goes on we put up work that they have just done. It's a general area for them hang up work, not a specific subject area but just for them to have as their own area. We do have our usual artwork bulletin board we change with their work. It can be seasonal or just themes that we're talking about, like a science area where we will have key words, pictures, and mind maps.

PLANNING AND ORGANIZING FOR DIVERSITY

There is no one magic way to organize classrooms so that all children's needs are met all the time. The key to effective classroom organization is flexibility in organizing materials, time, space, and children. The challenge of organizing an effective language arts program becomes even greater when we consider, as we discussed in Chapter 1, the diversity of learning needs and funds of knowledge in today's classrooms. The goal of language arts teachers should be to maximize the learning of *all* children in their classrooms. We have designed the balanced literacy framework in this book and its instructional components to support teachers in this endeavour. Moreover, we have maintained throughout that when children have been evaluated as having difficulties with their literacy achievement or when children do not fit the idea of the standard student, educators should critically appraise the context in which this evaluation is taking place, and they should question whose standard is being used, why, and with what effects. What we might always fight against is seeing literacy achievement difficulties or differences (as in the case of **English Language Learners—ELLs**) as a within-child pathology, that is, the view that the child is somehow "sick" or deficient and in need of a cure. Instead, we should see children as "at-promise" (Swadener & Lubeck, 1995) and recognize that our instruction, while it is certainly not the only variable that affects children's achievement, can and does make a difference.

Though the whole of *Constructing Meaning* has been created for all children, we would here like to highlight some considerations for children who are particularly vulnerable in schools, children who struggle with their literacy achievement, particularly their *reading achievement*, as it is such an important piece of **capital**, and ELLs. Accordingly, we have created Boxes 13.4 and 13.5 to collate and highlight significant considerations when you're planning for these children.

BOX 13.4 INSTRUCTIONAL PLANNING CONSIDERATIONS FOR CHILDREN WHO STRUGGLE WITH THEIR LITERACY

1. *Start at the classroom level.* The first, and perhaps best, line of support for all children is an effective classroom literacy program.

2. *Instruction in multiple modes and media.* Children must have the opportunity to express themselves and to allow the various language arts to support each other's development. As such, create opportunities for children to expand their language arts resources through exposure to and instruction in a wide range of modes and media (Heydon, 2007). A practical way to do this is to use the Language Experience Approach and other opportunities for children to represent their understandings of the world as instructional texts (see Chapter 3).

3. *Increased reading and writing time.* In terms of print literacy, whether in the classroom or in an interventionist setting, children need plenty of time to read and write. When children struggle with their literacy, they often spend far more time completing activities related to "bits" of language than actually reading or writing authentic materials (Heydon & Iannacci, 2008). It is through extensive reading and writing of connected texts (not isolated words or letters) that children consolidate reading and writing strategies and develop automaticity (Allington, 2006).

4. *Matching materials, instructional context, and students.* In terms of reading, be sure that children have ample opportunity to be matched with books that they can read independently and that match the instructional context (see Chapters 4 and 5) (Allington, 2007).

5. *Increased literacy instruction.* Teachers need to devote more time to explicit instruction for children who have difficulty with their literacy achievement. Rather than providing instruction in short time blocks once or twice per week, effective intervention involves consistent, daily reading instruction, which is the cornerstone of the popular print literacy intervention program, *Reading Recovery* (Clay, 1993).

6. *Instruction in fluency.* Children need ample opportunities to develop their reading fluency (Allington, 2007) and writing fluency. It may be helpful to build these from children's oral fluency (Bromley, 2007).

7. *Quality instruction.* Instructional time alone is not sufficient. For instruction or intervention to be most effective, quality of instruction is also important. Indeed it may be that "knowledgeable teachers are what matter most for students' literacy achievement" (Donnelly, Morgan, DeFord, Files, Long, et al., 2005, p. 336). Being knowledgeable means engaging in and developing an "awareness of the complexities of educational practice and an understanding of and commitment to a socially just, democratic notion of schooling" (Kincheloe, 2004, p. 50). This requires that teachers be "knowledge producers" and "knowledge workers who pursue their own intellectual development" within a "community of practice" (p. 51). That is, teachers need to work together and pursue ongoing professional development (Hibbert, Heydon, & Rich, 2007).

(Continued)

8. When intervention is needed:

   a. *Make it early.* Most educators agree that when intervention for literacy difficulties is needed, it should occur early. Children who are behind their peers can fall farther and farther behind. Prolonged failure has negative consequences for children's self-concepts, which in turn negatively affects their learning. By intervening in grade 1, the cycle of failure can be prevented, and this is how reading recovery (Clay, 1993) operates.

   b. *Make it individual or small-group instruction.* The most effective intervention involves instruction for individuals or small groups (no more than four or five children).

   c. *Coordinate with excellent classroom instruction.* Finally, intervention is more effective when the children's total program is taken into consideration. For maximum impact, children need to receive excellent and coordinated instruction both in their classroom and intervention programs (Allington & Baker, 2007).

BOX 13.5   **CONSIDERATIONS FOR PLANNING FOR ENGLISH LANGUAGE LEARNERS**

1. *Create opportunities for immersion, use, and feedback.* Culture and communication are closely linked, so learning a new language also involves learning a new culture (Winzer & Mazurek, 1998). Teachers must thus ensure that ELLs have great exposure to expert language users within context, opportunities to use the language, and feedback as to how well they are approximating the model (Sheppard, 2001).

2. *Not too much too fast and language in context.* Acquisition of a new language may be the result of **comprehensible input**, that is, exposure to the new language that is only slightly above where the child already is (Krashen, 1982). As this is not always possible for a teacher in a classroom, teachers must attempt different ways of presenting material and different opportunities to encourage language acquisition. The use of play, drama, poetry, and music within the classroom can offer teachers diverse ways in helping ELL students increase their linguistic competence, cultural understanding, and analytical thinking skills. Play is especially important as it helps to "establish bonds of friendship among children who could not communicate well in English" (Silver, 1999, p. 66), allows ELLs to exhibit a sense of confidence that, in many other areas, are "not otherwise evident" (p. 68), and permits ELLs to develop a sense of autonomy (Iannacci, 2005).

3. *Create a sense of safety.* Teachers must remember that ELLs might well be dealing with a host of stresses that can, of course, affect their learning. For instance, many ELLs, if they have just moved to a new country, may be feeling "fear," "confusion," and "alienation," including grieving for a lost homeland and culture (Gonzalez-Ramos & Sanchez-Nester, 2001). Consequently, teachers need to be patient with ELLs and allow them to participate in their own time and through structured choice in classroom activities. Teachers should give children the chance to prepare or rehearse contributions before they perform them in a whole-class setting and offer them choice over activities and texts. In this way, ELLs may have fewer unknowns and be able to better connect with, for instance, texts, and have a degree of control over the topic (Alford, 2001).

4. *Respect and build on ELLs' funds of knowledge, including first language.* ELLs are not working from a deficit. They come to school with a range of knowledge and skills that can facilitate their English language development and contribute to the classroom community. A strong first language better ensures an easier acquisition of a second language (Cummins, 1994). Teachers can build on ELLs' first language by encouraging students to use their first language and compare it to the new language and by using multilingual bulletin boards and books. As there is considerable overlap or interdependence across languages (Cummins, 2000), it can be extremely helpful for ELLs to have access to texts in their own language within the classroom. It is sometimes beneficial for students to be able to read the text in their own language prior to reading the English text; at other times, it is useful for students to be able to read the text in their first language as a follow-up activity in order to review the information from the English text. It is also an excellent idea to encourage parents to continue supporting their children in terms of reading, writing, speaking, and listening in their first language. Teachers need not worry that using more than one language at a time will confuse children. In fact, if a "program is effective in continuing to develop students' academic skills in both languages, no cognitive confusion or handicap will result; in fact, students may benefit in subtle ways from access to two linguistic systems" (Cummins, 2000, p. 39).

5. *Adjust assessment to reflect the unique language arts development of ELLs.* Different dimensions of the language arts can develop at different times in ELLs. Unlike typically developing English language users, with ELLs, it is not uncommon for print literacy to develop before oral language (Watts-Taffe & Truscott, 2000). In fact, many ELLs go through a normal period of silence where they are taking in what is going on around them. Unfortunately, many educators wrongly assume that this silent period is a problem (Iannacci, 2008b). Teachers therefore need to have an excellent grasp of second language acquisition before jumping to the conclusion that there is something wrong with a child. Teachers may also consult experts in second language acquisition if they are unsure of a child's development. Most schools have English as a Second Language (ESL) teachers or consultants through the school district.

6. As we described in Chapter 1, context-specific social language (e.g., what happens on the playground and at the water fountain) usually develops more quickly than academic language (e.g., what students need to understand content lessons). The first can develop in two years; the second may need five to seven years to develop (Cummins, 1984). Teachers should thus be patient with students' learning and provide necessary scaffolds for content area literacy. Connecting students' background knowledge and experiences with new content can assist with this (Ruiz, Vargas, & Beltran, 2002).

Planning for Aboriginal Children

The balanced literacy framework of *Constructing Meaning* has equally been created with the needs of Aboriginal children in mind. Still, Aboriginal children are also vulnerable in schools, and so let us pause to consider them specifically.

There is a great deal of evidence that literacy is related to sociocultural variables. Literacy levels are lower among the poor than the rich, among rural than urban populations, and among children who are seen as cultural and/or racial *minorities* even when, as in the case of many Aboriginal children in schools, they are the numeric *majority* (Shields, Bishop, & Mazawi, 2005). Several explanations have been given to account for the relative lack of success of children from non-mainstream homes in schools (Jacobs & Jordan, 1993). Most explanations lay the responsibility for low school achievement on the cultural groups themselves. One explanation, now widely discredited, claimed that social class and IQ were largely the result of genetic differences. A more widely held view is that the child's home and community may be at fault by failing to provide the experiences, attitudes, and values the child needs to succeed in school. As a result, proponents of this explanation believe that children arrive at school with deficient language and cognitive development.

Both of these views have been reflected in a century of Aboriginal education in the United States and Canada (Deyhle & Swisher, 1997). Although there is considerable research to show that Aboriginal children and their families are not inherently inferior, attitudes and beliefs of inferiority continue to contribute to a self-fulfilling prophesy for many of these children. The notion of *cultural deprivation*, a term that came into vogue in the 1960s, persists in the minds of many educators and has fuelled assimilationist solutions such as boarding schools and immersion of Aboriginal children in public schools.

To help redress these inequities, elders and educators from the Northwest Territories, Yukon Territory, British Columbia, Alberta, Saskatchewan, and Manitoba produced a curriculum based on what they refer to as an Aboriginal perspective (*Western Canadian Protocol for Collaboration in Basic Education: The Common Curriculum Framework for Aboriginal Language and Culture Programs*, 2000). This perspective reflects the view that survival is dependent upon respectful and spiritual relationships with oneself, other people, and the natural world. Teachers can draw on documents such as this one, as well as the principles of other documents developed expressively by and for teachers of Aboriginal children, to help them with their planning. The First Nations and Métis branch of Saskatchewan learning has a website with such resources (**http://www.sasked.gov.sk.ca/branches/fn-me/learning.shtml**) including *Aboriginal Languages: A Curriculum Guide for Kindergarten to Grade 12*. The principles of this document, while they refer to the acquisition of Aboriginal languages, are helpful to our consideration of language and literacy acquisition in general. These principles include:

- Second language acquisition must occur as holistically as possible.
- Language is used for meaningful purposes.
- The tenets of language acquisition are represented in the communicative approach and thematic base.
- The curriculum is resource-based.
- Language acquisition and communicative competence is supported by an anxiety-free environment.
- The teacher's role is one of observer, adapter, coordinator, facilitator, and motivator.
- Assessment and evaluation strategies and techniques take into account the gradual and ongoing nature of language acquisition: communicative competence and linguistic competence.

ORGANIZING FOR FAMILIES AS PARTNERS

The International Reading Association recommends that teachers implement effective strategies to include parents as partners in the literacy development of their children (Armbruster & Osborn, 2002). This is a recognition that school success begins at home, and that parents are the first and most important people in the education of their children. Research shows that parental involvement of almost any kind is positively related to school achievement in general and that there is a strong relationship between a child's home environment and success in learning to read and write at school. We would like to expand the notion of parents as partners to include family members as partners. We use the term "family" instead of "parent" to indicate that children are raised by a diversity of people, not just a mother and/or father. In fact, children's literacy development can be positively affected by a range of people in the community as well (Gregory, Long, & Volk, 2004). What seems to make an individual's influence particularly significant is if the child values and loves that individual (Hicks, 2002). As we've discussed in Chapter 3, however, school/family partnerships must be seen as a "doin'-it-with-em" rather than a "doin'-it-to-em" situation (Wink, 2005) where schools simply tell families what to do.

Building Partnerships with Families

Including families as partners in their children's literacy development is not a one-way relationship with information going from the teacher to the family. Families can provide valuable information to teachers regarding their children's home literacy practices and funds of knowledge.

One way to promote family involvement is by supporting families to engage in literacy activities at home that complement school literacy. Teachers should think of this as more than mere "homework." Be careful that any language arts work that you ask a child and/or family to complete be meaningful, authentic, and truly complement a balanced literacy program. Homework should never be done just for its own sake, and teachers must be vigilant that homework not place undue expectations or stress on the home and/or child. When thinking about how to support families and children at home, teachers can, for instance,

■ Encourage families to read to and with their children and to talk about books being read. Teachers can accomplish this by informing families of the importance of independent reading and by encouraging them to help their children get a library card and use their local public library. Library use, however, might not "just happen"; thus, schools can introduce children first to public libraries and teach children how to use their services. Reaching out to families and providing them with the resources to do what it is schools ask of them is crucial.

■ Provide materials and methods for families to use with their children. Book bags for home are one way of doing this (Christie, Enz, & Vukelich, 2003). Each bag contains three or four books and informal, interactive activities for extending children's language and literacy abilities. Each bag may also contain two response journals (one for the child and one for the family). For families who speak a language other than English, teachers might include a book on tape to accompany the print text and a tape recorder. Each bag includes an inventory so families and children can ensure that they return everything in the bag. A word of caution: In her own teaching, Rachel learned that some families find the book bag very stressful, as they worry that if something is lost they will not be able to pay to replace it. Teachers need to expect a certain amount of loss, and can help to defray some of the inconvenience and cost of this by working with school administration to budget for extra books, procuring multiple copies of books, using used books, and sending home paper "take-home" books that are teacher-, child-, or publisher-made.

- Build bridges between home and school literacy by including books in the bag from the family's culture, by having children interview older relatives in families with a strong oral tradition, and by inviting family members to the classroom to share their literacy traditions (Armbruster & Osborn, 2002).

- Set up a homework club or see if there are homework clubs in the community to provide support to children when families may be unable to help with homework because of academic challenges, shift work, etc.

Another way teachers can encourage involvement of families is by communicating with them about language arts instruction in their classroom. Family–teacher conferences and open houses are common ways to do this, but it is better to use the following strategies to keep families informed throughout the year:

- Invite families into the classroom as observers, guest speakers, and volunteers.

- Send home letters, newsletters, and students' work. Along with samples of a student's work, teachers send an explanation of the nature of the assignment and what it tells about the child's school progress. Linda Levely, like many other teachers, enjoys sending home a summer letter to the children who will be entering her classroom in the fall. This helps break the ice and defray some beginning of school jitters.

- Call or visit families. This will be most effective if at least some of the time the teacher is calling to talk about what the child does well at school (Armbruster & Osborn, 2002).

Teachers also need, as we discussed in Chapter 3, to see families as curricular informants— that is, as people who have some input into the curriculum. Making communication and resource sharing reciprocal is one of the ways to accumulate the information necessary to accomplish this.

TEACHER WISDOM

CATHERINE HUNTER AND CLOSING THOUGHTS ON BEING A LANGUAGE ARTS TEACHER

As a language arts teacher, what are the top three things you need to know, do, and value?

First, you have to value the child and appreciate that every child brings a different set of gifts to the learning experience and that each child will take away a different set of gifts. Second, you need to value yourself as a human being with all your imperfections and shortcomings and then as a teacher who is always a work in progress. Third, you need to really understand that there is no single right answer, no one way of teaching language arts. The answer doesn't come in a prepackaged kit—it comes from reflective practice. What this means for a teacher of language arts is that you need to use all your senses to understand your students and be open to using a variety of resources and tools to accomplish what you are trying to do.

SUMMARY

No organizational structure is best for all classrooms, Instead, teachers must use their professional decision making to take into account multiple aspects of the classroom as they plan, such as materials, time, space, and children. As veteran elementary teacher Catherine Hunter explains in the Teacher Wisdom box above this requires professional discernment.

Teachers must consider myriad factors when planning, including what resources to use. Traditionally, basal reading series have provided the material for language arts programs throughout Canada and the United States. More recently, there has been a movement to increased use of children's literature and nonbook materials as well. Whether or not teachers choose to use a basal series, we believe that it is important that teachers make a wide range of materials available. These materials need to reflect the range of cultural backgrounds and the knowledge and skill levels of the children. Many teachers select and organize materials according to themes, but the most important criterion to use when selecting any material, whether a book, magazine, videotape, or computer program is the extent to which it is consistent with the philosophy of the language arts program and will contribute to children's language learning.

When making decisions about the organization of time, space, and children, teachers need to provide for whole-class instruction, small-group work, and independent practice. Groupings should be fluid, temporary, and based on multiple factors, not simply a child's level of achievement. Ability groups have traditionally dominated language arts classrooms, but more educators are now recommending a range of grouping practices to meet the diverse abilities and interests of children. These include interest, research, special needs, and paired groupings. Cooperative learning rather than individual competition is perhaps best in keeping with a balanced literacy agenda. Learning centres are one way to encourage children to work in groups. It is also important that children have opportunities to use the language arts independently each day and that they have some structured choice within these opportunities. Allocating time for one or two large daily time blocks for language arts provides flexibility and facilitates integration.

One of the biggest challenges language arts teachers face is meeting the needs of all children in their classrooms. While all children are unique, educational research has provided us with some basic understandings for consideration for teaching children who struggle in their literacy achievement and for ELLs. Teachers must also be sensitive to the unique linguistic and cultural needs of Aboriginal children.

Another challenge for teachers is how to include families as partners in the language and literacy development of their children. Teachers build partnerships by supporting families to work with their children at home on literacy activities that complement school literacy, by communicating with parents about the language arts instruction in their classrooms, and by ensuring that the classroom literacy program builds on home literacy.

TALKING POINTS

Veteran upper elementary teacher Alison Ogilvie has this advice for teachers regarding classroom setup:

1. Students should know that they have entered a place where they can take risks and where they can trust their teacher to acknowledge what they know and who they are as well as appreciate their effort.

2. The teacher's support should be evident: time lines, word walls, subject charts, wall text that prompts, class code of student and teacher rights and responsibilities, and supportive quotes that help create this feeling.

3. Areas should be available to display work and spots where the students can personalize and "manage" the area themselves.

4. The space needs to be organized so the "choreography" of the classroom can occur for both effective teaching and support.

5. Teachers should consider including a teacher/student area that lists strategies and has exemplars, teacher-made and student-made models, and frameworks that are not commercially produced but very much related to the learning and can build throughout the year.

6. Supplies need to be obvious, central, and available so the learning "flows."

7. Teachers should display their passion for literacy with "in your face" choices of literature and ways of responding; strong encouragement of questioning and opinions; and many Read-Alouds.

8. Teachers should consider how to make connections to the students' lives and the larger issues around them evident in their choice of books, posters, music, technology, and creative use of space.

9. Desks should be easy to move into various configurations and the students should be trained in the first days of school to help make these moves quickly.

10. Planning needs to include reciprocal teaching and lots of opportunity for metacognition.

Now that you've read Alison's advice, think and then share with your colleagues:

1. Which aspects of Alison's list ring true for you? What might you add here? What might you change? Upon what experience and knowledge have you drawn in your evaluation of this list?

2. How might you organize your time, space, and students to accomplish the goals in the list you've identified as important?

3. Right now, which of these goals do you feel you could best accomplish? What more do you need to know or do in order to reach all of the goals you feel to be important?

PROFESSIONAL RESOURCES

Linda Levely recommends ...

Morrow, L. M. (2003). *Organizing and managing the language arts block: A professional development guide.* New York: The Guilford Press.

Going to workshops and talking with colleagues is one of the greatest professional development activities. This book is the next best thing. It gives us an account of 24 different teachers' classrooms and how they organize their classrooms for balanced literacy teaching.

Comber, B. & Kamler, B. (Eds.). (2005). *Turn-around pedagogies: Literacy interventions for at-risk students.* Newton, New South Wales: Primary English Teaching Association.

Like the book above, this terrifically friendly and readable little book is also like peeking into your next-door neighbour's classroom. It is written by teachers for teachers, and describes in the first person a special literacy-related professional development program where newer and more established teachers paired up to see what they could learn together about creating programs that could support the students they found hard to reach.

Ontario Ministry of Education and Training. (N.d.). *Many roots, many voices: Supporting English language learners in every classroom: A practical guide for Ontario educators.* Toronto: Author. Available at: http://www.edu.gov.on.ca/eng/document/manyroots/manyroots.pdf.

Ontario Ministry of Education and Training. (2001). *The Ontario curriculum grades 1–8, English as a second language and English literacy development: A resource guide.* Toronto: Author: Available at: http://www.edu.gov.on.ca/eng/document/curricul/esl18.pdf.

Both of these guides offer important information to help teachers assess, plan for, and understand English Language Learners. These are excellent companions for any curriculum document.

APPENDIX

CHILDREN'S LITERATURE BY GRADE LEVEL: FICTION AND NONFICTION FOR RECREATIONAL READING

Preschool to Grade 1

FICTION

Adoff, A. (1991). *Hard to be six.* New York: Lothrop, Lee & Shepard.

Ahlberg, J. and Ahlberg, A. (1978). *Each peach pear plum.* London: Kestrel Books.

Alborough, J. (1992). *Where's my teddy?* Cambridge, MA: Candlewick Press.

Brett, J. (1999). *Gingerbread baby.* New York: G.P. Putnam's Sons.

Brown, M. W. (1982). *Goodnight moon.* New York: HarperCollins.

Brown, R. (1985). *The big sneeze.* New York: Mulberry Books.

Browne, A. (1985). *Willie the champ.* New York: Knopf.

Carle, E. (1968). *The very hungry caterpillar.* New York: World Books.

Day, A. (1985). *Good dog, Carl.* New York: Simon & Schuster.

❧ Fernandes, E. (2000). *Sleepy little mouse.* Toronto: Kids Can Press.

Franco, B. (1994). *Tina's taxi.* New York: Scholastic.

❧ Gay, M. (1999). *Stella, star of the sea.* Toronto: Groundwood Books.

❧ Gay, M. (2002). *Stella, fairy of the forest.* Toronto: Douglas & McIntyre.

Gravett, E. (2005). *Wolves.* London: Macmillan Children's Books.

Harter, D. (2003). *Walking through the jungle.* [Text in English and Arabic]. London: Mantra Duets.

Hutchins, P. (1969). *Rosie's walk.* London: Bodley Head Press.

❧ Levert, M. (2001). *An island in the soup.* Toronto: Groundwood Books.

Lewis, J. P. (1990). *A hippopotamus's.* New York: Dial Books for Young Readers.

Martin, B, Jr. (1970). *Whistle, Mary, whistle.* New York: Holt, Rinehart and Winston.

❧ Morgan, A. (2001). *Matthew and the moonlight wrecker.* Toronto: Stoddart Kids.

Ormerod, J. (1981). *Sunshine.* Harmondsworth, UK: Puffin/Penguin.

Ormerod, J. (1982). *Moonlight.* Harmondsworth, UK: Puffin/Penguin.

Parr, T. (2003). *The family book.* New York: Little Brown.

Rathmann, P. (1994). *Goodnight, gorilla.* New York: G. P. Putnam's Sons.

Rosen, M. and Oxenbury, H. (1989). *We're going on a bear hunt.* London: Walker Books Ltd.

❧ Schwartz, R. (2001). *The mole sisters and the moonlit night.* Toronto: Annick Press.

Sis, P. (1998). *Fire truck.* New York: Greenwillow Books.

Sis, P. (2001). *Ballerina!* New York: Greenwillow Books.

❧ Vaage, C. (1995). *Bibi and the bull.* Edmonton, AB: Dragon Hill Press.

Waddell, M. (1992). *Can't you sleep, Little Bear?* Cambridge, MA: Candlewick Press.

Waddell, M. (1992). *Owl babies.* Cambridge, MA: Candlewick Press.

Wild, M. and Legge, D. (2001). *Tom goes to kindergarten.* Sydney, Australia: ABC Books.

NONFICTION

Bradley, K. B. (2001). *Pop! A book about bubbles.* New York: HarperCollins Children's Books.

Brown, R. (2001). *Ten seeds.* New York: Alfred A. Knopf/Random House Children's Books.

🍁 Everts, T. and Kalman, B. (1995). *Horses.* Niagara-on-the-Lake, ON: Crabtree Publishing.

🍁 Jocelyn, M. (2005). *ABC×3: English, Espanol, Francais.* Toronto: Tundra Press.

Rockwell, A. (1999). *One bean.* New York: Walker Publishing Company.

Rockwell, A. (2001). *Bugs are insects.* New York: HarperCollins.

🍁 Swanson, D. (2001). *Animals can be so sleepy.* Vancouver: Greystone Books.

Tafuri, N. (1999). *Snowy flowy blowy.* New York: Scholastic Press.

Kindergarten to Grade 2

FICTION

Alma, F. A. and Campoy, F. I. (2003). *Pio peep! Traditional Spanish nursery rhymes* [selected]. [Text in English and Spanish]. New York: Rayo.

🍁 Bailey, L. (2001). *The best figure skater in the whole wide world.* Toronto: Kids Can Press.

Bang, M. (1983). *Dawn.* New York: Mulberry Books.

🍁 Bedard, M. (2000). *The wolf of Gubbio.* Toronto: Stoddart Publishing.

🍁 Bennett, J. (1993). *Machine poems.* Don Mills, ON: Oxford University Press.

Berenstain, S. and Berenstain, J. (1964). *The bike lesson.* New York: Beginner Books.

🍁 Bogart, J. (1997). *Jeremiah learns to read.* Richmond Hill, ON: North Winds Press.

Brett, J. (Illus.). (1991). *The owl and the pussycat.* (Poem by Edward Lear). New York: G.P. Putnam's Sons.

Brown, M. W. (1977). *The important book.* New York: HarperCollins.

Brown, R. (1981). *A dark, dark tale.* New York: Scholastic.

Bunting, E. (1999). *Butterfly house.* New York: Scholastic Press.

Burningham, J. (1977). *Come away from the water, Shirley.* London: Cape.

Cole, B. (1988). *Prince cinders.* New York: G. P. Putnams's Sons.

Crews, D. (1978). *Freight train.* New York: Greenwillow Books.

🍁 Delaronde, D. (2000). *Little Métis and the Métis sash.* Winnipeg: PemmicanPublications, Inc.

🍁 Eyvindson, P. (1994). *The night Rebecca stayed too late.* Winnipeg: Pemmican Publications.

Edwards, P. (1996). *Some smug slug.* New York: HarperCollins.

Galdone, P. (1974). *Little Red Riding Hood.* New York: McGraw-Hill.

🍁 Gillard, D. (2001). *Music from the sky.* Toronto: Groundwood Books.

🍁 Gillmor, J. (2000). *Yuck, a love story.* Toronto: Stoddart Publishing.

🍁 Gilman, P. (1992). *Something from nothing.* Richmond Hill, ON: North Winds Press.

🍁 Gilman, P. (1998). *Pirate Pearl.* Markham, ON: North Winds Press.

Gramatky, H. (1939). *Little Toot.* New York: G. P. Putnam's Sons.

🍁 Gregory, N. (2000). *Wild Girl and Gran.* Calgary, AB: Red Deer Press.

🍁 Hartry, N. (2000). *Jocelyn and the ballerina*. Markham, ON: Fitzhenry & Whiteside.

Hoffman, M. (1991). *Amazing Grace*. New York: Dial.

🍁 Hundal, N. (1999). *Melted star journey*. Toronto: HarperCollins Canada.

🍁 Hutchins, H. (1997). *Shoot for the moon, Robyn*. Halifax, NS: Formac Publishing.

Hutchins, P. (1986). *The doorbell rang*. New York: Greenwillow Books.

🍁 Kusugak, M. (1998). *Arctic stories*. Toronto: Annick Press.

🍁 Leedahl, S. (1999). *The bone talker*. Red Deer, AB: Red Deer Press.

🍁 Leger-Haskell, D. (1990). *Maxine's tree*. Victoria, BC: Orca Books.

🍁 Lesynski, L. (1999). *Dirty dog boogie*. Toronto: Annick Press.

🍁 Little, J. (1991). *Once upon a golden apple*. Markham, ON: Viking.

🍁 London, J. (2001). *What the animals were waiting for*. Markham, ON: Scholastic Canada Ltd.

🍁 Manuel, L. (1997). *Lucy Maud and the Cavendish cat*. Toronto: Tundra Books.

Moser, B. (2001). *The three little pigs*. Boston: Little, Brown & Company.

🍁 Munsch, R. (1985). *Thomas's snowsuit*. Toronto: Annick Press.

🍁 Oberman, S. (1997). *By the Hanukkah light*. Toronto: McClelland & Stewart.

🍁 Oppel, K. (2001). *Peg and the whale*. Toronto: HarperCollins Canada Ltd.

Ormerod, J. (1990). *The frog prince*. New York: Lothrop, Lee & Shepard Books.

Parish, P. (1963). *Amelia Bedelia*. New York: Scholastic Book Services.

Parr, T. (2004). *The peace book*. New York: Little Brown.

Pilon, A. (1972). *Concrete is not always hard*. New York: Xerox Education.

Polacco, P. (1990). *Just plain fancy*. New York: Bantam.

Rand, T. (Illus.). (1990). *My shadow*. (Poem by Robert Louis Stevenson). New York: G.P. Putnam's Sons.

Rylant, C. (1986). *Night in the country*. New York: Bradbury Press.

🍁 Sadler, A. (2001). *Sandwiches for Duke*. Toronto: Stoddart Books.

Sanderson, R. (2001). *Cinderella*. Boston: Little, Brown & Company.

Sis, P. (2000). *Madlenka*. New York: Greenwillow Books.

Siebert, D. (1990). *Train song*. New York: T. Y. Crowell.

Seuss, D. (1957). *How the Grinch stole Christmas*. New York: Random House.

Seuss, D. (1960). *Green eggs and ham*. New York: Random House.

Teague, K. (1991). *Anna goes to school*. [Text in English and Chinese]. London: Magi Publications.

🍁 Thompson, R. (2000). *The follower*. Markham, ON: Fitzhenry & Whiteside.

🍁 Thurman, M. (1993). *One, two, many*. Toronto: Viking Kestrel.

🍁 Tibo, G. (2000). *The cowboy kid*. Toronto: Tundra Books.

Waddell, M. and Oxenbury, H. (1991). *Farmer duck*. London: Walker Books, Ltd.

🍁 Wallace, I. (2000). *Duncan's way*. Toronto: Groundwood Books.

Ward, H. (2001). *The animals' Christmas carol*. Brookfield, CN: The Millbrook Press. (All ages)

🍁 Wilson, B. (2001). *A fiddle for Angus*. Toronto: Tundra Books.

NONFICTION

Baker, J. (1987). *Where the forest meets the sea*. New York: Greenwillow Books.

Bernard, R. (2001). *Insects*. Washington, DC: National Geographic Society.

Bunting, E. (1993). *Red fox running*. New York: Houghton Mifflin Company.

Cole, H. (1998). *I took a walk*. New York: Greenwillow Books.

Cowley, J. (1999). *Red-eyed tree frog*. New York: Scholastic Press.

Davies, N. (2001). *Bat loves the night*. Cambridge, MA: Candlewick Press.

Demarest, C. L. (1939). *Firefighters A to Z*. Eau Clair, WI: E. M. Hale.

❦ Douglas, A. (2000). *Before you were born: The inside story!* Toronto: Owl Books.

George, T. C. (2000). *Jellies: The life of jellyfish*. Brookfield, CN: Millbrook Press.

Grindley, S. (1997). *Polar star*. Atlanta, GA: Peachtree Publishers.

Horenstein, H. (1999). *A is for...? A photographer's alphabet of animals*. San Diego: Gulliver/ Harcourt Brace.

Kessler, C. (2001). *Jubela*. New York: Simon & Schuster Books.

King, D. (1997). *The flight of the snow goose*. London: HarperCollins.

❦ Kusugak, M. (1996). *My Arctic 1, 2, 3*. Toronto: Annick Press.

Pfeffer, W. (2003). *The shortest day: Celebrating the winter solstice*. New York: Dutton Children's Books.

Posada, M. (2000). *Dandelions: Stars in the grass*. Minneapolis, MN: Carolrhoda Books/ Lerner.

Zuchora-Walske, C. (2000). *Leaping grasshoppers*. Minneapolis, MN: Lerner Publications.

Grade 2 to Grade 3

FICTION

Ahlberg, A. and Briggs, R. (2001). *The adventures of Bert*. Toronto: Penguin Books. Ltd.

Bagert, B. (2007). *Shout: Little poems that roar*. New York: Dial Books for Young Readers.

Bannerman, H. (1899). *The story of Little Black Sambo*. New York: Frederick A. Stokes and Company.

Bannerman, H. and Marcellino, F. (1996). *The story of Little Babaji*. New York: Michael di Capua Books (HarperCollins).

Bishop, C. (1938). *The five Chinese brothers*. New York: Coward, McCann & Geoghegan.

❦ Brownridge, W. (1995). *The moccasin goalie*. Victoria, BC: Orca Books.

❦ Brownridge, W. (1997). *The final game*. Victoria, BC: Orca Books.

Bunting, E. (1994). *Smoky nights*. New York: Harcourt Brace.

DiCamillo, K. (2003). *The tale of Despereaux: Being the story of a mouse, a princess, some soup, and a spool of thread*. Cambridge, MA: Candlewick Press.

❦ Eyvindson, P. (1996). *Red parka Mary*. Winnipeg: Pemmican Publications Inc.

Falconer, I. (2000). *Olivia*. New York: Atheneum.

Fox, M. (1989). *Wilfred Gordon McDonald Partridge*. New York: Kane Miller.

❦ Gilmore, R. (1999). *A screaming kind of day*. Markham, ON: Fitzhenry & Henry.

❦ Graham, G. (1998). *The strongest man this side of Cremona*. Red Deer, AB: Red Deer College Press.

Hoberman, M. A. (1978). *A house is a house for me*. New York: Viking Press.

Howe, D. (1996). *Bunnicula: A rabbit tale of mystery*. New York: Simon & Schuster.

❦ Hume, S. E. (2001). *Red moon follows truck*. Victoria, BC: Orca Book Publishers.

❦ Hundal, N. (2001). *Number 21*. Markham, ON: Fitzhenry & Whiteside.

❦ Jam, T. (1998). *The stoneboat*. Toronto: Groundwood Books.

🍁 Jam, T. (2001). *The kid linet.* Toronto: Groundwood Books.

🍁 Kulyk Keefer, J. (2000). *Anna's goat.* Victoria, BC: Orca Book Publishers.

🍁 Lawson, J. (1992). *The dragon's pearl.* Toronto: Stoddart.

🍁 Lawson, J. (1997). *Emma and the silk train.* Toronto: Kids Can Press.

🍁 Lawson, J. (1999). *Bear on the train.* Toronto: Kids Can Press.

🍁 Lebox, A. (2001). *Wild bog tea.* Toronto: Groundwood Books.

🍁 Lunn, J. (1979). *The twelve dancing princesses.* Toronto: Methuen.

🍁 McNicoll, S. (1996). *The big race.* Richmond Hill, ON: Scholastic Canada.

Median, J. (1999). *My name is Jorge: On both sides of the river.* Honesdale, PA: Boyds Mills.

🍁 Miller, R. (2002). *The bear on the bed.* Toronto: Kids Can Press.

🍁 Mollel, T. M. (1999). *My rows and piles of coins.* Markham, ON: Clarion Books.

🍁 Morck, I. (1996). *Tiger's new cowboy boots.* Red Deer, AB: Red Deer College Press.

Polacco, P. (1988). *Thank you, Mr. Falker.* New York: Philomel Books.

🍁 Munsch, R. (1980). *The paper bag princess.* Toronto: Annick Press.

🍁 Reynolds, M. (1999). *The prairie fire.* Victoria, BC: Orca Book Publishers.

🍁 Reynolds, M. (2000). *The magnificent piano recital.* Victoria, BC: Orca Book Publishers.

🍁 Richler, M. (1975). *Jacob Two-Two meets the hooded fang.* Toronto: Puffin Books.

🍁 Richler, M. (1987). *Jacob Two-Two and the dinosaur.* Toronto: Puffin Books.

🍁 Richler, M. (1995). *Jacob Two-Two's first spy case.* Toronto: McClelland & Stewart, Inc.

Rounds, G. (1993). *The three billy goats Gruff.* New York: Holiday House.

Sanderson, R. (1990). *The twelve dancing princesses.* New York: Little, Brown & Co.

Siebert, D. (1991). *Sierra.* New York: HarperCollins.

🍁 Simmie, L. (1995). *Mr. Got to go.* Red Deer, AB: Red Deer College Press.

Trivizas, E. (1993). *The three little wolves and the big bad pig.* London: William Heinemann Ltd.

🍁 Van Camp, R. (1998). *What's the most beautiful thing you know about horses?* Markham, ON: Children's Book Press.

Van Allsburg, C. (1988). *Two bad ants.* Boston: Houghton Mifflin.

Waddell, M. (1986). *The tough princess.* London: Walker Books.

🍁 Wilson, B. (1995). *Harold and Harold.* Porters Lake, NS: Pottersfield Press.

🍁 Wynne-Jones, T. (1992). *Zoom upstream.* Toronto: Douglas & McIntyre.

NONFICTION

Adler, D. A. (1999). *How tall, how short, how faraway?* New York: Holiday House.

Arnosky, J. (1996). *All about owls.* New York: Scholastic Hardcover.

🍁 Bateman, R. and Archbold, R. (1998). *Safari.* Toronto: Penguin Books Canada/Madison Press.

🍁 Berkowitz, J. (2006). *Jurassic poop: What dinosaurs (and others) left behind.* Toronto: Kids Can Press.

Bishop, N. (2004). *Forest explorer: A life-size field guide.* New York: Scholastic Press.

🍁 Hodge, D. (2000). *The kids book of Canada's railway and how the CPR was built.* Toronto: Kids Can Press.

Kalman, B. and Everts, T. (1994). *Butterflies and moths.* New York: Crabtree Publishing.

Kroll, V. (1994). *The seasons and someone.* New York: Harcourt Brace & Company.

Kudlinski, K. (1999). *Dandelions.* Minneapolis, MN: Lerner Publications.

Lehn, B. (1998). *What is a scientist?* Brookfield, CN: The Millbrook Press.

London, J. (1999). *Baby whale's journey.* San Francisco: Chronicle Books.

❦ Mackin, B. (2001). *Soccer the winning way.* Vancouver: Greystone Books.

McMillan, B. (1995). *Nights of the pufflings.* Boston: Houghton Mifflin Company.

❦ Milich, Z. (2001). *The city ABC book.* Toronto: Kids Can Press.

Montgomery, S. (1999). *The snake scientist.* Boston: Houghton Mifflin.

❦ Morton, A. (1993). *In the company of whales: From the diary of a whale watcher.* Victoria, BC: Orca Books.

Moss, M. (2000). *This is the tree: A story of the baobab.* London: Frances Lincoln Limited.

Pratt-Serafini, K. J. (2001). *Salamander rain: A lake and pond journal.* Nevada City, CA: Dawn Publications.

❦ Pringle, L. (1991). *Batman: Exploring the world of bats.* New York: Charles Scribner's Sons.

Pulley Sayre, A. (2001). *Dig, wait, listen: A desert toad's tale.* New York: Greenwillow Books.

Schlaepfer, G. (2006). *Animal ways: Butterflies.* New York: Marshall Cavendish.

Shapiro, N. (1999). *The Oxford picture dictionary.* (English/Arabic). New York: Oxford University Press.

Singer, M. (2001). *Tough beginnings: How baby animals survive.* New York: Henry Holt Books for Young Readers.

Walker, A. M. (2001). *Fireflies.* Minneapolis, MN: Lerner Publications.

Wallace, K. (1998). *Gentle giant octopus.* Cambridge, MA: Candlewick Press.

Yolen, J. (1998). *Welcome to the icehouse.* New York: G. P. Putnam's Sons.

Yolen, J. (2001). *Welcome to the river of grass.* New York: G. P. Putnam's Sons.

Grade 3 to Grade 4

FICTION

Ahlberg, J. and A. (1993). *It was a dark and stormy night.* London: Viking.

❦ Andrews, J. (2000). *Out of the everywhere.* Toronto: Stoddart Publishing.

Baker, J. (1995). *The story of Rosy Dock.* New York: Greenwillow Books.

Blishen, E. (comp.). (1963). *The Oxford book of poetry for children.* London: Oxford University Press.

Browne, A. (1983). *Gorilla.* New York: Alfred A. Knopf, Inc.

Bunting, E. (1991). *Fly away home.* New York: Clarion.

❦ Carrier, R. (1985). *The hockey sweater.* Montreal: Tundra Books.

Cassedy, S. (1987). *Roomrimes.* New York: Thomas Crowell.

Ciardi, J. (1989). *The hopeful trout and other limericks.* New York: Houghton Mifflin.

Cooney, B. (1982). *Miss Rumphius.* New York: Viking Penguin.

Dahl, R. (1961). *James and the giant peach.* New York: Puffin Books.

Dahl, R. (1982). *Revolting rhymes.* London: Jonathan Cape.

Dahl, R. (1991). *The Vicar of Nibbleswicke.* New York: Viking.

❦ Davidge, B. and Wallace, I. (1993). *The mummer's song.* Toronto: Groundwood Books.

Denslow, S. P. (2002). *Georgie Lee.* New York: Greenwillow Books.

❦ Einarson, E. (2004). *The moccasins.* Penticton, BC: Theytus Books.

❦ Elwin, R. (1990). *Asha's mums.* Toronto: Women's Press.

🍁 Fitch, S. (1997). *If you could wear my sneakers!* Toronto: Doubleday.

Florian, D. (1994). *Beast feast.* New York: Harcourt Brace.

Froman, R. (1974). *Seeing things: A book of poems.* New York: Thomas Y. Crowell.

🍁 Gilmore, R. (2000). *Mina's spring of colours.* Markham, ON: Fitzhenry & Whiteside.

Hyman, T. S. (1983). *Little Red Riding Hood.* New York: Holiday House.

🍁 Highway, T. (2001). *Caribou song.* Toronto: HarperCollins (In Cree and English).

🍁 Highway, T. (2002). *Dragonfly kite.* Toronto: HarperCollins (In Cree and English).

🍁 Highway, T. (2003). *Fox on the ice.* Toronto: HarperCollins (In Cree and English).

Hope, L. L. (1904). *The Bobbsey twins.* New York: Grosset & Dunlap.

Hopkins, L. B. (1987). *Click, rumble, roar: Poems about machines.* New York: Thomas Y. Crowell.

🍁 Jam, T. (1997). *The fishing summer.* Toronto: Groundwood Books/Douglas & McIntyre.

Juster, N. (1989). *As: A surfeit of similes.* New York: William Morrow.

🍁 Keens-Douglas, R. (1992). *The nutmeg princess.* Toronto: Annick Press.

🍁 Kusugak, M. (1990). *Baseball bats for Christmas.* Toronto: Annick Press.

🍁 Kusugak, M. (1992). *Hide and sneak.* Toronto: Annick Press.

🍁 Kusugak, M. (1993). *Northern lights: The soccer trails.* Toronto: Annick Press.

🍁 Laurence, M. (1979). *The olden days coat.* Toronto: McClelland & Stewart.

Lear, E. (1964). *The complete book of nonsense.* New York: Dodd, Mead.

Lester, J. (1996). *Sam and the tigers: A new retelling of Little Black Sambo.* New York: Dial Books for Young Readers.

🍁 McGugan, J. (1994). *Josepha: A prairie boy's story.* Red Deer, AB: Red Deer College Press.

Mitchell, A. (2004). *Daft as a doughnut.* London: Orchard Books.

🍁 Munsch, R. (1989). *Giant: Or, waiting for the Thursday boat.* Toronto: Annick Press.

Murpurgo, M. (2006). *The amazing journey of Adolphus Tips.* New York: Scholastic.

Norton, M. (1952). *The borrowers.* San Diego: Harcourt.

🍁 Provensen, A. (2001). *The master swordsman and the magic doorway: Two legends from ancient China.* Toronto: Simon & Schuster Books for Young Readers.

🍁 Roberts, K. (2001). *The thumb in the box.* Toronto: Groundwood Books.

🍁 Sanderson, E. (1990). *Two pairs of shoes.* Winnipeg: Pemmican.

Scieszka, J. (1989). *The true story of the three little pigs.* New York: Scholastic.

🍁 Spalding, A. (1999). *Phoebe and the gypsy.* Victoria, BC: Orca Book Publishers.

🍁 Van Camp, R. (1999). *A man called raven.* San Francisco: Children's Book Press.

🍁 Wallace, I. (1994). *Hansel and Gretel.* Toronto: Douglas & McIntyre.

🍁 Wallace, I. (1999). *Boy of the deeps.* Toronto: Groundwood Books.

🍁 Watts, I. M. (2000). *Remember me.* Toronto: Tundra Books.

White, E. B. (1952). *Charlotte's web.* New York: Harper & Row.

White, E. B. (1973). *Trumpet of the swan.* New York: Harper & Row.

Wiesner, D. (1988). *Free fall.* New York: Lothrop, Lee & Shepard Books.

Woods, A. (1982). *As quick as a cricket.* New York: Child's Play International.

NONFICTION

Bailey, D. (1990). *Animal world: Butterflies.* New York: National Education Corp.

Baker, J. (1991). *Window.* New York: Greenwillow Books.

Biesty, S. (2002). *Gold quest.* New York: Hodder Children's Books.

Collard, S. B. (2000). *The forest in the clouds.* Watertown, MA: Charlesbridge.

Dewey, J. O. (1999). *Antarctic journal: Four months at the bottom of the world.* New York: HarperCollins Publishers.

✤ Funston, S. (2000). *Mummies (Strange Science).* Toronto: Owl Books.

✤ Galloway, P. (2003). *Archers, alchemists and 98 other medical jobs you might have loved or loathed.* Toronto: Annick Press.

✤ Godkin, C. (1989). *Wolf Island.* Markham, ON: Fitzhenry & Whiteside.

✤ Godkin, C. (1997). *Sea otter inlet.* Markham, ON: Fitzhenry & Whiteside.

✤ Granfield, L. (1997). *Silent night.* Toronto: Tundra Books.

✤ Greenwood, B. (2001). *Gold rush fever: A story of the Klondike, 1898.* Toronto: Kids Can Press.

✤ Hancock, P. (1998). *The kids book of Canadian prime ministers.* Toronto: Kids Can Press.

✤ Harrison, T. (1992). *O Canada.* Toronto: Kids Can Press.

Hurst, C. O. (2001). *Rocks in his head.* New York: Greenwillow Books.

Kalman, B. (1998). *Pioneer life: From A to Z.* New York: Crabtree Publishing.

Levine, S. and Johnston, L. (2000). *The science of sound and music.* New York: Sterling Publishing.

✤ MacLeod, E. (2004). *Hellen Keller: A determined life.* Toronto, Kids Can Press.

Martin, J. B. (1998). *Snowflake Bentley.* Boston: Houghton Mifflin.

Maydak, M. (2001). *Salmon stream.* Nevada City, CA: Dawn Publications.

✤ Owens, A. M. and Yealland, J. (1999). *Canada's maple leaf: The story of our flag.* Toronto: Kids Can Press.

Redman, I. (2001). *The elephant book: For the Elefriends campaign.* London: Walker Books.

✤ Rhodes, R. (2001). *A first book of Canadian art.* Toronto: Owl Books/Greey de Pencier Books. (All ages)

✤ Skreslet, L. and Macleod, E. (2001). *To the top of Everest.* Toronto: Kids Can Press. (All ages)

✤ Szpirglas, J. (2004). *Gross universe: Your guide to all disgusting things under the sun.* Toronto, Maple Tree Press.

Truss, L. (2006). *Eats, shoots & leaves: Why, commas really do make a difference!* New York: G. P. Putnam's Sons.

Grade 4 to Grade 5

FICTION

Avi. (2000). *Crispin: The cross of lead.* New York: Hyperion.

Babbitt, N. (1975). *Tuck everlasting.* New York: Farrar, Straus and Giroux.

Balliett, B. (2004). *Chasing Vermeer.* New York: Scholastic Press.

Bauer, M. D. (1986). *On my honor.* New York: Bantam Doubleday Dell.

✤ Booth, D. (1989). *Till all the stars have fallen.* Toronto: Kids Can Press.

✤ Booth, D. (1995). *Images of nature: Canadian poets and the Group of Seven.* Toronto: Kids Can Press.

Browne, A. (1981). *Hansel and Gretel.* London: Julia MacRae Books.

Browne, A. (1986). *Piggybook.* New York: Alfred A. Knopf.

Browne, A. (1989). *The tunnel.* London: Julia MacRae Books.

Browne, A. (1998). *Voices in the park*. New York: DK Publishing.

Burnett, F. H. (1962). *The secret garden*. New York: Dell.

Byars, B. (1996). *Dead letter*. New York: Viking.

❦ Chamberlain, P. (2006). *Chasing the moon*. Winlaw, BC: Sono Nis Press.

Choldenko, G. (2004). *Al Capone does my shirts*. New York: G. P. Putnam's Sons.

Coerr, E. (1977). *Sadako and the thousand paper cranes*. New York: G. P. Putnam's Sons.

Coerr, E. (1993). *Sadako*. New York: G.P. Putnam's Sons.

Collington, P. (1997). *A small miracle*. New York: Alfred Knopf.

❦ Cumyn, A. (2002). *The secret life of Owen Skye*. Toronto: Groundwood Books.

Curtis, C. P. (1995). *The Watsons go to Birmingham—1963*. New York: Bantam Doubleday Dell/ Delacorte.

Dahl, R. (1983). *The witches*. New York: Farrar, Straus and Giroux.

DiCamillo, K. (2000). *Because of Winn-Dixie*. Cambridge, MA: Candlewick.

DiCamillo, K. (2006). *The miraculous journey of Edward Tulane*. Cambridge, MA: Candlewick Press.

Giff, P. R. (1997). *Lily's crossing*. New York: Delacorte Press.

❦ Godfrey, M. (1994). *Just call me Boom Boom*. Richmond Hill, ON: Scholastic Canada.

❦ Godfrey, M. and O'Keeffe, F. (1991). *There's a cow in my swimming pool*. Richmond Hill, ON: Scholastic Canada Ltd.

Graham, K. (1908). *The wind in the willows*. New York: Charles Scribner's Sons.

Hughes, T. (1968). *The iron man*. London: Faber and Faber.

Hughes, T. (2007). *Collected poems for children*. New York: Farrar, Straus and Giroux.

Jacques, B. (1987). *Redwall*. New York: Philomel.

Jeffers, S. (Illus.). (1976). *Stopping by woods on a snowy evening*. (Poem by Robert Frost). New York: Dutton Books.

Jeffers, S. (Illus.). (1982). *Wynken, Blynken and Nod*. (Poem by E. Field). New York: E. P. Dutton.

❦ Lottridge, C. B. (1992). *Ticket to Curlew*. Toronto: Groundwood Books.

MaCaulay, D. (1995). *Shortcut*. Boston: Houghton Mifflin.

❦ MacGregor, R. (1997). *The Screech Owls series*. Toronto: McClelland & Stewart.

❦ Major, K. (2000). *Eh? To Zed: A Canadian ABeCedarium*. Calgary, AB: Red Deer Press.

Mayer, M. (1989). *The twelve dancing princesses*. New York: Morrow.

❦ Mollel, T. (1990). *The orphan boy*. Toronto: Oxford University Press.

Montgomery, L. M. (1908). *Anne of Green Gables*. London: L. C. Page & Company.

❦ Morin, P. (1998). *Animal dreaming: An aboriginal dreamtime story*. Toronto: Stoddart Kids.

❦ Muller, R. (2001). *The happy prince*. Toronto: Stoddart Kids.

Naylor, P. R. (2003). *Bernie Magruder and the bats in the belfry*. New York: Athenium Books for Young Readers.

❦ Oberman, S. (1994). *The always prayer shawl*. Honesdale, PA: Boyds Mills Press.

❦ Oberman, S. (2000). *The wisdom bird: A tale of Solomon and Sheba*. Honesdale, PA: Boyds Mills Press.

Paterson, K. (1992). *The king's equal*. New York: HarperCollins.

Pearce, P. (1958). *Tom's midnight garden*. London: Oxford University Press.

❦ Pendziwol, J. (2005). *The red sash*. Toronto: Groundwood Books.

Prelutsky, J. (1983). *The Random House book of poetry*. New York: Random House.

Prelutsky, J. (1984). *The new kid on the block.* New York: Greenwillow Books.

✤ Priest, R. (1993). *Day songs, night songs.* Toronto: Groundwood Books.

Rand, T. (Illus.). (1993). *Arithmetic.* (Poem by Carl Sandburg). New York: Harcourt Brace.

Raskin, E. (1990). *The westing game.* Morton Grove, IL: Albert Whitman & Co.

Rosen, M. (2007). *Something's drastic.* London: Collins.

Sandburg, C. (1944). "Fog." In *Chicago poems.* New York: Harcourt Brace & Co.

Schwartz, A. (1981). *Scary stories to tell in the dark.* New York: HarperCollins.

✤ Scrimger, R. (1998). *The nose from Jupiter.* Toronto: Tundra Books.

✤ Scrimger, R. (2000). *A nose for adventure.* Toronto: Tundra Books.

✤ Sharmat, M. W. (2006). *Nate the Great talks turkey.* New York: Delacorte Press.

Siebert, D. (2002). *Motorcycle song.* New York: HarperCollins, 2002.

Silverstein, S. (1981). *A light in the attic.* New York: Harper & Row.

Snicket, L. (1999). *The bad beginning (A series of unfortunate events). Book 1.* New York: HarperCollins.

Snicket, L. (2002). *Lemony Snicket: The unauthorized autobiography.* New York: HarperCollins.

✤ Spalding, A. (1995). *Finders keepers.* Victoria, BC: Beach Holme.

Steig, W. (1976). *The amazing bone.* New York: Farrar, Straus and Giroux.

✤ Taylor, C. (1987). *The doll.* Toronto: Douglas and McIntyre.

Valentine, J. (1994). *One dad, two dads, brown dad, blue dad.* Boston: Alyson Wonderland Publications.

✤ Valgardson, W. D. (1996). *Sarah and the people of Sand River.* Toronto: Groundwood Books.

✤ Valgardson, W. D. (1997). *Garbage Creek.* Toronto: Groundwood.

Van Allsburg, C. (1987). *The Z was zapped.* New York: Houghton Mifflin.

Van Allsburg, C. (1992). *The widow's broom.* New York: Houghton Mifflin.

Whitman, R. (1968). "Listening to grownups quarrelling." In *The marriage wig and other poems.* New York: Harcourt Brace & Co.

Wiesner, D. (1991). *Tuesday.* New York: Clarion.

Winthrop, E. (1985). *The castle in the attic.* New York: Bantam Skylark.

Young, E. (Illus.). (1988). *Birches.* (Poem by Robert Frost). New York: Henry Holt & Company.

NONFICTION

Anholt, L. (1999). *Stone girl, bone girl: The Story of Mary Anning.* New York: Orchard Books.

Atkins, J. (1999). *Mary Anning and the sea dragon.* New York: Farrar, Straus & Giroux.

✤ Beatty, O., and Geiger, J. (1992). *Buried in ice: Unlocking the secrets of a doomed Arctic voyage.* Mississauga, ON: Random House.

✤ Brewster, H. (2004). *On Juno Beach: Canada's D-Day heroes.* Markham, ON: Scholastic Canada/Madison Press.

✤ Brewster, H. (2006). *At Vimy Ridge: Canada's greatest World War I victory.* Toronto: Scholastic.

✤ Bowers, V. (2004). *That's very Canadian!: An exceptionally interesting report about all things Canadian.* Toronto: Maple Tree Press.

Cone, M. (1992). *Come back salmon.* San Francisco: Sierra Club Books for children.

Emberly, R. (1989). *City sounds.* Boston, MA: Little, Brown and Company.

Goodman, S. E. (2001). *Claws, coats and camouflage: The ways animals fit into their world.* Brookfield, CN: Millbrook Press.

Goodman, S. E. (2001). *Seeds, stems and stamens: The ways plants fit into their world.* Brookfield, CN: Millbrook Press.

❦ Granfield, L. (1993). *Cowboy: A kid's album.* Toronto: Groundwood Books.

❦ Granfield, L. (1995). *In Flanders Fields: The story of the poem by John McCrae.* Toronto: Lester Publishing.

❦ Granfield, L. (1999). *High flight: The story of World War II.* Toronto: Kids Can Press.

Kerley, B. (2001). *The dinosaurs of Waterhouse Hawkins.* New York: Scholastic.

❦ Kuitenbrouwer, P. (2004). *Our song: The story of O Canada.* Montreal: Lobster Press.

❦ Levine, K. (2002). *Hana's suitcase.* Toronto: Second Story Press.

❦ Macleod, E. (2003). *Albert Einstein: A life of genius.* Toronto: Kids Can Press.

Napier, M. (2002). *Z is for Zamboni: A hockey alphabet.* Chelsea, MI: Sleeping Bear Press.

❦ Rainey, K. (1999). *Shooting hoops and skating loops: Great inventions in sports.* Toronto: Tundra Books.

Simon, S. (1999). *Tornadoes.* New York: Morrow Junior Books.

❦ Suzuki, D. and Vanderlinden, K. (1999). *You are the earth.* Vancouver: Greystone Books.

❦ Swanson, D. (1994). *Safari beneath the sea.* Vancouver: Whitecap Books.

❦ Tanaka, S. (1996). *Discovering the iceman.* Richmond Hill, ON: Scholastic Canada/Madison Press.

❦ Tanaka, S. (1997). *The buried city of Pompeii: What it was like when Vesuvius exploded (I was there).* Richmond Hill, ON: Scholastic Canada/Madison Press.

❦ Thornhill, J. (2006). *I found a dead bird: The kids' guide to the cycle of life and death.* Toronto: Maple Tree Press.

❦ Tripp, N. (1994). *Thunderstorm!* New York: Dial Books.

❦ Trottier, M. (2004). *Our Canadian flag.* Markham, ON: North Winds Press.

❦ Ulmer, M. (2001). *M is for maple: A Canadian alphabet.* Chelsea, MI: Sleeping Bear Press.

Zoehfeld, K. W. (2001). *Dinosaur parents, dinosaur young: Uncovering the mystery of dinosaur families.* New York: Clarion Books.

Grade 5 to Grade 6

FICTION

❦ Bastedo, J. (2001). *Tracking Triple Seven.* Calgary, AB: Red Deer Press.

❦ Buffie, M. (1987). *Who is Frances Rain?* Toronto: Kids Can Press.

❦ Clark, J. (1995). *The dream carvers.* Toronto: Viking.

Creech, S. (1994). *Walk two moons.* New York: HarperCollins.

Creech, S. (2001). *Love that dog.* New York: HarperCollins.

❦ Doyle, B. (1984). *Angel Square.* Toronto: Douglas & McIntyre.

❦ Dueck, A. (1996). *Anywhere but here.* Red Deer, AB: Red Deer College Press.

DuPrau, J. (2003). *The city of Ember.* New York: Random House.

❦ Ellis, D. (1999). *Looking for X.* Toronto: Groundwood Books.

❦ Ellis, D. (2000). *The breadwinner.* Toronto: Douglas & McIntyre.

❧ Ellis, D. (2002). *Parvana's journey*. Toronto: Groundwood Books.

❧ Ellis, S. (1997). *Back of beyond*. Toronto: Groundwood.

Farmer, N. (1994). *The ear, the eye and the arm*. New York: Puffin Books.

Fenner, C. (1991). *Randall's wall*. New York: HarperCollins.

Fine, A. (2002). *Up on cloud nine*. London: Doubleday.

❧ Freeman, B. (1998). *Prairie fire!* Toronto: James Lorimer & Company Ltd., Publishers.

French, J. (2001). *Hitler's daughter*. London: Collins.

Funke, C. (2001). *The thief lord*. New York: Scholastic.

❧ Galloway, P. (1995). *Aleta and the queen: A tale of ancient Greece*. Toronto: Annick Press.

❧ Galloway, P. (1995). *Atalanta: The fastest runner in the world*. Toronto: Annick Press.

❧ Galloway, P. (1997). *Daedalus and the minotaur*. Toronto: Annick Press.

❧ Harrison, T. (1987). *The cremation of Sam McGee*. (Poem by Robert W. Service). New York: Greenwillow.

❧ Horrocks, A. (1996). *Breath of a ghost*. Toronto: Stoddart Kids.

❧ Horrocks, A. (2000). *Topher*. Toronto: Stoddart Publishing.

❧ Horvath, P. (2001). *Everything on a waffle*. New York: Farrar, Straus and Giroux.

Hughes, L. (1950). "City." In *The Langston Hughes reader*. New York: Harold Ober Associates.

Hughes, L. (1960). "Poem." In *Don't you turn back: Poems by Langston Hughes*. L. B. Hopkins (Ed.). New York: Knopf.

❧ Hughes, M. (1980). *The keeper of the Isis light*. London: Mammoth.

❧ Hughes, M. (1998). (Ed.). *What if … ? Amazing stories*. Toronto: Tundra Books.

❧ Hutchins, H. (1997). *The Prince of Tarn*. Toronto: Annick Press.

Innocenti, R. (1985). *Rose Blanche*. Mankato, MN: Creative Education.

❧ Jocelyn, M. (2000). *Earthly astonishments*. Toronto: Tundra Books.

Kehret, P. (2003). *Escaping the giant wave*. New York: Simon & Schuster Books for Young Readers.

L'Engle, M. (1962). *A wrinkle in time*. New York: Farrar, Straus and Giroux.

Lisle, J. T. (1989). *Afternoon of the elves*. New York: Orchard Books.

❧ Little, J. (2001). *Orphan at my door: The home child diary of Victoria Cope*. Markham, ON: Scholastic Canada Ltd.

❧ Lottridge, C. B. (1997). *Wings to fly*. Toronto: Groundwood Books.

Lowry, L. (1989). *Number the stars*. Boston: Houghton Mifflin.

Lowry, L. (1993). *The giver*. Boston: Houghton Mifflin.

❧ Lunn, J. (1981). *The root cellar*. New York: Charles Scribner's Sons.

Macaulay, D. (1990). *Black and white*. New York: Houghton Mifflin.

❧ McLaughlin, F. (1990). *Yukon journey*. New York: Scholastic, Inc.

❧ McNicoll, S. (1994). *Bringing up Beauty*. Toronto: Maxwell Macmillan.

Newman, L. (1998). *Belinda's bouquet*. Anola, MB: Blue Heron Enterprises.

❧ Oppel, K. (1997). *Silverwing*. Scarborough, ON: HarperCollins.

❧ Oppel, K. (2002). *Firewing*. Toronto: HarperCollins.

Parks, R. (1980). *Playing Beatie Bow*. Ringwood, Australia: Penguin Books Australia.

Paterson, K. (1977). *Bridge to Terabithia*. New York: HarperCollins.

❧ Pearson, K. (1986). *The daring game*. Markham, ON: Puffin Books.

❧ Pearson, K. (1987). *A handful of time*. Markham, ON: Viking Kestrel.

❧ Pearson, K. (1989). *The sky is falling*. Markham, ON: Viking Kestrel.

🍁 Pearson, K. (1996). *Awake and dreaming.* Toronto: Viking.

🍁 Pearson, K. (1998). *This land.* Markham, ON: Viking.

🍁 Pratt, E. J. (1923). "The shark." In *Newfoundland Verse.* Toronto: Ryerson Press.

Roberts, W. D. (1988). *Megan's island.* New York: Macmillan.

Rowling, J. K. (1998). *Harry Potter and the sorcerer's stone.* New York: A. A. Levine Books.

Sachar, L. (2000). *Holes.* New York: Dell Yearling.

Shreve, S. (1987). *Lucy Forever and Miss Rosetree, shrinks.* New York: Alfred A. Knopf.

🍁 Silverthorne, J. (1996). *The secret of Sentinel Rock.* Regina, SK: Coteau Books.

🍁 Smucker, B. (1977). *Underground to Canada.* Toronto: Clarke, Irwin.

Spearman, B. (2005). *Barry, boyhound.* New York: Alfred Knopf Books for Young Readers.

Spinelli, J. (1990). *Maniac Magee.* New York: Little, Brown.

🍁 Sterling, S. (1992). *My name is Seepeetza.* Vancouver: Groundwood Books.

Stine, R. L. (1992). *Welcome to the dead house* (Goosebumps Series). New York: Scholastic.

🍁 Taylor, C. (1987). *The doll.* Toronto: Douglas & McIntyre.

🍁 Truss, J. (1977). *A very small rebellion.* Edmonton: J. M. Lebel Enterprises.

Twain, M. (1963 [1885]). *The adventures of Huckleberry Finn.* New York: Washington Square Press.

Van Allsburg, C. (1986). *The stranger.* Boston: Houghton Mifflin.

Van Draanen, W. (1998). *Sammy Keyes and the hotel thief.* New York: Alfred A. Knopf.

🍁 Walters, E. (2002). *Camp X.* Toronto: Viking.

Wild, M. (1991). *Let the celebrations begin!* Adelaide, Australia: Omnibus Books.

🍁 Wilson, E. (1995). *The Inuk mountie adventure.* Toronto: HarperCollins Canada Ltd.

🍁 Withrow, S. (1998). *Bat summer.* Toronto: Groundwood Books.

🍁 Wynne-Jones, T. (1993). *Some of the kinder planets.* Toronto: Douglas & McIntyre.

🍁 Wynne-Jones, T. (1994). *The book of changes.* Toronto: Douglas & McIntyre.

🍁 Wynne-Jones, T. (1999). *Lord of the fries and other stories.* Toronto: Douglas & McIntyre.

🍁 Yee, P. (1996). *Ghost train.* Toronto: Groundwood Books.

York, C. B. (1986). *Secrets in the attic.* New York: Scholastic.

NONFICTION

🍁 Batten, J. (2002). *The man who ran faster than everyone: The story of Tom Longboat.* Toronto: Tundra Books.

🍁 Bogart, J. (2003). *Emily Carr: At the edge of the world.* Toronto: Tundra Books.

Chorlton, W. (2001). *Woolly mammoth: Life, death and rediscovery.* New York: Scholastic, Inc.

Cummings, P., and Cummings, L. (1998). *Talking with adventurers.* Washington, DC: National Geographic Society.

Fisher, L. E. (1999). *Alexander Graham Bell.* New York: Athenium books for Young Readers.

🍁 Granfield, L. (1997). *Circus.* Toronto: Greenwood Books.

🍁 Granfield, L. (2001). *Where poppies grow: A World War I companion.* Toronto: Stoddart Kids.

🍁 Greenwood, B. (1998). *The last safe house: A story of the underground railway.* Toronto: Kids Can Press.

🍁 Graydon, S. (2003). *Made you look: How advertising works and why you should know.* Toronto: Annick Press.

🍁 Hodge, D. (2006). *The kids book of Canadian immigration.* Toronto: Kids Can Press.

Holler Aulenbach, N. and Barton, H. A. (2001). *Exploring caves: Journeys into the earth*. Washington, DC: National Geographic Society.

Kennett, D. (2000). *Olympia: Warrior athletes of ancient Greece*. New York: Scholastic.

Kodama, T. (1995). *Shin's tricycle*. New York: Walker.

❧ Littlechild, G. (1993). *This land is my land*. Emeryville, CA: Children's Book Press.

Maruki, T. (1980). *Hiroshima no pika*. New York: Lothrop, Lee & Shepard Books.

❧ Raskin, L and Pearson, D. (1998). *52 days by camel: My Sahara adventure*. Toronto: Annick Press.

❧ Ross, V. (2006). *You can't read this: Forbidden books, lost writing, mistranslations and codes*. Toronto: Tundra Books.

❧ Savage, C. (2001). *Born to be a cowgirl*. Vancouver: Greystone Books.

❧ Shoveller, H. (2006). *Ryan and Jimmy and the well in Africa that brought them together*. Toronto: Kids Can Press.

❧ Trottier, M. (2005). *Terry Fox: A story of hope*. Markham, ON: Scholastic Canada.

Webb, S. (2000). *My season with penguins: An Antarctic journal*. Boston: Houghton Mifflin Inc.

Wright-Frierson, V. (1999). *A North American rainforest scrapbook*. New York: Walker & Co.

Grade 6 to Grade 8

FICTION

Almond, D. (1999). *Skellig*. New York: Delacorte Press.

Almond, D. (2000). *Kit's wilderness*. New York: Delacorte Press.

Bagdasarian, A. (2002). *First French kiss and other traumas*. New York: Melanie Kroupa Books/ Farrar, Straus and Giroux.

❧ Barwin, G. (2001). *Seeing stars*. Toronto: Stoddart Kids.

❧ Brandis, M. (1996). *Rebellion: A novel of Upper Canada*. Erin, ON: The Porcupine's Quill.

❧ Brooks, M. (1998). *Bone dance*. Toronto: Groundwood Books.

❧ Buchan, B. (1975). *The dragon children*. Richmond Hill, ON: Scholastic-TAB.

Byars, B. (1997). *Death's door*. New York: Viking.

❧ Carter, A. (2000). *The girl on Evangeline Beach*. Toronto: Stoddart Kids.

Collins, S. (2003). *Gregor the Overlander*. New York: Scholastic Press.

Cooper, S. (1969). *The dark is rising*. New York: Collier Macmillan.

Creech, S. (2000). *The wanderer*. New York: HarperCollins.

❧ Demers, B. (1999). *Willa's new world*. Regina, SK: Coteau Books.

❧ Doyle, B. (2001). *Mary Ann Alice*. Toronto: Groundwood Books.

❧ Ellis, S. (1991). *Pick-up sticks*. Toronto: Groundwood Books.

❧ Fairbridge, L. (1995). *Stormbound*. Toronto: Doubleday Canada.

Frank, A. (1952). *The diary of a young girl: Anne Frank*. New York: Doubleday.

Freeman, S. (1997). *The cuckoo's child*. New York: Disney Press.

❧ Friesen, G. (1998). *Janey's girl*. Toronto: Kids Can Press.

❧ Friesen, G. (2000). *Men of stone*. Toronto: Kids Can Press.

Garner, A. (1967). *The owl service*. London: William Collins & Sons.

Gavin, J. (2001). *Coram boy*. New York: Farrar, Straus and Giroux.

Griffin, A. (1998). *The other Shepards*. New York: Hyperion Books for Children.

Herrick, S. (1999). *The spangled drongo*. St. Lucia, QLD: University of Queensland Press.

Herrick, S. (2002). *Tom Jones saves the world*. St. Lucia, QLD: University of Queensland Press.

Hesse, K. (2001). *Witness*. New York: Scholastic Press.

❧ Holeman, L. (1998). *Mercy's birds*. Toronto: Tundra Books.

❧ Hughes, M. (2002). *The maze*. Toronto: HarperCollins Canada Ltd.

❧ Johnston, J. (1994). *Adam and Eve and Pinch-me*. Toronto: Lester Publishing.

Kindl, P. (1997). *The woman in the wall*. Boston: Houghton Mifflin.

Konigsburg, E. L. (2002). *Silent to the bone*. New York: Aladdin Paperbacks.

❧ Korman, G. (2003). *Dive: Book one, the discovery*. New York: Scholastic Inc.

Lowry, L. (2000). *Gathering blue*. Boston: Houghton Mifflin.

❧ Lunn, J. (1997). *The hollow tree*. Toronto: Alfred A. Knopf Canada.

❧ Martel, S. (1980). *The king's daughter*. Vancouver: Douglas and McIntyre.

Morimoto, J. (1987). *My Hiroshima*. Sydney, Australia: Collins.

Nicholson, W. (2000). *The windsinger*. New York: Mammoth.

O'Roark, F. (2000). *Dovey Coe*. New York: Atheneum Books for Young Readers.

❧ Porter, P. (2005). *The crazy man*. Toronto: Groundwood Books.

Price, S. (2000). *The Sterkarm handshake*. New York: HarperCollins Children's Books.

Pullman, P. (1995). *The golden compass*. New York: Ballantine Books.

Rees, C. (2001). *Witch child*. Cambridge, MA: Candlewick Press.

Rowling, J. K. (2005). *Harry Potter and the half-blood prince*. Vancouver: Raincoast Books.

Rubinstein, G. (1995). *Galax arena*. New York: Simon & Schuster Books for Young Readers.

Silverstein, S. (1964). *The giving tree*. New York: Harper & Row.

❧ Slade, A. (2001). *Dust*. Toronto: HarperCollins.

❧ Stenhouse, T. (2001). *Across the steel river*. Toronto: Kids Can Press.

Thomas, G. and Crossley-Holland, K. (1985). *Tales from the Mabinogian*. New York: Overlook Press.

Tolkien, J.R.R. (1937). *The hobbit*. Boston: Houghton.

❧ Trembath, D. (1996). *The Tuesday Café*. Victoria, BC: Orca Book Publishers.

Wolff, V. (1993). *Make lemonade*. New York: Scholastic Inc.

Winton, T. (1999). *Lockie Leonard, scumbuster*. New York: Margaret K. McElderry Books.

❧ Wynne-Jones, D. (1998). *The lives of Christopher Chant*. New York: Greenwillow Books.

❧ Wynne-Jones, T. (1995). *The maestro*. Toronto: Groundwood Books.

❧ Wynne-Jones, T. (2000). *The boy in the burning house*. New York: A Melanie Kroupa Book/ Farrar, Straus and Giroux.

NONFICTION

❧ Ellis, D. (2004). *Three wishes: Palestinian and Israeli children speak*. Toronto: Groundwood Books.

❧ Graydon, S. (2004). *In your face: The culture of beauty and you*. Toronto: Annick Press.

GLOSSARY

aesthetic response is a term coined by American educator Rosenblatt (1989) to describe the enjoyment or appreciation a reader feels while reading a text. An aesthetic response is concerned, not with comprehension, word meanings, recall, or learning, but with the deep personal engagement of reader and text. Aesthetic responses are not necessarily pleasurable; some texts can be deeply moving and cause stress or discomfort rather than pleasure, but this is still considered to be an aesthetic response.

assessment involves collecting and analyzing information about students to help make decisions about what they know, value, and are able to do. The end goal of assessment is to inform future decisions about instruction.

automaticity is the ability to carry out a complex act rapidly and without conscious awareness or control. An important characteristic of automaticity is that an individual can perform a complex skill or act while at the same time performing another that may not be automatic. As readers become proficient and are able to identify most of the words in texts automatically, they are able to direct their mental resources to constructing meaning. Most experts feel that children need to engage in extensive reading to achieve automaticity.

basal reading series are sets of materials for teaching reading and language arts. These series generally consist of teacher guides, student anthologies, workbooks, and supplemental materials such as assessment materials, big books, correlated **trade books**, audiovisual aids, and computer software. Initially, basal series focused almost exclusively on reading, but in recent years they have included other areas of language arts as well. Basal series derive their name from the original intention that they form the basis of a program of instruction in reading.

basic interpersonal communication skills (BICS) refers to context-specific social language, such as what happens in the lunchroom or the playground. BICS is usually developed among second language learners within two years.

capital is a term coined by sociologist Pierre Bourdieu. There are three kinds of capital: economic (referring to financial resources), social (referring to social connections), and cultural (referring to academic and other qualifications).

challenged books are those that groups or individuals have attempted to censor by having them removed from the shelves of libraries, especially in schools. Not all challenges result in the removal of a book. Specific procedures are usually followed in dealing with a challenge to a book, and a committee of parents and teachers usually makes the final decision about whether a book should be removed from a school library.

chapter books are beginning novels for children that are designed to facilitate the reader's transition from a reliance on illustrations for creating meaning (as is done with **picture books**) to a stronger reliance on text. Many chapter books are available for young readers, and a number of publishing companies are producing specific series of chapter books (e.g., Hodgepog Books). Like **picture books**, chapter books include all of the major **genres** of literature. An example of a chapter book is *Harold and Harold* by Budge Wilson (1995).

children's literature is a term used in this book to refer to those print materials (fiction, nonfiction, magazines, and poetry) that possess an aesthetic quality, are written primarily with an audience of young readers in mind, are acknowledged by critics to meet high standards, are well written and illustrated, and provide children with pleasurable and challenging reading experiences.

cognitive academic language proficiency (CALP) refers to the academic language that students need to understand content area lessons and/or texts. Second language learners usually take five to seven years to develop this level of linguistic proficiency.

comprehensible input is used with regard to second language learning and refers to exposure to the new language that is only slightly above where the child already is.

constructivism is a theory of learning in which individuals use their knowledge to build or make meaning. Texts are viewed as providing cues to possible meanings rather than as containing meaning themselves. Readers are viewed as active meaning makers rather than passive receivers of meaning, and, because of variations in background knowledge, they construct variable meanings of the same text.

contemporary realistic fiction is imaginative writing that accurately reflects life as it is lived today. Events and situations in such stories might conceivably happen to people living in the real world. Young readers consistently select contemporary realistic fiction as their preferred **genre**. Stories are often about characters growing up in the world and their manner of coping with the problems and dilemmas of the human condition. Examples of contemporary realistic fiction are *Pick-Up Sticks* by Sarah Ellis (1991) and *The Maestro* by Tim Wynne-Jones (1995).

context cues are knowledge and linguistic cues that help a reader construct meaning when reading. Linguistic cues involve both syntactic (**grammar** or word order) and semantic (meaning) aspects of language. When children use context cues, they make predictions and monitor their reading in terms of what sounds right and makes sense.

conventions are "indicators of the way in which *time, space* and *presence* can interact and be imaginatively shaped to create different kinds of meanings in theatre" (Neelands & Goode, 2000, p. 4). Conventions may also be described as specific teaching strategies that can be adapted to engage students' belief and commitment to an imagined context in process drama.

critical literacy goes beyond providing students with conventional language arts skills to equipping them to critically examine how texts reflect power structures and inequalities. It involves interrogating texts from different perspectives and taking action to promote social justice.

cuing systems are the three systems of **semantics**, **syntax**, and **graphophonics** that are used by readers and writers to make meaning from printed symbols. Pictures, diagrams, and charts also act as cues for readers to construct meaning, but *cuing systems* usually refers to the text-based systems discussed in this book.

culturally and linguistically diverse (CLD) refers to students who are learning in a language that is not their mother tongue. This includes students coined as ESL (English as a second language), EAL (English as an additional language) or ELL (English language learner). The term *CLD* recognizes the ties between language and culture, and acknowledges that these learners bring with them to their learning a language and culture.

cursive writing is handwriting in which the letters are connected to one another with a continuous flow from one stroke to another. The most prevalent form of handwriting today is a combination of printing and cursive writing, with printed uppercase letters and cursive lowercase letters.

dialect is a variety of a spoken language used in a geographic region or by members of a social class. Every dialect has distinctive patterns, rules, and features. Regional dialects are much less pronounced now than they were 50 years ago, but speech in the southeastern United States, the north of England, the east coast of Australia, and maritime Canada are examples of dialects that remain distinct. The advent of radio, television, and movies has brought a more standard version of spoken language into our homes and schools.

differentiation in a lesson or activity can allow for children to perform differently on the same learning task. The teacher will not expect all students to make the same learning connections, as students are most likely at various stages in their literacy development.

directionality refers to the way print is written and read. More specifically, students learning to read learn that: (1) print begins at the top of a page and continues to the bottom, (2) we read and write from left to right on the page, (3) the front of a book opens on the right, and (4) directionality is important to the identity of letters.

discourse is a linguistics term used to describe a continuous stretch of spoken or written language longer than one sentence. Frequently, *discourse* is reserved for spoken language and *text* for written language. Discourse is also used to refer to specific topics or types of language (e.g., the discourse of high finance). As well, discourse can be perceived as process and text as product.

early literacy refers to the specific form of literacy practised by young children. This term respects the fact that young children communicate in various ways, and the fact that this communication is not a lesser form of adult communication but is meaningful in its own right.

efferent response is a term coined by American educator Rosenblatt (1989) to describe a response to literature in which the intent is to focus on what can be learned, observed, and taken away from the reading. Focused on gaining information, an efferent response is at the opposite end of the continuum from an aesthetic response.

emergent literacy is a term developed during the early 1980s to refer to the literacy development of young children. Sulzby (1985) defines emergent literacy as the reading and writing concepts, attitudes, and behaviours that precede and develop into conventional literacy. Emergent literacy begins early in children's lives at home, involves interactions with print, and is part of, rather than separate from, reading and writing development.

English as a second language (ESL) is an official term often used by the government or school board in relation to students whose first language is not English.

English language learner (ELL) refers to a student learning English in addition to his/her first language(s).

environmental print is print in the home and community, such as on restaurant signs and cereal boxes. The term is also used to refer to print in the classroom, such as labels, signs, calendars, charts, and lists used to organize the room.

episodes "The first step toward solving the problem of structure in process drama lies in conceiving of the development of the work in units or episodes" (O'Neill, 1995, p. 48). Each self-contained activity within a sequence of activities is an *episode*. Episodes are connected by a common focus or theme to constitute a process drama.

evaluation is a measurement of student performance on a particular skill or set of skills in order to make a judgment about their ability.

expository writing is a form of writing that provides information, detailed explanations, judgments, and supporting examples. It may be persuasive or argumentative writing.

expressive writing is a term used by James Britton (Britton et al., 1975) to describe one of the three **voices** of writing (the others being **poetic** and **transactional**). Expressive writing is found in diaries, journals, and personal letters, in which the writer's intent is to share personal points of view, ideas, thoughts, and questions. Expressive writing aims to communicate the personal identity of the writer.

fantasy is a **genre** of literature that engages and stimulates the reader's imagination and gives free rein to endless possibilities. The reader is taken to worlds where animals and toys can speak, where people can travel across time and into completely fictional worlds. Modern fantasy is rooted in folk tales, myths, and dreams. Examples of modern fantasy literature include *Charlotte's Web* by E. B. White (1952) and *The Dark Is Rising* by Susan Cooper (1969).

fluency is the ability to read text quickly, effortlessly, with appropriate intonation, smoothly, and automatically so that the reader's conscious attention does not need to be directed toward decoding.

funds of knowledge are the various resources students bring with them to school. These resources can be cultural, intellectual, physical, and the like.

genre refers to the different literary and linguistic forms and functions of various texts. **Narrative**, for example, is different in form and function from expository text, which is different again from persuasive or descriptive text. Genre also refers to categories of literature such as myth, fable, poetry, **fantasy**, and **contemporary realistic fiction**. Each of these genres meets different functions and uses a variety of different forms to achieve the intentions of the text.

grammar is an ambiguous term that has been largely replaced today by the term **syntax**. However, where "grammar" is used, it refers to three distinct perspectives on language: (1) systemic-functional grammar, a description of the choices made by language users based on context and intention in order to create meaning (e.g., see Halliday, 1969); (2) generative-transformational grammar, a description of how language actually works as a process and is based on language universals (e.g., see Chomsky, 1957); and (3) prescriptive grammar, focused on the rules of language and how language *should* work. Where most grammar taught in the first part of this century was based on perspective 3 (frequently dealing with inappropriate usage, e.g. of *seed* and *saw*), most grammar taught today is descriptive and functional, and more like perspective 1 or 2.

grand conversations are small group discussions of literature that are usually guided by students. With the careful assistance of their teacher, the students' thoughts and ideas are received and explored. Through listening and conversing, the layers of meaning possible in literature are uncovered and meaning making is enhanced.

graphophonics refers to the print–sound relationship of text. Graphic cues generally include letters, letter clusters, words, and parts of words. **Phonics** refers to the relationships between graphic cues and sounds. Graphophonic cues are one of the **cuing systems** that help readers identify words as they read. They identify words by relating speech sounds to letters and letter clusters.

high fantasy is a **genre** of literature usually involving a quest, elements of the mystical or magical, time travel, and time warps, and frequently takes place in a fictional setting and with a fictional language. Examples include *A Wizard of Earthsea* by Ursula K. Le Guin (1968) and *The Golden Compass* by Philip Pullman (1996). High fantasy is based on mythology (frequently Celtic). Elementary school children are aided in their reading of high **fantasy** when they have some familiarity with mythology.

historical fiction is a **genre** of literature set in a specific place and time in the past. It requires a great deal of research, descriptive detail, and authentic language to be credible. Good historical fiction is both an aesthetic and an efferent reading experience. The reader will learn history from it, and will also appreciate and identify with the lives and concerns of the characters.

hypertext is nonlinear writing. Text is linked so that the reader is able to go through a topic in any order. Readers of hypertext have greater control over what they read and the sequence in which they read it than with traditional texts.

improvise "[A]ctivities of an exercise nature, based upon a source, in which the teacher does not participate in role, but stays outside the action facilitating the work through side coaching" (Morgan & Saxton, 1987, p. 120). The use of this term within this chapter should *not* be confused with that of "improv" or theatre sports.

instructional reading level is the level of reading instruction a child needs in order to make maximum progress learning to read. The material must be just difficult enough to help children develop reading strategies with the support of instruction. On an informal reading inventory, this is the highest level at which a child is able to accurately identify 90 percent of the words and answer 70 percent of the comprehension questions.

intermediate role allows the teacher to convey information in a dispassionate way. It is useful when the imagined leader's goals or motives are inconsistent with the goals of the students in role. See also **opposer role, victim role, leader role**.

interpretation has been defined in many different ways within the field of educational drama. In the Chapter 12 context, the term refers to dramatic activities in which students work with some form of prepared, written text with the purpose of bringing meaning to someone else's words through drama.

intonation is a term most commonly associated with music or chanting. It refers to the vocal patterns created by rising and falling pitch.

invented spelling refers to a child's first attempts at transcribing spoken language into print symbols before learning the conventions of standard spelling. Children pay particular attention to the sounds of language, and invented spelling is a reflection of this focus.

leader role provides safety, familiarity, and guidance for students who are new to drama work. See also **opposer role, victim role, intermediate role**.

levelled text refers to reading materials that represent a progression from more simple to more complex and challenging texts. Some text progressions are based on readability formulas, others on letter–sound relationships, and still others on multiple criteria related to language predictability, text format, and content.

literacy is a term generally associated with reading and writing, but it has been defined in many different ways. *Basic* literacy is the ability to read and write. *Functional* literacy is frequently defined as those reading and writing skills needed by people to do everyday tasks such as writing cheques and reading instructions on a medicine bottle. **Critical literacy** goes beyond conventional reading and writing to an interrogation of texts and taking action to promote social justice. In recent years, *literacy* has been extended to other forms of representation, such as *media literacy* and *computer literacy*.

manuscript printing, sometimes called *manuscript writing*, is the first form of written language taught to children and consists of individual letters that are not connected. There are a number of styles of manuscript writing, but all of them are plain, easy to recognize, and easy for children to learn.

media (plural; singular *medium*) are the resources one uses to communicate meaning (e.g., pencil and paper, computer).

metacognition is awareness and control of the thinking processes involved in developing an ability. In reading, metacognition includes knowledge of factors that affect reading, of reading tasks, and of reading strategies. The regulative or control dimension of metacognition in reading involves planning and monitoring.

metafiction is a **narrative** mode used by authors to provide a constant and deliberate reminder that a book is something an author and reader create together, something that is not real but fictional and that is open to many interpretations. The device has been used by authors since the time of Chaucer. It is the opposite of literary realism. By drawing attention to how texts are structured, works of metafiction can show readers how texts "mean." Techniques used to this end include obtrusive narrators who directly address the reader, situations in which characters and narrators change places, the insertion of parodies of other texts, typographic experimentation, and the mixing of **genres** and **discourses**. Works of metafiction usually employ any number of these techniques in combination. *Black and White* by David Macaulay (1990) and *Piggybook* by Anthony Browne (1986) are examples.

metalinguistic awareness is the growing awareness and ability we have to think and talk about language as a formal code. With children, it refers to understanding terms such as *letter, word, sentence*, and *sound*.

miscues is a term coined by Goodman (1969) for errors during oral reading. Goodman believes that analyzing oral miscues gives insights into the reading process, since miscues result from the same cues and processes as correct responses.

modes are a set of resources that people in a given culture can use to communicate. Examples of modes include print, image, music, and speech. All modes relate to at least one dimension of the six language arts.

morphology is the study of the structure of words, specifically the ways in which morphemes (the smallest units of meaning in a language) combine to create meanings. An example of a morpheme is *s*, which denotes plural in English. Hence *dog* means one creature, and *dogs* means more than one. Suffixes and prefixes are also morphemes. Morphology is one of the essential **cuing systems** readers use to make sense of the printed word. Morphology is distinct from **syntax** in that syntax deals with the meaning of language at the level of sentences and phrases.

narrative consists of a story or a succession of related events. These events are frequently organized according to cause and effect or chronology. Narratives include descriptions of settings, events, and characters, as well as comments and observations. Narratives can have the structure of a story or a much looser structure without opening and closing sequences.

native speaker ability is the ability to use language in many situations to accomplish a wide range of purposes. Idiomatic language, **pragmatics**, and **dialect** are all important in native speaker ability.

new literacies refer to literacies that have recently emerged with the era of digitalization and the Internet. Being able to navigate a video game, surf the Internet, shop on eBay, or chat online all require particular literacy skills.

onset is the initial consonant or consonants in a syllable. The **rime** is the vowel and remaining consonants in a syllable after the onset.

opposer role challenges the students to assume leadership and argue for what they believe. This role should not be used until trust and relationship have been developed with a group of students. See also **victim role, intermediate role, leader role**.

performance assessment refers to assessment in which students demonstrate what they can do by actually doing it. Rather than using paper and pencil tests, teachers use their best judgment to evaluate performance along a continuum defined by increasingly demanding performance criteria. These criteria are written descriptions that capture quality performance at various levels of achievement. This form of assessment is frequently used for children's writing.

persuasive writing is used to persuade others to do something, buy something, or believe something. Advertising, editorials, political campaign literature, religious tracts, and much of the unsolicited junk mail that arrives in mailboxes consists of persuasive writing. Children use persuasive writing when they create a poster presentation about a favourite book they have read or write a letter asking the school principal to consider changing a school rule.

phonemes are the smallest units of meaningful sound in a language, e.g. "a" as in "cat." See also **phonemic awareness, phonetics, phonics, phonological awareness, phonology**.

phonemic awareness is the ability to segment spoken words into their distinct sounds, or phonemes. The spoken word "dog" consists of three separate phonemes, one for each letter in the written word, D-O-G. The spoken word "chin" has three phonemes, the two letters in "ch" representing one phoneme. See also **phonemes, phonetics, phonics, phonological awareness, phonology**.

phonetics refers to the way sounds are articulated and produced. The term is often used to describe the way children spell, sounding out a word so they can articulate individual sounds (phonemes) within a word and transcribe them into print symbols. See also **phonemes, phonemic awareness, phonics, phonological awareness, phonology**.

phonics is the relationship between letters and their spoken sounds. **Analytic** phonics is the association of sounds with larger clusters of letters such as phonograms or word families (e.g. *ight*). **Synthetic** phonics is the association of sounds with individual letters or letter clusters and the blending of these sounds to identify words. See also **phonemes, phonemic awareness, phonetics, phonological awareness, phonology**.

phonological awareness is an awareness of patterns of sound that create meaning in language. See also **phonemes, phonemic awareness, phonetics, phonics, phonology**.

phonology, sometimes called *phonemics*, is the study of the patterns of sound that create meaning in language. In any one language, a number of sounds (phonemes) combine to produce words and meanings. See also **phonemes, phonemic awareness, phonetics, phonics, phonological awareness**.

picture books are books in which illustrations play an integral role in creating meaning. Picture books are not the same as illustrated books, in which meaning does not depend on illustrations. In a picture book, text and pictures work together. Good examples of picture books are *Each Peach Pear Plum* by Janet and Allan Ahlberg (1976) and *The Tunnel* by Anthony Browne (1989).

poetic writing is a term used by James Britton (Britton et al., 1975) to describe one of the three **voices** of writing (the others being **expressive** and **transactional**). Meant to have an aesthetic element to it, poetic writing consists of poetry and also fictional writing, including **narrative** and description. The purpose of poetic writing is purely pleasure or satisfaction on the part of the writer and audience. (Poetic writing is not necessarily pleasurable to read; it can, in fact, cause distress or discomfort for the reader.)

portfolio assessment uses a compilation of work done by a child over a period of time. Frequently, the portfolio items are selected by the learner or by the teacher and learner together. Items included in a portfolio are chosen with deliberation in order to demonstrate what a learner can do. Teachers find portfolios useful in demonstrating a child's learning to parents and administrators, and in explaining to children what they need to focus on and what learning must be accomplished next. Portfolios also give teachers an opportunity to reflect on their teaching and the learning their students are engaged in. Portfolios provide children with an opportunity to see the range of work they have done over time and to assess what they are accomplishing.

pragmatics is the study of how speakers create meaning. The emphasis in pragmatics is on the context of language use and on the intentions and presuppositions of the speakers. The focus is on what an individual speaker means and on how that meaning is communicated. Pragmatics examines relatively short stretches of language compared with **discourse** analysis, which studies linguistic patterns in longer stretches of language.

predictable books, a term coined by Goodman (1969), are books that make reading easy for emergent readers. They have the following characteristics: the pictures support the text; large chunks of text are repeated; and the language has cadence, rhythm, or rhyme that supports the reading of the text. *Brown Bear, Brown Bear, What Do You See?* (Martin, 1972) and *Each Peach Pear Plum* (Ahlberg and Ahlberg, 1976) are examples of predictable books.

pre-text "refers to the source or impulse for the drama process … a reason for the work … the meaning of a text that exists before the event" (O'Neill, 1995, p. xv). In Chapter 12, this term is used interchangeably with *source*.

process drama is a larger unit of drama work built around a common theme from a "series of episodes or scenic units" (O'Neill, 1995). Unlike a traditional play, process drama focuses on creating an experience for the participants rather than performing for an audience.

reading recovery is an intervention program designed for struggling first-grade readers created by Marie Clay. The goal of reading recovery is to help readers to catch up to grade level. The program involves daily one-on-one tutoring that focuses on running record assessment, word study, reading, and writing.

reading series (See **basal reading series**.)

realistic fiction (See **contemporary realistic fiction**.)

retellings are an assessment strategy in which children are invited to retell their understanding of a text.

rime (See **onset**.)

running records are an assessment strategy that involves students reading aloud a short passage to the teacher. The teacher takes note of all reading miscues and calculates an oral reading accuracy percentage, which is used to place students in reading levels. Running records can also help to determine student strengths and weakness by noting trends in the types of miscues they make when reading.

scaffolding refers to the temporary supports teachers give to children to help them extend their skills and knowledge to a higher level of competence.

schemata (plural; singular *schema*) are organized mental frameworks that develop through repeated exposure to ritualized experiences such as playing baseball, eating in restaurants, or singing on car trips. Schemata influence our expectations and impose structure on the information we receive.

semantic map or web is a diagram that shows relationships among ideas. It consists of nodes containing key words, with connecting lines between the nodes. Teachers and students use semantic maps or webs to organize ideas about concepts, texts, or units of study.

semantics is the meaning component of language. It does not refer simply to the denotational meanings of words but also to the ways in which words are used, in both the actual choice of one word rather than another and the connotations created by those words. A semantic system includes idioms and compound words and the unique ways that words are used in different situations.

social constructivism is a model of learning developed by Vygotsky (1978). This model postulates that the ways people think are learned primarily through social interactions and that the ways we learn language develop as a result of our use of language in social contexts.

strategy is an overall, conscious plan for performing a task. One strategy can be used in several learning situations. In contrast, skills are more context-specific and used in the service of a strategy. Examples of strategies include predicting meanings, summarizing, and monitoring. In Chapter 12, *strategy* refers to specific teaching procedures or dramatic *conventions* (such as "still image" or "role on the wall") that teachers may use to engage students in a process drama. Strategies are the raw material or building blocks of a dramatic unit or episode.

syntax (formerly *grammar*) is a linguistic term that refers to the structure of sentences. In the English language, syntax consists largely of word order. English is a non-inflected language; it does not depend on specific inflectional word endings to denote the role of a word in a sentence.

teacher-in-role refers to the teacher's practice of assuming a role within the process drama so that he or she can model and encourage sincerity of role-play for their students. Teachers may make different choices of the kind of role they want to play, depending on their teaching objectives for the drama.

text structure is the pattern or organization of ideas in a text. There are two major types of texts: **narrative** (story) and expository (informational). Knowledge of text structure helps us to construct meaning for texts when reading and writing.

thematic organization is a way of organizing learning matter around a central concept (such as courage), the work of a particular author, or a topic (such as farms). The theory is that learning will be facilitated and deepened by connecting ideas to one another. Thematic units may be organized within language arts or extended across other areas of the curriculum as well.

time-slip fantasy is a **genre** of literature that involves the main character or protagonist in two eras. An object often enables the character to slip from one era to the other. In *Who Is Francis Rain?* by Margaret Buffie (1987), the object is a pair of spectacles. In *Playing Beatie Bow* by Ruth Parks (1980), the object is a piece of fabric on a dress. In time-slip **fantasy**, the protagonist explores issues in the past that lead to an understanding of current issues.

trade books are books published by publishing companies as works of literature and not as educational texts. Books published as part of an educational program and intended for use in schools are usually referred to as *textbooks*.

transactional theory, also called *transactive theory*, is based on the work of Louise Rosenblatt (1978). It posits that meaning comes from a transaction between a reader and a text in a specific context. Readers rely on the text itself and on their background knowledge, experiences, and world view to construct meaning while reading. The focus is on the reader's response to texts.

transactional writing is a term used by James Britton (Britton et al., 1975) to describe one of the three **voices** of writing (the others being expressive and poetic). Like **expository writing**, with which it is often used interchangeably, transactional writing is meant to accomplish a specific practical goal. Business letters, reports, term papers, report cards, recipes, and shopping lists are all examples of transactional writing.

victim role allows the teacher to provide a context where students may practice compassion and empathy as well as problem solving and leadership. See also **opposer role, intermediate role, leader role**.

voice is a term used in writing to refer to the combined effects of the writer's purpose, style, tone, and other intangibles, such as commitment, energy, conviction, and personality. Also used to refer to the three voices or types of writing: **expressive writing, poetic writing,** and **transactional writing**.

zone of proximal development, a term coined by Vygotsky (1978), refers to a level of difficulty just beyond that which a child can handle independently but at which he or she can manage with help from others. Providing children with the opportunity to work with others on problems or tasks at this level maximizes learning.

REFERENCES

Adams, M. J. (1990). *Beginning to read: Thinking and learning about print.* Cambridge, MA: MIT Press.

Adams, M. J. (1998). [Videorecording]. *What children need in order to read: Preparing young children for reading success.* Bellingham, WA: DeBeck Educational Video.

Adams, M. J. (2002). Alphabetic anxiety and explicit, systematic phonics instruction: A cognitive science perspective. In S. B. Neuman and D. K. Dickinson (Eds.), *Handbook of early literacy research* (pp. 66–80). New York: The Guilford Press.

Adams, M. J., Anderson, R. C., and Durkin, D. (1978). Beginning reading: Theory and practice. *Language Arts, 55,* 19–25.

Adams, P. (1987). Writing from reading: "Dependent authorship" as a response. In B. Corcoran and E. Evans (Eds.), *Readers, texts, teachers.* Portsmouth, NH: Boynton/Cook.

Afflerbach, P. (1998). Reading assessment and learning to read. In J. Osborn and F. Lehr (Eds.), *Literacy for all: Issues in teaching and learning* (pp. 239–263). New York: The Guilford Press.

Ajayi, L. (2005). Teachers' needs and predesigned instructional practices: An analysis of a reading/language arts coursebook for a second grade class. *Reading Improvement, 42*(4), 200–211.

Albers, P., and Murphy, S. (2000). *Telling pieces: Art as literacy in middle school classes.* Mahwah, NJ: Lawrence Erlbaum Associates.

Alberta Education. (1993). *Diagnostic teaching in a language learning framework 5.* Edmonton, AB: Student Evaluation Branch.

Alberta Education. (2000). *Language arts program of studies, K–9.* Edmonton, AB: Author.

Alberta Learning. (2005). *English language arts Grade Six provincial testing bulletin.* Retrieved June 22, 2007, from: http://www.education.gov.ab.ca/k_12/testing/achievement/samples.

Alberta Learning. (2000). *English language arts, K–9.* Edmonton, AB: Alberta Learning, Curriculum Standards Branch. Retrieved April 23, 2007, from: http://www.learning.gov.ab.ca/k_12/curriculum/bysubject/english/default.asp.

Alford, J. (2001). Learning language and critical literacy: Adolescent ESL students. *Journal of Adolescent and Adult Literacy, 45*(3), 238–242.

Allen, J. (2004). *Tools for teaching content literacy.* Markham, ON: Pembroke Publishers.

Allington, R., and Walmsley, S. A. (Eds.) (1995). *No quick fix: Rethinking literacy programs in America's elementary schools.* New York: Teachers College Press.

Allington, R. L. (2006). *What really matters for struggling readers: Designing research-based programs* (2nd ed.). Boston: Pearson/Allyn and Bacon.

Allington, R. L., and Baker, Kim. (2007). Best practices for struggling readers. In L. B. Gambrell, L. M. Morrow, and M. Pressley (Eds.), *Best Practices in Literacy Instruction* (3rd ed.) (pp. 83–103). New York: Guilford Press.

Anderson, J., Moffat, L., Shapiro, J. (2006). Reconceptualizing language education in early childhood: Socio-cultural perspectives. In B. Spodek and O. N. Saracho (Eds.), *Handbook of research on the education of young children* (pp. 135–151). Mahwah, NJ: Lawrence Erlbaum Associates.

Anstey, M., and Bull, G. (2006). *Teaching and learning mutiliteracies: Changing times, changing literacies.* Kensington Gardens, SA: Australian Literacy Educators' Association and the International Reading Association.

Applebee, A. (1978). *The child's concept of story.* Chicago: University of Chicago Press.

Armbruster, B. B., and Osborn, J. H. (2002). *Reading instruction and assessment: Understanding the IRA standards.* Boston: Allyn and Bacon.

Armbuster, B. B., Mitsakas, C. L., and Rogers, V. R. (1986). *America's history.* Peterborough, NH: Schoolhouse Press.

Ashton-Warner, S. (1986). *Teacher.* New York: Touchstone Books.

Atwell, N. (1987). *In the middle: Writing, reading, and learning with adolescents.* Portsmouth, NH: Heinemann.

Atwell, N. (1998). *In the middle: New understandings about writing, reading and learning* (2nd ed.). Portsmouth, NH: Boynton/Cook.

Bagdasarian, Adam. (2002). *First french kiss and other traumas.* New York: Melanie Kroupa Books/ Farrar, Straus and Giroux.

Baghban, M. (2007). Scribbles, labels, and stories: The role of drawing in the development of writing. *YC Young Children, 62*(1), 20–26.

Bainbridge, J., Coleman, W., and Gellner, J. (2004). Assessing children's growth in literature circles and discussion groups. *READ: Reading, Exploration and Discovery. The Journal of the Louisiana Reading Association, 25*(1), 21–32.

Balke, Eva. (1997). Play and the arts: The importance of the "unimportant." *Childhood Education, 73*(6), 355–360.

Ball, E. W., and Blachman, B. A. (1991). Does phoneme segmentation training in kindergarten make a difference in early word recognition and developmental spelling? *Reading Research Quarterly, 26,* 49–66.

Barnes, D. (1976). *From communication to curriculum.* Harmondsworth, UK: Penguin Books.

Barone, D., and Taylor, J. M. (2007). *The practical guide to classroom literacy assessment.* Thousand Oaks, CA: Corwin Press.

Barrs, M. (2000). Gendered literacy? *Language Arts, 77*(4), 287–293.

Barton, B. (1992). *Stories to tell.* Markham, ON: Pembroke.

Barton, B., and Booth, D. (1990). *Stories in the classroom: Storytelling, reading aloud and roleplaying with children.* Markham, Ont.: Pembroke Publishers.

Bear, D., Invernizzi, M., Templeton, S., and Johnston, F. (2004). *Words their way: Word study for phonics, vocabulary, and spelling instruction.* Upper Saddle River, NJ: Pearson/Merrill Prentice Hall.

Beard, R., and Oakhill, J. (1994). *Reading by apprenticeship? A critique of the apprenticeship approach to the teaching of reading.* Slough, England: NFER.

Beaver, J. (2001). *Developmental Reading Assessment* [Kit]. Parsippany, NJ: Celebration Press.

Beck, I. L. (2006). *Making sense of phonics: The hows and whys.* New York: The Guilford Press.

Beck, I., McKeown, M., Hamilton, R., and Kucan, L. (1997). *Questioning the author: An approach for enhancing student engagement with text.* Newark, DE: International Reading Association.

Beers, J. W., and Henderson, E. H. (1977). A study of developing orthographic concepts among first graders. *Research in the Teaching of English, 11,* 133–148.

Belliveau, G. (2004). Struggle to success: Collective drama on anti-bullying. *Canadian Theatre Review, 117,* 42–44.

Benson, B., and Barnett, A. (2005). *Student-led conferencing: Using showcase portfolios* (2nd ed.). Thousand Oaks, CA: Corwin Press.

Benton, M., and Fox, G. (1985). *Teaching literature: Nine to fourteen.* London: Oxford University Press.

Berk, E., and James, M. (1992). *The play's the thing: A community of students, teachers, and artists create theater.* New York: National Arts Education Research Center, New York University.

Beswick, J. F., Willms, J. D., and Sloat, E. A. (2005). A comparative study of teacher ratings of emergent literacy skills and student performance on a standardized measure. *Education, 126*(1), 116–137.

Biancarosa, G., and Snow, C. E. (2004). *Reading next—A vision for action and research in middle and high school literacy: A report to Carnegie Corporation of New York.* Washington, DC: Alliance for Excellent Education.

Bissoondath, N. (1998, September). No place like home. *New Internationalist,* 20–22.

Blair, H., and Sanford, H. (2003). *Rethinking literacy for boys.* Paper presented at the International Conference on Language, Education and Diversity, University of Waikato, Hamilton, New Zealand, November 26–29. Retrieved February 28, 2007, from: http://www.education.ualberta .ca/boysandliteracy/publications.html.

Blair, H., and Sanford, K. (2004). Morphing literacy: Boys reshaping their school-based literacy practices. *Language Arts, 81*(6), 452–460.

Blair, H. (2004). Let's study gender gap on reading. *Edmonton Journal,* A18.

Blessing, C. (2005). Reading to kids who are old enough to shave. *School Library Journal, 51*(4), 44–45.

Bloome, D., and Green, J. (1984). Directions in the sociolinguistic study of reading. In R. Barr, M. L. Kamil, and P. B. Mosenthal (Eds.), *Handbook of reading research* (pp. 395–421). New York: Longman.

Bolton, G. (1985). Changes in thinking about drama in education. *Theory into Practice, 24,* 3, 151–156.

Bolton, G. (1992). *New perspectives on classroom drama.* Hemel Hempstead, Herts: Simon and Schuster Education.

Booth, D. (1987). *Drama Words.* Toronto: Toronto Board of Education.

Booth, D. (1992). *Censorship goes to school.* Markham, ON: Pembroke Publishers.

Booth, D. (2005). *Story drama: Creating stories through role playing, improvising and reading aloud* (2nd ed.). Markham, ON: Pembroke Publishers.

Booth, D., and Moore, B. (1988). *Poems please! Sharing poetry with children.* Markham, ON: Pembroke.

Booth, D., and Neelands, J. (1998). *Writing in role: Classroom projects connecting writing and drama.* Hamilton, ON: Caliburn Enterprises Inc.

Bourdieu, P. (1984). *Distinction: A social critique of the judgment of taste.* (Trans. R. Nice). Cambridge, MA: Harvard University Press.

Bowen, L. (2006). Attracting, addressing, and amusing the teen reader. *ALAN Review, 34*(1), 17–23.

Brabham, E. G., and Villaume, S. K. (2001). Building walls of words. *Reading Teacher, 54*(7), 700–702.

Brabham, E. G., and Villaume, S. K. (2002). Leveled text: The good news and the bad news. *Reading Teacher, 55*(5), 438–441.

Braxton, B. (2007a). Read-alouds: Choosing the right book. *Teacher Librarian, 34*(3), 52–53.

British Columbia Ministry of Education. (1988). *Enhancing and evaluating oral communication in the primary grades: Teacher's resource package.* Victoria: British Columbia Ministry of Education.

Britton, J. (1970). *Language and learning.* Harmondsworth, UK: Penguin Books.

Britton, J. (1982). *Prospect and retrospect: Selected essays of James Britton.* G. Pradl (Ed.). Montclair, NJ: Boynton Cook.

Britzman, D. (1998). *Lost subjects, contested objects: Toward a psychoanalytic inquiry.* Albany, NY: State University of New York Press.

Britzman, D. (2003). *Practice makes practice: A critical study of learning to teach*. Albany, NY: State University of New York Press.

Bromley, Karen. (2007). Best practices in teaching writing. In L. B. Gambrell, L. M. Morrow, and M. Pressley (Eds.), *Best practices in literacy instruction* (3rd ed.) (pp. 243–263). New York: Guilford Press.

Brophy, J. (1985). Interactions of male and female students with male and female teachers. In L. C. Wilkinson and C. B. Marrett (Eds.), *Gender influences in classroom interaction*. Toronto: Academic Press.

Brown, J., and Fisher, P. (2006). Balanced literacy: One middle school's experience. *Principal Leadership, 7*(1), 38–40.

Bruner, J. (1986). *Actual minds, possible worlds*. Cambridge, MA: Harvard University Press.

Bruner, J. S. (1975). The ontogenesis of speech acts. *Journal of Child Language, 2*, 1–40.

Burns, B. (2006). *How to teach balanced reading and writing* (2nd ed.). Thousand Oaks, CA: Corwin Press.

Burns, M. (1992). *Math and literature (K–3): Book one*. Sausalito, CA: Marilyn Burns Education Associates.

Burns, M. (1995). *Writing in math class*. Sausalito, CA: Math Solutions Publications.

Burns, M. (2000). *About teaching mathematics: A K–8 resource* (2nd ed.). Sausalito, CA: Math Solutions Publications.

Burns, P. C., and Roe, B. D. (2002). *Informal reading inventory* (6th ed.). Chicago: Rand McNally.

Butler, A. (1992). *Exploring reading*. [Videorecording]. Crystal Lake, IL: Rigby Education.

Butler, A. (1993). *Phonics and spelling*. [Videorecording]. Crystal Lake, IL: Rigby.

Byrne, B., and Fielding-Barnsley, R. (1993). Evaluation of a program to teach phonemic awareness to young children: A 1-year follow-up. *Journal of Educational Psychology, 85*, 104–111.

Cadiero-Kaplan, K. (2002). Literacy ideologies: Critically engaging the language arts curriculum. *Language Arts, 79*(5), 372–381.

Calabrese, N. M. (2003). Developing quality sociodramatic play for young children. *Education, 123*(3), 606–608.

Calkins, L. (1986). *The art of teaching writing*. Portsmouth, NH: Heinemann.

Calkins, L. (1991). *Living between the lines*. Toronto: Irwin.

Calkins, L. (2006). *Units of study for teaching writing, grades 5–6*. Portsmouth, NH: FirstHand Heinemann.

Calkins, L. M. (2001). *The art of teaching reading*. New York: Longman.

Cambourne, B. (1988). *The whole story: Natural learning and the acquisition of literacy in the classroom*. New York: Scholastic.

Cambourne, B. (2002). The conditions of learning: Is learning natural? *The Reading Teacher, 55*(8), 758–762.

Campaign 2000. (2006). *Oh Canada! Too many children in poverty for too long: 2006 Report Card on Child and Family Poverty in Canada*. Retrieved February 13, 2008, from : http://www.campaign2000 .ca/rc/rc06/06_C2000NationalReportCard.pdf.

Campbell, J. (1988). *The power of myth*. New York: Doubleday.

Canadian Library Association. (1974). *Statement on intellectual freedom*. 29th Annual Conference, Winnipeg, MB.

Carlo, M. S. (2007). Best practices for literacy instruction for English language learners. In L. B. Gambrell, L. M. Morrow, and M. Pressley, *Best practices in literacy instruction* (3rd ed.) (pp. 104–126). New York/London: Guilford Press.

Carroll, J., Davies, P., and Richman, B. (1971). *Word frequency book*. Boston: Houghton Mifflin.

Cazden, C. (1988). *Classroom discourse: The language of teaching and learning.* Portsmouth, NH: Heinemann.

Cazden, C. B. (1988). *Classroom discourse: The language of teaching and learning.* Portsmouth, NH: Heinemann.

Cervetti, G., Pardales, M. J., and Damico, J. S. (2001). A tale of differences: Comparing the traditions, perspectives, and educational goals of critical reading and critical literacy. *Reading online.* Available at: http://www.readingonline.org/articles/cervetti.

Chard, S. (1998). *The project approach: Making curriculum come alive.* New York: Scholastic.

Chittenden, E., and Courtney, R. (1989). Assessment of young children's reading: Documentation as an alternative to testing. In D. S. Strickland and L. M. Morrow (Eds.), *Emerging literacy: Young children learn to read and write* (pp. 107–120). Newark, DE: International Reading Association.

Chorzempa, B. F., and Graham, S. (2006). Primary-grade teachers' use of within-class ability grouping in reading. *Journal of Educational Psychology, 98*(3), 529–541.

Christie, J., Enz, B., and Vukelich, C. (2003). *Teaching language and literacy: Preschool through the elementary grades.* Boston: Allyn and Bacon.

Citizenship and Immigration Canada. (2005). *Facts and figures 2005 immigration overview: Permanent residents.* Retrieved February 19, 2007, from: http://www.cic.gc.ca/english/pub/facts2005/permanent/19.html.

Clausen-Grace, N., and Kelley, M. (2007). You can't hide in R5: Restructuring independent reading to be more strategic and engaging. *Voices from the Middle, 14*(3), 38–49.

Clay, M. M. (1972). *Reading: The patterning of complex behaviour.* Auckland, NZ: Heinemann Educational Books.

Clay, M. M. (1975). *What did I write?* Portsmouth, NH: Heinemann.

Clay, M. M. (1993a). *An observation survey of early literacy achievement.* Portsmouth, NH: Heinemann.

Clay, M. M. (1993b). *Reading recovery: A guidebook for teachers in training.* Portsmouth, NH: Heinemann.

Cleary, L., and Peacock, T. (1998). *Collected wisdom: American Indian education.* Needham Heights, MA: Allyn and Bacon.

Clymer, T. (1963). The utility of phonic generalizations in the primary grades. *The Reading Teacher, 16*, 252–258.

Commaire, A. (Ed.). (Published annually since 1971). *Something about the author.* Detroit: Gale Research.

Conrad, D. (2004). Popular theatre: Empowering pedagogy for youth. *Youth Theatre Journal, 18*, 87–106.

Cooper, C. (1985). *Researching response to literature and the teaching of literature.* Norwood, NJ: Ablex.

Cooper, C., and Odell, L. (Eds.). (1999). *Evaluating writing: The role of teachers' knowledge about text, learning and culture.* Urbana, IL: National Council of Teachers of English.

Cooper, J. D., and Kiger, N. D. (2005). *Literacy assessment: Helping teachers plan instruction* (2nd ed.). Boston: Houghton Mifflin.

Council of Chief State School Officers. (n.d.) *The words we use: A glossary of terms for early childhood education standards and assessment.* Retrieved April 23, 2007, from: http://www.ccsso.org/projects/SCASS/projects/early_childhood_education_assessment_consortium/publications_and_products/2926.cfm.

Cox, C. (1999). *Teaching language arts: A student- and response-centered classroom.* Boston: Allyn and Bacon.

Culham, R. (2003). *6+1 traits of writing: The complete guide grades 3 and up.* Toronto: Scholastic Professional Books.

Cummins, J. (1984). *Bilingualism and special education: Issues in assessment and pedagogy.* Clevedon, UK: Multilingual Matters.

Cummins, J. (1994). The acquisition of English as a second language. In K. Spangenberg-Urbschat and R. Pritchard (Eds.), *Kids come in all languages: Reading instruction for ESL students* (pp. 36–62). Newark, DE: International Reading Association.

Cummins, J. (2000). *Language, power and pedagogy: bilingual children in the crossfire.* Clevedon, England: Multingual Matters.

Cummins, J., Bismilla, V., Chow, P., Cohen, S., Giampapa, F., Leoni, L., Sandhu, P., and Sastri, P. (2005). Affirming identity in multilingual classrooms. *Educational Leadership, 63*(1), 38–42. Retrieved February 15, 2007, from: http://www.ascd.org/authors/ed_lead/el200509_cummins.html.

Cunningham, P. M. (2007). Best practices in teaching phonological awareness and phonics. In L. B. Gambrell, L. M. Morrow, and M. Pressley, *Best practices in literacy instruction* (3rd ed.) (pp. 159–177). New York/London: Guilford Press.

Cunningham, P. M., and Allington, R. L. (2007). *Classrooms that work: They can all read and write* (4th ed.). Boston: Pearson/Allyn and Bacon.

Cunningham, P. M., and Cunningham, J. W. (1992). Making words: Enhancing the invented spelling-decoding connection. *Reading Teacher, 46*(2), 106–113.

Cunningham, P. M., and Allington, R. L. (2003). *Classrooms that work: They can all read and write* (3rd ed.). New York: Longman.

Cunningham, P. M., Hall, D. P., and Cunningham, J. W. (2000). *Guided reading the Four-Blocks way.* Greensboro, NC: Carson-Dellosa.

Cunningham, P. M., Hall, D. P., and Gambrell, L. B. (2002). *Self-selected reading the Four-Blocks way.* Greensboro, NC: Carson-Dellosa.

D'Arcy, P. (1989). *Making sense, shaping meaning: Writing in the context of a capacity-based approach to learning.* Portsmouth, NH: Heinemann.

Daniels, H. (2002). *Literature circles: Voice and choice in book clubs and reading groups.* Portland, ME: Stenhouse.

Davey, B. (1983). Think aloud—modeling the cognitive processes of reading comprehension. *Journal of Reading, 27*(1), 44–47.

David, T., Raban, B., Ure, C., Goouch, K., Jago, M., and Barriere, I. (2000). *Making sense of early literacy: A practitioner's perspective.* Stoke on Trent: Trentham.

Davies, H. (1983). An operational approach to evaluation. In C. Day and J. Norman (Eds.), *Issues in Educational Drama* (pp. 95–122), London: The Falmer Press.

DeBenedictis, D. (2007). Sustained silent reading: Making adaptations. *Voice from the Middle, 14*(3), 29–37.

DeFord, D. E. (1985). Validating the construct of theoretical orientation in reading instruction. *Reading Research Quarterly, 20*(3), 351–367.

Delpit, L. (1995). *Other people's children: Cultural conflict in the classroom.* New York: The New Press.

Delpit, L. (2006a). *Other people's children: Cultural conflict in the classroom.* New York: The New Press.

Department of Education and Training in Western Australia. (2006). *First steps (2nd ed.). Writing map of development.* Toronto: Pearson Professional Learning.

Department of Education and Training in Western Australia. (2006). *First steps (2nd ed.). Writing resource book.* Toronto: Pearson Professional Learning.

Department of School Education. (1991). *English profiles handbook.* Melbourne, Australia: Department of School Education.

Deyhle, D., and Swisher, K. (1997). Research in American Indian and Alaska Native education: From assimilation to self-determination. In M. Apple (Ed.), *Review of Research in Education* (pp. 113–194). Washington, DC: American Educational Research Association.

Diakiw, J. (1997). Children's literature and Canadian national identity: A revisionist perspective. *Canadian Children's Literature, 23*(3), 36–49.

Dillon, D. (1985). Editorial. *Language Arts,* 62(1), 9.

Dixon, N., Davies, A., and Politano, C. (1996). *Learning with reader's theatre.* Winnipeg: Peguis Publishers.

Doake, D. B. (1981). *Book experience and emergent reading behaviour in preschool children.* [Unpublished doctoral dissertation]. University of Alberta, Edmonton, AB.

Doake, D. B. (1988). *Reading begins at birth.* Richmond Hill, ON: Scholastic-TAB Publications.

Doctorow, R., Bodiam, M., and McGowan, H. (2003). *Comprehension attitude strategies interests 4 reading assessment.* Toronto: Thomson Nelson.

Doiron, R. (2002). *Lesson planning.* [Unpublished paper presentation]. University of Prince Edward Island, Charlottetown, PE.

Doiron, R. (2003). Boy books, girl books: Should we re-organize our school library collections? *Teacher Librarian, 30*(3), 14–16.

Doiron, R. (2003b). Motivating the lifelong reading habit through a balanced use of children's information books. *School Libraries Worldwide, 9*(1), 39–49.

Donaldson, M. (1978). *Children's minds.* New York: W. W. Norton and Co.

Donnelly, A., Morgan, D., DeFord, D. E., Files, J., Long, S., Mills, H., et al. (2005). Transformative professional development: Negotiating knowledge with an inquiry stance. *Language Arts, 82*(5), 336–346.

Dorn, L. J., and Soffos, C. (2001). *Shaping literate minds: Developing self-regulated learners.* Portland, ME: Stenhouse Publishers.

Dzaldov, B. S., and Peterson, S. (2005). Book leveling and readers. *The Reading Teacher, 59*(3), 222–229.

Easley, S., and Mitchell, K. (2003). *Portfolios matter: What, where, when, why and how to use them.* Markham, ON: Pembroke Publishing.

Eco, U. (1979). *The role of the reader: Explorations in the semiotics of texts.* Bloomington: Indiana University Press.

Education: Alberta Government. (2007). *Assessment practices of Canadian provinces: Kindergarten to Grade 12.* Education. Retrieved April 23, 2007, from: http://www.education.gov.ab.ca/k_12/testing/achievement/supporting_excellence/asses_practices.asp.

Edwards, J. (1992). Dialogue journals in math: Grades two, four and six. *Reflections on Canadian Literacy, 10*(1), 2–12.

Edwards, P. A. (2004). *Children's literacy development: Making it happen through school, family, and community involvement.* Boston: Pearson.

Eeds, M., and Wells, M. (1989). Grand conversations: An exploration of meaning construction in literature response groups. *Research in the Teaching of English, 23*(1), 4–29.

Egoff, S., and Saltman, J. (1990). *The new republic of childhood: A critical guide to Canadian children's literature in English.* Toronto: Oxford University Press.

Ehri, L. C., Nunes, S. R., Willows, D. M., Schuster, B. V., Yaghoub-Zadeh, Z., and Shanahan, T. (2001). Phonemic awareness instruction helps children learn to read: Evidence from the National Reading Panel's meta-analysis. *Reading Research Quarterly, 36*(3), 250–283.

El-Hindi, A. (1999). Beyond classroom boundaries: Constructivist teaching with the Internet. *Reading online.* Available at: http://www.readingonline.org/electronic/elec_index.asp?HREF=/electronic/RT/constructivist.html.

Elkonin, D. B. (1973). USSR. In J. Downing (Ed.), *Comparative reading: Cross-national studies of behavior and processes in reading and writing* (pp. 551–579). New York: Macmillan.

Farr, R., and Tone, B. (1998). *Portfolio and performance assessment: Helping students evaluate their progress as readers and writers* (2nd ed.). Fort Worth, TX: Harcourt Brace College.

Farrell, E., and Squire, J. (Eds.). (1990). *Transactions with literature: A fifty year perspective.* Urbana, IL: National Council of Teachers of English.

Fassler, R. (1998). "Let's do it again!" Peer collaboration in an ESL kindergarten. *Language Arts, 75*(3), 202–210.

Fawson, P. C., and Reutzel, D. R. (2000). But I only have a basal: Implementing guided reading in the early grades. *The Reading Teacher, 54*(1), 84–97.

Fischer, D., Brozo, W. G., Frey, N., and Ivey, G. (2007). *50 Content area strategies for adolescent literacy.* New Jersey: Merrill Prentice Hall.

Fish, S. (1980). *Is there a text in this class? The authority of interpretive communities.* Cambridge, MA: Harvard University Press.

Fitzgerald, J. (1999). What is this thing called "balance"? *The Reading Teacher, 53*(2), 100–107.

Fleming, M. (1994). *Starting drama teaching.* London: David Fulton Publishers.

Fleming, M. (2001). *Teaching drama in primary and secondary schools: An integrated approach.* London: David Fulton Publishers.

Flippo, R. (1998). Points of agreement: A display of professional unity in our field. *The Reading Teacher, 52*(1), 30–41.

Flippo, R. F. (2001). Points of agreement: A display of professional unity in our field. In R. F. Flippo (Ed.), *Reading researchers in search of common ground* (pp. 7–21). Newark, DE: International Reading Association.

Fountas, I. C., and Pinnell, G. S. (1996). *Guided reading: Good first teaching for all children.* Portsmouth, NH: Heinemann.

Fountas, I. C., and Pinnell, G. S. (1999). *Matching books to readers: Using leveled texts in guided reading, K–3.* Portsmouth, NH: Heinemann.

Fountas, I. C., and Pinnell, G. S. (2006). *Leveled books (K–8): matching texts to readers for effective teaching.* Portsmouth, NH: Heinemann.

Frager, A. (1994). Teaching, writing and identity. *Language Arts, 71*(4), 274–242.

Freebody, P., and Luke, A. (1990). "Literacies" programs: Debates and demands in cultural contexts. *Prospects, 5*(3), 7–16.

Freeman, E., and Person, D. (Eds.). (1992). *Using nonfiction trade books in the classroom: From ants to zeppelins.* Urbana, IL: National Council of Teachers of English.

Freire, P. (1970). *Pedagogy of the oppressed.* New York: Herder and Herder.

Freire, P., and Macedo, D. (1987). *Literacy: Reading the word and the world.* South Hadley, MA: Bergin and Garvey.

Froese, V. (Ed.). (1997). *Language across the curriculum.* Toronto: Harcourt Brace and Company Canada, Ltd.

Fulwiler, T. (Ed.). (1987). *The journal book.* Toronto: Boynton/Cook.

Gallagher, K. (2000). *Drama education in the lives of girls: Imagining possibilities.* Toronto: University of Toronto Press.

Gallant, R. (1970). *Handbook in corrective reading.* Columbus, OH: Charles E. Merrill.

Gambell, T., and Hunter, D. (2000). Surveying gender differences in Canadian school literacy. *Journal of Curriculum Studies, 32*(5), 689–719.

Gambrell, L. B., Malloy, J. A., and Mazzoni, S. A. (2007). Evidence-based best practices for comprehensive literacy instruction. In L. B. Gambrell, L. M. Morrow, and M. Pressley (Eds.), *Best practices in literacy instruction* (3rd ed.) (pp. 11–29). New York: The Guilford Press.

Gammill, D. M. (2006). Learning the write way. *The Reading Teacher, 59*(8), 754–762.

Gangi, J. M. (2004). *Encountering children's literature: An arts approach.* Boston: Pearson.

Garcia, C. L. (1998). No fun with Dick and Jane. *The Reading Teacher, 51*(7), 606–607.

Gentry, J. R. (1978). Early spelling strategies. *Elementary School Journal, 79,* 88–92.

Gentry, J. R. (1981). Learning to spell developmentally. *The Reading Teacher, 34,* 378–381.

Gertridge, A. (2002). *Meet Canadian authors and illustrators: 60 creators of children's books.* Toronto: Scholastic Canada.

Gillen, J., and Hall, N. (2003). The emergence of early childhood literacy. In N. Hall, J. Larson, and J. Marsh (Eds.), *Handbook of early childhood literacy* (pp. 3–12). London: Sage.

Gillet, J. W., and Temple, C. (1994). *Understanding reading problems: Assessment and instruction.* New York: HarperCollins.

Gillies, R. M., and Boyle, M. (2006). Ten Australian elementary teachers' discourse and reported pedagogical practices during cooperative learning. *The Elementary School Journal, 106*(5), 429–451.

Goffin, J. (1995). The collective creation in the classroom. In B. Warren (Ed.), *Creating a theatre in your classroom* (pp. 193–205). Toronto: Captus Press.

Golub, J. N. (1994). Cooperative learning. In A. C. Purves (Ed.), *Encyclopedia of english studies and language arts* (pp. 298–299). New York: Scholastic.

Gonzales, N., Moll, L. C., Floyd-Tenery, M., Rivera, A., Rendon, P., Gonzales, R., and Amanti, C. (1993). *Teacher research on funds of knowledge: Learning from households.* Tucson, AZ: National Center for Research on Cultural Diversity and Second Language Learning. Retrieved January 7, 2007, from: http://www.ncela.gwu.edu/pubs/ncrcdsll/epr6.htm.

Gonzalez-Ramos, G., and Sanchez-Nester, M. (2001). Responding to immigrant children's mental health needs in the schools: Project mi tierra/my country. *Children and Schools, 23*(1), 49–62.

Goodman, K. (1969). Analysis of oral reading miscues: Applied psycholinguistics. *Reading Research Quarterly, 5*(1), 9–30.

Goodman, K. S. (1970). Behind the eye: What happens in reading. In K. S. Goodman and O. Niles (Eds.), *Reading: Process and program* (pp. 3–38). Urbana, IL: National Council of Teachers of English.

Goodman, K. S., Watson, D. J., and Burke, C. L. (1987). *Reading miscue inventory: Alternative procedures.* New York: Macmillan.

Goodman, K., Shannon, P., Freeman, Y. S., and Murphy, S. (1988). *Report card on basal readers.* Katonah, NY: Richard C. Owen.

Goodman, Y. (1978). Kidwatching: An alternative to testing. *Journal of National Elementary School Principals, 574,* 22–27.

Goodman, Y. M. (1991). Informal methods of evaluation. In J. Flood, J. M. Jensen, D. Lapp, and J. R. Squire (Eds.), *Handbook of research on teaching the English language arts* (pp. 502–509). New York: Macmillan.

Gouvernement du Québec Ministère de l'Éducation. (2001). *Québec Education Program: Preschool Education, Elementary Education.* Quebec: Gouvernement du Québec Ministère de l'Éducation.

Grady, S. (2000). *Drama and diversity: A pluralistic perspective for educational drama.* Portsmouth, NH: Heinemann.

Graves, D. H. (1983). *Writing: Teachers and children at work.* Exeter, NH: Heinemann.

Green, P. (2001). Critical literacy revisited. In H. Fehring and P. Green (Eds.), *Critical literacy: A collection of articles from the Australian Literacy Educators' Association.* Newark, NJ: International Reading Association. Available at: http://www.reading.org/store/content/286c.html.

Greene, M. (1995). *Releasing the imagination: Essays on education, the arts, and social change.* San Francisco: Jossey-Bass Publishers.

Gregory, E., Long, S., and Volk, D. (Eds.). (2004). *Many pathways to literacy: Young children learning with siblings, grandparents, peers, and communities.* New York and London: RoutledgeFalmer.

Gregory, E., and Williams, A. (2000). *City literacies: Learning to read across generations and cultures.* London and New York: Routledge.

Gummersall, D. M., and Strong, C. J. (1999). Assessment of complex sentence production in a narrative context. *Language, Speech, and Hearing Services in Schools, 30*(2), 152–164.

Guskey, T. R., and Bailey, J. M. (2001). *Developing grading and reporting systems for student learning.* Thousand Oaks, CA: Corwin Press.

Halliday, M. A. K. (1969). Relevant models of language. *Educational Review, 22*(1), 26–37.

Halliday, M. A. K. (1975). *Explorations in the functions of language.* London: Edward Arnold.

Halliday, M. A. K. (1975). *Learning how to mean.* New York: Elsevier North-Holland Inc.

Handsfield, L. (2006). Being and becoming American: Triangulating habitus, field, and literacy instruction in a multilingual classroom. *Language and Literacy, 8*(2). Retrieved October 11, 2006, from: http://www.langandlit.ualberta.ca/current.html.

Hardy, B. (1975). *Tellers and listeners: The narrative imagination.* Dover, NH: Longwood.

Haynes, C., and McMurdo, K. (2001). *Structured writing: Using Inspiration software to teach paragraph development.* Eugene, OR: International Society for Technology in Education.

Heath, S. B. (1983). *Ways with words: Language, life and work in communities and classrooms.* Cambridge, MA: Cambridge University Press.

Heathcote, D., and Bolton, G. (1995). *Drama for learning: Dorothy Heathcote's mantle of the expert approach to education.* Portsmouth, NH: Heinemann.

Hedrick, W. (2006). Reading incentives don't necessarily grow readers. *Voice from the Middle, 14*(2), 77–78.

Heinig, R. B. (1993). *Creative drama for the classroom teacher* (4th ed.). Englewood Cliffs, NJ: Prentice Hall.

Hetzroni, O. E., and Shrieber, B. (2004). Word processing as an assistive technology tool for enhancing academic outcomes of students with writing disabilities in the general classroom. *Journal of Learning Disabilities, 37*(2), 143–154.

Heydon, R. (2003). Literature circles as a differentiated instructional strategy for including ESL students in mainstream classrooms. *The Canadian Modern Language Review, 59*(3), 463–475.

Heydon, R. (2007). Making meaning together: Multimodal literacy learning opportunities in an inter-generational art program. *Journal of Curriculum Studies, 39*(1), 35–62.

Heydon, R., and Hibbert, K. (Under review). Disrupting teacher candidates' habitus through a language arts curriculum: "The possibilities make my brain tingle."

Heydon, R., and Hibbert, K. (2006). [Pre-service language arts teaching and learning]. Unpublished raw data.

Heydon, R., Hibbert, K., and Iannacci, L. (2004). Strategies to support balanced literacy approaches in pre- and inservice teacher education. *Journal of Adolescent and Adult Literacy, 48*(4), 312–319.

Heydon, R., and Iannacci, L. (2005). Biomedical literacy: Two curriculum teachers challenge the treatment of dis/ability in contemporary literacy education. *Language and Literacy, 7*(2). Retrieved April 23, 2007, from: http://www.langandlit.ualberta.ca.

Heydon, R., and Iannacci, L. (2008). The biomedical approach to literacy: Pathologizing practices within early literacy. In R. Heydon and L. Iannacci, *Early childhood curricula and the de-pathologizing of childhood*. Toronto: University of Toronto Press.

Hibbert, K. (In press). Virtual communities of practice: A vehicle for meaningful professional development. In C. Kimble and P. Hildreth (Eds.), *Communities of practice: Creating learning environments for educators*. London: Idea Group Publishing.

Hibbert, K. (2005). [Students' perceptions of assessment and evaluation]. Unpublished raw data.

Hibbert, K. (2006). *Assessment strategies*. Unpublished course material. The University of Western Ontario, London, ON.

Hibbert, K., Heydon, R., and Rich, S. (In press). Beacons of light, rays, or sun catchers? A case study of the positioning of lead literacy teachers and their knowledge in neoliberal times. *Teaching and Teacher Education*.

Hicks, D. (2002). *Reading lives: Working-class children and literacy learning*. New York: Teachers College Press.

Hiebert, E. H. (1999). Text matters in learning to read. *The Reading Teacher, 52*(6), 552–566.

Hill, S. E., and Nichols, S. (2006). Emergent literacy: Symbols at work. In B. Spodek and O. N. Saracho (Eds.), *Handbook of research on the education of young children* (pp. 153–165). Mahwah, NJ: Lawrence Erlbaum Associates.

Holdaway, D. (1979). *The foundations of literacy*. Gosford, Australia: Ashton Scholastic.

Holland, H. (2007). Can educators close the achievement gap? *Journal of Staff Development, 28*(1), 54–75.

Horn, J. (1992). *An exploration into the writing or original scripts by inner-city high school drama students*. New York: National Arts Education Research Center, New York University.

Hoyt, L. (2002). *Instructional strategies for guided reading that enhance students' reading comprehension: grades 3–6*. [Videorecording]. Bellevue, WA: Bureau of Education and Research.

Huck, C. S., Hepler, S., Hickman, J., and Kiefer, B. Z. (2004). *Children's literature in the elementary school* (8th ed.). Dubuque, IA: McGraw-Hill.

Hunt, K. (1965). *Grammatical structures written at three grade levels*. NCTE Research Report Number 3. Urbana, IL: National Council of Teachers of English.

Hunt, L. C. (1970). The effect of self-selection, interest and motivation upon independent, instructional and frustration level. *The Reading Teacher, 24*(2), 146–151.

Huss, J. (2006). Gifted education and cooperative learning: A miss or a match? *Gifted Child Today, 29*(4), 19–23.

Iannacci, L. (2005). Othered among others: A critical narrative of culturally and linguistically diverse (CLD) children's literacy and identity in early childhood education (ECE). Unpublished doctoral dissertation, The University of Western Ontario, London.

Iannacci, L. (2008a). Asset-oriented approaches to cultural and linguistic diversity in early childhood education. In R. Heydon and L. Iannacci, *Early childhood curricula and the de-pathologizing of childhood*. Toronto: University of Toronto Press.

Iannacci, L. (2008b). The pathologizing of culturally and linguistically diverse students in early years classrooms. In R. Heydon and L. Iannacci, *Early childhood curricula and the de-pathologizing of childhood*. Toronto: University of Toronto Press.

Indrisano, R., and Paratore, J. R. (1991). Classroom contexts for literacy learning. In J. Flood, J. M. Jensen, D. Lapp, and J. R. Squire (Eds.), *Handbook of research on teaching the English language arts* (pp. 477–487). New York: Macmillan.

International Reading Association. (n.d.). *Phonemic awareness and the teaching of reading*. Retrieved March 9, 2007, from: http://www.reading.org/resources/issues/positions_phonemic.html.

International Reading Association. (n.d.). *Using multiple methods of beginning reading instruction: Summary*. Retrieved February 20, 2007, from: http://www.reading.org/resources/issues/positions_multiple_methods.html.

International Reading Association. (1999). *Position statement: High-stakes assessments in reading*. Retrieved April 23, 2007, from: http://www.reading.org/resources/issues/positions_high_stakes.html.

International Reading Association. (2000). Moving beyond the debate. *Reading Today, 18,* 1–9.

Invernizzi, M. (2003). Concepts, sounds, and the ABCs: A diet for a very young reader. In D. M. Barone and L. M. Morrow (Eds.), *Literacy and young children: Research-based practices* (pp. 140–156). New York/London: Guilford Press.

Irvin, J. J., Buehl, D. R., and Radcliffe, B. J. (2007). *Strategies to enhance literacy and learning in middle school content area classrooms* (3rd ed.). Boston: Pearson Education.

Iser, W. (1974). *The implied reader: Patterns of communication in prose fiction from Bunyan to Beckett*. Baltimore: Johns Hopkins University Press.

Jacobs, E., and Jordan, C. (1993). Understanding minority education: Framing the issues. In E. Jacob and C. Jordan (Eds.), *Minority education: Anthropological perspectives* (pp. 3–13). Norwood, NJ: Ablex.

Jenkinson, D. (1994). The changing faces of censorship in Manitoba's public school libraries. *Emergency Librarian, 22*(2), 15–21.

Jewitt, C., and Kress, G. (2003). Introduction. In C. Jewitt and G. Kress (Eds.), *Multimodal literacy* (pp. 1–18). New York: Peter Lang.

Jobe, R., and Hart, P. (1991). The basalization of children's literature. *Reflections on Canadian Literacy, 9*(3 and 4), 147–150.

Johnston, F. P. (2001). The utility of phonic generalizations: Let's take another look at Clymer's conclusions. *The Reading Teacher, 55*(2), 132–142.

Johnston, I., Bainbridge, J., Mangat, J., and Skogen, R. (2006). National identity and the ideology of Canadian multicultural picture books: Pre-service teachers encountering representations of difference. *Canadian Children's Literature, 32*(2), 79–96.

Johnston, P. (1998). The consequences of the use of standardized tests. In S. Murphy (Ed.), *Fragile evidence: A critique of reading assessment* (pp. 89–101). Mahwah, NJ: Lawrence Erlbaum Associates.

Jonassen, D. (1996). *Computers in the classroom: Mindtools for critical thinking*. Englewood Cliffs, NJ: Prentice-Hall.

Jones, J., and Leahy, S. (2006). Developing strategic readers. *Science and Children, 44*(3), 30–34.

Juel, C. (1988). Learning to read and write: A longitudinal study of 54 children from first through fourth grades. *Journal of Educational Psychology, 80,* 437–447.

Kaufman, M. (2002). Putting it all together: From one first-grade teacher to another. *The Reading Teacher, 55*(8), 722–726.

Kendrick, M. (2003). *Converging worlds: Play, literacy, and culture in early childhood*. Bern: Peter Lang.

Kincheloe, J. (2004). The knowledges of teacher education: Developing a critical complex epistemology. *Teacher Education Quarterly, 31*(1), 49–67.

Kinniburgh, L., and Shaw, E. Jr. (2007). Building reading fluency in elementary science through reader's theatre. *Science Activities, 44*(1), 16–22.

Knobel, M., and Lankshear, C. (Eds.). (2007). *A new literacies sampler*. New York: P. Lang.

Kohn, A. (2002). Poor teaching for poor kids. *Language Arts, 79*(3), 251–255.

Kong, A., and Pearson, P. D. (2003). The road to participation: The construction of a literacy practice in a learning community of linguistically diverse learners. *Research in the Teaching of English, 38*(1), 85–124.

Koskinene, P. S., and Blum, I. H. (1986). Paired repeated reading: A classroom strategy for developing fluent reading. *The Reading Teacher, 40*(1), 70–75.

Krashen, S. D. (1982). *Principles and practice in second language acquisition.* Oxford/New York: Pergamon.

Kress, G. (1997). *Before writing: Rethinking the paths to literacy.* London and New York: Routledge.

Kress, G. (2003). *Literacy in the new media age.* London: Routledge.

Kress, G., and Jewitt, C. (2003). Introduction. In C. Jewitt and G. Kress (Eds.), *Multimodal literacy* (pp. 1–18). New York: Peter Lang.

Lang, L. (2002). Whose play is it anyway?: When drama teachers journey into collective creation. *Youth Theatre Journal, 16,* 48–62.

Langer, J. (1994). Focus on research: A response-based approach to teaching literature. *Language Arts, 71*(3), 203–211.

Language and Literacy Researchers of Canada. (2006). *Draft position statement on literacy assessment.* Unpublished presentation at the annual meeting of the Canadian Society for the Study of Education, Toronto.

Language and Literacy Researchers of Canada. Home page. Retrieved February 16, 2007, from: http://www.csse.ca/CACS/LLRC/index.htm.

Lankshear, C., and Knobel, M. (2003). *New literacies: Changing knowledge and classroom learning.* Buckingham, UK: Open University Press.

Larson, J. (Ed.). (2001). *Literacy as snake oil: Beyond the quick fix.* New York: Peter Lang.

Leland, C., Harste, J., Ociepka, A., Lewison, M., and Vasquez, V. (1999). Exploring critical literacy: You can hear a pin drop. *Language Arts, 77*(1), 70–77.

Leppard, S. (1991). A reading–writing continuum. *Program continuity: The positive link.* Calgary: Alberta Educational Communications Corporation.

Lesesne, T. S. (2006). Reading aloud: A worthwhile investment? *Voices from the Middle, 13*(4), 50–54.

Leslie, L., and Caldwell, J. (1990). *Qualitative reading inventory.* New York: HarperCollins.

Leslie, L., and Caldwell, J. (2001). *Qualitative reading inventory—3.* New York: HarperCollins.

Lewis, C. (1989). *Partnership writing: Ten-year-olds talking and writing together.* MEd thesis, University of Alberta, Edmonton, AB.

Lewis, C. (1993). "Give people a chance": Acknowledging social differences in reading. *Language Arts, 70*(6), 454–461.

Lewis, M., and Wray, D. (1995). *Developing children's non-fiction writing.* Leamington Spa, UK: Scholastic.

Lewison, M., Flint, A. S., and Van Sluys, K., Henkin, R. (2002). Taking on critical literacy: The journey of newcomers and novices. *Language Arts, 79*(5), 382–392.

Lindfors, J. W. (1987). *Children's language and learning* (2nd ed.). Englewood Cliffs, NJ: Prentice-Hall.

Lipson, M. Y., and Wixson, K. K. (1991). *Assessment and instruction of reading disability: An interactive approach.* New York: HarperCollins.

Lipson, M. Y., and Wixson, K. K. (2003). *Assessment and instruction of reading and writing difficulty: An interactive approach* (3rd ed.). Boston: Allyn and Bacon.

Long, S., and Meyer, R. (2004). Passionless text and phonics first: Through a child's eyes. *Language Arts, 81*(5), 417–426.

Loveless, T. (1998). *The tracking and ability grouping debate.* The Fordham Report. Washington, DC: The Fordham Foundation.

Lundy, C., and Booth, D. (1983). *Interpretation: Working with scripts.* Toronto: Harcourt Brace Canada.

Lundy, K. G. (2007). *Leap into literacy: Teaching the tough stuff so it sticks!* Markham, ON: Pembroke Publishers.

Maaskant, F. (1989). *Children's perceptions of writing in a Grade One/Two classroom.* MEd thesis, University of Alberta, Edmonton, AB.

MacAlister, S., Kydd, G., and Jones, G. (1988). *Writing and primary science.* Calgary: Calgary Board of Education.

Malloy, J. A., and Gambrell, L. B. (2006). Approaching the unavoidable: Literacy instruction and the Internet. *The Reading Teacher, 59*(5), 482–484.

Mandlebaum, L. H., Hodges, D., and Messenheimer, T. (2007). Get students to read it again. *Intervention in School Clinic, 42*(5), 292–299.

Marzana, R., Pickering, D., and McTighe, J. (1993). *Assessing student outcomes: Performance assessment using the dimensions of learning model.* Alexandria, VA: Association for Supervision and Curriculum Development.

Massey, D. (2002). Personal journeys: Teaching teachers to teach literacy. *Reading Research and Instruction, 41*(2), 103–125.

Mayer, K. (2007). Emerging knowledge about emergent writing. *YC Young Children, 62*(1), 34–40.

McCoach, D., O'Connell, A., and Levitt, H. (2006). Ability grouping across kindergarten using an early childhood longitudinal study. *The Journal of Educational Research, 99*(6), 339–347.

McKenna, M. C., and Stahl, S. A. (2003). *Assessment for reading instruction.* New York: The Guilford Press.

McKeown, M. G., and Curtis, M. E. (Eds.). (1987). *The nature of vocabulary acquisition.* Hillsdale, NJ: Lawrence Erlbaum Associates.

McTavish, M. (2007). Constructing the big picture: A working class family supports their daughter's pathways to literacy. *The Reading Teacher, 60*(5), 476–484.

Median, J. (1999). *My name is Jorge: On both sides of the river.* Honesdale, PA: Boyds Mills.

Meek, M. (1988). *How texts teach what readers learn.* Stroud, UK: Thimble Press.

Mendelsohn, D. J. (1989). Testing should reflect teaching. *TESL Canada Journal, 7*(1), 95–108.

Merchant, G. (2005). Barbie meets Bob the Builder at the Workstation: Learning to write on screen. In J. Marsh (Ed.), *Popular culture, new media and digital literacy in early childhood.* London: Routledge Falmer.

Merriman, E. (1999). A lazy thought. In J. Simon (Ed.), *Days like this.* Cambridge, MA: Candlewick Press.

Meyer, C. (2002). *English corpus linguistics.* Cambridge, MA: Cambridge University Press.

Meyers, D. (1997, Fall). Dependent authorship: A dependable teaching activity for reading and writing critically and creatively. *Statement,* 20–22.

Michaels, A. (1996). *Fugitive pieces.* Toronto: McClelland and Stewart.

Millard, D. (1997). *Differently literate: Boys, girls, and the schooling of literacy.* London: Falmer Press.

Miller, C., and Saxton, J. (2004). *Into the story: Language in action through drama.* Portsmouth, NH: Heinemann.

Miller, G. (1977). *Spontaneous apprentices: Children and language.* New York: Seabury Press.

Miller-Lachmann, L. (1992). *Our family, our friends, our world.* New Providence, NJ: R. R. Bowker.

Ministry of Education. (2003). *Early reading strategy: The report of the expert panel on early reading in Ontario.* Toronto: Queen's Printer for Ontario.

Ministry of Education, Province of British Columbia. (2006). *English Language Arts, Kindergarten to Grade 7: Integrated Resource Package.* Victoria, BC: Ministry of Education, Province of British Columbia. Retrieved April 19, 2007, from: http://www.bced.gov.bc.ca/irp/ela_k7_2006.pdf.

Moffett, J. (1968). *Teaching the universe of discourse.* Boston: Houghton Mifflin.

Moffett, J. (1979). Integrity in the teaching of writing. *Phi Delta Kappa, 61*(4), 276–279.

Moje, E. B., Ciechanowski, K. M., and Kramer, K. (2004). Working toward third space in content area literacy: An examination of everyday funds of knowledge and discourse. *Reading Research Quarterly, 39*(1), 38–70.

Moll, L. (1992). Funds of knowledge for teaching: Using a qualitative approach to connect homes and classrooms. *Theory into Practice, 31*(2), 132–41.

Moore, J. (2000, 1995). *Writing with Results.* Calgary, AB: Books for Results, Inc.

Moray, N. (1969). *Listening and attention.* Baltimore: Penguin Books.

Morgan, N., and Saxton, J. (1987). *Teaching drama: A mind of many wonders.* London: Hutchinson Education.

Morris, D. (1993). The relationship between children's concept of word in text and phoneme awareness in learning to read: A longitudinal study. *Research in the Teaching of English, 27*(2), 133–154.

Morrow, L. M. (1989). Designing the classroom to promote literacy development. In D. S. Strickland and L. M. Morrow (Eds.), *Emerging literacy: Young children learn to read and write* (pp. 121–134). Newark, DE: International Reading Association.

Morrow, L. M., and Lesnick, J. (2001). Examining the educational value of children's magazines. *The California Reader, 34*(2). Available at: http://www.childmagmonth.org/learning/Research.pdf.

Moss, G. (2000). Raising boys' attainment in reading: Some principles for intervention. *Reading, 34,* 101–106.

Murphy, S. (1991). Authorship and discourse types in Canadian basal reading programs. *Reflections on Canadian literacy, 9*(3 and 4), 133–138.

Murphy, S. (1998). *Fragile evidence: A critique of reading assessment.* Mahwah, NJ: Lawrence Erlbaum Associates.

Murray, D. (1984). *Write to learn.* New York: Holt, Rinehart and Winston.

Muter, V., Hulme, C., Snowling, M., and Taylor, S. (1997). Segmentation, not rhyming, predicts early progress in learning to read. *Journal of Experimental Child Psychology, 65,* 370–396.

Nagy, W. E. (1988). *Teaching vocabulary to improve reading comprehension.* Urbana, IL: ERIC Clearinghouse on Reading and Communications Skills and the National Council of Teachers of English and the International Reading Association.

National Council of Teachers of English. (1982). *The students' right to read.* Urbana, IL: National Council of Teachers of English.

National Council of Teachers of English. (1998). *Rationales for challenged books* [CD-ROM]. Urbana, IL: National Council of Teachers of English.

National Council of Teachers of Mathematics. (2000). *Principles and standards for school mathematics.* Reston, VA: Author.

National Reading Panel. (2000). *Teaching children to read: An evidence-based assessment of the scientific research literature on reading and its implications for reading instruction.* Washington, DC: National Institute of Child Health and Human Development. Available at: http://www.nationalreadingpanel.org.

Neelands, J. (1984). *Making sense of drama: A guide to classroom practice.* London: Heinemann Educational Books.

Neelands, J., and Goode, T. (2000). *Structuring drama work: A handbook of available forms in theatre and drama* (2nd ed.). Cambridge: Cambridge University Press.

Neuman, S. B., and Roskos, K. A. (1993). *Language and literacy learning in the early years: An integrated approach.* New York: Harcourt Brace Jovanovich College.

Newkirk, T. (1987). The non-narrative writing of young children. *Research in the teaching of English, 21*, 121–145.

Nichols, M. (2006). *Comprehension through conversation: The power of purposeful talk in the reading workshop.* New Hampshire: Heinemann.

Nichols, W. D., and Rupley, W. H. (2004). Matching instructional design with vocabulary instruction. *Reading Horizons, 45*(1), 55–71.

Nieto, S. (1992). *Affirming diversity.* New York: Longman.

Nodelman, P. (1992). We are all censors. *Canadian Children's Literature, 68*, 121–133.

O'Neill, C. (1995). *Drama worlds: A framework for process drama.* Portsmouth, NH: Heinemann.

O'Neill, C., and Lambert, A. (1982). *Drama structures: A practical handbook for teachers.* Portsmouth, NH: Heinemann.

Oczkus, L. D. (2003). The four reciprocal teaching strategies. In L. D. Oczkus, *Reciprocal teaching at work* (pp. 13–28). Newark, DE: International Reading Association.

Ondaatje, M. (2007). *Divisadero.* Toronto: McClelland and Stewart.

Ontario Ministry of Education. (2004). *Me read? No way! A practical guide to improving boys' literacy skills.* Toronto: Queen's Printer for Ontario.

Ontario Ministry of Education and Training. (2003). *A guide to effective instruction in reading: Kindergarten to grade 3.* Queen's Park: Toronto.

Ontario Ministry of Education and Training. (2006). *The Ontario curriculum: Grades 1–8: Language.* Queen's Park: Toronto.

Opie, I., and Opie, P. (1963). *The Puffin book of nursery rhymes.* Harmondsworth, UK: Penguin Books.

Opitz, M. F. (2000). *Rhymes and reason: Literature and language play for phonological awareness.* Portsmouth, NH: Heinemann.

Owicki, G., and Goodman, Y. (2002). *Kidwatching: Documenting children's literacy development.* Portsmouth, NH: Heinemann.

Ozdoba, A. (1992). Writing to learn: Science journals in year one. MEd thesis, University of Alberta, Edmonton, AB.

Pahl, K. (1999). *Transformations: Children's meaning making in a nursery.* Oakhill, UK: Trentham Books.

Pahl, K., and Rowsell, J. (2005). *Literacy and education: Understanding the new literacy studies in the classroom.* London: Paul Chapman.

Pahl, K., and Rowsell, J. (2006). Introduction. In K. Pahl and J. Rowsell (Eds.), *Travel notes from the new literacy studies: Instances of practice* (pp. 1–15). Clevedon, UK, and Buffalo, NY: Multilingual Matters.

Palincsar, A. S. (1986). Metacognitive strategy instruction. *Exceptional Children, 53*(2), 118–124.

Pantaleo, S. (1994). *Teacher influence on student response to literature.* PhD dissertation, University of Alberta, Edmonton, AB.

Pappas, C., Kiefer, B., and Levstik, L. (1995). *An integrated language perspective in the elementary school: Theory into action.* White Plains, NY: Longman.

Paratore, J. R., Melzi, G., and Krol-Sinclair, B. (2003). Learning about the literate lives of Latino families. In D. M. Barone and L. M. Morrow (Eds.), *Literacy and young children: Research-based practices* (pp. 101–118). New York and London: Guilford Press.

Paris, S. G., and Hoffman, J. V. (2004). Reading assessments in kindergarten through third grade: Findings from the Center for the Improvement of Early Reading Achievement. *The Elementary School Journal, 105*(2), 199–217.

Parsons, L. (2001). *Response journals revisited: Maximizing learning through reading, writing, viewing, discussing, and thinking.* Markham, ON: Pembroke.

People for Education. (2005). Annual Report on Elementary Schools, 36. Retrieved August 2, 2006, from: http://www.peopleforeducation.com/tracking/summrpts/elem/2005/elem_2005. pdf.

Peregoy, S. F., and Boyle, O. F. (2000). English learners reading English: What we know, what we need to know. *Theory into Practice, 39*(4), 237–247.

Peregoy, S. F., and Boyle, O. F. (2004). English learners reading English: What we know, what we need to know. In R. D. Robinson, M. C. McKenna, J. M. Wedman (Eds.), *Issues and trends in literacy education* (3rd ed.) (pp. 103–118). Boston: Pearson/Allyn and Bacon.

Perel, D., and Editors of the Weekly World News. (2005). *Bat boy lives!: The weekly world news guide to politics, culture, celebrities, alien abductions, and the mutant freaks that shape our world.* New York: Sterling Publishing.

Peterson, R., and Eeds, M. (1990). *Grand conversations.* Richmond Hill, ON: Scholastic-TAB.

Peterson, S. (2001). Teachers' perceptions of gender equity in writing assessment. *English Quarterly, 33*(1 and 2), 22–30.

Petite Rivière Elementary School. (1993). *History of Crousetown.* Lunenburg County, NS: Petite Rivière Publishing.

Phenix, J. (2001). *The spelling teacher's handbook.* Markham, ON: Pembroke.

Piaget, J. (1962). *Play, dreams and imitation in childhood.* New York: W. W. Norton.

Pikulski, J. J., and Chard, D. J. (2005). Fluency: Bridge between decoding and reading comprehension. *The Reading Teacher, 58*(6), 510–519.

Pinnell, G. S., and Fountas, I. C. (1998). *Word matters: Teaching phonics and spelling in the reading/writing classroom.* Portsmouth, NH: Heinemann.

Pinnell, G. S., and Fountas, I. C. (2002). *Leveled books for readers: Grades 3–6.* Portsmouth, NH: Heinemann.

Pogrow, S. (2006). Restructuring high-poverty elementary schools for success: A description of the hi-perform school design. *Phi Delta Kappan, 88*(3), 223–230.

Preminger, F., Weiss, P. L., and Weintraub, N. (2004). Predicting occupational performance: Handwriting versus keyboarding. *American Journal of Occupational Therapy, 58*(2), 193–201.

Pugh, K. H. (2005). Peer tutoring dos and don'ts. *Phi Delta Kappa, 528*, 5–31.

Purcell-Gates, V. (1998). Growing successful readers: Homes, communities, and schools. In J. Osborn and F. Lehr (Eds.), *Literacy for all: Issues in teaching and learning* (p. 54). New York: The Guilford Press.

Purcell-Gates, V. (2001). What we know about readers who struggle. In R. Flippo (Ed.), *Reading researchers in search of common ground* (pp. 118–128). Newark, DE: International Reading Association.

Purcell-Gates, V., Jacobson, E., and Degener, S. (2004). *Print literacy development: Uniting cognitive and social practice theories.* Cambridge: Harvard University Press.

Purves, A. (1993). Toward a re-evaluation of reader response and school literature. *Language Arts, 70*(5), 348–361.

Purves, A., and Rippere, V. (1968). *Elements of writing about a literary work: A study of response to literature.* NCTE Research Report No. 9. Urbana, IL: National Council of Teachers of English.

Raphael, T. E. (1986). Teaching question-answer relationships. *The Reading Teacher, 39*(6), 516–522.

Rasinski, T. V., and Padak, N. D. (2001). *From phonics to fluency.* New York: Longman.

Rasinski, T. V., and Padak, N. D. (2005). Fluency beyond the primary grades: Helping adolescent struggling readers. *Voices from the Middle, 13*(1), 34–41.

Read, C. (1975). *Children's categorizations of speech sounds in English.* Urbana, IL: National Council of Teachers of English.

Reid, R. (2006). Comedy club: Read-aloud passages that young teens will find funny. *Book Links, 16*(2), 20–21.

Reid, R. (2007). Flying under the radar: Great read-alouds you may have missed. *Book Links, 16*(3), 32–33.

Reutzel, D. R., and Cooter, R. B., Jr. (2003). *Strategies for reading assessment and instruction: helping every child succeed* (2nd ed.). Upper Saddle River, NJ: Merrill Prentice Hall.

Rhodes, L. K., and Shanklin, N. L. (1993). *Windows into literacy: Assessing learners, K–8*. Portsmouth, NH: Heinemann.

Rigby [Imprint of Harcourt Achieve]. (n.d.). *What is balanced literacy?* Retrieved February 20, 2007, from: http://www.harcourtcanada.com/rigby/bal-lit.htm.

Riley, J. (2006). *Language and literacy 3-7: creative approaches to teaching*. London, Thousand Oaks, CA: Sage Publications.

Ritchey, K. D. (2006). Learning to write: Progress-Monitoring tools for beginning and at-risk writers. *Teaching Exceptional Children, 39*(2), 22–26.

Roberts, E. A. (1996). *A survey of censorship practices in public school libraries in Saskatchewan*. MLIS thesis, University of Alberta, Edmonton, AB.

Rog, L. J. (2003). *Guided reading basics: Organizing, managing, and implementing a balanced literacy program in K–3*. Portland, MA and Markham, ON: Stenhouse Publishers and Pembroke Publishers.

Rosen, B. (1988). *And none of it was nonsense: The power of storytelling in the classroom*. Richmond Hill, ON: Scholastic-TAB.

Rosen, H. (1984). *The importance of story*. Sheffield, UK: National Association for the Teaching of English.

Rosenblatt, L. (1978). *The reader, the text, the poem: The transactional theory of the literary work*. Carbondale, IL: Southern Illinois University Press.

Rosenblatt, L. (1989). Writing and reading: The transactional theory. In J. M. Mason (Ed.), *Reading and writing connections* (pp. 153–176). Boston: Allyn and Bacon.

Rosenblatt, L. M. (1978). *The reader, the text, the poem: The transactional theory of the literary work*. Carbondale: Southern Illinois University Press.

Roskos, K. (1995). *Linking literacy and play*. [Kit]. Neward, Del.: The International Reading Association.

Rossman, A. D. (1987). Reading automaticity: The essential element of academic success. *Principal, 67*, 28–32.

Rothenberg, C., and Fisher, D. (2007). *Teaching English language learners: A differentiated approach*. Upper Saddle River, NJ: Pearson.

Rothstein, R. (2004). *Class and schools: Using social, economic, and educational reform to close the black–white achievement gap*. New York/Washington, DC: Teachers College, Columbia University/Economic Policy Institute.

Routman, R. (1991). *Invitations: Changing as teachers and learners K–12*. Toronto: Irwin.

Routman, R. (2000). *Conversations: Strategies for teaching, learning and evaluating*. Portsmouth, NH: Heinemann.

Routman, R. (2003). *Reading essentials: The specifics you need to teach reading well*. Portsmouth, NH: Heinemann.

Routman, R. (2005). *Writing essentials: Raising expectations and results while simplifying teaching*. Portsmouth, NH: Heinemann.

Ruiz, N. T., Vargas, E., and Beltran, A. (2002). Becoming a reader and writer in a bilingual special education classroom. *Language Arts, 79*(4), 297–309.

Rumelhart, D. E. (1977). *Introduction to human information processing theory.* New York: John Wiley and Sons.

Saccomano, D. T. (2006). *A descriptive study of a classroom teacher and the conditions of learning and the dimensions of teaching reflected in practice with intermediate-level literacy students.* Unpublished doctoral dissertation, Central Connecticut State University.

Sampson, M. B. (2002). Confirming a K-W-L: Considering the source. *The Reading Teacher, 55*(6), 528–532.

Sampson, M. B., Rasinski, T. V., and Sampson, M. (2003). *Total Literacy: Reading, writing, and learning* (3rd ed.). Belmont, CA: Wadsworth/Thomson.

Samuels, S. J. (1979). The method of repeated readings. *The Reading Teacher, 32*, 403–408.

Sanford, K., and Blair, H. (n.d.). *Boys and literacy.* Retrieved February 26, 2007, from: http://www.education.ualberta.ca/boysandliteracy/index.htm.

Sanford, K., and Madill, L. (2006). Resistance through video game play: It's a boy thing. *Canadian Journal of Education, 29*(1), 287–306.

Sanford, K. (2005/2006). Gendered literacy experiences: The effects of expectation and opportunity for boys' and girls' learning. *Journal of Adolescent and Adult Literacy, 49*(4), 302–315.

Saskatchewan Education. (2002). *English language arts: A curriculum guide for the elementary level.* Available at: http://www.sasked.gov.sk.ca/docs/ela/speaking01.html.

Saskatchewan Learning. (n.d.). *Aboriginal languages: A curriculum guide for Kindergarten to Grade 12.* Retrieved August 30, 2007, from: http://www.sasklearning.gov.sk.ca/docs/indlang.

Sastri, P. (2005). Affirming identity in multilingual classrooms. *Educational Leadership, 63*(1), 38–42. Retrieved February 15, 2007, from: http://www.ascd.org/authors/ed_lead/el200509_cummins.html.

Schrader, A. (1996). Censorproofing school library collections: The fallacy and futility. *School Libraries Worldwide, 2*(1), 71–94.

Schwartz, S., and Bone, M. (1995). *Retelling, relating, reflecting: Beyond the 3 R's.* Concord, ON: Irwin Publishing.

Scollon, R., and Scollon, S.B.K. (1981). *Narrative, literacy and face in interethnic communication.* Norwood, NJ: Ablex Publishing Corporation.

Scollon, R., and Scollon, S. (1983). *Narrative, literacy, and face in interethnic communication.* Norwood, NJ: Ablex.

Scott, R. (1993). *Spelling: Sharing the secrets.* Toronto: Gage.

Serafini, F. (2001). Three paradigms of assessment: Measurement, procedure and inquiry. *The Reading Teacher, 54*, 384–393.

Shannon, P. (1998). A selective social history of the uses of reading tests. In S. Murphy (Ed.), *Fragile evidence: A critique of reading assessment* (pp. 75–87). Mahwah, NJ: Lawrence Erlbaum Associates.

Sheppard, S. (2001). Tips for teaching. *Preventing School Failure, 45*(3), 297–309.

Shiel, G., and Cosgrove, J. (2002). International assessments of reading literacy. *The Reading Teacher, 55*(7), 690–692.

Shields, C. M., Bishop, R., and Mazawi, A. E. (2005). *Pathologizing practices: The impact of deficit thinking on education.* New York: Peter Lang.

Silver, A. (1999). A fundamental equalizer for ESL children. *TESL Canada Journal/La Revue TESL du Canada, 16*(2), 62–69.

Simmons, J. (2002). *You never asked me to read: Useful assessment of reading and writing problems.* Boston: Allyn and Bacon.

Simon, R. I., and Armitage-Simon, W. (1995). Teaching risky stories: Remembering mass destruction through children's literature. *English Quarterly, 28*(1), 27–31.

Simpson, C. (1980). *The Scott, Foresman word study for spelling.* Glenview, IL: Scott, Foresman and Company.

Sinatra, R. C., Stahl-Gemake, J., and Berg, D. N. (1984). Improving the reading comprehension of disabled readers through semantic mapping. *The Reading Teacher, 38*(1), 22–29.

Slade, P. (1954). *Child drama.* London, UK: University of London Press Ltd.

Slavin, R. E. (1980). Cooperative learning. *Review of Educational Research, 50*, 315–342.

Sloan, K. (2007). High-stakes accountability, minority youth, and ethnography: Assessing the multiple effects. *Anthropology and Education Quarterly, 38*(1), 24–41.

Smilansky, S. (1990). Sociodramatic play: Its relevance to behavior and achievement in school. In E. Klugman and S. Smilansky (Eds.), *Children's play and learning: Perspectives and policy implications* (pp. 18–42). New York: Teachers College Press.

Smilansky, S., and Shefatya, L. (1990). *Facilitating play: A medium for promoting cognitive, socio-emotional and academic development in young children.* Silver Spring, Maryland: Psychosocial and Educational Publications.

Smith, F. (1983). Reading like a writer. *Language Arts, 60*(5), 558–567.

Smith, F. (1988). *Joining the literacy club: Further essays into education.* London: Heinemann.

Smith, J. L., and Herring, J. D. (2001). *Dramatic literacy: Using drama and literature to teach middle-level content.* Portsmouth, NH: Heinemann.

Snow, C. E., Burns, M. S., and Griffin, P. (Eds.). (1998). *Preventing reading difficulties in young children.* Ottawa: National Research Council.

Spandel, V. (2001). *Books, lessons, ideas for teaching the six traits of writing in the elementary and middle grades.* Wilmington, MA: Great Source Education Group (Houghton Mifflin).

Spandel, V. (2004). *WriteTraits classroom kit.* Wilmington, MA: Great Source Education Group (Houghton Mifflin).

Spence, C. M. (2006). *Creating a literacy environment for boys: Ideas for administrators, teachers, and parents.* Toronto: Nelson.

Stanovich, K. E. (1986). Matthew effects in reading: Some consequences of individual differences in the acquisition of literacy. *Reading Research Quarterly, 21*(4), 360–406.

Starrett, E. V. (2007). *Teaching phonics for balanced reading.* Thousand Oaks, CA: Corwin Press.

Statistics Canada, Census of Population. (2001a). *Aboriginal identity population, 2001 counts for Canada, provinces and territories-20% sample data.* Retrieved February 20, 2007, from: http://www12.statcan.ca/english/census01/products/highlight/Aboriginal/Page.cfm?Lang=E7&Geo=PR&Code=0&View=1a&Table=1&StartRec=1&Sort=2&B1=Counts01&B2=Total.

Statistics Canada, Census of Population. (2001b). *Population by mother tongue, by province and territory (2001 Census).* Retrieved February 19, 2007, from: http://www40.statcan.ca/l01/cst01/demo11b.htm.

Statistics Canada, Census of Population. (2001c). *Proportion of foreign-born population, by census metropolitan area (1991 to 2001 Censuses).* Retrieved February 19, 2007, from: http://www40.statcan.ca/l01/cst01/demo47a.htm.

Stooke, R. (1999). *Partnerships for children's literacy: The information needs and information seeking activities of concerned parents.* Unpublished master's thesis, University of Western Ontario, London, ON.

Straw, S. B. (1990). The actualization of reading and writing: Public policy and conceptualizations of literacy. In S. P. Norris and L. M. Phillips (Eds.), *Literacy policy in Canada* (pp. 165–181). Calgary: Detselig Enterprises.

Street, B. (1984). *Literacy in theory and practice.* Cambridge: Cambridge University Press.

Sullivan, M. (2004). Why Johnny won't read. *School Library Journal, 50*(8), 36–39.

Sulzby, E. (1985). Children's emergent reading of favorite storybooks: A developmental study. *Reading Research Quarterly, 20,* 458–481.

Sulzby, E. (1991). The development of the young child and the emergence of literacy. In J. Flood, J. M. Jensen, D. Lapp, and J. R. Squire (Eds.), *Handbook of research on teaching the English language arts* (pp. 273–285). New York: Macmillan.

Sutherland-Smith, W. (2002). Weaving the literacy web: Changes in reading from page to screen. *The Reading Teacher, 55*(7), 662–668.

Swadener, B. B., and Lubeck, S. (1995). (Eds.). *Children and families "at promise": Deconstructing the discourse of risk.* Albany, NY: Albany State University of New York Press.

Swearingen, R., and Allen, D. (2000). *Classroom assessment of reading* (2nd ed.). Boston: Houghton Mifflin Company.

Szymusiak, K., and Sibberson, F. (2001). *Beyond leveled books: Supporting transitional readers in Grades 2–5.* Portland, M A: Stenhouse Publishers.

Taberski, S. (1996). *A close-up look at teaching reading: focusing on children and our goals.* [Videorecording]. Portsmouth, NH: Heinemann.

Taberski, S. (2000). *On solid ground: Strategies for teaching reading K–3.* Portsmouth, NH: Heinemann.

Tarlington, C., and Verriour, P. (1991). *Role drama.* Markham, ON: Pembroke Publishers.

Taylor, B. M., Peterson, D. S., Pearson, P. D., Rodriguez, M. C. (2002). Looking inside classrooms: Reflecting on the "how" as well as the "what" in effective reading instruction. *The Reading Teacher, 56*(3), 270–279.

Thomas, V. (1979). *Teaching spelling: Canadian word lists and instructional techniques.* Toronto: Gage.

Thomson, J. (1987). *Understanding teenagers' reading: Reading processes and the teaching of literature.* Norwood, Australia: Australian Association for the Teaching of English.

Tizard, B., and Hughes, M. (1984). *Young children learning.* Cambridge, MA: Harvard University Press.

Tompkins, G. (2007). *Teaching writing: Balancing process and product* (5th ed.). Upper Saddle River, NJ: Prentice Hall.

Topping, K. (1987). Paired reading: A powerful technique for parent use. *The Reading Teacher, 40,* 608–614.

Tough, J. (1976). *Listening to children talking: A guide to the appraisal of children's language use.* Portsmouth, NH: Heinemann.

Tovani, C. (2000). *I read it, but I don't get it: Comprehension strategies for adolescent readers.* Portland, ME: Stenhouse Publishers.

University of Oregon. (n.d.). *Phonemic awareness in beginning reading.* Retrieved April 6, 2007, from: http://reading.uoregon.edu/pa/pa_features.php.

Unrau, N., and Schlackman, J. (2006). Motivation and its relationship with reading achievement in an urban middle school. *The Journal of Educational Research, 100*(2), 81–101.

Vacca, J. L., Vacca, R. T., and Gove, M. K. (2006). *Reading and learning to read* (6th ed.). Boston: Pearson/Allyn and Bacon.

Vacca, R. T., Vacca, J. L., and Begorary, D. L. (2005). *Content area reading: Literacy and learning across the curriculum* (Canadian ed.). Toronto: Pearson/Allyn and Bacon.

Valencia, S. W., Hiebert, E. H., and Afflerbach, P. P. (Eds.). (1994). *Authentic reading assessment: Practices and possibilities.* Newark, DE: International Reading Association.

Valli, L., and Chambliss, M. (2007). Creating classroom cultures: One teacher, two lessons, and a high-stakes test. *Anthropology and Education Quarterly, 38*(1), 57–75.

Vasquez, V. M. (2003). *Getting beyond "I like the book": Creating space for critical literacy in K–6 classrooms.* Newark, DE: International Reading Association.

Vasquez, V. M. (2004). *Negotiating critical literacies with young children.* Mahwah, NJ: Lawrence Erlbaum Associates.

Vaughn, S., Hughes, M., Moody, S., and Elbaum, B. (2001). Instructional grouping for reading for students with LD: Implications for practice. *Intervention in School and Clinic, 36*(3), 131–137.

Villaume, S. K., and Brabham, E. G. (2001). Guided reading: Who is in the driver's seat? *The Reading Teacher, 55*(3), 260–263.

Vogt, M. E. (1997). *Cross-curricular thematic instruction.* Retrieved August 21, 2007, from: http://www.eduplace.com/rdg/res/vogt.html.

Voke, H. (2002). What do we know about sanctions and rewards? *Infobrief, 31*, 1–10.

Von Heyking, A. (2002). *Teaching with Dear Canada Volume 1.* Toronto: Scholastic.

Von Heyking, A. (2004). *Teaching with Dear Canada Volume 2.* Toronto: Scholastic.

Von Heyking, A., and McConaghy, J. (2001). *Social studies though literature: A teaching resource for the early grades.* Markham, ON: Scholastic Canada.

Von Heyking, A., and McConaghy, J. (2003). *Teaching with Robert Munsch books.* Toronto: Scholastic Professional Books.

Vygotsky, L. S. (1978). *Mind in society: the development of higher psychological processes.* M. Cole, V., John-Steiner, S. Sribner, and E. Souberman (Eds.). Cambridge, MA: Harvard University Press.

Wagner, B. J. (1998). *Educational drama and language arts: What research shows.* Portsmouth, NH: Heinemann.

Walker, B. J. (2005). Thinking aloud: Struggling readers often require more than a model. *The Reading Teacher, 58*(7), 688–692.

Walker, L. (1989). *Instant puppets for kids.* Markham, ON: Pembroke Publishers.

Walker, L., and Walker, H. (1989). *The instant puppet resource book for teachers.* Markham, ON: Pembroke Publishers.

Wanzek, J., and Haager, D. (2003). Teaching word recognition with blending and analogizing. *Teaching Exceptional Children, 36*(1), 32–38.

Ward, Angela. (1990). Communicative inequality: The participation of native Indian and non-Native children in instructional dialogue in a cross-cultural kindergarten class. *Reading-Canada-Lecture, 8*(1), 22–29.

Wason-Ellam, L. (2002). Interwoven responses to critically conscious stories. *Query, 31*(1), 21–26.

Watts-Taffe, S., and Truscott, D. M. (2000). Using what you know about language and literacy development for ESL students in the mainstream classroom. *Language Arts, 77*(3), 258–264.

Way, B. (1967). *Development through drama.* London: Longman Group Ltd.

Weaver, C. (1996). *Teaching grammar in context.* Portsmouth, NH: Boynton/Cook.

Weaver, C., Gillmeister-Krause, L., and Vento-Zogby, G. (1996). *Creating support for effective literacy education.* Portsmouth, NH: Heinemann.

Weber-Pillwax, C. (2001). Orality in Northern Cree Indigenous worlds. *Canadian Journal of Native Education, 25*(2), 149–165.

Wells, C. G., and Chang-Wells, G. L. (1992). *Constructing knowledge together: Classrooms as centers of inquiry and literacy.* Portsmouth, NH: Heinemann.

Wells, G. (1986). *The meaning makers.* Portsmouth, NH: Heinemann.

Western Canadian protocol for collaboration in basic education: The common curriculum framework for Aboriginal language and culture programs. (2000). Governments of Alberta, British Columbia, Manitoba, Northwest Territories, Saskatchewan, and Yukon Territory. Retrieved August 30, 2007, from: http://www.wcp.ca.

Whitin, P., and Whitin, D. (2000). *Math is language too: Talking and writing in the mathematics classroom.* Reston, VA: NCTM.

Wiener, R. B., and Cohen, J. H. (1997). *Literacy portfolios: Using assessment to guide instructions.* Des Moines, IA: Merrill Prentice Hall.

Wilkinson, L. C., and Marrett, C. B. (1985). *Gender influences in classroom interactions.* Toronto: Academic Press.

Wilkinson, Louise C., and Silliman, Elaine R. (2000). Classroom language and literacy learning. In Kamil, M. L., Mosenthal, P. B., Pearson, P. D., and Barr, R. (Eds.), *Handbook of reading research.* Vol. 3. Mahwah, NJ: Lawrence Erlbaum Associates.

Wilson, L. (2002). *Reading to live: How to teach reading for today's world.* Portsmouth, NH: Heinemann.

Wink, J. (2000). *Critical pedagogy: Notes from the real world* (2nd ed.). New York: Longman.

Wink, J. (2005). *Critical pedagogy: Notes from the real world* (3rd ed.). Boston: Pearson/Allyn and Bacon.

Winzer, M., and Mazurek, K. (1998). *Special education in multicultural contexts.* Upper Saddle River, NJ: Merrill.

Wolf, M., and Katzir-Cohen, T. (2001). Reading fluency and its intervention. *Scientific Studies of Reading, 5*(3), 211–239.

Yopp, H. Y., and Yopp, R. H. (2000). Supporting phonemic awareness development in the classroom. *The Reading Teacher, 54*(2), 130–143.

Young, J. P., and Brozo, W. G. (2001). Boys will be boys, or will they? Literacy and masculinities. *Reading Research Quarterly, 36*(3), 316–325.

INDEX

A

Ability groups, 483–84

Aboriginal Canadians
children's literature by, 427–28

Aboriginal children
planning for, 495–96
reading assessment, 127–29

Aboriginal Languages: A Curriculum Guide for Kindergarten to Grade 12, 496

Aboriginal peoples, storytelling by, 372

Aboriginal students, discourse patterns, 43–44

About Teaching Mathematics: A K-8 Resource, 242

Accountability
standardized tests and, 131
time blocks and, 486

Achievement tests
in Alberta, 313, 315–16
provincial curricula, 129

Adams, M. J., 80, 81, 99, 120, 187, 202, 408

"Adventures of Isabel, The" (Nash), 373

Adventure stories, 166

Advertisements, 383, 408

Aesop, 372

Aesthetic reading, 123, 392

Affective behaviours in oral communication, 42

Affixes, 197

Afflerbach, P. P., 143

Ahlberg, J. and A., *Each Peach Pear Plum,* 354, 358

Ajayi, L., 474

Albers, P., 10

Alberta Education
analytic assessment, 313–16
ICT Program of Studies, 342
Kaleidoscope Conference, 352
language arts, curriculum documents, F14
Language Arts Program of Studies, 60
Provincial Achievement Tests, 313, 315–16

Al Capone Does My Shirts (Choldenko), 365

Aleta and the Queen (Galloway), 371

Alford, J., 494

Allen, D., 139

Allen, J., 229

Allington, R. L., 136, 155, 157, 162, 173, 178, 189, 190, 194, 195, 197, 202, 227, 475, 488, 493, 494

Alliteration, 375

Almond, D. (*Skellig*), 367–68

Alphabet games, 329

Alphabetic principle, 81

Amelia Bedelia (Parish), 35

Amelia Francis Howard-Gibbon Award, 412

Anderson, J., 78

Anderson, R. C., 120

And None of It Was Nonsense (Rosen), 373

Anecdotal records, 65, 83, 299

Anecdotes, writing of, 269

Anholt, L., *Stone Girl, Bone Girl,* 230, 232

Animal stories, 166

Anne Frank: The Diary of a Young Girl (Frank), 167

Anstey, M., 262

Applebee, A., 265

Arbus, Diane, 48

"Arithmetic" (Sandburg), 377

Armbruster, B. B., 158, 497, 498

Armitage-Simon, W., 167, 168

As: A Surfeit of Similes (Juster), 375

Ashton-Warner, Sylvia, 109

As Quick as a Cricket (Woods), 375

Assessment
analytic scales, 311–16
balanced, 133–47
checklist for, 125
content, of, 313
conventions, of, 316
drama, of, 458–61
early literacy, of, 82–97
early reading, 93–94
English language learning, of, 495
general impression marking, 309
high-stakes, 130–33

H

Haager, D., 192
Haiku, 376
Hall, D. P., 174, 176, 177, 195
Hall, N., 6, 75
Halliday, M. A. K., 44, 45, 46, 47, 224, 244, 288, 405, 446
    functions of language, 46–51
Hamilton, R., 208
Hana Project, The: Writings Inspired by the Novel *Hana's Suitcase,* 49, 50–51
Hana's Suitcase (Levine), 47–49, 61
Handful of Time, A (Pearson), 367
Handsfield, Lara, 21
Handwriting
    cursive, 338, F339
    left-handed writers, 341–42
    letter forms, teaching, 339–41
    printing, 338
    teaching of, 337–42
    and word processing, compared, 343
Hansel and Gretel (Browne), 371
Hansel and Gretel (Wallace), 371
Hardy, Barbara, 265
Harold and Harold (Wilson), 361
Harry Potter and the Sorcerer's Stone (Rowling), 367, 415
Harste, J., 421
Hart, P., 475
Haycock, Kati, 17
Hazzard, Ben, 237–38
Head-Smashed-In Buffalo Jump drawings, 233
Heath, S. B., 44, 56
Heathcote, D., 437, 441, 452
Hedrick, W., 175
Henderson, E. H., 320
Henkin, R., 8
Hepler, S., 373
Herrick, Steven, 272
Herring, J. D., 446
Hetzroni, O. E., 343
Heuristic language, 46, 47, 51
Heydon, R., 2, 6, 7, 25, 119, 132, 493
Hibbert, K., 2, 25, 115, 119, 134, 476, 493
Hickman, J., 373
Hicks, D., 17, 77, 497
Hide and Seek (Kusugak), 427

Hiebert, E. H., 143, 474, 476
Highest Level of Achievement Tests (HLATs) (Edmonton), 311–13
High-stakes tests, *see* Standardized tests
Highway, Thompson
    Caribou Song, 427
    Dragonfly Kite, 427
    Song of the North Wind, 427
"Highwayman, The" (Noyes), 373
Hill, S. E., 79, 80
Hippopotamusn't, A (Lewis), 376
Hiroshima No Pika (Maruki), 359
History of Crousetown, 52–54
Hitler's Daughter (French), 365
Hobbit, The (Tolkien), 367
Hodges, D., 204
Hoffman, J. V., 131
Holdaway, D., 101, 103, 201, 354
Holistic scoring, 309–10
Home, *see also* Families; Parents
    literacy practice, 76–77, 86–87
    school success, 497
Hope, L., *The Bobbsey Twins,* 418
Hopeful Trout and Other Limericks, The (Ciardi), 376
Hopkins, L. B., *Click, Rumble, Roar,* 375
Horn, J., 459
Horn Book, The, 414
Horn Book Magazine, The, 380
Horror stories, 166
Hot-seating, 405–406
Huck, C. S., 373
Hughes, I., *The Iron Man,* 400
Hughes, Langston
    "City," 375–76
    "Poem," 376
Hughes, M., 52, 53, 56, 483
Humour stories, 166
Hungry Thing, The, 109
Hunt, K., 37
Hunt, L. C., 363
Hunter, Catherine, 498
Hunter, D., 18
Hunter, Jennifer, 82
Huss, J., 483
Hutchins, P.,
    The Doorbell Rang, 226
    Rosie's Walk, 355, 356